In loving memory of all
our ancestors.

'Ignorance of our history, we fear, is the cause of all our misunderstandings and discords. In breaking with the past, ignorance deprives us of the lessons of wisdom which are always drawn from earlier misfortunes. It is ignorance again which makes us indisposed towards one another and leads us to throw ourselves into the arms of every new stranger for the sake of good fellowship. In a word, it is ignorance which breaks the links of fraternity which exist naturally between children of the same country. No matter what has been said, it is not by erasing history that we arrive at unity. The more we lose the trace of our first steps, the less will we achieve our goal.'

— *Pierre-Gustave-Louis Borde*
'The History of the Island of Trinidad Under the Spanish Government',
Vol. II (1498-1622), 1876.

J Stewart Del.

1. Bar-Tailed Humming Bird.   2. Stoke's Humming Bird.   3. Underwood's Humming Bird.
4. Gould's Humming Bird.   5. Topaz-Throated Humming Bird.

J. Bishop Sc.

THE BOOK OF TRINIDAD

Gerard Besson
&
Bridget Brereton

ISBN - 976-8054-36-0

Second Edition

Produced and
designed by
Paria Publishing Co. Ltd.
66 Woodford Street, Newtown, Port of Spain,
Republic of Trinidad and Tobago, West Indies.
Printed by Caribbean Paper & Printed Products

Boundary Road, San Juan, Republic of **Trinidad & Tobago**

Contents

Contents

Preface

This publication, The Book of Trinidad has had a fairly long genesis (about five years) and on behalf of Dr. Bridget Brereton, who is presently Reader in Caribbean Social History as well as Head of the History Department of the University of the West Indies, St. Augustine and myself I would like to thank all those who have contributed of their time and their resources and their positive encouragement in making it a reality.

Words cannot express the gratitude we feel towards Mr. Andre Lange who with a spontaneity and an act of, to us, unsurpassed generosity made the printing of this work possible. Quite taken by it I asked Andre one day, "How come?" and he looked at me with mild surprise and then perhaps a little shyly he pointed up to the heavens and said "for the ancestors;". Therefore we have dedicated this body of work to all the ancestors of all our people in loving memory.

Because nothing is more unfair than to judge men and events of the past by the ideas of the present, we have attempted to assemble in this book as wide as possible a collection of paintings, lithographs, and photos in the hope of bringing to light visual truth about the way we were. Beyond this we have created an anthology, excerpts from the writings of travellers and administrators local men and women who knew Trinidad in those formative years. It would be useful to point out at this stage that often what some of them had to say about the conditions of the place and the nature of people is not always complimentary, History however is about truth, therefore in the spirit of history we have not censored their writings. Also running through these pages is a chronology of events great and small. In fact there are four chronologies these being the works of Daniel Hart who published in the 1869; José Bodu who produced *Trinidadiana* in the 1900's; The Port of Spain Gazette Special Centenary Issue, 1826-1926 and Harry Pitts One Hundred Years Together. And then there are the marvellous recipes of Jean de Boissiere to bring a rich and pungent flavour, a spicy tang a fragrant memory of Creole cooking.

We would like to express our thanks to Mrs. Olga Mavrogordato for making available to us her large collection of old photographs and for allowing us access to Conrad Bismark Franklin's collected papers; these yielded special gems such as the *Discovery of Trinidad* by Ferdinand Columbus the son of Christopher Columbus and an account of the Discovery of the Island by the Admiral himself; a judgement by John Nihell Trinidad first Chief Judge; The Great Fire of 1808 and much more. Her generosity of spirit and active critical faculty was of considerable help in the formulating of the original draft. Our grateful thanks must also go to Mrs. Hélène Farfan who very kindly allowed us to reproduce her father's collection of photographs. Thanks as well to Gregor Duruty who in the weeks before he died having reached the great age of 95, made available his archives, his prodigious memory and with loving kindness guided and encouraged us. Gregor made one request and that is that the memory of those who served and of those who fell in the Great War should not be forgotten and space permitting we have endeavoured to keep our promise to this grand old man. A special thanks to Miss Mildred Cambridge who gave us permission to reproduce many objects from the Tom Cambridge Collection. To my dear friend Peter Shim who painstakingly reproduced many of the very old engravings and rendered in pen drawings the old estate houses, my grateful thanks. Our gratitude must also go to Professor Carl Campbell for his kind help and contributions and also to Mrs. Marianne Ramesar for hers. These two fine academians together with the articles written by Andrew Carr and Andrew Pearse served to bring into a better perspective the historical and cultural processes at work in the society during the 19th and early 20th century.

We have made every effort to source and acknowledge and seek permission for the material reproduced herein and in anticipation of any lapses sincerely extend our sincere apologies. In closing we would like to say thanks to our friend Sue-Anne Gomes for the writing, collecting, arranging, editing, helping and encouraging that she so readily did and to Simon Lee and Candyce Kelshall for the help in proof-reading this work, also to Jo-Anne Ferreira and Elizabeth Mowser.

Both Messrs. Albert Hadeed and Joe Sabga were of invaluable help to us and so to was Mr. I.P. George. To the former Chief Librarian of the University of the West Indies Dr. Alma Jordan, and to the staff of the University's Library and especially Dr. Margaret Rouse-Jones we would like to express our grateful thanks. We truly appreciate the tireless dedication and patience shown by Mrs. Angela Greene in doing the typesetting for The Book of Trinidad.

And to my wife Sheelagh for her help and encouragement during the period in which The Book of Trinidad was produced I would like to say thanks for everything.

G.A.B.

Introduction

'. . . Yea, the first morning of creation wrote what the last dawn of reckoning shall read'. The words of Omar Khayyam, the great poet of Persia evoke a sense of awe and one feels caught by the idea of being perpetually, in a great state of stop . . . but not a stillness, for patterns pervade the human condition and history tends to repeat itself.

Another poet an Englishman by the name of John Donne perceived time and man's place in it thus: 'Creatures of an inferior nature are possessed with the present', he went on to declare 'man is a future creature'.

In doing this Donne sensed one of the basic distinctions between man and practically all other animals. The human being has an ingrained sense of memory and anticipation of the future. In the pursuit of order mankind created a framework of past, present and future. And in so doing realized that the chief enemy of life is not death, but forgetfulness and stupidity. The simple fact is we lose direction too easily. This is the great penalty that life has paid for descending into matter; a kind of partial amnesia.

History is about organising the past, preserving in commonality the memory of shared experiences, many of which are not our own nor in fact those of our immediate antecedants. In preparing this book that we have boldly called 'The Book of Trinidad' we have acted, not necessarily as historians generally do, which is to record and illustrate events and ideas of the past, but rather we have attempted to correct ingrained perceptions and to introduce new views in the hope that our present stage of development may be more readily assessed and that we do not fall victim to past mistakes. We *must* remember . . . and we must remember everything.

The collective experience of the people of Trinidad is a relatively short one when compared to the other islands in the Caribbean. It is also a very multi-faceted one full of irony and surprises. From the very beginning while other islands may have had one or two tribes of native people Trinidad appears to have had several. After the period of the European discovery, while other islands – Tobago for example – were being developed socially and economically, Trinidad remained virtually neglected. With the exception of the myths of El Dorado and the exploits of Sir Walter Raleigh and the Spanish Conquistadors, dimly flickering like old gold or fools' gold, the period from the arrival of Columbus in these waters, to the time of the French Revolution some three hundred years later, is one when the changing of the seasons was the only constant in an otherwise timeless world. Timeless, that is, in the European sense but not so for the tribal peoples, who with the advent of the foreigners entered into the twilight of their age.

The introduction of the Cedula of Population in 1783 quickened the pace of change and introduced cosmopolitanism. Hundreds of Catholics, mostly of French descent both black and white sought to establish themselves on this beautiful, scarcely populated Spanish island. The introduction of the system of African slavery opened up the land to agriculture which flourished. By the time of the British conquest the French were firmly established. As a consequence of all this, Trinidad a former Spanish possession populated by mostly French speaking inhabitants became a British colony in the unique position of maintaining a Spanish legal code for over three decades, in the beginning of the 19th century.

The remarkable thing in the development of Trinidad has been the make up of its population, perpetuated perhaps by the legal precedent of the Cedula of Population. Literally, people from all over the world found a home in the island by virtue of their Catholicism, or other considerations. Truly antique strains, such as the Rada from West Africa and Maronite Christians from the Ottoman Empire, Brahmins from India, French aristocrats; Corsican revolutionaries, Portuguese converted to Protestantism from Madeira, Chinese peasants, liberated Africans and Shi'ite Muslims who have continued to the present to celebrate Muharrum (Hosay) were all poured into the mould of British colonialism and stamped by the prejudices of the time.

The occupying British felt no need to retain the memory of Amerindian, Spanish or French experiences and the very nature of slavery lent itself to the eradication of religious beliefs, tribal affiliations, original names and such like. The process of forgetting our past commenced on a grand scale and was institutionalized by colonial fiat. The history of the island was not taught.

Despite this the collective memory of the people continued to survive serving to produce a distinctive culture, which was remarkably unique. This predominantly Afro-French Creole culture dominated 19th century Trinidad. All the while a steady flow of immigrants from the Indian sub continent continued to pour in, having been brought to work in the cane fields abandoned by the freed negro slaves. The very nature of the colonial system perpetuated 'an apartness' between these new arrivals and the older inhabitants. In this way we became increasingly 'a nation of minorities' bound together by loyalty to the British Crown.

Over a period of time, as Arnold Toynbee remarks in 'A Study of History'

> 'This state of mind takes practical effect in an act of self-surrender to the melting pot; and in the process of social disintegration an identical mood manifests itself in every province of social life in religion and literature and language and art as well as in the wider and vaguer sphere of manners and customs'.

With the advent of Independence after some 150 years of Crown colony rule it is remarkable that the history of these islands has hardly been studied in itinerary and far less, been passed on to the young. The era of Independence seemed to mean the forgetting of our collective past and in fact the whole scale dereliction of the colourfully quilted national fabric. The shared experience of all the 19th century and half of the 20th has been debunked as colonial and useless.

That this nationally institutionalized amnesia has created in Trinidad's body politic, a sense of loss, is to say the least. A yearning to 'bring back the old time way' is not at all surprising.

In the Book of Trinidad we have attempted not so much to bring back the old time days but to provide a collection of metaphors that could serve as catalysts to help us catch a glimpse of our true selves, in that infinity of mirrors that reflects both our past and future, all at the same time.

Gérard A. Besson
September 2nd, 1991

TRINIDAD
THE LAND OF BEGINNINGS

Gérard Besson

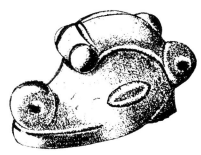

Bottle heads
Prehistoric objects from a shell heap at Erin Bay
collected by J. Walter Fewkes.

The island of Trinidad has about it many unique and special qualities — placed as it is in the mouth of one of South America's great river systems – Trinidad has the continental climate of the Coastal Guianas; the placid Gulf of Paria on our Western Coast is made sweet by the mighty Orinoco at its flood and the great chain of the Andean Mountains coming out of South America turns sharply to the right into Venezuela, then to cross like so many stepping stones, the islands in the Dragon's Mouth - to form a miniature of itself in the beautiful mountains of our own Northern Range.

It was from this vast and ancient wilderness that the first visitors to our shores arrived, perhaps as early as 7,200 years ago. These early people inhabited the Banwari Hill at the edge of the Oropouche Lagoon in South-West Trinidad. They were the earliest inhabitants of Trinidad of which we have proof, thus making Trinidad the oldest settled island in the West Indies. The Banwari people were fishermen, hunters of small game and collectors of wild edible fruits, vegetables, nuts and shell-fish. The Meso Indians, as they are called by archaeologists, had developed a great familiarity with the sea: developing the skill to build boats and the ability to navigate, enabling them to explore and settle the islands of the Caribbean archipelago. These ancient inhabitants occupied this site at Banwari Hill for some 1,500 years. Remembered now only by the scattered shards of broken pottery – some striped red and white, and by the place-names left behind, silent momentoes in a book now forever closed.

Closed, but not completely lost, for the names, as given to rivers, bays, towns, points and districts in our island and the broken bits of pots and heaps of shell tell a story. In so far as place-names are concerned, there are no less than 150 of these in Trinidad that are actually of Amerindian origin. Some of them are:- Erin, Mucurapo, Piarco, Mayaro, Cumana, Chaguaramas, Moruga, Ortoire, Oropouche, Nariva, Guayaguayare, Maraval, Tunapuna, Curepe, Ariapita, Couva. Many of these place-names represent Amerindian names of plants, trees, and animals. For instance, Mucurapo (formerly Cumucurapo) is derived from *apo* ("place of") and *kumaka* ("silk cotton tree"), hence "place of the silk cotton tree". Chaguaramas includes the Amerindian name for the Palmiste palm, *chaguaramo,* as well as Mayo, Bejucal, and Los Charros-the names of particular plants. Tunapuna is derived from *tona* ("water") and *pona* ("on"); the name thus simply means "on the river".[1]

The story they tell is that this island is a land of beginnings, the first step in a vast migratory trek that would take these children of the high woods and rivers of the Mainland first to Trinidad and then to all the islands of the Caribbean Sea.

These first peoples contributed to Trinidad its first and to this day, most unique characteristic; its sense of cosmopolitanism. For as P.G.L.Borde notes in his seminal work 'The History of Trinidad Under the Spanish Government': "The other islands of the Antilles, even the largest, were inhabited by only one or two, or at the most three Amerindian tribes. Trinidad had an agglomeration of the greater part of those found on the neighbouring continent within a radius of more than two hundred and fifty miles". It would appear that at the time of its discovery by Christopher Columbus in 1498, it was occupied by several tribal peoples, speaking dialects belonging to two major Amerindian language families: Arawakan and Cariban. Columbus thinking that he had discovered India, called the aboriginal people he found living in the Caribbean area Indians, hence the name American Indians or Amerindians for short.

Who were the Amerindians of Trinidad and Tobago at the time of the discovery and how did they actually live? According to the earliest written records, Trinidad was inhabited by some 40,000 Amerindians, belonging to different tribes. The south coast was occupied by the *Shebaio* and *Arawak (Lokono)* tribes of which the Arawak also inhabited the lower Orinoco area and the coast of Guyana. The *Nepoio* lived on the south east and east coast of Trinidad. They, too, inhabited parts of the lower Orinoco valley. Amerindians of the Yao tribe had settled along the south west Trinidad coast.

Whereas the Shebaio and Arawak spoke Arawakan dialects, the Yao and Nepoio spoke forms of Cariban. Finally, the *Carinepagoto,* who occupied north west Trinidad, probably belonged to the Cariban language family as well.

At the time of the discovery several other Amerindian tribes must have resided in Trinidad, but their names have not been preserved. It is likely, for instance, that Cariban-speaking groups occupied most of north east Trinidad circa A.D. 1500. During the early seventeenth century Tobago was inhabited by the Cariban-speaking *Kalina;* afterwards *Kalinag* (Island-Caribs) occupied the island. Contrary to their name, these Island-Caribs spoke a basically Arawakan dialect.

The Trinidad Amerindians are described by the sixteenth century Spanish chroniclers as well-proportioned and of lighter complexion than the Island-Caribs of the Lesser Antilles. They went entirely naked except for girdles and headbands of multi-coloured cotton cloth. They wore their hair long and parted in the middle. Bodies were painted red and feathers were used for decoration. Tribal headmen wore a golden crown and wore golden eagle-shaped ornaments on their breasts.

The Amerindians used all sorts of beads of stone and bone, carved stone amulets, pearls, and animal teeth for decoration. Stone for making axes and other implements were obtained from Paria and the Guianas. Golden objects and other products of South America were bartered with the Orinoco Indians for pearls, salt, and, probably, tobacco. The Gulf of Paria formed the main link in the Amerindian trade routes which were confined to the waterways.

Subsistence was based on the cultivation of cassava, maize, tobacco, beans, squashes, and peppers. The Amerindians practised shifting cultivation. At the end of

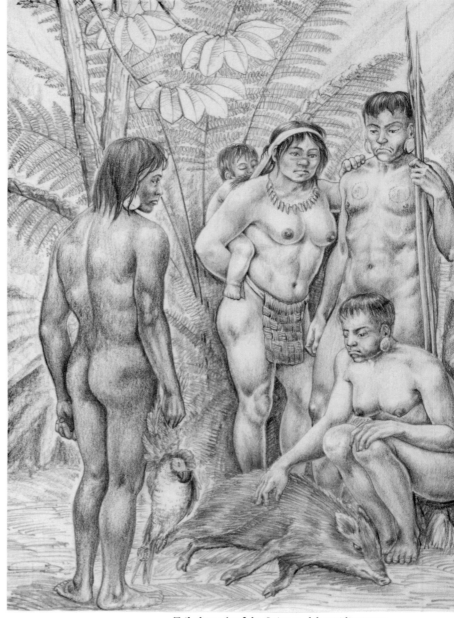

Tribal people of the Orinoco delta with parrots and wild pigs. After Rugendas by Peter Shim.

Opposite:

Early 18th century engraving of tribal people dancing. A herb possibly kohiba, being smoked in a long pipe called a tavaco, is being blown into the faces of the dancers. This pipe, a tavaco, later gave its name to tabaco and to the island of Tobago, which may have been originally called La Magadalená by the earliest cartographers.

the dry season they burned their fields in the forest and planted them at the beginning of the wet season. Plots were abandoned after a couple of harvests when the soil had become depleted.

The Amerindians cultivated cotton for clothes and hammocks, and annatoo for body paint. Fishing, hunting, and the gathering of shells, crabs and turtle eggs still accounted for an important part of their diet, especially to supplement the cassava-based meals with protein rich food. Division of labour was simple and confined to that between man and woman. The men cleared the forest for gardens, they hunted and fished, whereas the women planted, weeded and harvested the manioc roots; they also prepared the meals.

The Amerindians lived in villages consisting of at most several hundred inhabitants. Their houses, described as bell-shaped, were moved frequently. Society was loosely organized. The village headman (the "chief") was elder kinsman and relative by marriage to most of the village people, he did not have much power. Chiefs were chosen by the village people for their prowess during war expeditions; they were the only men with more than one wife.

Feasts were held on the occasion of ceremonies like the initiation of chiefs or their burials, and as part of the preparations for a war expedition. Religion was characterized by a universal belief in spirits of nature; deities were not worshiped. Medicine men served as curers and advisors due to their ability to contact spirits. Chiefs were often medicine men as well.

Trade and war were expressions of the same phenomenon. Villages often formed alliances against villages of other tribes. Men fought with darts thrown

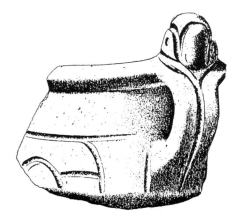

Sections of Vessel with animal heads.
Prehistoric objects from a shell heap at Erin Bay
collected by J. Walter Fewkes.

An Amerindian family on the island of St. Vincent in the later half of the 18th century, drawn by Agostino Brunias and published in Brian Edward's 'History of the West Indies'.

from atlatls having hooks on the back, with sling stones, and with bows and arrows. The Trinidad Amerindians are said to have been excellent bowmen. Their arrows were feathered, tipped with bone points, and poisoned. Warriors also used shields. War parties signalled with drums and shell trumpets. The medicine men took snuff to communicate with the spirits, so as to predict the best time to attack.

The other tribes' villages were raided by surprise. The older people were killed and the young men and women brought home as slaves but a few of the war prisoners were ritually killed. However, most war expeditions ended in just a skirmish, after which both parties went home, without any casualties.

The Amerindian warfare never interrupted the mutual commerce between otherwise hostile tribes. The Island-Caribs, for instance, kept a lively trade with the Arawaks of Trinidad in the golden breast ornaments which were worn only by chiefs. The Arawaks exchanged them for their own products on the Orinoco river. They received these ornaments from tribes who had obtained them as far west as the highlands of Colombia."[2]

Although these different tribes had their own dialects it seems that Cariban/Arawakan was the dominant language of the island, much as English is today. Trinidad appears to have been a polyglot country from its very beginning - for even now, close on 500 years after its discovery, there are remnants of Spanish, French, Chinese, Portuguese and Hindi speaking people. There are groups of Islamic speaking people from both the Far and Middle East and memories of African dialects, especially Yoruba, contained in song and religious ritual.

Sources for material used:
(1) From Articles Published by Dr. Arie Boomert
in the Trinidad Naturalist.
(2) Id. Ibid.
Reproductions of Carib implements from the Tom Cambridge collection.
Prehistoric objects Reprinted from the American Anthropologist
Vol. 16 No. 2 April - June 1914.
History of Trinidad under the Spanish Government by
Pierre Gustave Louis Borde Book 1 1883.

The reconstruction of an Amerindian village
by Peter Shim from 'Sketches of Amerindian Tribes'
by Edward Goodall 1941.

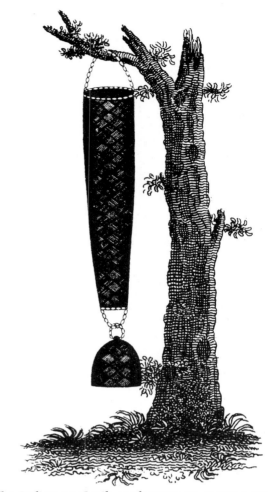

The Indian or Carib couleccure or manioc strainer
and the weights hung on it.

Carib girl Arima late 19th century, photographed by Marshall.
The Book of Trinidad T.B. Jackson 1904.

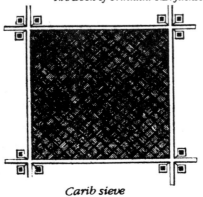

Carib sieve

Carib pannier

Carib carbet left open to show the hammocks.

Bacassas with one mast.

Carib paddle.

Pirogue without a mast.

Carib man, Stark's Guide to Trinidad, late 19th century,
and most probably of Guyana or Venezuela.

"The Child awakes
What does she see?
Where are the woods,
Where is the sea?"

Sainte Marie de Teteron
from Russel's 'Legends of the Bocas'

Carib Mace or Club

From objects engraved for the
American Antiquarian Society.

THE ORIGIN OF CARIBS
Collected by Walter E. Roth

The water - Camudi had an Indian woman for a sweetheart. During the day he took the form of a snake; at night, he was a person like myself. The couple used to meet at the water side, and hence the girl's parents knew nothing about their being so fond of each other. After she became pregnant, a baby Camudi was born. The little one used to appear when she reached the river bank, swim about, and after a time return to its nesting place. Now, as she stayed so long each time at the water's side, the old father said to his two sons, "What is the matter with your sister, why does she take so long to bathe?" Accordingly, the brothers, watching her go down to the stream, (videt serpentum parvan exire atque serpentum magnam intrare). They also saw the huge Camudi bring his infant son something to eat and saw the baby take the father's place when the latter left. When they arrived home, the sons complained to the old man about what they had seen: he told them to kill both the snakes. So on the next occasion they killed the huge Camudi, and seizing the baby serpent, carried it far away, back into the bush, where they chopped it up into small pieces. Some months after when hunting in the neighbourhood, the brothers heard a great noise and the sound of voices coming from the very same direction, and going to ascertain the cause, found four houses in the identical spot where they had cut up the baby Camudi, all occupied by Indians who had grown out of the fragments of the snake. In the first hut the house-master said he was glad to welcome his two uncles, but in the other three, the occupants wanted to kill them for having destroyed their sister's child from whom they had all sprung. But the first house-master said, "No, don't do that, because these two visitors are uncles to all of you and you must not have a bad mind towards them". Thus, it happened that the two brothers got away without further molestation, and on arriving home told their old father how the snake fragments had grown into people. When he expressed a wish to see his grandchildren, his two sons led the way into the bush, and he was very glad to see his numerous progeny, with whom he made good friends, and they all drank paiwarri. Thus the Carib nation arose from the water - Camudi.

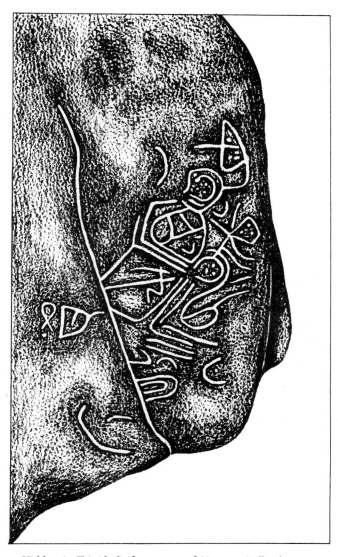

Hidden in Trinidad's forest, east of Maracas Valley lies a rare haven of archaeological finds. The rock drawings of Caurita. They are of unknown age and their meanings are equally as mysterious. The actual rocks are large eched and chiselled Amerindian drawings across the surfaces of the rocks highly likely to be rendered of or depicting their existing culture.

The Prehistoric Amerindians left their mark not in written material but in the form of petroghyphs. It is virtually impossible to interpret stones with any accuracy at all since traces of Amerindian religion, magic and mythology is unknown. This has not detered archaeologists from theorizing over the rock drawings. They have been seen as tribal boundary markers, symbols of heavenly bodies and constellations, recording devices, Amerindian dance masks, direction marks and illustrations of myths and tales. These are a few of the more serious philosophies of the rock culture.

The reason for our prehistoric forebearers engraving these petroghyphs remains a well chiselled mystery, but these artifacts also remain to be one of Trinidad's most revered and oldest monuments.

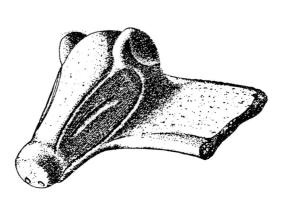

Bottle heads from a prehistoric shell heap from Erin Bay Trinidad collected by J. Walter Fewkes.

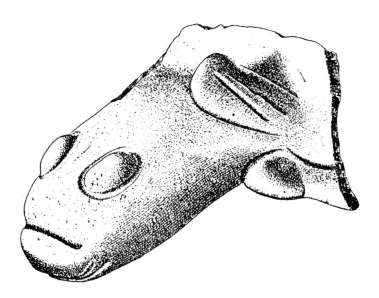

Early 18th century engraving of a Carib religious festival.

THE SHREWD LITTLE BOY AND THE HEBU

Collected by Walter E. Roth

A woman, having to make starch out of the Ite (Mauritia) tree, left her little children - two girls, behind the house. While she was away, Kan-Nassa, a bush spirit, came along, disguised as their grandmother, and said "Come along my little girls, I will take you to your mother". But instead of doing that the Hebu led them far away into the bush, till they reached a creek where the old woman sat down and made a basket. When it was completed, she told the youngsters to get inside; once they were in, she closed the top and threw it into the water, where the children were soon drowned. Kan-Nassa then went to another house, where a little boy and girl had been left in charge during their parents' absence, and similarly disguised as their grandmother, repeated her story. She led the children as before to the creek, where she proposed making another basket and they started playing around her. "You children," she said, "must not play behind my back. Play in front of me where I can see you." Now, the very fact of being told not to go behind her made the boy all the more anxious to do what had been forbidden. So while playing in front with his sister, he made an excuse to slip away behind and then he saw the lower part of the old woman's back, which was all aglow with the fire that she carried there. He now knew that she was a Hebu, and getting back to his little sister, carried her home. But before going he called out: "Kan-Nassa, Kan-Nassa!" So angered and dismayed was the spirit at being discovered and hearing her name called out that she burst into wind and flame and flew away.

THE SONG OF THE TURTLE

An Amerindian Tale retold by Gérard Besson

Once, a long, long, time ago, when the Great Spirit Yacahuna ruled over all living things, there appeared in a village on a high hill in the centre of the island, two boys, twins. When they were grown they climbed the highest mountain on the island in search of wisdom. At the very top of the mountain they discovered a great cave and in this cave, an ancient woman who tended a fire that never died. she had as a companion a giant snake, so long that no one in living memory had ever seen the whole of it. It had a great red stone in the middle of its head and as she tended her fire it would rise up and hover above her. From this wise woman and her terrible companion the boys acquired great knowledge and after several years returned to the people on the high hill in the centre of the island. The boys grew into men and were the teachers and the healers of their people. After many years had passed and they had become very old, they left the village one day, walking hand in hand down the high hill and upon reaching a wide lagoon that lay at the foot of the hill, they waded into it and began slowly to swim towards the other side. A party of people on the opposite bank saw the old men enter the water and saw them swimming across. Much to their surprise, when the two old men approached the bank they were no longer men at all, but two giant turtles that pulled themselves up on the sand and from the shells of those great turtles there emerged two beautiful boys who ran hand in hand into the high woods – made by the Great Spirit Yacahuna, young and innocent again, to go in search of the old woman and her giant snake to acquire wisdom so that they might bring healing and knowledge to their people.

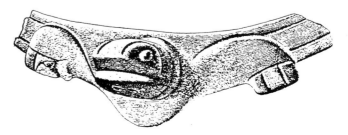

Section of rim of vessel
Prehistoric objects from a shell heap at Erin Bay collected by J. Walter Fewkes.

An old engraving of Caribs eating human flesh. Paria Prints

The Discovery Of TRINIDAD

Ferdinand Columbus

On Tuesday, the last day of July 1498, the Admiral having sailed many days west insomuch that in his judgement the Carribe Islands were north of him, he resolved not to hold that course any longer but to make for Hispaniola not only because he was in great want of water but also because all his provinces perished and he was afraid lest during his absence some mutiny or disorder had happened among the people he left there, as in effect there had, as we shall show hereafter.

Thereupon altering his course from the west, he stood north, thinking to light on some of the Caribbe Islands, there to refresh his men and take in wood and water of which he had great want.

As he was then sailing one day about noon, Alonzo Perez Nirando, a sailor of the Town of Gullva, going up to the round top saw land to the westward at about 15 leagues distance and there appeared three mountains all at the same time but not long after they perceived the land stretched out towards the north east as far as the eye could reach and that did not seem to be the end.

Having given thanks to God and said the Salve Regina and other prayers the seamen use in time of distress and joy, the Admiral called that land the Island of the Trinity as well because he had before thoughts of giving that name to the first land he found as in return because it had pleased God to show him three mountains all together as has been said.

He sailed due west to make a cape that appeared to south of him and making for the south side of the Island till he came to anchor five leagues beyond a point which he called de la Galera or of the Galley because of a rock that lay near the point and at a distance looked like a galley under sail.

Having now but one cask of water for all his ship's crew and the other ships being in same condition, there being no conveniency here to take in any, on·Wednesday

CHRISTOPHER COLUMBUS

following in the morning he continued his course still west and cast anchor at another point which he called de la Playa or of the Strand where the people landed and took water in a delicate brook without seeing any town or people there though along the coast they left behind, they had seen many houses and towns.

True it is they found the tokens of fishermen who had fled leaving behind them some of the fishing tackle. They also saw the prints of the feet of beasts which seemed to be of goats and saw the bones of one but the head being without horns they thought it might be some catamountain or monkey as they afterwards found it to be, seeing abundance of those cats in Paria.

The same day being the first of August, sailing between Cape Galera and that of la Playa, they discovered to the southwards the Continent about 25 leagues distance as they guessed but they, thinking it to be another island, called it the Isla Santa or Holy Island. The land they saw of the Trinity between the two points was thirty leagues in length, east and west, without any harbour but all the country very pleasant with trees down to the sea and abundance of towns.

This space they ran in very short time because the current of the sea set so very violent westward that it looked like a rapid river both day and night and at all hours notwithstanding the tide flowed and ebbed along the shore about 40 paces as happens at St. Lucar de Barrameda when there are floods for though the water rises and falls never so much yet it never ceases running towards the sea.

CHAPTER LXIX.—*How the Admiral sailed to the Cape called Punta del Arenal and a canoe came out to talk to him.*

Perceiving that they could have no account of the people at this Cape, and there was no convenience for taking water without excessive labour and that there was no convenience for careening the ships and getting provisions, the next day being the 2nd August, the Admiral went on to another point of land which seemed to be the most westerly in that Island and called it del Arenal where he came to anchor thinking that the easterly winds which reign there would not be so troublesome to the boats in going backwards and forwards.

On the way before they came to the point, a canoe began to follow them with 25 men in it and stopped at a cannon shot distance calling out and talking very loud. Nothing could be understood though it was supposed they enquired who our men were and whence they came as other Indians used to do at first.

There being no possibility of persuading them with any words to come aboard, they began to show them several things that they might covet to have, such as little brass basins, looking glasses and other things the rest of the Indians used to make great account of. But though this drew them a little, yet they soon stopped again and therefore the more to allure them, the Admiral ordered one to get upon the poop with a tabor and pipe and some young fellows to dance. As soon as the Indians saw this, they put themselves into a posture of defence laying hold of their targets and shooting their arrows at those who danced who, by the Admiral's command that these people might not go unpunished or continue, the Christians leaving this dance, began to shoot with their crossbows so that they were glad to draw off and made to another caravel clapping close to its side without any apprehension. The pilot of this ship went over into the canoe and gave them some things they were well pleased with and said if they had been ashore they would have brought him bread from their houses and so they went towards land nor would they stop in the ship, ere one displeased the Admiral.

The account they gave of them was that they were well shaped people and whiter than those of the other islands and that they wore their hair long like women bound with small strings and covered their privities with little clouts.

CHAPTER LXX. — *Of the danger the ships were in entering the mouth of the channel they called boca del Drago or the Dragon's Mouth and how Paria was discovered being the first discovery of the Continent.*

As soon as the ships had anchored at Punta del Arenal, the Admiral sent the boats ashore for water and to get some information of the Indians but they could do neither that country being very low and unpeopled. He therefore ordered them to dig trenches on the Island and by good luck they found them ready made and full of excellent water and it was thought the fishermen had made them. Having taken what they wanted, the Admiral resolved to proceed on to another mouth or channel which appeared towards the northwest which he afterwards called Boca del Drago or the Dragon's Mouth to distinguish it from that where he was to which he had given the name of Boca de la Sierpe or the Serpent's Mouth.

These two mouths or channels like the Dardenelles were made by the two westernmost points of the Trinity Island and two others of the Continent and lay almost north and south of one another. In the midst of that where the Admiral anchored was a rock which he called El Gallo, that is the Cock.

Through the mouth he called Boca del Sierpe, the water continually ran so furiously northwards as if it had been the mouth of some great river which was the reason for giving it that name because of the fright it put them into. For as they lay very securely at anchor there came a stronger stream of water than usual with a hideous noise running through that mouth northward. And another current running out of the Gulf now called Paria opposite to that before mentioned, they met with hideous roaring and caused the sea to swell up like a high mountain or ridge of hills along that channel which mountains soon came towards the ships to the great terror of all the men fearing they could be overset. But it pleased God, it passed under or rather lifted them up without doing them any harm though it drew the anchor of one of them carrying the vessel away but by help of their sails they escaped the danger not without mortal fear of being lost.

That furious current being past, the Admiral, considering the danger he was in there, stood for the Dragon's Mouth which was between the north point of the Trinity Island and the east point of Paria yet went not through it at that time but sailed along the south coast of Paria westward believing it to be an island and hoping to find a way out northwards to Hispaniola. And though there were many ports along the coast of Paria, he would put into none, all the sea being a harbour locked in with the Continent.

CHAPTER LXXI. — *How there was some gold and pearls found in Paria and a people of good disposition.*

The Admiral being at anchor on the 5th of August, it being his particular devotion never to weigh on a Sunday, he sent the boats ashore where they found an abundance of fruit of the same sort they had seen in the other Islands, great numbers of trees and signs of people who had fled for fear of the Christians. But being unwilling to lose time he sailed down the coast 15 leagues further without going into any harbour for fear he should miss the wind to bring him out.

Being at anchor on the coast at the end of these 15 leagues, there came out a canoe to the Caravel called El Correo, with three men in it; the pilot knowing how much the Admiral coveted to receive some information from the people he pretended to talk to them and let himself into the canoe and the Spaniards in the boat took these three men and carried them to the Admiral who made very much of them and sent them ashore with many fights where there appeared an abundance of Indians.

These, hearing the good account the three gave them, came all in their canoes to barter for such things as they had which were much the same as had been seen in the islands before discovered only that here they had no target nor poisoned arrows which these people do not use but only the cannibals. Their drink was a sort of liquor as white as milk and another somewhat blackish, tasting like green wine made of grapes not quite ripe, but they could not learn what fruit it was made of. They wore cotton cloths well wove of several colours about the bigness of a handkerchief, some bigger and some less; what they most valued of our things was brass and especially bells.

The people seem to be more civilised and tractable than those of Hispaniola. They cover their nakedness with one of the cloths above-mentioned and have another wrapped around the head. The women cover nothing not even their privities; the same they do in Trinity Island. They saw nothing of value here except some little plates of gold hung about their necks for which reason and because the Admiral could not stay to dive into the secrets of the country, he ordered six of those Indians to be taken and continued his voyage westward believing the land of Paria, which he called Holy Island, was no continent. Soon afterwards another island appeared towards the south and another no less than that towards the west, all high land and well peopled; the Indians had more plates of gold about their necks than the others and abundance of guanins which is very low gold. They said it was produced in other western islands, inhabited by people that eat men.

The women had strings of beads about their arms and among them very fine large and small pearls in strings some whereof were got in exchange to send their

The six ships of Christopher Columbus third voyage set sail from Spain on the 30th May 1498 making for the island of Gomera in the Canary Islands. Here the fleet divided, three ships were to sail for Hispaniola with men and supplies. The other three under the command of the Admiral were to sail further south than they had ever. The 'Santa Maria de Guia' described as a noah which is said to have been about two thirds the size of the original Santa Maria the Caravels 'La Castilla' and 'La Gorda' sometimes called 'Correo'. Above, the 'Santa Maria' of the first voyage after a drawing by Columbus from Nelsons West Indian Histories Book I.

*The fourth voyage of Christopher Columbus
illustrated by Jeffrey Pataysingh.*

The Admiral of the Ocean Sea Christopher Columbus being greeted by an Amerindian Casique on the island of Cuba. Where he had landed on October 28, 1492 at a place called Gibara. He was impressed by its size and the beauty of its forest. Columbus spent some time exploring it in the hope of finding gold. Lithograph by Agostino Brunias from Brian Edwards. History of the West Indies – second edition 1805.

Catholic Majesties as a sample. Being asked where they found these things they made signs to show that in the oister shells which were taken westward of that land of Paria and beyond it towards the north, they were found.

Upon this the Admiral stayed there to know more of that good discovery and sent the boats ashore where all the people of the country that had flocked together appeared so tractable and friendly that they importuned the Christians to go along with them to a house not far off where they gave them to eat and a great deal of wine. Then from that house, which it is likely was the King's Palace, they carried them to another which was his son's and showed them the same kindness.

They were all in general whiter than any they had seen in the Indies and of better aspect and shape with their hair cut short by their ears after the Spanish fashion. From them they understood that land was called Paria and that they would be glad to be in amity with the Christians. Then they departed from them and returned to the ships.

CHAPTER LXXII. — HOW THE ADMIRAL PASSED THROUGH THE BOCA DEL DRAGO AND THE DANGER HE WAS IN THERE.

The Admiral holding on his voyage westward, they still found less and less water insomuch that being come through four or five fathoms, they found but two and a half at ebb, for the tide differed from that at Trinity Island; for at the leagues to westward, it ran but one and then always whether ebb or flood, the current ran west and here upon the ebb they ran east and upon the flood west; there the water was but brackish, here it was like river water.

The Admiral perceiving the difference and how little water he found, dared to proceed no further in his ship which required three fathoms of water being of 100 tons and therefore came to anchor on that coast which was very safe, being a port like a horseshoe locked with that land on all sides.

However he sent the little caravel called El Cerreo or the Post, to discover whether there was any pass westward among the islands. She having gone but a little way returned the next day, being the 11th August, saying that at the westernmost point of that sea there was mouth or opening two leagues over from north to south and within it a round bay with four other little bays, one towards each quarter of heaven; that from each flowed a river whose water made that sea so sweet which was yet much sweeter further in, adding that all that land which seemed to be island, was on the same continent and that they had everywhere four or five fathoms of water and such abundance of weeds that they hindered the sailing.

The Admiral therefore, being certain that he could not get out westward, that same day stood back to the eastward designing to pass the straight which he saw between the land the Indians call Paria and the Trinity. In this straight there are four little islands next the point of the Trinity which he called Cape Boca because it was blunt, west upon the point of the continent which he called Cape Lapa and in the middle.

The reason why he called this the Dragon's Mouth was because it is very dangerous by reason of the abundance of fresh water that struggles to get out there into the sea and makes three boisterous channels extending from east to west of the strait. And because as he was sailing through, the wind failed him and he was in danger of being drove on some sand or rock, therefore he with reasons gave it a name answerable to that of the other mouth where he was in no less danger

Columbus landing in Hispaniola from a wood cut of 1494. Nelsons West Indian Histories, Vol. II.

as we said above.

But it pleased God that what they most dreaded should be their greatest safety, the strength of the current carrying them off. Therefore on Monday the 17th August, he began to sail westward along the coast of Paria in order to stand over afterwards for Hispaniola giving thanks to God who delivered him from so many troubles and dangers, still showing him new countries full of peaceable people and great wealth especially that which he certainly concluded to be continent because of the great extent of that Gulf of Pearls, of the rivers which ran from it, of the sea which was all sweet water and by the authority of Esdras in the 8th chapter of the 4th Book where he says – That dividing the globe into seven parts, only one of them is covered with water — for all the Indians of the Caribbee Islands had told him that there was a vast land southward.

Source:— 'The History of the life and actions of Admiral Christopher Columbus and of his discovery of the West Indies called the New World now in possession of His Catholic Majesty'. Written by his own son D. Ferdinand Columbus. From Churchill's "Collection of Voyages and Travels." Vol. II, 1704 Chapter LXVII. How the Admiral discovered the Island of the Trinity and saw the Continent.

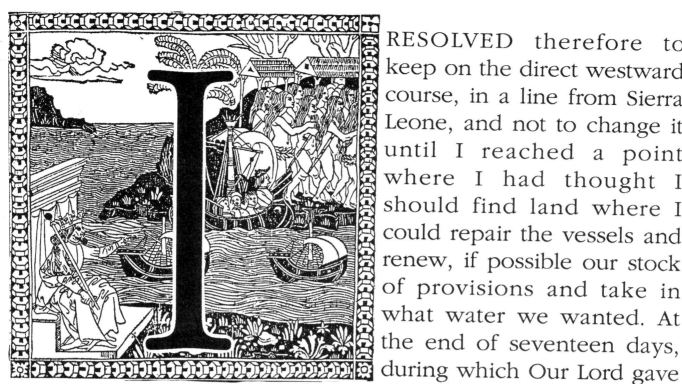

RESOLVED therefore to keep on the direct westward course, in a line from Sierra Leone, and not to change it until I reached a point where I had thought I should find land where I could repair the vessels and renew, if possible our stock of provisions and take in what water we wanted. At the end of seventeen days, during which Our Lord gave me a propitious wind, we saw land at noon of Tuesday the 31st July. This I had expected on the Monday before and held that route up to this point; but as the sun's strength increased and our supply of water was falling, I resolved to make for the Caribee Islands and set sail in that direction; when by the mercy of God which he has always extended to me, one of the sailors went up to the main-top and saw to the westward a range of three mountains. Upon this we repeated the "Salve Regina" and other prayers and all of us gave thanks to Our Lord.

I then gave up our northward course and put in for the land; at the hour of complines we reached a cape which I called Cape Galera, having already given to the Island the name of Trinidad, and here we found a harbour which would have been excellent but there was no good anchorage. We saw houses and people on the spot and the country round was very beautiful and as fresh and green as the gardens of Valencia in the month of March.

Christopher Columbus

Left: Christopher Columbus with his sons Diego and Ferdinand. The lady in the picture may be Columbus' wife Doña Felipa Perestrello y Moniz, mother of Diego, the older of the two boys or Beatriz Enriques, de Araña, who bore him Ferdinand, later to become his biographer. Diego, whose mother was of the royal house of Braganca, was later to become the governor of Santo Domingo. Beatriz is remembered with gratitude and loving kindness in Columbus' will. Lithograph by Agostino Brunias from Brian Edwards. History of the West Indies – second edition 1805.
A letter signed by Columbus El Alminante the Admiral, as he signed himself from the time of his landing on the far shore of "the ocean sea".

The natives are very numerous and all handsome in person and of the same colour as the Indians we had already seen; they are moreover very affable and received our men who went on shore most courteously seeming very well disposed towards us. These men relate that when the boats reached the shore, two of the chiefs whom they took to be father and son, came forward in advance of the mass of the people and conducted them to a very large house with facades and not round and tent-shaped as other houses were; in this house were many seats on which they made our men sit down, they themselves sitting with them. They then caused bread to be brought with many kinds of fruit and various sorts of wine, both white and red, not made of grapes but apparently produced from different fruits. The most reasonable inference is that they use maize which is a plant that bears an ear like that of wheat, some of which I took with me to Spain where it grows abundantly; the best of this, they seemed to regard as most excellent and set a great value upon it.

The men remained together at one end of the house and the women at the other. Great vexation was felt by both parties that they could not understand each other for they were mutually anxious to make enquiries respecting each other's country. After our men had been entertained at the house of the elder Indian, the younger took them to his house and gave them an equally cordial reception; after which they returned to their boats and came on board.

I weighed anchor forthwith for I was hastened by my anxiety to save the provisions which were becoming spoiled and which I had procured and preserved with so much care and trouble as well as to attend to my own health which had been affected by long watching; and although on my former voyage when I went out to discover terra firma, I passed thirty-three days without natural rest and was that all time without seeing it, yet never were my eyes so much affected with bleeding or so painful as at this period.

These people, as I have already said, are very graceful in form, tall and lithe in their movements and wear their hair very long and smooth. They also bind their heads with handsome worked handkerchiefs which from a distance look like silk or gauze; others use the same material in a longer form wound round them so as to cover them like trousers and this is done by both the men and the women. These people are of whiter skin than any I have seen in the Indies. It is the fashion among all classes to wear something at the breast and on the arms and many wear pieces of gold hanging low on the bosom.

Their canoes are larger, lighter and of better build than those of the islands which I have hitherto seen and in the middle of each they have a cabin or room which I found was occupied by the chiefs and their wives.

I called this place "Jardines", that is the "Gardens", for it corresponded to that appelation. I made many enquiries as to where they found the gold, in reply to which all of them directed me to an elevated tract of land at no great distance on the confines of their country lying to the westward; but they all advised me not to go there for fear of being eaten and at that time I imagined by their description they wished to imply that they were cannibals who dwelt there but I have since thought it possible that they meant merely to express that the country was filled with beasts of prey.

But after I had passed the meridian or line which I have already described, I found the climate become gradually more temperate; so that when I reached the island of Trinidad where the north star rose five degrees as night came on, there and in the land of Gracia I found the temperature exceedingly mild; the fields and foliage likewise were remarkably fresh and green and as beautiful as the gardens of Valencia in April. The people there are very graceful in form less dark than those whom I had before seen in the Indies and wear their hair long and smooth; they are also more shrewd, intelligent and courageous. The sun was then in the sign of Virgo over their heads and ours; therefore all this must proceed from the extreme blandness of the temperature which arises, as I have said, from this country being the most elevated in the world and the nearest to the sky.

The town of Isabella and the colony formed by Columbus from a wood cut of 1494.

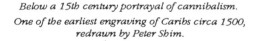

Below a 15th century portrayal of cannibalism.
One of the earliest engraving of Caribs circa 1500,
redrawn by Peter Shim.

The Legend Of "El Dorado"

Sue-Anne Gomes

The legend of El Dorado begins with gold, that precious metal eagerly sought after by man for centuries. Men the world over have fought and conquered each other in their quest for the ever illusive El Dorado, the city of gold. The arrival of Christopher Columbus in the new world opened the flood gate for these treasure seekers which resulted in whole native civilizaaations being wiped out.

The exploitation and ravaging of the Indies for treasure lasted for centuries, the Conquistadores, and pirates alike relentlessly searching for the fabled cities built entirely of gold, and the golden men said to exist in the steaming, seething jungles of South and Central America.

The Conquistadores dauntless iron clad men, heroically battled against nature itself to win the golden civilization for the Spanish Crown. They were told by the Amerindians of the vast riches to be found up the Orinoco; they were told of "El Dorado". These tales fuelled the raging fire that burned deep into the souls of the early Conquistadores. The fear of the savage jungles filled with mammoth dangers flickered dim against the unquenchable vision of the golden city of "El Dorado".

The Europeans came to the West, led only by dreams, ignorant and unprepared, having neither sufficient supplies nor men. They came with horses and they came in armor. However they were soon to learn of the perils of the jungle, the vast flatlands filled with miles of grass, the scorching heat, the rivers that appeared like oceans, the snakes that were mistaken for logs, the jaguars, the swamp, the twenty-foot long crocodiles that lay in wait and moved with lightning speed. Many soldiers died, quickly succumbing to strange jungle fevers. They were bitten by bats and tiny insects laid eggs in their flesh. They met the horrors of hell head on, wholly unprepared for the relentless wrathful form it displayed itself in. They journeyed up the Orinoco, they went into the Andes, it grew very cold, they died of pneumonia.

Apart from the elements, many Indian tribes waged war with these tall, fair men dressed in iron. The few Amerindian tribes who welcomed the Europeans were interrogated about the golden ornaments they wore, and the cups of pure gold from which they drank. The strangers were told of the men of gold of the sacred golden lakes that were to be found higher up river. And the Europeans never considered the possibility of ritual, or the distortion of the Indian's stories, they listened to only what they wanted to hear — gold and El Dorado.

So it was that the Spaniards were convinced of the existence of untold wealth waiting to be tapped just higher up the Orinoco. This idea was even further concretised with Pizarro's and Cortes' discovery of Mexico and Peru and the enormous treasures found in those lands. The Spaniards wished to secure the newly found and untapped wealth of the Indies. Trinidad therefore became a very strategic position, it became the port of the Spaniards, the starting point for the journey up the Orinoco river. It would be these Spaniards who would lay the foundation for the development of Trinidad and Tobago, for they brought their laws and government in the form of Trinidad's Illustrious Cabilldo, however this would not happen for another several hundred years. Trinidad would be used merely as a stepping stone for the many heroic men who would die filled with the passion of conquering the splendid treasures of the golden city — El Dorado.

The 'El Dorado' or 'Golden Man' being covered with resin and sprayed with gold dust. Taken from an old engraving redrawn by Peter Shim.

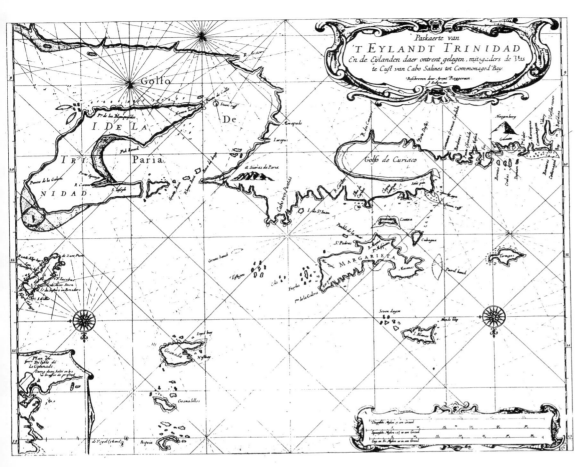

*A chart showing the island of Trinidad and Tobago
and Margarita published by Roggeveen in 1675.*

Ever since the first discoveries of the Indies, there
has been talk of the provinces called El Dorado and it has
been said that they are peopled by great numbers of
Indians and contain vast riches and are very prosperous.

In the year 1531, Don Diego de Ordas, Knight of the
Order of Santiago, attempted to make an entry into these
lands in the hope of discovering them and having the
Faith extended there. But nothing came of it and no
better success attended the efforts of others who
continued this enterprise until Captain Antonio de Berrio
undertook it by virtue of the agreement made with him as
to the discovery of the lands lying between the two rivers,
Pauto and Papamene, at the exit of the New Kingdom of
Granada.

He began to enter and to discover, so they say, the
said lands called El Dorado. He travelled as far as the
Island of Margarita and founded a settlement in the Island
of Trinidad whence he intended to form an expedition
and enter the said El Dorado by way of the Orinoco to
Guayana.

From Trinidad he sent his Maestro de Campo,
Domingo de Ibargoyen y Vera, to give an account of the
whole matter to the King, Our Lord, that he might achieve
this glory and to obtain men, arms and ammunition. In
the year 1596 orders were given for a thousand settlers
consisting of 600 bachelors and 400 married men with
their wives and children to be supplied to the said
Maestro de Campo. His Majesty also thought well to make
a loan to the said Antonio de Berrio from his Royal
Treasury with which to buy and fit out a number of fly
boats to convey the said men and supplies and other
things for which he had asked.

With all this the said Domingo de Vera set out from
these Kingdoms for the Island of Trinidad. When he
arrived there with these people, his lack of foresight and
his bad government were such that the greater part were
wasted and perished without having achieved any of the
objects for which they were sent and without having
gained any positive knowledge of what these lands
contained, for their opinions differed.

The said Antonio de Berrio having died in the year
1597, his son Fernando who succeeded him, remained
there, having with him the said Domingo de Vera and the
remanants of the people who escaped. They are still
insisting on continuing the exploration of these lands and

for that purpose have asked the Governor of Venezuela to
help them with cattle and other supplies. He writes to
report that he is sending them and approves of this
venture.

During the time when the said Domingo de Vera
was in these Kingdoms and Antonio de Berrio was
waiting in the Island of Trinidad, some English arrived
there and landed and entered by the Orinoco River. They
left an Englishman in the country whom our men
afterwards captured there and who was sent to Seville
and on to this Court. He had remained there as a hostage
for certain Indians whom the English had taken away
intending to bring them back and return and settle in
these lands.

Ever since this, the Council has taken great pains to
find out whether the enemy had found an entrance to
these lands by way of the Orinoco and they regard this as
of great importance still.

According to the letters of Alvaro Mendez de Castro,
an honourable man known to the Council, written from
Lisbon and enclosed herewith with a Castilian translation
of a report which he also sent, the English have
discovered a land between Brazil and Peru which they
call Guiana. This is a land rich in gold into which,
according to the said Alvaro Mendez de Castro, the
English have entered by the River Maranon and are taking
away much gold.

Certain things in the Flemish reports seem to
corroborate the accounts of the discovery of Guayana, or
El Dorado, brought by the Maestro de Campo. If the
enemy should settle and people it this would be very
dangerous and much expense would be required to drive
them out.

The Council having taken these matters into their
consideration together with the inferences which are to
be drawn from the papers sent by the said Alvaro
Mendez de Castro, it has seemed fitting that endeavour
should be made to find out the exact truth of the matter
which can be determined by writing to all the Governors
of the districts and provinces contained in the said
reports, and in the discoveries of Antonio de Berrio,
requiring them to use their utmost endeavours to
ascertain what truth there is in these claims, for the
Indians of their districts are in communication with all the
others.

The Council is also of the opinion that the Governor
of Brazil should be required to enquire and advise us of
any information which exists there about these provinces
and those bordering them and whether any English,
French or Flemish have made any entrance through those
parts and if so, in what place and whether any have
remained, in what numbers and with what defences.

Likewise it appears that it would be well to send two
intelligent persons by sea and land who should go in a
vessel for the special purpose to ascertain the truth of this

*A very early engraving of tribal people
redrawn by Peter Shim.*

matter as well by sea as by land. They should bring a very particular account of every detail whereby better deliberation may be made as to what should be provided in a matter of this urgent importance.

In any case it would be necessary to put into some measure of defence, that part of Trinidad where the enemies usually come and are accustomed to use as a port in order to pass to the River Orinoco which is the principal entrance for El Dorado which has been so far discovered.

News has now come that 12 ships from England are going there which may result in great trouble unless in the meantime all possible measures for defence have been resolved and executed.

It would be very helpful to all if the decision which was reached many days ago, to send the Armadilla to the Islands of Barlovento, was put into effect.

May it please Your Majesty to consider this report and provide what is necessary.

Madrid,
    30th January, 1599.

ENDORSED.

On things concerning El Dorado. Let every effort be made promptly to secure a thorough investigation into the whole matter contained in this report recommending it to the attention of intelligent and trustworthy persons.

As regards the fortification of the Island of Trinidad, it would be well for the Council to say how, when and how much is necessary and to whom this can be entrusted.

As to the Armadilla, when the ships which are now being fitted out for patrol work during the coming summer have sheltered for the winter, the most convenient method may be considered and orders given accordingly.

A Report by the Council of the Indies to the King.

Madrid,
January 30th, 1599.

*Bartolomé Las Casas from West Indian Histories
by Edward W. Daniel.*

provinces which are of the character described above and that we shall pacify and conquer. Our General and Governor is Antonio de Berrio, by faculty and authority granted by His Majesty. He will divide the lands between us as was done in Peru and New Spain which were settled in this way.

If we pacify a province of 100 pueblos with 1,000, 2,000 or 10,000 Indians more or less, these pueblos will be granted to each according to his labour, merit and efficiency. These pueblos will be granted for three lives which are those of the conquistador, that of his son and his nephew. These supply the rents which His Majesty and Ministers have decided and published and are in conformity with the riches, abundance or sterility of the lands.

The Indians for their labour will gain instruction in the matters of Our Holy Faith and shelter and protection, as though our children, so that they may recognise and appreciate the great work which our Commander does in bringing them to the obedience and protection of His Majesty. From this, those who wish to go will learn that we intend to populate these lands and not to depopulate them; to develop them and not to exploit them; to control them and not destroy them. Those who do not accept this are warned that they will suffer the anger of God who has clearly shown that those who rob and maltreat the Indians, perish in the land they try to desolate and their riches, acquired by deceit and tyranny, are lost in the sea and their families perish and are forgotten.

Of this at the present moment in the Indies, are obvious examples.

CHRONOLOGICAL TABLE FROM 1577 TO 1866:—

Daniel Hart

1577 Don José de Oruña founded what he called the City of San José (St. Joseph).—6 miles from Port-of-Spain.

1584 Don Antonio de Barrero was appointed Governor of Trinidad.

1595 Sir Robt. Dudley in a vessel called the Bear, of 200 tons, together with 2 Caravels which he had captured off the island of Palma, entered the Gulf of Paria and landed at Trinidad were he remained 40 days.

1595 Sir Walter entered the Gulf by the Serpent's Mouth with two sails; they anchored off Punta de Gallo; he afterwards caused his vessels to move further up the Gulf, and they anchored off Point La Brea where he caused his vessels to be newly paved with the pitch of the Lake.

1596 Captain Lawrence Keymis touched at Trinidad.

---

*Report of the Discovery of El Dorado by Domingo de Vera,
1595 Madrid.*

For 70 years in those parts many Captains with many people, horses and cattle have sought on many occasions to find the entrance to these New Provinces because of the reports by neighbouring Indians of their great size, fertility and riches, but without avail because of the surrounding mountains which are very high and steep and of the large rivers which surround it and which may more properly be described as fresh water seas.

At last our Commander in the year 1593 conceded this venture to me, the Maestro de Campo, as general of this expedition. With 35 soldiers I found the way very easily and without difficulty and got through into the lands which in these parts are called Guayana, a matter of 35 leagues, in which I saw many large settlements of Indians of good disposition and well built who, both men and women, went naked, only covered in the parts which one does not honestly mention.

The country is healthy, temperate and pleasant. It is fertile for the products of the Indies and above all is well favoured and covered with eternal forest. There is much game and fish and in all parts that I have seen, it is well suited for recreation and pleasure. It is very rich in gold and the Indians are ready to show me the place whence they get it but I said that my journey was not to seek gold (so as not to appear avaricious nor to let them know) but only to make friends with the people of these lands. I only took 17 pieces of worked gold which I sent to His Majesty and three battle axes of stone which alone they showed me. Though these people are barbarians they do not lack ability to give that up if good priests were sent to them.

They told me that 7 days further on there is endless quantity of gold; that in these mines no one may take it but the Caciques and their women and that it is collected with great superstition, first fasting for 3 days. In the rivers they find much gold being able to take it anywhere only giving as tribute to the Cacique such nuggets as are as large as the grain of maize or larger.

The people are amicable, courteous and liberal. They treated and supplied us well. As I had but few people, I returned to the Island of Trinidad whence I had gone at the order of our Captain General and Governor, Antonio de Berrio.

This province bounds on the one side with Tierra Firma opposite to the Island of Trinidad, on another with the Government of Cumana, Margarita and Venezuela and also with the New Kingdom of Grenada and with the Government of Popayan and Quito. It is one of the nearest lands which have been discovered in the Indies so that one can go there from Spain in less than 30 days.

Report on what may be expected by those who go on this expedition.

It should be known that we go to settle and and occupy these

THE CONQUISTADORS OF TRINIDAD

Edited by Sue-Ann Gomes

Trinidad was to see several conquistadors, whose imaginations had been fired by the idea of vast riches in the upper reaches of the Orinoco. In 1511 Diego Columbus, the son of the governor of San Domingo was instructed by the King to set sail for Trinidad and explore the island for gold. Despite the dreams of wealth which abounded in the period the precious commodity repeatedly eluded the gold seekers. Despite destroying the hopes of the gold seekers, Trinidad remained important for its apparently unending supply of Indian slaves. The pearl industry which rapidly developed in 1506 catapulted Trinidad into the limelight as the primary source for the all important Indian labour.

In 1520 the title of Adelantado was granted to Captain Roderigo de Bastidas by the King of Spain. However, Bastidas' governorship was strongly opposed by Diego Columbus. As a result of this de Bastidas waived his rights to claim the island due to the developing conflict and took up another appointment in Santa Marta where he was subsequently to become a hero to the Indian population of the province. Due to his partial treatment of the Indians de Bastidas was fatally wounded in an assassination attempt by one of his lieutenants, in 1527 Roderigo de Bastidas died as a result of treacherously inflicted wounds.By the time of his death he had become famous for his great affection for the native Indian population.

It is interesting to speculate on the fate of Trinidad and its eagerly sought after Indian population if Bastidas had in fact taken up his appointment. Undoubtedly the treatment meted out to the native Indian population would have been infinitely better.

In 1528 Don Antonio Sedeno formerly applied for the title of Governor and Captain General of Trinidad. Two years later, on July 12th 1530, Sedeno was granted the post he longed for and given instructions to construct a fort for the defence of the island in the name of Charles V, King of Spain. In addition to this task, he was given an even greater one by the King, who charged him with the responsiblity for the conversion of the native Indians to Christianity. This was a mammoth task bearing in mind the nature of the primitive natives who inhabited the island thousands of leagues away. Two months later the first of those brave Conquistadors to play a role in Trinidad's colourful history set sail from Spain to begin his adventures on the island of Trinidad.

Despite the treacherous seas, the long and dangerous voyage across the Atlantic passed without incident and Sedeno landed at Punta de Las Palmas where, as was the custom, he read his commission to his followers and they accepted him as Governor of Trinidad. Sedeno subsequently set sail for the peninsular Paria on the South American mainland. Thereupon Sedeno met and enlisted the help of the Indian cacique known as Turpiari to assist him in the peaceful conquest of Trinidad. The friendship that blossomed between these two men endured until their deaths.

Sedeno's expedition to Trinidad was joined by Cacique Turpiari and a small party of his native people. They first landed at Chacomare, the southern province, ruled by Marnana. Here they found that the province had an excellent port facing the gulf. This is believed to have been San Fernando where much evidence has been found to support the idea that several native Indian settlements existed. Present evidence supports the view that there were several bush trails which began in San Fernando and led to the interior of the island.

After gaining much goodwill from Cacique Marnana and his people, Don Antonio and Turpiari once again took to the sea and set sail for the northern province of Camocorabo now known as Mucurapo. This settlement of Indians was led by several chiefs and although they appeared to be friendly, Sedeno was not fooled. He was beginning to learn the vagaries of the native Indians and how easy it was for their allegiance to be bought by the highest bidder. In times past these Indians had been exposed to mistreatment by the Spaniards and they distrusted the intentions of these strangers. The time was clearly not yet right for Sedeno to peacefully conquer the north and erect the fort which the King had commanded him to.

Don Antonio returned with Cacique Turpiari to Paria where, with the consent of his new found friend, he finally erected a fort. The fort afforded the men protection from the naked jungle and the alien insects which inhabited it. Don Antonio left some soldiers under the charge of Juan Gonzalez and proceeded to San Juan where he had previously been the commander. Sedeno desperately needed to obtain fresh supplies and additional manpower since both were dwindling rapidly. The jungle was taking a toll on the Spaniards, many of whom had never faced its perils before. They ate and drank with avaricious appetites no doubt affected by the climate. As fate would have it a famous captain Diego de Ordas who had been on Cortez's marvellous expedition to Mexico obtained the rights to Guyana including Paria. Upon landing at Paria and learning of the existence of Sedeno's fort, Ordas promptly engaged the men Sedeno left behind and took possession of the fort capturing the fort's defenders who were perhaps only too happy to see other Spaniards. Undoubtedly their misery and isolation would have made them willing prisoners. Don Antonio could not have been aware of this turn of events and sent men and supplies ahead of him from San Juan. When these new recruits arrived at Paria and learnt of the situation at the fort they retreated quickly, setting sail for the island of Trinidad where they landed at Cumucurapo. Upon their arrival in Mucurapo the Indians greeted them with apparent civility; it was the same false civility which had greeted Sedeno on his previous arrival there. The new recruits however were simply inexperienced and they were easily fooled by the two faced Indians. Eight days later these 24 Spaniards were murdered, three men who were on the ship at the time were the only survivors. They fled to Cubagua, and sent word upon their arrival there to Don Antonio Sedeno.

With revenge burning deep within his heart at the callous cold blooded murder of his men, Don Antonio equipped himself anew with men and supplies and set forth to launch a surprise attack on the rebel Indians. They would be taught a lesson about the might of Spain. Except for a few Indians who had escaped, the entire village was burnt to the ground and the inhabitants of the village perished painfully. One can picture the mayhem which must have ensued with an entire Amerindian village engulfed in flames and the killing of all the inhabitants by bloodthirsty Spaniards bent on revenge. Although the Spaniards were victorious, their search for food proved fruitless and they were forced to retreat to the island of Margarita.

One year later, Sedeno left Margarita with 92 men and 8 horses and set sail for Paria Upon his arrival there, Agustin Delgado and 34 of his people joined forces with him. On June 8th 1533 this party landed and settled at the Indian pueblo of Cumucurapo. The Spaniards spent their time strengthening their position, and making themselves ready for the impending battle with the Indians of the north. The following is the translated account of this attack as written by Don Antonio Sedeno to the King of Spain.

"Thus we waited on watch until four o'clock in the early morning of September 13th, 1533, as dawn was breaking upon the pueblo and before the guards were relieved or the rounds made, a great number of Indians, all clothed, swept down upon us with loud cries contrary to their usual mode of attack. They at once surrounded the pueblo on all sides and launched the attack with great courage and persistence as though they had been Turks, and in half-an-hour about 15–20 of our men had

been wounded..

So many were the arrows that they covered the ground. As the horses were stabled in the middle of the pueblo, the Indians were not able to get at them through the defences, but by shooting arrows high up they managed to wound five out of the eight before steps were taken to cover them. These horses were the principal reserve and would be urgently required later, as we felt certain that without them we should all be killed. We all agreed that if these horses were lost, that day or soon after, it would be necessary to abandon the Island with the loss of everything.

We then sent out the horses to resist and break up this furious attack. As soon as the first horseman was seen, the Indians began to shout loudly, 'Horses, Horses, Horses,' and to turn and flee. As the other horsemen followed and wounded and killed the Indians, they broke completely and fled to the hills, leaving in their flight on the battlefield many bows, arrows, shields and war clubs.

We killed about 30 Indians and captured three alive, from whom we learnt that many tribes had united to make this assault. They had agreed to take arms to kill the Spaniards and drive them out of the Island. If this attempt were not successful they had agreed to return again in eight days in still greater numbers to make the Island free of us.

This was sure to happen sooner or later and our men were depressed at this news, for the punishment inflicted by the horsemen was not sufficiently great. We searched the battlefield and collected our wounded, about 20 or more. Amongst these was the Teniente of Paria who had been one of the horsemen; his horse had been killed by two arrows tipped with poison, so that it died raving mad.'

The battle was long and hard and the victory dearly bought. The remaining handful of Spaniards were now less than twenty-five, and many of their horses lay strewn around the battle field poisoned by the arrows of the Amerindians.

Don Antonio Sedeño

The food supply was critical and the morale of the men was even lower. Dissention in the ranks caused Sedeno much concern and forced him into a position where he had to depend upon Cacique Maruana in the southern provinces, and Cacique Turpiari in Paria for food supplies. Although the Indians were never able to organise themselves sufficiently to dislodge Sedeno the real problem faced by the indomitable Conquistador was the question of food supplies. This shortage was exacerbated by a renewed interest which had developed with Pizarro's discovery of Peru, the result being that ships from Cubagua and San Juan were no longer be diverted to Trinidad.

In March 1534 Sedeno's men mutinied, tired of the dangers and hardships of life in the jungle. Apart from this, their fear of the uncertain natives and the prospect of virtual starvation confirmed their desperation to escape from the island. Death's nearness was enough to dim their dreams of glory. Despite this, Sedeno remained loyal to his mission and was eventually released by his captors. Without adequate food supplies however, the future seemed very dim. The mutineers secured one of Sedeno's two emergency caravels and deserted the island leaving their governor to the sweltering heat and unfriendly forest with only one ship.

Only 20 devoted followers remained with their leader, uncertain as to their fate but confident that Don Antonio Sedeno would deliver them to safety. Finally Don Antonio gave up in utter desolation due to the fact that his food supply was becoming critically short. The men who remained with him had convinced him that a prolonged stay would undoubtedly lead to further death and disaster. Shortly after he left the island with his remaining followers, never to return again.

During the next forty years or so, Trinidad saw only the slave hunters in search of Indians for the gold mines of other islands or as pearl divers. Adventurers in pursuit of the Gold of El Dorado, their names like dusty memories, float in the pale light of half-remembered histories, dimly flickering, old, antique gold, in pursuit of the new Garden of the Hesperides, somewhere in the upper reaches of the Rio Meta. Sebastian de Belalcozar, Don Gonzalo Ximenes de Quesada, Orillana, Pedro de Ursua – sailing the northern coast of Hierro, dying in the swamps of no return. These men of Old Spain sought the Golden Man in his City of Gold; and Trinidad, a Puerto de Los Hispanioles, was the threshold of this dream.

Don Juan Ponce de Leon

hen came the second Conquistador of Trinidad - Don Juan Ponce. He had been granted a Royal Permit, good for 'tres vidas' - three generations - and in 1571, he embarked his men and set sail. The splendid expedition arrived in Trinidad after a successful voyage. It is not known where exactly they landed although it has been suggested that it was near to the present capital of Port of Spain.

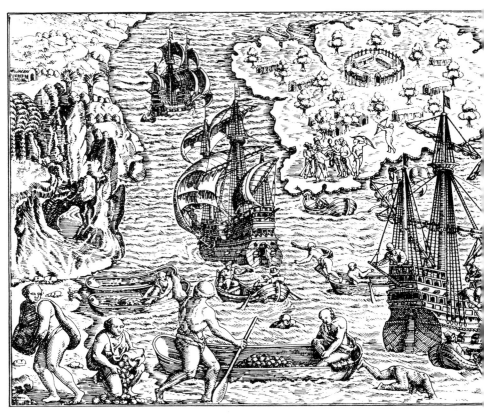

Early engraving of pearl fishing in the Gulf of Paria, by de Bry redrawn by Peter Shim.

According to the custom of the period his powers were restricted to those of a mere governor during the conquest, but extended to that of an adelantado after reducing the Indians to a life of Christianity and building a fortified town. They were the same powers as those accorded to Don Antonio Sedeño, with the added advantage of being hereditary for some time. The Royal Command also granted him the right to take a dozen priests among his followers. The fact that he took so many priests would indicate de Leon intended a peaceful conquest and the concession of hereditary authority, the importance Spain attached to the conquest.

Having completed his negotiations, Don Juan Ponce immediately set to work. He asked for priests from the order of the Observants of Granada, and collected them at Seville under the commissionership of R.P. Fr. Juan A. Dios who was provided with the necessary powers to found a convent and parish in the colony. He also collected a great number of *pobladores* or emigrants.

Unfortunately they did not meet with success. Given a bad welcome by the Islanders, they had to suffer their hostilities from the very start. They were also pestered by mosquitoes and jiggers (a kind of flea which inserts itself between the skin and flesh to lay its eggs). Soon overwhelmed by sickness and sores the unfortunate Spaniards did not have the strength to work in the fields. They ran short of food and nearly all died of hunger. The few who were sufficiently strong to resist all these miseries, lest they follow their unfortunate companions, had to leave the unhealthy coast of the Island; some for Spain and others for the continent and the realm of new Granada. Among the former was the commissariat Father Juan A. Dios and several priests. Another priest, Father Diego Ramirez accompanied those who left for the continent. It is not known what became of the conquistador.

These are the only details which have been handed down to us of this second attempted conquest. It was just as unsuccessful as the first and the island remained as it was in the past, solely in the hands of the Indians without any prospect of colonization in the near future.

Don Antonio de Berrio y Oruña

Antonio de Berrio was born in 1520. At the age of fifty-four he married the niece of the wealthy Adelantado, Conquistador Don Gonzalo Ximenes de Quesada. When Quesada died De Berrio's wife inherited several of his lucrative estates in New Granada. In 1580, the veteran soldier and his family came out west to retire. De Berrio had fought in many battles by the time of his retirement. His adventures had taken him to clashes with the Barbary pirates of Sierra, to Granada where he fought the Muslims and to wars in Germany and the Netherlands. The quiet life in New Granada however came too soon for the restless de Berrio. He was destined to spend the rest of his days in tireless search for the elusive El Dorado. The following is an extract taken from a despatch sent by Antonio de Berrio to the Council of the Indies:– "and seeing the insistence with which the Adelantado in a clause of his will commands me to continue and complete this expedition that he had commenced, this alone and my inclinations sufficed to impel me and so I determined to hasten and set out in search of it and I collected at once a number of men and a great quantity of horses and cows and plenty of munitions and other necessary supplies; and with this equipment which cost me a large sum of gold I set out from the New Kingdom and crossed the llanos and marched more than 300 leagues through them where no Spaniard had ever entered until I came to the cordillera on the other side of them which has been so sought for and desired by twenty-three Captains who have begun this conquest. I had skirmishes with some of the Indians and the captives and many others who came peaceably gave me a great deal of information about the land and all were very much agreed as to the great multitude of the people and the great riches that were beyond those cordilleras which I tried to pass several times in different parts, and with light armed men and on foot and I was never able to find any way that the horses and cattle could pass and it was impossible to attempt to take supplies and provisions such a long way on men's backs; and the troops seeing this clearly were so anxious and desirous to pass through and see part of what had been

told us that they drew strength out of weakness and laboured beyond their powers so that nearly all of them fell sick of fever so violently that they forthwith became delirious; so for this cause and because I knew that the Indians seeing us so ill were uniting to attack us I decided to depart at the end of seventeen months after I had entered the plains."

Antonio made three remarkable and costly voyages during his adventure filled lifetime. His last and most spectacular was made when he was about seventy. His son Fernando who was just sixteen at the time accompanied his father . Fernando would later have his own claims to glory, following in his fathers footsteps. On this journey up the Orinoco, de Berrio had to deal with much hardship and many of his men deserted or fell ill. The strangeness of the jungle and the alien way of life it enforced was too much for the men to endure for any length of time. Several of his canoes were lost and in order to banish any thought of returning to New Granada Antonio killed all the horses which were later eaten by the expedition. De Berrio and his remaining men journeyed down the Orinoco until they came upon Trinidad where they landed. Antonio de Berrio described Trinidad as an island very well populated with friendly Indians and soil which was rich, fertile and promising.

By 1592 the town of San José de Oruna in Trinidad was settled by Sedeno and his party. Domingo de Vera, Antonio's Lieutenant returned from his journey up the Orinoco with proof of the riches and the promise of El Dorado. The following is extracted verbatim from a letter to the King of Spain from Domingo de Vera.

"Moreover, Senor, the events of the last few years clearly confirm what has already happened from the far off times of the ancients, whether gentile or christian, that when one person undertakes an enterprise and it comes within the power of another to be able to help it, he does not do so because he envies the glory which redounds to he one who does it. This is particularly true of this enterprise for El Dorado, for all speak ill of it and yet each one tries it by special ways.

The land is always what has been said of it as regards grandeur and fertility, for merely in those parts which have been seen from the coast and the rivers in

Europeans making contact with Caribs from an old engraving redrawn by Peter Shim.

the interior, there are more than 500,000 Indians. As a proof of this consider the great numbers who have died in entering this land and where there are people there is wealth.

Furthermore in previous times, a great sum of gold has been obtained by barter, though the Devil now protects them so well that he has made them understand that they must not give it in exchange for anything. Consider also that the way thither is by a cold and lofty region where the people eat maize and not roots and other foods which produce effeminate races and that the Indians of this land gave news of clothed people with abundance of coined gold and of their fighting with javelins as in done in the New Kingdom.

This is true and corresponds with the accounts given by the Indians for a hundred, two hundred and three hundred leagues. It cannot fail nor can there be any doubt of its being an easy thing and that little profit accrues to me save in following the direct path of truth."

The condition in which we now find ourselves is as follows; we have 300 or more men at arms, 80 horses with cattle and a certain number of pigs with which to maintain the town of San José which is in the Island of Trinidad and that of San Thome which is at the entrance of the districts bordering El Dorado. We are sufficient to make some explorations into these lands but not to reach the heart of this country nor to subdue it. If we had control of Venezuela we should hold all these lands because they are in the hands of friends of mine. Indians who come to the Orinoco to see me.

Many of the Indians of this Island are submitting to Your Majesty's service. They are within Your Majesty's territory which they plough and make fruitful. All those on the rivers and the coast have already given their obedience."

By this time Antonio de Berrio was in desperate need of more men to continue on his great quest. The sticky heat of the jungle and its attendent dangers had taken their toll on de Berrio's ranks. Worse yet, men were reluctant to sign up for such an uncertain expedition. The fear of death was far greater than the call of gold and the great unknown. Antonio de Berrio and his son took several years to recruit men for these expeditions. As a result they never quite achieved the necessary quantities of recruits or supplies because the neighbouring Spanish governors were envious of de Berrio and so offered him very little assistance. In 1595 the English captain, Sir Walter Raleigh, launched an attack on San José and captured the vitally important location. The Spanish crown quickly retaliated and by April 10th 1596 a Spanish ship was anchored off the Bay of Paria. One year later Fernando, de Berrio's son, returned to San Thomé only to discover his father was at death's door and about to depart on his final expedition to the great unknown.

The following is an excerpt from "Historical Sketches" Vol. II, 1936 Dr. K.S. Wise.

"Thus in June 1597, Fernando de Berrio, at the age of 21 became the Governor of the Island of Trinidad, and of the Provinces of Guayana, by far the youngest of a long line of successors. This was due not to Royal appointment but to the usual Spanish colonial practice of granting patents for exploration to Conquistadors and Governors which included the right of nominating a successor for one, two or three lives as the case might be. Antonio de Berrio exercised his legal right of appointing his 21-year-old son, Fernando, as his successor as Governor.

It is true that Antonio's Lieutenant Domingo de Vera claimed to have a cedula from the King of Spain to administer the Government on the death or absence of Antonio de Berrio. Domingo, however, freely wrote to the King of Spain in October, 1597: "He showed so much wisdom and consideration and was so careful in setting guards and in other necessary precautions and above all was so good a Christian, and so disposed to act well, that I considered I should not take over the Government. I did not leave him during the day and remained at his side; he was so ready to take advice as to what should be done and showed that he was the master. All this being so, I gave him the Royal Cedula saying that I did not wish to make use of it."

The King of Spain loyally confirmed the dying act of Antonio de Berrio and Fernando was duly proclaimed as Governor of the Island of Trinidad, and of the province of Guayana, and as such succeeded to the wreck of his father's fortunes."

Don Antonio de Berrio had left the legacy of finding El Dorado to his son Fernando, and it was with much fervour that he picked up the gauntlet. Success was not to be had, however for these first settlers were subjected to endless attacks by the native Indians. Combined with this was the slowly dawning suspicion that the quest for the fabled El Dorado, city of gold, would lead only to empty pockets and empty dreams. The explorers were beginning to wonder if the desperately sought after El Dorado was in fact only an illusion never to be realised. By 1609, Don Fernando de Berrio's search for El Dorado was not his priority, rather he recognised in order to make these provinces of Trinidad and Guyana successful there was a need to live off the fruit of the land and not depend on a windfall such as the discovery of gold or precious stones.

Trade in Guyana and Trinidad had been developed by Fernando by 1611. However the Council of the Indies ordered that a residencia be taken upon the Governor of the Island of Trinidad., to investigate Fernando for trading illegally with Spain's enemies.

'The residencia was a unique feature of Spanish administration. Governors and other high officers were required to submit themselves every five years or at the end of their term of office, to an open enquiry at which anyone might appear and lodge a complaint. Any such complaint the Governor was required to answer and pending the final issue, the salary of his office and the bonds of his guarantors were held in suspense."

The Council of the Indies wrote to the King of Spain on the 28th March 1611, as follows:-

"About seven weeks ago there arrived at London, a ship with Juan Munoz having on board sixteen thousand pounds (libras) of Tobacco from the River Orinoco. This had been supplied by the Governor and the inhabitants at six reals the libra.

This ship left in the River Orinoco, two Dutch and one English ship; two other English ships were met entering the River Orinoco.

At the Island of Trinidad there were four or five ships trading there and another four were met on the way there."[1]

Another letter to the King dated 15th May, 1611, stated in summary:-

"Don Alonzo de Velasco, Ambassador in England, reports on the trade that the English carry on with Trinidad.

Quite lately three ships have arrived in England with Tobacco from Trinidad and the least was valued at five hundred thousand ducats.

At the time there were preparing in London four ships for the trade at Trinidad. The Governor of that Island should be punished.'[1]

Don Fernando was found guilty of illegal trading with the enemy and as such was ordered to pay a fine and to relinquish his governorship of the Island of Trinidad and the Province of Guyana. Fernando promptly left the West Indies for Spain where he made a petition to the King of Spain. His appeal was successful except that Don Fernando de Berrio had to obtain a licence from his Majesty in order to be reinstated as Governor. This attempt met with a repeated lack of success and Don Diego Palemeque de Acura eventually became the new Governor of the Island of Trinidad and the Province of Guyana. Don Fernando's link with Trinidad however, was not yet ready to be severed.

1. Historical Sketches, Vol. II, 1936, Dr. K.S. Wise.

necessaries to the Island and to carry back the produce.

In September, 1614, a register ship did actually pass between Spain and Trinidad, carrying out necessaries including linen and clothing, fifty muskets, ten hundred weight of powder, six hundredweight of gun matches and six hundredweight of lead and returning laden with tobacco.

Such ships became rare and irregular and in spite of the Royal Pardon to the inhabitants of San José and San Thomé, evidence still appeared of trading with the enemy and the Governor of Trinidad was instructed by the Cedula of November 8, 1615, to investigate and punish any who had dealings with the enemy after the promulgation of the pardon.

Tribal people pouring molten gold into the mouths of Europeans, from an early 16th century engraving by de Bry redrawn by Peter Shim.

THE FINAL EFFORTS OF DON FERNANDO (1618-1622)

Dr. K.S. Wise (Historical Sketches, Vol. II, 1936.)

By November of 1615 Don Fernando de Berrio had been dismissed by his government. By this time Don Diego Palameque de Acuna had reached the Island of Trinidad, and taken up his duties as the new Governor. Once on this island he fully apprised himself of the poor condition and scanty supplies of the towns of San José and San Thome.

The situation had become critical. The cessation of the tobacco trade and the forcible exclusion of foreign ships had ruined Trinidad and Guyana and though the Dutch and English made efforts to continue this trade even under force of arms, by 1614, trade was at an end.

In January, 1613, the Licenciado Pedro de Beltranilla, Procurator General of San Josef, reported to the Council of the Indies that for the past 18 years no Spanish ship had appeared at Trinidad to trade. The people had thus been forced by necessity to trade with enemy ships from which had flowed so many troubles and difficulties as was well known. He urged that the Casa de Contratacion should be ordered to send two register ships of 200 tons each to the Island of Trinidad every year so as to bring

To encourage and assist the dispirited settlements in Trinidad and Guayana, the King approved the grant of freedom from the Alcavala and Almoxarifazgo taxes (trading and custom dues) for six years on all tobacco shipped from these places to ports in Spain. Here was still another attempt to direct the Colony's trade into proper channels but the scarcity of Spanish vessels was not the only difficulty which discouraged the people of Trinidad, since on November 21st, 1617, one of the register ships, a patache full of tobacco from Trinidad, was lost off Cape St. Vincent, being captured by the Turks.

Just at this time Sir Walter Raleigh made his second attack on Trinidad and the Orinoco. He arrived at Cedros, on December 17th, 1617, and left Trinidad on February 8th, 1618, having sacked and burnt San Thome, during which Don Diego Palameque de Acuna had been killed. By June 21st, Sir Walter Raleigh was back at Plymouth, and on October 29th, was executed at Westminster in London.

The Island of Trinidad and the Province of Guayana, was once again without a Governor and as the Province of Guayana was within the jurisdiction of the Audiencia of Santa Fe, it appointed Don Geronimo de Grados, as Teniente, at San Thome, who took up duty from the Alcades on August 19th. As the Island of Trinidad was within the jurisdiction of the Audiencia of San Domingo, this Audiencia appointed Don Juan de Viloria y Quinones, as Teniente, at San Josef, where he assumed duty in high dudgeon at being rejected as Teniente by the people of San Thome.

Don Fernando de Berrio had persisted in his special pleading with Spain, and by means of family interests and other influence had at last succeeded in obtaining re-appointment as Governor of Trinidad and Guayana, after the end of the term of duty of Don Diego.

During 1617, Don Fernando had returned to the Indies and gone to his estates, at Pauto, about 200 miles from Santa Fe. Here in April, 1618, the news of the destruction of San Thome and the death of Don Diego Palameque de Acuna reached him whereupon he found himself once again Governor of these provinces.

In May, 1618, the Audiencia of Santa Fe, instructed him to go to Guayana and take up his duties and by July Don Fernando had gone to Casanare at the head of the Orinoco and had asked the Audiencia for 100 men and suitable supplies without which he could not go to Guayana.

The Audiencia authorised a loan of 2,000 ducats from the Royal Treasury to help the people of San Thome, and provided for 25 men. As the men did not materialise Don Fernando de Berrio was still at Casanare, when the President, on December 21st, 1618, threatened him with severe penalties for disobedience if he did not proceed forthwith.

Again on January 17th, 1619, the Audiencia had to repeat this order but this time the Audiencia supplied him with 2,000 ducats worth of supplies for the people of San Thome and with 20 men.

As usual Don Fernando reported nothing and up to June the Audiencia was still unaware of his movements. On this occasion however, Don Fernando had really gone and by May 11th, 1619, had arrived at San Thome with the supplies and 44 men having collected 24 of his own.

Don Fernando reported his arrival and his assumption of the duties of the Government to the King of Spain and complained strongly of his treatement by the Audiencia, stating that they would not supply him with the requisite men and supplies and had expected him to go undefended and without assistance to San Thome. He claimed to have collected 44 men by his own efforts and to have spent another 2,000 ducats of his own money and to have found the Spaniards at San Thome, threatened by a Carib fleet of 30 pirogues from which he saved them.

Don Fernando emphasised the importance of keeping Trinidad and of placing a fort there with 100 men as a garrison as well as at Guayana. He also asked for an annual register ship for Guayana as well as that now granted to Trinidad.

He complained bitterly that while Guayana had readily received him as Governor, the people in the Island of Trinidad had refused to accept him since Don Juan de Viloria y Quinones was there by orders of the Audiencia of San Domingo; and this after being Governor for 22 years and never during all that period receiving a cent of pay. He begged the King to grant him 4,000 pesos of gold from the Treasury at Santa Fe and that the 2,000 ducats loaned for supplies for San Thome be written off or placed against his arrears of pay. He finally prayed for permission to go to Spain to represent the urgent needs of his government.

The King by his cedula of May 12th, 1620, at once commanded the people of Trinidad to receive Don Fernando, as Governor. He also gave orders for the supply of military material, granted the annual register ship to Guayana, not to exceed eighty tons and extended the freedom from custom dues for another four years.

The King, however, had 'under consideration' the need for a fort in each place, the request for a grant of 4,000 pesos of gold and a petition for the title of Adelantado. The leave to return to Spain was definitely refused 'because your presence is very necessary in your Government.'

The Audiencia of Santa Fe had treated Don Fernando badly, the people of Trinidad had insulted him, San Thome was in ruins, trade had been reduced to almost nothing, the Caribs had taken the offensive, the Truce of Antwerp was ended and the Dutch were settling the Guayana coast and seriously threatening his own provinces. Don Fernando de Berrio felt that he had to go to Spain and convince the authorities that efficient defence and active support were vitally necessary. And go he did, without permission and in defiance of the Royal refusal.

On the way, unfortunately, like the patache with tobacco from Trinidad in 1617, his vessel was captured early in 1622, near the coast of Spain by the Moors, and Don Fernando, the Governor of Trinidad with his nephew, Don Martin de Mendoza y Berrio, were taken as prisoners to Algiers.

Don Fernando died in prison, shortly after being taken prisoner while Don Martin was more fortunate and was ransomed four years later. In 1642, he himself became the Governor of Trinidad.

Thus Don Fernando de Berrio had played his part in the affairs of the West. He had dutifully searched for El Dorado, he had rebuilt the towns of San Josef and San Thome, he had developed the pastoral and agricultural resources of his government and developed what was at the time, a thriving trade in hides and tobacco employing 40-50 ships a year.

But alas, he had not reckoned with the blindly rigid mercantilism of the day. This was perhaps more strongly held in Spain than elsewhere, and an economic expression of militant nationalism which was unable to conceive any mutual advantage in trade between one country and another. To the Spanish authorities trading with foreigners was anathema, more especially when it allowed access to their private empire in the Indies.

The residencia was held, Don Fernando and his people were adjudged guilty and condemned; the foreign trade was checked and the exports of Trinidad and Guayana dwindled to almost nothing, the freight of two or three small register ships a year.

Don Fernando had learnt from actual experience that the wealth of Trinidad and Guayana lay not in undiscovered and probably non-existent gold and precious stones but in the development of pastoral and agricultural resources. When he returned to his government in 1619, and viewed with sorrow the wreck of that prosperity which he had left in 1612, he quickly made plans for a revival.

He clearly realised that the first necessity was security from his enemies, obtainable only by a fort and garrison at each centre and that the second necessity was ample shipping communication with Spain. The Royal Cedula of May 12th, 1620, demonstrated to Don Fernando only too well the timid procrastination of the authorities and the entire lack of understanding of the local problems.

A man of action, a man of foresight, a man of courage, heedless of administrative restrictions, regardless of the consequences when paramount issues were at stake, he seized the sole hope of retrieving the position of his government and forthwith took passage for Spain evidently to demand in person and possibly to obtain, the two major necessities for his people in Trinidad and Guayana.

Alas, a disastrous misfortune led Don Fernando to close confinement at Algiers. Instead of achieving his objective in Madrid and starting Trinidad upon that extensive agricultural development for which it had to wait many a long year and which remains to this day its greatest asset, Don Fernando died unhonoured and unsung in prison at the early age of forty-six.

1. Source:– Addition Mss. 36319. British Museum.
    Published by courtesy of the Trustees of the British Museum.
    Translated from the Spanish.

2. The Council of the Indies to the King.
    Source:– Additional Mss. 36319. British Museum.

Sir Walter Raleigh

The inland town of San José de Oruña and the little port which was called Puerto de los Hispanioles began by the end of 1594 to be the focus for European dominance in the New World. England's expansion in the West Indies was purely economical. There was a need to find a new market for their goods, somewhere outside of Europe where there was money. By the 1560's trade between the early colonists and privateers such as Francis Drake and John Hawkins was established. These Englishmen began to wage attacks upon the closely guarded Spanish treasure ships. During this period 'might was right' in the Caribbean, as the courageous privateers and pirates attempted to break the Spanish monopoly in the West.

While peace reigned in Europe, the English corsairs were already infesting the Antilles Sea and the Gulf of Paria, intercepting Spanish galleons laden with riches from the New World. When Queen Elizabeth decided to take up the cause of the United Provinces of Holland against Philip II of Spain, she knew that the West Indies was the seat of his power and at the same time the most vulnerable part of his Empire. Because of this, one can form an idea of the vast number of British armaments sent to America. There was a veritable overflow of transatlantic expeditions in 1594 and 1595, among which the most celebrated are those of Richard Hawkins in the south, and those of Sir Francis Drake and Sir John Hawkins in the Antilles Sea. The two latter captains sacked and burnt the growing towns of Caracas, Santa María, Río Hacha, Puerto Bello etc., etc.

Of all these bold mariners with whom England fought Spain in America we have only to deal here with Sir Walter Raleigh, Captain of the Queen's Guards. A warrior as well as a writer, possessed perhaps of too romantic a character, this man was endowed with a noble heart and chivalrous bravery. If it is true, as it is so affirmed, that Elizabeth bestowed her favours on him, it is also necessary to recognize that his great influence at court was always used only to further the glory of his sovereign and the power of his country. He was one of the stalwarts upon whom England built her mighty empire and was therefore instrumental in England's development as a hemispheric power. Her wealth and navy were the two major factors that contributed to her phenomenal rise. Sir Walter Raleigh was a part of both those worlds.

As soon as war was declared, it became his stated intention to lead an expedition to America. It was whilst carrying out this very goal that his fevered imagination carried him beyond the realms of possibility. Influenced by the wonderful stories then current of the wealth of Guyana, he disregarded the methods of the other English captains and evolved the daring plan of seizing this province, thinking that the loss of this beautiful country Trinidad, would be a much greater loss to Spain than the burning of a few towns on the American coast.

In order to attract colonists Raleigh needed to use the lure of gold as motivation. The problem was to select an area that was known for its riches but which had not been secured by the Spanish Crown. The search for the elusive El Dorado began afresh with Raleigh's limitless imagination spurring him on. Hot on the trail of gold Raleigh sent captain Jacob Whiddon to explore the approaches to Guyana in 1593. By June of that same year Whiddon anchored in the Bay of Paria, and quickly established a relationship with Don Antonio de Berrio. In exchanging pleasantries, Whiddon learned from the Spanish Governor, information about Vera's journey up the Orinoco and about the treasures of El Dorado. Armed

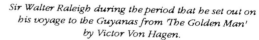

Sir Walter Raleigh during the period that he set out on his voyage to the Guyanas from 'The Golden Man' by Victor Von Hagen.

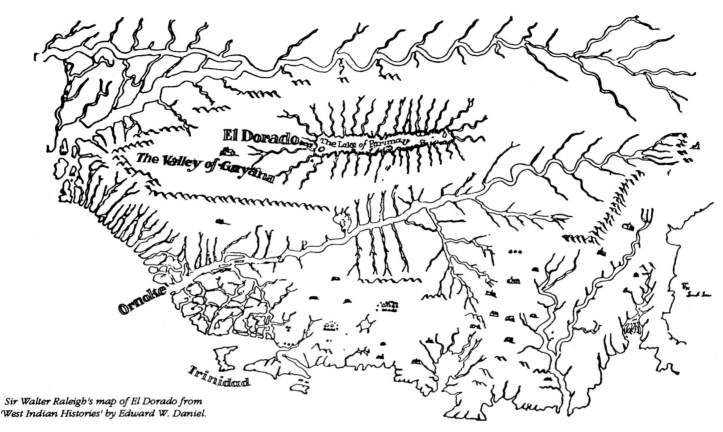

*Sir Walter Raleigh's map of El Dorado from
'West Indian Histories' by Edward W. Daniel.*

with the very information he came in search of, Jacob Whiddon returned to England to tell Raleigh about the stories told to him by Vera.

The stories that came back were incredible: stories of a man, a great King, covered in gold; of houses, huge buildings made of gold; of vast forests towering high; of a mountain of crystal that sparkled in the sun, washed over by a waterfall in whose vast basin, golden nuggets as big as fists — were found, and emeralds and sapphires in abundance.

There were also tales of man-eaters, and Caribs, who ate other Indians and who seized and killed white men in the most cruel ways possible and when these were not available, nourished themselves with negroes whom they also castrated and held in perpetual servitude, until they too were eaten.

There were also stories of Anthropohagi and men whose heads grew beneath their shoulders. The jaguars, the swamps, the mosquitoes, the silence and 'hardships so dire and grave when they are known, appear fables in the telling.' But always, there were the thoughts of gold — gold beyond their wildest dreams of avarice. Raleigh's action was decisive. His enthusiasm drove him to make hasty preparation for his departure from England. Yet despite Raleigh's haste, Sir Robert Dudley just 20 years old, managed to set sail before Raleigh on the 6th November 1594 and landed in Trinidad on January 31. Here the youthful Dudley befriended the Aruacs of the south and set forth on his great gold expedition. He too was set for disillusionment however. After discovering Marcasite he wrote to England 'all is not gold that glistereth.' His Indian helpers continued to perpetuate the gold myth however, and drove him on with stories of the great riches yet to be discovered further up the mysterious Orinoco River. It was about this time that Dudley met with Captain George Popham in the Bay of Paria. Popham had captured a Spanish vessel the previous year which fortuitously carried among its other precious contents a timely report by Domingo de Vera to Antonio de Berrio about the riches discovered up the Orinoco.

In Dudley's mind this was confirmation enough that great treasures lay awaiting discovery in the Guianas. With this news uppermost in his mind Dudley returned to England in May 1595.

Raleigh, on the other hand, weighed anchor in England on February 6th 1595 and arrived at Icacos, Trinidad, on March 22nd. Dudley had been well into his discovery by this time, but Raleigh made a unique and most important discovery of his own while in Trinidad.

He spent five days surveying the island and discovered the magnificent pitch lake, never knowing that this was the real gold. The movement of the English was being monitored by de Berrio closely and suspiciously all this time. By April 4th when Raleigh dropped anchor off Cumucurapo, Berrio sent four men and twenty-five Indians under his nephew's command to investigate the British presence. This party was invited on board where they were made welcome – Raleigh writes 'for these poor soldiers having been many years without wine, a few draughts made them merry, in which mood they vaunted of Guyana and of the riches thereof and all what they knew of the ways and passages, myself seeming to purpose nothing less than the entrance and discovery thereof, but bred in them an opinion that I was bound only for the relief of those English which I had planted in Virginia.'

Berrio sent two more soldiers on the 6th of April and yet another two soldiers the next day. They were all greeted warmly. Don Antonio felt satisfied that the English were obviously en route to the pearl fisheries of Margarita and thus not a threat to the Spanish holdings. Having alleviated the suspicions of the Spanish by the hospitality extended their way, Raleigh was able to safely survey the extent of the Spanish defences. He acted quickly and decisively, with one swift signal the nine Spaniards on board Raleigh's flagship were murdered and over 100 Englishmen landed on the island.

At 4.00 a.m. on Friday 8th April the English took the town of San José. The Spanish soldiers fled into the jungle with their women and children, terrified. Some reached as far as the Pitch Lake and the rest wondered around the dense jungles for days until reaching the southern end of the island. Don Antonio de Berrio, Alvaro Jorge and nine other Spaniards were taken prisoner during the mêlée. Twelve soldiers were killed, sixteen others including several women and a Fransiscan father escaped. By April 12th they had reported the tragedy to the Governor of Margarita who was unable and perhaps unwilling to help in any way.

The English plundered the town of San José taking everything of value and as a final act set the town of San José, built of thatch and tapia, on fire. The English then made their way to Cumucurapo where all the Indians were gathered together. Raleigh then placed them and the island of Trinidad under the protection of his beloved Queen Elizabeth. Such was the fate of San José de Oruña in the third year of its foundation. Don Antonio de Berrio, brave as all the gallant knights of that chivalrous age, put up a strong defence; but overwhelmed by numbers, had the misfortune to fall prisoner to Sir Walter Raleigh. Thus vanished the dreams of splendour and power of our illustrious conquistador.

Sir Walter Raleigh wrote 'We then hastened away towards our purposed discovery and first I called all the Captains of the Island together that were enemies to the Spaniards for here were some which Berrio had brought out of other countries and planted there to eat out and waste those that were natural of the place. By my Indian interpreter which I carried out of England, I made them understand that I was the servant of a Queen who was a great Cacique of the North and a Virgin and had more Caciques under her than were trees in the Island; that she was an enemy to the Castellani in respect of their tyranny and oppression and that she delivered all such nations about her as were by them oppressed and have freed all the coast of the northern world from their servitude, had

sent me to free them also and withal to defend the country of Guyana from their invasion and conquest. I showed them Her Majesty's picture which they so much admired and honoured as it had been easy to have brought them idolatrous thereof.'

Raleigh returned to Los Gallos. Here he erected a post which carried the arms of the Queen and built a fort before proceeding in his attempt to acquire more details and information about the treasures said to be found up the Orinoco. Raleigh interrogated Berrio, who in turn was as uncooperative as possible. After all the travails he had experienced in trying to get to El Dorado, he would not give this English pirate 'El Conde Guaterral' any information about his El Dorado. Antonio de Berrio played a game of time, knowing that the flood water of the Orinoco would soon make the river impassable. However Raleigh wrote 'Berrio was stricken into a great melancholy and sadness and used all the arguments he could to dissuade me and also assured the gentlemen of my company that it would be labour lost; and that they should suffer many miseries if they proceeded. First he delivered that I could not enter any of the rivers with any barque or pinnance nor hardly with any ship's boat, it was so low, sandy and full of flats and that his companies were daily grounded in their canoes which drew but twelve inches of water. He further said that none of the country would come to speak with us but would all fly and if we followed them to their dwellings, they would burn their own towns. Besides that the way was long, the winter at hand and the rivers were beginning to swell; it was impossible to stem the current and that we could not in those small boats by any means carry victuals for half the time and then (which indeed most discouraged my company) the Kings and Lords of all the borders and of Guiana had decreed for gold because the same would be their own overthrow and that for the love of gold and

Sir Walter Raleigh at the Pitch Lake Trinidad drawn by Peter Shim.

Christians meant to conquer and dispossess them of all together.' On May 2nd Sir Walter Raleigh led his expedition up the River Orinoco disregarding all that de Berrio had told him.

In his journey Raleigh met an old Indian Cacique Topiawarri, chief of the Nepuyo tribe. Sir Walter pledged the Crown's protection of the Indians from the tyranny of the Spaniards. From Topiawarri Raleigh learned of the riches to be found in the north. The expedition continued on in its quest but the rainy season threatened the party. Raleigh wrote:- 'for that the fury of the Oronoque began daily to threaten us with dangers in our return for no half day passed but the river began to rage and overflow very fearfully and the rains came down in terrible showers and gusts in great abundance.'

Raleigh sought advice from his friend Topiawarri. He was told that it was not a wise decision to make any attempt up the river, especially without the help of the Indians. The Englishman and the Indian Cacique then made a pledge. They agreed to meet one year later when Raleigh would bring 1,000 men to join with the Indians in the invasion of El Dorado. Topiawari gave his son Cauorako to Raleigh for protection against the Spaniards, and with that the expedition made its way back up the Orinoco.

On arrival at Punta de Piedras, Alvaro Jorge was put ashore. He was to arrange a ransom of 1,400 ducats for Don Antonio de Berrio and his lieutenant. The Spanish Governor at Margarita intervened, and did not allow the transaction to take place. Raleigh's ships were driven off with de Berrio still on board. Sir Walter promptly set sail

Sir Walter Raleigh captures the town of San Josef de Oruna and captures its Governor Antonio de Berrio. redrawn from an old engraving by Peter Shim.

to launch an attack on Cumara where he was badly defeated and three of his English captains killed. Much of Raleigh's precious cargo was lost to Neptune's locker during these vicious sea battles. Antonio de Berrio was finally released in the hope that the captured English prisoners would be allowed to return to their ship.

Sir Walter Raleigh returned to England in August 1595, the expedition not bringing the monetary return expected. The journey however had served to confirm Raleigh's belief in the riches of Guyana.

The following is an excerpt from Dr. K.S. Wise's Historical Sketches of Trinidad and Tobago Vol. II:

'Sir Walter Raleigh was now rapidly reaching the zenith of his career and became deeply immersed in the political movements in England so that the Guayana project had to fade into abeyance while he faced the rivalry of Essex and lost his intrigue for the favour of James Stuart.'

Raleigh was able however to arrange for a small expedition under Laurence Keymis to locate more definitely the Inca capital, to maintain contact with the Indians and to prepare the way for more extensive operations. The ship *Darling* and the pinnace *Discoverer* left Portland, on January 26th, 1596, but the latter was soon lost to view in foul weather during the voyage across the ocean. The *Darling* with Captain Keymis on board passed the Canaries and Cape Verde and 'fell so far to the southwards by Your Lordship's direction' that they reached the South American coast on March 14th to the west of the Amazon Delta.

From here, Captain Keymis surveyed the whole Guayana coast before reaching the Orinoco, exploring the Aprowaco River for 40 miles but not entering the

CHRONOLOGICAL TABLE FROM 1577

1644 The Society called the Santa Hermandad which existed since the first settlement of San José, was incorporated by a Royal Charter.

1677 The Marquis de Mantenon, in the Socière frigate, aided by some buccaneers, from the island of Tortuga, who had escaped from imprisonment at Cadiz, ravaged Trinidad; their plunder amounted to 100,000 pieces of eight.

1701 A Treaty was entered into between His Most Christian and His Most Catholic Majesty, by which it was agreed to allow the Royal Company of Guinea, established in France, to supply the Spanish Colonies with 48,000 slaves, commencing on the 1st May, 1702, at the rate of 4800 negroes per year. The inhabitants of the island, consequently, availed themselves of the Treaty to obtain the number of slaves they required. Several ship-loads were therefore landed at Trinidad, and Cocoa began to be extensively planted.

1716 Edward Tench, commonly called Black Beard, committed sad depredations in the Gulf of Paria.

1725 The whole of the Cocoa Crop failed and the greater part of the Cocoa trees died.

1730 Lieutenant Governor Colonel Don Bartolome de Aldunate y Rada was sworn in as Governor.

1731 A small vessel, belonging to Teneriffe, with six sailors was driven to the island, she was laden with wine.

other rivers. Along the coast he learnt from the Indians that they were expecting Raleigh to return. They also learnt that the Spaniards were expecting large reinforcements from Spain to arrive shortly in Trinidad and also that the Caribs were preparing to drive the Aruacs out of the Orinoco region so as to deprive the Spaniards of their source of food and therefore cause their withdrawal.

Still more importantly, Captain Keymis learnt of a great lake at the head of the Essequibo River where he was certain the famed golden town of Manoa was located. This lake could be reached directly by ascending the River Essequibo, and in this way the treacherous and difficult passage through the shoals of the Orinoco Delta could be avoided, as well as any settlements which the Spaniards might have on the Orinoco River.

By April 6th Keymis had reached the delta and entered the Orinoco River. His arrival was soon discovered by Indians in pirogues collecting food who disclosed information on the whereabouts of the Spaniards. Proceeding up river he captured a boat carrying letters from Don Antonio de Berrio to Trinidad asking for men to be sent at once. Captain Keymis continued up river to the mouth of the Caroni where he found Don Antonio settled with 55 men determined to dispute any entry to the hinterland. In addition to this settlement on the bank, the Spaniards had made a strong fort on an island nearby.

Here Keymis learnt that Don Antonio was expecting daily the arrival of a large force from Spain which would bring him men from Trinidad and horses from Caracas.

Realising the danger of being trapped in the river Keymis started to return on the 16th, dropping rapidly down stream and making contact with the Indians, from whom he learnt they were gradually deserting the area due to their mistreatment by the Spaniards. They asked urgently for protection by the English and reported that the Spaniards now found great difficulty in getting food supplies. The Indians showed Keymis where gold could be found and assured him that all the Indians were ready to rise against the Spaniards.

Keymis also discovered that the long expected expedition from Spain had arrived in Trinidad and that there were 16 ships prepared to repulse any fleet brought by Raleigh. These ships were to wait until June when the Orinoco in flood would be impassable and the danger avoided for at least a year.

On April 24th, Keymis reached the mouth of the Orinoco and was overjoyed to find there the pinnace *Discoverer* which had caught up with him after exploring four of the Guianese rivers. The men and stores were transferred to the *Darling* and the pinnace burnt as unserviceable.

From here Captain Keymis did not dare to enter the Bay of Paria and attempt to pass through the Bocas because of the presence of the Spanish Fleet. By anchoring during the flood and drifting with the current during the ebb, Keymis managed to work his vessel to the east along the south coast of Trinidad. Whereupon reaching to windward Keymis managed to clear the north-east point and arrived in Tobago. After sailing through the West Indies he finally arrived at Plymouth on June 29th 1596.

Engraved for Drakes Voyages.

Sir Walter Raleigh captured the island of Trinidad from the Spanish Governor Don Antonio Sedeno. After his victorious battle Raleigh set free five of the Amerindian Caciques who had been put into irons by the Spaniards. Their names were Wanawanare, Caroaori, Maquarima, Torroopanama and Aterima.

Sir Walter Raleigh sets at Liberty five Indian Kings, who were all linked together.

While Captain Keymis brought to Sir Walter Raleigh further and encouraging news of El Dorado he also brought a clear warning that the Spaniards had settled in force on the Orinoco near to the mouth of the Caroni, and were determined to prevent any entrance into their rich provinces. In 1597 as a direct consequence of this Raleigh sent Captain Leonard Berry to explore the possibility of entering Guyana by a more easterly route altogether avoiding the River Orinoco.

This third expedition left the Thames in a pinnace on October 14th, 1596. However for all their enthusiasm they remained stuck in the channel due to contrary wind till near the end of the year. They finally reached the Guyanese coast on January 27th. Captain Berry spent 9 days exploring the Wiapoco River, 17 days in the Marowyne and 20 days up the Corentyne River. He did not continue up the Corentyne beyond the Great Falls because he did not wish to antagonise the Accowoio Indians 'which would turn to our great hurt when Sir Walter Raleigh should come thither having occasion to use this river.'

He was told that the Spaniards were still present in force in Trinidad, on the Orinoco and also on the Essequibo and Captain Berry evidently feared to follow the coast further to the west to thoroughly explore the Essequibo as he had almost certainly been instructed. He left the Corentyne River, turned his course to the north, on May 8th, and reached Plymouth on June 20th, 1597.

With the reports of Keymis and Berry before him, Sir Walter Raleigh proceeded to try and carry out his original scheme to settle and exploit the natural resources of Guyana and as a secondary consideration to gain the treasures of El Dorado. Unfortunately, political intrigues increased and his star began to wane. The accession of James I led to the trial of Raleigh who was subsequently imprisoned in the Tower of London in 1603.

Having been left behind by Raleigh in Cumana in 1595, Don Antonio de Berrio, Governor of Trinidad, remained ever loyal to his obligations and hurried to Margarita, where he gathered together the remnants of his troops who had escaped from Trinidad. He returned with 10 men to view the ruins of San José. He decided to return to the Orinoco and occupy the port of Morequito at the mouth of the Caroni where he could guard the entrance to El Dorado and watch over his interests.

The Council of the Indies was greatly disturbed by the invasion and exploration of Guyana by Raleigh. It realised the grave and serious danger to the Spanish Empire in the West if European nations were to make permanent and growing settlements in the Indies.

Don Antonio de Berrio had long urged the conquest and settlement of Trinidad and now that Raleigh had raided the Island and had announced his intention of returning the next year with 1,000 men to occupy both Trinidad and Guyana and make permanent settlements, all the neighbouring officials pressed the urgent necessity of immediate action to secure those provinces.

Upon learning this the Council of the Indies was thoroughly convinced and urged the King to recognise Berrio's claims and send forth Domingo de Vera (then in Spain pleading on behalf of Berrio) at once.

Thus on February 23rd, 1596, Domingo de Vera, left San Lucar with 1,500 men, women and children on six vessels. This was part of a fleet bound for the West Indies which had received every facility for their departure including a loan of 70,000 ducats from the Royal Treasury and of 5,000 ducats from the City of Seville.

The ships dropped anchor at the Island of Trinidad, on April 10th, while the rest of the fleet sailed on. Ten additional vessels remained at the Five Islands, or Las Cotorras as they were called, to repulse the dreaded Sir Walter Raleigh. By July, any danger of invasion had passed and these ten vessels sailed on to their destination.

It is clear therefore that Captain Keymis only escaped from the Orinoco just in time, as within a week of his departure from that river, the Spaniards were passing up the river in force and by the end of May, Berrio had some 400 men at San Thomé.

The Council did not rest content with this effort. As reinforcements were always necessary in new settlements, one hundred families were embarked at Cadiz in June, 1596 ready to follow Vera's expedition to Trinidad and Guyana. Unfortunately they were never to depart from Cadiz. A combined English and Dutch fleet commanded by Walter Raleigh captured Cadiz shortly before the planned departure and destroyed 40 of the outward bound merchant vessels. Before the fleet could be reformed, the disastrous failure of Vera's adventure caused the intended reinforcements to be withdrawn.

The Spaniards, however, still remained in strength on the River Orinoco, and Captain Berry was correctly informed, when the Indians warned him in April, 1597, that the Spaniards were on the Essequibo. This was merely an exploring party and no permanent settlement by the Spaniards ever appeared to have been made in Guyana east of the Orinoco.

While the efforts of Spain to repel Sir Walter Raleigh and to prevent his settlements definitely failed, political events in England interfered to arrest the progress of the gold seeking expeditions. Raleigh only found opportunity to send out small exploring parties to keep in touch with the Indians of Trinidad and Guyana and twenty-three years elapsed before he made any further attempt in this direction.'

Daniel Hart's Chronology Continued

1733   Lieutenant Governor Bartolome de Aldunate y Rada died, the Government was administered by José Orbaii and Pedro Ximenes, Alcaldes in Ordinary.
A Census of the Island was taken and every free man's name was entered into the books of the Cabildo—it appears that there were 162 adult males, out of these 28 only were white. Indians were not considered inhabitants. No account is taken of the slaves. From these inhabitants a revenue of 231 dollars was raised, a part of which was taken to pay the Caroni Guard, consisting of a Corporal and three Privates.

1734   The Cabildo consisted of 2 Alcaldes, 3 Regidores, a Procurador General, an Alcalde of the Santa Hermandad, and a Quadrillon, the Governor was the President.

1735   Colonel Estevan Simon de Liñan y Vera was appointed Captain General of the Island. The Royal Revenue was this year 9737 reals (8 reals to the dollar).

Sources
History of Trinidad under the Spanish Government
by Pierre Gustave Louis Borde Book I 1883.
History of Trinidad, E.L. Joseph, 1840.
Loss of El Dorado, V. Naipaul, 1969.
The Golden Man, the Quest for El Dorado, Victor von Hagen, 1974.
Trinidad Historical Society Papers, Volume II and III
Historical Sketches of Trinidad & Tobago, Dr. K.S. Wise,
Volume II and III, 1936 and 1938.

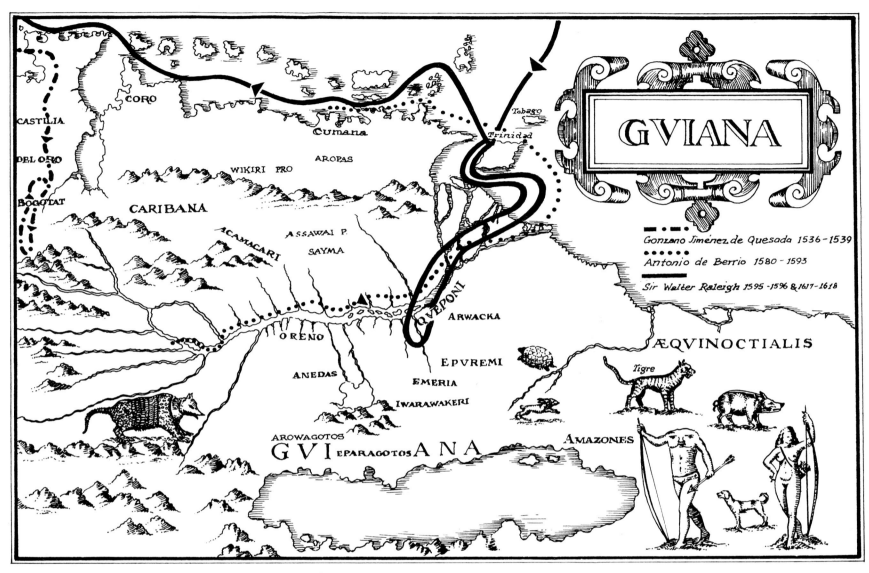

A map reconstructed to show the voyages of the Conquistadores Quesada, de Berrio and Raleigh.

Daniel Hart's Chronology Continued

1739 A general meeting of the inhabitants took place to prevent the introduction of Small Pox then raging on the Continent.

1740 The inhabitants petition their Sovereign to send them a Guard of 50 men in addition to the 20 stationed at the Caroni.

1746 The Taxes made payable in provisions (see Tariff herein).

19 June, 1746 The Treasury of the Island, counted by the proper officer; result 9735 reals plata ($1216 7 reals).

1759 Colonel Pedro de la Moneda arrived as Governor and took up his residence in Port-of-Spain.

1760 A schoolmaster appointed to instruct the children of the Island at the following rates: Teaching the Alphabet, $1/2$ real per month. Reading, 1 real. Writing and Arithmetic $1^1/_2$ real.

1760 All weights and measures regulated by a particular Standard.

1760 Order made that all boys of sufficient age be put apprentices to trades.

1764 Great alarm respecting the small pox which was raging on the neighbouring continent. Guards of 4 men each were put at Point Gourde, Point Chaguaramas and Point La Brea.

1766 Monsr. Jacques D'Alburquerque appointed Surgeon of the island.

1774 The seat of Government temporary made in Port-of-Spain.

1777 The island of Trinidad separated from the Vice-royalty of the New Kingdom of Granada, and added to the Captain Generalship of Caracas.

1780 The Cabildo empower the Alcalde of the first election to go to the French islands, and induce French and Irish settlers to come to Trinidad.

1780 The Royal Cedula of Privilege granted by His Catholic Majesty to encourage foreigners to colonize this island, was ordered to be translated into French and English.

1782 The Otaheite cane, the breadfruit tree, and the bamboo introduced into the island by St. H. Begorrat from Martinique.

1783 Port-of-Spain permanently became the Capital of the island, (21st August), and the Cabildo first held their sittings in that town.

1787 M. Picot de Lapeyrouse established the first sugar estate in the island.

TRINIDAD 1592 TO THE 1770'S
Bridget Brereton

With the foundation of San José de Oruña (St. Joseph) in 1592, Trinidad had been given the formal structure of a Spanish colony. But for nearly two centuries it remained undeveloped and isolated. Spain was too weak as a colonial power in this period to be able to develop a small remote island that possessed no gold or silver and lay far from the main shopping routes of her Empire. Instead of plantations producing tropical crops for export to Europe, worked by gangs of slaves, creating great fortunes for some planters and businessmen, Trinidad was the scene of a little cultivation by a few Spaniards, Indians, mestizos and slaves, preoccupied with survival and subsistence on scattered clearings in the forests.

Tobacco cultivation began on a small scale early in the 17th century, but this small export industry withered away with competition from North America. Cocoa became important later, and it was Trinidad's major industry between about 1670 and 1725; but in 1725 the cocoa crop failed, probably as a result of disease, and it never really recovered from this disaster. Of course there was always some food crop production for maintenance by the Indians on their conucos (gardens), and by the Spanish settlers. But up to the 1770's, agriculture was a very small-scale, primitive business and the colonists lived close to the margin of subsistence. In any case, the white population in this period was always very small, for Spain could not provide the manpower to develop her vast empire yet would not contemplate permitting foreigners to settle there. After the cocoa disaster in 1725, the Island's non-Indian population declined to a mere 162 adult men, of whom only 28 were described as 'white', that is Spanish. From then until the 1770's, though there was some recovery, the Spanish population was never large enough to become a viable Creole settler community. By 1765 Trinidad's population was estimated at 2,503, but 1,277 of these were Christianized Indians.

Indeed, up to the 1780's Trinidad remained essentially an Amerindian society, though the Indian population declined rapidly after the initial contacts with Spaniards in the early 1500's. The Indians were first parcelled out in encomiendas, large estates or villages in which the resident Indians had to work for, and pay tribute to the encomendero, the privileged Spaniard who had been given the grant. Four were established: Acarigua (San Juan), Arauca (Arouca), Tacarigua and Caura. Outside the encomiendas, where some 600 Indians may have been living in 1712, were many more living in the forests in independent settlements. To bring these 'wild Indians' under Christian influence and Spanish control, Capuchin missionaries were given the task of converting them between 1687 and 1708, and they established mission settlements some of which survived as Indian villages well into the 1700's (notably, Savanna Grande, Guayria, Savanetta and Montserrate). The missions were abolished in 1708 and the encomiendas in 1716, but by then the great majority of the Island's Indians had become 'Hispanised'; that is, Christian, Spanish-speaking, and organized into villages under some degree of control by the church and the Government Spanish Settlers used them as labourers on their farms. Their numbers steadily declined, though they remained the majority of the island's population until the 1770's.

For the Spanish settlers, life was precarious, and especially so in the middle decades of the 1770's. After the cocoa failure in 1725 and a smallpox epidemic in 1739, St. Joseph, as reported by a governor in 1757, was a derelict collection of mostly roofless mud huts. The citizens were indolent, impoverished and quarrelsome (in 1745 the Cabildo members had arrested and imprisoned the governor for nine months). In 1757 the governor took up residence in Port of Spain, then a small but growing fishing village and port of call. The Cabildo itself did not follow suit until 1784, but one can say that St. Joseph's day was effectively over when the governor left the impoverished little town to its own devices and went to live in the Port, the city that would come into its own in the 1780's and 1790's.

By 1765 the Spanish Empire came under the influence of the reform-minded Bourbon Kings. Trade within the Empire was liberalized and important administrative reforms were carried out. Of most direct significance to Trinidad, however, was the decision to allow foreign immigration (under certain controls) to the island. A 1776 decree authorized foreign Catholic settlement in Trinidad and other colonies. It was under this decree, in May 1777, that Roume de St. Laurent visited the island.

THE SPANISH GOVERNORS OF TRINIDAD

1530 – 1538	Antonio Sedeno
1571 – 1591	Juan Ponce de Leon
1592 – 1597	Antonio de Berrio y Oruna
1597 – 1612	Fernando de Berrio
1612	Sancho de Alquiza
1615 – 1618	Diego Palomeque de Acuna
1619 – 1622	Fernando de Berrio
1624 – 1631	Luis de Monsalves
1631 – 1636	Cristoval de Aranda
1636 – 1641	Diego Lopez de Escobar
1641 – 1657	Martin de Mondoza y la Hoz
1657 – 1664	Juan de Viedma
1665	Jose de Aspe y Zuniga
1670 – 1677	Diego Ximenes de Aldana
1677 – 1682	Tiburcio de Aspe y Zuniga
1682 – 1688	Diego Suarez Ponce de Leon
1688 – 1690	Sebastian de Roseta
1692 – 1698	Francisco de Menez
1699 – 1700	Jose de Leon Echales
1700 – 1705	Francisco Ruiz de Aguirre
1705 – 1711	Felipe de Artieda
1711 – 1716	Cristoval Felix de Guzman
1716 – 1721	Pedro de Yarza
1721 – 1726	Martin Perez de Anda y Salazar
1726 – 1731	Agustin de Arredonda
1731 – 1732	Bartholome de Aldunate y Rada
1734 – 1746	Estevan Simon de Linan y Vera
1746 – 1752	Juan Jose Salcedo
1752 – 1757	Francisco Nanclares
1757 – 1760	Pedro de la Moneda
1760 – 1762	Jacinto San Juan
1762 – 1766	Jose Antonio Gil
1766 – 1773	Jose de Flores
1773 – 1776	Juan de Dios Valdez y Varza
1776 – 1779	(Manuel Falques (Military Governor) (Martin de Salaverria (Civil Governor)
1779 – 1784	Martin de Salaverria
1784 – 1797	Jose Maria Chacon

Source: Voices in the Street, O. Mavrogordato, 1977.

The Coloniser of Trinidad

Edited by Sue-Anne Gomes

Don Manuel Falquez took over the government of the island on 30th December 1776, less than three months after the date of the regulation on immigration. His first concern was to have this regulation translated into French and English and distributed throughout the Antilles. One can understand that it was in Grenada, which is the nearest island and which had received the worst treatment of all the French islands ceded to the English, that its receipt was the best, and was acted on without delay. At once, Philippe-Rose Roume de St. Laurent, one of the most highly recommended creoles, made a plan to visit Trinidad in order to come to an understanding with the Governor about the details of the advantages which were offered to foreigners who wished to establish themselves there, and also to render an account of the resources which he found. Born on the 13th October 1743, he was at that time thirty-three years of age. His ancestors originated in Germany, and were of a very old noble family. His coat of arms was on a field of azure, three golden short cloaks accompanied by three golden stars, two in the centre and one at the point. The escutcheon was surmounted by a crest in front defended by five helmets and decorated by scallops in gold and azure, but without supporters. These external ornaments were worn by the cavaliers who were the banner bearers. Having emigrated to France from time immemorial, this family was settled first at Auvergne and later at Bourgogne where, by direct or indirect alliances, they were joined to Canillac, Bissy, Thairre, Guanay and others among the most distinguished families in the country. His grandfather Philippe Roume, had come to the islands in the position of a sub-delegate in the administration of Martinique, and later moved himself and family to Grenada, where he carried out the duties of a judge and a councillor to the Royal Court. His father, Laurent Roume, had also filled the post of councillor to the Royal Court in Grenada, and there he had married Rose de Gannes de la Chancellerie, who later made a second marriage with the Marquis de Charras. Roume's

first visited France when he was in his twenties. It was there that he met Anne Holmes who would later become his wife in 1765. After the marriage, Roume and Anne went to Grenda, it was on this tiny island that this section of the St. Laurent family would come to a tragic end. They had three children Francoise Elizabeth who was born in 1766, she died twenty years later, their second child, a boy, died in infancy and Celeste Elizabeth their third was born in 1770, she died at the tender age of four. The relationship between Roume and his wife Anne also withered away and they were eventually divorced in 1799.

Although Roume did not take up any public position he enjoyed a moderate income, and having no official attachments, he lived in complete independence, surrounded by the respect and esteem of his countrymen. He had a phlegmatic temperament, and beneath a simple and modest exterior, he concealed a great talent and vast knowledge. By limiting his desires to the ordinary needs of his family and to the well being and esteem of the public, he lacked nothing to prevent him from enjoying a happy and quiet life. However tension among his fellow Grenadian settlers soared, for France ceded the island to Great Britain in 1763 by the Treaty of Paris. The colonists on the island lived precariously, never knowing which way the tide would flow, constantly being used as pawns in European war games. This situation in Grenada was reflected throughout the other West Indian islands for these Caribbean settlers fervently desired to make their islands viable not withstanding the vagaries of the European powers. This was the birth of the West Indian spirit. The uncertainty of life in Grenada made Roume's heart bleed for his fellow countrymen. His ambition to remedy the situation was awakened, and when the regulation of Charles III was published in Grenada, at the expense of his own peace, he decided to dedicate

Overleaf: *The only known picture of Roume de St. Laurent is this cartoon drawing which was published in Carlton Ottley's 'Histories of Trinidad'. Roume de St. Laurent's signature from a document on Tobago, Tom Cambridge Collection.*

himself to the work of deliverance.

Roume de St. Laurent came to Trinidad in May 1777, and in order to study the natural resources of the island as well as its topography, he set himself the task of visiting all the coastline and of exploring the forests in every way. Like all visitors to Trinidad from the time of Christopher Columbus, he was filled with wonder at the island's geographical position, and at the happy and rich condition of its soil. He also delighted in the view of its peaceful gulf, its serene sky, its smiling valleys and fertile plains, and he was overcome by the fascination which the island always exercised on visitors. As a consequence, his devotion to his compatriots was doubled by a great desire to colonize this island which he had resolved to turn into his second home. To this double sentiment which was born in his breast, he determined to dedicate both his time and fortune. The history of the foundation of French establishments in America is full of such generous acts. To attain his ends, he found the regulation of Charles III insufficient, and at the interview which he had with Governor Falquez after he had explored the island, he pointed out the deficiencies. He said that there was no doubt that the French families in the islands which had been handed over to England, and even those which had remained French which were ravaged by ants, were anxious to abandon these places which had become so unliveable. However, they would not emigrate, except to places where they would find more advantages. He went on to say that, since the Declaration of Independence of the United Provinces (1776), the eyes of the colonists were turned to the north, where they could purchase fertile lands at a paltry price, and where they hoped, by their activity and industry, and the remains of their fortunes, together with the experience which they had achieved at the expense of their health, to repair their losses in a few years. The three provinces of Georgia, Carolina and Florida, especially, offered this advantage, that they would be able to engage in cultivations with which they and their slaves were familiar. The liberty which they enjoyed was another attractive feature which lured them. To persuade these people against settling in those provinces, already well populated and civilized, and to induce them to establish themselves in Trinidad which was still a savage desert, it was absolutely essential to offer them a form of compensation, which was not accorded by the Spanish Court which offered only the concession of free lands. This compensation could not be found but in sound material advantages and in serious legislative guarantees. Therefore, in order to avoid the inconveniences brought about by the state of war between the new American Federation and England, the heavy expenses involved in such a move, the risks of a change in climate, it was only on the conditions mentioned that they would consent to emigrate to the island.

Passing on to political considerations, Roume de St. Laurent then informed the Governor that Spain's commerce which was threatened by the new American Federation as well as by England, could not be saved except by a prompt and strong colonization of her desert islands, to which should be given the most generous franchises for their exchange. He also added that the island which needed the most prompt re-population was Trinidad, because of her commercial and exceptional position on the coast of the South American continent; following on, he stressed the military importance of her position for the defence of the continental Spanish

colonies, and he was of the opinion that this island constituted for Spain, a possession of inestimable price. Finally, he pointed out that up to that time, such a large colony had never been protected against the blows inflicted by the power in these parts, except by the ignorance of people as to her natural advantages. With this gift of being able to look into the future, which is only shared by men of genius, he was of the opinion that the re-population of the country by foreigners attracted by the regulation of Charles III, would certainly soon make Trinidad well known and appreciated, and the Spaniards would not be able to keep it any longer, except by a strong and rapid colonization, which would protect them from an outside desperate attack. During the course of these interviews which he had with the Governor and where he gained his esteem and confidence, it was decided that he would set out his views about colonization in a memorandum to be addressed to the Court of Spain. Before taking leave of Don Manuel Falquez, and in order to give proof of his affection for his new home, he purchased some land in the beautiful valley of Diego Martin.

Such is the remarkable plan which was carried out by Spain, very late for Trinidad (1784) and even later still for Puerto Rico (1815), which assured for these two colonies, and especially for Trinidad, an important and rapid colonization. As soon as his memorandum had been written, in the same year 1777, Roume de Saint Laurent returned to Trinidad and submitted it to Governor Falquez, who approved of it and sent it on to the Spanish Court. By good luck he had the opportunity of sending it direct to Spain. Just then there were in Port of Spain, two superior officers, Brigadier General Don Agustín Cranc and Lieutenant Colonel Don Juan de Catilla, on their way back from inspecting Spanish strongholds between Vera Cruz and the mouths of the Orinoco. The memorandum was entrusted to Lieutenant

Colonel Don Juan de Catilla, who was leaving for Spain immediately. For his part, Don José de Abalos, the Intendant of Caracas, had not been sleeping, and a few months later, in July 1778, he sent to Trinidad, Don Martín de Salaverría (who was the commandant of the company of coastguards), as a sub-delegate, with particular instructions for the advancement of agriculture and commerce, and the re-population of the island.

On his return to Grenada, Roume de St. Laurent urged his compatriots to give up their project of emigrating to the United Provinces and like him, to go and settle in Trinidad, which he painted a most attractive picture; he stressed its commercial and agricultural importance, and praised to the skies its beauty and fertility. He particularly urged his relatives and intimate friends not to delay in going and establishing properties there, and he succeeded in communicating his enthusiasm to all concerned. What really succeeded in winning the desire for emigrating to Trinidad was the prospect of obtaining from the Spanish Court, the guarantees and franchises for foreign colonists which were necessary to attain the desired result. Roume de Saint Laurent from that time onwards, undertook the drawing up of his memorandum. Whilst on this, he also got all the information he could concerning the number of families who were prepared to leave the French islands, either because they were devastated by ants, or because they had come under the power of England. From three of these islands he obtained definite figures. The families from Martinique numbered 286 with 24,710 slaves; from Dominica, 40 families with 3,647 slaves, and from Grenada, 57 families with 4,965 slaves. There is no question here that these families were all whites, and it was estimated that each one had an average of four persons, and thus we arrive at the total of 1,532 white colonists owning 33,322 slaves. Reckoning at even half the figures from the other islands of Tobago, St. Vincent, St. Lucia and Guadeloupe, we arrive at a sum total of 2,300 white colonists with 50,000 slaves, without counting the coloured families and their slaves. Such was the considerable population, for the time, which this able coloniser was anxious to settle in Trinidad. One can well understand the great interest which the Spanish Government had in attracting this elite population to their desert island.

Roume had already sent most of his slaves over, when the American War of Independence broke out and Grenada was re-taken by the French. This unforeseen happening presented an obstacle to his plans. Seeing that Spain was allied to France against England, he understood that she would not have the time to be concerned about the colonization of her American islands, and that it would be necessary for him to be patient until the declaration of peace. The return of his island to France, and the long delay with which he was threatened, could easily have changed his mind about the colonization of Trinidad. But nothing of the sort happened. On the contrary, it seems that the accidents and difficulties which obstructed his plan only rendered him more determined. So although Roume was driven with the desire to populate and settle in Trinidad in 1779 with the recapture of Grenada by France, he accepted the position of Governor to his native island. So dynamic was this man's execution of his duties that when his tenure was up the English settlers wanted to subscribe among themselves a hefty salary of £1,600 so that he would remain. Not even this would induce him to give up his dreams of Trinidad and four months later

upon his departure from Grenada the settlers presented him with a laudatory address in which they stated 'you have always maintained the reputation of an upright man, of a good son, of a good husband, of a good father, of a good neighbour, of a good master.' They praised him for his humanity in dealing with runaway negroes, and for the fact that he had never needed to bring anyone to court.

In the meantime, the Governor Don Manuel Falquez breathed his last in Port of Spain on 11th July 1779, and as usual, the two Alcaldes in service took charge of the government of the island.

As soon as he had been relieved of his duties as a judge, Roume de Saint Laurent hastened to proceed to Trinidad in order to supervise the work on his properties, and in consultation with the Governor, to try to urge by all possible means, the colonization of the island. On this occasion he was accompanied by a good many of his compatriots, among whom were three of his intimate friends, Mr. Dominique Dert, Mr. Étienne Noël and Mr. Picot de Lapéyrouse. It was the last of these who established the first sugar factory in the island, on lands which today form the cemetery in Port of Spain, and which continues to bear his name.

As was to be expected, Spain had not yet made any decree on the memorandum of the coloniser, but she had however, taken administrative measures which proved her preoccupation with the interests of the colonists of the island. She had doubled the administration of government, and had appointed two governors, one of whom was concerned entirely with civil and commercial matters, and the other with purely military affairs. The civil governor was entirely independent of the military governor, and consequently he was concerned only with the progress of the colonisation of the island. Spain had appointed to this superior post Don Martín de Salaverría, who was the sub-delegate of the Intendant at Caracas, and only the sinecure of military government was left on the 13th April 1779 to Don Manuel Falquez. But on the arrival of the despatch on the 21st August 1779, Don Manuel Falquez had already been dead for over a month, and therefore Don Rafael Delgado, who was commanding the troops, took over the military government. The new civil and commercial governor was a gentle and affable man, and at the same time, he was extremely able and had the prosperity of the island very much at heart. In the negotiations which this Governor had with Roume de Saint Laurent, the latter had no trouble in winning him over to his ideas. The one difficulty however, was to get the metropolitan government of Spain to accept their proposals, and this, in the opinion of the Governor, was a considerable one. To overcome this, he considered that the aid of the Intendant at Caracas was indispensable, and he urged Saint Laurent to go to Caracas to explain the details of his plan, and to get him to approve it. As a preliminary step, and in order to gain the confidence of this high official, it was agreed that Saint Laurent should go in person to the smaller islands with the object of recruiting the inhabitants to come to Trinidad. Complying with this arrangement, Philippe Rose Roume de Saint Laurent was appointed Alcalde of the First Election for the year 1780, and in this capacity he was authorized by a decree from the Governor, dated 29th April 1780, to proceed to the French islands, and furnished with a copy of the Royal Decree granted by His Majesty the King of Spain, which was translated into French and English, he was to invite the French and Irish inhabitants to establish themselves

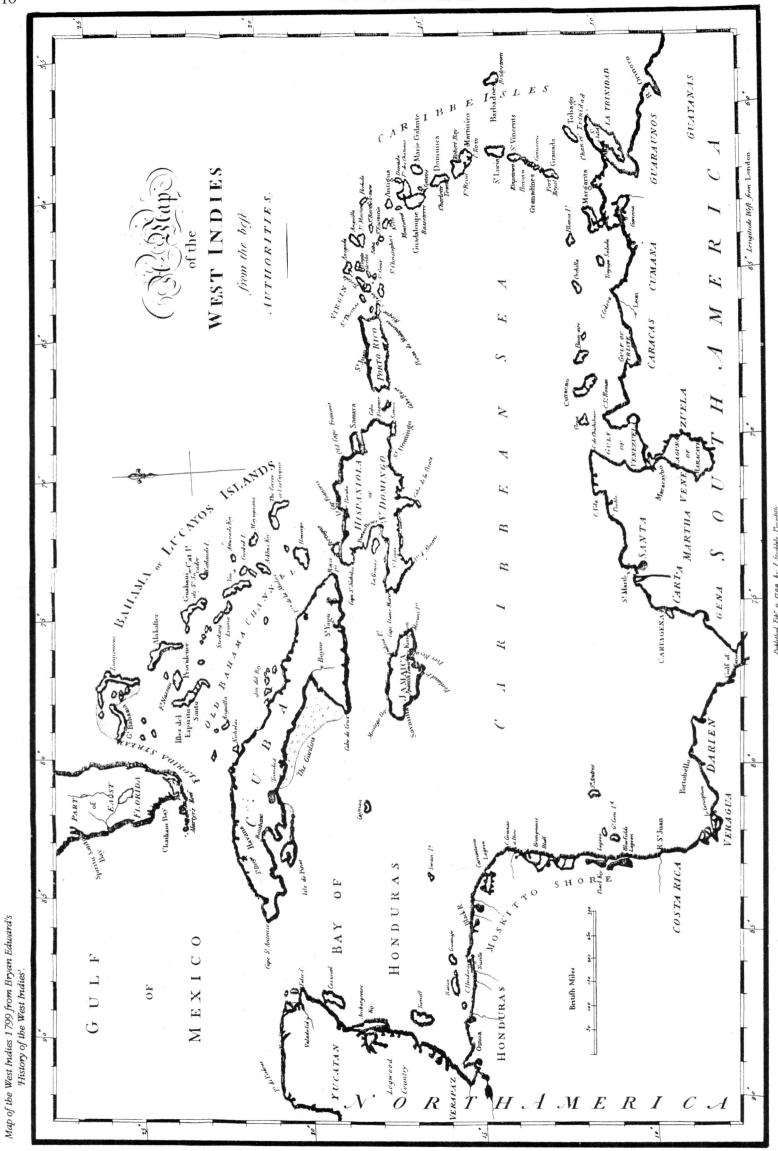

Map of the West Indies 1799 from Bryan Edward's 'History of the West Indies'.

in Trinidad.

On returning from his voyage, which had not resulted in matters of much importance to the country, he had however, been able to recruit a number of French families over and above the previous ones. When he arrived in Trinidad, he received the sad news that during his absence his friend Mr. Dominique Dert had been put into prison. Mr. Dert had set up a coffee plantation near to the sugar factory of Mr. de Lapéyrouse on a site which is today occupied by the road which bears his name (Dere Street, formerly Dert Street). One night his young coffee trees were destroyed by a horse belonging to the military Governor. He impounded the horse and refused to return it without receiving compensation for the damage which the animal had caused. Don Rafael Delgado refused to consider such a just claim, and Mr. Dert persisted in retaining possession of the animal. Thereupon, he was arrested by the military Governor, in spite of protests from civil Governor don Martín de Salaverría. Roume de Saint Laurent found great public indignation aroused by this arbitrary act, and in consequence the colonization of the island was seriously compromised. Owing to his friendship with Mr. Dert, and actuated by a desire to settle such a delicate matter, he took the affair in hand, but without success. The bad-tempered and brutal military Governor would not consent to release the prisoner unless he apologised very humbly, and the prisoner, considering that he had done nothing reprehensible, refused to submit to this humiliation. Having reached this point, the difficulty could not be settled except by the superior authority of the Captain General in Caracas, and Roume de Saint Laurent, on the advice of Governor Salaverría, took the opportunity of going to Caracas and submitting to the Intendant, Don José de Abalos, his plan for colonization, and asking for his approval of it.

The Coloniser left for Caracas accompanied by his friends Mr. Noël and Mr. de Lapéyrouse. He had no difficulty in obtaining full and entire justice from the Captain General. Don Rafael Delgado was thrown out and declared incapable of occupying any other appointment in government. Don Juan Francisco Machado was appointed to succeed him on 31st March 1781. With the Intendant, the Colonizer had equal success. The writer whom we follow here says that Saint Laurent had such a very strong and attractive personality that it was easy for him to communicate his enthusiasm to such a benevolent man as Don José de Abalos. With an easy eloquence, he showed how Trinidad, which was so important for the military establishment and commerce of Spain, was an island which was gradually stagnating. He also pointed out the dangers and privations which would have to be endured by foreign colonists who were to establish themselves there, and the necessity of offering them advantages to cover the risks and perils which they would be undertaking. He said that it was only under such conditions that one could hope to colonize the island within a reasonable time. The Intendant, who was already impressed by these ideas, studied the memorandum with much care. He was struck by such a splendid project, and promised to give it his support when sending it to the Court in Spain, seeing that it already had the approval of the two Governors, Falquez and Salaverría. However, he raised two objections which Saint Laurent felt that he had to agree in order to obtain the approval in principal for his plan. The objections raised were on the subject of the introduction of French priests, and about the equality of advantages granted to foreign colonists, both white and coloured.

Roume de Saint Laurent returned to Trinidad with the hope that the support given to him by the Intendant would finally lead to the acceptance of the plan of colonization which he had drawn up and submitted to the Court in Spain, at least four years before. Nevertheless, nothing happened, and after he had waited anxiously until the end of that year, he decided with the approval of Don José de Abalos, to proceed to Spain for the purpose of stimulating the colonial zeal of the Minister, and for coming to an understanding with him. In order to get together the necessary funds for such a long voyage, he was obliged to dispose of all his possessions and turn them into money, and he left his family in the charge of his mother. No consideration of personal interest was allowed to be an obstacle in his devotion to his new country. He paid a second visit to Caracas in order to get letters of recommendation from the Intendant, and also to obtain favourable reports on his project, and following this, he embarked for Europe in the beginning of 1782. After a successful voyage, he arrived in France and proceeded to Paris where he submitted his colonisation plan to the Spanish Ambassador, with a view to obtaining from him as well, his approval and recommendations. It will be seen that the Coloniser neglected nothing which might help the success of his enterprise. The Spanish ambassador at that time, was the illustrious Count d'Aranda, the previous minister who had advised the King to adopt a liberal political attitude towards this matter in view of the coming independence of the New England Provinces, and the revolutionary influence which this independence brought about in the Spanish possessions in the New World. He gave a very favourable welcome to the project of the colonisation of the Spanish islands through the admission of foreign Catholics, and gave his support to the Coloniser. He advised him about the line of conduct which he should follow in order to conciliate the Minister in Spain, and to get him to agree to his plan without losing too much time. It is said that he carried his good will to the point of urging him to lose no time in taking these steps, because he knew that in the peace treaty which was about to be negotiated, England was proposing to demand the island of Trinidad in exchange for Gibraltar.

Armed with these recommendations and information, Roume de Saint Laurent arrived in Madrid in 1782. There he had no difficulty in getting an interview with the Minister, and it did not take him long to gain his interest with the same facility with which he had been able to get approval from all others to whom he had submitted his plans. All the advantages which had been agreed upon with the Intendant at Caracas were liberally granted in support of foreign Catholic emigration, and particularly those accorded to the French colonists, which as was right, was his particular aim. In a short time there was not much more to be done than to undertake the legal recording of these advantages, but the Minister would not consent to give them the force of law until after the conclusion of peace.

While waiting for the Peace Treaty, which was being negotiated at Versailles, St. Laurent occupied his time in establishing business relations between Europe and Trinidad. To this end he visited the principal towns of commerce, both in France and Spain, where he succeeded in establishing business connections in favour of many of his friends in the island. Everywhere he spoke so favourably about the commercial and agricultural advantages of the country, that he persuaded many wealthy European merchants and others to acquire land there. However he became totally frustrated by the delays on the part of the Spanish court, and in addition to this he also began facing serious financial difficulties. He had made some financial decisions as well as spent a fortune in going to Europe to plead his memoranda, his only option was to return to Paris. At last the Peace Treaty was signed on 3rd September 1783 at Versailles, and immediately after this, the Court at Madrid took up the duty of making the necessary administrative changes for the new colonial organisation in the island. By a ministerial decree dated 18th October 1783, the Governor Don Martín de Salaverría was promoted to another post, and Governor Don Juan Francisco Machado was appointed to administer provisionally, both the civil and military government of the island, whilst awaiting the arrival of the naval captain Don José María Chacon, who had been appointed Captain General, and whose mission it was to carry out the plan of colonisation which had been adopted by the Royal Court of Spain. In Paris Roume's financial situation worsened and he faced total bankruptcy. It is more than likely that the Spanish court had not yet offered him a position for the colonisation of Trinidad and the desperateness of the situation prompted him to apply for the position of Ordonnateur of Tobago.

On the 28th April 1786, the French Government issued an order to Roume to take up the post of Commissary-General of the Navy and Ordonnateur of Tobago. He took pleasure in informing the Spanish monarchy of this, and in addition he would, with the permission of the French King, continue to pursue the idea of developing Trinidad. Madrid's response was prompt, they suddenly realised the great loss they would suffer in not having this man act on their behalf in the Caribbean. They sent letter after letter finally making him the offer of Commissary of Trinidad with a renumeration of 10,000 livres. This Roume considered highly insulting for they in fact owed him 300,000 livres, he did not honour this offer with even so much as a reply.

On the 30th July 1786 Roume de St. Laurent Ordonnateur and Comte de Dillon Governor of Tobago arrived on the island. These two men immediately went to work. Under their zealous and tireless administration they were able to set up systems by which the once crippled Tobago economy was able to flourish. While on the island he met a young coloured woman Marianne Elizabeth Rochard they had a daughter on the 6th July 1788. Roume and his lover were eventually married in 1799 in Santo Domingo in the presence of Toussaint L'Ouverture. It was the friendship between these two men that would save Roume's life some years later.

Dillon and Roume had achieved a great deal during their administration of Tobago however the English planters on the island still had large unmanageable debts with the London merchants. This problem became insurmountable and legal difficulties arose and the French Government found it necessary to recall Dillon and Roume. During that same period France began facing the possibility of losing their very valuable colony St. Domingue as faith would have it Roume was chosen as one of the three Commissioners to be sent to the island.

On 29th November 1791 Roume arrived in St. Domingue. The situation there was explosive each social group at loggerheads with the next. France was dealing with a Pandora's box and over the next five years they made four attempts to grapple with worsening social problems in their prized colony. Roume by this time was no longer in St. Domingue; he had since been commissioned as Governor to Santo Domingo (the other side of the colony). Toussaint L'Ouverture a dynamic black leader soon rose to the position of Governor and Commander-in-Chief of St. Domingue. He recognised the sincerity of Roume's feelings for the blacks and over the years they developed an amiable working relationship.

This friendship however came to a bitter end, when Roume acting under direct order from Napoleon disregarded a request made by Toussaint. Roume and his family were placed under arrest, and Toussaint reported to Napoleon that Roume had plotted against him. Napoleon was totally insulted by the black leader's action and in 1808 the fourth and final attempt was made to control St. Domingue. This ended in total disaster, France's position in that colony was mortally wounded. Roume however retained his respect for Toussaint for he believed that this man once treated properly by the French would remain loyal to the crown — Roume had in fact advised against the attack. Toussaint released Roume and his family.

After Roume's narrow escape in St. Domingue he returned to France where he died in 1805. Although he had been awarded a handsome pension of 3,500 francs this came to an end upon his death leaving his widow and daughter destitute. Initially Napoleon refused to award Marianne even a pittance because she was coloured he eventually relented and she was given 600 francs a year.

Phillippe Rose Roume de St. Laurent was a most outstanding man, truly a Caribbean man who dedicated his life to the betterment of the West Indies, whose successes impacted on many lives. Ironically though Roume himself never settled in Trinidad, his mother Rosa de Gannes de la Chancellere lived at Champ Elysées for many a year. It was through his persistence and dedication that he achieved for Trinidad the acceptance of the Cedula of Poplation in 1783. It is this document which has made Trinidad so unique with a cultural mix to be found no where else in the West Indies.

Happily the memoirs of the work of Roume de Saint Laurent have been preserved for us in the archives of the French navy. The title of the record is *Considerations on the Establishment of a French Colony in the island of Trinidad which belongs to the Spanish Court*. The style is quite clear and concise and the arguments are carefully kept short. It is not the work of a crafty diplomat, but of a man of action, which carries with it conviction. To start with, the question of the emigration of French colonists to the Spanish islands is treated in a general manner. Their material sufferings in the islands of Martinique, Guadeloupe, Dominica, St. Lucia, St. Vincent and Grenada, are catalogued in great detail and Roume shows how in order to escape these, they were reduced to the decision of expatriating themselves. Why should Spain, Roume argues whose islands of Santo Domingo, Puerto Rico, Margarita and Trinidad being depopulated, not attract this population which was still rich, and above all, experienced and able, in order to re-establish her American trade which was on the point of expiring? Trinidad, above all, as the nearest of these islands on the West Coast, could easily benefit by the presence of these colonists who knew that the soil there was healthy and fertile, that there was plenty of building material, and that the island enjoyed the inestimable advantage of being free from the hurricanes of the Antilles sea. It is true that

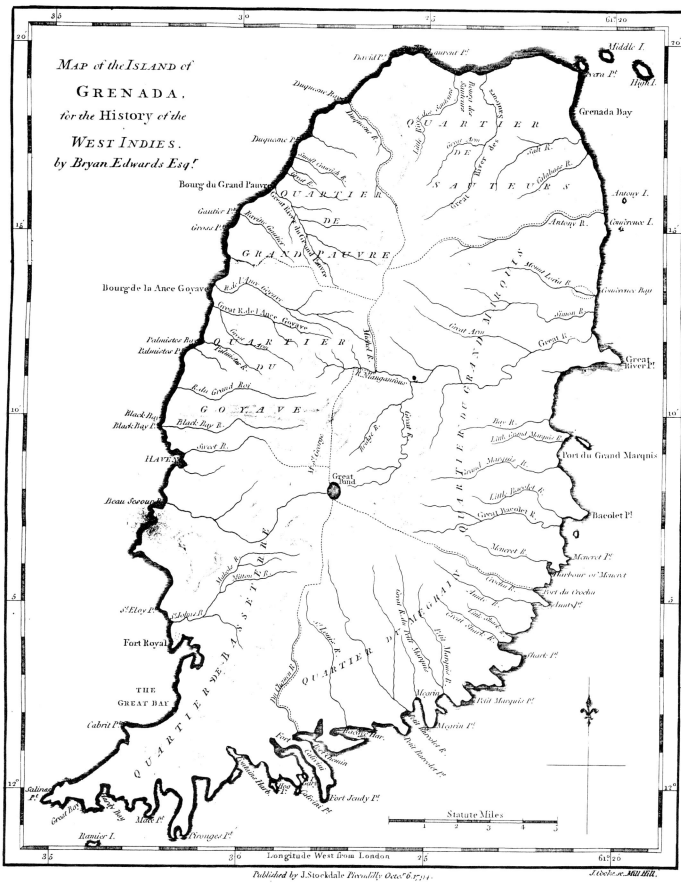

Map of Grenada from Bryan Edwards History of the West Indies.

Spain, on her own initiative and without foreign aid, could have re-populated her islands in order to revive her trade but how was she to create the desire for commercial and industrial enterprises among people who looked upon them with disdain? Furthermore, how much time would have to be wasted in trying to inculcate the necessary knowledge in these people so that they could successfully administer their affairs? In the absence of her own nationals, Spain could not think of attracting to her

islands the Dutch and English who, being of a reformed religion, were not acceptable to the Catholic faith. In addition, the English by their preponderance in the Antilles sea, could not fail to put Spain in the shade. There remained therefore, no one but the colonists from the French islands. But the United Provinces of New England attracted these people, and if Spain were to succeed in using them to her own advantage, it was necessary that she should give them compensation of two kinds: i.e. (1) compensation to France for the loss of her nationals, and (2) advantages granted to the colonists for the services which they would be called upon to render. Joined as she was to France by an agreement known as the *Pacte de Famille,* these just obligations would not in any way, disturb her internal politics. If, however, Spain on the contrary, abandoned the benefits of this important emigration to the United Provinces of New England, she was bound to suffer a double loss, namely that of having abandoned an assured gain, and that of increasing the power of a rival government which, according to the forecast of our political Coloniser, could before long, play an important part in the balance of power of the two continents.

According to the terms of the memorandum, the compensation for France would be the complete franchise of her flag in the ports of the Spanish islands for a period of twenty years. At the expiration of this term, the colonial produce loaded in these ports under the French flag, would be subject to an export tax which would have the double result of increasing the colonial revenue, and of raising the price of French goods, thus enabling Spanish merchandise to enter into competition. As regards the advantages which were to be given to the French emigrants, the Coloniser declared that it was not possible for him to indicate in advance all the conditions which might be required for the foundation of a colony, and in order to get clear information on this point, he invited the Spanish Court to select a governor of easy and gracious manner, who could talk to the colonists and get from them their just demands and the matters about which they were distressed. However, he was able to indicate certain conditions in advance which it was important for him to submit for the consideration of the Spanish Court. These are as follows, and are quoted verbatim:

The conditions for the Cedula of 1783

1. The French people belong to the same religion as the Spaniards, but they do not practise their religion with the same rigidity. It will therefore, be necessary to allow them the liberty of conducting themselves in this regard as they do in the French islands. In the parishes where they will reside, they must be allowed to have French priests under the jurisdiction of the Spanish ecclesiastical superior.

2. The new French colonists must have the liberty to make wills in favour of their relatives and friends who are residents of the other islands, and in the event of their dying intestate, their properties must pass without difficulty to their legitimate heirs who are domiciled elsewhere.

3. The new French colonists must be admitted without discrimination to serve as magistrates, in military appointment and in other honourable places without any other consideration than their merit and qualifications.

4. The French colonists must be given the right, with the approval of the Governor, to return to the French islands in order to recover debts or other effects which they may have left there, or to follow up the process of cases they may have had in those islands.

5. It will be necessary to establish tribunals in Trinidad which would be subject to the superior courts of Madrid.

6. It will be necessary to establish a code for the management of negroes, and the more educated of the colonists should be directed to state the details. The Spanish Court however, must recommend to their commissioners to consult with the colonists in this matter on humanitarian principles, and try to render the condition of the slaves as happy as is possible. The Court must also lay down that one of the clauses of the code must be that every inhabitant must have a properly planted and well cultivated piece of land in the proportion of one cavalière of land for every seventy negroes. The Governor should have the power to order the other Spanish governors to return to Trinidad such slaves as might have escaped.

7. It will be necessary to pay great attention to the fact that the colonists who bring negroes to Trinidad must feed them well, until the time when they have got the necessary means of life to feed themselves on the 'cavalière' of land well cultivated by seventy negroes.

8. It will be necessary to establish in each parish, commissioners who will inspect goods imported from the islands which are infested by ants, especially sugar cane plants, so as to prevent the entry of these ants into Trinidad.

On the 24th November 1783 the colonisation plan was legally formulated and was duly stamped with the Royal Seals at the Palace of San Lorenzo. The foreword of the Cedula states that, in the instructions given on the 3rd September 1776 to Captain Don Manuel Falquez on his nomination as Governor of the Island of Trinidad *de Barlovento,* and in the commission delivered to Don José de Abalos when he was invested as Intendant of Caracas, regulations were then established and privileges accorded for the advancement of the population and commerce of the island. Now, on the demand of the said Intendant, and on the representations of foreign colonists who were already established in the island, as well as for those who were desirous of establishing themselves there, it had become necessary to make more complete regulations. This declaration of intended policy is followed by a document of twenty-eight articles as follows:

The Royal Cedula of Population

The first prescribes that every new colonist of a foreign friendly nation, already established in the island or desirous of doing so, should prove his quality as a Roman Catholic. Those exempted from this regulation are the Spaniards, either from Europe or the Indies, as in their case no doubt exists about their religion.

The second insists that foreign colonists shall take the oath of allegiance to the King of Spain, and undertake to obey the laws of the Indies. In return for this, they are to be given a free and perpetual title to lands which they are authorised to possess under the provision of the following article.

The third provides that every white colonist of either sex has a right to four fanegas and two sevenths or ten squares of land (or 32 acres in English measurements), and half of this amount for every slave which he shall bring into the island. It recommends an equal distribution of these lands so that the good, middling and bad shall be equally divided among all; and it prescribes the recording of each one of these concessions of land in the *Libro Becerro de Poblacion,* (the Register of Population), together with the name of the concessionaire colonist, the date of his admission, the number of members of his family, his profession and the place from which he has come. An authenticated copy of each of these records is to be handed to the concessionaire as a title to property.

The fourth grants the same privileges to black or coloured colonists, but only one half of the quantity of land given to the white colonists. The lands given to the slaves remain practically the same.

The fifth stipulates that the foreign colonists after a stay of five years in the island, and on their promise to continue to live there, will enjoy all the rights and privileges attached to nationalisation, which will include the children whom they have brought with them and those who have been born since. In consequence, they will be admitted to honourable appointments in the administration and militia, according to their aptitude and ability.

The sixth exempts all the white colonists from all head or personal tax, however after a period of ten years in the island, they are to pay a tax of one strong piastre (or a dollar) per head per annum, but the cost of this is never to be increased.

The seventh grants to the Spanish and foreign colonists, after a period of five years from the date of their arrival in the island, the facility to leave, together with the valuables which they have brought with them, without any export tax. The valuables acquired during their stay in the island will be subject to an export tax of ten percent, and the lands which have been granted to them, will be returned to the Crown.

The eighth grants to the already established and new colonists who have no natural heirs in the island, the facility of making wills in favour of their relatives and friends abroad, and such heirs from abroad who come to

establish themselves in the island, are to enjoy the same privileges as their benefactors. If they prefer to transfer their inheritance elsewhere, they will have to pay an export duty of ten percent, and if they stay over five years, they will have to pay an export duty of fifteen percent. The same privileges are granted to natural heirs who are established abroad in the case of their relatives in Trinidad dying intestate.

The ninth also grants to the colonists established in the island, the power to bequeath in accordance with Spanish laws, their real properties which are not capable of division either to one or many of their children, provided that this does not result in any prejudice to the legitimacy of others and to that of the widow of the Testator.

The tenth permits the colonists on account of legal processes or because of other urgent private affairs, to leave the colony to go to Spain, to Spanish colonies and to foreign countries, provided they are not enemy countries, after having obtained permission from the Governor.

The eleventh exempts the Spanish and foreign colonists from the payment of tithes during ten years from the 1st January 1785, and from the expiration of this period, their contribution is fixed at half tithes or five percent.

The twelfth also exempts these said colonists from payment of the 'alcabala', which is the tax payable on the sale of their produce and merchandise, during the same period of ten years. On the expiration of this time, a tax of five percent is payable on all exports, except those sent to Spain in Spanish ships, as these are freed from all taxation in perpetuity.

The thirteenth in peace time imposes a duty on all colonists to keep themselves armed in order to control their slaves and to resist any attack from pirates, and for these purposes they are to be formed into corps of regular militia. In time of war, or if there should be a revolt of slaves, their obligation is to rally to the defence of the island.

The fourteenth imposes on both former and recent colonists who are the owners of vessels of any size and make, the obligation to put these under the Spanish flag, in addition to those which they might have purchased abroad up to the end of 1786. This is to be done without cost of registration or naturalization. Those of the colonists who wish to build vessels in the island, are granted permission to cut timber free of charge from the Crown forests.

The fifteenth permits free of any franchise, the introduction of black slaves and the trade in them, for a period of ten years from the 1st January 1785. On the expiration of this term a duty of five percent will be payable on slaves imported into the island, and six percent on those who are exported to other Spanish colonies.

The sixteenth permits colonists to leave for the purpose of selling their produce in the foreign but friendly islands, provided that an export tax of five percent is paid, and also provides that the profits from these ventures should be used for the purchase of slaves. The same tax is imposed on merchants who import slaves, but this does not include the import tax from which the colonists alone were exempt.

The seventeenth grants an absolute free franchise on all direct commerce between Spain and Trinidad and also on the produce of the island shipped to Spanish possessions in the Indies, during the period of ten years as from the 1st January 1785. At the expiration of this term the only articles which were declared free are to be those in the final schedule of commerce which were all exempted.

The eighteenth grants during the same period of ten years the same free franchise on all importations from Spain of materials and merchandise, Spanish and foreign, also provisions and liquors from Spain, and of all these imports no export is allowed to the other colonies except of Spanish articles. These are subject to the taxes in the schedule of commerce recently published.

The nineteenth, during the same period of ten years, authorizes Spanish vessels to accept cargoes for Trinidad in the French Consular Ports. In Trinidad, cargoes for the said ports paid a tax of five percent on entry and the same on export of produce, except on those whose export is prohibited.

The twentieth in cases of urgent necessity grants permission to give all colonists the same privileges for the French islands in America, on payment of the same tax of five percent on entry and exit, of provisions and merchandise.

The twenty first promises the colonists that orders will be sent to the Captain General at Caracas to supply them at current prices, with the necessary cattle for their food and industries and agriculture, up to the time when the colonists themselves have been able to breed sufficient for their own requirements.

The twenty second also promises to the colonists that similar orders will be sent to allow them to import flour during the period of ten years from the 1st January 1785. In the case of scarcity, they will be allowed to go elsewhere to buy under the Spanish flag, and in payment they must export produce which will be charged a five percent duty, similar to that imposed on flour received in exchange.

The twenty third also promises to the colonists the sending of similar orders to the factories in Biscay, so that during the same period of ten years, they can be supplied with agricultural tools, and in case they should not arrive, they are authorised to procure them from the foreign and friendly islands, on the same conditions established for flour in case of scarcity.

The twenty fourth also promises to newly arrived colonists, that two priests who know foreign languages will be sent to them as parish priests, and to these will be given sufficient income so that they can live according to their character, as without this, they will have to have recourse to the purses of their parishioners.

The twenty fifth obliges all colonists to submit to the King, through the Governor, the regulation which seems to them to be the best for the conduct of their slaves, on condition that this regulation is in accordance with instructions which the Governor will receive regarding this matter, and this must be based on the principle of the restitution of fugitive slaves from the foreign islands.

The twenty sixth recommends a very severe surveillance in order to prevent the introduction from neighbouring islands of destructive ants. It orders a rigorous inspection of vessels and also of luggage and effects of new colonists who arrive from the ant-ridden islands.

The twenty seventh promises to give the colonists the right to establish sugar refineries in Spain when the sugar crops in Trinidad have become sufficient for them to make a profit. They will enjoy the same privileges and liberties granted to foreign nationals. It also promises, but later on, the establishment of a Consular Court or

Commerce Court in the island, in order to extend protection to agriculture, shipping and commerce. It also recommends that in the meantime the Governor and other judges should undertake an administration which is just and prompt and humane, so that justice can be done to all inhabitants, both Spaniards and foreigners.

The twenty eighth gives the right to all inhabitants of the islands, to petition the King through the intermediary of the Governor. They are also granted the facility to go to Spain in person for the purpose of obtaining relief from the wrongs which they may suffer. A final paragraph stipulates, as is usual, that all provisions of the law which are contrary to the present Cedula remain in abeyance, and the officials of the American colonies and the Consuls in the Consular Ports in France, are hereby ordered to obey.

In order to understand the complete plan for colonisation adopted by Spain, we must remember, following the Cedula of Population, the Code Noir, drawn up by Roume de Saint Laurent, and promised by the twenty fifth article of the Cedula, even though it did not come into force until six years later. It is actually dated at Aranjuez, the 31st May 1789, and carries the title of the Royal Cedula for the Protection of Slaves in the Spanish Colonies. This work undertaken by the new colonists in Trinidad, plainly gives effect to the noble thoughts of Roume de Saint Laurent who said that he wished to make the life of the slaves as happy as their state would allow, because he was well known for his great humanity. The honour of preparing this Cedula was confided to Mr. Joseph de la Forest, a French colonist from Grenada who was the Syndic Procureur (or Attorney-General) of the Cabildo in 1785. This duty could not have been entrusted to anyone with more philanthropic ability. The regulations are preceeded by a long preamble which states that, many abuses having been introduced into the education, treatment and work of slaves by their masters or owners, it had become necessary to remedy these matters, particularly at this moment when liberty having been granted to Spanish subjects by a Royal Order dated 28th February 1785, it had become necessary to regulate the treatment of the blacks, as the number of slaves in the Americas was bound to increase considerably. The regulations are divided into fourteen articles as follows:

The Code Noir

This Code for the Regulation of Slaves was proposed by de St. Laurent, one of several proposed at various times in the West Indies. It was ignored by the Spanish Government of Trinidad on the advice of the planters and was never put into effect, being considered far too lenient and permissive. A subsequent Code far more severe was imposed by the British after the conquest by Col. Thomas Picton.

1. Education — Every slave proprietor, whoever he may be, is obliged to instruct them in the precepts of the Roman Catholic religion in order that they may be baptised within the year of their instruction; he is also bound to grant them rest on public holidays, except at harvest time. On those days, as the slave will have to attend Mass, a priest will be provided at the expense of the master. Every day after working hours, they will have to say the rosary with devotion, in the presence of the master or his steward.

Map of the island of Trinidad showing the bibitations from Pierre F. M'Callum's Travels in Trinidad 1805

A MAP OF THE ISLAND OF TRINIDAD. 1805

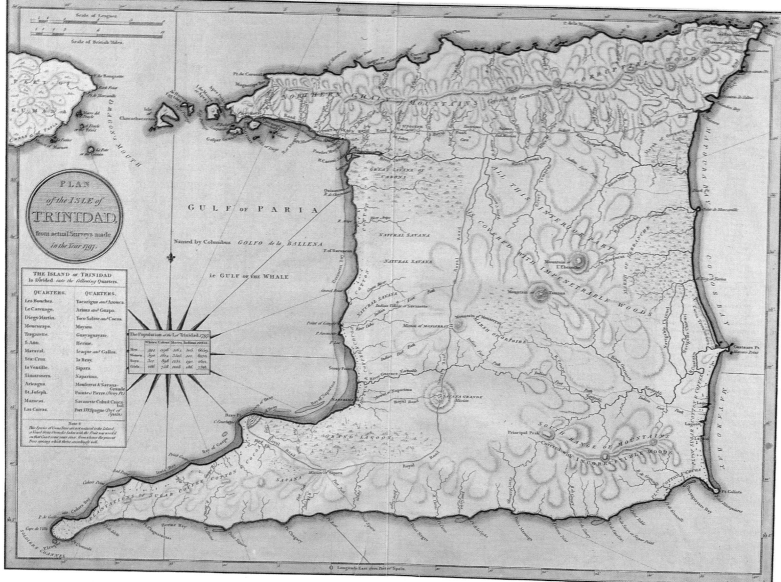

2. Food and Clothing — The master is under the obligation of feeding his slaves, as well as their wives and children, slaves or free, the latter up to the age when they can earn their keep, which is fixed at twelve years for girls and fourteen for boys. As there is no other fixed rule as to the quality and quantity of food and clothing on account of the difference of climate, it is stipulated that the magistrate or syndic appointed for the protection of slaves will decide the quality and quantity of food and clothing to be allowed to them according to their age and sex. This regulation shall be fixed upon the door of the Town Hall and of the church of each district so that everyone may be informed.

3. Work of Slaves — The slaves will be principally employed in agriculture. In order to make their services profitable to their masters and to the state, their tasks will be regulated by the magistrates and syndics in the manner as said in the foregoing chapter. The rule is that for two hours each day they will be free to do whatever work they want to their own personal interests, and every year they will receive from their masters two dollars for the use of their families; over sixty years and under seventeen years they will not be at the service of these masters, and women will not be employed in any work which is not conformable to their sex.

4. Relaxation — On public holidays, after attending Mass followed by religious instruction, the slaves will be allowed to relax in the presence of the master or steward, men and women separately, excluding those of neighbouring estates. Attention must be paid that there should be no excessive drinking and that their amusements should end before evening prayer.

5. Housing and Infirmary — All slaves will be accommodated in suitable houses to protect them from all types of weather, unmarried men apart from women, and each house will be provided with beds, blankets and other necessary objects; each man will have his bed and there shall be no more than two beds in each house.

Another house, warm and comfortable, will be for the sick, and there they ought to receive all that will be necessary for them. If they have to be sent to the hospital due to lack of space or the proximity of a town, the master will be bound to pay their daily hospital fees decided upon by the magistrate according to what was stated in Chapter 2. In case of death, the master will have to reimburse the hospital the funeral expenses.

6. The Aged and Infirm — Those who due to old age or illness are incapable of work, as well as children of both sexes, must be provided for by their masters. Such people cannot be given their liberty in order to get rid of them unless a sufficient amount of money be given to them to ensure their subsistence; the sum to be decided upon by the magistrates and syndics.

7. Marriage of Slaves — The master must not allow

concubinage but must encourage marriage among his slaves. Neither must he hinder them from marrying the slaves belonging to other masters; in the latter case, if the estates are distant from one another so that the newly-married couple are unable to fulfill the object of marriage, the master shall purchase the wife or the husband at a price fixed by two experienced arbitrators nominated by the two parties, and in case of disagreement, a third will be chosen by the two arbitrators. If the husband's master refuses to buy his wife, the wife's master will have the right to buy the husband.

8.   Duties and Punishments of Slaves — As masters of slaves are obliged to maintain them, to educate them and to employ them in useful work proportional to their strength, age and sex, without forsaking their children and those who are old and sickly, so on the other hand there is an obligation on the part of the slaves to obey and respect their masters and stewards, to perform the work which is given to them to do according to their strength, and to respect them as heads of their family. Consequently those who fail to fulfill those duties will be punished in the measure of the seriousness of their offence. The punishment will consist of imprisonment, chains, or whip, the latter not to exceed the number of twenty five lashes so as not to cause any contusion or bleeding. These punishments cannot be imposed on slaves except by the master or his steward.

9.   Applying Greater Punishments — When slaves commit crimes which deserve a more severe punishment, the master, his steward or any other witness will have the culprit arrested and will inform the court so that in the presence of his master and his defender he will be judged and punished in accordance with the seriousness of his offence. The same procedure as applied to common criminals will be also applied to the slaves. If the slave is condemned to pay a third of the expense of the trial, and even if the corporal punishment inflicted on him according to the seriousness of his crime,goes as far as death or the mutilation of his limbs, the master will be responsible for it.

10. Omissions or Excesses of Masters and Stewards — the master or his steward who fails to provide education, food, clothing, relaxation, housing etc. for slaves or who should forsake their children and those among them who are sick,will pay a fine of $50 for the first time, $100 for the second time and $20 for the third time. These fines will be paid by the master even when his steward is at ·fault. If the latter is not in a position to pay them, one third will be for the informer, one third for the judge, and one third for the Fines Chest which will be mentioned later. In case these fines do not produce the desired effect, the Queen will be informed so that she may decide whatever she may wish. If the masters or their stewards are guilty of excess in punishing their slaves causing wounds, bleeding or mutilation of limbs, beside paying fines, they shall be prosecuted as criminals and will be punished in proportion to their crime. The slave shall be taken away and sold to another master if he is able to work. The amount of the sale shall be put in the Fines Chest. If the injured slave is no longer able to work and therefore cannot be sold, he will not be returned to his master but the master will be bound to provide a daily sum which shall be fixed by the magistrate for his subsistence, and this for the rest of his life, paying every month in advance.

11. Of Those who injure Slaves — Slaves can only be punished by their masters or their stewards, therefore no other persons will be permitted to ill-treat, chastise, wound or kill them without incurring the punishment enacted by the law against those who commit the like excesses towards free people. The master of the slave who has been thus ill-treated, has the right to file a law suit against the criminal which will be defended by the Attorney, the Protector of Slaves.

12. List of Slaves — The slave masters are bond to provide the magistrate of their district with a list of the slaves they possess, mentioning the age and sex of each one, so that the Notary of the Town Hall may enter them on a separate register which will be kept in the said Town Hall to this effect. Each master whose slave runs away is bound to inform the magistrate within 3 days so that mention will be made of it in the register to avoid suspicion of murder. Should the master not fulfill this obligation, he will be obliged to produce proof either of the absence or the natural death of his slave; failing which he will be brought to court.

13. Method of Investigating the Excesses of Masters and Stewards — As it will be difficult for slaves to bring their complaints to the lawful authority, it will be necessary to find out how they are treated by their masters. To this effect the priest responsible for the religious instruction of slaves on each estate, will seek information about the treatment they receive. Should there be reason to complain, he will secretly let the Attorney General know, and it will be the duty of the latter to open an enquiry. If the complaints are unfounded, the priest will not be held responsible for informing the Attorney, as the mission of the latter will be only to notify the magistrate to open the enquiry and to pursue whatever procedure he may have begun. Besides these means,it will be necessary that trustworthy persons be appointed by justices and magistrates to visit estates three times a year and to report whatever they will have observed contrary to the regulations of the foregoing chapter; it is also declared that the denunciation of every infraction of these regulations is a public law which gives the privilege of secrecy to every informer, and that no one will be charged for his information.

Finally it is declared that the justices and Attorneys as Protectors of Slaves will be answerable for any neglect of theirs in making use of any necessary means to enforce these Royal Resolutions.

14. Chest of Fines — In the towns and villages where the forementioned regulations will be enforced and wherever there will be Courts of Justice, a Chest with three keys will be put and kept in the Town Hall, one of which will be delivered to the Justice of the Peace, another to the Governor, and the third to the Attorney-General. In this Chest will be kept the amount of fines received from those who have not obeyed the Royal Orders. The money will be used as a means of enforcing these same orders, and cannot be touched without an order signed by the three entrusted with the keys, who will be responsible for what ever may be missing and are obliged to replace it so that the yearly accounts which have to be presented to the Intendant of the Province may be approved of by him.

Then comes the final required section where it is stipulated that every law or custom opposed to the present Cedula, is and remains cancelled, and that the Supreme Council of the Indies and the American public servants are obliged to conform and have it enforced.

Such is the collection of regulations of colonization adopted by Spain on the recommendation of Roume de Saint Laurent. These regulations applied to all the

different colonial classes of the time including whites, people of colour and the slaves, and they became the basis of our public laws. They did not, however, apply to the Indians who were still confined in their missions and subject to the double tutelage of the priests and the magistrates.

Sources
P.G.L. Borde *History of Trinidad Under the Spanish Government* for the main text which was supplemented with information from Marquise de Charras, *Naturalización, ms., 1787.*
Beard, *Life of Toussaint-Louverture, ch. VII, p. 66.*
Abbad y Lasierra, *historia de Puerto-Rico.*

Natives of the French speaking Caribbean islands who would have immigrated to Trinidad at the time of the Cedula of Population by Peter Shim after the original lithograph drawn by Agostino Brunias.

Saint-Laurent, *Considerations sur l'établissement d'une colonie,etc., ms., 1777.*
Meany, *Abstract of the Minutes of Cabildo, 1733-1813, ms.,*
E.L. Joseph, *History of Trinidad, 1838.*
Bryan Edwards, *History of the B.W. Indies, t. IV., p. 299, art.*
Michael Pocock's unpublished manuscript, *Out of the Shadows of the Past.*
Free Mulatto, Address to Earl Bathurst, p. 4 et seq.

THE BRITISH INCURSION ON SPANISH TRINIDAD

Compiled by Candyce Kelshall

Sources
K.S. Wise, 'Historical Sketches'.
P.G.L. Borde, 'History of the Island of Trinidad Under the Spanish Government'.

Between the 17th and 18th centuries the West Indies had been the favorite bone of contention among the European powers. With respect to Trinidad very incidental events, created by overzealous egos frequently brought the European powers close to declarations of war. One such colourful incident occurred in May 1796.

Captain Vaughan of the Frigate Alarm was a persistent scourge and relentless opponent of the Republican privateers, many of whose ships he had captured or destroyed. On this day he landed at Port of Spain with the third Lieutenant, the Purser and the Surgeon and had gone to pay his respects to Madame de Mallevault at Coblentz whom he had known well with her husband in Martinique. It was on his return to Port of spain that the Republicans in considerable numbers met him and forced him to take refuge in the house of Madame Griffith whence he eventually escaped and reached his ship.

He immediately decided to carry out a signal vengeance. That same night he ordered the call to arms to be sounded, and made the necessary preparations for landing at day break. The boats from the ships were launched and armed, and the men, both sailors and soldiers numbering 250 were placed in order of battle on the bridge with their officers at their head. Before day break the order was given and they embarked in boats and were given their marching orders.

This flotilla advanced in silence, and at the first signs of day break, all the men from the frigate landed, armed to the teeth. It is said, that in his anxiety to increase the number of his fighting men, he committed his second imprudence by depleting the number of those left on the frigate to a point where it would have been easy for a detachment of his adversaries to capture it without a blow being struck.

As soon as the English had landed, a picket of four men commanded by the officer on duty in the fort of the harbour went towards them in order, if possible, to stop their advance, or at least to protest against the violation of international laws. Captain Vaughan, who was still inflamed with fury, was deaf to those remonstrances, and replied that he had only come to chastise the French scum who had ill treated his officers and sailors. The Spanish officer replied that 'as the four men under my command are powerless to prevent the outrage which you are about to carry out against my flag, I can only constitute myself your prisoner, and I hand you my sword.' These noble words did not have any effect in calming the hot-headed captain, who disdained to take the officer's sword, and gave the order to advance on the town. The little Spanish force was pushed aside, and the English started on the march, headed by the band and with flags flying. At this moment the whole town was on foot, having heard of the landing of the English. The French sailors armed themselves in haste in order to meet force with force, and the French, English and Spanish notables of the town, appeared before the aggressor in order to try to stop him in this dangerous enterprise. The Irish and English showed themselves to be particularly sadly afflicted by the violation of the territory of the island. They pointed out the great harm that his conduct would bring to them and their families if the French sailors decided to carry out reprisals after he had gone, and they pressed him to abandon his enterprise and to return to his ship. But this wise advice had no more effect than the noble words of the Spanish officer. The Commandant of the Alarm was inflexible. Whilst his nationals were making their representations, he ordered a roll of drums to be sounded which drowned their voices, and resuming his march, he entered the town and covered its length and breadth.

During these negotiations the French sailors, accompanied by their friends and compatriots, indignant at the attack which the English had made on neutral territory, had had time to put themselves in battle order outside the town on the right bank of the old course of the St. Anns river. This position was very well chosen so that they could protect themselves in case of a bayonet charge. This party consisted of three or four hundred men who were resolved to await the enemy, and they were flying the French flag and had decorated themselves with the tricolour cockade. On his side, the Governor had also had time to collect a company of soldiers, and he put himself at their head with the object of stopping what looked like an inevitable battle. By a clever manoeuvre, and passing through a cross road, he arrived in time to put himself between the two enemy bands just at the moment when they were about to come to blows. He faced the English, and in order to make himself well understood, he addressed Captain Vaughan in the English language. He reproached him for his outrageous conduct against the Spanish flag whose neutrality he was violating. He then spoke of other considerations, and reminded Captain Vaughan that the whole island, both in the towns and in the country, was almost entirely inhabited by French people, and that the first shot fired by the English ranks could well be the signal for a general massacre of the English and Spaniards. The English, because the French had been attacked by their compatriots contrary to the rights of men, and the Spaniards because they were considered to be accomplices of the English, not having joined with the French to fight against them. He finished up by saying: "I will not suffer a province of my King which is confided to my care to become the field of battle of two nations who are at war with each other. As my troops are very inferior in number, I declare to you that we shall not allow you to attack the French except over our dead bodies."

This sensational little speech, made in a voice full of emotion, created a visible hesitation amongst the English who, up to that time had been so resolute. The officers of the 'Alarm' surrounded their Commander and spoke to him in low voices. It was evident that the determined attitude which Chacon had taken up in placing himself between the two parties who had prepared for combat, was very embarrassing for the aggressors. After a short conference they decided to retire, and Captain Vaughan, saluting the Governor with his sword, but without saying a word, ordered his troops to about turn, and they returned to their boats. When they saw the English beating a retreat, an immense clamour arose from the ranks of the French; there were jeers, shouts and hooting which followed them up to the moment of their re-embarking under the protection of the Spanish troops. On the return to his ship, Captain Vaughan was covered with confusion and immediately set sail and abandoned the field of his sad exploit. A short time later it became known that he had blown out his brains as Sir Lawrence Keymis had done in 1617. These two captains met the same violent fate on account of their similar conduct. If Vaughan, like Keymis, had not made war on the Spaniards in time of peace, he had at least decided to make war on the French in Spanish territory, and at a time when they were at peace with Spain. Both of these men, by foolish enterprises, had the misfortune to compromise the politics of their governments, and both took their own lives in order to escape what would have been their just punishment.

Gerard Besson

On the 1st September 1784 Don José Maria Chacon arrived as Governor. he was to be the last Spanish administrator of this island, the thirty-eighth in a succession that had run some two hundred and fifty years. He carried titles: Captain General and Governor of the island, Sub-Inspector of troops in his garrison and Judge Conservator of mails and postages, whose Royal Vice Patron he was.

The Chevalier de Colatrava, Don José María Chacon is remembered by chroniclers as a man of easy and gracious manner, well educated and able to express himself with facility in French as well as English.

His attention was directed first to the implementation of the Cedula of 1783 and during the next five years of his office a steady stream of immigration was established and the population increased from under 3,000 to 10,422.

As Port of Spain was expanding rapidly, the roads being insufficient, it became necessary to open up new areas for development. To make land available for expansion to the West, Chacon diverted the course of the St. Ann's River from its course in the West of the town to the foot of the Laventille Hills in the East. He developed the wharf and water-front area (Plaza del Marina) and built a Battery there, a small fort in the shape of a Crescent which he called Fort St. Andres.

He constructed Government Buildings for the Public Services — and built a road to St. Joseph and a military Barracks there. He created the Town of San Juan. On the 25th October 1786 he instituted the Parish of San Fernando. He divided the Territory into districts, which are still in existence today, now known as Wards.

He created a Police Service and a Fire Department as well as the first Medical Board and first Port Health Doctor. These and many others were the works done by this able and devoted Governor during the early years of his office.

He is today remembered by the National Flower the Chaconia, and the Street in Port of Spain that still bears his name.

Don Jofeph Maria Chacon Sanchez de Sotomayor, Cavallero del Orden de Calatrava Capitan de Navio de la Real Armada, Gobernador, Comandante General è Intendente de esta Yfla de Trinidad de Barlovento y fus aggregados   Infpector General de las Tropas de fu Guarnicion, Comandante del Cuerpo Veterano de Infanteria de ella, Juez Protector de Real Renta de Correos y Poftas por S. M. Vice Patrono Real, &c. &c. &c.

CONCEDO   e y Seguro pafaporte à
para que
— — y a fin de que no fole ponga impedimento alguno en fu viage y antes bien fe le de la afiftencia y favor que necefitare pido à los Senores Gefes de las Efquadras Comandantes de Embarcaciones de guerra y Corfarios à fi de fu Magd. como de las demàs Potencias Amigas fe lo Franqueen, y lo mifmo à todos los Miniftros de guerra y jufticia de los paifes por donde tranfitaré por convenir a fi al Real Servicio. Dado y fellado con el Efcudo de mis Armas en el Puerto de Efpana de la citada Yfla de Trinidad à 28 — de enero de 1792

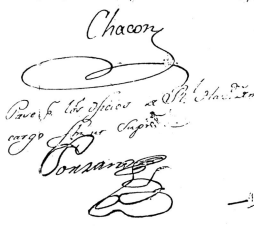

Governor José María Chacon's accreditation or Passport, bearing his signature. Reproduced with the kind permission of Micheal Joberty.

1795   Freemason's Lodge, Les Freres Unis, founded by Benoit Dert, who was the first W.M.

1796   Sugar estates established at Tragarite and La Brea.

1797   Charter granted from Grand Lodge of Pennsylvania, and recorded as No. 77, by Brother De Lannay.

1798   William Hardin Burnley arrived in the colony, and in 1802 took up his abode permanently and entered into mercantile transactions. In 1813 he was appointed a member of the Legislative Council.

1 August, 1799   First Newspaper published in the island by M.. Gallagher, entitled *The Trinidad Weekly Courant.*

10 August, 1800   H.M. ship Dromedary wrecked on the Parasol Rock, north point of Huevas.

1802   The Union Lodge, No. 60, under the registry of the Grand Lodge of Ireland, was opened by Brother Leonard, W.M.

27 May, 1802   Mr. Canning moved for an address to His Majesty, praying him not to alienate any of the uncleared lands in Trinidad, unless upon the condition that they were not to be cultivated by negroes newly imported from Africa.

The French Creoles of Trinidad

Gerard Besson

On the 24th November, 1783, the legal documentation making possible the colonization of a Spanish possession by a largely French population was formulated, and duly stamped with Royal Seals at the Palace of San Lorenzo in Spain.

Trinidad de Barlovento (which means the Windward) was to become the safe haven in a region torn by war and revolution. This had been achieved largely through the efforts of M. Roume de St. Laurent, a man of extraordinary vision, talent and energy.

The Royal Cedula of Population welcomed the Catholics of the region to the island and they, largely people of French descent, both white and free coloureds, took advantage of the offer.

Prior to this, Trinidad had been almost completely under-populated and undeveloped. In 1773, for example, the population amounted to the insignificant figure of approximately 1,000 of all conditions and all colours. By 1797 however, the figure stood at 18,627 inhabitants of which 2,500 were whites, 5,000 free blacks and people of colour, 10,000 slaves and 1,082 Amerindians, who were mostly indigenous.

They had arrived from both the French and English islands. At first, in the 1780's mostly, from Grenada, Martinique, St. Lucia and Dominica. Then a second wave of immigrants began to arrive, as a result of the terrible events that were taking place in Santo Domingo in 1790's

Thus it happened that a colony which had never belonged to France became largely peopled by persons of French descent, many of them holding diametrically opposite political views. To this hostility of opinions may be traced much of the turbulence and excitement and many of the actual disturbances which marked the closing years of Spanish rule in the Island.

The original colonists, known as the new colonists of Trinidad to distinguish them from the old Spanish settlers, were mainly drawn from the lesser aristocracy of France, the cadet branches of the ancient and noble houses and to some extent several of these had their origins in the South of that country. Many had left the land of their fathers several generations before, and had helped to colonise French possessions in other parts of the New World. Some families began their colonial experience in Acadia, in what is now Canada, in the 17th century, others in Louisiana and New Orleans.

In their migrations, subject as they were to changes political, economic and climatic, they found themselves at times completely uprooted; their circumstances substantially altered, often having to start afresh; and because of the fortunes of war, families would find themselves distributed among several islands whose ownership would change hands from one year to the next, while in reality they would continue to share identical interests and a way of life that had evolved as a result of living in the tropics, on cocoa and sugar plantations operated by slave labour for, in some cases, several generations. All the while they maintained the language and traditions of the land of their origins.

All these factors contributed to the fostering of a West Indian spirit, a West Indian or Creole way of life, as well as to produce a community of opinion between the colonists of various islands, in spite of the strict application of French, English or Spanish colonial laws.

To quote the French researcher F.P. Renault: 'In fact the French inhabitants of the islands considered themselves as brothers, jointly responsible to each other and hardly coming to care for a nationality which they would probably never employ for long. Also they were more attached to the islands where they had established themselves, to the islands in which they were united by memories and interest, than to a mother country which they had left with no thought of returning.' It was because of this that the all-powerful tradition of kinship developed and became central to the French Creole character.

In the twelve years covered by 1785-1797, which followed the distribution of the Royal Cedula of Population in the islands of the Antilles Archipelago, the population of Trinidad had been increased by about 1,500 souls per year. During that period, on an annual basis, there arrived approximately 214 whites (mostly French), 428 free blacks and people of colour - Patois and French-speaking - and about 856 slaves - Patois-speaking and often being second or third generation West Indian born. The whites were mainly proprietors and so too were approximately a quarter of the blacks and free people of colour. On the average, each proprietor, black or white, possessed three to five slaves.

These French and upper class French-speaking coloured families, formed an elite population. As one writer of the period put it:— "more recommended by their quality than their numbers. They were distinguished particularly by their energy and their agricultural and commercial knowledge. Having been driven away from their former houses by the misfortunes of the time, they emigrated with their slaves and their tools of labour, and they offered to Trinidad the fruits of their experience and talents in exchange for the hospitality which they received from the Spaniards".

Trinidad during this period, seemed like a French island. Every thing was French: morals, customs and language. The sweet Creole Patois from the French

The above lithograph possibly by Richard Bridgens was done in 1820. Champs Elysées by that time had become the property and residence of John Boissiere Esq.

islands, seasoned by Spanish words strangely pronounced, often punctuated with words and phrases of West African origin, was the popular tongue. All business was carried out in French. The Spanish laws and local ordinances were never promulgated without a French translation. The very name of the Capital was not known abroad except in the form of French translation. Admiral Harvey, dating his dispatch regarding the seizure of the Island in 1797, did not write from the harbour of Port of spain, or Puerto de España, but it was from the harbour of Port d'Espagne.

In the words of the famous historian P.G.L. Borde: "A distinctive style of dress had developed, especially among the ladies. They always wore white, highlighted sometimes by foulards at their necks and handkerchiefs from the Indies on their heads, in the same manner as the gracious ladies of Bordeaux. So far as the men were concerned, those of middle age and older, continued to wear short trousers to the knee and stockings, a queue and powdered hair. The young men, however, wore the new long trousers called pantaloons.

One general aspect of their character is sufficient to describe the creoles - they were all excessively sensitive, and duels of honour were more frequent than they were in France. They were so very sensitive on the point of honour, that the slightest offence or a word sounding unpleasant, or a doubtful look, often provoked meetings at which blood was shed which was noble and generous.

There was the easy intimacy of family - a feeling of equality. Once admitted you had access to the very

CHAMPS ELYSÉES

The beginning of the Champs Elysées estate came on the 18th April, 1779 when Philippe Rose Roume de St. Laurent signed an agreement to purchase the small estate of St. Xavier in Maraval, comprising 3 fanegas of land, from Dons Miguel and Francisco Lezama. Soon afterwards, his mother, Rosa, the Marquise de Charras, née de Gannes de la Chancellerie, came to Trinidad from Grenada. She consequently acquired La Prudence estate, 5 fanegas in area, from Pierre Michel Jacques Pouchet, on the 5th February, 1782, for a price of 35 moedes, the equivalent of 350 piastres. Later she was granted a large tract of adjacent uncultivated land amounting to 85 fanegas, five solares, less one hundred and thirty-one varas standard measurements of the island, by the Governor, Don Martín Salaverría. She named the whole 'Les Champs Elysées'. The area chosen for the house was a twelve acre site at the entrance to Maraval, near the southern boundary of her lands, on a slight eminence with a commanding view northwards across her domain to the hills of Saut d'Eau in the distance. A large wooden house with a thatched roof was built on the site of the present building, approached by the carriage way that exists to this day from the Long Circular Road, at the entrance to which she placed the imposing stone gates which still stand.

Subsidiary buildings were also erected by Rose Marquise de Charras, the mother of Roume de St. Laurent, at Champs Elysées for the successful operation of the estate. There was a structure of 70 feet by 50 feet, of local wood, to accommodate the slaves (of which she had about 80); a sugar usine, also of local wood 54 feet by 27 feet, covered with 'texamani from the North', which housed 4 coppers and 4 spares, with their 'limandas' and scum removers, and all the utensils and instruments for the manufacture of sugar; a mill with iron wheels and drums; a house 27 feet by 27 feet to accommodate a boiler with a capacity of 300 gallons; a storehouse for coffee, and a mill to extract the

'*Cutting Canes', St. Clair Farm, Trinidad. The property and residence of Robert Grey Esq., St. Clair Farm bounded on the North by what is now Rapsey Street, on the South by Tragarete Road, on the East by Maraval Road and on the West by Maraval River. It was after this family that Grey Street was named. The family residence being, 'Sweet Briar House'.*

bosom of the family. The criteria were strict: one had to be white, Catholic, of legitimate descent, of an aristocratic family in the old country and preferably land owning - for it was above all, a land owning society.

One could however, be assimilated into this elite group through marriage if Irish, German, English or Corsican. By the time of the British conquest in 1797 French Creoles society was in the process of becoming one large family dominated by the 'old families' to whom P.G.L. Borde refers as 'étaient nobles, car on sait que ce furent des gentils hommes qui peuplèrent en grande partie les éstablissement de Français en Amérique'.

One is constantly reminded that the tone of the society was not only cordial but of a very high standard, it could not be otherwise for so many of the families came from the old nobility of France who had founded the establishments of the French people in the Americas.

The white French Creole population, who by the system of slavery had become accustomed to command and who had been authorized by Louis XIV to carry a sword, formed in the colonies an aristocracy of blood. In this way there was no line of demarcation among the white families, the closest relations joined them together, cemented as it was by the statutes enshrined in the

'*cereza' from the coffee; a store for bagasse and a stable for the mules, cattle and sheep; there were two kitchens, each with an oven, and, in addition, a bread oven and two kitchen gardens.* Michael Pocock.

Cedula of Population and in the practical pursuit and control of the economic base of the island: sugar, its processing and export. The French Creole families controlled this especially in the early years. The sons of this first generation were sent to France for their education and for those who could afford it, the experience of the grand tour.

Like most Franco-West Indian populations of the period, the French Creoles of Trinidad were known for their open, easy and polite manners. Having a somewhat haughty view of themselves, both as achievers and carriers of that almost sacred quality 'the old blood', they felt it important to adopt, especially with the stranger, a gesture of noblesse oblige, often offering the hospitality of their homes and introductions to their friends and family.

The European stranger having passed the test of

The Old Sugar Mill'. Richard Bridgens, an Englishman, served in Trinidad in the early 19th Century. He was an engineer and erected buildings such as the first Red House and the Police Barracks at St. James. He also made drawings of the people and places around him. This old mill and shed is thought to have been situated at Champs Elysées Estate in Maraval, and to have been drawn by him after 1820.

polite manners at the table and in the drawing room could quite easily make the rounds of the extended group of families made up of no more than seven or eight families. During the period before the English conquest, in the town and the countryside, he would quite possibly see a truly lavish dinner party where excellent wines and delicious meals would be served in large, high-ceilinged rooms, by silent and ubiquitous black servants dressed in dark blue and gold livery, their white gloved hands moving with the surety of practice in the art of service, gained by many years of experience, their bare feet making whispering sounds on the highly polished floors. He would glimpse, perhaps, the iron discipline with which a great house or a large estate would be run and he may well have marvelled at the quality of the silver with which he ate his breakfast and the crystal from which he drank his wine. If he was capable, he would notice the polished grace of his hostess and wonder at how such charm and beauty could flourish in such a wild and inhospitable clime. Never being told, of course, that she was the third generation born in these islands — a testament to a resilient race who had kept its culture intact.

It was in fact the dining room table, large and of mahogany, with its thick carved legs and shining brass castors that stood at the centre of the retention of French culture. It was in the dining room where the family met daily that life in the old style was maintained — with its traditions of politeness, humour, good conversation and a gentle consideration for the comfort of the ladies, an appreciation for good food and wine, where the traditions and the history of the family would be passed

CRAB MATETE

Clean three large crabs and dismember them, smashing the shells. Season them strongly and well with chives, thyme, garlic, onions and pepper. Let that stop while you grate three coconuts and strain the liquid from them after adding some water to the grated nut. Put this into an iron pot and let it boil down to pure oil. Remove the crabs from the seasoning and stew them in the oil complete with its sediment. Add some water to this and throw in the seasoning to let that cook. Then slowly add cassava farine, turning it vigorously all the time until it assumes the consistency of a cuckoo. Just after adding the water to the stewing crab put in a whole hot pepper but do not burst it. Serve with plain boiled ochroes. Whilst this is the simplest of dishes to prepare and one of the easiest of creole foods and its only fault lies in the combination of being too tempting and at the same time so rich. Unless you are a strong minded epicure you are likely to suffer from surfiet.

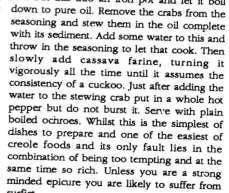

La Chance property and residence owned by
Gaston de Gannes.

on to the young. Under the eye of La Chatelaine and where everyone dressed for dinner, the strict code of good table manners would be inculcated: thus setting the foundations of style in place for the future ladies and gentlemen who would conduct themselves with grace in salons and boudoirs anywhere in the world, and who would give to La Trinidad, the reputation of having the most cultured society in the West Indies. And so it has remained to this day.

In the country our visitor would have stayed in large, plain wooden houses covered with wooden shingles, built sometimes several feet off the ground, standing on thick arched foundations made of river stone or ballast brick. The basement would be used to ripen fruit and vegetables and sometimes as a store room. These one storied houses of the first Creoles would have six or even eight bedrooms down one side and across another, all opening onto a wide gallery that would entirely surround the house; the drawing room and dining room adjoining each other, would have entry to each of these rooms. The partitions would never reach to the high ceilings but would be topped by a delicate filigree woodwork which would be perhaps the pride of the young men of the household. The furnishings of these estate houses would be few, quite often very old and sometimes with a remnant of gilt on their edges, and because of their antique elegance they would seem a little out of place in such a rustic setting.

The house would seem constantly full of children and there would invariably be one or perhaps two families overnighting or spending a day or two. The children, watched constantly by several Das (nannies) would have spent their days — if sunny — in the large gardens and grounds shaded by the many fruit trees that would surround the estate house; splashing in the stream or river that invariably ran nearby. The Da would have complete control over the children and often would exert considerable discipline. In many cases she would be with one family for several generations, setting into ringlets with her strong black hands, the golden tresses of a little girl who would never quite forget her and who would move slowly and inexorably away into another world one day, but would return to place her own little girl into those hands that she herself had known and had loved so well.

The estate, as had the ancestral chateau in France, became the centre of economic and social life of the district. The slave, and later the free labourers, looked to the "seigneur" in the big house as his lord and master and sometimes as his friend. Under Chacon they had been the established ruling class. With the capitulation to the British, however, things began to change.

In those days the course of the absentee landlord was still unknown and the colonists who lived permanently in the country were known as 'habitants de la campagne'. Our visitor would have moved from one 'habitation' to the next and in so doing would have seen much of the island. So easily were invitations handed out, many writers of the period who visited Trinidad in that time before the British conquest, have commented on the generous hospitality practised by the colonists of the island.

We must be on our guard against a tendency natural in Borde's description to idealise French society in Trinidad, but there are clear indications that its members, emerging from their homes, or entertaining therein, sought and found recognition amongst their peers by excelling in elegance, sophistication and ability in the arts, conversation, dress, music and hospitality, according to provincial French standards, rather than regarding the West Indian colonies as places to be tolerated for the sake of a quick fortune, the fruits of which might be enjoyed in the metropolitan country, as was often the outlook of the English planter or absentee owner. It was characteristic of the French through most of the nineteenth century, that they should send their children to school in France *at all costs*. Certainly Port of Spain seems to have had blossoming pretensions to a gay and cultured urbanity during the first three decades of the nineteenth century, based on a considerable prosperity. Eckstein, some of whose notes were published posthumously in the *Port of Spain Gazette* during 1840, speaks facetiously of this development as follows: 'At this period of the history' (approximately 1806) of our Experimental Island, the town Society could not yet boast of sufficient stock of elegants to assume a *bon ton* and the *haut ton*, to which it has since so rapidly aspired, and was scarcely suspected. The seductive soirées at Mademoiselle Annie's — the fascinating Ninon of Trinidad, collected at this time the male beau-monde round her sofa, or the harpsicord . . . Of the 1820's he notes "satiated with the ordinary indulgences of the human appetite, the relish of higher society became so exquisite, that while scores of old pianofortes stand silent . . . nothing less will now soothe the modern ear than Parisian-tuned harps, from the Atelier of an Ekhard. None other must touch the bosom of the finished boarding-school Miss, except a pedal lyre . . . By the sacred honour of the lovely muses I aver, that the Apollos and Amphions of Musical Antiquity never consumed so many strings as are snapped at one soirée of the tight-laced dilettantes of our Port of Spain".

There was about the island in those times, a sense of adventure, a pioneer spirit. It was, in fact, a frontier town. Master and slave shared the hardships of carving out of the living forest a great estate, the dangers of the high woods, the giant snakes, the alligators, the fevers, the terrible insects, the bad food and of course, death. There are those who today like to think that slavery as it existed in Trinidad was benign, paternal, kindly, even generous. One must, however, bear in mind that slavery is slavery and at the end of the day, or for that matter the end of the work of building a great house, the master proceeded to enjoy the fruit of his labour, while the slave was expected to be content with his lot, which for all intents and purposes wold hardly have altered. There was the overseer's whip that was cracked loudly at the break of day - perhaps giving rise to the saying 'the crack of dawn'. There were the stocks in which men and women were chained and a range of tortures and punishments, deprivations and pain constantly inflicted.

Only a few memoirs of those times exist today. There are the history books of course, often seeking to promote one point of view over another, and then there are the actual memories of the very old who remember their mothers and grandmothers telling of long ago when some of the French Creoles still lived in the 'old style' of the huge wooden plantation houses surrounded by giant forest trees, the candles flickering in the crystal chandeliers, lighting the eyes in the portraits of ancestors long dead on other islands, the tropic night closing

Gaston de Gannes who built La Chance was born in Trinidad in 1838. In the 1860's he married Miss Sophie Cipriani "and took his young bride up the Caroni by corial, or dug out canoe". On the banks of the river, just south of the village of Arima, he developed a large cocoa estate. A few years later he acquired some 50 acres on the O'Meara Road to the south of the old Arima Railway Station and there he built La Chance.

round. The great feasts when hundreds of slaves dressed in spotless white, would line the drive to the Estate house, holding high lighted flambeaux to guide the way for the carriages, while an ox would be roasted whole on an open spit. Inside, up on the polished floors, the Minuet and Waltz would be danced with grace and charm and for a night or perhaps a moment, amid the laughter and champagne, the memory of another time and of another age would be evoked.

It became the fashion among the French planters to have a coloured mistress, to keep a 'belle affranchise', a beautiful metisse or 'sang mêlée' with sea green eyes and red hair, very nearly white. It is said that in the old days a Grand Ball would be given to which only the most beautiful 'filles de couleur' would be invited so that the young men could choose a mistress from among them.

The term French Creole was by no means restricted to persons of purely French parentage born in the West Indies. French Creoles also included free people of colour, the children of the French planters of the early

Perseverance estate.

times and their African slaves and later, their mulatto, quadroon and octaroon mistresses. Some of these children were recognised by their fathers and legitimized, receiving educations at French universities and inheriting land and property. Several of these families settled in the south of Trinidad, many in Port of Spain, their children becoming in turn the doctors, lawyers and school masters in the latter part of the 19th century. They were however a minority, almost a curiosity in the socially structured colonial society. Very little has come down to us today, of the nature of the relationships between the French planter and the women of colour who surrounded him, who were often remarkably beautiful and sometimes power-seeking.

The fascination of these beautiful women prompted special laws such as Article 9 in the Code Noir of 1665 of the French islands, enacting first: that free men who should have one or two children by slave women, as well as the slave owners permitting the same, should be each condemned to pay two thousand pounds of sugar. An exception, however, was made to the effect that if the father was unmarried during the period of his concubinage, he could escape the provisions of the penalty by marrying the female slave according to the rites of the Church. She would thereby be enfranchised and her children "rendered free and legitimate". Few men

married their mistresses and those who did were no longer accepted into white French Creole society. There were exceptional cases. For example, the old French Comte who lived with a young lady of colour for many years after his wife's death, was persuaded by the Priest to marry her and so save his soul from the everlasting fires of hell. In later days, Governor Ralph Woodford would do all in his power to prevent those deathbed marriages. However, some men sometimes felt themselves bound in honour to secure the freedom of their own blood. It was not a rare thing to see legitimate wives taking care of the natural children of their husbands — becoming their godmothers (s'en faire les marraines). There is still the memory today of the men who kept their mistresses on the grounds of their estates,their children — both legitimate and illegitimate — growing up together, becoming friends in adulthood and standing godfather for each other's children and acting as executors to the other's estate upon death.

Only too often it is presumed that estate owners of this time were automatically on the royal road to riches, but the margin between success and failure was small, and only skilful management and unremitting labour brought profit to the planters. In fact the surprising thing is that so many of these French soldiers - turned - farmers,who settled in Trinidad just before or after the

British conquest succeeded in their agricultural pursuits.

As the French 'Founding Fathers' went inland into the cool river valleys of the northern range and along the coasts to carve out their estates from the jungle, they never forgot their aristocratic background and the fact that they were here to re-establish their lost fortunes. They considered themselves the social élite and the natural ruling class. As they established themselves on their estates they built their country houses surrounded by pastures for the grazing of their stock and planted their samaan trees for shade.

The stranger, however thoroughly he made the tour, would have met only the polished charm of his well mannered host and hostess. He would hardly ever have penetrated the privacy of the family; the inner sanctuary was reserved for the cousinage, the brothers, the sisters, the children — for above all, the French Creole was private; to survive they had long ago created a world within a world, closely guarded by the tenets of their religion and the retention of the French language and culture. I was told by a very old French Creole lady that in her mother's household not even the servants were allowed upstairs after lunch. A most exclusive entity, the French Creole family. As Mr. Pat O'Connor mentions in his book 'Some Trinidad Yesteryears':—

"And this was good old Trinidad
The Land of the Red Cocoa Pod
Where the Ganteaumes spoke only to the de Verteuils

Sophie de Gannes née Cipriani wife of Gaston de Gannes

opposite — Perseverance Estate House Trinidad. In Spanish times (before 1797), the estate known as Moka (Mocha) in the upper reaches of the Maraval Valley was owned by Don Francisco Mendez. It is not clear whether Perseverance formed a part of that property. However, from early 19th century records, we know that Perseverance was owned by the Chevalier Hippolite Borde and comprised some 340 acres. It was later owned by M. Paul Latour who built the Great House in 1850 and whose son Dr. Georges Louis Latour and his half sister Paula Louisa Leoniza Ultima Latour was born there in 1851.

The house passed into the hands of Albert (Baba) Cipriani who, by the 1920's, added many embellishments. He lived there in extravagant style until, faced with business reversals, he too was forced to sell. In 1926, Perseverance was sold to an Englishman, James Evans, and later it was owned by one Frederick Williams. He then rented it to Ethel Taylor in 1934, who operated a small private club for dinner and dancing.

Other owners of this beautiful property have been Mr. & Mrs. Simpson in 1939, and Marshall Ian Campbell, whose wife furnished it with furniture from White Hall. Later, the Estate passed into the hands of the Battoo family in 1943. The Perseverance Estate was eventually divided into house lots and by 1987 the once grand, old house, the pride of former days, had fallen into disrepair and finally collapsed.

CHICKEN GUMBO
Cut fowl in two and boil in two quarts of water in which you have placed fumity and seasonings, for a half hour. Remove chicken strip off the flesh (which can be used to make chicken au gratin, mayonnaise or rissoles) return skin and bones to liquid; boil for two or three hours on a slow fire. Strain through cloth. Boil ten ochroes separately, throw away their water and add to strained chicken consomme.

FRENCH EMIGRÉS & THE BRITISH ARMY
Bridget Brereton

Right from the start of the French Revolution, in 1789, priviledged Frenchmen, and especially members of the noblesse, fled from their native land to the comparative safety of exile. This exodus stepped up during the first half of the 1790's, when the Revolutionary régime was at its most extreme. Although the emigrés included thousands of clergymen and members of the Third Estate (commoners), it was the noble exiles who gave the emigrés as a group their main characteristics: royalist, fiercely Catholic, and bitterly opposed to the Revolution and all its works.

Since many of the noble emigrés had been military officers (the Army being one of the few acceptable careers for young noblemen), it was natural that they would want to serve the great counter-revolutionary military alliance spearheaded by Britain, Austria and Prussia. And of these, large numbers did enlist in the armed forces of these three powers as officers, to such an extent that special French units were organised in each Army. The British military authorities allowed many emigrés to raise regiments for regular service with the Army, such as the Chasseurs Britanniques, only one of many. Royalists emigrés often bought commissions in regular British companies or regiments.

Many of these emigrés serving as officers with the British armed forces fought in the Caribbean campaigns of the 1790's. As early as 1792, before Britain was at war with Revolutionary France, plans were being hatched among emigrés in Britain with property in Ste Domingue (Haiti) to ship an army of emigrés to the Caribbean, presumably to crush the revolution in the French colonies. This came to nothing, but many French emigrés from the French West Indies — Ste Domingue, Martinique and Guadeloupe — served in the British forces as officers in the Caribbean war. For instance, in 1798, a number of French emigrés from the Antilles received commissions in the 9th, 10th, 11th and 12th West India Regiments, which were raised in Guadeloupe and Martinique and were taken into the British Establishment (i.e. as regular British troops) in 1798. White French Creole officers serving with British-raised black troops in Ste Domingue during the British occupation (1794-1798) often remained in the British service after the occupation was over. Many emigrés without Caribbean connections, who had received commissions in regular British troops, took part in the West Indian campaigns of 1793-1797, in one of which Trinidad was conquered.

LISTE *des colons français titrés établis dans l'île antérieurement à la capitulation.* — *Voir le Libro Becerro de población, Registre de population, tenu sous le gouvernment de Chacon en vertu de la cédule royal de colonisation, et les* Parlimentary Papers, Report on titles to lands in Trinidad, *ou Documents parlementaires, Rapport sur les titres des terres á la Trinidad, imprimés par ordre de la Chambre des communes, le 18 février 1823.*

1. Comte Louis-Nicolas de Percin la Roque, chevalier de Saint-Louis, ex-gouverneur de l'île de Saint-Vincent.
2. Comte Benjamin de Castelet, chevalier de Saint-Louis, ex-lieutenant-colonel de S.M.B.
3. Comte Philippe-Vincent de Saint-Pern.
4. Vicomte Jean Martin de Fouquet, chevalier de Saint-Lazare.
5. Vicomte Louis-Sylvestre de Nesmond.
6. Vicomte Jean de Crény.
7. Chevalier Pierre de Crény.
8. Chevalier Gabriel de Crény.
9. Chevalier Philippe-Rose Roume de Saint-Laurent.
10. Chevalier François Roume de Saint-Laurent.
11. Chevalier de Gannes de la Chancellerie.
12. Chevalier Antoine de Jacques de la Bastide.
13. Chevalier de la Sauvagére, ex-governor français de Tobago.
14. Chevalier François-Régis de Rampont-Sommercour.
15. Baron Joseph-Paul-Augustin de Cambefort.
16. Baron Thomas de Paussadet.
17. Antoine Lefaye de Beaubrun, écuyer.
18. Christophe Le Gendre, écuyer, seigneur de la Bretesque.
19. Michel du Pont du Vivier de Gourville, chevalier de Saint-Louis, ex.lieutenant de vaisseau.
20. Pierre du Pont du Vivier de Gourville.
21. Louis-Charles-François Malleveault de la Varenne.
22. Guillaume Faure de Chabrac.
23. Pierre-Guy Gallet de Saint-Aurin.
24. Louis Hodebourg de Brosse.
25. Nicolas Hodebourg de Brosse.
26. Alexandre-François-Jacques-Guy-Abdon de Failly.
27. Antoine Charbonné de Bampart.
28. Nicolas de Saint-Pré.
29. Jean-Baptiste de la Gaudiére.
30. Jean de Poulaine.
31. Jean-Baptiste d'Albuquerque.
32. Haycinthe de Gournay.
33. Jérome de Gournay.
34. Jean-Baptiste de Saint-Didier.
35. Louis Maury de la Péyrouse.
36. Picot de la Peyrouse.
37. Claude de Deshayes.
38. Jean de la Forest.
39. Joseph de la Forest.
40. Jean d'Anneville.
41. Thomas de Thomaseau.
42. Jacques Prioteau de Coudrée.
43. Joseph de Guillaume de Rochebrune.
44. charles du Bochet.
45. Jean de Saint-Martin.
46. Charles de Lanoz.
47. Nicolas-Pierre-Louis-Charles le Mercier de Beauvoisin.
48. Pierre Carcenas de la Beissière.
49. Jean-Baptiste de la Grange-Platellet de la Tuilerie.
50. Charles-César de la Barquerie.
51. Jean-André-Martin de la Dence.
52. Élie-François Rabocon de Combes.
53. Joseph-François des Rieux.
54. Antoine Rigault de Rozée.
55. Philippe de la Hante-Belisle.
56. Charles de la Hante-Belisle.
57. François de Kersozie.
58. Duval des Rivières.
59. Dubuc du Gallion de Vitry.
60. Albert de Lâtre.
61. durand de Beauval.
62. De Germont.
63. De Lauréal.
64. Jean-Charles de Castaing.
65. De Vailoux.
66. De la Barrére.
67. Christophe de Sainte-Catherine.
68. Masson de la Coulommiére.
69. Roget de Belloquet.
70. Valleton de Boissière.
71. De Léry.
72. Le Mort.
73. De Cournand.
74. De Launay.
75. De Villars.
76. De Molé.
77. Mme la marquise de Cahrras, née de Gannes de la Chancellerie.
78. Mmme Thérèse d'Ayron.
79. Mme Marie-Madeleine Lefébvre de Bonneterre.
80. Mme Anne-Maarie — Guillaumine Pinel du Manoir.

Cette liste ne peut être que fort incomplère, parce que: 1. il n'existe aucun registre de population antérieur au gouvernement de Chacon; 2. celui tenu sous l'administration de ce gouverneur ne contient qu'une faible partie des con-concessions de terres faites aux nouveaux colons; et 3. le rapport sur les titres des terres à la Trinidad ne s'occupe uniquement que des beins en litige. À cette liste imparfaite nous ajoutons les noms titrés de quelques-uns de ceux qui sont venus s'etablir dans l'île, soit á la conquête anglaise á la quelle ils ont concouru,soit peu de temps après cette conquête; ce sont:

1. Comte de Loppinot et ses quatre fils.
2. Comte de Montalembert.
3. Général des Sources.
4. Colonel Gaudin de Soter.
5. Chevalier de Verteuil.
6. Chevalier de Bruny.
7. Marquis de Montrichard.
8. Vicomte de Bragelonne, etc., etc.

Liste des colons Français, noir et de couleur, inscrits au
Libro Becero de Población

1. Louis Philippe.
2. Louis Sabanne.
3. Jean Chrisante Clozier.
4. Charles Bideau.
5. Jérémie Piloge.
6. Joachim Ferret.
7. François Richard.
8. Jérome Richard.
9. Joseph Dubois.
10. Florentin Tocti.
11. Guillaume Renaud.
12. Jean Dumas.
13. Louis Mondésir.
14. François Boudin.
15. Honoré Vincent.
16. Louis Marcel.
17. Pierre Joseph
18. Alexandre Boutier.
19. Lambert François Boudin.
20. Louis François.
21. Michel Bétan.
22. Louis Florent
23. Jean-Pierre Durand.
24. Henri Déterricourt.
25. Michel Louison.
26. Michel Latraille.
27. Barthélemi Darquantin.
28. Louis Chevron.
29. Jean-Baptiste Léveillé.
30. Jérémie Beauruisseau.
31. Joseph Vatellier.
32. Hippolyte Martial.
33. Jean-Louis Patience.
34. Lot Libe.
35. François-Louis Fermenton.
36. Jean Baptiste
37. Louis Plet
38. Mme Veuve Marianne Lapoupe.
39. Mmes Marie Foucade.
40.   Suzanne Philippe.
41.   Cécile Parfaite.
42.   Marie Catherine.
43.   Rebecca.
44.   Madeleine.
45.   Julienne.
46.   Madeleine Joseph.
47.   Élizabeth.
48.   Marthe-Rose.
49.   Patience Napia.
50.   Marie Louise.

List of Proprietors of land in the island of Trinidad March 20th 1797. Made by the order of Sir Ralph Abercromby K.B. by F. Mallet Captain of the Surveying Engineers. These lands were all granted by the Crown of Spain 'since the first Establishment'.
Note the spellings of names and districts are reproduced here as they appeared on the original document.

ICAQUE
Capeville

NAPARIMA
V. Pechier
Loreille
Rochard
Mongonge
Salvador
Dubois
Vincent
Pilatre
Picou
Blondel
Juillet
Bontour
Caille
Clairmen
Bordénave
Treit
Deravine
Clarek
Nugent
Bernard
Sipriani
Renau
Borde
Bouler
Gracien
Rambert
Oliver
Sr. Martin
Francique
D'Coll
Serrat
Anfries
Cupet
Sardien
Crivel
Thelor
Hudes
Langtan
Morin
Godinee
Polesias
Fifague
Pradon
Letrain

TROIS
La Mote
Long
L'Patiance
Honore
Marsiany
Qorge

ERIN
Lesado

BREA
Vatable
Boucau
Durignee
Boye
Oditto
Dandon
Vance
Cadue
Dubois
Dance
Gougon
Deprace
Coander
Lesier
Papin
Fortin

CARENAGE
Sippiuni
Mercie
Traiton
Elic
Dert
Bodin
D'guspar
Percin
Joycn
Nicol
Noel
Simon
Gardin
Betteran
Rochard
Duvivur
Ozelet
Dumas
Gelino

AROUCA
Chaumet
Teblau

TOCO
Narcise
Jacquis
Traille
Guiro
D'Godet
Ponne
Guiro
Dupi
Monique
Rotan

DIEGO MARTIN
Mingot
Petiete
Sicar
Duran
Audier
Rolan
Roche
Du Couron
Dominique
Bergere
Olivier
Sorre
Labarene
Dufally
Teansie
Semian
Moro
Felicite
Audiber
Gealtroi
Audiber
Pouchet
Desoon
Portel
Julien
Gros

ST. JOSEPH
Morel
Norare
Felix
Farfas
Cazenove
Lapargan
Ulorte
Gardien
Indare
Miane
Cajeton
Novari
Topez
Silier
Greny
Lunch
Farfan
Gaspar
Legendre
Purtel
Magnemar
Lufay

QUIAOUANE
Mulispine
S. Aurin
Purre

SAVANETA	STA. CRUZ	CASAHAL
Dyckson	Porlet	Pilard
Codet	Black	Diguine
Jantis	Sousane	Ramsay
Favel	Charbon	Henitson
Samerson	Nugent	Ignius
Duchaleau	Clark	Nugent
Aluson	Courville	Waldrop
Farfan	Martin	Warner
V. Safon	Farfan	Robertson
Cofine	Cosle	
General Cuyler,	Laforet	
Commander in		MARAVAL
Chief, 1920	MAYARO	Mendes
Acres.	Radia	Winderflet
	Guias	chapel
TRAGARETE	Thomaso	Pecennin
Dert	Mahan	Devauch
Danglade	Allatre	Loton
Fayelle	Duchatel	Ludeves
Huet	Huet	Gousales
Gignon	Mer. Huet	Peschier
Vignon	Mahan	
	Hugues	GUAYAGUAYARE
MARACAS	Duitron	Pedre
Roblos	Juan Radin	Guide
Jermin	Selier	Rose
Farfan	De Burel	Louis
Mosquire	Ruanet	P. Martin
Lesaine	Suranpar	Lignes
Gama	Cardoniere	Martao
Tourn	Dupuch	Robert
Rivnin	Fronlin	Lignes
Guerino	h'Lahai	fontin
Gene	Ipolite	Blans
Miver	Romain	Palanquin
Aralby	Desten	Rigo
	Redou	Copstus
TACARIGUA	Rose	Rigo
Geugnon	Raphad	Copstus
Solger		Rigo
S. Pern	SIPARIA	Durefor
Dauson	Trabau	S. Martin
Joseph	Poleric	Desqueruche
Obrien	Oroser	Me. Robert
Robinson	Voisin	Biasque
Mucarti	Toulisier	Guide
	Hilaire	Tenebre
POINT A		Balan
PIERRE		Rogie
V. Benfils		Ruanel
Mandillon		Bernard
Le Fevre		Moncreau
Belgent		Godin
V. Pechier		Gilulau
Letain		
D'Vineta		

SOME OLD FAMILIES OF TRINIDAD

The Farfan Family

The Farfan Family if not the oldest is certainly one of the oldest of the Spanish families in the country. The first settler of the name was Don Manuel Farfan de los Godos, who arrived in Trinidad in 1644 and founded the Hermandad del Santissimo Sacramento, or Confraternity of the Blessed Sacrament at St. Joseph. From him are descended the Farfans of today, in a direct line.

The distinctive epithet "de los Godos" indicated that they belonged to one of the Gothic Families, so many of whom perished in the disastrous battle of Guadaletee (otherwise named Xeres de la Frontera) in 711 A.D., where Rodrigo, the last of the Gothic Kings of Spain, was slain by the victorious Saracens. In 1566 Pedro Huarex Farfan emigrated to New Granada, and it is from that branch, that Juan Manuel Farfan, of whom mention is made as having settled in Trinidad is descended.

The Family of Don José Mayan

On the fourth day of the Capitulation, Don José Mayan was appionted to the important post of Teniente de Justicia, Mayor of St. Joseph, an office which appears to have been created at the time the seat of Government was removed to Port-of-Spain in 1784, a step which gave mortal offence to the old Spanish settlers. The nomination of the honourable office of Teniente, a kind of Lieutenant Governorship, was always reserved for one of them as a concession to their wounded dignity.

Don José Martiniano Mayan, was a native of Trinidad, the son of Don Matias Mayan, who emigrated from the Province of Galicia in Old Spain early in the previous century. He settled at St. Joseph and married Augustina Prieto de Posada, daughter of Don Juan Antonio Prieto de Posada and Doña Josefa Gonzales, both settlers of a date prior to his arrival. On the 7th April, 1777, Don José Mayan married Doña Antonio de Salas by whom he had issue, one daughter, Trinidad de los Angeles. In 1797 she married Don Pablo Giuseppi. The descendants of this marriage are numerous and widespread. Apart from the direct line represented by Mr. Leon Giuseppi and the children of his younger brother Eugene Giuseppi, they are to be found among the Ciprianis, Fitts, Frasers, Monagas, and others more remote. It was at the house of Don José Mayan, on the Valsayn Estate, St. Joseph, that the Articles of Capitulation under which Don Chacon surrendered the Island to the British Crown, were signed on the 18th February, 1797.

The Sorzano Family

The Sorzano Family has been connected with Trinidad for more than two hundred years, its founder Don Manuel Sorzano having occupied the important post of Contador de Real Exercity under the Spanish Government for some years before the capture of the Island by Abercromby. As it was necessary for him to give an account of his administration of that Office he went to Spain with Chacon and was one of the officers mentioned in the last paragraph of the Despatch in which the Spanish Governor announced the disaster which had befallen him. As he was the owner of considerable property in the Island he determined to take the oath of allegiance to its new Sovereign, and with a view to making his family position perfectly clear, took occasion whilst in Spain to collect all the necessary documents to prove his descent from a long line of distinguished ancestors.

After his return to Trinidad, Don Manuel Thomas Sorzano de Tejada enjoyed the fullest confidence of the British Government which he served loyally and faithfully for many years. In 1803 Sir Thomas Hislop named him Assistant Commandant of Arima, and ten years later he was given a seat on the Board of Council by Sir Ralph Woodford.

The family of Sorzano is a very ancient one. One coat of arms was bestowed upon don Sancho Martinez Sorzano de Tejada by Alphonso III King of Asturia for his distinguished gallantry at the battle of Clavijo, 872 where he and his thirteen sons gained a great victory over the army of Abdullah, the Arab Caliph of Cordova. The thirteen green pennants, each having on it a crescent, which surround the coat of arms, are commemorative of this. The services of this same Don Sancho were formally recognised by Ferdinand and Isabella immediately after the conquest of Granada in 1492 which led to the expulsion of the Moors from Spain. The Sovereigns, by a solemn Act, confirmed the privileges granted to him to his descendants.

This solemn confirmation was renewed by Charles V in 1527.

The Basanta Family

Don Valentine de Basanta at the time of the Capitulation held the first office of Commissary of Population to which he had been appointed by the King of Spain in the year 1792. He had held a commisison in the Spanish Navy and, like Don Manuel Sorzano owning property, and having married in the colony, decided to remain after the Conquest, taking the oath of Allegiance to the King of England. The name of de Basanta is that of a very ancient family of Castille and occurs frequently in the chronicles of the 14th and 15th centuries as having taken part in the wars with Navarre under Pedro the Cruel and in those waged by Ferdinand and Isabella against the Moors. The arms of the family are a shield of four quarters; dexter, a field chief vert charged with an oak proper balzoned or; sinister chief a field azur charged with a fountain argent; dexter base, a field argent charged with a goat azur couped; sinister base a field sable charged with a triangle and eye or and four crosses argent. The whole is surmounted by a closed helmet turned to the right in proof of legitimacy, lined gules, ornamented and barred or. The father of Don Valentine Basanta, emigrated to Cartagena in 1775, and the latter, as has already been stated, after serving for some years in the Spanish Navy settled in Trinidad where he left numerous descendants.

THE FAMILY OF DON SIMON AGOSTINI, A CAPITULANT

Don Simon Agostini was a Corsican by birth. There is no exact date to prove when he arrived here but all the records show that some years before the capture of the Island by the British there was a considerable immigration of Corsicans to Trinidad. Those acquainted with the History of Corsica will remember that Pascal Paoli maintained for 13 years the struggle for the

Independence of Corsica against Genoa, and that when at last, the latter found it impossible to conquer the Islanders, he sold Corsica to France, he resisted the French with as much energy and ardour as he had done the Genoese. At last, in 1769, beaten by Devaux he took refuge in England. In 1790 his compatriots who in the meantime had become accustomed to the French rule, urged on him to return to Corsica, and on his consenting, Louis XVI named him Governor of the Island with the rank of Lieutenant General. He showed himself a warm partisan of the Bourbons, and when cited to appear before the Bar of the Convention preferred handing Corsica over to England in 1794. For this he has been blamed by some and praised by others. It was just about this period that the Corsican Immigration to Trinidad commenced, but whether it had any connexion with Paoli's acts there is no record to show. Don Simon Agostini was a Capitulant, and one among the first to take the oath of allegiance to the King of England. This is clear from the Exhibit which is a certificate dated 5th March 1797 a fortnight after the Capitulation, and signed by Picton, to the effect that Don Simon Agostini had subscribed the oath of allegiance. Permission was granted to Don Simon Agostini to own and carry two pistols, he having taken the oath of allegiance. Perhaps one of the most curious and valuable articles in the families possession is the large silver cup which belongs to Mr. Edgar Agostini. The family tradition is that this cup was a present from Picton to his great friend, Don Cristoval de Robles. Don Cristoval had two daughters, one of whom married a Mr. Charles Dancla and the other a Don——— Truxillo. The father of Mr. Edgar Agostini married a daughter of this Mr. Dancla and in the course of events the cup found its way back into the family. There are two shields on this cup, one bearing three trefoils, the other a nondescript animal, a tiger or a lion courant, but there is no inscription.

THE DE BOISSIERE FAMILY

The de Boissiere Family is one of the oldest in the Island, of those who were at the time called the 'New Colonists' to distinguish them from the old settlers. Jean de Boissiere left France, his native country, at a very early age in 1792 or 93 and after a few years of wandering, finally settled in Trinidad previously to 1797, as his name appears amongst the capitulants. The de Boissieres belong to a family of the ancient noblesse of Perigord, the patronymic name of which is Valleton, the senior branch being the family of Fontenelle. According to the custom of those days, the various branches were known as the de Boissieres de Valleton, the de Garrandes de Valleton, &c. &c. In the year 1847 the oldest representative of the family in France was a lady then nearly 96 years of age who remembered the Court of Louis XVI and the troublous times of the French Revolution. A young man, then some 17 years of age, a native of Trinidad, was travelling in the South of France at that time and presented himself to this old lady and to the rest of the family, and after giving his history was most warmly received by them, the old lady remembering his great grand-mother as her cousin and most intimate friend. That young man who subsequently served the British Crown as a Medical Officer both in the Crimea and in India and later on as a member of the Legislative Council of this Island. He inherited the Champs Elysees Estate, Dr. J. Valleton de Boissiere a Trinidadian of whom the Colony has every reason to be proud. The first settler, the grandfather of the Doctor, who lived until 1853 always called himself Jean Boissiere, having dropped the particule 'de' for a reason which shows that he was a man of great practical common sense. He saw that so long as he was engaged in commerce of any kind, however honourable, it was absurd to bear a title of nobility. At the same time he never forgot the race from which he sprang. On one occasion he was twitted by some one with claiming to be a 'noble' on which the old man replied "C'est vrai Monsieur, mais contrairement a ceux qui ne peuvent se faire passer pour nobles, qu'a l' étranger, je ne suis, et je ne passe pour noble, que dans mon pays." Mr. Boissiere however felt that he had no right to prevent those who were to follow him from the enjoyment of what he professed to esteem so lightly, and in the year 1836 he registered here by a notarial act drawn up from documents certified by the Mayor of Bergerac, the particulars of his claim to the name of "de" Boissiere. Jean Boissiere's career was an eminently successful if not a brilliant one. He held the office of President of the Cabildo, and commandant of the Quarter of Maraval. he was also a major in the Militia. At the beginning of the century Mr. Jean Boissiere was joint proprietor of the Champs Elysees Estate which had been founded by the Marquise de Charras, becoming its sole owner in 1817. His son, Mr. Henry Boissiere, married the daughter of a Royalist French Officer belonging to a very old family of Alsace, the Rogets de Belloquet. This officer had held a commission in the English Army and had served in the 1st West India Regiment and settled in Trinidad early in the Century. His uncle, the Baron Roget de Belloquet had given his adhesion to the Republic and was a General commanding a division under Massena at the celebrated battle of Zurich (1799.)

CARACCIOLO-PANTIN FAMILY

Count Joseph (Giuseppe) Caracciolo who died in Trinidad on the 6th of August 1819, was the direct descendant of Domenico Caracciolo, Marchese de Brienza, who had several children, of whom the eldest, named like himself Domenico, married a lady of the family of Ruffo, by whom he had but one son who appears to have borne the somewhat peculiar name of Literis, who was born in 1725, and who is registered under the name of Giuseppe Literis Caracciolo in the Libro d'Oro of Naples. He was twice married, and by his second wife, who was also of the Ruffo family, he had four sons, the third of whom, Luigi Giuseppe, married Mariana de la Porte Strabia. Their son Giuseppe was born in 1779 and at the age of 18 was named to a Sub-Lieutenancy in the Royal Cavalry. Impatient to earn military fame in the following year he joined the Russian Army under the famous Suwarov who was then engaged in aiding the Austrians to fight the French under Massena and Macdonald. He served for about a year and then for some reason not mentioned returned to Naples. Subsequently, finding his safety, perhaps even his life, endangered, in consequence of his having taken service with the Russians, he determined to emigrate and arrived in Trinidad about 1801. On the 5th of May 1805 he married Marie Josephine Amphoux by whom he became the father of two sons the elder of whom, Luigi married, and had several children.

One son, the eldest, married Henrietta Pantin de Mouilbert, the other, Alfredo, married Barbara Almandoz. Of these two marriages there are many descendants still living.

THE PANTIN FAMILY

Mr. Lewis Pantin the descendant of a French Huguenot Family which left France and settled in Yorkshire at the Revocation of the Edict of Nantes, 1685. Mr. Pantin made a fortune in the East Indies and eventually returned to England. The ship in which he sailed was threatened with quarantine at some port the name of which appears to have been forgotten by his descendants in Trinidad. All they know is that the vessel put out again to sea and was never again heard of. Mr. Pantin must have had some official connection with the Government, for all his children were educated at the public expense. One of them Lewis, entered the Royal Navy at the age of 14 and served in the Dictator 80, Captain Stewart, in the Baltic and North Sea squadron under Admiral Reynolds, where he saw a good deal of fighting. He was afterwards appointed Secretary to Admiral Sir P.C.H. Durham, Commander-in-Chief of the West Indian Squadron, and was on board the Venerable (the Flagship) 74 at the reduction of the French Islands. He assisted at a remarkable interview between Admiral Durham and the Comte de Vaugirard, the Governor of Martinique. The two had met before during the unfortunate Quiberon expedition and Admiral Durham for some reason or another was under the (erroneous) impression that Vaugiraud who was then amongst the French Officers serving with the English Army, had acted treacherously when piloting the English vessels. On meeting Vaugiraud at Martinique Durham taxed him with this supposed treachery and in a moment of anger threatened to hang him from the yard arm. Fortunately, calmer councils prevailed, explanations were given and nothing more was said. A friendly intercourse of civilities commenced between the Admiral and the Ex-Governor, who was a prisoner of war, which ended in the Secretary of the former falling in love with and marrying the niece of the latter, Mademoiselle de Mouillebert. When Admiral Durham struck his flag Mr. Pantin returned from the Service and on the invitation of Sir Ralph Woodford whose acquaintance he had made during a visit of the fleet to this colony, settled in Trinidad where he remained until the day of his death which occurred on the 31st October 1803. He filled several responsible posts in Government Service during his lifetime. He left numerous descendants.

PUMPKIN AND OCHRO SOUP
Cut up a quarter pound of salted beef that has been soaked in cold water overnight into small pieces. Put them in a pot with a slice of salt pork and sliced onion, two tomatoes, a clove of garlic crushed, some thyme and chives. Simmer thin in butter for five minutes and add enough water to boil two pounds of pumpkin. Peel and cut up the pumpkin and boil until soft. In a separate saucepan boil ten ochroes until soft. Remove from slimy water and put into pumpkin soup cut in inch long pieces. Simmer on slow fire until the pumpkin has melted completely and soup is smooth. Salt to taste.

*Above: Fort Chacon, The Observatory at Laventille built in 1792.
Photograph — O. Mavrogordato.*

Fort Chacon at Laventille was originally built by Don José Chacon as an
Observatory for the use of Don Cosmo Damien Charruca in 1792. It
was there that on the 2 January 1793 he observed 'the immersion of the
third satellite of Jupiter in the disk of the moon, and also that of the first
satellite'. From his observations he fixed for the first time an accurate
meridian in the new world. Upon returning to Spain Don Cosmo
completed his experiment by observing from Cadiz on the 23 October
1793 the entrance of the star Aldebaran into the disk of the moon, with
its exit. This, with his observations in Trinidad in January of that year
enabled him to link up the New World with the old and to fix an
absolute longitude, the first one so fixed in the New World. Observatory
Street in Port of Spain commemorates this remarkable event. Don
Cosmo who was born in 1759 and married Doña María Dolores Ruiz
de Apodaca, niece of Don Sebastian Ruiz de Apodaca, Admiral of the
Spanish fleet, settled at Chaguaramas in 1797. In 1805 while in
command of the 'San Juan Nepocumeno' he was killed at the battle of
Trafalgar at the age of forty-six.

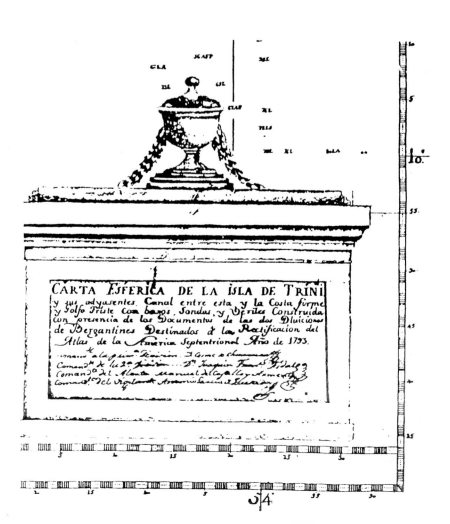

Scène Nocturne, Antilles.
As war and revolution swept through the French colonies the old order
vanished, the slaves now not only free and republican often fought over
the spoils. In the lithograph below the turn of a card has decided the
fate of a young woman, the daughter of a planter whose habitation has
been sacked by the rebels and whose daughters are now fair game. It
was against such a background that the settlement of Trinidad which
in the 1780's began as a trickle, by the 1770's became a torrent.

NEWSPAPERS

The following is a list of the several Newspapers that have
from time to time been published in the Island:—
The Trinidad Weekly Courant.   (1799).
The Trinidad Courant and Commercial Gazette.
The Trinidad Gazette.
The Port-of-Spain Gazette.   (1825.)
The Guardian.
The Observer.
The Trinidad Standard.
The Spectator.
The Trinidadian.
The Examiner.
The Free Press.
The Trinidad Reporter.
The Herald.
The Palladium.
The San Fernando Gazette.
The San Fernando Reporter.
The Sentinel.
The Chronicle.
The Colonist.
The Star of the West.
The Trinidad Chronicle.
The registration of Newspapers commenced in 1834.

SOME OLD SPANISH AND FRENCH MEASUREMENTS
FROM REPORT
by MADDOCK & DWARRIS 1827
TITLES TO LANDS IN TRINIDAD
Prepared by A.D. JARDINE

PASO OR PACE	=	54.8491	Inches	or	6.9254	Links
PULGADA	=	0.9142	Inches	or	0.1154	Links
PIE	=	10.9698	"	or	1.3851	"
VARA	=	32.9095	"	or	6.9254	"
ESTADAL	=	329.0948	"	or	41.5523	"
ESTABONE	=	109.699	Inches.			
ESTADAL (QUAD)	= 100. VARAS QUADRADAS		or 1726.6 Sq. Links			
SOLAR	= 25 ESTADALES QUADRADOS		or 43165 Sq. Links			
SUERTE	= 4 SOLARES		or 172660 Sq. Links			
QUARREE	= 3 1/5 Acs. (3.2 Acs).		or 320,000 Sq. Links			
FANEGA	= 4. SUERTES		or 690640 Sq. Links			
FANEGA	= 40000. VARAS QUADRADAS		or 690640 Sq. Links			
HECTARE	= 2.54 Acs.					
40 ACS.	= 1. Sq. Mile.					
CHAIN	= 100 Lks. or 66 feet.					

When converting feet to links. **x** by 100 & divide by 66.
When converting links to feet **x** by 66 & divide by 100.

The Capitulation

P.G.L. Borde

As soon as he had dealt with the Dutch establishments, and had pacified or conquered the French islands, with the exception of Guadeloupe which resisted all attacks, General Abercromby collected his available forces at Martinique so as to open the campaign of 1797 against the possessions owned by England's new enemy. The orders which the General had were to attack Trinidad first because of its size and fertility, and especially because of the facilities it offered for great commerce owing to its proximity to the continent.

The expeditionary squadron was commanded by Rear Admiral Henry Harvey and consisted of twenty sails and nearly nine hundred pieces of armament. There were seven ships of the line, two frigates, eight corvettes, a bomb vessel and two transports. The seven vessels were:

'Prince of Wales', 100 cannons, Captain J. Harvey. The Flag Ship.

'Bellona', 74 cannons, Captain Wilson.
'Vengeance' 74 cannons, Captain Russell.
'Invincible' 74 cannons, Captain Cayley.
'Alfred', 74 cannons, Captain Totty.
'Scipio', 68 cannons, Captain Davers.
'Dictator', 68 cannons.

The two Frigates were:
'Arethusa', 44 cannons, Captain Woolley.
'Alarm', 40 cannons, Captain Fellones.

The eight Corvettes were:
'Anna', 20 cannons.
'Thom', 20 cannons, Captain Hamstead.
'Favourite', 20 cannons, Captain Wood.
'Zebra', 20 cannons, Captain Skinner.
'Zephyr', 20 cannons, Captain Laurie.
'Victorious', 16 cannons, Captain Dickson.
'Bittern', 16 cannons, Captain Lavie.
'Pelican', 20 cannons.

The bomb Vessel was the "Terror", Captain Westbeach.

The two Transports were:
'Surrett Castle', 58 cannons.
'Ulyssees', 50 cannons.

The troops which were to land consisted of 6,750 men, and were commanded in person by General Abercromby. These consisted of 4,050 English Foot Soldiers as follows:

2nd or Queen's Regiment	700 men
14th Foot	650 "
3rd or Buffs	650 "
38th Foot	730 "
53rd Foot	680 "
60th Foot	640 "
	4,050

They also had 1,500 German Light Infantry Soldiers:

Lowensteins	500 men
Hompesch's Reg. of German Jaegers	1,000 "
	1,500

They also had: Gunners	500 "
Snappers, artificers etc	700 "
	1,200
	6,750 men

A large number of French royalists who were serving with the English forces were part of this expedition. This very considerable force could be increased in case of necessity, by the sailors from the Squadron.

The expedition left Fort de France on the 12th February, destined for Carriacou, which is one of the small Grenadine islands and which was their rallying point. On the morning of the 15th, they set sail for Trinidad, and on the morning of the next day they were in sight of the Dragon's Mouth. In a very short time the news of the presence of the English squadron in the waters of the island reached Port of Spain where Admiral Apodaca was, who having discussed the situation with the Governor, went back on board his ship. No one knows exactly what passed at this secret interview, but everything points to the fact that the Governor and the Admiral considered the position to be desperate, Governor Chacon because he had, for a long time, determined that he would not defend the colony against the English, and Admiral Apodaca because he found himself placed between a shameful flight through the Serpent's Mouth, or else facing a very unequal naval battle, which was too much for his courage. He therefore, returned to his ship, and believing that he could avoid both of the shameful extremities, he called a council of war, consisting of the five captains of his squadrons, who unanimously decided to burn their ships so as to prevent them falling into the hands of the enemy. But this was a false move, because the hasty destruction of such a squadron was more shameful to their military honour than if they had run away.

During this time, the English squadron, piloted by an African named Sharper, had to battle with the currents in the Grand Boca before they could enter the Gulf, and they did not succeed in passing through until three thirty in the afternoon. On entering and sailing towards the town, Admiral Harvey discovered the Spanish squadron in Chaguaramas Bay, but as it was already late, he decided not to engage battle with them until the next morning. He disposed of his forces in the following manner: The frigate 'Arethusa' and the corvettes 'Thorn' and 'Zebra' were ordered to approach the town and to anchor, together with the transports, probably in the region of the Parrot islands. The frigate 'Alarm' and the corvettes 'Favourite' and 'Victorious', were ordered to remain under sail for the whole night, and to station themselves between the transports and the town, so as to prevent the ships which were in the harbour from going out. At the end of the day, the Admiral anchored all his vessels of the line in order of battle before the enemy squadron, within reach of projectiles from the fort and from the vessels, so as to survey the enemy squadron and prevent it from sailing off during the night. We have

General Sir Ralph Abercromby

The distinguished soldier to whom Trinidad surrendered belonged to an ancient and honourable Scotch family.

Born in 1738, he was given a cornetcy in the 2nd Dragon Guards, in May 1756. In 1781 he was in command of the 103rd Regiment and served in Holland under H.R.H. The Duke of York. In 1797 he was named Commander-in-Chief in the West Indies and the expedition by which Trinidad was captured was commanded by him. In 1801 he was in command of the army in Egypt and at the battle of Alexandria on the 21st March of that year was severely wounded. He contrived, however, to conceal the fact until after the defeat of the French, and this was probably the cause of his wound proving fatal. He was taken on board the vessel of the Admiral. Lord Keith and lingered until the 28th of May.

Lord Hutchinson, afterwards Lord Donoughmore, on whom devolved the command in reporting his death, said: "It is some consolation to those who loved him that as his life was honourable so was his death glorious." He was buried in malta, but a magnificent monument to his memory was placed in St. Paul's Cathedral, where Nelson and Wellington also repose.

already seen how unnecessary these precautions were. The able plans which he made, bore witness that he had perfect knowledge of the territory.

We can well understand that the next day in Port of Spain was one of great anxiety. Although the day of attack on the colony by the English had been forseen for more than a year, when it finally arrived, the Governor had not carried out any of the works or taken any measures for the defence of the island. Contrary to the undertaking he had given, he had done absolutely nothing even after he had retained the troops of the Spanish squadron; the building of the batteries and redoubts for the protection of the town, had not yet even been started. The French colonists, who had no intention of delivering themselves bound hand and foot to the English, wished to defend themselves, and a big crowd of them appealed to the Governor to, at least, begin to organise some defensive measures. To all of them he gave the same short reply: "Little by little gentlemen, little by little." To the French Consul who went to see him to advise him to arm the population, and others who asked that the militia should be armed, he replied in the same way: "Little by little gentlemen, little by little." Being a disciple of the lawyer Patelin, he thus avoided giving replies which might compromise him, as he had evidently already decided not to move in the matter. Faced by this vexatious immobility of the Governor, and in view of the imminence of the danger, the general population displayed a feverish panic. Loud cries of "To arms" and "We are betrayed" were heard on all sides. The roads were filled with indignant men and women and weeping children. At this moment a thousand tumultuous

voices were heard, and among the imprecations and threats were mixed complaints and lamentations. In the midst of all this violent excitement, only Chacon remained unmoved. Due to his fear of the Republicans, he was resolved to throw himself into the arms of the enemy, and when the population became more and more turbulent, it strengthened him in his determination. As a precaution, he decided to send the archives and the treasure to Don José Mayan, who was the Justice of the Peace at St. Joseph, and these were buried under the cocoa trees on a plantation. He also secretly advised the English and Spanish inhabitants of the town, to remove themselves with their families and precious valuables to the old capital of the island. This was an entirely useless precaution because, let it be said to the honour of the British that no violence was committed against persons or properties.

The same tumultuous agitation continued during the night of the 16th to 17th. To the comings and goings of those who were running about the town seeking to organize some kind of resistance against the enemy, were added the steps of those who were fleeing to try to find a refuge at St. Joseph, and of those who were crossing the town carrying their money and jewelery and precious objects for the purpose of hiding them somewhere against possible pillage. Whilst the population was completely engaged in these painful occupations, around two o'clock in the morning a great glow suddenly appeared behind Pointe Gourd, and this created consternation in the breasts of all. Everybody realized at once what had happened to the beautiful Spanish squadron, and they understood that on the sea as well as on land, the authorities had abandoned any idea of an

The British Fleet off the coast of Diego Martin

Peru Estate owned by the Devenish family where the British landed in 1797, now called Invaders Bay. A watercolour by Captain Wilson 1837. Cambridge Collection.

offensive. It was indeed these superb vessels which, with all their sails spread were being slowly burnt during one of the calmest nights of our region. Apodaca himself presided over the arrangement of inflammable materials on the bridge of his own flag ship, and it was he who gave the order to set the fire, and all his subordinates followed his shameful example. For three hours the English squadron remained astonished spectators of this conflagration which did away with the necessity for a combined sea and land attack, and removed all difficulties for the capture of the island. When daybreak came, the whole Spanish Squadron had been consumed, with the exception of the vessel San Damaso, where the fire had not caught properly, and the English ships presently towed her into their lines. At the same time, a detachment of the Queen's Regiment peacefully occupied the battery on the island of Gaspar Grande, which had been abandoned during the night, as the Spanish vessels had been.

Immediately after this, General Abercromby, who had been relieved of the anxiety of having to engage in a naval battle, went on board the frigate 'Arethusa' which was anchored with the transports, so that he could supervise the landing of the troops, which took place at Mucurapo. This was a small suburb of Port of Spain, on which there was a sugar factory called 'Peru', which belonged to an Irish family named Devenish. The spot could not have been worse chosen. In this locality, a big marsh extended some distance into the sea and along the coast, and so prevented the approach of the boats.

Therefore, they had to stop at a considerable distance from the beach, and the troops had to carry out a very laborious march of several hundred paces through mud up to their knees. At this moment, the slightest resistance would have been fatal to them, but no one made any move, and the troops arrived on the beach without any danger, and under the protection of the guns of the corvette 'Favourite'. At the same time, and in order to create a diversion, the frigate 'Alarm' fired some shots at the battery in the roadstead, which replied with a few shots, but without any success. This was the only pretence of opposition which the English troops encountered. It is related that on arrival at the Peru sugar factory, the English troops, very fatigued owing to their forced march through the mud, found an ingenious method of recovering their strength. Into the pits of the sugar factory, they emptied two casks of sugar and three casks of rum. This grog was raised by means of pulleys suspended on ropes, and emptied into casks, and it served to refresh the whole of the expeditionary force.

Governor Chacon, quite evidently, had decided to capitulate without fighting, which is what the Dutch governors in Guyana had done. But Chacon was a little anxious about the news of the landing of the English troops without any previous consultation with him, and he was afraid to submit the town which, through his own fault, would have the appearance of having been taken by force. He therefore decided to make a demonstration, the real object of which was to enable him to discuss conditions with the invaders. A crowd of inhabitants had besieged the government, night and day, asking that they be supplied with arms. The Governor finally ordered the arsenal to be opened, and a short time later he ordered Lieutenant Don Juan Tornos, who was commanding one of the Spanish frigates, to collect a detachment of troops to make a reconnaissance. This detachment did not get under way before five o'clock in the afternoon, and was supported by the rest of the battalion which was commanded by Lieutenant Colonel Don Francisco Carabano. They very shortly met the advance guard of the English forces which was marching on the town, and they immediately fell back on the battalion, which by order of the Governor, had placed itself under the protection of the redoubt No. 1, which was behind the Dry River, and where they arrived at 5.30. Such then, was the only military action taken by Don José María Chacon, and the real reason for this was the hope that he could make the enemy believe that he had decided to resist them, and by this military ruse to obtain the object of his desire, which was capitulation. As regards the volunteers who had been armed at the eleventh hour, and who consequently were without organisation or leaders, they had accompanied the Spanish troops in their reconnaissance. They were then being led by Lieutenant Pio Ponte, and having retreated, they did not think it was any use to join the Spanish troops under the protection of the redoubts. They therefore spread out through the countryside as guerillas in order to harass the enemy. Only French ships continued to remain associated with Spanish troops.

The German soldiers who formed the advance guard of the English forces, scaled the easy grades of the small hills of Laventille without any opposition, and they established themselves, both infantry and artillery on the flat ground which dominated the position of the Spaniards and threatened their rear. The rear guard of the English army corps for their part, entered the town and encountered not the slightest resistance. They seized the rear side of the redoubt in the harbour, and thus cut off all communication between this redoubt and the one on Laventille. The centre part of the army established itself on the outskirts of the town in order to guard the approaches. At the same time, the frigates and the corvettes of the squadron, were tacking about in the harbour, and were ready to fire on the town in case that became necessary. Alas! there was nothing to oppose them but the small French corsair 'Patriot'. Thus, by eight o'clock in the evening, all the Spanish forces found themselves completely encircled. General Abercromby having taken up these positions, was now certain that his opponents could not escape him, and he therefore sent an officer to the Governor under a flag of truce, to deliver the following message: "Tell the Governor that I regret to see that he has no hope whatever of obtaining what he desires. The superiority of the forces under my command has made me master of this town, and has enabled me to encircle both the land and sea forces in such a manner that, by taking possession of the heights, they have been cut off from all communication and all help; that with such unequal forces as he has at his disposal, there is no possibility of making any resistance. Rather than spilling blood uselessly, I request that he

The Spanish Fleet under the command of Vice-Admiral Don Sebastian Ruiz de Apodaca on fire in Chaguaramas Bay, from a painting entitled 'Capture of Trinidad by the British', by Nathanial Pocock. Crown copyright.

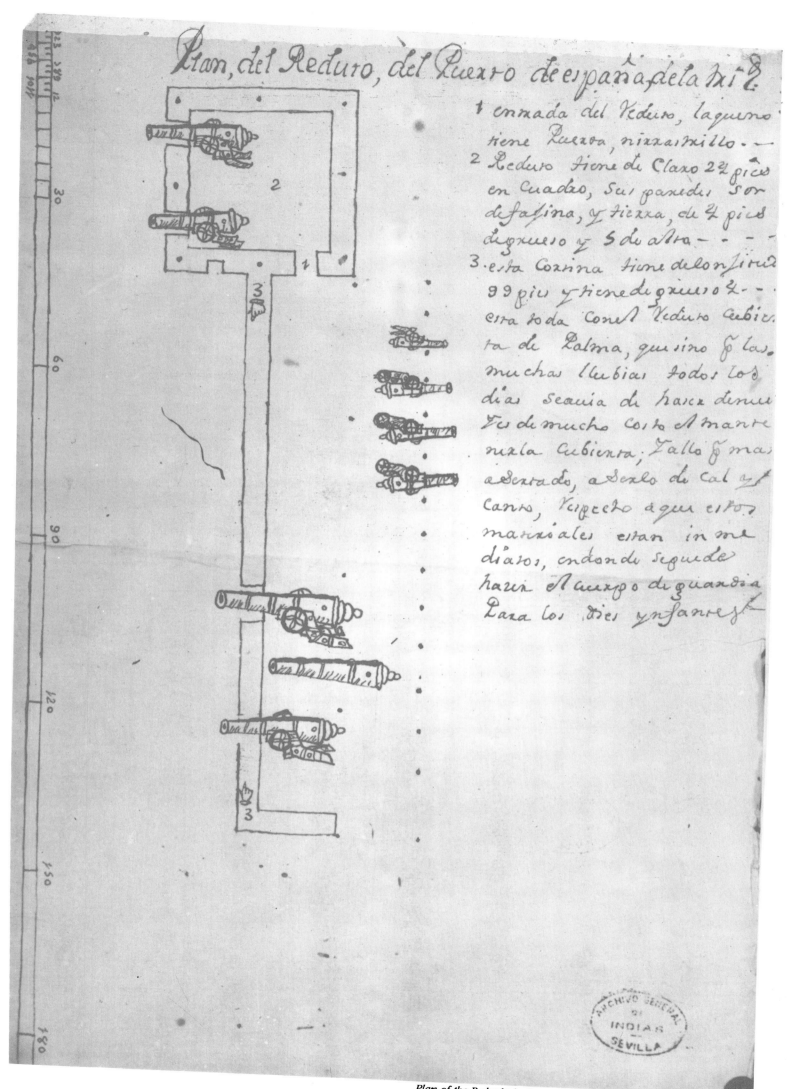

Plan of the Redoubt built in 1730 to defend the western approaches of the town of Puerto de Los Hispanioles under the Spanish Governor Agustin de Arrendonda 1726-1731. By permission of the Archivo General de Indias – Sevilla –

should appoint a place where we can confer together and where I can offer him the most honourable capitulation which it is possible to give to good and faithful soldiers who otherwise would be uselessly sacrified." One cannot say how he could have been so able and so courteous at the same time.

After two long days of anxiety, Governor Chacon finally succeeded in getting what he had wanted all the time, that is, the capitulation of the island without any fighting. He called together a council of war consisting of the Lieutenant Governor and the officers commanding the various corps, so that they could discuss the proposal of the English general. All of them, taking into consideration the desperate position of their affairs, necessarily decided to agree to suspend all armed action immediately, and a conference was arranged for eight o'clock the next morning the 18th, to discuss the terms of capitulation. At the appointed hour the next day, General Abercromby, Admiral Harvey and Governor Chacon met in one of the houses in the town, and the following fifteen articles of the Capitulation were recorded and signed by them:

1.   The officers and troops of His Catholic Majesty and his allies in the island of Trinidad, are to surrender themselves prisoners of war, and are to deliver up the territory, forts, buildings, arms, ammunition, money, effects, plans and stores, with exact inventories thereof, belonging to His Catholic Majesty; and they are hereby transferred to his Britannic Majesty in the same manner and possession as has been held heretofore by His said Catholic Majesty.

The troops of His Catholic Majesty are to march out with the honours of war, and to lay down their arms at the distance of 300 paces from the forts they occupy, at five o'clock this evening, the 18th February.

3.   All the officers and troops aforesaid of His Catholic Majesty are allowed to keep their private effects, and the officers are allowed to wear their swords.

4.   Admiral Don Sebastian Ruiz de Apodaca, being on shore in the island, after having burnt and abandoned his ships, he, with the officers and men belonging to the squadron under his command, are included in this capitulation, under the same terms as are granted to His Catholic Majesty's troops.

5.   As soon as ships can be conveniently provided for the purpose, the prisoners are to be conveyed to Spain, there remaining prisoners of war until exchanged by a cartel between the two nations, or until peace, it being clearly understood that they shall not serve against Great Britain or her allies until exchanged.

6.   There being some officers among His Catholic Majesty's troops, whose private affairs require their presence at different places of the continent of America, such officers are permitted to go upon their parole to the said places for six months, more or less, after which period they are to return to Europe; but as the number receiving this indulgence must be limited, His Excellency Don Chacon will previously deliver to the British commanders a list of their names, ranks, and places which they are going to.

7.   The officers of the royal administration, upon the delivery of stores with which they are charged to such officers as may be appointed by the British commanders, will receive receipts, according to the custom in like cases, from the officers so appointed to receive the stores.

8.   All the private property of the Spanish inhabitants, as well as those as may have been naturalized, is preserved to them.

9.   All public records are to be preserved in such courts or offices as they are now in; and all contracts and

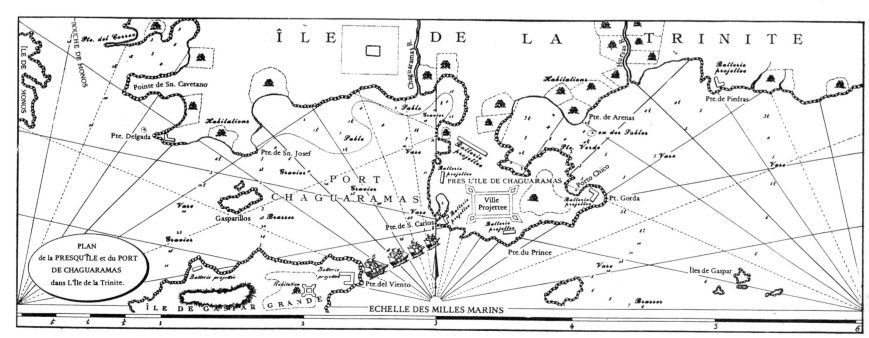

An old French map showing the position of the Spanish ships sunk between the island of Gaspar Grande and the Predes Carlos. It also shows the displacement of various fortifications and habitations. The Spanish squadron under the command of Rear Admiral consisted of four vessels of theline and one frigate. The troops which the squadron carried came up to seven hundred men. The four vessels were as follows: "San Vincente" of 84 cannons, Captain don Geronimo Gonzales de Mendoza, this was the flagship. "Gallardo" of 74 cannons, Captain don Gabriel Diundo. "Arrogante" of 74 cannons, Captain don Rafael Rennazar. "San Damaso" of 74 cannons, Captain don José Jordan. The frigate was the "Santa Cecilia" of 36 cannons, Captain don Manuel Urtuzabel.*

Slaves were pivotal to the prosperity of the sugar plantation. 'Planting Sugar Cane' was illustrated by Richard Bridgens circa 1830 — Tom Cambridge Collection.

purchases between individuals, which have been done according to the laws of Spain, are to be held binding and valid by the British Government.

10. The Spanish officers of administration who are possessed of landed property in Trinidad, are allowed to remain in the island, they taking the oaths of allegiance to His Britannic Majesty, and they are further allowed, should they please, to sell or dispose of their property, and to retire elsewhere.

11. The free exercise of their religion is allowed the inhabitants.

12. The free coloured people who have been acknowledged as such by the laws of Spain, shall be protected in their liberty, persons and property, like other inhabitants, they taking the oath of allegiance, and demeaning themselves as become good and peaceable subjects of His Britannic Majesty.

13. The sailors and soldiers of His Catholic Majesty are, from the time of their laying down of their arms, to be fed by the British government, leaving the expense to be regulated by the cartel between the two nations.

14. The sick of the Spanish troops will be taken care of, but to be attended to and be under the inspection of their own surgeons.

15. All the inhabitants of Trinidad shall, within thirty days from the date hereof, take the oath of allegiance to His Britannic Majesty to demean themselves quietly and faithfully to his government, upon pain, in case of non compliance, of being sent away from the island.

Apart from the articles concerning the war, we can see that his capitulation did not guarantee anything to the inhabitants except the validity of contracts and engagements which had been concluded under Spanish laws, and the freedom to exercise their religion. No mention is made about the maintenance of the Spanish laws or even the Cedula of Colonisation and the Code Noir. Nevertheless, such as it was, the capitualtion was accepted by the population, if not with satisfaction at least without dislike, seeing that the population was not diminished by the fact of the English conquest by hardly more than a thousand inhabitants. At this time, England possessed all the islands of the Lesser Antilles except Guadeloupe.

The population which the Island passed to British hands was 18,627 — 2,500 whites 5,000 free mulattoes and negroes, 10,000 slaves and 1,127 Indians. There were 159 sugar plantations, 130 of coffee, 130 cotton, 6 cocoa, 70 tobacco and a few of indigo. Their expanses covered 85,268 1/5 acres and from them were gathered the colony's exports, then consisting of 9,356,952 pounds of sugar, 330,000 pounds of coffee, 224,000 pounds of cotton, 96,000 pounds of cocoa and small quantities of both tobacco and indigo. The approximate value of these exports was $1,000.000.

There was a complicated system of currency, both gold and silver. In gold there were Doubloons (value: $16), with divisions of half, quarter, eighth and sixteenth. In silver were Large Piastres and Small Piastres (value: $1.00 and 80¢ respectively) and divisions of half, quarter, tenth and twentieth. These coins and their divisions were for many years known locally by various French or French Patois names. There being at one time an insufficiency of change, pieces were stamped out of the dollars and circulated, at the value of 10¢ each, under the name of 'escalin clou.' Even these were not sufficient, however, so shop-keepers began to issue their own tokens; called 'marks' locally, of very small value. When these private tokens along with other confusing coinage were later replaced by sterling at the instance of Sir Ralph Woodford, some traders whose total value of outstanding tokens were swollen by counterfeits, were reduced to near bankruptcy. One such merchant, a M. François Declos, whose tokens were stamped "F.D.," was called upon to cash an amount estimated as high as 500 percent over that which he had issued.

The weights and measures were the Spanish Pound of 16 ounces; 'Arrobas', 25 lbs.; 'Quintal,' 100 lbs,; 'Fanega,' 110 lbs.; 'Varas,' 33 inches; 'Estabal,' 10 x 10 'Varas;' 'Solar,' 5 x 5 'Estabals,' Fifteen 'Fanegas' of land was equal to 112 acres and one 'Suerte' was 2 x 2 'Fanegas.' One 'Fenega' when referring to measures of capacity was equal to eight gallons; one 'Almide' was a gallon; and four 'Millares' equalled one 'Almide.'

The Government at the time of British conquest was made up of a Governor and Captain-General, a Lieutenant-Governor and Chief Justice, both of these being appointed by the Crown, and, in addition, a Treasurer and Administrator of the Royal Revenues, a Receiver of Taxes, Collector of Customs, Harbour Master, Chief of Police, and two Wardens, these being appointed by the Governor.

The centres of population were the new capital Port D'Espagne (Port of Spain), St. Juan D'Aricagua (San Juan), the old capital San José de Oruña (St. Joseph), San Fernando de Naparima (San Fernando), and the four Indian Missions of Arima, Toco, Siparia and Savannah Grande. Port of Spain with 500 to 600 houses and a population of between 5,000 and 6,000 was the largest town and was principally inhabited by the French and other foreigners. St. Joseph, with between 500 and 600 residents, contained the residences of most of the Spanish population. San Juan and San Fernando were merely represented by a few houses surrounding the plazas or public squares. The best houses were built of wood and tapia with shingle coverings.

The following schedule of prices, approved by the Governor, will give some idea of the cost of living in those days.

Fresh Beef	..	3½	cents per lb.
Salt "	..	5	" " "
Fresh Pork	..	5	" " "
Quarter of Mutton	..	60	"
Quarter of Goat	..	40	"
1 Quenk (Salted)	..	30	"
1 Large Lappe. .	..	20	"
1 Agouti	..	10	cents
25 lbs. Salt Fish	..	60	"
25 lbs. Cod Fish	..	$ 1.20	"
4 Red Fish (length of the elbow)		10	"
1 Large Turtle	..	$ 1.20	"
1 Small Turtle	..	30	"
1 Morocoy	..	10	"
1 Tatou ..	..	10	"
1 Large Turkey	..	$ 1.60	"
1 Large Capon	..	30	"
1 Large Fowl	..	20	"
2 Large Pigeons	..	20	"
4 Ramiers	..	10	"
12 Eggs ..	..	10	"
2 Gals. Milk	..	10	"
1½ lbs. Cheese	..	10	"
1½ lbs. Flour	..	10	"
1 lb. Bread	..	10	"
110 lbs. Corn	..	80	"
110 lbs. Cocoa	..	$12.00	
110 lbs. Rice	..	$ 3.00	
110 lbs. Peas	..	$ 4.00	
1 lb. Coffee	..	10	"
100 Plantains	..	30	"
12 Bots. Brandy	..	90	"
12 Bots. Old Rum	..	40	"
12 Bots. Olive Oil	..	90	"
1 lb. Butter	..	40	"
1 Bar Soap	..	15	"
2 Melons	..	05	"
6 Soursops	..	05	"
24 Avocado Pears	..	10	"
24 Oranges	..	05	"
1 Pineapple	..	05	"
1 Papaw	..	05	"
6 Sweet Potatoes	..	05	"
25 lbs. Tobacco	..	30	"
Ordinary Calico	..	50	" per vara
Osnaburgs and Checks	..	20 to 30	" per vara
1 Small Knife	..	20	"
5 Sheets Paper	..	05	"
Fine Calico	..	80	" per vara
1 Ordinary Handkerchief	..	40	"
1 Fine Handkerchief	..	80	"
12 Reels Cotton Thread	..	15	"
1 Good Axe	..	80	"
1 Good Cutlass	..	80	"

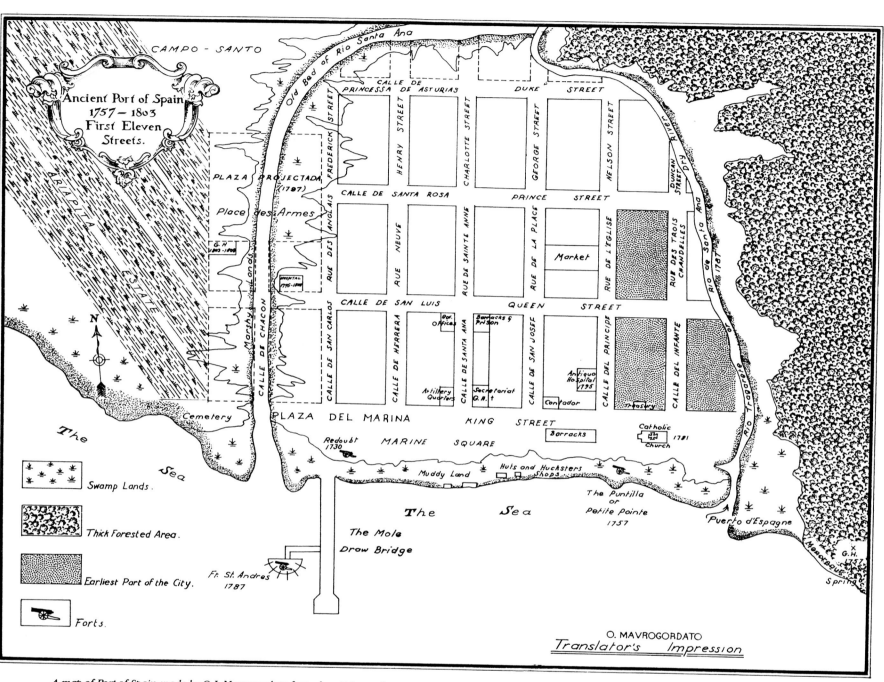

Ancient Port of Spain 1757 – 1803 First Eleven Streets.

O. MAVROGORDATO
Translator's Impression

A map of Port of Spain made by O.J. Mavrogordato from descriptions of the town as contained in the first edition (French) of P.G.L. Borde's 'History of Trinidad' under the Spanish Government.

The state of our currency at that time could not be described otherwise than as chaotic. French, Spanish and American gold and silver coins passed just as currently as the British. We had 5, 10, 20, 25, 50 and 100 cent coins, both Spanish and American, 20 and 25 centimes French coins, which passed for 4 and 5 cents, and 25 francs French, which passed for 90 cents. In gold coins we had 1, 2/12, 3, 6, 10 and 20 dollars American; 1, 2, 4, 8 and 16 dollars Spanish and Mexican and 25 franc, French which passed for $3.60. There were also in circulation Spanish silver dollars with a hole cut out in the centre, which were called Cut dollars and passed for 90 cents. British coins, both gold and silver, were conspicuous by their absence. The copper coinage was mostly British pennies and half-pennies, with a sprinkling of French 10 centime pieces. A bitt, was the unit of computation and all prices were quoted in "Dollars" and "Bitts". The bitt being of the

A few days after the capitulation Don Chacon left Trinidad, never to return.

"Abercromby, after making the best arrangements that the extremely confused state of the colony allowed, and banishing some of the most notoriously corrupt of the Spanish lawyers departed two months after." He left as Governor, Colonel (later General) Sir Thomas Picton, his A.D.C. and protegé A force of only 520 soldiers remained to hold the island.

One of Picton's first acts was to drive away "the worst and most worthless part of the republican inhabitants;" Hundreds, perhaps even thousands, left Trinidad and settled in and around Guiria, Venezuela. Bribery and corruption being rife, the new Governor threatened to hand the first public officer taking a bribe, a method which met with quick success. He was firm and formidable but nevertheless well liked.

When the Governors of Caracas and Guayana offered $20,000 for Picton's head the gentleman in question politely invited them by letter to come over and take it, and burlesqued a proclamation offering in return $20 in full settlement for either of their heads.

Picton instituted a council of advice consisting of Don Christoval de Robles (a Spanish creole), Messrs. John Nihell, John Black and John Nugent (Irishmen) and M. St. Hilaire Begorrat, a French creole. On 1st June, 1797, the commission of His Majesty arrived, officially appointing Picton Governor.

Historical Notes from H.C. Pitts '100 Years Together'.

General Account of the POPULATION and AGRICULTURE of the ISLAND of TRINIDAD,

MADE BY QUARTERS IN JULY, 1797.

Name of Quarters.	MANUFACTURERS.						WHITES.				COLOUR.				SLAVES.				INDIANS.				Total.
	Water Mill.	Wind Mill.	Mills worked by Mules.	Coffee Mills.	Cotton Mills.	Rum Distillers.	Men.	Women.	Boys.	Girls.	Men.	Women.	Boys.	Girls.	Men.	Women.	Boys.	Girls.	Men.	Women.	Boys.	Girls.	
Las Bocas – – – – –	–	–	–	1	42	–	19	6	2	4	6	9	6	8	84	49	9	11	–	–	–	–	213
Le Carenage – – – –	–	–	10	5	18	5	29	11	12	12	40	54	24	13	250	219	72	66	–	–	–	–	804
Diego Martin – – – –	–	–	19	12	4	9	63	42	12	24	76	85	65	33	323	256	93	62	–	–	–	–	1134
Mucurapa – – – – –	–	–	8	2	–	3	11	12	–	1	13	26	11	13	92	81	21	28	–	–	–	–	309
Tragarette – – – – –	–	–	3	–	–	2	7	9	3	1	4	11	–	1	109	87	25	19	–	–	–	–	276
St. Anne – – – – –	1	–	5	24	16	2	21	9	12	6	52	58	36	41	164	167	39	39	–	–	–	–	644
Maraval – – – – – –	1	–	2	7	1	4	21	8	5	2	36	49	31	25	200	119	59	56	–	–	–	–	611
Santa Cruz – – – – –	–	–	–	5	–	–	7	5	7	11	64	58	46	43	48	39	24	22	–	–	–	–	374
La Ventille – – – – –	–	–	1	16	25	–	9	7	–	1	33	52	24	25	103	93	43	29	–	–	–	–	419
Simaronero – – – –	–	1	4	5	1	3	5	1	–	–	16	14	10	11	140	69	33	24	–	–	–	–	323
Aricagua – – – –	–	–	6	7	–	2	14	13	6	12	46	44	47	27	162	123	50	45	–	–	–	–	589
St. Joseph – – – –	–	–	13	7	4	2	57	45	26	14	63	59	27	28	169	130	60	50	–	–	–	–	728
Maracal – – – – –	–	–	3	4	–	1	18	14	12	2	23	18	20	13	66	31	16	15	–	–	–	–	248
Las Coiras – – – – –	1	–	–	–	–	–	2	–	–	–	2	2	–	–	40	14	2	2	–	–	–	–	64
Tacarigua and Arouca	–	–	14	2	–	8	18	9	8	–	58	49	31	26	282	172	69	80			–	–	802
Arima and Guanapo – –	–	–	–	5	–	–	13	9	2	5	16	7	10	14	56	40	23	27	110	184	105	96	717
Toco, Salibia, and Cumana	–	–	1	–	59	–	7	7	7	7	7	12	19	24	51	56	27	20	57	50	20	28	399
Mayaro – – – – – –	–	–	1	–	65	–	28	12	6	2	13	16	9	6	146	84	40	41	–	–	–	–	401
Guayaguayare – – – –	–	–	1	–	74	–	26	10	15	10	6	17	14	9	132	79	56	34	–	–	–	–	410
Erin – – – – – –	–	–	–	–	1	–	1	1	1	2	20	14	15	12	8	4	1	–	–	–	–	–	79
Icaque and Gallos – – –	–	–	5	–	3	–	27	18	6	4	47	41	11	6	116	79	8	11	–	–	–	–	375
La Brea – – – – –	–	–	20	3	–	6	31	16	1	10	38	40	13	11	171	137	46	41	–	–	–	–	555
Siparia – – – – – –	–	–	–	–	–	–	1	–	–	–	–	–	–	–	–	–	–	–	50	49	26	14	140
Naparima – – – – –	–	–	20	25	28	8	69	32	36	28	128	74	85	59	385	293	90	100	–	–	–	–	1379
Monserrat & Savana Grande	–																		88	118	39	48	293
Pointe à Pierre – – – –	–	–	6	–	3	1	12	18	9	2	24	10	6	6	73	76	26	30	–	–	–	–	292
Savanetta, Cuba & Cascajal	–	–	13	–	–	3	25	6	3	1	44	34	30	33	227	152	35	27	–	–	–	–	617
Puerto d'Espana – – –	–	–	–	–	–	1	453	270	110	105	321	771	308	271	567	856	264	229	–	–	–	–	4523
Total – –	3	1	155	130	344	60	994	590	301	266	1196	1624	898	758	4164	3505	1232	1108	305	401	190	186	17718

Abstract of the Account

	Whites.	Colour.	Slaves.	Indians.	Total.
Men —	994	1196	4164	305	6659
Women —	590	1624	3505	401	6120
Boys —	301	898	1232	190	2621
Girls —	266	758	1108	186	2318
Total —	2151	4476	10009	1082	17718

by F. Mallet Captain of the Surveying Engineers.

value of ten cents. The half-bitt or 5 cent piece was the most popular coin, and half of that called a "stampee" or "tampay" in patois, was the smallest quantity you were supposed to buy in any shop. To facilitate this, as there were no farthings, the 5 cent piece was cut in half and the mutilated coin passed current as a "stampee". Some went further and cut the 10 cent pieces into four and these triangles were also cheerfully accepted as stampees. As time went on and the money market became tighter, the necessity for a half stampee, "dimi tampay" was felt and a popular shop-keeper named Francois Declos, fell upon the expedient of stamping his initial F.D. upon a half-penny and giving and receiving it from his customers, as a half-stampee. This was quite a patriarchal way of adapting the currency to the need of the population. After a time the Government woke up to the necessity of putting their house in order and straightening out the chaos surrounding the currency. An Ordinance was passed, calling in all foreign coins, and making British money the only legal tender thenceforward. The fashion of counting in bitts survived for a long time after the bitts and half-bitts had disappeared and the present generation knows them no more.

CASCADURA MATETE

Steam the cascadura for a few minutes, then take off the skins and clean thoroughly. Season well with onions, garlic, thyme, chives and pepper. Boil the milk of two grated coconuts until it becomes oil. Put in the seasoned cascadura and simmer for five minutes. Then add cassava farine by the spoonfuls turning the meanwhile to make the whole into a coo-coo. If wanted very hot burst a whole red hot pepper in it. This is the dish which has the legend about after having eaten it the person would always have to return to the island. While we don't know if this is true, we certainly know that since having eaten it the person must return to the pot.

Lieut. General Sir Thomas Picton, K.B.

Thomas Picton was born at Poyston in Pembrokeshire, in August 1758, and from his youth showed a strong prediliction for that career in which he was to become so distinguished. In 1773 he obtained an ensigncy in the 12th or East Suffolk Regiment of Foot, then commanded by his uncle, Lieutenant-Colonel Picton. He remained in it for seven years, but anxious to see active service he applied for and obtained an exchange into the 75th Highlanders. In 1783 the Regiment was disbanded in one of the fits of economy which has so often proved disastrous to England, and Captain Picton was placed on half pay. When in 1793, war was declared, after the death on the scaffold of Louis XVI, he sought for re-employment but for some time in vain. Towards the end of the year

1794 he joined the troops surviving under Sir John Vaughan in the West Indies. Vaughan, who knew his merit, at once appointed him to a company in the 17th Foot and placed him on his own staff. He was shortly after promoted to a majority in the 68th and appointed Deputy Quartermaster-General with the brevet rank of Lieutenant Colonel. Vaughan died in 1795 and was succeeded by General Knox who superseded Picton. He was about to return to England when General Sir Ralph Abercromby, who had just arrived in the West Indies in supreme command, appointed him to his own staff. He was present at the capture of St. Lucia and St. Vincent, on both of which occasions he greatly distinguished himself. He accompanied Abercromby to England and early in 1797 he returned with that distinguished Officer to the West Indies as Lieutenant Colonel of the 57th Foot, to which Regiment he had been appointed on 1st May, 1796. He still held his staff appointment and accompanied the General on the expedition against Trinidad. When Abercromby quitted the island in April he left his Aide-de-Camp as Governor and Commandant. He announced the appointment in the following remarkable words:-

"I have placed you in a trying and delicate position nor to give you any chance of overcoming the difficulties opposed to you, can I leave you a strong garrison; but I shall give you ample powers; *execute Spanish law as well as you can;* do justice according to your conscience, and that is all that can be expected of you. His Majesty's Government will be minutely informed of your situation, and no doubt will make all due allowances."

An excerpt taken from M'Callum's 'Travels in Trinidad'.

Head-Quarters, PUERTO DE ESPAÑA, MARCH 1803.
Dear Sir,

Dr. Blair somewhere remarks, "that the history of mankind has ever been a continued tragedy, — the world a great theatre, exhibiting the same repeated scene of the follies of men shooting forth into guilt, and of their passions fermenting by a quick process into misery."

Thomas Picton, being the leading character, claims our first attention. He was born of obscure parents somewhere on the mountains of *South Wales*. I am totally unacquainted with his early progress in life, or with his relations, any farther than that he has a sister married in *New York*, to a peddling broker of the name of Bette, who was originally an itinerant showman or player in the *United States of America;* at other times a sailor, &c. He came here about two years ago to pay a visit to his brother-in-law, who being elevated in most extraordinary manner to the appellation of "Excellency," *which none of the family ever enjoyed before or since the days of Caractacus, it was some time before little Bette* could be recollected in the pomp and grandeur of coldness, which manifested a treasonable abuse of friendship, and an inward perplexity, the constant comparison of pride, with a sort of secret sense of unworthiness that sunk him amidst his triumph and fancied greatness.

There are some pitiful wretches, who having just emerged, by a perverse partiality of fortune, from the lowest condition, conceive that the only way of shewing themselves qualified to maintain their new character, is to manifest an extreme scorn for their old one; and that, to evince an elevation of mind proportioned to their rise of fortune, they have only to discard the associates and witnesses of their humble beginnings; which puts me in mind of the poet's account of the metamorphosis of Atlas into a mountain; "his beard and hair shot up into a huge forest; his shoulders and hands became ridges; his head supported the place of a pinnacle; his bones were converted into rocks; and his whole person swelled out to a monstrous size, and which all the stars of heaven reposed." Bette returned (as I am informed) disgusted at the change in his brother-in-law's deportment, as well as his morals, who mistook pride for dignity, giving himself airs of importance, and behaving to all as if haughtiness were his exclusive prerogative, as though civility belonged only to private men; yet instead of being respected, he was the reverse. Sensible that his conduct provoked laughter, and deserved ridicule, he told him one day at table, that, with all his greatness, he was sure his situation was much more enviable when they lived in *Wales* on twenty pounds a year, than as he was then

TRAVELS

TRINIDAD

DURING the MONTHS of FEBRUARY, MARCH, and APRIL, 1803,

IN A SERIES OF LETTERS,

ADDRESSED TO

A MEMBER OF THE IMPERIAL PARLIAMENT

OF

GREAT BRITAIN.

ILLUSTRATED

WITH

A MAP OF THE ISLAND.

By PIERRE F. M'CALLUM.

No power of words,
No graceful periods of harmonious speech
Dwell on my lips—the only art I boast
Is honest truth, unpolish'd, unadorn'd,—
Truth that must strike conviction to your heart!
MURPHY's ZENOBIA.

Liverpool,

PRINTED FOR THE AUTHOR BY W. JONES, 56, CASTLE-STREET, AND SOLD BY THE BOOKSELLERS IN LONDON, EDINBURGH, GLASGOW, &c. &c.

1805.

governor of *Trinidad.*

He came here as Lieutenant-Colonel when the island was conquered under the command of the much lamented Sir Ralph Abercromby, who appointed him governor. He, like many others, entered upon public life too early; was invested with the supreme authority of a commercial colony, before he obtained the knowledge of governing himself, consequently formed systems in haste, upon false premises,—on erroneous theories, erected upon the chimerical fabric of a treacherous foundation.

Elated with his elevated situation, he vainly imagined he should find favour in the eyes of his Sovereign (who is, literally speaking, the father of his people), by pushing authority much farther than had hitherto been attempted by delegated majesty. In this island Sir Ralph found a considerable number of British runaways, or more properly speaking, if I may use the expression, *'scapehemps,* from the other West India Islands; men who would disgrace, if possible, either the soil of *America* or *Botany Bay.* The Spaniards encouraged, and their laws protected them; hence, before it was captured, it was like *America,* a rookery for fugitive vagabonds of every description. Dreams of avarice, and its proximity to the main, held out delusive prospects at a distance to mercantile men, who came with their articles to realize the golden dreams. To the planters they sold on credit under the idea of probity, little dreading that the laws of the colony were in the hands of those of whom I have, in my preceding letter, attempted to give a faint delineation.

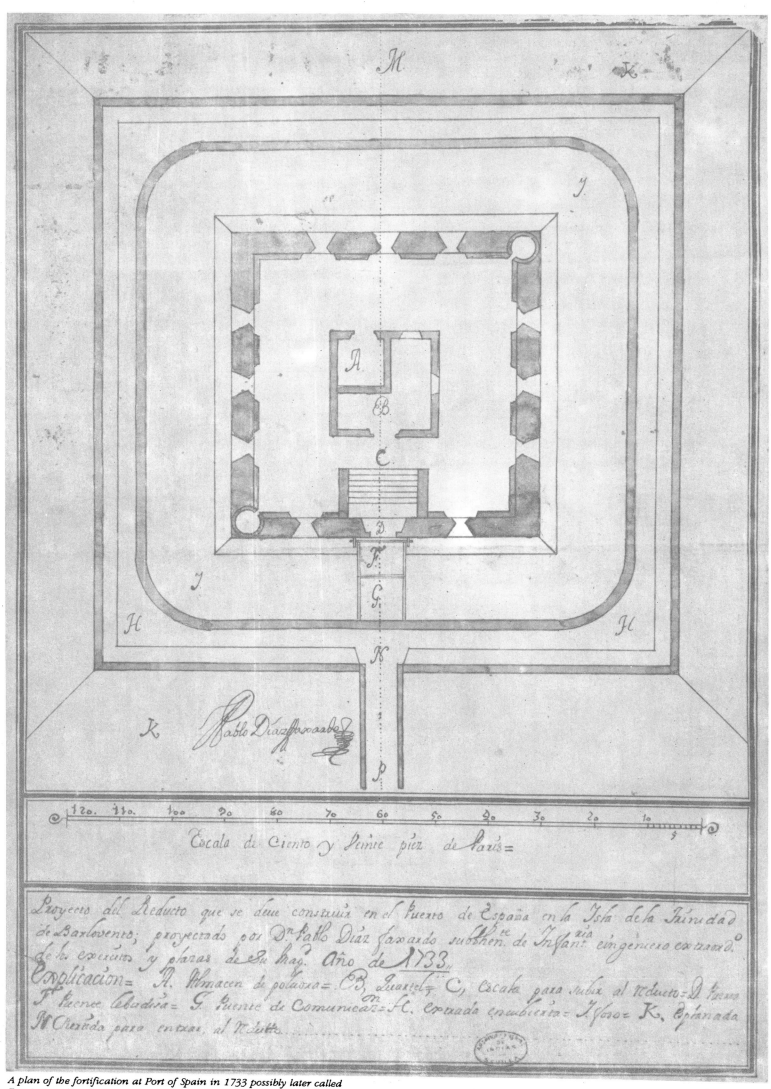

A plan of the fortification at Port of Spain in 1733 possibly later called Fort San Andres. By permission of the Archivo General de Indias Sevilla.

Betrayed by these circumstances, it could not be expected, after the unfortunate merchant was precipitated into the snare of villainy, his credit would maintain itself at home without making returns, which could not be made, as the laws of *Trinidad* prevented the planter being honest, at least they would not oblige him, if he was inclined to avail himself of their protection; the consequence was, as might be anticipated, the merchant became insolvent; some returned home to give an account of their misfortunes, and others remained overwhelmed with *ennui*. Elated with the dazzling refulgence of his elevation, with the mark of the beast distinctly evident on his forehead, Picton was ready, upon all occasion, to authorize, if not to foment any measure, however scandalous and mischievous, which tended to the augmentation of his fortune; finding himself firmly fixed under the auspices of the Inquisition, he began to look around him, designing to make his reign as profitable as possible. The tools he selected to put his designs into execution, were like himself, corrupt by constitution, and had their origin in filth, whose lives might as well be measured by their crimes as by their days, making a jest of fame, and laughing at virtue;— he found them ready to second any iniquity with greediness. With such exhalations, drawn from the rankest fens and foulest ditches, he began his career in this island.

Among the first things that attracted his attention, was the *vendue* office, which yielded monthly five hundred dollars, if not more. Gambling-houses, of which there are many, afforded considerable gain; every billiard table paid,

and now pays monthly sixteen dollars. The custom-house, I was told, was a profitable concern, but what share he had of its enormous fees, I have not been able to learn, however, it is of no consequence,– the following statement will enable you to form some idea of the lucrative situation of the custom-house *rats*. You have plenty of such vermin at home, who are, like those that are here, preying on commerce. When the evil is accounted legitimate at the fountain-head, we should not complain of its nuisance at this remote distance: to be upon a par with those at home, the fees ought to be doubled. The captain of the British schooner, Eclipse, (Parker), of seventy tons burthen, in the service of the contractor, Mr. Cruden, of *Barbadoes,* entered 300 barrels of flour, and cleared forty head of cattle.

In addition to this, may be reckoned the fandango licences, which cost eight dollars a-piece. In short, every thing that was capable of being made lucrative, he turned to his advantage, so that the first year of his government yielded more than £15,000, most of which sum however, I am well informed, was obtained by oppression and peculation. The oppressor and peculator, I have always considered the pest of society. The plea of a series of national services (even where there is a colour for it), cannot palliate the charge of having made thousands miserable; but, I cannot find that this opressor and peculator has any such plea to urge, unless indeed we explode truth for a while, to give credence to his panders, when they boast of his false exploits, in frustrating invasions, insurrections, witchcraft, mighty magic, etc.

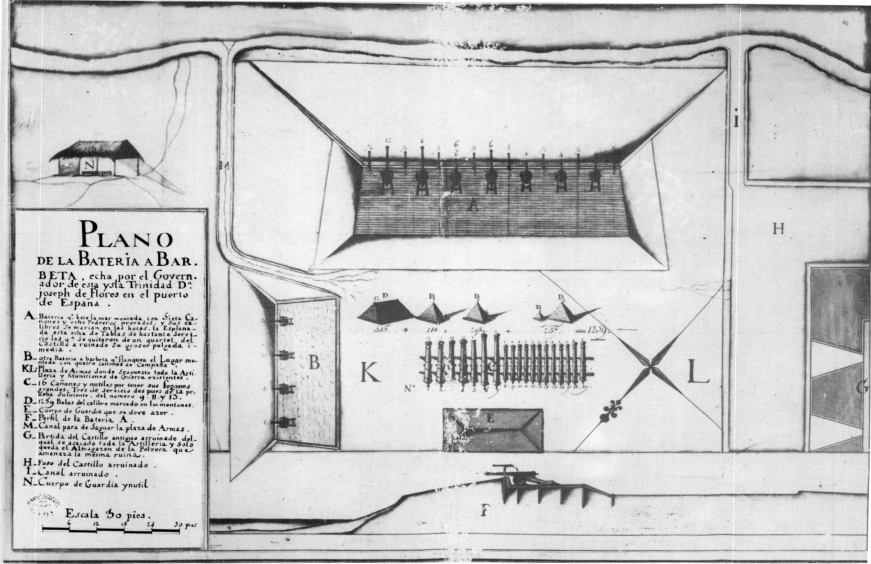

A plan of the fortifications at Port of Spain during the administration of Don José de Flores 1766-1773, by permission of the Archivo General de Indias – Sevilla

which they have been in the habit of trumpeting so long, that they now firmly believe the reality of what was orginally the child of imagination. Supposing their empty assertions were really well founded, will it for a moment diminish the crimes and the cruelties laid to his charge which I am about to develop?

Under a rod of iron Trinidad prospered under Picton, commerce and agriculture improving with rapidity. The Spanish inhabitants petitioned him that if and when peace was made Trinidad should not be exchanged for any consideration. He backed their petition and later Trinidad emerged a British possession from the Treaty of Amiens.

Settlers (British) began now to crowd into the island; they were all obliged, as soon as theylanded, to be introduced to him, according to the usual custom of the *West India islands,* when he never failed (if he disliked the appearance of any of the strangers) to usher them to his mirador; and after pointing out to them a gallows which he had caused to be erected in an oblique direction from his house he used thus to accost them: "Look at that gallows, Sir! if you do not behave yourself properly, you may depend on being hanged,–go about your business, and let me not hear any complaint about you."

What a salutation for a British subject from a British governor, in a British island! One would be apt to suppose, though born and bred among the goats on the mountains of *Wales,* that he might have had a little more sense, than to make use of such language to the meanest

This historic building was first built in 1788, later destroyed by fire in 1808, it was soon rebuilt. Now no longer in existence, it stood at the corner of Charlotte Street and Independence (Marine) Square. It served as the Governor's Residence for both the last Spanish Governor, Chacon, and the first English Governor, Picton. It was from the upstairs gallery that Governor Picton would point out to the newly-arrived, the gallows erected in the square below, remarking to them that that the wind would pass beneath their feet if they did not comply with his absolute authority. Photograph: O. Mavrogordato.

1800: In the year 1800 Picton put into being a "Code" to govern the slaves of the island – a set of rules which, with some modreation, remained law until 1824 when it was greatly improved.
The population totalled 22,850.
Historical notes from H.C. Pitts 100 Years Together.

of His Majesty's subjects, who are taught, by the constitution of *England,* to believe that they were not created to be the sport of any tyrant whatever, within the pale of that immortal fabric! A reception so harsh, so blasphemously absurd, did not fail to gain Governor Picton a formidable host of enemies. At this early period of his career, he was very lonely for want of a domestic partner to share his amorous embraces, to ease his mind of the arduous duties of his station; but no one could be conveniently found suitable to his taste, which, *e n passant,* is not very refined. Hence, it is said of him as was of a late Antigua governor (Park), who was put to death by the inhabitants for his cruelties, that *"he neither spared a man in his rage, nor a woman in his lust."* How far he merits this assimilation, it will be soon in your power to judge. These repeated acts of brutality did not fail to rouse the indignation of many whose minds were yet in an oscillatory state respecting his conduct. The British viewed him as a ferocious barbarian; the French and Spanish inhabitants, habituated to oppression and crimes, seldom gave his actions any serious consideration; – however, his panders were now alarmed. Fearful that reports of his conduct would reach the thrones, they advised him to procure some female to prevent a repetition of such crimes: in the meantime, he had several pimps who foraged for him,–black or livid-coloured were equally welcome to his depraved embraces. After much trouble and many vexatious efforts, a loving fair one was found congenial to his mind, of the name of Rosetta Smith, of whom I made honourable mention in my preceding letter. She was solicitied to leave her husband and her children, to become Lady Governess. Allured by ambition, she abandoned every thing dear to the imagination of a female, to share the pillow and power of the greatest man in the colony; and as he is called "the most potent governor in His Majesty's dominions." Soon after the honeymoon was over, he presented her with the fuel contract for the garrison, saying, *"Accept of this bagatelle, my darling; the profits of it will enable you to buy trinkets, &c."* The profits of this *bagatelle,* as he was pleased to call it enabled Rosetta to bribe almost all the kept ladies in the colony to reveal the secrets of their paramours, and thereby he became acquainted with the sentiments of the inhabitants generally. Those who unguardedly insinuated their disapprobation, or animadverted on his tyrannical conduct, became the immediate objects of his vindictive rage, were arrested and confined in the bastille,amongst negroes afflicted with loathsome distempers; their friends and acquaintances were denied the satisfaction of visiting them and even the common comforts of life frequently denied. I intreat you to pause for a moment, while you give a full scope to your imagination, to anticipate, if possible, the feelings which must necessarily occur under such a degrading predicament. Incarcerated in a nauseous prison, without a breath of fresh air, respiring the putrid exhalation copiously emitted from your fettered fellow-prisoners, the clangour of their chains, together with their hideous yells, must assimilate your situation to that of the infernal regions. Your mind would be either racked with horror, or corroded with despair and resentment against him who thus hell-doomed you; but, all this was extremely gratifying to Governor Picton, whose sole delight was to torment indiscriminately.

Rosetta, though not tinctured with humanity, was however, prompted by avarice to visit the recesses of horror, to tender her services, and for a few doubloons wold set them at liberty; so that it appears that this method of "raising the wind" was too lucrative not to be followed with peculiar attention. Her influence over his mind increased the more he discovered her talents of accumulating wealth, consequently nothing was resorted to that would tend to embarrass her financial operations.There is hardly a store or shop in this town but she regularly visited;–any article that took her fancy (particularly toys) she would carry away without paying for it; indeed it would be death to take notice of her. I have heard only of one person who dared to resist her encroachments. Whereupon she flew in a rage to government-house, and complained to Governor Picton of this gentleman's insolence in refusing her some

The Trinidad term "Picong" (meaning to give someone a hard time) has its origins in a form of torture once carried out, on Picton's orders, at the Royal Gaol on Frederick Street. Louisa Calderon was tortured some say to make her admit to the theft of money, others say that she was privy to the whereabouts of a buried treasure. At left holding two keys is Valot the gaoler. On his right is his able assistant Porto Rico. One of the gentlemen on the left is St. Hilaire Begorrat.

trinkets. A file of soldiers were instantly dispatched for the offender, and he was ignominiously dragged to government-house, when Colonel Picton thus accosted him: "You are a pretty fellow, a d------d insolent Jacobin rascal; I'll make an example of you, to shew the rascals I govern; that I will be obeyed." One of his judges made his appearance, and after a few minutes private conference, the gentleman was ordered to the bastille for sedition.

It is customary with him never to hear both sides of a question. If any malicious individual of his junta, or their dependants, had taken the least umbrage against another person, however modest and innocent his deportment, by giving a fee to Rosetta now regulated the government commanded the military,[*] held her *levee* twice a week, which was numerously attended by a crowd of sycophants, male and female panders, &c. Those who did not pay their *devoirs,* might apprehend trouble, if not destruction. An instance of this nature soon followed. Mrs. Griffiths, and two amiable daughters, never attended the *levee,* therefore, Rosetta marked them out for destruction. It is unnecessary to remark, that if they did attend the *levee* of this MEDEA, their conduct would be deemed no less than extremely reprehensible by those who hold virture in esteem; for, without that inestimable jewel, the fair sex would present nothing but a disgusting shadow of uniform depravity, the baneful effects of which we strongly exemplified in the case before us. Dr. Johnson says, that "virtue is merely local. In some situations the air diseases the body, and in others poisons and mind."[†] That as it may, I am not going to dispute the matter with the doctor, but to assert that it is a crime to be virtuous in this island, and for that reason, these ladies experienced implacable resentment. They inhabited a house belonging to themselves in Queen Street,–Rosetta sent a message to them, which imported that she wanted to purchase the house. They took no notice of the impudent wretch, nor her message, as they did not want to part with their property. Rosetta (having the power of torturing at her command), persisted in her former demana,–was resolved to have the house right or wrong,–sent a guard of soldiers with her diabolical orders to confine the old lady and her daughters, together with their attendants, to a small apartment in the house, to prevent every intercourse with either their friends or their neighbours, and the necessaries of life from being conveyed to these distressed females. One gentleman, of whose compassionate heart I have seen repeated instances, and who is an honour to the country which gave him birth *(England)*, was stimulated by the god-like feelings which gave him a distinguished pre-eminence over the rest of his countrymen in this place. Being in the neighbourhood, he contrived some means to relieve them, but his beneficent wishes were soon defeated, by his being detected in conveying a kettle of hot water to them at the back of the premises, to make a little tea for themselves. They were besieged so closely afterwards, both in front and rear of the house, that they were ultimately obliged to capitulate to Rosetta's forces. She has held the conquest ever since (say four years), which brings her in eight hundred dollars *per annum!* Now, whether this money goes into Picton's pocket, or is added to the profits of the fuel contract, to purchase Rosetta more trinkets, &c. is a question I am not able to elucidate; however, it is of no consequence, since the act itself will rouse your indignation, and make you exclaim with the poet—

"Calmly to practice injuries pre-designed,
Argues the baseness of a villain's mind."

I have been told that some gentlemen remonstrated with Picton on this shameful prostitution of authority and robbery, and at the same time urged that his partiality for Rosetta had been already too conspicuous in many instances. To some he alleged he did not interfere with Rosetta's business, but one gentleman in particular, he was pleased to answer in the following romantic strain. "What is life without love, without that tender union of hearts, which is accompanied with thrilling transports never to be described? And must this amiable creature, whose extreme sensibility is so delightfully depicted in every glance of her sentimental eyes,–in every feature of her lovely countenance,–replete at once with beauty, benevolence, wisdom, and truth, be denied any favour in my power to bestow? No, Sir, I am determined not to interfere, therefore your further animadversions shall be considered as an insult." It is well for mankind that Picton has not a wiser field to sport in; if he had, he would shine like *Tarquinius Superbus*, who did not attain the latter appellation, until the imperious spirit, for which he was so justly branded, and the disposition to enrich himself, became evident by his plundering excesses; his walk to tyranny was, however, slow, and by degrees, but in the end he ruined his country. An ordinary genius might have gone the lengths Picton has done by slow gradations, but his superior spirit scorns to arrive at the

1802: On 27th March, the final peace treaty was signed at Amiens.

In July Colonel Fullerton, of the East India service, was appointed over General Picton's head as "first commissioner" of Trinidad. Picton was second commissioner and Samuel Hood, a Captain in H.M. Navy, third commissioner. This commission was responsible for the government.

1803: Fullerton arrived by H.M.S. Ulysses on 4th January and Hood by the "Blenheim" on 22nd February. Bad relations immediately sprang up among the commissioners and on 20th July, Fullerton left the island as had Hood and Picton a little while before. A gold sword, subscribed to by the inhabitants, was sent to Picton after he had left.

On the departure of the last of the commissioners, Brigadier-General Sir Thomas Hislop took over as Governor.

Population reached 28,427.

Historical notes from H.C. Pitts 100 Years Together.

goal of tyranny by progressive steps; he vaulted the moment he assumed the command, into the seat of the stern oppressor and cruel tyrant. He and his friends, I am aware, will attribute to me a considerable portion of presumption for collecting materials, in order to exhibit to you, and (I trust in the end) to the world, a view of the crimes of so great a personage, as he himself supposes he is. I have only to observe, it is a privilege which every British subject has an undoubted right to exercise as well as myself, had leisure and inclination prompted them. In the progress of the business, I hope I shall have observed both candour and decency. I found my authority on the testimony of my respectable witnesses, who voluntarily step forward to assist in the performance of this my sacred duty to my country, and mankind at large. Whoever doubts the purity of my efforts, I shall not hesitate to consider an enemy to His Majesty, from whose feeling bosom oppression of any kind does not emanate. Ministers are, ere now, in possession of a catalogue of his crimes; and no doubt, they are making arrangements to have him taken home to be tried. The first criminal trial will be for executing a serjeant of the Royal Artillery without any previous trial, civil or military. The circumstance has been frequently related to me as follows:— Some men belonging to the Royal Corps of Artillery committed some trifling depredation in the house of an unprotected woman, who it seems, impeached them with having taken away a couple of handkerchiefs. The whole corps were exposed to her view, but she was not able to point out a single individual of the party she alleged had been at her house. She pretended to recognize one of her handkerchiefs about the neck of this serjeant,who was brought before Picton. He thus accosted him:— *"Did you see the sun rise this morning?"* "Yes," said the serjeant. *"Then you shall not see it set."* Though the woman did not assert that the poor serjeant was one of the number who had been in her house, yet he was hanged the same day in the presence of Picton. The unfortunate man persisted he was innocent till the last moment. This and the two succeeding instances, will clearly proved that he spared no man in his rage. A Spanish peasant, and an inhabitant of *St. Joseph d'Oruña,* was disorderly one day from being disguised in liquor;–the commandant of the quarter of district sent him to Picton, probably with a view to receive a gentle flagellation. Without any further accusation or trial, he was hanged next morning, notwithstanding one of his panders remonstrated against his proceedings. In the south part of the island, resided a French gentleman planter of respectability, well known to have supported an unblemished reputation and discreet sentiments during the late revolution. It so happened that he had his enemies,–one of them maliciously insinuated to Picton (and likely enough enforced the argument by feeing his *(bonaroba),* that this gentleman was in the habit of harbouring the crews of some French privateers. Accordingly, an armed launch was dispatched to bring the gentleman to head-quarters. The commander of the launch, it is said, before he went on shore dressed himself in the uniform of a republican officer, thinking thereby he might meet with a flattering reception;–to his astonishment, he met with an opposition contrary to his anticipation, in as much as being shot at several times, but on making himself known, he was received with the greatest cordiality. The commander then related the purport of his visit; and the French gentleman, who well knew his own innocence, accompanied him back without hesitation. When he appeared at head-quarters, Picton

ordered him to the Bastille, and next morning about daylight, he was marched down to the gallows, on which he was instantly hanged, also, without trial. It was but a very few days after that his innocence was proved beyond a single doubt—Alas! it was too late. These executions, together with many more (I learn in all thirty-six) were perpetrated before the trial of Governor Wall, whose fate did not meliorate his oppressive and malignant spirit. He has been contaminated so long by his late ministerial friends, and had also an idea that the island would be ceded to *Spain* at the conclusion of the war, which supported his predilection in the commission of crimes, and left no stone unturned to gain as many Spanish friends as possible: he even went so far as to

This historic building on the corner of Pembroke and Keate Street was the residence of Colonel Fullerton, one of the Commissioners to Trinidad and so could be regarded as a former Government House. Photograph O. Mavrogordato.

send a confidential friend to *Madrid,* to intercede for him a case of recession, that he might be continued Governor; other urgent reasons were added privately to ensure him success. We are informed he was accordingly successful. It was not long after a promise so flattering to his ambitious but cruel vanity, that he was constantly heard exclaiming againt the British consitution and English laws, adding, that "*Those who had framed them were fools.*" No one but a knave, a tyrant, or a madman, would be guilty of uttering such language; it is, however, Sir, the language of Thomas Picton governor of *Trinidad,* who has been too long supported in swaying the cruel sceptre of despotism over a considerable portion of His Majesty's dutiful and loyal subjects. If government knew of these repeated acts of cruelty, they are extremely culpable for continuing him in the government of this unfortunate colony. Had he been removed when the first complaint of his conduct reached them, his subsequent acts of cruelty would not now be the subject of my investigation; it is, therefore, your business to inquire into this affair, and let the censure be properly applied. As I have nothing to do with that part of the business, I shall proceed:— Picton issued orders to the commandants of the different quarters to send all runaway slaves to the Bastille of head-quarters. What became of these poor wretches afterwards, is best known to Rosetta and her co-adjutor Vallot. It is said, more than three thousand were taken up during the period of six years, allowing five hundred to have died. What became of the rest – two thousand five hundred?–Were they restored to their legal owners?–Why, sir, they were sent to the Spanish main, and there sold. This is founded on the evidence of a Spaniard, the master or mate of a Spanish

1807. The British abolished the Africans slave trade. When the first rumours were heard large numbers of Africans were rapidly brought to the island and sold, even for credit.

Historical notes from H.C. Pitts 100 Years Together.

1805. On 7th June, Nelson's fleet, pursuing a squadron of French and Spanish ships, appeared off the North Coast on which a lookout tower stood. The officer stationed at this tower mistook Nelson's fleet for the enemy, blew up the tower, threw away his solitary gun, and retired to spread the news. This action also led Nelson to believe that Trinidad was in enemy hands and he sailed his fleet into the Bocas expecting a battle. Meanwhile the Governor proclaimed Martial Law and everyone of the inhabitants capable of bearing arms marched along with the troops of the line and the militia to Fort George after Hislop had decided that Port of Spain was untenable. The fort was stocked with provisions and valuables when the mistake was discovered. Nelson, without stopping to send ashore any message whatsoever, put about his ships and departed in pursuit of the real enemy.

During December of this year a plot for the overthrow of the Europeans was discovered to be brewing and promptly terminated by vigorous punishments including some executions.

Historical notes from H.C. Pitts 100 Years Together.

launch, who was hanged or burnt as soon as it was found that he had divulged the secrets of this important and lucrative branch of traffic. Rosetta managed the business with great dexterity, and confided very much in the fidelity of this man, consequently was as confounded as if she had been thunderstruck, when she heard that the peculation was no longer an arcana. In this, as in other cases, there was no form of trial observed. Picton, like the famous Justice *Twistum* of *Coventry,* hears (as I have already insinuated) only one side of the question, and is ready to condemn even before he hears any part of the trial. Strange he should be so disposed, but he has contracted such a habit of so doing, it is not very likely he will depart from it while he remains in power. I hope for the benefit of my fellow-subjects the period is not far distant when he will be obliged to exclaim:-

"Fate o'er my head suspends disgrace and death."

Rosetta imagined that the destruction of the poor Spaniard would obliterate any further knowledge, and restrain inquiry:— the case was otherwise. Two or three independent gentlemen, who were not terrified, though the gallows, which had been constantly occupied lately by both whites and blacks, stared them in the face every day, were stimulated to inquire into this clandestine trade carried on to the inquiry of the planters; I mean those planters who did not attend her levee, and approve of his mode of governing. These gentlemen quickly found the truth of what the unhappy Spaniard advanced;–the consequences was that they became the victims of oppression in their turn.

I imagine I have now entered far enough into an elucidation of Picton's conduct. Do not think that I take a pleasure in dwelling so long on the dark side of this great man. I wish to God, for his own sake, he had two sides, that I might turn the corner of horrors. After diligent inquiry, I lament my inability to point out a single train in his character during the time he has been governor of this island, which a candid writer would deem praiseworthy,–even with his own panders I have been disappointed; however, the inclosed panegyric will, I trust, convince you how eager I have been in my researches in order to transmit to you any thing that I imagine will tend to shew you the delectable side of his conduct–if he has any.* I sincerely hope the foregoing elucidation of his governorship will not lead you to apprehend that my pen is either influenced or prejudiced; I am sure you are convinced, nothing would afford me more real satisfaction than to depict a favourable view of him, if it was in my power to embrace a glance so desirable to my feelings. As that is totally beyond my practicability, I shall proceed with an inquiry, which I anticipate will be deemed one day or other interesting to my fellow-subjects in *Great Britain,* and inform them what a portion of their fellow-Britons have endured at this remote distance from the source of justice.—Here let me drop the curtain for a while over scenes that bring reviving anguish to my heart.

FRANKLIN'S TRINIDAD
Select Documents
1803-1854
by
C.B. Franklin

A JUDGEMENT OF JOHN NIHELL, CHIEF JUDGE, 1808.

The accompanying extract of a Judgement delivered in the Courts of this Colony in 1808 by our first Chief Judge, John Nihell, is of special interest, in that it is probably one of the last delivered by the gentleman who held this distinguished office, as his term of office, gathered from old records, show that he was Chief Judge from 1797 to 1808. The firm tone of the Judgement shows him a strong man, such as was needed in those early and trying times of the newly conquered colony. He had lived in this Colony twenty-two years from 1786 to 1808 and was, therefore, doubtless a resident 11 years before the Capitulation. The Attorney-General in question, who was complimented by the Chief Judge, was Archibald Gloster. (From "The Barbados Mercury and Bridge-Town Gazette", 6th August, 1808.)

In the Court of Vice-Admiralty of Trinidad. Briarly (qui tam) vs. Ship Adams and Cargo.

In my sentence in the cause of the schooner Gipsy, I endeavoured to explain my ideas of the meaning which the statutes appear to give the word importation. I then declared, that I considered importation contrary to law to be a coming into port for the purposes of illicit trade, and with an intent, which must be clearly proved, of breaking the law. In fact, I meant, and now express, that independent of bare bringing in of goods, there must be a manifestation by the papers on board, or the overt acts of the Captain, of design or direct intention to land goods contrary to the known laws of the mother country, or of the colony. Nothing of this kind has been shown in the case of the Adams, by proof or otherwise. She brought here a mixed cargo of articles occasionally permitted to be landed, of others constantly admitted. When the wants of the colony were not urgent, the articles not used were admitted for exportation. I do not conceive that the voyage to this place and the desire to trade under such circumstances, criminal or smuggling. Here was a fair trader conforming to the admitted usage and practice, not only of this colony but of all the neighbouring British Islands. It has been indeed insinuated and pressed by the Counsel for the prosecution, that Captain Tubbs meant to run his tobacco, his beef, and his port clandestinely; but no proof of such fraudulent intentions has appeared.

On the contrary, he reported his whole cargo at the custom-house; what was usual was not disputed entry, and the articles not usual were entered for exportation, as it appears without any guile or bad intentions. Finding afterwards that tobacco was in demand in the Colony, a petition was framed and signed by many British merchants, requesting the Governor to permit the landing of it, and sale for the benefit of the colonists. With this

his Excellency complied, after consulting his Council. He was not satisfied with his own opinion, but referred to those gentlemen, with whom he is instructed to advise, when any matter is in agitation involving interests of the Island. In addition to which, it is also to be remarked, that the Collector of His Majesty's Customs was duly referred to, and the entry inwards, and intended landing of the tobacco, sanctioned fully by his knowledge and permission.

The whole charge against the ship then is, having put out of the Adams into a boat alongside, a few hogsheads of tobacco, authorised by the Governor and the Custom-house to be admitted, and that not clandestinely, but openly in the face of day-My God! is this an offence for which I am called upon to condemn a valuable ship and cargo, and reduce an honest unoffending neutral to beggary and ruin Heaven forbid! that I should charge my conscience with so evident, so shocking a piece of injustice, or lend my assistance to what I conceive so decided an act of oppression.

It was contended by the Counsel for the prosecution, that the Governor and Custom-house, generally speaking, have no right by law to give such a licence to the Master, that the Intercourse Bill between America and the West India Islands is prohibitory, and the Order of Council of the 17th September, 1806, decisive, and tobacco inadmissable; but he was pleased to say in the same breath, that if the occasion was great and urgent, the Governor might authorise the entry and landing of any article in spite of the Acts of Parliament-the Colony is much obliged to him for this concession; if it were not so, every one knows that we should be reduced at times to the miseries of absolute famine in this new settled Colony. But if he admits the Governor's discretion to travel out of the prohibitory law in cases of necessity, I should be glad to know who is to limit or control his power, or decide when he is authorised or not to deviate from Acts of Parliament? He certainly will not pretend to say that the power is lodged elsewhere than in the breast of the Representative of the Sovereign, and who acts upon his own responsibility. If, therefore, the Governor has judged a case to be that of necessity, as I presume he did in this, can I be persuaded that it is in the breast or power of any petty Officer of the Navy to step forth and tell him-"No, Sir. Although on shore, I am under your Government and subject to your jurisdiction, yet, as I am Commander of a Prison Ship in your port, I am the best judge of the wants of your Government;–you shall not determine this to be a case of necessity, but I WILL-you shall not relieve the distresses or wants of the poor and miserable inhabitants, entrusted to your care by your Sovereign, by your Commission, but it is I; and particularly so when I have so good an opportunity of relieving MY OWN WANTS by the seizure of so rich a ship and so rich a cargo!" Can anything be more monstrous than this view of the question? Or is it possible for a moment to imagine such contradictory authorities existing in the same Government? Are British Governors, appointed by the King, and in his confidence, to be liable to the capricious, or perhaps corrupt control of the most insignificant Officers of the British Navy? The Counsel for the prosecution has pressed forward the entry for the beef and pork into the harbour, but it does not appear by the evidence that such articles were by the Governor and Custom-house admitted to an entry, and to be landed and sold: nor does it appear by the evidence that they were ever attempted to be landed and sold by the claimants-it was only the article of tobacco, and that

upon the representation of respectable merchants.

To beef and pork, both legal and political objections might apply. In the Order of Council they are expressly prohibited and excepted. These commodities are ordinary exports from the mother country and its colonies in America, but unmanufactured tobacco cannot, I conceive, prejudice the British trade in the most trifling degree. It grows in no part of the British territories so as to be made an object of export for the purposes of commerce. It would not therefore interfere with or molest those who were not concerned in that article. The imports in British vessels, from neutral countries into this colony in the course of the year, are comparatively trifling. It would injure therefore, neither the general interests of Great Britain, or those of individuals; and that I presume, might have operated on the minds of the Governor and Council to admit the article, independent of their knowledge how important it was to the health and comfort of the poor slaves. Much has been urged to prove that tobacco is not food or clothing for the negroes or the indigent white and coloured population of Trinidad I do not say that it is either; but this I will say, that twenty-two years experience in the colony has taught me that it is an essential article of life, contributory in the highest degree to the health of the unfortunate white and coloured settlers, and particularly so to the slaves; and as necessary in the rainy season (July and August), when the Adams was here with these Articles as food and raiment.

Advocates do not speak the sentiments of their hearts, but I am bound from my oath and station candidly to speak mine and I do therefore say, that the seizure of this ship and cargo was not, in my opinion, warranted by law, on the contrary that it was wanton and vexatious. It appears to me further, to be violently flying in the face of His Majesty's governor and Collector of the Customs, tending to disturb the peace of the colony, and to create if possible, distress among the poorer inhabitants and negroes: I therefore ACQUIT the SHIP and CARGO. And I cannot help adding, that I most decidedly disapprove of the warmth and violence with which the suit was argued on Friday last, on part of the prosecution; and I beg it may not be repeated in this court. The moderation and calmness of the Attorney-General for the Claimants did him honour and calls for my approbation.

JOHN NIHELL

From "The Barbados Mercury and Bridge-Town Gazette," Saturday August 6, 1808.

THE THREATENED REVOLT OF THE SLAVES IN 1805.

From a further perusal of the newspaper files in the Barbados Public Library we are again enabled to record detailed accounts of important happenings in the Island of Trinidad, as reproduced in the Barbados newspapers in those early days.

The incident recorded in the Document happened so long ago, and conditions of life have since changed so materially, that it is almost impossible to conceive that such a diabolical plot, as was intended to have been put into execution on Christmas Day 1805, could ever have been contemplated.

Joseph, in his History of Trinidad, calls attention to this plot, and states that the revolt was to have commenced on Shand's Estate, and appears to have originated among some French and African negroes.

In Fraser's History mention is also made of this terrible incident, but very meagre details are given, for the reason, doubtless, that full particulars were not available at the late date at which he wrote. He, however, states that at that time there were in the island 20,000 slaves, whilst the white and coloured inhabitants together did not amount to even one half of that number. He points out that some of the members of the Board "had actually witnessed the horrors of a servile insurrection," and to all, the awful details of the revolt of the slaves in St. Domingo were familiar. It was also felt that if they would save, not only the properties of themselves and their fellow colonists from fire and pillage, but the lives of all near and dear to them, they must act promptly and with decision. This incurred, but appends in a footnote that the Governor and Council of Trinidad were criticised for having acted in that manner. Fraser, in error places this incident in 1808.

The recovery of this Document from the ancient archives in the Sister Colony with its fuller details, throws a light on the methods employed by these would-be rebels in forming themselves into regimental units, while at the same time it reveals the names of those early settlers who were slave owners.

TRINIDAD

By His Excellency Thomas Hislop, &c.,

PROCLAMATION

Whereas there are strong reasons to apprehend that this Colony is threatened with internal dangers from the nefarious machinations of ill-disposed negroes and slaves in this community: And His Majesty's Council of the said Island having recommended me to adopt the measure of Martial Law, I have therefore thought fit, by and with the advice of His Majesty's said Council, to issue this my Proclamation, and do hereby declare that from and after the publication hereof, Martial Law shall be and is hereby in full force, until further orders of which all his Majesty's liege subjects are required to take due notice, and govern themselves accordingly; and all His Majesty's good and loyal subjects, of all descriptions and of all colours, are hereby called upon to make every possible exertion to defeat the diabolical plans supposed to be in agitation; and as the purpose of this my proclamation is for the more speedily and effectually suppressing such dangers only, I do hereby, by and with the advice of His Majesty's said Council, authorize all civil courts of Justice to remain and continue in force, notwithstanding Martial Law.

All Commandants of Quarters and Alcades de Berrio, are hereby ordered to put their INSTRUCTIONS into full force, and to give every possible effect to them.

And whereas, under the present circumstances of the Colony which involves its very existence, it is proper and expedient that all persons must suffer temporary and individual inconvenience for the general welfare of the community, and that the most exemplary and summary punishments should be inflicted on all offenders, notice is hereby given that the several patrols will be ordered to take up all negro and other slaves, who shall be found in any of the streets of Port-of-Spain, after eight o'clock at night and to lodge them in security during the night and

that such negro or other slave or slaves who may be found to have offended against any of the ordinances now in existence will be immediately punished with DEATH, or otherwise, according to the regulations of the said ordinances: And in order to give the most public notice of the hour of eight o'clock in the evening not only the gun at the Sea-battery will be fired as usual, but the bells at the Spanish Catholic Church will be rung for the space of five minutes; and all such negro or other slave or slaves attempting to escape from the patrols, will be immediately shot; all persons concerned are therefore required to make the same known to their several slaves.

Given under my hand and seal at arms, in council, at Governor-House, this 14th day of December, 1805, and in the 46th year of His Majesty's reign.

THOMAS HISLOP.

By His Excellency's command,

W. HOLMES, Sec.

GOD SAVE THE KING

Extracted from "The Barbados Mercury and Bridge-Town Gazette," February 1st, 1806.

THE COUNCIL TAKES IMMEDIATE STEPS TO DEAL WITH THE ATTEMPTED RISING OF THE SLAVES

The following extract from the Minutes of Council, which speaks for itself, shows the reasons for the urgent and imperative operation of the law in order to save the situation and thus render nugatory the machinations of the attempted slave-rising of 1805:-
Extracts from the Minutes of His Majesty's Council published by order of His Excellency and the Board.

Council-Chamber, 20th Dec., 1805.

"Pain c'est Viande Beque, Vin c'est sang Beque; nous va mange Pain Beque nous va boir Sang Beque" et les autres compagne repondivent avec le refrain St. Domingue.

Puts it beyond a doubt that (the insurrection having once broken out) measures had not been neglected to prepare the minds of the slaves in general for such an event.

One of the prisoners now in custody has become King's evidence, by whose testimony it appears that he was invited to join with his regiment those of the Carenage on Christmas-day for the purpose of rising against the whites; that having effected their purpose there, they were to proceed to town to set it on fire, after which a general massacre of the whites and free coloured people, and those blacks who refused to join the insurgents was to take place.

By command of the Board

W. HOLMES, Dep. Clerk of Council

Ibid., February 1st, 1806.

LIST OF PERSONS FOUND GUILTY OF CONSPIRACY IN CONTEMPLATED OUTBREAK OF SLAVES.

This Document gives full details of the various persons who were charged with taking part in the general conspiracy, together with the punishment meted out to each. Our discovery of the details in the Barbados paper gives such full particulars as to make it a Document of value to be preserved, particularly as the sentences are but briefly recorded by Joseph and Fraser, though the latter deals more fully with this matter than the former.

The sentences recorded appear very severe, but one must recall that the conditions of life then were different from what they are today, and strong measures were necessary in order to strike terror into the hearts of the rebellious slaves. It is well known that at that period even in England men were hanged for stealing and many minor offences for which nowadays a small fine is imposed.

List of negroes sentenced by the Supreme Tribunal (the Lieutenant-Governor and Council) to punishment, for being concerned in the late intended insurrection.

Roo-Colonel in the Cocorite Regiment (belonging to C. Melville, Esq.) to have both his ears cut off, to receive as severe a flogging as the Surgeon attending may think he can bear, without injuring his life; and to be banished from the Colony, not to return to it under pain of death.

Jean Pierre-Colonel in the Macaque Regiment, belonging to George Cruden, Esq.

Gabriel-General in the Sans-peur Regiment of the town, belonging to L. Littais, Esq.

Gabriel-Colonel in the Macaque Regiment, belonging to Duvivier, Esq.

Edward-King of the Sans-peur Regiment Carenage, belonging to P. Noel, Esq. to have both their ears cut off, to receive one hundred lashes and to be banished from the colony, not to return to it under pain of death.

Cuffy-Colonel of the Macaque Regiment belonging to E.M. Noel Esq.

Gaspard-Major in the Danish Regiment, belonging to P. Noel, Esq.

Jean Baptiste-Colonel in Sans-peur Regiment in the town, belonging to J.M. Belliard, Esq.

Bastian-Colonel in the Sans-peur Regiment, Carenage (belonging to Duvivier, Esq.) to receive one hundred lashes and to be returned to their owners, first having an iron ring of ten pounds weight affixed to one of their legs, to remain thereon for the space of two years.

Avril-Colonel in the Danish Regiment, belonging to E.M. Noel, Esq.

Michel-Treasurer in the Danish Regiment, belonging to E.M. Noel, Esq.

Pancras-Major in the Macaque Regiment, belonging to Madame Joyeux to receive fifty lashes and to be returned to their owners, first having an iron ring of ten pounds weight affixed to one of their legs, to remain thereon for the space of two years.

Florentin-General in the Sans-peur Regiment of the town, belonging to J.M. Belliard, Esq.

Scipio-Secretary in the Sans-peur Regiment, Carenage, belonging to George Rochard, Esq. to have both their ears cut off, to receive one hundred lashes, and to be banished from the Colony, not to return ot it under pain of death.

Joseph-Prince in the St. George's Regiment, Carenage, belonging to Lachancelerie, Esq.

Louis-Admiral in same regiment, belonging to E.M. Noel, Esq.

Simon-King of the same regiment, belonging to George Rochard, Esq.

Paul-King of the Danish Regiment, belonging to P. Noel, Esq.

Monday-Prime Minister in the same regiment, belonging to John Gloster, Esq.

Pompey-General in the same regiment, belonging to John Gloster, Esq. to have the tip of their ears cut off and to be banished from the colony not to return to it under pain of death.

Adelaide Dixon-Alias Buzotter, free woman-Queen of the Macaque Regiment, to work in chains for life, with an iron ring of ten pounds weight affixed to one of her legs.

Dominique Rivierre, Free man-General in the Sans-peur Regiment of the town (or more emphatically by some called the Factotum of the regiment), to have both his ears cut off, to be returned into slavery, and sold for the benefit of the Colony, and to be banished therefrom, not to return to it under pain of death.

Dick-Belonging to Mr. M'Comie, of no rank or belonging to any particular regiment, but labouring under strong suspicions, from certain seditious and rebellious expressions, to receive one hundred lashes, and to be returned to his owner, first having an iron ring of ten pounds weight affixed to one of his legs, to remain thereon for the space of two years.

Harold, a free man-King of the St. George's Regiment of the town, to be banished from the Colony, not to return to it under pain of death.

The Lieutenant-Governor and Council have also thought proper to issue orders for the following punishments to be inflicted by the respective owners upon the following slaves:-

Marcelle-Dauphin in Sans-peur Regiment, town, belonging to Mr. Robin.

Pedro and Charles-Aid-de-Camps in Sans-peur Regiment, town, belonging to T. Bray, Esq.

Tom-of Sans-peur Regiment, Carenage belonging to Mr. Castor.

Valere-Valet of King Edward belonging to-Duvivier Esq.

Petit Dominique-Aid-de-Camp in Sans-peur Regiment, town, belonging to Madame St. Laurent.

Modeste, Atanaze Eustace, in the St. George's Regiment Carenage, belonging to-Duvivier, Esq.

Sayman-in Sans-peur Regiment, Carenage, belonging to P. Noel, Esq.

Louis-in St. George's Regiment, town, belonging to Madamoiselle Luce.

Nero-Colonel in St. George's Regiment, Carenage (belonging to Madam Joyeux) to receive thirty-nine lashes, and to have an iron ring of ten pounds weight affixed to one of their legs, to remain thereon for the space of two years.

Marie-Queen in the same regiment, belonging to Madame Bona Vita.

Marie-Queen in the same regiment, belonging to Madame Allou.

Marie Ursule-in same regiment, belonging to J.M. Belliard, Esq.

Jean Rose-in same regiment, belonging to John Black, Esq. to receive twenty-five lashes.

Extracted from "The Barbados Mercury and Bridge-Town Gazette," Feb. 1, 1806

DEATH OF SIR THOMAS PICTON

Simon Lee

Picton left Trinidad on 14 June 1803 after hearing that his resignation as Junior Commissioner on the Civil Commission responsible for governing the island, had been accepted. He returned to London to face accusations laid by the Senior Commissioner Colonel Fullarton of his 'cruelties and excesses while Governor . . and principally that he had permitted the application of torture to a girl, Louise Calderon, in order to extract a confession about a robbery.'

Public opinion already sensitized to the horrors of slavery by a growing Abolitionist lobby, was inflamed against Picton by Fullarton's vitriolic attacks. As V.S. Naipaul points out in 'The Loss of El Dorado' Picton was being tried for being the Governor of a slave colony. Although a second trial in 1810 overturned the guilty judgement of the first trial, (a verdict based on the unchallenged evidence of the Spanish speaking witness Vargas who erroneously testified that Spanish law did not allow torture) no judgement was given and the spectre of 'The Trinidad Affair' was to remain with Picton for the rest of his life. In a society whose laws upheld the principle of 'guilty until proven innocent', Picton was held morally responsible for torture prior to trial — the fact that according to the Spanish laws then in effect that torture was permitted during preliminary investigations was conveniently overlooked. The image of Picton as a cruel tyrant does not really accord with what we learn of him in later years, it is more likely he was 'a rough hard man who used forceful methods to impose a very considerable degree of order on a lawless, turbulent and largely disaffected community.

Picton was essentially a military man, eager for active service and in the Peninsular Campaign against Napoleon which climaxed in the Congress of Vienna he was to impress the English Commander Wellington. By the time he returned to England in March 1813 to take his seat as member of Parliament for the Tory pocket borough of Pembroke 'he had achieved a considerable amount of fame and glory and had caught the fancy of both the army and the public. Anecdotes about him were legion, many knew all about the fighting general whose stolid courage, blue frock coat, civilian hat, cob (horse) and astounding flow of strong language became legend.' Significantly Picton was appointed a knight of the Grand Order of the Bath in 1814 in recognition of his services.

When in March 1815 Napoleon showed his contempt for the Armistice and the Congress of Vienna and marched on Paris where he was able to raise a powerful army within a few weeks, Wellington realizing the gravity of the situation began mobilizing the allies and on 26 May summoned Picton to join him. There is a macabre story which underlines Picton's strong presentiment that he would not survive the coming campaign. After receiving Wellington's summons at his Welsh country seat where he lived the life of a country squire, he drove out with friends past a cemetery; seeing a freshly dug grave he leapt into it and lying down remarked it was just his size! Picton arrived in Brussels on 15 June accompanied by Gronow, a young Guards officer. In what Gronow notes was a brief and oddly cold meeting, Wellington gave Picton command of 'the troops in advance'. Wellington's coldness can possibly be understood in the

light of an assessment he later made of Picton both socially and professionally: 'Picton was a rough foul-mouthed devil as ever lived, but he always behaved extremely well; no man could do better in the different services I assigned to him.'

Napoleon's plan for the coming campaign hinged on splitting the allied forces who were drawn up in an irregular V shape which joined just above Charleroi; he planned to force his way through this junction or to head for Brussels, whose capture he reasoned would both strengthen his prestige and weaken allied morale. On 15 June the French crossed the frontier passing North through Charleroi. Blücher, the Prussian commander, on the eastern allied flank decided to concentrate his forces around Sombreffe. Wellington meanwhile on the allied western flank ordered his forces to concentrate on the Brussels – Charleroi road, just south of the forest of Soignies. Thus Napoleon succeeded in separating the allies.

By the early morning of 16 June while still at the Duchess of Richmond's Ball in Brussels, Wellington received news that the French had reached Quartre Bras. Picton's 'troops in advance' – the 5th Division were ordered South to support the Dutch Nassau troops holding off the French at Quartre Bras. That same morning Napoleon decided to attack the Prussians with his right wing while Marshal Ney advanced up the Brussels road with the left wing. The Prussians were forced to retreat to Wavre and confident that the Prussian threat was now over Napoleon headed confidently for Brussels.

Ney arriving at Quartre Bras delayed his attack long enough for Picton's leading battalions to arrive and when Ney finally launched his attack at 2 p.m. with 6,000 infantry and all the available cavalry and guns after initially pushing back the Dutch he ran straight into Picton's division coming down the road from Brussels and Wellington's forces arriving simultaneously from Ligny. Picton's leading battalions were dispatched to seize Pireaumont in order to keep a line of communication open to Blücher and the Prussians; unable to do so the riflemen took up position in Cherry Wood. The remainder of Picton's battalions were drawn up facing south along the Namur road. Ney now launched a full scale attack and although he made advances on the left his cavalry were bloodily repulsed by Picton's division. Renewed French cavalry attacks were repulsed by the famous British square formations of infantry under Picton. Despairing of an allied cavalry counter-attack Picton ordered his troops to march south directly into the midst of the astonished French cavalry, in order to drive them off. At one stage Picton's square was attacked on 3 sides simultaneously 'there was a breathless pause as the French horsemen approached until Picton, sitting composedly on his cob roared in his hoarse voice "28th – remember Egypt!" Then the muskets came up, the volleys rolled out, and the galloping French squadrons dissolved into a bloody shambles of dead men and wounded horses'. The battle thus far had been exhausting but Wellington and Picton 'by hard riding, gallant leadership and judicious use of successive reinforcements . . . succeeded in holding their ground.'

At some point during 16 June Picton had been struck by grapeshot – the blow broke several ribs, caused heavy bruising and internal injuries; realizing a second great battle was imminent he concealed the injury and spent the night in considerable pain.

Next morning on 17 June Wellington decided to

retire to Mount St. Jean and stand and fight; Picton accompanied his division back still in great pain. After a detailed reconnaissance of the new positions he retired to the cottage he had been billeted in and re-dressed his wounds.

Wellington had chosen a position well suited to the type of defensive battle he was a master at. The allies formed up facing south along the reverse slope of a long ridge running East-West. On 18th June Picton supervised as his division formed up with their right on the Brussels road. The commander of the 52nd regiment passing Picton heard him remark he had just galloped along the whole allied line – a remarkable feat in his wounded condition.

Napoleon still labouring under the misapprehension of the Prussian's flight decided on a simple plan of attack: soften the enemy with artillery, attack with the cavalry to get them to reveal their positions and then when sure of their exact location, destroy them with the élite Guards. Refusing to heed the advice of his generals about the fighting qualities of the British at 11.30 a.m. 18 June he ordered a diversionary attack on Hougoumont to weaken Wellington's centre. At 2 p.m. under cover and heavy artillery fire he launched his main attack.

Under the French advance Bijlandt's Dutch Brigade wavered and Picton immediately deployed Kempt's Brigade to fill the gap. The French were now only 30-40 yards away and after firing their first volley the British charged with fixed bayonets. Picton rode alongside them urging them on until a bullet fired by the retreating enemy hit him in the brain and he slumped dead in his saddle. Sadly Picton did not live to see the fast approaching and decisive victory: the French cavalry attack was once again repulsed by the British square formations until the arrival of the Prussians. Napoleon launched his middle and young guards unsuccessfully at the British right centre and as the Prussians closed in the British line advanced with a great roar driving the French from the field.

The surgeon who later examined Picton's body, opined that the wounds he had received at Quartre Bras might well have eventually proved fatal and it is a 'measure of his fortitude that he had been able not only to remain on his feet but actually to command his division in a great battle.'

OLD TRINIDADIAN FAMILIES continued
THE DE VERTEUIL FAMILY

This family cannot be counted amongst those of the capitulants, it is however co-eval with the existence of the Island as a British possession, as the Chevalier de Verteuil was a cadet in Lowenstein's Regiment which formed part of the expedition commanded by Sir Ralph Abercromby to whom the Island capitulated.

The early history of the Chevalier is most interesting and might form the groundwork for such a novel as Dr. Conan Doyle or the author of 'Under the Red Robe' now and again produced for the instruction and amusement of the world. At a very early age he entered the Royal Navy of France serving as a midshipman *(éléve de Vaisseau)*. After a cruise of three years' duration he returned to France and was horror struck to find that the King, Louis XVI., had been guillotined. The de Verteuils like all the La

Vendée Nobles were imbued with the most intense devotion to their Church and to their King, and the young naval officer at once decided to quit France and devote his life and his sword to the service of his Sovereign. he accordingly managed, not without difficulty, to reach Coblentz where the brothers of the late King held a kind of Court and from where they directed intrigues which however justifiable had undoubtedly hastened, if they had not provoked, the tragedy of the 21st of January, 1793, and certainly led to the execution of Marie Antoinette and the ill-treatment of the Dauphin in the gloomy prison of the Temple. He there joined the 'Armée des Princes' as it was called, and served with it until it was disbanded. Republican France had declared war against Great Britain and the Stadtholder of Holland and the young de Verteuil after the dissolution of the Armée des Princes went to the Netherlands and took service on board a Dutch vessel of war, 'Les Etats Generaux' which was under orders to co-operate with the British Fleet then blockading Toulon. The blockade having been abandoned he returned with his ship to Holland and with a large number of other French Royalists took service in the special regiments composed of French emigrés raised and paid by the British Government who had taken refuge in England. He formed part of the unfortunate and disastrous Quiberon Expedition in which the Count d'Artois, afterwards Charles X., showed himself so unworthy of the devotion of his adherents and of the name he bore. The Royalists finding themselves deserted by their leader were disheartened and were easily defeated by Hoche who commanded the Republican Army. Every prisoner taken was executed as a traitor to the country. De Verteuil was rescued by a boat from an English frigate belonging to the fleet which under the command of Admiral Warren had conveyed the cowardly Prince and his brave followers to France. On board of this vessel he found his uncle the Count de Vaugirard. He joined the Royalist Army which in 1794-5 was under the orders of the celebrated Georges Cadoudal, but when the dissensions arose between the Vendean generals and the emigrant officers, which for a time brought the movement to a standstill, he left France for England, in which country he arrived in a state of absolute destitution. However the English were at the time doing all in their power both as a nation and as individuals to aid the unfortunate refugees and in a very short time he was appointed to the Regiment known as Lowestein's German Jægers. As already stated he took part in the capture of the Island and returned with Sir Ralph Abercromby to Martinique. His name however seems to have been mentioned during his stay in Trinidad, for shortly after reaching Martinique he received a letter from a Baron de Gourville, then the proprietor of Le Vivier Estate, St. Joseph. In this letter the Baron inquired whether the young soldier was any relation to his, as his sister had married a Chevalier de Verteuil, who had served in Canada under the famous Marquis de Montcalm. This last named turned out to be the father of the young officer serving under Abercromby and, on learning this, M. de Gourville at once wrote to his newly discovered nephew, suggesting that he should leave the somewhat uncertain career in which he had embarked and settle down in Trinidad as a planter. The nephew took that advice and lived here until he died at the advanced age of 92 years and some months. He was named by Sir Ralph Woodford, who held in him very great esteem, Commandant of Arima and Corregidor (Controller) of the Indians of that Mission.

FRANKLIN'S TRINIDAD
Select Documents
1803-1854
by
C.B. Franklin

GOVERNMENT HOUSE, BELMONT HILL

The original manuscript of Franklin's Papers was made available to us by Olga Mavrogordato.

The old Government House at Belmont Hill, pictured overleaf, can be seen on the elevation at centre, the two small buildings nearby are outhouses. The Government House is distinctly marked by a road winding up to the summit. The St. Ann's hills are clearly seen in the background. The large building to the right of the picture, also on an elevation, might possibly be the Great House of the 'Belmont' Estate.

The Belmont Government House, which has long since fallen into decay, and which can only be located to-day by the mason-work which forms its foundations, was a house of some pretensions in days gone by. We are indebted to Sir Norman Lamont, Bart, for the preservation of this picture. The drawing, the original of which has been in the possession of his family, is entitled 'Belmont', country residence of His Excellency Major General Sir Thomas Hislop, Governor of Trinidad 1803-1810.

It will be interesting to record some of the facts regarding the construction of this old building as well as some information concerning it given to the Editor in 1920 by the late Mr. Thomas James St. Hill (six months before his death at the age of 90) who as a boy played around it and had frequent opportunities of roaming about its rooms. In describing it he said the house had no pretensions to architectural beauty, but the interior was nicely furnished. The ceiling and sides were of plaster of Paris; the walls were of tapia made from black pick-mock roseau, grown in the forest, split into three, with the pith scooped out and tapia laid between. The tapia was covered with white lime plaster, and plaster of Paris was laid over all. There was a chandelier in each of the two large rooms, the drawing room and the ball room. Stucco work was around the Chandeliers, while a gilt frieze ran around the rooms at the top. The doors were of cedar and nicely worked in design; the locks were brass ones about 8 or 9 inches wide, the staircase was six feet wide, the balustrade of which was of mahogany with turned rails. A marble stair ran from the ground floor to the landing, comprising twelve steps of black and white. There was a front gallery twelve feet wide, and, apart from the two large rooms described above the interior was not otherwise large, so this gallery was often used as a dining verandah for balls and other purposes. the principal doors were of glass; there were no jalousie windows, but glass sashes; the reception room was marble tiled and the staircase to the West, leading from the dining room to the garden was of red tiles. The upper part that ran to the north was two-storied, otherwise it was a one-storey building.

The Government House on Belmont Hill was situated on its crest. Today Hilton Hotel is on this very site which overlooks the city and harbour of Port of Spain. This painting was done by Peter Shim after an unknown painter.

Mr. St. Hill further stated that this building, which had at one time been used as a Government House, was occupied for a good many years by the Hon. Ashton Warner, Chief Judge of the Colony, until his decease in 1830. Mr. Warner was the last occupier of this building, and from that time it fell into decay and ruin. On being asked why it was never tenanted subsequently he remarked that it was supposed to be situated in an unhealthy locality, being greatly exposed to the north winds and that someone had died there of a malignant type of fever.

When giving the information recorded above he also drew the ground plan of the building from memory. These measurements were duly checked by a local architect and found to be correct in every detail. This plan, however, has unfortunately been misplaced by the architect. it would have been interesting to reproduce it along with this photograph and the description of the interior. It would also be of interest to find out from what point this view was originally sketched. Mr. St. Hill further stated that when the Prince's Building was being built in 1861 this old property was demolished in order to obtain bricks to be used in the construction of the new building.

From 'Parliamentary Papers relating to the Island of Trinidad, 18th February 1823' we gather that the Belmont lands were leased to the Government from January 1803 and that these were the lands 'on which the Government House and buildings and the negro houses are erected.' And further 'at the time of the original contract for lease of land by colonial government there was only a small house 36 ft x 18 ft. built of American timber, shingled and floored and a small hut covered with straw upon the said lands: the former building was new shingled and repaired by the Government previous to its occupation of the property'.

As 'Paradise Estate' was bought by the Government in 1825 and the Great House thereon used as Government House, we think it could safely be averred that the Governors who occupied this house were Governors Hislop, Munro and Woodford from 1803-1825.

We are glad to be able to place on record these important facts regarding this historic building about which, until now, little has been publicly known. Indeed, there is one common theory about this place that this document explodes and that is that, the building on the Belmont Hill was never a Government House. There is abundant evidence to disprove this. Trinidad is thus greatly indebted to Sir Normal Lamont and the late Mr. T.J. St. Hill.

We are further indebted to Mr. T.I. Potter for the information regarding this property and the section taken at law by claimants to the land, as subjoined:—

The old 'Government Cottage' on Belmont Hill.

The history of the old ruins to be seen on the crest of the hill which overlooks the city and the harbour of Port of Spain from what is now called Belmont Pasture is interesting.

The 'Belmont Estate,' which apparently did not comprise much more than the present pasture and the ridge to the North East of it, although the whole district to the South has taken the name, was a very old occupancy held by a Spaniard whose name is not recorded, because very probably, he was a squatter. In 1780 this man sold his holding to one Riviere, an immigrant to this island from St. Vincent. Riviere, in his turn, sold the occupancy to Don Francis Pasqual de Soler, who conveyed it to Edward Barry (a member of the firm of Barry & Black) on the 16th December, 1784 for the sum of "$900 of eight bits," (whatever that may be).

Edward Barry died some time after the purchase and the representative of his estate leased the lands and

The ruins of Government House on Belmont Hill.

buildings, the cultivation (only 'provisions and plantains') having been abandoned, to the Governor of the island as a site for a country residence, at a yearly rental of $1,200, and gave him a preferential option of purchasing the property at a fair valuation whenever the heirs of Barry could give a legal title to the lands. The residence was erected the same year, and Governor Hislop was the first tenant of it.

In the year 1811, the heirs of Barry got into financial difficulties, and Messrs. Park and Heywood took the Belmont property in Execution. The Court ordered an appraisement to be made, and the Governor, Major-General Monro, was notified of it. He objected to the inclusion of the Governor's residence in the appraisement, and it appears that nothing was done until the 30th April 1814, when notice of the order for appraisement was served on the new Governor, Sir Ralph Woodford, who at once referred the matter to the Attorney-General (Henry Fuller) in order that the interest of the Crown in the property might be represented in the suit. On the 24th May, 1814 he directed the Attorney-General to limit his objection to the valuation of the buildings.

The title of Belmont Estate was then raised, and the matter came into the Court of First Instance before the Chief Judge (John T. Bigge), who after hearing the arguments of the Attorney General and the representatives of the heirs of Barry, dismissed the claim of the Crown, and held that this title of the heirs of Barry to Belmont Estate was good, and he warranted it.

The Attorney-General appealed against this decision to the Court of Civil Appeal, which, at that time, was the Court of Intendant as regards matters relating to lands of the Colony. This Court had very large powers there. The Governor was the President of this Court, and he had as his legal assistant a Judge of the Colony, who was called the 'Assessor'.

After hearing both sides, the President reversed the decision of the Chief Justice, and decreed that the act of a servant cannot forfeit the right of the lord paramount, that no grant had been issued to any one, of the lands forming the Belmont Estate, and that there was no prescription against the Crown in the Colony, therefore His Majesty had never been divested of the ownership of the lands which formed Belmont Estate; but that the heirs of Barry could sue for compensation under a recent British Proclamation dealing with Crown Lands and lands occupied in the island, which gave compensation in land to occupiers, in certain cases, where lands were resumed from them for public purposes; and that the rent received by the heirs of Barry would be taken into account in considering the question of compensation.

The representative of the heirs of Barry applied for leave to appeal to the Privy Council, which was granted, and the vexed question was submitted for final decision to that tribunal.

The case of the Claim of the Crown to the lands of Belmont, and the alleged arbitrary action of Sir Ralph Woodford in the matter formed one of the many grievances of the Committee of Landholders of Trinidad, headed by the late Joseph Marryat, M.P., in their petition in 1816 to the Secretary of State against what they considered to be the aggressive and tyrannical administration of the Government of the Colony by that Governor.

'Belmont Estate' eventually became Crown Land, and the 'Government Cottage' was occupied by the Governors of the Colony until the 'Great House' of the 'Paradise Estate,' (which property had been purchased from the Peschier family and was converted into the

Botanic Gardens and the Queen's Park) was fixed up as a Governor's Residence. It was then apparently abandoned and fell into decay.

Drawing of African women in Trinidad by Richard Bridgens in the early 19th century and published by him in his book 'West Indian Scenery 1834'.

Translation of the will of Michael Loreilhe

This is the Will of a French Planter who died at an early age on his estate at Marabella South Trinidad. It provides us with a good idea of the relationships between various types of people that existed in those times.

"In the name of God the Father, the Son and the Holy Spirit etc.

1st.   I commend my soul to God, etc., etc.

2nd.   I declare that I am the proprietor of the estate (Marabella) and its appurtenances in partnership with Mr. Thomas Smith (which property has been valued at £36,000 Stg.) and the estate called Union in partnership with Governor Picton, also in the estate in Grenada called Thelsaide, formerly planted in coffee, but at present abandoned, also a parcel of land (in Grenada) consisting of 90 acres situated in the same quarter used as a garden for the Negroes of the Corinth estate.

I declare that it is my wish that this parcel of land be given to the Proprietor of Corinth Estate in exchange and for the balance of my total debt realizing the impossibility of adjusting otherwise having lost my books and papers at the time of the Revolt.

3rd.   I wish also that the Negro called Sampson and the two Negresses called Jeannette and Marguerite be given to Messrs. Alysen (or Alefssan) directing that, for all that, the said agents should sell the said slaves to the owner of best repute in the Island or give them the opportunity of choosing their own Master.

4th.   I declare that I have two Natural children by the Mulatress Luce living at present in my house, the boy was baptized in Grenada by the Minister of the Parish on the 3rd April, 1792 under the name of Charles Barclay and the girl was born in this Island on the 26th November last and baptized under the name of Marie-Anne.

5th.   I declare that I give to my Mulatress, Eliza, her liberty and my wish is that she enjoy all that is possible after my decease; I give to her and bequeath fifty portuguesas which are to be paid to her by my testamentary Executors (whom I will name hereafter) as soon as the state of my affairs will permit.

6th.   I give and bequeath to my Mulatress Magdelaine, a negro named Jean Francis at present employed on Union estate which negro I have deliberately not included in my various partnerships because he belongs to my nephew.

7th.   I declare to give to the Widow Dognon, widow of the deceased lawyer Dognon in the Island of Grenada, the sum of six thousand silver pounds of the Islands which amount I received in Grenada to repay to him (or her?) in Marseilles which the outbreak of war has prevented me from doing.

8th.   I give and bequeath to the Mulatress Luce the sum of five hundred portugesas payable in three equal instalments ..... the sale of Union estate.

9th.   I give and bequeath to my son Charles Barclay the sum of one thousand portuguesas which sum is to be paid to him on his majority and which is to be guaranteed by all my properties bearing interest at the rate of six percent for his upkeep and education.

10th.   I gave and bequeath to the girl Mulatress, Marie-Anne, his sister, the sum of three hundred Portuguesas which sum is to be paid to her at her majority and which is to be guaranteed by all my properties bearing at interest at the rate of six percent for her upkeep and education.

11th.   I appoint for Tutor to my above mentioned children M. Salvador Dominici, my neighbour and friend, entrusting him to undertake this task.

12th.   I give and bequeath to the child to be born in two or three weeks to the wife of Lieutenant Colonel Balfour commanding the 57th Regiment the sum of £300 Stg. payable a year after my death on the demand of its mother.

13th.   I give and bequeath to Governor Picton a cask of Madeira wine and a cask of Rum which are at present in my store with his mark.

14th.   I give and bequeath to the Mulatress Luce, all my clothes and household furniture which have been declared to belong to me by the District police.

15th.   I appoint my testamentary Executors Mr. Robert Prentis and M. La Sourd Mardither giving to each of them personally the sum of five hundred portuguesas, entreating them to accept this trust which I give to them full of sorrow. They have the power to act together or separately, but I assert that I have chosen them in the firm belief that three are no others who are able to put my affairs in order which are truly in confusion. No account is make up for Union estate, everything is in two notebooks which I consider can be put in order in a few days. I beg my Executors to examine my papers with care and by this means draw up an account. In general they will find my papers in a safe place waiting to be found. They are not to destroy any document after they have examined it in case they have to be re-examined. My friend Prentis has knowledge of many Chattels which I have in Port of Spain in various places.

16th.   I declare to have sold to Messrs. Peschier the Coppers and Mill of one hundred and fifty portuguesas payable at the next crop. I have received on account nine portuguesas from the Mother of these Gentlemen.

17th.   I commend to Governor Picton my Mulatto children to obtain for them everything which is possible following the satisfactory sale of Union.

18th.   I the undersigned bequeath as my residual heir and legatee my brother Zacharie Loreilhe, residing at present at Bergerac in France.

Done and signed at my Marabella estate, Island of Trinidad, the 12th day of September 1800.

Michael Loreilhe

Witnesses: J.J. Derneyere (or Demeyere)
                Alexandre Williams, Doctor
   Polustre   John Delly (or Relly)
   James Gamayan (or Gabayan)
                    N. Le Sucur

1808: At about 10 p.m. on March 24th, a certain Doctor Schaw (apothecary) in Frederick Street, was reported to have started the famous fire of Port of Spain by dropping, when not quite sober, a brand of fire on some wood shavings in an out-house. With the aid of a brisk breeze the fire quickly spread through the wooden houses of the town. Bells were rung, drums beat and troops summoned; robbery was rife during the disorder. Three-quarters of Port of Spain was destroyed and thousands rendered homeless and penniless. A Grenadier of the 37th Regiment was severely burnt and later died through saving the life of an infant. A Negro in Frederick Street also lost his life through burns; other casualties were only minor.

When at 8 a.m. on the 25th the flames subsided, damage was estimated at £500,000. Martial Law was proclaimed and the authorities erected tents and temporary huts for the relief of the homeless. On 28th March the Cabildo met to consider further relief measures and several merchants asked permission to rebuild their stores below Fort George, this request, however, meeting with denial.

Historical notes from H.C. Pitts 100 Years Together.

The AFRICANS, Slavery and Emancipation

Bridget Brereton

Trinidad was a 'late developer' in Plantation America. Not until the island was opened up by French immigrants in the 1780's did it begin to establish a flourishing export economy based on plantations. Up to that period, African slavery was not significant to the island's economy (such as it was) and only a few people of African descent lived here along with the Spanish settlers and the majority Amerindians. But as soon as plantations were established and sugar and cotton production began, the cry was for slaves, slaves and more slaves. Africans arrived with their owners from the French and British Caribbean, and some came directly from Africa via British slave ships. By 1797, when the island was conquered by Britain, there were just over 10,000 slaves.

African slavery and European colonization in the Caribbean are inseparable. Africans or Spanish-born blacks arrived in the islands along with Columbus and the earliest Spanish settlers, and enslaved Africans soon became the major work force for the mines, plantations and ranches established in the Hispanic Caribbean in the 16th century. In the 17th and 18th centuries, as the British, French and Dutch set up flourishing plantation colonies, the use of African slave labour was vastly extended. Whenever an island moved towards plantation development based on the production of export crops — above all, King Sugar — then African slave labour soon became the basis of its social and economic structure.

The first years of British rule saw a massive influx of Africans: between 1797 and 1802 the slave population rose from about 10,000 to nearly 20,000, doubling in five years. After 1802, when the island was formally ceded to Britain by peace treaty and the government in London decided to check its development as a slave colony, the rate of increase of the slave population slowed down considerably. In 1806 the slave trade to the newly acquired colonies, including Trinidad, was prohibited and there was a gradual but marked decline in the island's slave population between 1806 and 1834. Nevertheless, Trinidad had become a slave colony and African slaves had come to constitute the majority of her population.

Trinidad's African born population came from a very wide geographical spread, from Senegambia in the north to Angola ('Congo') in the south. As late as 1813, the majority of Trinidad slaves were African born, unlike the situation in older colonies such as Barbados. In that year, the slaves from the Bight of Biafra formed the largest single group (39.4% of the African born slaves). Gradually, between 1813 and 1834, as the older Africans died, the balance shifted in favour of the Creoles, those born in Trinidad or in the other Caribbean islands.

1809: A certain M. Le Bis flogged one of his slaves to death 'before settling down to enjoy a good breakfast.' Due to certain technical submissions by his lawyer he was only fined $50 for 'treating his slave unskillfully in his capacity of surgeon.'
Historical notes from H.C. Pitts 100 Years Together.

This is one of a series of plates, in which it is proposed to exhibit the various kinds of stocks directed by Government* to be used in the Crown Colonies before the Abolition Act passed. It may be seen, from the care taken for the ease of the prisoner, that no punishment is attempted in the Bed-Stock beyond confinement of the person. They are generally placed in some of the outhouses belonging to the estate, where the offender may be denied the society and encouragement of his friends or accomplices. The Bed-Stocks are usually, indeed, employed in cases of drunkenness, when the individual is callous to the shame of exposure. As the Negro is often unwilling to bear the pain caused by a dressing, which may have been applied to a wound or sore, it is requisite on such occasions to confine the hands behind the back, to prevent him from removing the bandages. A plentiful provision of warm clothing is rendered necessary by the total inability of the Negro to bear cold, without serious injury to his health.
*An Order in Council, dated Sept. 2nd, 1831, restricts the use of the Bed-Stocks in these terms: 'For the confinement of the feet, during the day; only provided, that for each offence the period of confinement shall not exceed six hours.'
Richard Bridgens was the Superintendent of Public Works and was responsible for the building of several public buildings such as the Police Barracks at St. James and the first Red House. His illustrations which were published by him in 1834 give a dramatic picture of life in Trinidad in the period 1808-1830 and are in fact the earliest portrayals of places and people in Trinidad. This drawing is reproduced with the kind permission of Mrs. Clair Broadbridge.

Here is a representation of one of the various modes of tattooing in use among the native tribes of the West coast of Africa. The operation is performed in infancy. The desired figure having been pricked on the skin with a sharp instrument, a dyeing liquid is rubbed into the wound. The impression is indelible, and expands with the growth of the features. These are the distinctive badge of the Mocha tribe, who are reproached with the horrid crime of cannibalism. some are willing to suppose the charge may have arisen from their disfiguring practice of filing the teeth to a point, which they consider a great beauty.
Richard Bridgens 1820

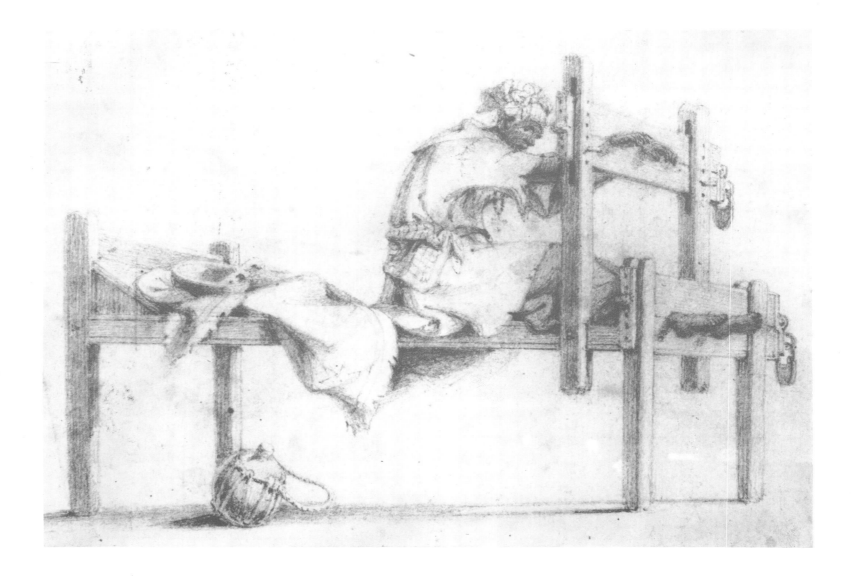

There was one remarkable group of Africans living in Trinidad before Emancipation that we know something about: the Mandingoes. These people came from the region of West Africa between the rivers Gambia and Senegal and they were Moslems. Although they had been enslaved and brought to Trinidad some time before 1806 they never lost their sense of identity, their religion or their longing to go home to Africa. Under the leadership of Jonas Mohammed Bath, they formed a distinct association, acquiring property in Port of Spain and cocoa estates in the country, and they systematically bought the freedom of all their 'countrymen' — fellow Moslems from the Senegambia. This remarkable group of Africans could proudly state that virtually all of them had been freed by August 1834 when the Act of Emancipation became law. However this was not enough: their real goal was to go home. This was not to be, but their pride, their industry and their strong belief in self-help were important qualities for Trinidad's African descended population in the post-slavery period.

1812: The Royal Jail was opened.
   A Royal decree dated 26th March provided for the establishment of a registry of slaves in Trinidad.
Historical notes from H.C. Pitts 100 Years Together

A slave in the Stocks by Richard Bridgens; this drawing is reproduced with the kind permission of Mrs. Clair Broadbridge.

PETITION OF MANDINGO EX-SLAVES FOR RETURN TO THEIR OWN COUNTRY, FORWARDED THROUGH LT. GOVERNOR HILL

Trinidad No. 4

12th January, 1838

To the Right Honourable Lord Baron Glenelg,
Her Majesty's Principal Secretary of State for the
Colonial Department,
London,
ENGLAND

The Memorial of the undersigned African Subjects of Her Most Gracious Majesty the Queen of Great Britain and Ireland humbly sheweth unto Your Lordship:

That Your Memorialists are natives of Africa and of the Nation or Tribe called Mandingo; that during the existence of the Slave Trade Your Memorialists were torn from their beloved Country, their friends and relations, delivered into the hands of Slave Merchants, who imported Your Memorialists into the West Indies and sold them as Slaves.

That Your Memorialists, resolving to extricate themselves and others of their Nation, from the cruel and degraded state to which they had been reduced, formed themselves into a Society in this Island; and as the earnings of their honest industry accumulated, gradually redeemed themselves and their Countrymen from the House of Bondage; hence on the memorable first day of August one thousand, eight hundred and thirty-four, a day which will always live in the Annals of Nations, and which will ever be remembered with feelings of the highest gratitude by the black man — Your Memorialists can safely, and with truth, assert, very few, if any of their Tribe in the Island of Trinidad remained in Slavery to partake of the beneficient and humane achievement of the British Nation. —No!—Your Memorialists had long before unfettered themselves, their tribe and their families, by the fruits of their joint and industrious efforts.

That Your Memorialists have always behaved themselves as quiet and peaceable members of this Community; that they are proud of the name of British

Subjects and feel grateful for the protection and benevolence which they had experienced from the Government.

That many generous and praiseworthy attempts have been made by the enlightened of Europe to introduce and establish civilization in Africa, but that such attempts which have hitherto proved vain or but partially successful. That Your Memorialists feel confident that could they but reach the shores of the land that gave them birth, their efforts, as heads of their tribe, would ensure success in propagating Civilization, the benefits of which they so deeply feel themselves, and would give them an opportunity of proclaiming to their Nation the liberality of the British Government.

That there are no means of direct communication between this Island and any of the British Settlements on

The Sable Venus — a very romantic view of the slave trade which can only be compared to the reality of it as seen in the picture on the opposite page — A drawing by Richard Bridgens of a Slave in the Stocks. Lithography by Agostino Brunias from Brian Edwards.

the Coast of Africa, and if there were, the great number of Your Memorialists have not the means to defray the necessary expenses attendant upon going there; besides which, Your Memorialists are greatly afraid, that if they were to venture upon the open seas, in any other than a British armed vessel, they would be exposed to the imminent danger of being captured and again sold into the Iron Hands of bondage by the Nations that still carry on the Slave Trade.

Upon these grounds, and under these fears, and also upon the assurance of their Countryman Mohommed Houssa, otherwise called Philip Friday, who visited England last year and was then introduced into the presence of Her Most Gracious Sovereign the blessing of a long, happy and prosperous reign is and ever will be the prayer of Your Memorialists.

Leonas Bath, for self, wife and children
   Signature in

Arabic Characters
Salhin, commonly called Charles Alexander
  "   "

Mahommed Waatra, commonly called
   Auguste Bernard for himself
  "   "

Mohommed Habin, commonly called
   Mohommed Littledale
  "   "   "

Mahommed Sisari, commonly called
   Felix Ditt
  "   "   "

Eonta Torre, otherwise called
   Sampson Boissière
  "   "   "

Aboouberika Torre, commonly called
   Joseph Sampson
  "   "   "

Brahima, commonly called
   Adam Balthazar
  "   "   "

Hammedi Torrouke called
   Louis Modeste
  "   "   "

Mahommed Bailiah, commonly called
   Christopher Picka
  "   "   "

Samba Jaiih, commonly called
   Michael Sylvestre
  "   "   "

Malick Job, commonly called
   Thomas Jones
  "   "   "

Port of Spain
11th January, 1838

Witness: Edward Schack.
Source: Public Record Office, State Papers, Colonial C.O.
      295/12.
      T.T.H.S. Pub. (811).
This petition was not granted.

These qualities pride, self-help, industry were also often to be found among Creole slaves as well as those born free in Africa. For instance, Mrs. A.C. Carmichael, the wife of a Scottish planter who owned Laurel Hill estate in the late 1820's, describes — with grudging respect — several men and women on the estate who were independently minded and self-assertive. From the slave-owner's perspective, of course, these were the difficult slaves, the 'uppity niggers'. Mrs. Carmichael's cook was a formidable lady who could not be got to work in the fields and made trouble whenever anyone tried to make her; but she cultivated her garden plot energetically, kept a little 'shop' on the estate, organized pay fêtes and could always lend her mistress respectable sums of money. 'C' wouldn't work for Massa, but she worked hard for herself, and bought her freedom well in advance of Emancipation in 1834.

Slavery was a harsh and oppressive system, degrading to all who were a part of it. After the abolition of the Slave Trade in 1806-07, the British moved slowly to remove some of its worst features and then to end it altogether in two stages between 1834 and 1838. These efforts to reform the slave system by legislating for 'Amelioration' (improvement in the slaves' conditions) provoked strong reactions from the slave-owners, especially in Trinidad where the new laws were first introduced on an experimental basis.

The Trinidad planters objected strenuously to any attempt by the British Government to interpose their authority between master and slave. In their view, the owner's authority over his property must be absolute (short of a right to actually murder his slave) and the slave must feel that every kindness, every 'privilege' that he received, was an act of pure benevolence by his owner — not a 'right' guaranteed by law and enforced by a third party, the government.

Moreover, the planters feared (with some justification) that the reforms were only the first round in a campaign that would end in complete emancipation. And this was almost unthinkable for men and women born and bred into slave-holding, as it were. How could estates be run without slave labour? Would the master become the 'slave' of his former property because he couldn't make sugar without labourers? No wonder that the last decade of British slavery (1823-34) was a tense, anxious period for the planters who mounted an almost hysterical propaganda campaign, in the West Indies and the Britain, aimed against the abolitionists and all their sympathisers.

This campaign failed, of course, and the hopes and fears of slaves and slave-owners were finally realized when Parliament in Britain enacted the formal end of slavery in August 1834. But this did not mean 'full free': all slaves over the age of six were to be 'apprenticed' to their former owners and would still have to give 45 hours a week unpaid, forced labour to their 'masters'. This 'Apprenticeship' was to last six years for field slaves (the great majority) and four years for others, such as domestics. No wonder that a body of ex-slaves, now apprentices, converged on Port of Spain in August 1834 to protest: 'Point de six ans!', they shouted, as well they might.

A near riot ensued, but it was suppressed, a few ringleaders were punished and the rest went (sullenly, we may suppose) back to their estates to sweat out their 'Apprenticeship'.

Four long years were to pass before the Apprenticeship was abolished for all categories of ex-slaves and full freedom was granted on August 1, 1838.

Continued from page 88 M'Callum's 'Travels in Trinidad'.

On the arrival of the European, his first object is, to look out for a mistress, either of the black, yellow, or livid kind. As there are plenty in the market, he has no difficulty to encounter. After pleasing his taste, he bargains for her, in the same manner you would for a colt in Smithfield, either with the mother or the proprietor, for a certain sum of money. He supports this wretched companion of his solicitude in all her extravagance; she denies him nothing, and he is equally generous in return; —free from the trammels of all moral restraint, he is at once launched into the labyrinth of guilty fascination.

Misled by the facinorous disposition of others, and those false doctrines, which grant an unlimited licence to follow the depravity of inclination, vice soon becomes so familiar, as to be considered a virtue. The important duties of religion are banished from the mind; so that God is forgotten in the riot betwixt Lust and Mammon.

The traveller can see no signs whatever of such a day as Sunday,—no trace of christianity,—no respect for morality. On the day called Sunday, the stores are open for the transaction of business till dinner time,—the rest of the day is spent in dancing, playing, billiards, etc. Instead of christianity, he is shocked at the constant display of brutality; and in the room of morality, he sees vice arrayed in putrefaction. To me, nothing evinces the folly and frailty of human nature more, than a shameful neglect of all moral and religious duties. What a benign idea does a religious conduct excite! It stimulates the

exaltation of human nature; inspires the love of truth and benevolence; and enforces the practice of charity. Religion also teaches us to love our fellow-creature, whether black or white, to refine our passions, and reduce them to the obedience of reason. It will

1829
SLAVE REGULATIONS
Public notice is hereby given that the Illustrious Cabildo in order to prevent, as far as possible, the disorders and robberies which have generally taken place, resolved that notice be given to all owners of slaves that they are by no means to suffer their slaves to sleep out of their premises by night, and are to compel them to be at home by eight o'clock in the evening. Slaves are absolutely forbidden to hire houses from any proprietor or tenant . . . . . . while proprietors or tenants are in general hereby warned against such practices under penalty of $25 for each default . . . Owners who wish to send their slaves to work out are required to furnish them with a written permission; in default of which the slave will be apprehended as a runaway and publicly flogged, and the owner fined a sum of $25.

(Sgd.) Antonio Ardila,
Escribano de Cabildo.
('Gazette,' 7th March, 1829).From the Port of Spain Gazette. Special Centenary issue.

1831. A slave ship having been wrecked on the Anegrada reef on 10th July, the slaves were seized by the Customs officers of Tortola and 150 of them sent to Trinidad. Subsequently, several shipments of slaves were condemned by Cuban authorities and sent to Trinidad where they were apprenticed.
Historical notes from H.C. Pitts 100 Years Together.

A stick fight between West Indian Negroes.

encourage and increase the energies of friendship, and add tenderness to the ties of conjugal affection. Whatever our great philosophers may advance, as De Mably very justly observes, all depends upon the morals; and the deeper you search into the operation of politics, the more you will be convinced of it. But now, Sir, I find such an habitual negligence of every thing that is good, and such a superior inclination for that which is evil, that the reformation of them would be more than Herculean labour.

> Vice, is a monster of so frightful mien,
> As, to be hated, needs but to be seen;
> Yet soon, too oft, familiar with her face,
> We first endure, then pity, them embrace.
>
> POPE

. . . . Every lad who comes out bound to serve in a store, hires a prostitute, with whom he shares his bed; and, between salacity and intemperance, debilitates his constitution before it has time to arrive at maturity. As for the native creole, a female companion is provided for him from among the slaves of the family, at an early age, to prevent his going astray to increase the stock of his neighbours, to the manifest injury of his own property.

I have somewhere seen a calculation, which went to prove, that out of 100 living men, we must expect 28 to die every year. Let us apply this ratio to Trinidad. For instance; out of every 100 white men that arrive in the course of a year, we shall suppose 20 will die of course within the year. Well, Sir, I have made a calculation, which I firmly believe, is a correct one, that so perish in that period, by various diseases, which ramify from the deleterious and maniacal effects of salacity and intemperance.

Most (if not all) of the West Indian planters are, more or less, addicted to this social, festive vice, and a vice, beyond any other, apt to draw in people by the example. The planter collects his circle, and that circle naturally spreads, so that they all emulate each other in corrupting every new comer. The frequent duels you hear of in the West Indies are, *en passant,* owing to this deleterious vice. I have seen persons addicted to excessive drinking, in the intervals of sobriety, labouring under the oppressive *circa pracordia,* which exceeded the ordinary patience of human nature to endure. It is no way relieved but by a repetition of the same excessive libation.

Though the new imported negroes do not indulge the vice of drunkenness, yet I find they perish in greater proportion than the unseasoned Europeans. A young medical gentleman, a nephew of the celebrated Dr. Jenner, informed me, during his attendance at a plantation in the district of *Naparima,* that out of 270 field negroes, 80 died the last year. This is surely a great mortality, and a great loss to the planter, which is neither the fault of bad food nor bad care, as this planter has studied, in a great degree, the comforts of his slaves. The most *regnant* malady among them is, what the French call *mal d'estomac.* No method has been found out to prevent their indulging a depravity of taste; it prompts them to devour, with the most sensual avidity, almost everything that falls in their way, particularly lumps of clay,—it begins with an *ennui,* and ends in a marasmus, that baffles the knowledge of the sons of Esculapius*.

Mal d'Estomac, Cachexia Africana, or the stomach disease of the negroes.

It is astonishing how little medical men are informed respecting this disease, and how slovenly it is passed over by medical authors. Dr. Hunter passed it over with a

Title page from 'Travels in Trinidad', Pierre F. M'Callum, 1805.

Pierre F. M'Callum

M'Callum was a British writer who visited Trinidad in 1803 and wrote a book denouncing Colonel Thomas Picton, Governor of Trinidad since 1797. His book, published in 1805, was part of the campaign undertaken in Britain to bring Picton to justice for the many atrocities committed under his regime in Trinidad. M'Callum was a warm supporter of William Fullerton, who was appointed First Commissioner (Picton being superseded to Second Commissioner) over Trinidad in 1802, and who soon became a dedicated enemy of Picton's

M'Callum belongs to the humanitarian tradition which was gathering strength in Britain at the turn of the 18th century. He supported the movement to abolish the Slave Trade which was successful in 1807 and he was plainly shocked by the horrors of slavery. The point was that by 1803, atrocities against slaves and free coloureds which would have hardly troubled anyone's conscience, back, say in the 1750's, were now coming under challenge by the spokesmen of the new humanitarianism and the new doctrine that colonial powers had an obligation to protect their subject peoples. If Picton had committed his 'acts of severity' in 1760 or 1770 no one would have taken note, but by 1800 ideas had changed and his actions had become an embarrassing liability to the British Government, especially when publicized by a clever writer like M'Callum who appealed to the conscience of all 'free born Britons'.

As a figure of the 18th century enlightenment, M'Callum was a rationalist who had little belief in magic or the super-natural, hence his attitude towards obeah by the slaves is sceptical and he does not believe that obeahmen were, in fact, dangerous people; quite unlike Picton's own attitude and that of the French Creole slave-owners who advised him on slave affairs.

dash. The authors of the Medical and Physical Journal, vol. ii, 172, merely stated the symptoms, and a sort of cure loosely; and Mr. Edwards, in his History of the West Indies, treats it in the like manner, adding, 'the best and only remedy is kind usage and wholesome animal food—*Perhaps a steel drink may be of some service!!* Lastly, Dr. Winterbottom:—he ought to be excused, for in Africa he had no opportunity of observing the disease, but among the children, which might be seen in England among even our grown up misses. The reader, if a medical one, I hope will pardon me, should I presume to hazard an opinion on the origin of it in the male negroes, when I say, that it is owing to the constant, cruel castigation they experience in the field and elsewhere, from the inhuman task-master, causing an *ennui*, or marasmus of the *Nostalgia* kind, which creates this preternatural taste for dirt-eating. On recurring to the MS. of my travels through the United States of America, I find I have noticed this disease under the head of *Maladie Ecossois*, which proceeds from an ardent desire in the Highlanders of Scotland to re-visit their native hills. I have seen many of them in several parts of America labouring under the affliction of this disorder, occasioned by disappointed hopes, and the barbarous usage of the

slave-master, to whom they were originally sold for the payment of their passage, and from whose infernal gripe they were never able to extricate either themselves or their children. The thoughts of being thus held in had and hopeless bondage, together with the brutality of their tyrants, brings on a gradual *ennui*, which tempts them to end their miserable existence by suicide, when dirt-eating, and a constant libation of *Yankie*-rum, does not speedily effect their liberation from their ill-fated

"
Prisionier levez, mettes lumiere bai Congo Barra
Deux eslave courri sortie Tunapun'
Congo ba yo bois fair yo devire.

Prisoners wake up and put a light for Congo Barra
Two slaves run away from Tunapuna
Congo beat them with a stick and make them return.

Excerpts of calypsoes rendered over the centuries. The above dates
from the 1830's – 'Atilla's Kaiso', Raymond Quevedo, 1983.
"

The deed for Cleaver Lands was made in 1825 and was one of the new
deeds coming into existence during this period. These new deeds
replaced the old Spanish land grants which were employed during the
Spanish Colonial period.

captivity. It is the same with the negroes, but far more violent from the nature of their bondage. I could really wish to pursue this important inquiry further, and elucidate the subject properly, but, I am precluded, from the nature of the situation in which this note appears.

FOR SALE

An excellent washerwoman and ironer, a native of Barbados; price, — Three hundred perfect dollars. Apply to the office of this paper. *(14th January, 1826). Port of Spain Gazette, Special Centenary Issue.*

THE CON-CON

This dish of African origin is eaten from two bowls. In one is the Sususumber Callaloo with crab, in the other is a cuckoo made with cassava farine. The callaloo is made with small pieces of salt beef and pigtail, chives, onions, garlic and thyme, to which is added a quantity of ochroes cut small and a few handfuls of sususumber berries. Then put in two crabs and allow to cook without touching until it has dissolved into a gooey callaloo. The cuckoo is made by grating three or four sweet cassava, squeezing out the water and adding the result to a quart of boiling water in which there is salt, pepper and butter.

SIR RALPH ABERCROMBY

Apart from his illustrious career as a Governor General Sir Ralph Abercromby was also known as the Father of Amphibious warfare . During his military career his amphibiuos landing tactics gained him fame amongst his peers for his successful ingenuity. Abercromby joined the US army in 1756 and retired in 1783 in protest against the US war of Independence. He returned to the army in 1793 at the beginning of the Napoleonic wars and served in Holland and the Caribbean between 1794–1797. While in the Caribbean Abercromby captured Grenada, St. Lucia, St. Vincent and Trinidad; the latter of which he remained in for a while and in fact by virtue of his brilliance as a leader, went on to become one of the most revered governors of the period. The year 1798 found him in command of the British forces in Ireland. One year later in 1799, at the age of 60, a respected and admired General, Abercromby commanded an amphibious landing in Holland and had 2 horses shot from under him. He returned to Britain in 1800 and 1801 found him the Commanding officer of the British army in the Mediterranean. On the 2nd January Abercromby sailed from Malta to Turkey in pursuit of new victories and on the 22nd February he arrived in Aboukin Bay, Egypt where he commanded yet another trademark amphibious landing. On the 21st March Abercromby was hit in the thigh by a musket ball and was transferred to Lord Keith's flagship where he died on the 28th March 1801, thus ending a colourful and intrepid career in the army of Great Britain.

General Sir Ralph Abercromby was in command of the British Army in Egypt in 1801, where at the battle of Alexandria he was severely wounded. By Peter Shim after an old engraving.

FRANKLIN'S TRINIDAD
Select Documents
1803-1854
by
C.B. Franklin
THE GREAT FIRE OF 1808

Between ten and eleven o'clock on the night of the 24th March, the inhabitants of this town were suddenly awoke by the drums beating and bells ringing the alarm. Fire was soon found to be the cause, and the house of Dr. Schaw, in Frederick Street, one of the narrowest, most populous, and built altogether of timber, the focus from whence the conflagration issued, threatening, by its impetuosity, devastation all around.

The fire from the inflammable and combustible materials of Dr. Schaw's shop, in which were stored quantities of nitre, sulphur, ether, and other rectified spirits and essential oils, soon raged with inconceivable violence: and diverging from that focus in every direction, the whole of that street, together with Henry Street on the East, Chacon Street on the west, and King and Queen Streets on the North and South, were soon enveloped in the devouring element; and to those who had time to reflect, afforded a melancholy presage of the total destruction of the town. The terror which took possession of the unfortunate tenants and proprietors of this neighbourhood is not to be described nor can fancy paint a scene of such astonishment and dismay.

They were roused from their sleep to behold the very flames bursting into their chamber windows, and had but sufficient time to abandon all and save their lives. The screams of the women and children running distractedly through the streets in search of a place of safety-the neighing, or rather squealing of the horses and mules, many of which were burnt to death in their stables; and the loud frequent reports of butts of spirituous liquors and of gunpowder, as the fire reached them altogether formed an assemblage of horror, as awful as it was terrific. Of lives, we have not heard of any being lost, except a negro of Mr. Sandes, the Vendue-master, whose house was contiguous to the spot where the fire originated, and a Grenadier of the 37th, who generously devoting himself to save the life of a child, succeeded in the attempt, but was so scorched as since to have died of his sufferings.

The Pump Company with the water engines did everything that could be expected from them, to stop the progress of the flames; but from the number of years that the town, through a variety of hazards, had escaped and the late uncommon wet weather, which had lulled the inhabitants into security, people were off their guard, and the machinery of every class attached to that establishment had been neglected-the want of water was another difficulty, the wells only furnishing the little that was procured, and those were soon drained, or became inapproachable by the excessive heat of the houses and palings on fire around them. We will venture to affirm, however, that the quantity of water a dozen such engines as ours, well served and well furnished, could have thrown, would have been totally useless and unavailing to extinguish or even arrest the impetuosity of a conflagration such as we have been a witness to, after it once got ahead.

His Excellency the Governor, with the officers of his staff, and working parties from the 37th and 8th, were early at the scene of action; and although their efforts were vigorous, and behaviour orderly and meritorious under his Excellency's orders, it was all ineffectual; human art or exertion could do nothing against the progress of such a torrent of fire, continually renewed and excited by fuel of such inflammable matter.

When day broke, and the clouds of smoke which lay on the ground and could not ascend from its own density, had cleared away by the morning breeze, a scene of desolation presented itself to us not to be described–a large and populous town, which but a few hours before bore the second rank in our Windward Island possession, had vanished, and nothing remained but stacks of chimneys and walls in ruins; not an atom of anything inflammable escaped, and in many places bottles and glassware, and even pot metal, were found to be in a state of fusion.

On taking an account of the extent of the damage with the plan of the town in hand, we find that 12 squares or blocks have been entirely consumed, and 49 partially, making an ensemble of 435 principal houses or stores with the fronts to the streets, besides back stores and out-offices, which may be estimated at four times that number at least, and the whole, at a moderate calculation, worth 3,500,000 dollars, the lodging or property about 4,500 persons, who are now in the streets, and numbers of them totally destitute; of the value of merchandise, produce, and effects destroyed, we can at present form no idea. Government has called for the account of every person's loss upon oath-it will however exceed, we think, half a million sterling.

Of the public buildings not one has been saved-Government-house, the Custom-house, the Hospital, the Protestant Church, the Town-hall, and a part of the Public archives' and Treasurer's Offices, have fallen a sacrifice to the flames; most fortunately the Commissaries' Stores and King's provisions were by great exertion saved, and to this source of life many now owe in a great measure their subsistence-it having pleased his Excellency to proclaim Martial Law, and with his usual goodness and humanity, to order rations to be issued to the Militia as in times of actual warfare; and all the tents which could be spared in the Garrison have been pitched in Brunswick Square, to lodge the unfortunate sufferers who have neither house nor home, and they are numerous.

On the part of the Government, every measure that could contribute to alleviate the public misery has been taken with a precision and promptitude which does his Excellency infinite honour. Expresses have been sent to the neighbouring Colonies, to the Spanish Main, and to the United States, for supplies; a Committee of His Majesty's Council, and of the notable inhabitants has been appointed to receive donations of every kind that can be useful, and distribute to those who are in need, rations of bread, flesh and fish salted, and even fresh beef to the infirm, which are purchased up by the Committee, from a private subscription opened for the relief of the sufferers, at the head of which stands his Excellency's name, and that of His Majesty's Collector of Custom, Charles Grant, Esq., for £1,000 sterling each, an example of munificence, worthy the imitation of the charitable and humane to whom it has pleased God to dispense the blessings of wealth or independence.

With respect to the source of this dreadful calamity, we have not only the contiguous to the flames, but of Dr.

A Plan

of The Town of Port of Spain Island of Trinidad
in Which it is pointed out the Houses Burnt down by the fire
of The 24th & 25th March 1808

— Shows the Part of the Town Burnt
— The part remaining of the Ancient Town
— Houses built in the New Town Since the Year 1802.
— Vacant Lots
— Where The Fire Began

A Government House
B Hospital
C Church
D Town Hall
E Public Goal
f Custom House

A true Extract from the Original
Plan of The Town of Port of Spain
lodged in the office of the Surveyor General

J. E. Maingot
Dept Surveyor General

Schaw himself, who has confessed before authority, that the first knowledge that he had of the fire was its bursting in at the windows of his back gallery from the out-offices in his yard; but by what means his out-offices caught fire is all conjecture. We firmly and religiously believe, that there was no design immediate or premeditated in the affair; it was undoubtedly owing to accident, and that is the best face we can put upon it. A town opulent and flourishing, and an immense property, have been destroyed; it is of little consequence to the sufferers to be informed how it happened, the mischief is done and there is no remedy, but it is at least satisfactory to be assured, that evil design had no hand in it. – 'Trinidad Weekly Courant', 1st April 1808.

STORY OF THE TOWN HALL PORTRAITS

SIR RALPH ABERCROMBIE AND SIR THOMAS PICTON

On the 24th and 25th of March 1808, a great calamity befell Port-of-Spain. A devastating fire destroyed the whole of the town. The houses in those days were built mainly of wood, were covered with shingles or thatch, and therefore became an easy prey to the consuming conflagration.

Among the public buildings destroyed was the Cabildo Hall, but fortunately there were saved from it the Cabildo Records and two portraits – one of Sir Ralph Abercrombie, who captured Trinidad and was its first Governor, and one of Sir Thomas Picton, his faithful Aide-de-camp, whom he left as Governor of Trinidad on his departure in 1797, and who continued to govern the island until 1803. Picton was the first English President of the Illustrious Cabildo. The Town Hall at the time of the fire was situated in Charlotte Street, a little way from Queen Street on the right going up.

The salved portraits were entrusted to the care of two of the leading citizens of the town, Mr. St. Hilaire Begorrat and Mr. F. Lecadre

The Records consisted of Minutes of the Cabildo extending back to the early days of the Spanish occupation-precious documents, many of which have, alas! since disappeared. the portraits were crayon coloured portraits painted by John Russell, who in those days was an eminent portrait painter and favourite of the Court. He was known by the title of "Painter to the King and the Prince of Wales".

In 1815 the Cabildo purchased a house in Brunswick Square and wishing to hang their pictures in the meeting hall of their new Town Hall got them back from the gentlemen who had so kindly taken care of them.

The crayon portraits by Russell would be permanent if well taken care of. There are many of then in existence to-day in public and private galleries. But the Cabildo portraits had gone through many vicissitudes, climate, fire, removal, etc., Cabildo ordered the portraits "to be packed and sent to England for the purpose of being copied in oil, and when completed to be sent back to ornament the Hall of Illustrious Board".

The Cabildo in those days did not do things in a mean or niggardly manner. they desired to have the portraits of their Presidents to ornament the walls of their Town Hall and they insisted that these portraits should be painted by the best artist of the day. The crayon portraits of Generals Abercrombie and Picton were the work of the great artist Russell, whose crayon portraits were all the vogue at the time. When the crayon portraits were sent to London in 1815 the Cabildo had already commissioned Sir Thomas Lawrence, the most eminent artist of the day, to paint General Hislop's portrait, of which more will be said later on.

When Sir Ralph Woodford came as Governor to Trinidad in 1813, he brought with him as his Private Secretary, Mr. Philip Reinagle. mr. Reinagle belonged to a highly artistic family. His grandfather, Joseph Reinagle, was a musician of repute; his father, Philip Reinagle, was a well known animal and landscape painter. His brother, Ramsey Richard Reinagle, was a portrait painter of merit, who had attained to the dignity of President of the Society of Painters in water colours, which he held for many years.

Pictures by him are to be found to-day at the South Kensington Museum and the National Gallery of Scotland. The Governor's Secretary was himself a gifted architect who was mainly responsible for the building of our two Cathedrals, and later on became the Town Surveyor of Port-of-Spain, now the City Engineer.

Mr. Reinagle was in London in 1815, and the Cabildo commissioned him to get the crayon portraits of Generals Abercrombie and Picton copied in oils by Sir Thomas Lawrence. It is to be regretted that Mr. Reinagle did not carry out strictly the commission entrusted to him. On the plan that Sir Thomas Lawrence's charges were too high, he took it upon himself to have the work done by another artist and, as would be expected, selected his brother Ramsey Richard Reinagle.

The portraits are very fine paintings, admired by all artists who have seen them; in spite of over one hundred years of the tropics with their powerful fading and bleaching light, and other accidents and changes, they have preserved their fine colouring. But one can't help feeling that it would have been better to have the walls of the Town Hall adorned by two Lawrences than by two Reinagles. What happened to the two Russell crayon portraits no one knows. They were not returned to Trinidad. They were valuable pictures, and probably to-day adorn the walls of some public or private gallery.

SIR THOMAS HISLOP

General HISLOP was Governor of Trinidad from 1803 to 1811, and followed after the troublous times of Picton and Fullerton.

It was customary to vote to have the portrait of the President of the Cabildo painted when the Address of Good-bye was presented to him. The Cabildo must have decided in 1811 to have General Hislop's portrait painted.

In 1815 it is on record that the portrait had been ordered and that Sir Thomas Lawrence was the painter selected; furthermore, the money for the payment had been sent to a Mr. Gardner who, unfortunately had died. In 1817 Mr. Reinagle made enquiries of Sir Thomas Lawrence who informed him that "such a portrait had been painted by him and that he presumed it was duly delivered". The executors of Mr. Gardner knew nothing about it. The portrait had been painted by Lawrence, paid for, and then disappeared".

It was six years after in 1823 that Sir Ralph Woodford when in London started a search and discovered that General Hislop himself was in possession of the portrait. The General had no good feeling for the Cabildo as after his retirement he had made a claim against the Cabildo for over £900-which was disallowed by the then Secretary of State for the Colonies, Lord Bathurst. He had got the pictures from Sir Thomas Lawrence and decided to keep it as an offset to his disallowed claim.

Anyway Sir Ralph Woodford paid the General for the frame got the picture, had it cleaned and sent it back to its rightful owners in Trinidad. The picture is on the walls of our Town Hall. It has recently been cleaned again in England and put in a new frame. The cleaning of old masters has resulted lately in great damage to pictures, especially in the case of the portrait in the National Gallery of Phillip IV. by Velasquez. the picture of Sir Thomas Hislop, however, does not seem to have been much affected by the cleaning it has gone through.

SIR RALPH WOODFORD

Sir RALPH WOODFORD was one of the greatest Governors that Trinidad ever had. At any rate he was in high favour with the Cabildo who did not wait for his departure and the usual valedictory address, to order his portrait. In 1822 when he was going on leave they expressed the desire that he should sit to Sir Thomas Lawrence for his portrait. On his return in 1823 he reported to the Cabildo that he had been fortunate enough, notwithstanding some difficulty, to succeed in inducing Sir Thomas Lawrence to draw his portrait, that the head had been finished previous to his departure and that Sir Thomas had promised to complete the body during the year".

In 1828, after the death of Sir Ralph Woodford, the Hon. Mr. Ashton Warner informed the Cabildo "that the portrait of Sir Ralph Woodford is so nearly finished that very little time and attention would enable Sir Thomas to finish it, but that he is so much engaged that unless urged on the subject, the picture may remain in his gallery for years to come". The necessary presurement have been exercised, for in May 1829 Mr. Warner was requested "to obtain the portrait of H.E. Sir Ralph Woodford from Sir Thomas Lawrence, and to send it out to the Colony," the Board authorising a remittance of 80 guineas to meet the cost of the frame, packing case, etc". Sir Ralph Woodford's portrait, a fine life-size picture by Sir Thomas Lawrence, adorns the fine Chamber of the Legislative Council of the Colony. The picture is too large for the meeting hall at the Town Hall and the City Council lent it to the Government. At first it was at Government House, St. Ann's, but it was felt that only a limited few would have the opportunity of seeing it, and it was transferred to the Legislative Council Chamber to which the general public has easy access.

The picture has been lately cleaned and renovated and it is fortunate that it has not suffered in any way by the process, as has been the care with some masterpieces, and, especially with the great picture of Phillip Iv. by Velasquez in the National Gallery.

SIR ARETAS WILLIAM YOUNG

Sir ARETAS W. YOUNG acted as Governor of Trinidad during the absence of Sir Ralph Woodford in 1820 and again from 1821 to 1823. His relations with the Cabildo must have been of the pleasantest because when his acting appointment came to an end they voted him a very eulogistic address, gave him a present of £150 to purchase for himself a service of plate when he got home and requested him to sit for his portrait.

It is to be regretted that he did not wait until he got to England to sit for his portrait, which would have been the work of Sir Thomas Lawrence, who was still at the time the great portrait painter. The portrait was painted by a local artist named John Eckstein. Mr. Eckstein was a versatile gentleman who followed other pursuits than that of painting. In 1822 he had offered the Cabildo to translate the Spanish laws into English at the rate of £250 a volume. He also induced the Illustrious Board to take chances in a lottery of two paintings-a rather peculiar procedure on the part of a public body. The Cabildo took ten chances at the cost of £20 and must have drawn blanks as there is no record of their having won either of the pictures.

Mr. Eckstein was paid 100 guineas for the picture of Sir A.W. Young. The frame was imported and cost £50. The portrait may be an early example of the impressional school of painting, but the æimpression" made on those who inspect it is the reverse of agreeable.

LORD HARRIS

Lord HARRIS was a very able and popular Governor. One of his important public acts was the bringing of water to Port-of-Spain from the Maraval River. He introduced the first Education Ordinance. he was a very successful President of the Town Council, as evidenced by the usual eulogistic address presented to him by the Municipality on his leaving Trinidad.

The portrait in the Town Hall was painted by a local artist, E.D. Faure, but there is no record of when it was done. The artist was a Councillor of the Municipality. This portrait is not standing the ravages of time very well, and, after its comparatively few years of existence, is showing evident sings of decrepitude and decay, unlike the other pictures by its side on the walls. It is to be feared that it won't have a long life.

EXPEDITION TO ATTACK ANGOSTURA SEEN IN GULF OF PARIA

This is but barely a note regarding those stormy times when the Republic of Venezuela was then in the throes of the revolution which ended in the formation of the Republic in 1821.

The following has been communicated to a most respectable Mercantile House in this Town, in a letter dated Trinidad, 13th February:– 'The Expedition which sailed some time back from Cumana, destined against the Cronoko, has at last arrived in the Gulph, and was seen yesterday on its way to the mouth of the river:– it consists of 25 sail (all small craft) and about 500 men. – They expect to be joined by great numbers, and there is every probability of their succeeding in the attack of the City of Angostura, and the Province of Guiana.'

Barbados Mercury and Bridge-Town Gazette,
10th March, 1812.

The original manuscript of Franklin's Papers was made available to us by Olga Mavrogordato.

THE STORY OF ST. ANNES

Compiled by Candyce Kelshall

The Saint Ann's valley has a most colourful history. It is particularly so because it even had a very small part to play in an event which at the time, almost brought a declaration of war between France and England. There are essentially two families who figure most prominently in the history of the valley these are the de Mallevault and the Peschiers families.

During the early 1930's the Coblentz estate in St. Ann's was in the words of K.S. Wise, limited to the spacious house at Coblentz and surrounded by a comparatively small piece of land. When first established however, it was a large and profitable estate covering a considerable amount of this valley. It included part of the Fondes Amandes and Cascade Valleys and lands now occupied by the St. Ann's Mental Hospital, the Errol Park area, part of the Government House lands and the present Coblentz House and gardens.

It was in the year 1794 that this estate was developed and the land cleared and planted. This was due to the enterprise and energy of a French Royalist from Martinique Monsieur de Mallevault, captain of the French Frigate Calypso, which boasted 32 guns. The Frigate was stationed in Martinique at the time and it was common practice for captains of vessels to own and work thriving estates ashore of the island in which they were based. When revolutionary troubles broke out in Martinique in 1793, the Aristocratic party had decided not to attempt to oppose the forces sent by French Republican .

As a result of this decision, Monsieur de Behague, the French Governor of Martinique, retired to Grenada while the Vicomte de Riviere, the Admiral of the French Squadron and Commander of the Ship La Firme; 74 guns and Monsieur de Mallevault in the Calypso and Monsieur D'Ache in the Frigate, Mareschal de Castries, took their ships to the island of Trinidad.

Monsieur de Mallevault lost all his properties in Martinique during the revolutionary disturbances. However he transpoted to Trinidad a quantity of settlers, mostly from the French colonies, particularly after the French Revolution. The terms of the Cedula of Population of 1783 encouraged foreign persons to settle in Trinidad provided that they were subjects of nations friendly to the Spanish Crown, were of the Roman Catholic persuasion and would take an oath of loyalty to the Crown of Spain. Those qualifying would each be granted four and two-sevenths fanegas (32 acres) of land and half of that amount for every negro or coloured slave they introduced into the Island.

This picture entitled 'The Doo Di Doo Bush' or 'Which is thief' by Richard Bridgens. This drawing depicts a ceremony by which an obeah man extracts the truth from a fellow slave. — Tom Cambridge Collection.

He therefore took the opportunity to transport his family and his property to Trinidad with the intention of taking advantage of the exceptional terms offered to colonists by the cedula of 1783. On arrival in Port of Spain Monsieur de Mallevault pursued his intention of settling in Trinidad and after careful examination of various lands available in the country, applied for a grant of land in the St. Ann's valley.

Together with the Compte de Rieviere and the other French officers, he also offered his ship for service to the Spanish crown. Shortly after this the officers learned of resistance to the republicans and left Trinidad in an effort to join forces with Admiral Gardners' British fleet which was enroute to capture the French islands. The British offered protection to ships of war sailing under the old French royalist flag.

A plan to attack the island on the 18th June in conjunction with royalists on the island was foiled and the British made arrangements to assist the royalists and escape the wrath of the republicans. The British ships took off 600 people including people of colour and slaves and landed them at Barbados. The French ships, La Firme, Calypso and Mareschal de Castries, carried 1,000 people from Bay St. Anne in Martinique to the island of Trinidad.

Some of these people managed to obtain small parcels of land in the St. Ann's valley, hence the reason for its name Monsieur de Mallevault having returned succeeded in obtaining his original request of 436 quarrees (about 1395 acres) in St. Ann's mainly in the Fondes Amandes and Cascade Valleys. Much of the land consisted of precipitous slopes extending to the highest ridges of the valleys while some were valuable and fertile vega. To this area other sections of land were added later by purchase from adjacent owners. Due to de Mallevault's service with the Spanish government the management of his property had to be left largely in the hands of his wife, Madame Anne Pinel de Mallevault.

De Mallevault began to realize that he had acquired too large an area of land in the valley and did not have sufficient capital to develop the property. He therefore sold a half share to Monsieur Jean Charles, Baron de Montalembert whose wife was Madame Anne Magdalene Penel du Manoir. This gentleman was also a French royalist who, however, had settled and developed valuable estates in the Island of San Domingo. With the spread of revolutionary troubles to that island many people were forced to leave including the Baron de Montalembert. He transferred all that he had saved of his property in San Domingo to Trinidad and in 1801 joined with Monsieur de Mallevault in developing the Coblentz estate.

In 1802 Monsieur de Mallevault left Trinidad for good and the Baron became the sole owner. Monsieur Auguste Monier de Laguerre was brought to Trinidad to assist in the management while the Baron identified himself closely with the interests of the Island and took an active part in organizing and promoting the Militia.

"COBLENTZ ESTATE, TRINIDAD". This property was originally developed in 1794 by a Monsieur de Mallevault, who, seven years later, sold our to Monsieur Jean Charles, Baron de Montalembert. Coblentz House was situated at the confluence of the St. Ann's and Cascade Rivers, and is said to be named after the German town of the same name, which stands near to the junction of the Moselle and the Rhine. The Great House at Coblentz in the St. Ann's Valley, dates back to the 1870's. In those days it was the property and residence of Capt. the Hon. John Bell-Smythe; from him it passed to his brother-in-law, Leon Agostini, who made many improvements and in 1880 entertained Prince Albert and Prince George, sons of the Prince of Wales. The property was later owned by Leon Centeno and in 1900 by Mrs. Beatrice Gregg. In 1925, she in turn, sold it to Sir George Huggins who cultivated a beautiful collection of orchids.

The year 1803 proved to be very fatal for the Coblentz estate as the Baron de Montalembert lost 70 out of 150 slaves in a period of nine months; an unprecedented mortality which led to a strong suspicion of the use of poison. In 1804 Colonel Hislop, the Governor, commissioned Mr. St. Hilaire Begorrat, a member of the Council of Government and Monsieur Louis Francois Sergent, a French Notary from Martinique to enquire into the circumstances of this tragedy at Coblentz estate. Eventually the principal driver, the hospital orderly and three slaves of the estate were convicted and executed. During the enquiry it became known that amongst the slaves on the estate were some who had been brought by Monsieur de Mallevault with him from his estates in Martinique, where in 1793 a similar excessive mortality had occurred and the use of poison also strongly suspected.

In this report the property is described as one of the most healthy, airy and well watered in the Island of Trinidad. As long ago as 1794, in less than six months Monsieur de Mallevault had lost a number of slaves at Coblentz the cause of which had never been definitely discovered. In 1802 the Baron de Montalembert had imported 150 well seasoned slaves from Jamaica and for six months all had been well. Later on, however, this excessive mortality had occurred again in spite of all the attention and treatment by the best physicians and special domestic care. During this same period the slaves on the neighbouring estates were quite healthy and well.

The Commissioners went on to report 'Every experienced planter knows that the negro doctor obeah-men are nothing but poisoners who profit by the ignorance and credulity of their comrades. They sell them some insignificant powders to which they attribute miraculous virtues and after carrying on this trade for some time to acquire reputation, always finish by selling poisons extracted from plants with which they are well acquainted and can always find. The police can never be too vigilant of these sort of doctors as they are dangerous from their principles and from the consequences they produce.'

The loss of these slaves at Coblentz is reported to have brought the Baron de Montalembert to the brink of ruin with little hope of recovering his financial position. The records certainly show that shortly afterwards (1806) he sold his town house in St. James Street (now the section of Frederick Street from Brunswick Square to Park Street) and by 1808 he had sold large portions of his property in St. Ann's Valley. In this same year, 1808, the Baron died and the estate passed into the hands of his son René who was a Captain in the 69th Regiment of the British Army. Monsieur Auguste Monier de Laguerree carried on the management of this property as Attorney for the heir and continued to sell out portions and realise the capital value of the estate.

The property consisted of five separate sections. The original grant included the Fondes Amandes Estate at the mouth of that part of the St. Ann's Valley and the St. Elizabeth Estate at the mouth of the Cascade Valley.

The second large landowner in the Cascade/St. Ann's area was Henri Peschier, who originally settled in Grenada but was forced to leave that island due to a series of misfortunes that caused unrest on the island. Grenada was politically unsettled and this situation was exacerbated by the effects of a scourge of bachac ants which devastated the Grenadian sugar plantations in 1770. By this time Henri Peschier had decided to try and seek his fortune elsewhere due to his building

disenchantment with Grenada. With hopes of finding a new home Peschiers cast his eyes southward towards the large and under-developed Spanish island of Trinidad.

No doubt Henry was influenced in this by a fellow resident of Grenada, Philippe Rose Roume de St. Laurent. At the time he was taking a great interest in Trinidad and encouraging settlers to migrate there and at the same time trying to persuade the Spanish Government to open the Island to these settlers on more liberal terms than before. His efforts were finally rewarded when the Spanish Crown issued its famous Cedula of Population in 1783.

Spain had done little to develop the island and in 1777 five years before the Peschiers arrived and 250 years of so called colonization the population of Trinidad was a mere three thousand, four hundred and thirty-two persons. By 1797 the population had risen to seventeen thousand, seven hundred and eighteen and this increase after only 20 years was mainly due to the Cedula.

However, before the Cedula of 1783, the Spanish Crown had, as early as 1766, passed legislation permitting foreign immigration into the island under certain restrictions, in form somewhat similar to the terms of the Cedula of 1783. As a result of this legislation in 1782, the Governor, Don Martin de Salaveria, on behalf of King Charles IV granted Henry Peschier, his wife Celeste Rose and his widowed mother-in-law, Marie Madeleine de Beltgens, various parcels of land on the island.

Henry received lands at Pointe-a-Pierre along with fifty-six quarrees and eight hundred and sixty-seven square paces (approximately 180 acres) to the north of Port of Spain; his mother-in-law was also granted land at Pointe-a-Pierre as well as sixteen and eleven-eighteenth quarrees (approximately 53 acres) in St. Anns, immediately to the north of Henry's grant, while his wife received another twelve and a half quarrees to the north of her mother's grant.

The 1780's must have been difficult years for Henry, having had to clear the lands, plant the cane, construct factories for the processing of his sugar and build quarters for his labour as well as a home for his family; but the hardest year of all for him must have been 1786, when his two eldest sons died, aged thirteen and fourteen respectively. Unfortunately, Henry did not live to enjoy the fruits of his labour as he died in 1791, shortly after the death of his mother-in-law, the Dowager Marquise de Beltgens.

It would appear that up to the time of Henry's death the de Beltgens-Peschier lands at St. Anns, which had been worked as a single sugar plantation called 'Paradise', had been a successful venture. After the death of the Marquise, her land in St. Anns was bought by the Baron de Montalembert and afterwards ownership passed to his son Mark René and the Abbe de la Quarree and was known as 'Hollandais'.

The years immediately following the death of Henry could not have been easy for his widow, a mother of seven, the eldest Elizabeth aged sixteen the youngest Marie Celestine, just one year old. Apart from her own problems, the widow obviously could see the political situation in Trinidad steadily deteriorating. The island was inundated by the French, royalist and republican, both sides seeking asylum from the confused state in the French West Indian island that had developed as a result of the French Revolution, and these two factions were constantly warring amongst themselves and flouting the authority of Spain. Therefore, Celeste Peschier must have been very relieved when British forces under

Abercromby invaded the Island on the 18th February of 1797, and even more so in 1802, when the Island was ceded to Great Britain, as she had already lived most of her adult life under British rule while resident in Grenada.

It was probably in 1795 that Celeste Rose Peschier was joined in Trinidad by her sister, Elizabeth Rose Peschier, the widow of Jean Peschier, who brought along her children with her, one of whom, Joseph, would one day marry the youngest daughter of Celeste Rose, Marie Celestine Peschier.

The widow Elizabeth Peschier acquired lands in St. Anns on which she built her home and portions of these lands remained as the property of her descendants for many generations.

Following the death of Celeste Rose Peschier in 1817, her heirs sold the two parcels of land which comprised the fifty-six quarrees granted to Henry Peschier, to the Illustrious Cabildo by Registered Deed No. 1219/1817 for the sum of six thousand pounds currency. This was to be paid in three instalments of two thousand pounds each over the years 1817 to 1819; but excluding a small portion containing six thousand, six hundred square feet 'in which the ancestors of the said Family of Peschier are interred.'

Two years afterwards the Illustrious Cabildo made another purchase, this time from the Baron de Montalembert and the Abbe de la Quarree of 'Hollandais' estate of approximately fifty-three acres for the sum of one thousand, six hundred and sixty-one pounds and 2 shillings.

In order to regularize the situation, Sir Ralph Woodford in 1825 had these two portions of land, which today comprise the Queen's Park Savannah, transferred from the ownership of the Illustrious Cabildo to H.M. The King.

The old Peschier home was renovated and became the residence of Woodford and remained as the residence of successive governors for many years, until it was destroyed by fire in 1867. This building was situated a little to the south of the building that is now known as President's House. The Peschier family's association with St. Anns did not end here however, because Francis Peschier the son of Jean and Elizabeth Rose was appointed Commandant of St. Anns by Sir Ralph Woodford.

The Commandant of a district was a man with wide ranging powers and authority. He was the chief and sole magistrate and was at the same time police justice of the peace and administrator of his district, charged with the return of population and property and the collection of taxes. He held petty sessions and had the power of fining and condemning to prison. He also acted as coroner.' Francis must have been a very capable man and highly thought of by Sir Ralph Woodford, a man who would not suffer fools gladly. On 1823 he was further honoured when he was appointed a member of the Council of Government by Woodford, a post he held until December 1833, when he resigned at the age of seventy years.

He was succeeded by Philip D. Souper, who was the owner of a property in that Quarter called 'The Hermitage', which in 1942 became the home of Joseph Peschier's great-great-grand-daughter, Audrey Jardine and her family.

Francis was a very staunch member of the Roman Catholic faith. His devotion to the Roman Church is evident when it is seen that in 1814 he was appointed by Governor Woodford as a member of a committee to safeguard certain rights and privileges of that Church in the island, and again, in 1844, when he acted as a pall bearer at the funeral of the Right Reverend Dr. MacDonnell, Bishop of Olympus and Vicar Apostolic of the British West Indies.

After relinquishing the post of Commandant of St. Anns and retrial from the Council of Government, he remained active as a planter until his death at the advanced age of eighty-nine years. He had been the part owner of 'Plein Palais' estate in the quarter of Pointe-a-Pierre, along with his youngest brother, Charles Peschier. At the time of his death he also owned property in St. Anns, adjacent to the Governor's residence. It was bounded on the south, while on the east by the St. anns Road, and on the north by what became known as St. Anns Avenue. The driveway that led to the house from St. Anns Road is now known as La Fantasie Road.

Sources
P.G.L. Borde's *'History of the Island of Trinidad Under the Spanish Government'*, Vol. II.
K.S. Wise, *'Historical Sketches'*.

1813. A plot was secretly laid in Trinidad for the liberation of Columbia (Venezuela). Señor Santiago Marino, with a wealthy planter named Manuel Valdez, J.B. Bideau, two of the Bermudez family, Pial, Armurio, Azcue and a few others, collected a sum of money and without the knowledge of the local government gathered and armed wit muskets some 200 volunteers. Preparations were made to cross the gulf on or about 6th January.

1814. The English language was first introduced to the courts of the colony on January 1st. Spanish lawyers, however, were permitted to address the court in their own language.

From August to December as a result of disturbances on the South American mainland, many fugitives fled from the wrath of Spanish Royalists to Trinidad. In an enquiry before Parliament it was charged against Sir Ralph that he had denied admission to a great number of these fugitives, causing them to turn back and be butchered by their enemies, but His Excellency had no difficulty in disproving this charge.

1815. The foundation stone of the Church of St. Joseph was laid by the Governor on 18th March.

In a proclamation of 7th November, 1815, a law was passed requiring landowners to own at least one slave for every five quarrés (16 acres) of land under pain of forfeiture. This proclamation also enforced payment of five shillings, quit rent, for each quarré of land.

The News Room was opened.

1816. Sir Ralph Woodford laid the foundation stone of the Roman Catholic Cathedral on 26th March and that of Trinidad Cathedral on 30th May.

1817. The Eastern Market was built by the Cabildo.
Dr. O'Connor arrived in the colony as Assistant Surgeon to the Artillery stationed at Fort George.

Trinidad, the neighbouring islands and part of South America were ravaged by an epidemic of yellow fever.

1818. The Church of St. Joseph was consecrated on 26th March. On 1st May the greater part of San Fernando (so called by Chacon in honour of the Prince Infante of Austrias — born in Madrid on 1784) was destroyed by fire. The damage was very substantial, rendering many persons homeless and causing great suffering to estate owners who through the destruction of their warehouses were obliged to stock their produce in the open. A liberal subscription was raised in Port of Spain but little if any of the money collected ever reached the sufferers: it was afterwards discovered that the person in whose charge the sums were left for distribution had used it for his own ends.

1819. During April of this year a detachment of about 100 of the Militia, under Captain Taylor, was sent into the woods in search of a maroon camp formed by runaway slaves.

Three of the slaves were shot and about 25 captured when the camp was discovered to the east of Mount Tamana. Another camp was found during the following month and 27 more runaways were captured.

Historical notes from H.C. Pitts 100 Years Together.

Sir Ralph Woodford Governor of Trinidad 1813-1828. Woodford's Government House was once the home of the Peschier family. After being acquired it was remodelled. Bridgens who might have had a hand at it describes it thus:

This estate is situated about half a mile from Port of Spain, the capital of the colony, at the foot of the picturesque chain of hills which run along the Northern side of the Island. Being the official residence of the Governor, it possesses on that account a claim to notice, which it does not merit from any superiority in the style of architecture of its buildings. The grounds are beautifully wooded, and the garden contains fine specimens of the choicest plants brought from the most distant parts of the world. The collection has been formed under the direction of the late Sir Ralph Woodford, and their culture is superintended by Mr. Lockhart.

A few notices may enable the reader to understand better the objects in view. On the left is seen a colonnade, or portice, which leads to the principal entrance. This affords an agreeable shade during the heat of the day, and commands a view of the Circular, which is the favourite drive of the inhabitants of Trinidad. The more lofty part of the house in the background is occupied as bed-rooms. The advanced portion in the centre are the public reception rooms of the Governor. In the drawing-room are the portraits of Sir Ralph Abercrombie, General Picton, Colonel Young, General Hislop and Sir Ralph Woodford, the two latter by Sir Thomas Lawrence. A portion of the low continuation towards the right, open at the sides to admit a free circulation of air, is a dining room, or hall, which is agreeably refreshed by the constantly falling water of a handsome fountain in the angle formed here with the body of the house. Conveniently adjoining, a more lofty building contains the kitchen, servant's hall, &c., a covered gallery leads thence to a Chinese bath on the extreme right of the spectator. Nearly the whole of these buildings are constructed of wood, which from its lightness and tenacity, is found to resist better than stone the frequent violent earthquakes to which most of the Islands are subject. This advantage, however, is nearly counter-balanced by the facility with which the walls and roof absorb and transmit the intolerable heat of a West Indian sun, for ever precluding the delightful coolness enjoyed in the more solid structures of other climates.
Richard Bridgens 1828.

1823. Sir Ralph Woodford returned to the colony on 18th February. A slave named Isifore was tried and convicted for the murder of a man called Boatswain. The trial was remarkable because it was the first to be held here in an open court. Place was set aside for newspaper reporters but the gentlemen of the local Press very seldom availed themselves of this favour for many years.

A tread-mill, the first machine of its kind in the West Indies, was set to work in Trinidad.

Trinity Cathedral was consecrated on 25th May, Trinity Sunday.
Historical notes from H.C. Pitts 100 Years Together.

An excerpt taken from 'Six Months in the West Indies',
Henry Coleridge

We weighed anchor with the morning breeze, and stood down gently before its refreshing breath to the modern capital of the colony. I shall not be weak enough to attempt a detailed description of the enchanting scenery which presented itself to us; nothing but painting could hope even faintly to convey an image of it to the inhabitants of the Temperate Zone. Its parts may be just mentioned, and the imaginations of my readers may combine and colour them as they please, sure that, let them conceive as deeply and as richly as they may, they will never attain to an adequate notion of the unspeakable loveliness of the original. The Gulf of the purest ultramarine, just wreathed into a smile and no more; on the right hand the mountains of Cumana with their summits lost in the clouds; on the left the immense precipices of Trinidad covered to the extremest height with gigantic trees which seemed to swim in the middle ether; the margin fringed with the evergreen mangroves, which were here hanging with their branches bathed in the water, and there themselves rising out of the midst of the soft waves; behind us the four mouths of the Dragon

SIX MONTHS

IN

THE WEST INDIES

IN

1825

HENRY NELSON COLERIDGE

SECOND EDITION
WITH ADDITIONS

LONDON
JOHN MURRAY, ALBEMARLE STREET

MDCCCXXVI

Above: Title page from 'Six Months in the West Indies', H.N. Coleridge, 1825. The extract at left is taken from that book.

Below: A view of Port of Spain painted by Richard Bridgens in the 1820's from the Tom Cambridge Collection. What follows is a description of a visit to Trinidad by a young English gentleman who was a guest of the governor Sir Ralph Woodford in 1825, and travelled to various parts of the island.

of Columbus with the verdant craggy isles between them: before us Port of Spain with its beautiful churches, the great Savannah, and the closing hills of Montserrat. Meanwhile the Eden gracefully bent beneath the freshening wind, (no other ship should ever sail on this lake of Paradise;) the long dark canoes glanced by us with their white sails almost kissing the sea, and enormous whales ever and anon lifted their monstrous bodies quite out of the water in strange gambols, and falling down created a tempest around them, and shot up columns of silver foam. We came to anchor two miles from shore, and had a boat race in the evening.

Port of Spain is by far the finest town I saw in the West Indies. The streets are wide, long, and laid out at right angles; no house is now allowed to be built of wood, and no erection of any sort can be made except in a prescribed line. There is a public walk embowered in trees and similar in all respects to the Terreiro in Funchal, and a spacious market place with a market house or shambles in excellent order and cleanliness. The Spanish and French females, their gay costume, their foreign language, and their unusual vivacity give this market the appearance of a merry fair in France. The Protestant church is beautifully situated, with a large inclosed lawn in front of it, which is surrounded on two sides by the best houses in the town. The church itself is one of the most elegant and splendid things in the empire; it is wainscotted with the various rich woods of the island, and the pews are arranged with not more regularity than with a liberal consideration of the feelings of the coloured people. These last sit in the area towards the western end, and the difference of their accommodation from that of the whites is scarcely perceptible. This circumstance is creditable to the colony, and might well be imitated in some other of the islands. There are no aisles, the roof sweeping in an elliptical arch from side to side; the altar, the western door, the organ and staircase, are all in a corresponding style of richness and propriety. It is more than worthy of the town, as it now is; it will be fit for it when it has become a city. When viewed from without it seems to want height, and though they say it cannot be better than it is, I must own I think the coup d'oeil of the building and Port of Spain itself would be much improved by a greater elevation of the tower. There wold be no impiety in such a thing here as in Barbados, for the hurricanes have never ventured so low as Trinidad. In another part of the town is an unfinished church for the Romanists; there is no roof as yet, but what is perfected is of even a still more costly and exquisite character than our own. The lateral walls certainly appear too thin to be able to support any weight laid upon them, but Abbé goffe has no fears on that head, and the facetious Ab. is a competent judge. At present the Romanish serv. is enacted in a very rude chapel of wood, from which they are obliged during Lent to extend awnings into the street to afford a temporary receptacle for the worshippers who crowd in from the country.

The Boiling House on a sugar estate by Richard Bridgens.
— Tom Cambridge Collection.

St. Anne's the residence of Sir Ralph Woodford, stands on a very gentle slope about half a mile from the town; the mountain forests rise almost immediately behind it, whilst the lawn and shrubbery give much of an English air to the whole place. There are some rare and valuable plants here, introduced by the governor, such as the nutmeg, which was flourishing in great vigor, the cinnamon and the clove. The nutmeg is a tree, and uncommonly beautiful; the others were bushes. The house, though plain, is beyond measure comfortable, and it will be some time before I forget the luxury of its matchless bath. The town, the church and the gulf lie in sight, and within a mile is the entrance of the famous valley of Maraval, and still farther on the coast the less celebrated but hardly less beautiful vale of Diego Martin with its single silk-cotton tree prevailing over it in desolate majesty. I hope that noble ornament of the place will never be cut down; it is but one, and let it remain amidst the softer cultivation around it, to show hereafter what harvests the earth once bore upon its bosom there. At about twenty feet from the ground the trunk of the silk-cotton tree diverges into buttresses of great prominence and size, so that if a covering were thrown over them, a very tolerable set of barracks might be organized for one man each round the enormous stem.

I live to recollect the days which I spent in Trinidad, and would fain record some of their events whilst the impressions which they made are still fresh upon my mind. Gentle reader, whilst thou pokest thy coal fire, and cleavest to the grate as if Satan were at thy back, think, O! think of the mercury at 94° of Fahrenheit!

On a morning of such a temper, the elixir cup of coffee being first duly quaffed, we, that is to say, the governor, the bishop, the lordship's two chaplains, your poor bookmaker and an honest man, Sainthill by name, started in landau and four, and in gig and one for La Pastora the residence of Antonio Gómez. First we stopped at the governor's grog shop, the trival name of a crystal spring which has been taught to gush forth from a rock on the way-side into a neat stone bason, whereat under the shade of a spreading evergreen the dark ladies of the country rejoice to lave their dusty feet, and indue the snowy stocking and the coloured shoe or ever they enter the gallant streets of Puerto de España. Then we rambled on between hedges and trees, now in lanes and now in roads, leaving the little village of San Juan on the right, and crossing many a clear and brawling brook till we arrived, well toasted, at the sweet spot where we were to breakfast.

Antonio Gómez' plantation of cacao is one of the finest in the island. It lies on a very slight declivity at the bottom of a romantic amphi-theatre of woody mountains. His house, together with the works of the estate, is situated at the edge of the trees, and a quieter or more lovely spot no hermit ever chose to count his beads in for eternity! The cocoa, which grows from ten to fifteen feet in height, is a delicate plant, and like a lady, cannot bear exposure to the direct rays of the sun; for this reason a certain portion of the wood is thinned and appropriated, the tall and umbrageous trees are left, and these form with their interwoven branches and evergreen leaves a sun-proof screen, under cover of which the cacao flourishes in luxuriance and preserves her complexion. At a distance the plantation has the appearance of a forest advantageously distinguished by the long bare stems of tropic growth being shrouded with the rich green of the cacaos below, and here and there

MARROW ON TOAST
Boil some marrow bones and remove marrow. Cook in a little butter with salt, pepper and a crushed clove of garlic or a piece of onion. Serve very hot on crisp freshly made bread.

burning and flashing with the flame-coloured foliage of
the glorious Bois Immortel. One main road led through
the plantation, and numberless avenues diverged from it
to every other part. These alleys, as well as the whole
plantation itself, were fringed with coffee bushes, which
with their dark Portugal laurel leaves, jasmine blossoms
and most subtle and exquisite perfume refreshed the
senses and delighted the imagination. Water flowed in
abundance through the wood, and gentle breezes fanned
us as we sauntered along. If ever I turn planter, as I have
often had thoughts of doing, I shall buy a cacoa
plantation in Trinidad. The cane is, no doubt, a noble
plant, and perhaps crop time presents a more lively and
interesting scene than harvest in England; but there is so
much trash, so many ill-odoured negroes, so much scum
and sling and molasses that my nerves have sometimes
sunken under it. 'The sweet negociation of sugar,' as old
Ligon calls it, is indeed a sweaty affair; and me thinks it
were not good for that most ancient and most loyal
colony, Barbados, that her sons should often visit the
sylvan glades, the deep retreats, the quiet and the
coolness of the cacao plantations in Trinidad. But
planters are not poetical. Sugar can surely never be
cultivated in the West Indies except by the labour of
negroes, but I should think white men, creoles or not,
might do all the work of a cacao plantation. The trouble
of preparing this article for exportation is actually
nothing when compared with the process of making
sugar. But the main and essential difference is, that the
whole cultivation and manufacture of cacao is carried on
in the shade. People must come between Cancer and
Capricorn to understand this.

I was well tired when we got back to Antonio's
house. What a pleasant breakfast we had, and what a
cup of chocolate they gave me by way of a beginning! So
pure, so genuine, which such a divine aroma exhaling
from it! Mercy on me! what a soul-stifling compost of
brown sugar, powdered brick and rhubarb have I not
swallowed in England instead of the light and exquisite
cacao!

I love the Spanish ladies to my heart; after my own
dear and beautiful countrywomen I think a señorita
would be my choice. Their dress is so gay yet so modest,
their walk so noble, their manners so quiet, so gentle
and so collected. They have none of that undue vivacity,
that much ado about nothing, that animal conceit which
disgusts me in the Gauls. A Spanish woman, whether her
education has been as finished or not, is in her nature a
superior being. Her majestic forehead, her dark and
thoughtful eyes assure you that she hath communed with
herself. She can bear to be left in solitude; yet what a
look is hers, if she is animated by mirth of love! Then,
like a goddess, she launches forth that subtle light from
within,she is poetical if not a poet, her imagination is
high and chivalrous, and she speaks the language in
which romance was born. It is a favorite subject of
exultation with me that twenty-two millions of people
speak English or Spanish in the New World. Their
grammar and accent are perfectly pure in Trinidad, but,
like all the South Americans, they have deflected from
the standards of Castilian pronunciation.

Soledad! thou wilt never read this book; few of those
who will can ever know thee, and I shall never see thee
again on this side of the grave. Therefore I write thy
name whilst I yet remember thy face and hear thy voice,
thou sweet and ingenious girl! And so having shaken
hands with kind Antonio and his lady, with Patricia, and
Dolores, and Lorenza, and all of them, we mounted our
horses and took our leave.

El Honorable Don Antonio Gómez.

We returned by another route through the woods,
ascended a narrow pass called the Saddle, if I recollect
right, and came in at the head of Maraval. We rode quite
through this most lovely valley, and got back to St.
Anne's tired, delighted and burnt to brick dust.

La Pastora Estate House, Santa Cruz. Originally the property and residence of Don Antonio Gomez, Senior Judge at the time of Governor Sir Ralph Woodford, 1813 to 1828. La Pastora was later acquired by Hippolyte Borde, Esq.

1823

CONSECRATION OF TRINITY CHURCH

The solemn and interesting services in connection with the consecration of our new Church to the Most Holy Trinity took place on Sunday last, being Trinity Sunday, the 23rd May. As early as 9 o'clock, the temporary building erected for the reception of the ladies and public bodies and leading to the west entrance was fully occupied. At half past ten, the Illustrious Board of Cabildo proceeded from Cabildo Hall to the new church. . . . .

There together with the members of His Majesty's Council, and the public officers, drawn up on the right and left of the principal entrance to the Church, they awaited the arrival of His Excellency the Governor and the clergy. His Excellency, Sir James Ralph Woodford, accompanied by the Revd. J.H. David Evans, garrison chaplain, and the Revd. George Cummins, arrived about a quarter before eleven, in His Excellency's state carriage, and four, with his servants in their state liveries, and escorted by a detachment of the Royal Trinidad Light Dragoons. A procession was at once formed to enter the Church as follows:-

The Alguacils
The Chief of Police
The Alcaldes of Barrios
The Illustrious Board of Cabildo
(in the order above given)
The Clerk
The Consecrating Clergyman
The Assisting Officiating Clergy
The Public Officers
His Majesty's Council
The Alguacil Mayor
His Excellency the Governor, Sir Jas. R. Woodford
The Governor's A.D.C.'s and suite
The Beadle
The Keeper
The Beadle
The Architect
The Churchwardens

His Excellency and members of His Majesty's Council were conducted to the pews by Henry Graham, Esq., and the Clergy to the vestry by George Sherlock, Esq. (Churchwardens). A large, respectable and very numerous congregation, to whom tickets had been issued by the Churchwardens, then assembled and took their seats, which were all decorated with evergreens in honour of the occasion.
(28th May, 1823)

1824

MARTIAL LAW FOR CHRISTMAS

Agreeably to custom in this colony at this season of the year, martial law, by a proclamation contained on the outer part of this paper, was this afternoon declared to be in force from three o'clock. . . . .
(24th Dec. 1824).

. . . . .In the days of fathers, West Indians, in imitation of their countrymen, in Great Britain, indulged in the barbarous customs of those times and made the holy festival of Christmas one continuous scene of noisy mirth, revelry and inebriety. Martial law was then obviously necessary to control the white population and prevent a total relaxation of military discipline . . . The times since then have changed. The noise, the mirth, the revelry, and the inebriety are now found chiefly amongst the slaves and lower classes . . . Martial law has ceased to be necessary for the purposes for which it was originally instituted, but it has become necessary under the new and perilous circumstances in which we are now placed . . . . By this proclamation, every person is bound to deliver himself up to be enrolled, or in default is liable to be condemned to 6 months' hard labour on the public works and then to be banished from the island as a person inimical to the peace and good government thereof. Every owner of a house is made responsible for the good behaviour of the inmates; every landlord for the good conduct of his tenants; . . . . exhibiting a state of society in a British colony during a period of profound peace not to be paralleled in English history since the occupation of the country by the Danes. . . . .
(29 December, 1824.)
Port of Spain Gazette. Special Centenary Issue.

The Circular Road as it passes in front of the Champs Elysées estate, Maraval. A watercolour by Captain Wilson 1837 — Tom Cambridge Collection.

Everyone who goes to Trinidad, should make a point of visiting the Indian missions of Arima and Savana Grande. They are wholly unlike anything which I had ever seen before, and differ as much from the negro yard on the one hand as they do from an European-built town on the other. The village of Savana Grande consisted chiefly of two rows of houses in parallel lines with a spacious street or promenade between them, over which there was so little travelling that the green grass was growing luxuriantly upon it. Each house is insulated by an interval of ten or fifteen feet on either side; they are large and lofty, and being beautifully constructed of spars of bamboo, and thatched with palm branches, they are always ventilated in the most agreeable manner. A projection of the roof in front is supported by posts, and forms a shady gallery, under which the Indians will sit for hours together in motionless silence. They seem to be the identical race of people whose forefathers Columbus discovered, and the Spaniards worked to death in

Hispaniola. They are short in stature, (none that I saw exceeding five feet and six inches,) yellow in complexion, their eyes dark, their hair long, lank and glossy as a raven's wing; they have a remarkable space between the nostrils and the upper lip, and a breadth and massiveness between the shoulders that would do credit to the Farnese Hercules. Their hands and feet, however, are small-boned and delicately shaped. Nothing seems to affect them like other men; neither joy or sorrow, anger, or curiosity, take any hold of them; both mind and body are drenched in the deepest apathy; the children lie quietly on their mothers' bosoms; silence is in their dwellings and idleness in all their ways. Our party was sufficient of itself to have attracted some attention, even if the Padre had not welcomed us with a furious salute from his two tin-kettle bells. The Indians were all summoned forth, and the alcalde and the regidores stood in front with their wands of office. These were nearly the only signs of life which they displayed; they neither smiled or spoke or moved, but stood like mortals in a deep trance having their eyes open. The governor gave a piece of money to each of the children, which was received with scarcely the smallest indication of pleasure of gratitude by them or their parents. They were much more completely clothed than the negroes; the decency of the female dress was conspicuous, and both the maiden's and the mother's bosom were modestly shrouded from the gaze of man. The bestial exposure of this sacred part of a woman's form is the most disgusting thing in the manners of the West Indian slaves. The planters might and ought to correct this.

The amazing contrast between these Indians and the negroes powerfully arrested my attention. Their complexions do not differ so much as their minds and dispositions. In the first, life stagnates; in the last, it is tremulous with irritability. The negroes cannot be silent; they talk in spite of themselves. Every passion acts upon them with strange intensity; their anger is sudden and furious, their mirth clamorous and excessive, their curiosity audacious, and their love the sheer demand for gratification of an ardent animal desire. Yet by their nature they are good-humoured in the highest degree, and I know nothing more delightful than to be met by a group of negro girls, and be saluted with their kind "How d'ye, massa? how d'ye, massa?" their sparkling eyes and bunches of white teeth. It is said that even the slaves despise the Indians, and I think it very probable; the latter are decidedly inferior as intelligent beings. Indeed their history and existence form a deep subject for speculation. The flexibility of temper of the rest of mankind has been for the most part denied to them; they wither under transportation, they die under labour; they will never willingly or generally amalgamate with the races of Europe or Africa; if left to themselves with ample means of subsistence, they decrease in numbers every year; if compelled to any kind of improvement, they reluctantly acquiesce, and relapse with certainty the moment the external compulsion ceases. They shrink before the approach of other nations as it were by instinct; they are now not known in vast countries of which they were once the only inhabitants; and it should almost seem that they have been destined by a mysterious Providence to people a third part of the globe, till in the appointed time the New World should be laid open to the Old, and ceaseless and irresistible stream of population from the East should reach them and insensibly sweep then from off the face of the earth.

Drawing by Richard Bridgens of a woman and child at the 2nd Company Village circa 1820, redrawn by Peter Shim.

*The number of Indians at Savanna Grande, is:

Men	43
Women	56
Boys	64
Girls	66
at Arima . . . Men	60
Women	77
Boys	81
Girls	60
Total	507

The Trinidad Almanac for 1824 states the total amount of Indians in the island thus —

Men	218
Women	234
Boys	222
Girls	219
Total	893

giving an excess of only 13 females over the males, which I believe is not according to the due proportion in countries where population is on the increase.

In this place were assembled by the governor's order a division of free negro settlers, a part of that body of slaves who were excited to insurrection in some of the southern states of the North American Union by a British proclamation during the last war, and upon the ill-success of the expedition against New Orleans, were received on board the squadron commanded by Sir Alexander Cochrane, and finally dispersed about the West Indies, but chiefly, I believe, established in Trinidad. It was a deed mali exempli, and one which may be very easily played off hereafter against ourselves. This settlement comprises about three hundred persons, and a very fine and jovial set of Yankees they are. It happened to rain hard at the time, and the padre of the mission was courteous enough to proffer the use of the chapel, into which accordingly we all entered with one consent. The Americans being after some time tolerably composed, their men on one side and their women and children on the other; the bishop standing before the altar, (the pyx being first duly removed), the padre on the right hand, the chaplains on the left, myself in a corner, los señores regidores, the alcaldes and cacique of the Indians bearing their wands of office, and las señoras their wives with their patient babies, both awaiting in deep resignation the explanation of this mystery, Sir Ralph Woodford, in Windsor uniform, took his Leghorn hat off his head, vibrated his silver-studded Crowther with the grace of a Cicero, and, as the Spaniards say, con gentil donayre y continente, in hunc modum locutus est.

"Silence there! . . . What for you make all dat dere noise? Me no tand dat, me can tell you. I hear that there have been great disturbances amongst you, that you have been quarrelling and fighting, and that in one case there has been a loss of life. Now, me tell you all flat . . . me no allow dat sort of ting . . . me take away your cutlashes, you savey dat? What for you fight? Because you nasty drunk with rum. You ought to be ashamed; you no longer now slave . . .King George have tak you from America, he make you free . . . What den? Me tell you all dis (What for you no make quiet your piccaninny*, you great tall ting dere? . . .) me tell dis . . .if you free, you no idle; you savey dat? You worky, but you worky for yourselves, and make grow noice yams and plantains. . . den your wives all fat, and your piccaninny tall and smooth. You try to make your picnies better and more savey dan yourself. You all stupid . . .what den! no your fault day . . . you not help it. Now but you free, act for yourselves like bukra, and you love your picnies? yes . . . well den, you be glad to send dem to school, make dem read, write, savey counting and able pray God Almighty in good words, when you no savey do so your selves.

Now de bishop is come to do all this; His Majesty King George have sent him from England to take care of you and all of us; he is very must gentleman and he king, you savey, of all de parson. He savey every ting about you, he love you dearly, he come from England across the sea to see your face . . no you den very bad people, if you no obey him? Yes, you very bad, much wicked people if you don't*."

Finierat Woodford; his harangue, of which the above is an imperfect sketch, produced a great effect, and a murmur of applause arose from the assembled Yankees; then the bishop addressed them, and as the governor had laid down the law civiliter, so he spoke to them spiritualiter; his manner was affectionate and impressive, his matter simple and cogent, and he concluded by solemnly blessing in the name of God the whole congregation. The padre was very complimentary in Andalusian, the negroes elated in negro tongue, and the poor dear Indians quiet, and as cognizant of the nature of what was going on as of the proceedings of the House of Commons. It was altogether a strange contrast of different natures and a theme for passing smiles and lasting thoughts.

Amerindian heads drawn by Richard Bridgens at the Mission of Savanna Grande in 1820 and published by him in 1834.

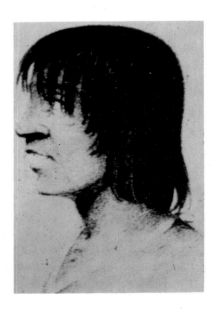

According to appointment at nine the next morning, Mr. Mitchell's house was surrounded by a noisy multitude of men, women and children. Some came to be baptized, some to gossip, and some to be married. Many of the latter brought in their arms smiling arguments that the prayers of the church for fecundity would be superfluous. They all entered the house with perfect nonchalance, roamed about in every part of it, and laughed and grabbed in as unrestrained a manner as they would have done in their own huts. Mrs. Mitchell's parlour, where I had slept, was constituted baptizery and altar. A white cloth was spread on the table, and a large glass vase, filled with pure water, was placed in the middle. After about a quarter of an hour's arduous exertions on the part of the governor and commandant, these light-hearted creatures were reduced to as low a degree of noise, as their natures would admit. The bishop then read the first part of the service, the whole party kneeling on the floor; but when the rite of immersion came to be performed, there had like to have been a riot from the mothers struggling for the honour of first baptism at the bishop's hand. The two chaplains ministered till they screamed, and never did I hear such incessant squalling and screaming as arose from the refractory piccaninnies. I think seventy were baptized and registered, which was the most laborious part of all. We had some difficulty in collecting them for the conclusion of the service, but upon the whole the adult negroes behaved exceedingly well, and displayed every appearance of unfeigned devotion.

And then came Hymen! Bless thine eyes, sweet divinity, how I love thee! Thou that camest so easily to those poor votaries, when wilt thou come to me? When wilt thou with a spark from thy golden torch set fire to political economy, and reduce to ashes the relation which sexagenarians have created between population and the means of subsistence?

About a dozen couples were agreed, but seven or eight more were influenced by the sweet contagion, and struck up a marriage on the spot, as we see done at the ends of the old comedies. One woman, I remember, turned sulky and would not come to the scratch, but Chesapeak her lover was not to be so done; "Now yo savey, Mol," said he, "mee no tand your shim shams; me come to be married, and me will be married; you come beg me when I got another;" still Mol coquetted it; Chesapeak went out, staid five minutes, and, as I am a Christian man, brought in a much prettier girl under his arm, and was married to her forthwith. I have known cases in England, where something of this sort of many conduct would have had a very salutary effect. Now a grand difficulty arose from there being no rings; those in the women's ears were too large by half. Hereupon I took . . .not thy hair, my Eugenia! oh no . . .but a gold hoop which my good father bought for me from a wandering Jew; this I preferred for the service of the sable bridegrooms, and I now wear it as a sort of charm as close as possible to Eugenia's hair. It noosed thirteen couples. I gave away most of the brides; one of them, a pretty French girl of the Romanish faith, behaved very ill; she giggled so much that the clergyman threatened to desist from the ceremony, and her mate, a quiet and devout Protestant, was very angry with her. When she was kneeling after the blessing, I heard her say to her husband, - "diton, Jean! hooka drole manière de se marier! he! he! he!" I'll warrant she leads her spouse a decent life of it.

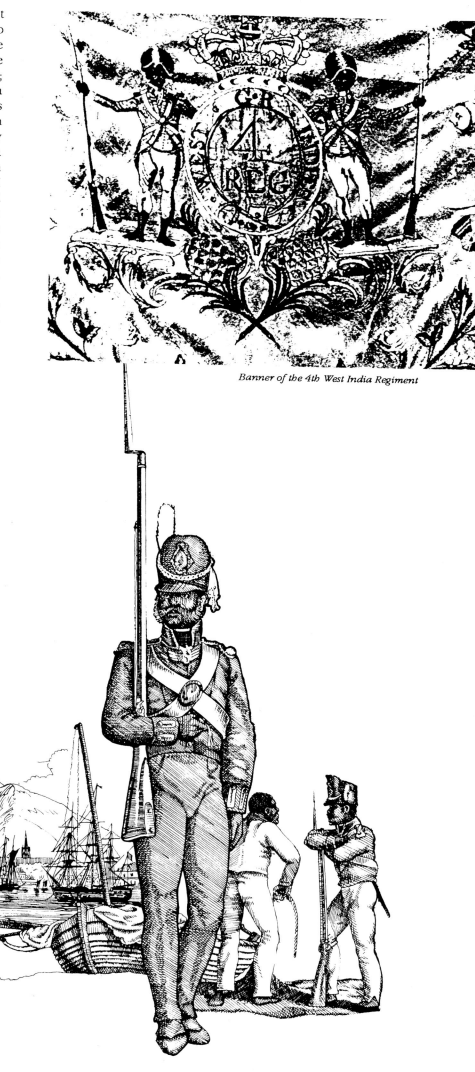

Banner of the 4th West India Regiment

In 1812, War blazed across the the western territories; land-hungry men fought the Red Indian and eventually over the border into Canada. The British, whose forces thinned by war in Europe against Napoleon, raised companies of men, European and Free Black Men, and joined by the Red Indian tribes bordering the Ohio under their last great Warrior Leader, Tecumseh, fought the American Union Armies to a halt.

Before long, the British had occupied Detroit and captured Fort Deer Horn where the city of Chicago now stands.

Out of the war between Britain and its former colony, America, comes an interesting slice of Trinidad and Tobago history. For it was in the year, 1815, that fifty free black men, heroes of that war, arrived in Trinidad from America. The following year, another batch of 34 men, 15 women and 7 children landed; they were members of the military companies which had helped the British in the American war of 1812.

Members of five companies came to settle in Trinidad at the expense of the Colonial Government. One company, the 2nd, is said to have been wrecked off Tobago. The members swam ashore and settled in that island.

The others in Trinidad, named their villages after their respective companies. Today, their descendants still live in these settlements near Princes' Town.

Before coming on the estate, we had been told the general character and disposition of each individual. Among others, we were informed that C., a female, was a personage next to impossible to manage. She appeared to us a clever superior person, with not a disagreeable countenance; neat, and civilized looking. She had been a domestic at one time to a former master; but being in this capacity quite inefficient, she was transferred to the field with her own acquiescence in the change. About ten days after our arrival, while the negroes were holing a piece of canes near the foot of the hill, I suddenly heard a very angry voice, which became louder and louder; but as Mr. C. was in the field, I paid no more attention to it. In the evening, when the driver came up to get his orders for the next day, Mr. C. said, "F., I never say such a woman as that; is she quiet now that she is in the stocks? – "Quiet, massa! no, noting will ever stop her. Massa, she bad too much." – "Can she work, F." – "Yes, for hersel, massa; fine grounds she have; but she'll neber work for you nor any massa; me tink de Jumbee in her." Mr. C said, "Come, we must try; I find kindness won't do, for I've stocks will do." F. shook his head; "Massa, tock neber do good to nigger; dem who make dat new law do very bad, to make massas keep bad heart to niggers." "But why do you suppose that is a sign of keeping bad heart?" "Cause, massa, all da time a nigger is in da tock afroe he be punish, massa heart burn gainst nigger, and nigger heart burn gainst massa, – dat's all bad massa; dem who made dat law no know a we." "But F., those who made that law say, that negroes were often and unjustly and severely flogged; because, at the moment their master was in a passion: and by giving time, they think the master will cool, and the negro repent." – "Bless you, me massa, den de know noting at all about it; for afore time massa had no time for he heart to burn; and nigger neber like noting so bad as for he massa to keep bad heart to him." – "Well, F", I did not make the law. I must keep it, and try whether it will do good or not." – "Me massa, hear me; I know black nigger better eber dan you; it do no good; it do very bad, massa."

To return for a moment to C., the negro who gave rise to this colloquy: in the stocks, or at work, it was all the same to C. she was the torment of everyone, – she poured forth abuse upon her master, the overseer, the driver, and her mother. She often came to sell articles to me, – poultry, fruit, and vegetables; and was very civil and polite. I took no notice of her bad conduct on the estate; whether it was that she had expected I would have done so, and therefore was pleased at my forbearance, I cannot tell; but she always looked graciously upon me.

The cook at this time wished to change for the field; and I proposed to C. to take her place. I thought that, by removing her from those with whom she had been accustomed to quarrel, and by flattering her self-esteem (for to cook well is no small pride in a negro), I might change her character. She accepted the place, and served me faithfully and well; and became, under my eye, a most exemplary person; and she served us until the day we left Laurel-Hill; and cried for days before we went away. I asked her if she would like to go home to England with me? She said, "Yes, misses, me like to see England, if you bring me back." I said, "That is very natural, C.; your mother is here, and all your friends." – "Yes, misses, and me grounds." She might well say "me grounds," for C.'s grounds were indeed a source of riches to her: she had them in beautiful order, and was altogether a money-making personage. She kept a

DOMESTIC MANNERS

AND

SOCIAL CONDITION

OF THE

WHITE, COLOURED, AND NEGRO

POPULATION

OF THE

WEST INDIES.

BY MRS. CARMICHAEL,

FIVE YEARS A RESIDENT IN ST. VINCENT AND TRINIDAD.

Title page of Mrs. Carmichael's account of her visit to Trinidad, the following is an extract from her book during the period of slavery.

" C'est la meme moen perdi gangan moen.
C'est la meme yo blesse mun one moen.
Ambas pons Marabella
C'est la meme moen perdi gangan moen.

Under the Marabella bridge
It's there I lost my grandmother
It's there I lost my grandmother
It's there they wounded my uncle. "

A photograph taken in the 1870's of a freed African slave. Photograph – O. Mavrogordato

complete hackster's shop on the estate; and many, both on Laurel-Hill and the adjoining properties, bought thread, tapes, candle, soap, and pins, &c. from her. She had always plenty of money, and could at any time change a doubloon for me; or, if I was short of a few dollars, C. always produced whatever sum I required at once; I giving her an acknowledgement for the sum borrowed, which she kept until I repaid her, when it was torn up. She had no ostensible husband. I often advised her to marry, and settle like a respectable girl - for, in spite of her temper, she had two great attractions: she had money, and was handsome; and I knew she had many admirers. She would not hear of marriage, however, but said, that "when nigger come good, like white man, den she might marry." She gave dances, and made a great deal of money by them: she paid for everything - supper, liquor, and music, and each negro paid half a dollar for admission. The refreshments were in the house, which was particularly neat; the dance was in front of her house, with seats surrounding a space large enough for the dancing; the musicians being placed at the end. Yet, inconsistent as it must appear, this young woman was a perfect savage in many respects: if any one contradicted her, she was like a frantic person, and always began to bite furiously.

I had told the grown-up negroes, that I should be very happy to see them come up, and hear the children instructed; and some, now and then dropped in; while others were very frequent in their attendance. Among these was C., who listened with great attention. I often tried to convince her how improper her violent conduct was; but she always defended herself; and said, "Misses, when me say bad to you, no curse me:" by which she meant, that if when she abused the other negroes they

A freed African slave. Photograph — O. Mavrogordato.

In the early days of slavery, when the day's labour was done, the gang that had produced the most would sing to announce their success. With big drum and iron beating, they would dance to the work songs of their African forebears. Kaiso! someone shouts, well done!

would not return the abuse, she would sooner restrain her temper. No sooner had we left the estate, than she was as bad as before we had come to Laurel-Hill - no one dared to speak to her. She freed herself, I believe, in 1830, or thereabouts.

I have already, when speaking of the negro population in the first volume of this work, treated upon negro recreations. On looking back to these slight notices, I find that I have yet wherewithal to fill a short chapter upon this subject; which, besides being an interesting one, is not without its importance in devising a plan of instruction and civilization for the negroes. The habits of a people, in their hours of relaxation, may not be barren of a lesson.

It may almost be said, that negro recreation is comprised in the one word, dancing. I have spoken of the entertainments given by negroes, and of the handsome style in which they provide refreshments: but as an every day amusement, the dance is not accompanied by supper, or refreshments; and on these occasions there is little other music than the drum, – which is a barrel, having the top covered with sheep-skin, and tightly fastened down.

Christmas and Easter are the two grand seasons of negro recreation. Before speaking of the feasts of these gala days, let me just notice another recreation of the negro; not an every day, or universal amusement, like dancing, – but one in which he frequently indulges; more, however, from the love of gain, than from the greater pleasure it affords him. I allude to field sports – shooting and running down game. Among the wild animals most commonly the subject of negro prowess are the ramier, the tourterello, the perdrix, the wild boar, the lappe, and the wild deer, all of which are abundant. The wild boar and the lappe of Trinidad are excellent; the deer is, however, greatly inferior to the venison of England or Scotland. I have seen the wild deer so abundant at Laurel-Hill, that, on one occasion, I remember one of them having put its antlers in at the window. They are not the light, graceful, elegant creatures, one sees in the parks of the nobility and gentry at home: – on the contrary, they are tumble down, awkward, calf-looking animals. When a deer is caught, upon a moderate sized estate, which sometimes occurs twice in a week, the person who catches it, sends up a quarter to the master; and sells, or makes use of the rest as he pleases. They also catch the armadillo, and the agouti; both of which are excellent for the table. The armadillo is as white and delicate as a chicken; the agouti very much resembles the hare. In some parts of Trinidad there are wild turkeys, which are considered a great delicacy. All those animals are often caught at night; and on a moonlight night, some one or other of the negroes is always on the look-out. Excepting deer, the master always pays for game to the negro who catches it. I paid a quarter dollar for an agouti, and half a dollar for an armadillo; for a lappe, two bitts per lb.; and for wild boar the same; tourterello, ramiers, and perdrix, from a dollar to a dollar and a half per couple.

Negroes have an inclination for gambling; and pitch and toss is a game for which they have an early predilection; but which I always tried to discourage. Sitting outside their doors, in the fine night of a tropical climate, – cooking, and eating their suppers, telling stories, and singing songs, is also a common negro recreation.

The children, besides dancing, have many games; some of which have a resemblance to those of Britain.

The mask is used as a punishment and preventive of the practice of dirt-eating, a disease peculiar to the Negro, and for which no satisfactory cause has hitherto been assigned. Richard Bridgens 1820.

1827. St. James' Barracks completed on 11th June at a cost of £80,000. Dr. Jean Bertrand Lubet, Surgeon of the Royal Artillery, died on Sunday, 18th October.
Historical notes from H.C. Pitts 100 Years Together.

'Through-the-needle-eye, boy,' I found very common; also 'French and English,' and a game resembling 'the hounds and the hare,' which all little masters and misses in Trinidad know by the name of 'I'm fishing, I'm fishing all night, and what did I catch but a grouper;' and the chase begins.

Let me return to the festival season and its galas. The first Christmas I was at Laurel-Hill, I had an invitation to go and see a ball given by F., as a return from the St. Vincent people, for the civilities of those of Laurel-Hill, upon their arrival on the estate. We had a cold dinner at three o'clock, that our negroes might have the sole use of our kitchen and oven, which were soon filled with good things – hot and cold roast fowls, pork roasted and soused, and plenty of pies, both of meat and of fruit; cakes from St. Joseph's, and fruit in every variety. Mr. C. gave them some wine an porter; besides which, they had bought some. I went about nine o'clock, and found them all well dressed. The prevailing costume was thin muslin, and some had coloured slips on. Shoes were not universal; but many had handsome necklaces and earrings. Their head handkerchiefs were gracefully put on; and the whole was managed with an attention to politeness and decorum, that was certainly very creditable. The music consisted of four female singers, one drum, and three women with calabashes hollowed out, so that a few stones may be put in them; this they flourish up and down, and rattle in the same way as a tambourine. There was no drinking or fighting; they supped very late, and kept it up until near sunrise; and danced the next night, as long, and as merrily elsewhere.

The tin collar is a punishment for drunkness in females'
Richard Bridgens 1820.

1828

DEATH OF SIR RALPH J. WOODFORD
His Excellency Sir Ralph Woodford died on board his Majesty's packet the 'Duke of York', on the 16th May last at 2 a.m., attended by his faithful steward, Mr. Benjamin Combes. The letter of Captain Snell leaves no doubt of the care which that gentleman's high consideration for his illustrious passenger has manifested under this deplorable catastrophe. The bells of both churches have been tolling mournfully since morning. At 12 o'clock minute guns were firing, we believe 49, the number of the years of our deceased Governor; and both churches will be hung with mourning. (26th July, 1828).
Port of Spain Gazette. Special Centenary issue.

THE FIRST CENSUS
Under date of the 21st July, 1826, is set forth in tabular form a concise statement of the results of the first census ever taken in Trinidad. The total number of whites is returned at 3,310, comprising 1,302 males, 1.020 females, 490 boys and 498 girls. Of free blacks there were 14,933; including 4.503 males, 5,076 females, 2,740 boys and 2,674 girls.
There were also 727 Indians; 12 Chinese; 8,225 African slaves and 15,108 creole slaves: total population of 42,262. During the three years 1823-25 there were reported to have been only 2,476 deaths in the Island, an annual number of 828, or, as the compiler of the census returns says, 'only about 2 percent of the total population'; and this included 14 deaths from drowning.
Port of Spain Gazette. Special Centenary issue

Negro Figuranti

A series of drawings of dancing figures by Richard Bridgens in 1820. Note the figure in the top left, he is wearing the Jupe costume worn by slaves both male and female during the earliest times-— Tom Cambridge Collection.

The Free Blacks and People of Colour

Bridget Brereton

From very early in the history of European settlement and colonization in the Caribbean, a new group began to emerge: people of mixed European and African ancestry, the result of sexual contacts between European settlers and visitors and African slaves. These were the people of coloure *(gens de couleur),* many of whom eventually became legally free. In addition there came to be people who were not necessarily of mixed racial origins, people who were definitely black, but who had in one way or another acquired manumission. These were the free blacks *(affranchis).* Together the free blacks and people of colour constituted an increasingly important class in the slave societies of the Caribbean. They were an intermediate group, placed between the whites and the slaves. They were legally free, yet they lacked most of the legal and political rights of free people. As an English Governor put it, they were 'unappropriated people': they did not belong to any one master but as a group they were defined as subordinate to all whites. Neither slave nor free, between black and white, the free blacks and people of colour occupied a difficult, ambivalent position in Caribbean slave society.

Their origins lay in the earliest days of colonization in the Spanish, French and British Caribbean. Once the process of clearing the forest began in earnest, and the establishment of plantations on a large scale began in earnest, hundreds of thousands of African slaves were brought to the Caribbean between the 16th and the 19th centuries. This development was most marked in the British and French colonies from the mid-17th century, less so in the Spanish colonies which did not develop large-scale plantations until the later 18th century. With the arrival of vast numbers of Africans, sexual contacts between them and the Europeans–predominantly male–who came to exploit the new colonies were inevitable. One can say that miscegenation has been a central feature of Caribbean society from those early days

A pure black, 'La Belle Affranchie', 1870.
Photograph — Maureen Hanton.

of Spanish conquest when a new man–the mestizo-was created from Spanish-Amerindian sexual unions. The mulatto was the product of European-African unions.

The people of colour or mulattoes developed in all the Caribbean colonies, but it is, perhaps, in the French Antilles that this class became most characteristic and most important. The Spanish, as the original colonizers of the New World, had long ago begun to produce their own half-caste off-spring, but in the Spanish Caribbean colonies there were relatively few African slaves until the late 18th century or even the 19th. Certainly a class of free coloureds and free blacks had emerged in the British Caribbean colonies by 1780, but it was quite small and not yet of great economic, social or political significance. Perhaps because most Englishmen in the Caribbean were transients, longing only to return to Britain, perhaps because of their more rigid racial attitudes, the growth of the free coloured class was slower in the colonies under their domination than in the French islands.

By contrast, Frenchmen who emigrated to the major Caribbean colonies of France-St. Domingue (Haiti), Martinique, Guadeloupe, Cayenne, St. Lucia, Grenada and Dominica (up to 1763)–intended to become true settlers. They put down roots, they built comfortable estate houses and civilized towns, they created lively social and cultural institutions. They became *Creoles.* and as men of the Mediterranean (an area where race mixture had been the norm for thousands of years), they were fascinated by the beautiful black and coloured women. Slavery made these women only too available to French settlers, young and old, and so the people of colour as a class increased rapidly in the French Antilles. Typically, a French or French Creole man would make an attractive *tille de couleur* his mistress; normally he would free both her and her children. If he was upper class and reasonably well-off (and many French settlers in the colonies

belonged to the old *noblesse)*, his children by his coloured mistress might receive a privileged upbringing. They might live in the great house of the estate, benefit from a good education, and even enjoy higher education in France. By the 1780's, an elite group of free coloureds had emerged in all the French colonies, but especially in Ste. Domingue, the richest sugar colony in the world by then. These people owned land and slaves, they spoke good French and were educated and cultivated, and they had much in common with their French or French Creole counterparts. But, because they were not white, and because they represented a threat to *grands blancs* and *petits blancs* alike, they came under increasing discrimination from the colonial authorities and from the whites. This was true both in the French and British colonies by about 1780. No wonder that the free coloured elites of the Caribbean were restless and dissatisfied, insecure and offended by the *apartheid*-like regulations against them. No wonder that many were attracted by the idea of emigration to Trinidad.

The Cedula of Population (1783) offered important incentives to free coloureds from the French colonies. First, every free coloured settler would receive free grants of land: five quarrees (about 16 acres) for each man, woman and child and half of that for each slave brought in by the emigrant. Even though the coloured settler was entitled to only half the grant that the white emigrant received, this still represented a most attractive offer. Article 5 of the Cedula also promised that all settlers (it made no distinction between whites and coloureds) would enjoy rights of citizenship after five years'. residence, including the right to hold public office if qualified. All in all, the Cedula offered coloureds who could bring money and slaves' with them a new deal, a promise of far better social, economic and legal conditions than experienced by free coloureds and blacks in either the British or the French colonies.

MOROCOY
Kill the morocoy the day before it is to be used and take it out of the shell. Clean it well with limes and season with garlic, onion, tomato, thyme and cloves. Add some rum to the seasoning. In the morning put into the pot without the seasoning and brown in fatpork, oil and butter. Add a little water continuously for three hours until the meat is tender. Add a pint of claret and some garlic. Stew for another hour. Place in the shell which has been thoroughly cleaned and scraped in layers with sliced hard boiled eggs in between, cover the tops with three beaten eggs and bake for a few minutes.

Many French free coloureds responded by emigrating to Trinidad from Martinique, Guadeloupe, Ste. Domingue, Grenada (British after 1763) and St. Lucia. Leading families such as the Philippe, Cazabon, Saturnin, Beaubrun, Patience, Boudin, de la Grenade, Vincent, Louison, Latraille and Mortel families, to name but a few, were established. Bringing money, slaves, expertise in tropical agriculture, other skills and a tradition of enterprise and endurance, the free coloured settlers contributed in no small way to the development of Trinidad in the post-Cedula period. These elite free coloureds spoke excellent French, were often cultivated people, established estates of cocoa, cotton and sugar, owned slaves, practised professions in a few cases, and held officers' commissions in the island militia. For as long as Trinidad was Spanish, the leading coloured families were treated with dignity and courtesy by Chacon's administration, and no real attempts were made to enforce the kinds of discriminatory laws or regulations that existed in the French and British colonies. No wonder that Chacon's regime (1784-97) was looked back to by Trinidad's free coloureds as their 'Golden Age'.

Although most of Trinidad's free blacks and free coloureds were probably very poor and uneducated, they were very important as landowners and cultivators. Many hundreds came to own small parcels of land and were small farmers growing cocoa, coffee and provisions, using family labour and perhaps one or two slaves. Some families were able to establish sugar plantations, especially in the Naparimas. Illegitimate coloured children of white fathers often inherited land and slaves as well as money. Moreover, many free blacks and coloureds were skilled artisans working either for the estates or in the island's growing towns. A few were shopkeepers or merchants. The elite coloured planters were able to have their sons educated in Europe and a few of these were professional men. For instance, Louis Philippe emigrated to Trinidad from Grenada and was able to acquire several properties in the Naparimas. He became the wealthiest coloured planter in the island by about 1800, two of his sons, St. Luce and Jean-Baptiste, obtained medical degrees in Europe and practised as doctors in Trinidad in the early 1800's.

The conquest of Trinidad by Britain in 1797 led to an immediate deterioration in the position of the free coloureds and blacks. The British military Governors, Picton, Hislop and Monro, were determined to enforce all the anti-coloured rules and regulations that existed elsewhere in the Caribbean. Humiliating laws were enacted, quite new to Trinidad though familiar enough elsewhere. For instance, free coloureds and blacks had to carry a lighted torch when out at night; they could not carry a stick or cane to protect themselves in the city streets (for Port of Spain was dangerous then as now), a 9.30 p.m. curfew was imposed on them, they had to pay a special tax and get police permission to hold a private dance and so on. Picton stripped all the coloured militia officers of their commissions and forced them to serve under white sergeants. A European-trained doctor like St. Luce Philippe was refused a militia commission as a surgeon while untrained white 'doctors' (self-styled) were granted the distinction. Coloureds were forced to serve as alguacils (unpaid policemen) performing humiliating duties like guarding the homes of white magistrates. One can easily imagine how offensive such duties were to proud, well-educated coloured gentlemen.

These new laws and regulations, designed to humiliate and degrade the free coloureds and blacks,

Camille Dedierre, a Martiniquian mulatto half black half white, who settled in Trinidad after the volcanic eruption of 1902 - Photograph P. Pitman.

were imposed after 1797 for two main reasons. First, the British governors were far less sympathetic than Chacon to the aspirations of the free coloured elite and this class was treated far less generously in the British colonies than in the Spanish Empire at this time. So, in part, the campaign against the coloureds was an inevitable consequence of the British conquest of Trinidad. Secondly, both the British authorities and the French planters were convinced that the free coloureds were dangerous revolutionaries who had to be firmly suppressed. The French never forgot that in Ste. Domingue, the civil war which ended in the independence of Haiti and the destruction of the planters began with a rising by free coloureds to gain civil rights. They never forgot either that among the coloured and black emigrants to Trinidad in the 1790's were many republicans and supporters of

1832

SLAVE RISING

We yesterday received the distressing intelligence that the negroes of the Plein Palais Estate, in the quarter of Pointe-à-Pierre, had struck work under the pretence of demanding three days holiday in the week; and that when the magistrate of the district appeared to investigate the affair, the whole gang seized their cutlasses, having already laid hold of their hoes, and threatened to take his life. This threat was accompanied by the most horrible and diabolical imprecations from both the male and female slaves; when it became necessary to send for a detachment of the 19th Regiment, upon whose appearance upwards of 60 of the deluded beings marked off to the woods, first destroying the growing ground provisions they could tear up by the roots. . . . The affair has led to a hasty assemblage of His Majesty's Council for the purpose of sending forth the order for the punishment of offending slaves which was prepared in compliance with the orders of the Secretary of State, but was held back for motives which we are not prepared to disclose. *(26th May, 1832).*

From the Port of Spain Gazette Special Centenary issue.

Clothide Henderson née Escallier, her husband kit and their children Audrey and Dennis with their friend and neighbour Miss Ella Louisa Boissière.

A member of the well known Auguste family of Arima whose origins as free people of colour go back to 1800's. Photograph — Jeffrey Pataysingh.

This lovely Octoroon lady is thought perhaps to be a member of the Innis Family of Trinidad. Photograph — Maureen Hanton.

A Quarteroon lady of the 1880's,   Photograph O. Mavrogordato.

the revolution. These fears, almost hysteria in fact, that the free coloureds in Trinidad were a potential source of violent revolution, dominated policies and attitudes towards them well into the 1820's. They became the victims of fears which were really unfounded: unfounded because nearly all of the genuine revolutionaries in the island left voluntarily, or were deported, soon after the Conquest; and because the coloured leadership was a landed, salve-owning elite hardly likely to risk everything they possessed in the cause of revolution. Nevertheless, these fears continued to dog the free coloureds well into the period of international peace (now 1815) and the regime of the first civilian governor, Ralph Woodford (1813-28).

Dr. Carl Campbell sums up the difference in aims between the military governors of 1797-1813, and Woodford, in these terms: "The soldier governors of the period 1797-1813 used military terror to keep the fragmented population of Trinidad in order, but Woodford, the first civilian Governor, de-emphasized military force in favour of the institutionalization of racial prejudice — His intention was to establish a settled society institutionally fixed, racially defined and graduated in terms of social rank. To Woodford, the free coloureds had been allowed to get out of control. They were too numerous, too rich, too immoral, too intimately associated with whites, too insubordinate and too ungrateful. If it had not been for the British government he would have undermined their economic position by setting legal limits to their land ownership." In this he was stopped, but he did not hesitate to bring severe social pressure on the upper levels of free coloured society. He refused to grant commissions in the militia even to respectable and educated coloureds, he tried to prevent marriages between coloureds, and whites, he never addressed coloureds by the titles 'Monsieur' or 'Madame'. Of course lesser whites were only too glad to follow the Governor's lead. When the Anglican Church was opened—and it had been built with public funds —

coloured church-goers had to sit on special, inferior benches along with the slaves at the back. Even the coastal boat, again paid for by taxpayers, featured segregated seating. The last straw, for the coloured elite, was a 1822 law which wold make it possible for a free coloured or black to be flogged for a minor offence (a breach of police regulations) on the sole word of a city magistrate or alcalde — who was invariably a white slave owner. For the coloureds, this was tantamount to re-enslavement. It was time to fight back: and at this point a leader emerged. He was Jean-Baptiste Philippe, by far the most interesting coloured Trinidadian of the first half of the 19th century.

Jean-Baptiste took up the political leadership of the free coloureds in the early 1820. His education, his profession and his wealth (his family were the leading coloured planters of the island) all qualified him for this role. In 1823, taking advantage of a new liberal attitude at the Colonial Office, the coloured leaders petitioned the Secretary of State for their rights. They asked for the repeal of all laws that discriminated against free citizens who were coloured as against those who were white, and the right to hold public offices and militia commissions. In other words they wanted legal equality and civil rights. To back up the petition, Jean-Baptiste wrote, and published in London, a book which was a statement of the free coloured case addressed to Earl Bathurst, the Colonial Secretary. It would have been dangerous to have published it under his real name, so the title page stated that it was by 'A Free Mulatto of the Island', and it is generally known as A Free Mulatto, Jean-Baptiste's authorship, however, is beyond doubt, and the book is an extremely important document in Trinidad's history, the first sustained expression of political dissent and political protest.

Although Woodford was, as we might expect, quite hostile to the coloureds' campaign, the Colonial Office was sympathetic, and they instructed Woodford, in January 1826, to repeal some of the more obnoxious laws

Phillip Pitman. A coloured gentleman of the late nineteenth century. A descendant of the du Pont du Viviere de Gourville family who came to Trinidad in 1784. A land owner he held property in the Belle Eau Road area of Belmont, east Port of Spain. Photograph — P. Pitman.

discriminating against the free coloureds. This was only a partial victory, and the coloured leadership continued to fight for complete equality. Finally, in March 1829, an Order in Council was issued from London giving full legal equality and civil rights to Trinidad's free coloureds and free blacks. Trinidad was the first British Caribbean colony where free coloured gained their civil rights. And the main leader in their campaign, Jean-Baptiste Philippe, lived only long enough to hear that the order in Council had come into force. He died in July 1829, still in his early thirties.

Sources:

P.G.L. Borde, *History of the Island of Trinidad Under the Spanish Government*, Vol. 2.

L.M. Fraser, *History of Trinidad.*

B. Brereton, *A History of Modern Trinidad, 1783-1962.*

J. Millette, *Society and Politics in Colonial Trinidad.*

Several articles by Dr. Carl Campbell.

La Petite Mam'selle, well dressed in embroidery and lace zepingue tremblant, collier-choux and zanneaux chemilles. Photograph — O. Mavrogordato.

Sources
Lorna Mc Daniel – a research paper done on the Philip family.
Jean-Baptiste Philip, *'Free Mulatto'*, republished by Paria 1987.
P.G.L. Borde, *'History of the Island of Trinidad Under the Spanish Government,* Vol. 2.

LAPPE BOUNCANEE
Cut the lappe in large joints and season well after washing it with lime. Cook on gridiron over an open fireplace or very large coalpot with a brisk fire. To make the smoke continuously feed the fire with wet leaves. Pour some melted butter in which chipped parsley has been put over the pieces before serving or serve with sauce vinaigrette.

Jean Baptiste; Philip

1796-1829

Edited by Sue-Anne Gomes

Jean-Baptiste Philip is one of the foremost names in the history of Trinidad and belongs in the company of those responsible for creating its historical milestones – men like Columbus who named the island; Fernando de Berrio who perceived its true potential and Rose Roume de St. Laurent who masterminded the 1783 Cedula of Population which made large scale colonization possible. It was this same Cedula which set out the rights of the free blacks and people of colour and it was Jean Baptiste Philip who led the fight to ensure that these rights and privileges were upheld.

Jean Baptiste Philip's family was among the wealthy elite coloured sugar planters of the Naparimas. Research shows that during the 18th century the Philip family owned land in Cariacou, Grenada, as well as the entire island of Petite Martinique in the Grenadines. By 1790 the coloured landowning group in Grenada began taking an active part in island politics, forming a group to improve their social and economic conditions. This group became the backbone of the Fedon Rebellion and it was one Joachim Philip who came to prominence as the military leader and chief emissary of the rebellion. (The spirit of social consciousness being a Philip family hallmark).

In the wake of the upheavals in the French colonies of Haiti and Grenada, Michel Philip was one of many immigrants to Trinidad who took advantage of the favourable conditions of the 1783 Cedula of Population. Arriving between 1793-96, Michel purchased land in Laventille as well as the Concorde and Phillipine estates in Naparima. Jean-Baptiste, Michel's grandson, born in the period of discord between the English government and Spanish and French settlers, emerged as the leader of the coloured landowners in their struggle for both civil and social rights.

The following is based largely on excerpts from Carl C. Campbell's essay 'Man from the Naparimas' in the 1987 republication of Jean Baptiste 'An Address to the Right Honourable Earl Bathurst by a Free Mulatto', originally published in 1824.

'It was said that his father Louis Philip perceived in Jean-Baptiste the potential for higher education; but not wishing to educate him to the point where the injustices and indignities of Trinidad slave society would injure his

*Emma Clarke 1880. A mulatto of Port of spain who ran
a Boarding House on Broadway, then Almondwalk.
Photograph — O. Mavrogordato.*

feelings on his return, Jean's father was reluctant to send
him to Europe. But his mother, who was herself unable
to write, prevailed, and young Jean-Baptiste himself was
eager to go. . . he travelled first to England where he
studied Literature. One of his teachers was so impressed
that he reportedly predicted that Philip would one day be
a great man. Afterwards he entered the University of
Edinburgh in 1812. Fortunately for him there were at that
time no regulations governing the age of entry. Jean-
Baptiste remained there until 1815 when he graduated as
a doctor at the youthful age of about 19 years.

It was said by one of his Trinidad admirers, the Rev.
Francis DeRidder, that Philip had distinguished himself as
a medical student. As was customary Philip wrote a thesis
in Latin, the subject 'Hysterical Moods' suggesting that he
possibly had an interest in Psychiatry. After graduating
Philip toured Europe, possibly attempting the 'Grand
Tour', the traditional 'finishing' experience to the higher
education of the wealthy. He attended the lectures of
famous professors of medicine, especially at Montpelier
and Leyden.

In a Europe at peace after Napoleon, Philip found
time for his second love, literature. He struck up an
acquaintance with a Dr. Pichot in Montpelier who
claimed that Philip introduced him passionately to the
poetry of Byron. Philip was said to be uneasy at first in
the company of whites, but when accepted he would
speak like a superior. It is not known what degree of
racial mixture Philip represented, but it appears that he
was sufficiently removed from white to be easily
recognised as a man of colour. While on his tour Philip
fell in love with an European girl; thought of marrying
her, but heeded the advice of a friend who warned him
of the impolicy of taking a white wife back to Trinidad.'

Dr. Jean-Baptiste Philip returned to his native land
about 1816.

The free people of colour through the Cedula of

population 1783 had become considerable property
owners in Trinidad in the early years of the 19th Century.

'According to this Cedula any national of a state
friendly to Spain being a Roman Catholic, who took the
oath of allegiance to Spain would be entitled to free land.
If a white male or female the personal entitlement was 10
quarrees (1 quarree = 3 1/5 acres), with an additional 5
quarrees for each slave brought into the colony. Free
black and free coloured settlers were entitled to a half of
the white people's entitlement to land. Children and
other relatives, or even friends, could inherit the land of
grantees, provided they resided in the island. The result
was that between 1783 and 1797 when the English
captured the island about 42,090 quarrees were
distributed; a further sharing out of land under the
English between 1805 and 1812 distributed 26,453
quarrees, largely to persons already settled. It has been
calculated that of this latter distribution at least 6% went
to free coloureds, some of whom had already received
land under the previous distribution by Chacon. The total
effect of these two different periods of land distribution
was to provide a solid foundation of land ownership for
many free coloured families. Some had only received
small farms on which they grew cocoa, coffee and
provisions. Others had come into possession of enough
land to establish sugar plantations, particularly in the
Naparimas. Of course free coloureds through purchase or
gift came to possess land which had been granted to, or
purchased by, whites. By the time Jean-Baptiste Philip
returned a second generation of free coloured owners
had already inherited or purchased land. . . .'

The first Governors Picton, Hislop and Munro were
not too concerned with organizing the society as much as
they were with safeguarding it both from within and from
outside threats. With the arrival of Governor Sir Ralph
Woodford in 1813, pressures were brought to bear on

*A lady of the 1880's four parts black one part white.
Photograph O. Mavrogordato.*

the free coloureds. Dr. Jean-Baptiste Philip became their leader in the struggle against Colonial prejudice. A struggle that took him to the House of Lords where he presented possibly the first civil rights case fought and won in the western world for the cause of black people.

In 1823 Philip headed a two man delegation to London to present the grievances of the free coloureds to the Colonial Office. There followed a lengthy petition dated November 1823 outlining the abuses of the governors from Picton to Woodford. This petition influenced the British government to widen the terms of reference of a Judicial commission already on its way to the West Indies to investigate a number of problems. The commissioners were then instructed to conduct in Trinidad a special inquiry into the case of the free coloureds. Philip returned to Trinidad in time to help formulate other supporting petitions and evidence presented to the sitting commissioners. These commissioners then reported to the British government, which asked James Stephen Jr. of the Colonial Office to report on the commission's findings. The result was instruction from the British government in 1825 to Woodford to begin the dismantlement of legal discrimination against the free coloureds. This process was begun decisively in January 1826, but what was done then failed to satisfy Philip and the free coloureds, leading to a further petition to the British government in 1828, which finally elicited a complete elimination of legal inequalities in March 1829. Before this stage was reached, and notably by 1825/6, another branch of the free coloured movement, located in Port-of-Spain, not led by Philip, but under his inspiration, had developed. But this branch took a novel form and was more concerned with turning the paper equality of the free coloureds – for this was all that had been achieved by the Philip group up to that point – into a real equality.

The question arises where does the book 'Free Mulatto' fall in this line of development from 1823 to 1829. There is a sense in which it stands outside the mainstream of development: the free coloureds' case was based essentially on petitions; the November 1823 petition which came before the book, and the subsequent petitions which came after the book. The investigations of the free coloureds' case by the Judicial commissioners and James Stephen Jr. were based on these petitions. 'Free Mulatto' was addressed to the Secretary of State for the Colonies, Lord Bathurst; it is not known who else in the Colonial Office read it. If the book had not appeared the outcome of the struggle would in all probability have been the same. None of the other contemporary free coloureds' struggle in the other islands was adorned by an accompanying book. In so far as 'Free Mulatto' reiterates the grievances and arguments of the free coloureds about their lost rights it must certainly have strengthened their case generally, and as an achievement of one outstanding free coloured it gave the lie to the theory that no intellectual creation could emanate from anybody but the whites. The point is that 'Free Mulatto' as a book was not at the centre of the deliberations about the fate of the free coloureds, only the kinds of information to be found in it; but a great deal of this information was already in the petitions.

What was Dr. Jean Baptiste afraid of? A considerable part or 'Free Mulatto' recites the grievances of the free coloureds and repeats the claims of the petitions. But the book is not a petition. It constitutes the boldest expression of free coloureds' sentiments in a literary style unsuitable for petitions. It must rank as one of the earliest pieces of indigenous polemical literature by a non-white in the British Caribbean. Philip was devastatingly critical of the whites, particularly of certain powerful whites who were still alive: Commandant Robert Mitchell; Attorney-General Henry Fuller, Governor Sir Ralph Woodford. Several other whites had their names called in connection with overbearing social behaviour, financial corruption, judicial chicanery or governmental mismanagement. Could Philip be sure that Fuller, or Mitchell or Woodford would not sue him for libel in an all white Trinidad court? At any rate could he hope to escape the organised malice of the white power structure after his bitter exposure of white racism? He had good reasons to be fearful of the consequences; and it remains a moot point how much Philip did suffer from the whites between 1824 and the hour of his death July 1829. There was a suggestion that his last years were saddened by social harassment and frustration.

'Free Mulatto' of course reveals many things about Philip himself; and the reader is specially invited to ferret out his attitude to slavery, to Haiti and to the prospect of free labour in Trinidad. He employs the English language with more than ordinary skill although his family came from the French oriented sector of the society. He was a gentleman; a moderate reformer. He expected education and virtue regardless of colour or race to be regarded with social recognition. He was angry and shocked by the failure of the whites to distinguish in their public policy between the various classes among the free coloureds. He envisaged that persons like himself, wealthy, well educated, well bred would be among the social and political leaders. Not all the coloureds were fit to rule; nor all the whites. The whites were severely criticised, but Philip really believed that they too were the victims of a system of colonial customs and habits which adversely affected everybody in the society.

There is no mistaking the heroic quality of the life and achievement of Dr. Jean Baptiste Philip. There was youthful intellectual talent; a providential appearance when needed by an underprivileged social group; courage in the face of dangers; sacrifice of a professional career which could have supported a quite financially rewarding life; a book, mature beyond the years of the author, as a personal testament to a principled struggle, and finally an early death at about age 33, just before the moment of triumph. Philip died two weeks before the proclamation of the law granting full civil equality to the free coloureds. His entire adult life was consumed by the free coloureds' struggle. He did not live long enough to disillusion his admirers; or to sully his record by immersion into the politics of conversion of paper rights into actual reality. Even so the issue of slavery, the fact that his family owned slaves as well as he himself, the absence of a clear call for the abolition of slavery from the man who saw the injustices done to his own social group – this, slavery, was the first major stumbling-block to his acceptance as a hero by blacks and coloureds, especially the former, who had been slaves during the time of Woodford. As slavery became more a memory than the actual experience of many living persons the conditions were created for the commencement of a more generous estimate of the work of the Naparima doctor. No monument was built to his memory as was suggested by a sympathiser in 1842, but some 30 years later there was a torch-light procession to his grave in San Fernando, and speeches in praise not of a leader of the free coloureds, but of a hero of the underprivileged people.'

The wedding of Yolande Sellier and Leo de Lapeyrouse. Their children were Marie Amélie, Claire, Marie Ange.

The French in Trinidad

Jean de Boissiere

BEFORE a group of French emigres set out to colonize the Spanish Island of Trinidad they had the good sense to secure the political rights that would ensure their future in a foreign country. Before sailing for the new world they went to Madrid where they secured from the King of Spain a charter for the colonization of the Island.

The following year they arrived in Trinidad with hundreds of slaves they had purchased in the other West Indian Islands. With these and intense work they laid the foundation of the agricultural economy of the Island in a few short years.

They had not been in Trinidad ten years when the English seized it. While the new regime wisely allowed the existing criminal and civil law to remain as it was under Spaniards they took care to deprive the French planters of their political privileges.

The articles of capitulation were full of the high sounding phrases of all such documents; but in the last analysis, only meant that those who signed them gave up all the advantages they had held under the rule of Spain.

Nearly all signed and continued to build their plantations, relying on an apparent political leniency to protect their interests. The first disillusionment came

A. Beatrice Sellier married
   Louis Pantin.
B. Berthe Sellier married
   Michael de Verteruil.
C. Valentine Sellier married
   Roderick Clarke.
D. André Sellier married Carl
   de Verteuil.
E. Odette Sellier married
   Joseph d'Abadie
F. Louis Sellier killed in World
   War I.

These are the children of
Ernest and Josephine Sellier
née Agostini
   The three eldest, Yolande,
Caroline and Adhemar were at
school in England at the time
this picture was taken.

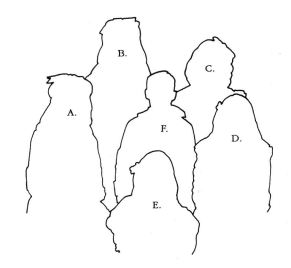

when the financial interest of the City of London decided
to absorb and develop the sugar industry of the West
Indies.

There was a new technique for the manufacture of
sugar. It involved the building of huge factoriès, the
acquisition of tremendous tracts of sugar lands to ensure a
supply of canes to feed the hungry jaws of these
machines; and most difficult of all a cheap labour market.

But the estates belonged to French planters and the
labour too. The estates the English were willing to
purchase, but the slaves were a different problem. They
could not afford to buy slaves at twenty to fifty pounds
sterling a head and then feed them for the rest of their
lives. It was cheaper to free them even at the expense of

compensating the planters with ten million pounds. It would have cost them more buying them outright and having to feed them forever afterwards.

So the first blow was delivered to these French settlers of Trinidad by a hand of iron that was encased in a glove of silk. The hand of iron was England's political domination of the island supported by a navy that was the most powerful in the world. The glove is known in terms of history as the emancipation of the slaves.

Some of the planters took their compensation, sold their estates for what they could get and went to the

the island with educators, doctors and men in public office who were as a shining example to some of the badly-trained English Civil Servants sent to administer the place.

At the end of this period of hard struggle the elder generation lay back for a while and left the management of affairs to their children and grandchildren.

These had had none of the bitterness of being robbed of the early work of their people. They had to do none of the work of building estates out of snake-infested jungles. They were educated at the best schools

---

KERNAHAN TOWN HOUSE — 5 QUEEN'S PARK EAST

William Kernahan was born in 1860 and educated at QRC. He joined the civil service and rose to the rank of Receiver General. He was a Protestant who refused to learn French, merely picking up enough patois to control the estate labourers. He married a Catholic French creole but was later completely ruined by his brother A.T. Kernahan who had pledged his estate and property as security for one of his businesses which had failed. For years the furniture in his home consisted of packing cases and barrels and whatever money he could spare went to the education of his children.

His son Andrew eventually became the wealthiest of the family and was the proprietor of the San Quentin and Le Pommier coconut estates in Cedros. He was reputably one of the founding members of the Union Club, an English rather than a French creole institution. The Kernahan

William Kernahan

men and women married throughout the social and cultural stratum. Andrew married a Grenadian, Isabel Harford and they adopted a daughter. By 1900 the Kernahans were one of the largest Trinidadian Irish families.

The Kernahans' house was situated at Queen's Park East which was originally the road from Port of Spain to the Indian mission at St. Ann's. When the Savannah was acquired from the Peschier family and the 'pitch walk' laid down, the sites around the Savannah were chosen by the rich for their comfortable and sometimes palatial homes. The house pictured must have been built around 1870 and reflects possibly the style of the second empire. Set well back from the road it combined privacy with easy accessibility to the Port of Spain business section. Its wide verandas and high ceiling lent a spaciousness and coolness that is lacking in modern buildings. The classical type portico is rather unusual for Trinidad.

French Islands. Those who remained had no finance to tide them over the violent transition period that took place after the emancipation and the local agents of London banks took good care to see that they did not get it either. Most of them went bankrupt and the London-promoted stock companies took over the estates.

Undaunted and now reluctant to leave the country of their adoption these dispossessed planters hewed their way into the interior forests of the islands and by the dint of hard work for fifty years made the cocoa they planted the first industry of Trinidad.

While doing this they still had the energy to supply

in England and the continent where instead of learning the management of the cocoa plantations their parents were building, they learnt to emulate the nobility of Europe who would inherit estates ten times the size of their whole island.

From 1880 to 1900 these indolent, European-educated French Creoles revelled in the prosperity their forebears had won from the jungle. They built hideous ginger-bread mansions in Port of Spain and entertained in a manner that outstripped any of the parvenus who visited them.

They forgot in the midst of this terrifically vulgar dispaly that the most important condition for the safety of their fortunes was the political power in the land. And it was no longer theirs. Even as they drank their champagnes nightly the tentacles of London inspired finance were again preparing to strangle them.

This time it was not necessary to perform an historical act of great moral value in order to dispossess a class. London merely loaned money to banks, merchants and shops that showered these Creole sybarites with cheap clothes, vulgar furniture and foul champagne at prices that would have shamed a war time profiteer.

The bills piled up. The mortgages followed and by 1910 the hurricane they had prepared with their stupid extravagance swept them right out of the economic life of Trinidad. A few exceptions who had arrived late on the scene and were working while their compatriots were living riotously escaped the debacle of foreclosures. They survived to amass fortunes from the dubious money that was being poured all over the place during the world war.

But the social process in the instance of these late French arrivals in Trinidad repeated itself. It took but a few short years of the 1920's to lay low those strugglers from a class that was now as dead economically as it had been politically for a century and a quarter.

As they declined they grew grander and grander. Most of them had for ancestors Petite Noblesse, or the exiled bureaucrats of the French Monarchy and ruined merchants of the seaport towns of France. When a M. Marigot arrived he purchased a sugar estate of 2,000 acres

present but in order to do so they had to become so anglicized that they were indistinguishable from Anglo-Saxon Creoles except for their names and a persistent love of gaiety.

Today nothing remains of the French in Trinidad except a couple of families who are only recognizable as such because of their names. As a people they have passed from the scene completely. But before doing so they gave to the West Indies its most glamorous social figure, its most brilliant educator and at the apex of its decline the man who was to arouse the political consciousness of its working class.

A. Thelma married Joseph Goddard from Barbados.
B. Angela married Adhemar Sellier.
   Their children were Trevor and Jean
C. Irene married Errol Maingot.
   Their children were Pelu, Cynthia, Sonia, Earle.
D. Irma married Connor O'Connor (no children).
E. Eileen married Brian O'Connor.
   Their children were Richard, Leary, Patricia.
F. Claire married Ralph Herrera.
G. Eric married Violet Turcher. Their two children were Elvin and Honor.

These are the children of Raul Maingot and his wife Ange née Gomez.

with the money he had managed to smuggle out of Republican France. His grandson lost half the estate and for compensation attached the aristocratic de to the former Bourgeois name of Marigot. When his grandson finally lost everything but his job as a tally clerk with its miserable pittance of pay he insisted on talking about the title of Marquis which was his by right to everyone he met.

A few outstanding individuals held to what rights they had, their property, and kept up the illusion that the French were still an influence in the island up to the

*Captain the Honourable Arthur Andrew Cipriani in
court dress.*

The Ciprianis of Trinidad

Gérard Besson

To this day there is a strong recall of the name of Cipriani in the collective memory of Trinidad, long after the demise of the ascendency of Trinidad's 19th century dominant minority, the French Creoles, who through marriage and cultural assimilation the Ciprianis had become very much apart of. This is of interest, especially when one considers that there is a city boulevard and a Labour College by that name, a public statue in the heart of Port of Spain and a call, from time to time, that Piarco Airport should be renamed 'Mikey Cipriani' Airport.

The Cipriani family is of truly antique origin and they are recorded as being members of the Florentine Consulate of the 12th century.

In the wars of the Guelphs and the Ghibellines that racked Italy through the 12th century the Ciprianis name is mentioned often in the chronicles as possessors of towers and fortified places. When victory was won by the Guelph family, in order to consolidate the popular Government, the Guilellini family and their supporters, who included the Ciprianis, were submitted to the deprivation of public representation and the confiscation of land and wealth. In 1292 rather than change their name and give up their status as nobles, as was being demanded, the Ciprianis preferred exile in a foreign land.

The sons of Antonio de Lapo de Cipriani, Giovanni and Picoli, were declared revolutionaries and sentenced to death. They, together with their wives and children and the remnants of their retainers, fled to the island of Corsica to the town of Contini, the home of the powerful feudalist Simon Pietro La Mare and 'there retained in born nobility and military pride'. Their service to this Lord re-established the family and their fortunes were recreated. It was during this period that the Ciprianis were allied through marriage to the famous Bonaparte family.

The early 17th century saw the descendants of Juvenale de Cipriani d'Contini emigrate to Marseilles, France and establish themselves. Tornelio de Cipriani and his son Simone presented to King Louis XIII (1610-1643) a memorandum strengthened by proof that they were the legitimate descendants of 'the great noble illustrious family of Cipriani of Florence' who had been obliged to emigrate on account of the wars between the Guelphs and the Ghibellines and that they were the descendants of the Lords of the Feifs of Cabres and Nebellian in Provence.

The earliest record found of the name of Cipriani in Trinidad is in the list of proprietors in the island on the 20th March 1797 by F. Mallet. Their name was spelt with an 'S', and showed them holding lands at Naparima 'since the first establishment'. The second record is that of J.A. Cipriani who signed a petition for the enactment of British laws in 1803.[6] Sabastian and Cipriano Cipriani were established in Port of Spain by 1823, Sabastian serving as Regidor and Field Executor in the illustrious Cabildo. Twenty-seven years later he would have the honour of being one of the last and longest serving members of that board as it was transformed from Cabildo to Town Council in 1840, his last position was that of Field Alcalda. He married, in the opening years of 19th century, a daughter of Don Paul Guiseppi, whose wife, Trinidad de Los Angeles had been the only child of Don José Mayan a senior member in the Administration of the island's last Spanish Governor. It was in fact at the Guiseppi Estate house 'Valsayn' at St. Joseph that the articles of Capitulation were signed on the 18 February 1797, between Don José María Chacon and Sir Ralph Abercrombie thus ceding Trinidad to England.

The Guiseppi family had come to Trinidad prior to the capitulation. Don Paul was one of the leading members of a considerable Corsican emigration to Trinidad which took place in the 1780's and 90's. They benefited from the Catholic clause in the Spanish Cedula of Population of 1783. Many of them were seeking refuge from Corsica's 13 year old struggle for Independence from Genoa. These Corsicans were the countrymen of Pasquale Paoli, Corsica's great nationalist freedom fighter, who had held out against first the Genoese, then later the French, and who, after the French had purchased the island from Genoa in 1768, became its administrator. He defeated the then Brigadier Napoleon Bonaparte at Ajacca in 1793. He expelled the Bonaparte family and their allies from Corsica. Paoli was later to hand the island over to the British in 1794. The Corsicans formed alliances with the Spanish and French families of Trinidad there circumstances may have led to the Corsican influx. Both Cipriano and Sabastian along with other Corcicans signed the subscription list for the farewell of Lt. Col. Aretas William Young, as well as other petitions in support of British causes.

Sabastian's daughter Sophia Cipriani married Gaston de Gannes de La Chancellerie and became the mistress of the great house 'La Chance' at Arima. Sabastian Cipriani's three sons were José Emmanuel Cipriani, Albert Henry Cipriani and Leon Cipriani. José Emmanuel first married Lucie Gantaume de Monteau, the daughter of P.A. Gantaume and Adele Besson, with whom he had three daughters. His second wife was Helen Lange, they had two sons and one daughter. José Emmanuel became a Solicitor and later, Mayor of Port of Spain for seven years, 1875-1882, 'the most distinguished member of his family in his generation' wrote C.L.R. James in 1932. He goes on to say 'José Emmanuel Cipriani played a great part in the lighting of the city and the laying out of Tranquility, and it is after him that Cipriani Boulevard is named. He not only spent time on Port of Spain, but also much of his personal fortune, giving largely to charitable courses'. He died at the age of 45. His son Leonetto Paul became a solicitor and married Helen Sellier and had five children. Among them was Andre Cipriani who was to distinguish himself later in the field of science. Another of Sabastian's sons, Albert Henry, married Alice Agostini. Alice was the daughter of John, son of Don Simon Agostini and Alix Gantaume, daughter of P.A. Gantaume and his first wife Eliza la Quarree.

Albert Henry Cipriani and his wife Alice Agostini had three sons. Edward the eldest married Catherine

Andrea and had no issue, Albert Henry (Baba) Cipriani was qualified as an engineer, but made a fortune for himself in cocoa. He bought Perseverance estate from Dr. George Latour and in the 1920's added many embellishments to it, living there in extravagant style. As a businessman he was apparently quite astute, diversifying out of cocoa just in time to avoid the collapse of the cocoa economy in 1919. He had also invested in the sugar industry and became a millionaire many times over. He speculated unwisely and eventually lost Perseverance estate to an Englishman, one James Evans.

Albert Henry's third son Arthur Andrew Cipriani, known to his friends as 'Tattoo', was born on the 31 January 1875. By the time he was six he had lost both his parents in a typhoid epidemic that swept Trinidad in the 1880's. He was brought up by his aunt Mrs. Dick and attended St. Mary's College. He spent a lot of time on the family's cocoa estates at Santa Cruz and at Grand Couva and from an early age demonstrated a way with animals, especially horses. He left St. Mary's College at about sixteen years of age and turning down various offers to study abroad decided to raise and train horses. He obtained a trainer's licence and travelled in the West Indies as a rider and trainer with some considerable success. His friends described him as a solitary sort of man who never married.

Today at the foot of Frederick Street in the middle of Independence Square stands a statue of Captain A.A. Cipriani 'The Captain' as he was known to one and all. This statute was erected by the Government which was being led at the time by Prime Minister Eric Williams. A Government that took this country from virtual British Crown Colony rule to Independence. As a mark of respect and in keeping with the wishes of the vast majority of people, the statue was erected. Called the champion of the barefoot man, Arthur Cipriani was a renowned sportsman as well as a turfite. A spokesman in the Legislative Council for the people, acting at times almost like an Ombudsman, his contribution to the Legislative process cannot be overstated. He was regarded by his peers as an officer and a gentleman; he was also undoubtedly a born leader and is acknowledged as a moving spirit in Trinidad's fledgling Workingman's association. He was many times Mayor of Port-of-Spain, and a supporter of many causes. He was presented at Buckingham Palace on more than one occasion. He retained the common touch all his life. He was a man of such personal prestige that he could raise five contingents of volunteers to fight in the first World War. He himself left with the 3rd elements of which went into action against a superior Turkish force in the Damay sector of the Jordan Valley in 1917 with considerable success — 'No public man is more widely known in Trinidad', wrote C.L.R. James, 'many West Indians (and a few Englishmen too) have worked for the emancipation of the West Indies. Their story will be told in time but none has worked liked Captain Cipriani'. The impact of Arthur Cipriani on the hearts and minds of Trinidadians up to the time of his death in 1945 is difficult to estimate. That he was revered by the basically black and coloured middle-class intelligentsia that assumed power in the fifties from the played out French creole minority is an indication of the stature of the man.

Another of Sabastian's sons was Leon Cipriani, he was probably the eldest, he had a relationship with a coloured slave woman remembered only as de Rose. This took place on one of the families estates. He may have had several children with her; among them was

Jules de Rose also known as Cipriani de Rose but who, later with his father's consent, took the name Cipriani. Leon Cipriani established L. Cipriani and Co at 41 Marine Square and operated as a Commission Merchant. Leon Cipriani appears not to have married. His son Jules Cipriani prospered as a businessman and built a remarkable mansion on Abercrombie Street known as Cumberland House. He married Louise Ultima Latour the daughter of M. Paul Latour of Perseverance Estate Maraval. Louise Ultima was Paul Latour's illegitimate daughter and is remembered for her beauty. She was brought up in his household together with his wife and other children. His wife was Jeannie Marie née Besson. Jules Cipriani had seven sons and seven daughters, one of his son's was Michael (Mikey) Cipriani. A solicitor by profession, he was one of Trinidad's pioneer aviators. A popular sporting hero, he was known as 'Marvelous Mikey' by Trinidad's sporting fraternity, and was at one time champion cyclist and athlete of Trinidad and of the West Indies.

Michael Cipriani aviation pioneer of Trinidad. Photograph — Trinidad Guardian.

A West Indian hero during the first European war in which he served as a gunnery Sergeant in the Second Life Guards, in 1917, he was attached, as a machine gun Sergeant to the French troops defending the Fortress of Verdun at which time he acquitted himself well. He became very interested in aviation and flew on several missions over the western front during the closing years of the war. He represented Trinidad in international cricket and also in football and 'shone in every position on the field'. 'Marvelous Mikey', as he was known, was considered during the 1920's and 30's as the 'greatest athlete Trinidad has ever known'. He was very popular among the people at large, he was one of their own, a born Creole. He moved at every level of society. When he died at the age of 40 a victim of a plane crash in the northern mountains of Trinidad, the entire country devotedly mourned his death. His body was taken from the wreckage of his aeroplane 'Humming Bird' and brought to Port of Spain. Thousands of people attended his funeral, people of every class, colour and creed, from the representative of the British Crown to the barefoot people in the street.

Andre Cipriani, son of Leonetto Paul, José Emmanuel's son with his second wife Helen Sellier, demonstrated from an early age an interest in science which grew after he entered St. Mary's College. His sister Louise wrote of him:-

'Realizing Andre's great potential, Papy started to

gear him from an early age for the scholarship class, unfortunately Papy died the year before Andre was successful in obtaining the Science Scholarship. Andre left for Canada and McGill University in 1928 to take up studies in Electrical Engineering, but when he arrived at McGill he was encouraged into the field of Mathematics and Physics. He took his B.Sc. and M.Sc. with first class honours and finally with the encouragement of the great neurologist Dr. Penfield took his M.D. in the field of Obstetrics and Gynaecology.' After the war, Andre entered the field of Atomic Energy. He became director of Biology and Radiation Hazards at the Atomic Energy Plant at Chalk River in Canada. He became a scientist of international reputation in this field of research, creating a unique laboratory. Through his pioneering efforts Andre Cipriani and his colleagues and staff at Chalk River developed 'the first highly active cobalt sixty sources' which were made for the treatment of malignant diseases. Several hundred cobalt therapy units have since been produced by the commercial products division of Atomic Energy of Canada Limited and sold worldwide, bringing relief to thousands of suffering patients.

At his death at 48 in 1956 the BBC gave him a 3 minute obituary describing him as the most knowledgeable man in the world on radiation hazards. He was married and had four daughters.

His success in the field of atomic research for peace is not known in Trinidad, nor the fact that he was a victim of his own research.

The Cipriani family produced outstanding figures, especially in the fields of business civic administration, sport, the military and finally in science.

Sources
Cipriani family papers presently in the possession of Louise Cipriani.
Map Collectors Guide.
'Travels in Trinidad', P. McCullums 1903.
'History of Trinidad', Fraser.
'Franklyn's Year Book', 1915.
Victoria Institute Centenary Exhibition Historical Catalogue 1897.
'Substance of Speech', Mariat 1822.
C.L.R. James' Captain Cipriani and Cipriani family tradition.
Louise Cipriani, Olga Mavrogordato, and Gregor Duruty — sources of oral history.
Besson Family Papers.
Trinidad Guardian.
'Atoms at your Service', David A. Keys, exhibition Royal Ontario Museum January 29, 1960.

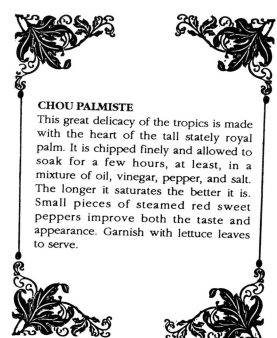

CHOU PALMISTE
This great delicacy of the tropics is made with the heart of the tall stately royal palm. It is chipped finely and allowed to soak for a few hours, at least, in a mixture of oil, vinegar, pepper, and salt. The longer it saturates the better it is. Small pieces of steamed red sweet peppers improve both the taste and appearance. Garnish with lettuce leaves to serve.

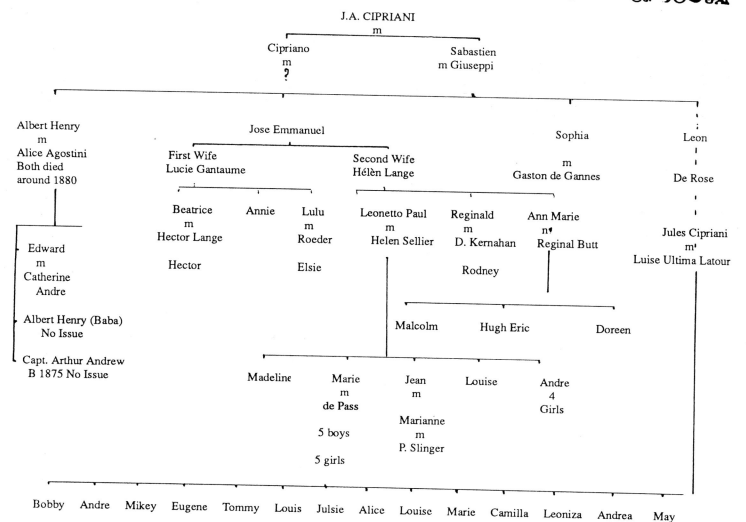

The Honourable Charles William Warner.

THE ENGLISH IN TRINIDAD

Bridget Brereton

Long before the British conquest of the island in 1797, several English families had settled in Trinidad. Most of them were merchants of one type or another who took up residence in Port of Spain and organised the developing colony's import-export trade in the post-Cedula years (1784-97). Some were probably Roman Catholics, others were Protestants (and therefore banned by the terms of the Cedula) who benefitted from Governor Chacon's rather generous interpretation, or perhaps merely lax enforcement, of the law. Quite a few Irishmen also settled here in this early period, men such as John Nihell who became Chief Judge under Picton. Of course most Irishmen were Catholics.

Naturally, the British conquest in 1797 and the formal cession of Trinidad in 1802 led to a considerable influx of settlers from England or from the English colonies of the Eastern Caribbean. Many planters left the exhausted soils of the 'old' sugar islands to seek their fortunes in Trinidad with its vast expanses of virgin land. Of course they brought their slaves with them, and this was quite legal up to 1824. An example is Burton Williams, a large proprietor from the Bahamas who brought many slaves here and settled in Central Trinidad (Williamsville is named after him). Another is A.C. Carmichael who emigrated from St. Vincent with his slaves and bought Laurel Hill estate in Tacarigua. His wife wrote an interesting account of their experiences in St. Vincent and Trinidad.

11 Wellington Terrace, facing the Queen's Park and No. 4 Tranquillity Lands was the home of the Hon. Frederick Warner,
It was designed by George Brown Esq. in 1882 but was sold by Frederick Warner to a group of local businessmen for the setting up
of a Hotel, to be called the Queen's Park Hotel. Edgar Tripp, a forward thinking businessman was the prime mover behind the venture.

Besides the fairly well-to-do planters, many Englishmen came to Trinidad after 1797 in the hope of making a quick fortune through commerce and business. A rapidly expanding frontier colony naturally attracted more than its fair share of adventurers and hustlers. Of course, many of the immigrants were respectable people: tradesmen and artisans, businessmen, merchants, lawyers and doctors, printers and journalists, estate overseers and mechanics to service the sugar machinery. Most of the new arrivals, once they established themselves (and if they didn't succumb quickly to disease and drink), soon accepted the norms of a slave-holding society and acquired at least a few domestic slaves themselves, if not a brown 'housekeeper' like Governor Picton's notorious Rosetta Smith.

As the English community developed and grew in the middle decades of the 19th century, it became more complex. We have to distinguish between the 'expatriates', the Britons who came to the island to work but not to settle, the colonial officals, the sugar company managers and some of the merchants; and the English Creoles, the families of English descent who had developed strong roots in the island. Often the Creoles (French as well as English) accused the expatriates of looking down on them, of snubbing them because they has the misfortune to be born on the wrong side of the Atlantic.

There were also religious distinctions. Not all of the English Creoles were Protestants. A minority belonged to the Roman Catholic Church, and these families often intermarried with the French Creoles and were assimilated into their society. An example was the English born historian L.M. Fraser, who married into a prominent French Creole family. The Irish Creoles too, who were mostly Catholics, were often assimilated into French Creole society; names like Devenish, O'Connor and O'Halloran come to mind.

Most English Creole families however were Anglican, and the divide between the 'English' and the 'French' in the mid-19th century was as much religious as national. Religion was the great barrier to inter-marrriage and closer social relations between the English and French Creoles, and at least up to the turn of the 19th century the two groups were quite separate and distinct as far as their private social lives were concerned.

The Hall
Home of the Warners

Sir Thomas Warner was born in 1575. He was one of the earliest Englishmen to conceive of colonising any island in the Caribbean. His rudimentary ideas lead him to go sea-faring to other climes. First Guiana which he found unsuccessful then St. Christopher. Despite much initial hostility from the native caribs of the island and the turmoil and the battles of would-be French and Spanish settlers; Sir Thomas Warner still persisted in his ambition to create a British settlement. The renowned pioneer became the first Lieutenant Governor of the Caribbean islands. He died in March 1649 and was buried in St. Kitts' middle island.

His sons and grandsons were also later established in the British West Indies territories. Sir Thomas Warner of Barbados, Colonel Phillip Warner, Governor of Antigua, William Warner of Dominica and Edward Warner who arrived in Trinidad in 1807 and purchased lands. The Warners were a predominant family and each became significant in the Commonwealth of nations in some way. As in the case of Charles Edward Warner, the only son of Colonel Edward Warner. He was born at sea between England and Barbados on 19th October 1805. At twenty-four he migrated to Trinidad with his wife whom he had recently wed on a visit to his cousin Ashton Warner, who was the Chief of Justice of the colony during the Governorship of Woodford. He was very attracted by the surroundings and the lifestyle so Trinidad remained there on his well loved home. Charles William Warner grew in stature like his relatives. He became one of the most prominent Attorney-Generals in the history of Trinidad, from 1844 to 1870. He so influenced the period while in office that 'Warnerism' became a synonym for the policy of the local Government. He married twice. Once to Isabella Ann Carmichael with whom he had six children and his second wife Ellen Rosa Cadiz with whom he had twelve children. The well known sons of Charles Warner were Aucher, Attorney-General and Sir Pelham a world famous cricketer. Charles Warner died in 1887 and was buried in the cemetary in the Royal Botanical Gardens.

In 1873 Charles Warner built his home called 'The Hall'. The building was a beautiful two storied property where his children grew up. It spanned the full block of Chancery Lane West. The house comprised of a splendid garden which included a swimming pool. The interior was composed of spacious foyers and huge rooms and verandahs which were used to entertain guests on occasions. The home was later sold in 1886 to one Carlos Damaso Siegert.

The original Tranquility Methodist Church on Stanmore Avenue was erected in 1886 and was built from corrugated iron sheets. It was erected on lands previously owned by ARchdeacon Cummings. This property known as Tranquility Pasture occupied the area between Borde Street and Cipriani Boulevard with the savannah at its northern boundary with Tragarete Road on the south. It is said that this entire area was covered with guava trees with Archdeacon Cummings house standing in the middle of the Pasture. Photograph — U.W.I. Library.

Just as the French Creoles had the de Verteuils who spoke only to God, so the English Creoles had their 'first family', the Warners. This large West Indian family was first represented in Trinidad early in the 1800's, and Ashton Warner served as Chief Judge in this period. But its most distinguished Trinidad member was definitely Charles Warner who served as Attorney-General between 1842 and 1870. Much more than simply Attorney-General, however, Warner was the most powerful man in Trinidad between the 1840's and the 1860's, the 'real ruler' of the island during these years as Governors came and went. He was the most important influence behind the 'anglicisation' policy of this period and he became the bete noire of the French Creoles and the Catholics. His cousin, Frederick Warner, was a prominent barrister who served as an Unofficial Member of the Legislative Council for many years from 1861. His son, Aucher Warner, also held high office in the closing years of the century and scored quite a coup by marrying the daughter of Sir William Robinson, Governor between 1885 and 1891. Warners seemed to proliferate in Trinidad's top positions in the 19th century, along with a few other prominent

English Creole familes. Many of them got their first 'break' from Lord Harris who governed the island between 1846 and 1854, and so their enemies called them the 'Harristocracy'. Heading the Harristocracy was John Scott Bushe, Lord Harris' brother-in-law and Colonial Secretary between 1861 and 1887; the Bushes were, perhaps, only second to the Warners in the English Creole pecking order. Another prominent family was the Cummings; Harris married a daughter of Archdeacon Cummings in Trinidad (they honeymooned on one of the Five Islands). Other leading English Creole families included the Fitts and the Stones.

Relations between English and French Creoles deteriorated markedly with the policy of 'anglicization', embarked on between 1840 and 1870 under Warner's guiding influence and with the blessings of the Colonial Office. Its aim was to make Trinidad more English in its institutions, values, language and 'feeling'. Naturally, the anglicizers were anxious to reduce the influence of the French Creoles and of the Roman Catholic Church, which was seen as a foreign, essentially French, institution. Hence, the spread of Anglicanism at the expense of Roman Catholicism, the spread of the English language at the expense of both French and Patois, and the fostering of English prestige through education, were all aims of the movement. French Creoles were squeezed out of top government posts and seats on the Council, the Church of England was established in Trinidad even though the great majority of the people were Catholics, public education exclusively in English and using British textbooks and methods was inaugurated, and the island's laws were completely assimilated to those of England. All these developments caused much anxiety and resentment among the 'foreign' Creoles, who saw themselves shunted aside in the island their ancestors had transformed from a wilderness in the century before.

Governor K.M. Jackson 1904 – 1909 in top hat at the opening of the new Railway station at Port of Spain. Second on the left is Col. Swain, Chief of Local Forces at the time. Photograph — Mr. and Mrs. Peter Stone.

Edward Lester Atkinson, manager of the Colonial Bank and his family. He was born in England in 1851, the son of the Rev. Cannon Atkinson, D.C.L. of Yorkshire he was educated at Rossal Grammar School and at Repon School Derbyshire. Became a banker in 1872 and served in several islands in the British West Indies as an employee of the Colonial Bank. He became Manager of the Colonial Bank, later Barclays, in Trinidad in 1883 upon the retirement of Mr. Samuel Kerton. he was the father of Dr. E.L. Atkinson who accompanied Scott on his world famous expedition to the South Pole. Photograph — Mr. and Mrs. Peter Stone.

The more aggressive aspects of anglicization, however, were ended in the late 1860's, symbolized by the disestablishment of the Anglican Church (1870) and the beginning of the 'dual' system in education by which Church Schools could receive State aid. Gradually French Creoles re-entered top posts in the Legislative Council. One could say that the period in which English families had a virtual monopoly over government - the period of Warnerism - ended in 1876, the year in which Charles Warner was forced to resign as Attorney-General because of alleged mishandling of a client's money. After 1870 relations between English and French Creoles slowly improved: an entente, even if not always an entente cordiale. The English Creoles were forced to share power and influence with the French Creoles, newly revitalized by the cocoa boom. Their period of sole ascendancy was over, but the English Creoles continued to form an important element in Trinidad's white elite.

ROAST BEEF

Choose a T-bone roast with sirloin on one side and tenderloin on the other side of the T. Season well with salt, pepper, thyme, chive and onion. Put in the iron pot with some oil and butter and very little water. Cover the iron pot with a piece of tinning on which live coals are heated. Cook for half an hour, lifting the tinning every now and again to baste the roast. Of course this is for people with simple arrangements; but if you have stoves with ovens you just have to put it in the heated oven and regulate it to medium.

Above: In the 1880's the Government purchased this property and several others in the immediate vicinity. The Boys and Girls Training Schools were built, the Government Printing Office and a Drill Hall for Volunteers. The remainder of the lands was divided in lots and sold at auction with leases of 199 years at a very small rent. The streets laid out were Victoria (named for the Queen) and Stanmore Avenues named for the Hon. Hamilton Gordon, later Lord Stanmore, Cipriani Boulevard named after Eugene Cipriani, the mayor of Port of Spain, Tranquillity Street (named after the estate), Cummings in memory of the Archdeacon whose daughter married Lord Harris 1845-1854, Albion the poetic name for England and Melville for a fellow cleric, a contemporary of Archdeacon Cummings, the pastor at St. Margaret's Church at Belmont.

A party of friends at Monte Cristo estate St. Ann's, fourth from right is Aucher Warner. Photograph — O. Mavrogordato.

1830.

YET ANOTHER THEATRE

The Creole Theatre, in Chacon Street, was opened on Saturday last. Owing to the limited time the performers had in which to get up their parts, some traits of imperfection were discovered in the latter part of the programme; but this was due to the desire to have the play staged before the closing of the theatre during the Lenten season.
(24th February, 1830).

THE WOODFORD MONUMENT

At a meeting of the Committee appointed for the erection of a monument to the late Sir Ralph Woodford, it was decided to abandon the decision arrived at the last meeting to erect a statue in bronze owing to the excessive cost which would considerably exceed the amount contemplated. The Chairman then proposed that the subscriptions received be applied to the purchase of an appropriate monument to be erected in Trinity Church, and a similar monument in the new Roman Catholic Church. This proposal was approved by the Committee
(11th August, 1830).

DEATH OF MR. ASHTON WARNER

Died, on Saturday last, the 4th instant, the Hon'ble Ashton Warner, Esq., His Majesty's Chief Judge, and a member of His Majesty's Council for this Island, aged 50 years. Mr. Warner, a barrister of Lincoln's Inn, was appointed Attorney-General of this Island in 1810. He resigned in 1811, and retired to St. Vincent. In May, 1818, he was nominated by Sir Ralph Woodford to fill the office of Chief Judge of the Island, and was confirmed in this office by the late King, a post which he held, with that of Judge of the Court of Vice-Admiralty, for a period of nearly 13 years, till the day of his death.
(8th September, 1830).

Mr. Edward Charles Mercer Stone seated in the company of his six daughters whose names were Violet, Amy, Anne, Nellie, May and Aileen. E.C.M. Stone and his brother Hubert Cockerton Stone came out to Trinidad in the 1830's. They were the nephews of Henry Fuller, then the Chief Justice of Trinidad. Both brothers became civil servants holding several positions of trust. They served as Stipendiary Magistrates of Port of Spain and variously as Registrar General and Protector of Immigrants. Photograph — Mr. and Mrs. Peter Stone.

Mr. Hubert Cockerton Stone, his wife Eliza and children Kenwin, Rosalie, Eulalie, Stanley and Harvey. Both brothers married into the Gibbon family and so did a sister as well. E.C.M. Stone lived at 54 Edward Street and it was largely through his efforts that the records in the Registrar General's Office were saved during the fire that destroyed the Red House during the water riots of 1903. Mr. H.C. Stone lived at the Rookery at Maraval, a property belonging originally to John Nicholas Boissière. Photograph — Mr. and Mrs. Peter Stone.

1832.

START OF THE 'ROYAL GAZETTE'

The *'Port-of-Spain Gazette'* begs to inform the inhabitants of Trinidad that it has pleased His Excellency the Governor to withdraw from this paper the whole of the Government printing and all advertisements Economy is the plea. An Unknown individual, self-styled 'The Government Printer,' takes leave to inform the public that he has started a public newspaper called the 'Royal Gazette.' We understand that this paper will have the Government patronage which we formerly enjoyed, and the Government assigns as a reason that it will thereby be saved £170 sterling per year. This new printer says that the use of a colonial newspaper is merely to compress the news received by the mail. *(21st January, 1832.)*

On the 1st February, 1832, the 'Port-of-Spain Gazette' writes editorially as follows:— 'The far famed Junius said that the man who can neither write common English nor spell well, is hardly worth attending to. This remark is so applicable to the 'Royal Gazette' that we shall in future be guided by it. But our readers may be assured that we shall watch it and its secret director closely; that upon the slightest misrepresentation calculated to injure your cause with those from whose hands you expect redress,—we should rather say justice for the cause of the planters, merchants and other inhabitants,—we will crush the viper even though we perish in the act.' *(1st Feb., 1832).*

1836

PUBLIC HOSPITAL

We are able to announce that the public hospital so long wanted, and the funds for which have been for so long awaiting appropriation, is now about to be commenced and carried on with the greatest possible expedition.

Mr. N.P. Blanchard committed to prison for one month and fined £10 for assaulting G. Knox, barrister-at-law, July, 1836.

Above: A house at St. Anns from Stark's Guide to Trinidad. It is possible that this house was one that stood at La Fantasie Road and was sometimes used by the islands Colonial Secretaries. Photograph — Stark's Guide to Trinidad.

Below: Some dance cards that once belonged to Miss Nellie Stone. Photograph — Mr. and Mrs. Peter Stone.

TRINIDAD

CONSTABULARY.

Programme

SERGEANTS' MESS DANCE.

Prince's Building,

TUESDAY,
26th NOV. 07.

Programme

Dance

MARYCLARE.

......

20th August, 1908.

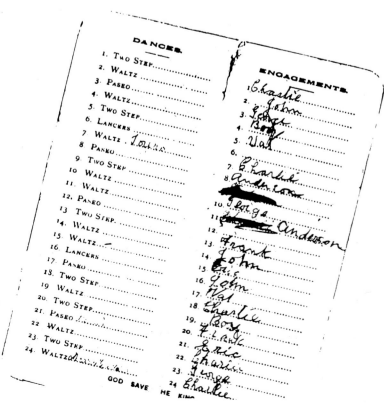

DANCES.		ENGAGEMENTS.
1. Two Step		1. Charlie
2. Waltz		2. John
3. Paseo		3. George
4. Waltz		4. Bob
5. Two Step		5. Nat
6. Lancers		6.
7. Waltz		7. Charlie
8. Paseo		8. Anderson
9. Two Step		
10. Waltz		10. George
11. Waltz		11. Anderson
12. Paseo		12.
13. Two Step		13. Frank
14. Waltz		14. John
15. Waltz		15. Eric
16. Lancers		16. John
17. Paseo		17. Nat
18. Two Step		18. Charlie
19. Waltz		19. Bob
20. Two Step		20. Frank
21. Paseo		21. Frank
22. Waltz		22. Eric
23. Two Step		23. George
24. Waltz		24. Charlie

GOD SAVE THE KING

A young English boy. Photograph — Mr. and Mrs. Peter Stone Esq.

1836

WRECK IN THE BOCAS

On Thursday last a vessel named the *Ruby* left this port for Tobago, and at 5 p.m. was running out through the first Bocas when she was drifted by the current onto a submerged ledge of rock known as the Parasol Rock close under the cliffs. Immediately after striking a huge wave threw the ship so high on to the cliffs that she was left dry; and all on board, save one lady, a Mrs. Sevarall, the owner of the vessel, were able to jump off on to dry land. This lady had swooned and was lying on the deck insensible, and in a moment more was washed overboard into the sea. Her son-in-law, Mr. Devignes, and the master of the vessel sprang overboard to rescue her, and after a short struggle they all three sank. The other passengers remained on the rocks till next morning when they were taken off and brought up to town by a fishing boat. *(22nd March, 1836).*

The house of the Misses Stone, daughters of E.C.M. Stone of Picton Street, Newtown. All three ladies lived with the exception of one who died in her eighties, well into the ninth decade of their lives and were unmarried.

1838

THE ORIGIN OF IMMIGRATION

A Committee of the Council on Saturday last passed several resolutions upon which an ordinance is to be immediately founded authorising the Government to appoint an agent for immigrants in this island, and to establish agencies in other places for the purpose of procuring immigrants used to field labour in tropical countries,—the Government paying the whole expense which, including the agent's fee, it is said will amount to 52/- sterling each. The Government is to do this gratis; that is, it will resign now and forever all claim to repayment, either from the immigrant or his employer. If this bounty, for such in fact it is, upon immigration should not be productive of the results anticipated from it, we know not by what other means,—more liberal they cannot be,—the necessary supply of labour can be obtained.

(13th November, 1838).

The ordinance for facilitating immigration of labourers into this colony came into force on Saturday last. *(4th December, 1838).*

1839

NEW MASONIC LODGE

Although we do not appertain to the fraternity, yet it gives us much pleasure to be able to state that the members of the Royal arch Chapter No. 48 and the Lodge United Brothers, No. 327, are now building a very handsome Temple at Mount Moriah, which solutely and for ever became a British possession. *(8th March, 1839.)*

In the issue of the 26th March is the announcement that the Queen has appointed Sir H.G. MacLeod to be Lieut-Governor of the island.

Photo Mr. and Mrs. Michael Brierley.

Frank Eccle

**CASUALS TEAM 1908 —
WINNER OF BONANZA CUP**

C. Ramon

BACK ROW: Mr. Smith   Don Anderson,   J. Day   Frank Brierley   Manager Casuals
(Managing Director Bonanza Stores)

MIDDLE ROW: B. Mc Craken, Eric Legge,

FRONT ROW: W. Eccles, G. Owen, L. Newbury, G. Rochford, George Brierley

1839

OPENING OF THE NEWSROOM

The Newsroom on the King's Wharf as announced was opened to the members this morning. It is really an elegant, spacious and airy building, and fitted up for the purpose in a neat and becoming manner, and it is a great ornament to that part of the town. Another table, for which there is space enough, on which to place the French papers would we think be a considerable improvement. (1st March, 1839).

DEATH OF THE GOVERNOR

It becomes our very painful duty to announce the decease this morning at nineteen minutes past six o'clock of His Excellency Sir George Fitzgerald Hill, Lieut-Governor of this island. He had attained his seventy-seventh year, and preserved until within a few hours of his death all his faculties clear and unimpaired. His remains will be deposited this evening beside those of his late amiable and lamented lady in the vault at St. Ann's. It is rather remarkable that Sir George is the only Governor of this island who has died in Trinidad since it became a British possession. (8th March, 1839).

1840

The Cabildo changed its name to Town Council, January, 1840.

The young people of the Stone, Gibbon and Atkinson families with friends. Photograph — Mr. and Mrs. Peter Stone.

1841

THE FIRST ELECTION HELD IN TRINIDAD

The first election under the ordinance which has converted the Illustrious Board of Cabildo into the Town Council of Port of Spain took place on Saturday last. There was no contest or struggle for the vacant seats, and consequently no excitement. Out of nearly 400 burgesses, about 60 appeared to exercise their privilege of recording a vote. The following gentlemen are the new member:

Thomas Hinds

Antoine Radix

William S. Paul

P. Blanchard

And Messrs. J.G. Arnavon and G.A. Rousseau were chosen as elected auditors of accounts for the new Council.

(23rd February, 1841).

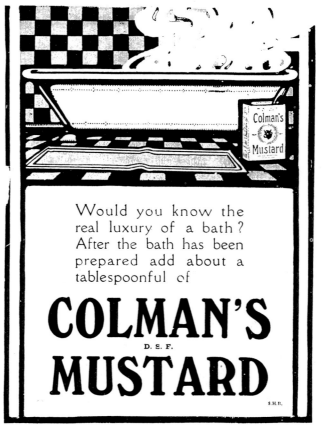

MANICOU

This delicious meat tastes very similar to chicken. Like a fowl you do not skin it, singe the hair over a flame. Scrape the skin well and cut it up as you would a fowl for fricassee. Wash with lime and season strongly. Melt a little bacon or fatpork in some oil and butter and brown the manicou in it. Add a little water and cook slowly for an hour and a half to two hours.

1843

GREAT COMET

A comet of extraordinary size and brilliancy has been visible for five successive nights in the south-western sky. Though its rays are by no means of that fiery hue which is the general characteristic of these meteors, being, on the contrary of a silvery appearance like the moon, and though its tail, as it is termed, does not extend so far across the heaven as in some previous comets, yet it is still by far the largest and most lustrous object that has visited this globe within the memory of man. *(7th March, 1843)*.

1844

NEW GOVERNMENT BUILDINGS

Yesterday afternoon His Excellency the Governor laid the corner stone of the new Court House in the presence of a numerous concourse of spectators. The following inscription printed on parchment, was read aloud by the Assistant Secretary, Mr. Johnston, and then deposited in a glass vessel, which was placed in a cavity prepared in the stone for that purpose:

In the 7th year of the Reign of
Queen Victoria
On the 15th day of February, in the
The Corner Stone of these Public Buildings
To be Erected at the Expense of the Colony
viz:
Government House, containing the Public
Offices of the Government, with the
Council Chamber and the
Court House,—containing the Public Offices
of the Judicial Establishment, and Hall of
Justice was laid by His Excellency
Colonel Sir Henry G. MacLeod, K.H.E., K.S.W.,
Governor and Commander in Chief of the
Island of Trinidad and Its Dependencies.

Architect: Richard Brigens
Engineer Officer: Captain Chaytor.
Builders: G. de la Sauvagère and A.A. Pierre.

His Excellency then took the trowel, and having spread the mortar, the stone was lowered into its place, after which His Excellency addressed the spectators as follows:— 'I believe it is quite necessary for me to mention my earnest wishes for the welfare of Trinidad and I lay this stone with the prayer that the officers who may preside in the respective buildings may perform the duties entrusted to them with firmness and integrity, and to the advancement of the colony.' Three cheers were given by the assembled crowd for Queen Victoria and one cheer more for His Excellency the Governor.
(16th February, 1844).

Sir H.E.H. Jerningham, K.C.M.G.

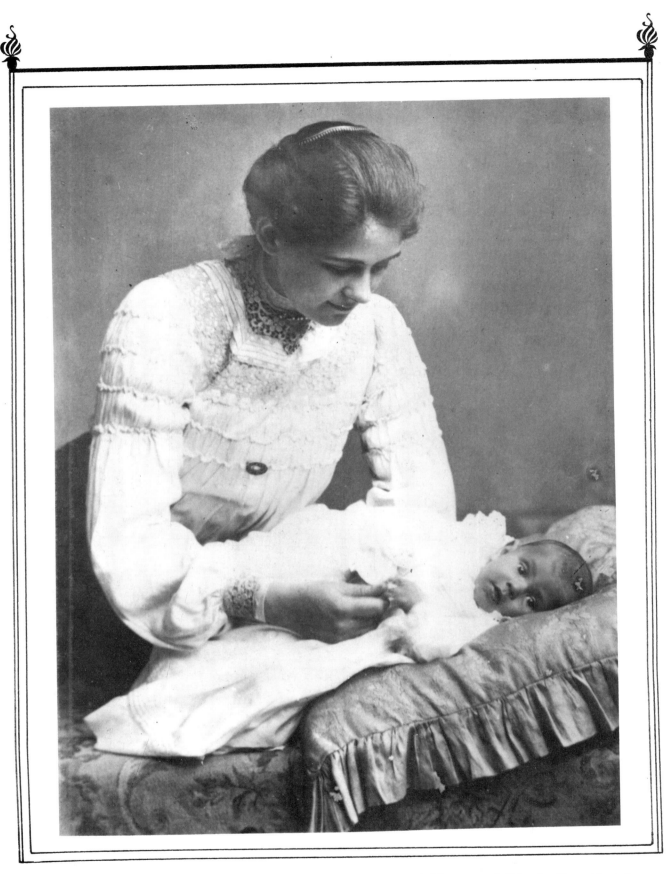

A friend of the Stone and Gibbon families and her baby.

1844

The first cargo of Ice, imported for the Ice House, arrived from Boston in the brig 'Allen King', consigned to D.P. Cotton, on the 26th December, 1844, just too late for Christmas, but in time for the New Year. Since that date the island has received a continuous supply of ice and iced delicacies from the United States, and always through the same channel. The firm of D.P. Cotton & Co., of which the Trinidad branch does business under the style and firm of C.L. Haley & Co., supplies, to the present day, Barbados and our own island with the luxuries of the temperate zone, and is at present one of the wealthiest houses of business in the British West Indies. From time to time, the firm has had to meet with competition which it has always managed to successfully overcome; and their good faith in catering to the requirements of the public have caused their name to be regarded as a household word in our community.

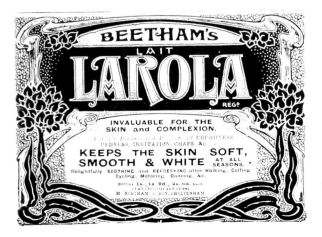

Polly Gibbon who gave his life in the Great War 1914-1918.
Photograph — Mr. and Mrs. Peter Stone.

1844

CAPTURED AFRICANS AS IMMIGRANTS
The brig. Lord Grey arrived here on Saturday evening last with 216
immigrants (captured Africans) from Rio de Jañeiro of which 98 were
females. They are principally young people, and were landed in good
condition, and found immediate employment. *(9th January, 1844).*

We understand that 300 more may be immediately expected from
the same source. It is a matter of congratulation that our agent at Rio was
enabled to charter this vessel at a low rate, and that these people will
therefore stand the colony considerably less than the rate fixed by the
Council, for the passage of Rio immigrants. *(9th January, 1844).*
the Port of Spain Gazette.
Special Centenary issue.

MUTINY AT ST. JOSEPH.

One of the most serious alarms to which the inhabitants of the town of St. Joseph have ever been subject, was raised on Sunday morning last, by a report that the companies of the 1st West India Regiment stationed there had mutinied during the preceding night and had attempted to massacre all their officers. The report, though much exaggerated, was so far founded on fact that the liberated Africans who were lately brought here from Grenada and Dominica as recruits to the Regiment had risen upon their officers at 3 a.m. that day with the determination of putting them to death. Providentially, one of the mutineers departed from the plan laid down and the mutiny has been suppressed within a few hours of its breaking out, but not without the most determined activity on the part of the Colonial Militia, and a fatal encounter between them and the mutineers. *(20th June, 1837)*.
Port of Spain Gazette, Special Centenary Issue.

Court martials held at St. James' Barracks on the mutineers of the 1st West India Regiment are concluded, but their sentences will not be made public until after they are confirmed by the Commander-in-Chief at Barbados.
(28th July, 1837).

The sentences passed by the Court Martial and confirmed by the Commander-in-Chief on the St. Joseph mutineers are as follows: William Satchell to be transported for life; Stewart, Gregson and Coffin to be shot to death by musketry. The execution of the sentence on these three men was ordered to take place at St. Joseph Barracks on the morning of Wednesday last. Donald Stewart belonged to the race of Yarabas, and entertained a rooted hatred for all white men. He it was who incited his companion to mutiny, promising to take them back to Guinea. Col. Donerty, who is well acquainted with the numerous tribes of Africans, would never admit into the West India Regiment any man of the race of the Yarabas, whom he pronounced irreclaimable savages. *(18th Aug., 1837.)*
Port of Spain Gazette, Special Centenary Issue.

An illustration of the execution of Makhandal Daager from a description of the event contained in Charles Kingsley's, 'At Last a Christmas in the West Indies'.

Established 1825

THE PORT OF SPAIN GAZETTE

Emancipation Day August first 1834.

Friday, the never to be forgotten 1st of August, — the day on which, for the first time in centuries, the sun rose on the British West Indies without lighting a single slave to labour, the day upon which 850,000 human beings, who had gone to their rest the previous night suffering under the weight of slavery and wretchedness insupportable, arose a free and happy people ..... The orders in Council, proclamations and ordinances had been carefully explained relating to the grand scheme of emancipation, both by the Government and by the slave owners, and had been as generally laughed at and rejected by the very people for whose benefit they were so humanely concocted. It was decided by the slaves that the King had freed them right out, and that the apprenticeship was a job got up by their masters and the Governor. Their masters were 'dam tief' and the Governor 'an old rogue', and the King was not such a fool as to buy them half-free when he was rich enough to pay for them altogether. These were the feelings universally and unequivocally expressed by the slaves whenever the topic of apprenticeship was ventured upon, and it was consequently thought wise to adopt some means of convincing them of their error more forcibly than mere explanation and reasoning; and four companies of militia were ordered to hold themselves in readiness for permanent duty. The morning of the 1st of August had scarcely dawned when the apprentices were found moving into town in numerous groups and gangs wending their way to Government House; and long before His Excellency the Governor arrived in town the courtyard and surrounding neighbourhood were peopled by the happy and free, who had come to inform His Excellency that they had resolved to strike work. His Excellency, and afterwards Captains Hay and McKenzie, justices of the peace who had arrived specially from England, explained to them their new condition, the obedience still due to their masters, and the risks they ran by their riotous conduct. The mob would listen to none, and became still more turbulent and insolent each moment. The Militia were ordered to muster, and in a space of time, scarcely credible, the whole of the town corps were under arms in a force and state of appointment gratifying to every man who beheld them.

We are sorry that we cannot speak in the same terms of the regulars. Col. Hardy brought forward several objections to bringing his men into town, such as the lack of accommodation, the heat of the sun, etc., etc. Ultimately, however, the ·guard was increased ..... The negroes continued to swarm Government House until a later hour in the evening without the slightest exhibition of the least inclination to return to their estates to which they were attached; and the Governor, upon taking his departure for his residence, was assailed with every kind of abuse that apparent immunity could suggest. The accounts received in the districts in the neighbourhood of Port of Spain represented that the estate gangs had ceased work almost without exception; but not a single instance of violence was heard of. For the further protection of the town during the night, pickets and patrols of the militia, cavalry, artillery and infantry were posted round the town. After dark, the negroes dispersed. Saturday produced a repetition of Friday with increased insolence on the part of the negroes. The muster round Government House continued. The magistrates tried 17 of the most prominent ringleaders and sentenced them to stripes and hard labour. It was thought, as these men were being led to gaol, that the sight would have a salutary effect on the rioters; but it

Of the emancipated slaves, few stayed on the estates. Many came to Port of Spain and many more squatted on Crown Lands. Photograph — Maureen Hanton.

only increased their fury. Captain Hay then read from the platform of Government House, the clause in the Royal Order in Council, declaring the assemblage of three or more apprentices to be a riot if continued for ten minutes after notice to disperse, and the display of a flag. It was read by him in both English and French, and the King's colours were displayed. This had no effect; and after twenty minutes, the order was given to clear the streets. The charge was made under the immediate supervision of the special magistrates from England, who, finding all other efforts to disperse the mob unavailing, sanctioned at the last hour the introduction of military force; and personally headed the charge. The mob fled and scattered. There were features in the bearing of the rioters which are sufficiently marked to point to a conspiracy amongst the agricultural population. They had been taught the power of passive resistance; not a cutlass, not even a *bois stick* was to be seen amongst them, not a single individual was intoxicated, and not an act of personal violence or robbery was heard of. Sunday presented a different scene. Not a country apprentice was to be found in the streets, but reports from the country were unsatisfactory. Two councils were held to determine upon the propriety of reading the martial law, for which a requisition had been presented to the Board signed by all the special magistrates, most of the public officers and influential men, and members of all classes of the community. Like their other deliberations, these ended in their rejecting the only measure at all available without being able to substitute any other in its place. Monday morning brought a return of the mob, while our guard houses were filled with prisoners who stopped the preceding night. Those condemned underwent their punishment this morning, in the Royal Gaol 19, and in Marine Square 33, the town corps of militia being present. We are happy to say that the reports from the Naparimas and the populous quarters adjoining are most favourable, which is universally attributed to the Regiment commander who is stationed there in command of the militia and regular troops, and who has also been appointed Special Justice for that neighbourhood.

(5th August, 1834).

1834. Martial Law was not proclaimed and only one life was lost — that of a Negro who was shot at Band de l'Est, his murderer escaping to the opposite coast of Colombia.
Historical notes from H.C. Pitts 100 Years Together.

PANCHOO CAMPBELL
A free African of Tobago

Commander Alford
(Published in 1948, 'Guide to Tobago'.)

It is with much regret that I have to relate that Panchoo Campbell, who lived at Speyside, and whose photograph is shown on the opposite page, died in December 1938, at Batteaux Bay, where he had been cared for by Mrs. Edna Whiteley, an American lady who owns Batteaux Bay, after having seen over eleven decades pass on this earth! Although he has gone, I cannot leave him out of this book for his history is too interesting and his name deserves to live on in Tobago.

As a boy, and young man, he lived in a village in what is now the French Congo. Then came one dreadful day in 1850 when Portuguese slave-traders descended on

The Faces of Freedom

Free at last, the former slaves planted subsistence crops, hunted in the forest or involved themselves in various forms of manual labour. Some became craftsmen, tin smiths, shoe-makers, fitters, carpenters; some simply did nothing. Photograph — O. Mavrogordato.

the village. With many others, Panchoo was driven down to the coast in misery and degradation, a slave to be sold like so much cattle.

The unfortunate men were herded on board a slave runner and shipped in despair towards America. The slaver, however, was unlucky. A sail appeared on the

Panchoo Campbell.

horizon, then the hull of a ship. The stranger altered course and bore down upon the slaver with all sail set. There was no escape, for the stranger was a British Frigate of War

One can imagine the feelings of the slaves on board. Would they be dumped overboard from the lee side, with weights attached to their legs (common trick to try and prove that they were not carrying slaves), or would they be rescued and set free?

Fortunately for Panchoo the former ghastly procedure was not carried out. The slaver was captured and all the slaves were taken off in safety.

As they stepped on board the frigate they became free men, protected by the Flag of England, but they were not returned to their own land. The policy adopted

A freed Creole Slave. Photograph — Maureen Hanton.

Britain and Emancipation
The Act of Parliament abolishing slavery (1833) provided for a free grant of £20 million – an enormous sum in that day – to be distributed among all the colonial slave-owners as compensation for the loss of their 'property'. This money, of course, came from the British tax-payers. Naturally there was some resentment at this burden, and the British public (long-suffering John Bull) tended to feel that both the former slave-owners and the former slaves had extracted all that could be expected from British coffers and should now settle down and behave in a decent, orderly fashion; above all, they should make no further demands on old John Bull.

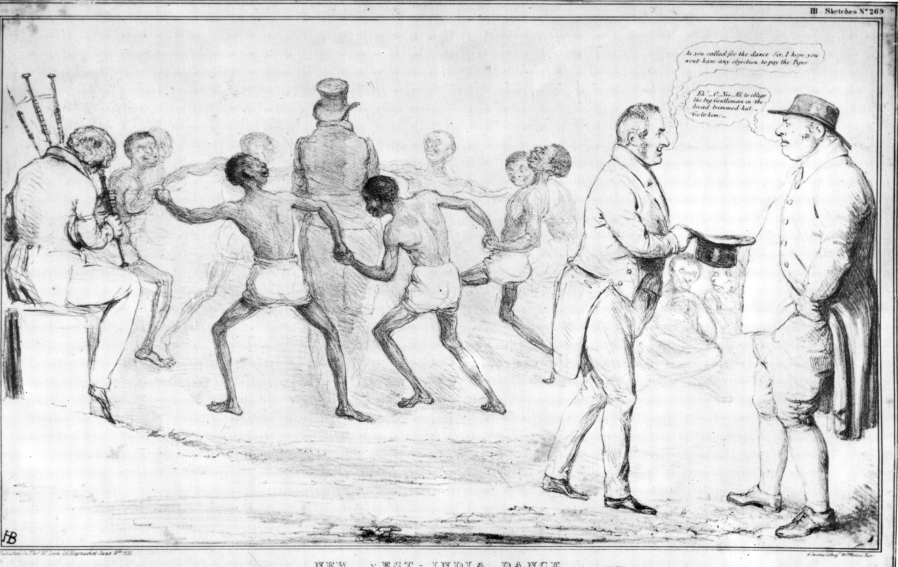

NEW WEST-INDIA DANCE.

at that time of sending slaves rescued from slavers to the West Indies has been questioned and is much too long a subject to discuss here. One of the most obvious reasons for this procedure, however, was that if they were landed on African soil at some port, they would almost certainly be recaptured long before they could ever return to their own villages, even if they knew how to get back there.

Consequently Panchoo journeyed to St. Helena, where he remained but a short while before being shipped to the West Indies. He came to Tobago, where he lived ever since, and adopted the Christian name of Campbell.

Panchoo Campbell, shown in the photograph on page 170, arrived in Speyside in 1871. He saw the water-wheel, the machinery and the housing erected. Panchoo outlived the mill, for the wheel is rust-riddled.

King Sugar died, but Panchoo lived on. He saw sugar change to rubber, and then to cocoa and coconuts.

Three times did Panchoo Campbell enter into the bonds of matrimony (no one can accuse him of lack of courage!), the last time in 1931 to a young girl of six decades.

Here is a little incident that may make some of us who drive about in a car think! When H.M.S. Rodney came into Man-O'-War Bay in 1931, Panchoo Campbell set out from Speyside and walked up Back Hill (which has a gradient of 1 in 5) to Man-O'-War Bay, a distance of about five miles there and back, in order to see one of His Majesty's Ships of War!

You will know therefore that this 'old-timer' was not by any means bed-ridden nor was he blind, deaf or

An illustration of a Trinidadian slave by Richard Bridgens from his book 'West Indian Scenery', 1820.

dumb, in fact all his faculties were standing the passage of years well, including his memory. There is one other thing that time did not erase, and which serves as a reminder of the horrors of the past. On his chest one could still see the cruel marks of the ghastly branding-iron whereby Man marked Man as his property.

Panchoo died peacefully at the age of 115 years.

An illustration of the Main Street, Scarborough, Tobago by Captain Wilson 1825 — Tom Cambridge Collection.

TOBAGO.

1st. AUGUST 1834.

SCHEDULE

THE RETURN of *Margaret Campbell of the Parish of St. Andrews*

of the total number of all *predial & non predial* **apprentices** Labourers of of Six years and upwards to whose services *she is* entitled.

NAMES		EMPLOYMENT	PREDIAL UNATTACHED.	NON PREDIAL.	REMARKS.
MALES.	FEMALES.				
Richard	"	Field	predial unattached		
Prince	"	Do.	Do. 1		
Tom Williams	"	Do.	Do. 1		
Daniel	"	Do.	Do. 1		
Alexander	"	pasture	Do.		
Diamond	"	no work			
	Mary	Domestic		non predial	
	Jinnett	Field	Field do 1		
	Teddy	Field	Do. 1		
	Jerry	Field	Do. 1		
	Madlain	Do	Do. 1		
	Kitty	Domestic	"	non predial	
	Charlotte	no work Trade	"	"	
	Amber	Domestic	"	non predial	
females 6	8		"		
	8		9	5	her

Sworn to before me this *30th* day of *August 1834* to be a true and distinct account, according to the Act in each case made and provided.

Henry Yeates Registrar

Margarate X Campbell mark

*A document which listed the name and status of apprentices
on an estate in Tobago for the 6-year period following emancipation
Margarite Campbell was a free black proprietress. Tom Cambridge Collection.*

EX SLAVES, VILLAGES, SQUATTING, AGRICULTURE 1838~1900.

Bridget Brereton

After complete Emancipation in 1838, the ex-slaves could for the first time exercise some freedom of choice about their place of residence, their employers, their occupations and their lifestyles. There was no immediate, large-scale 'exodus' from the sugar estates as so many planters had feared. Nor did the ex-slaves, or most of them have any objection to seeking employment on these estates after 1838. What they did object to, however, was any condition of dependence on the sugar estates. They wanted to be able to bargain with the planters. If they took jobs on the estates, it would not be solely on the planters' terms as before 1838, and if at all possible the ex-slaves wanted to have some other source of income besides the estate job: a bit of land or a craft or trade. Real freedom meant for them independence from the plantation, achieved by securing a plot of land on which to build a hut and cultivate food crops, which was usually combined with estate work at certain times of the year to meet the family's cash needs.

The result of these aspirations of the ex-slaves was a steady stream of freed men leaving the estates to live in new villages and settlements. This stream was on a fairly modest scale between 1838 and 1846, but it accelerated from then on as wages on the estates fell and so full-time wage labour (along with residence on the plantation) became less attractive. The new villagers often continued to take jobs on the near-by estates, but they did so when it suited them, and they certainly did not

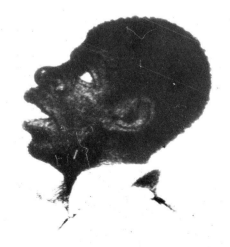

provide the type of steady, manageable labour force available all year round that the planters had got accustomed to.

Villages sprang up in close proximity to existing estates and settlements, for the creoles showed little interest in going into 'the bush,' which they left to the few surviving Amerindians and the 'peons' from Venezuela. For instance, a string of post-1838 villages developed along the Eastern Main Road between Port of Spain and Arima. Other villages grew up around Port of Spain and San Fernando (now absorbed as suburbs). Later, the cocoa boom after 1870 opened up new villages in Central and North-East Trinidad, or gave fresh life to older settlements like Arima.

Probably most of the ex-slaves aspired to combine a peasant life-style with occasional or even regular estate work for wages. But to achieve this ideal, access to land was essential. Some ex-slaves did manage to buy land when estates sold off marginal areas in small lots, though the price tended to be very high. But the amount of land coming on to the market in reasonably small parcels was never anything like enough to satisfy the ex-slaves' land hunger. On the other hand, Trinidad had abundant reserves of Crown Lands, made quite inaccessible to the ex-slaves, legally, by rules which forbade the sale of lots smaller than 340 acres. Squatting was the inevitable result. All over the island ex-slaves (and post-1838 immigrants of various races) occupied portions of Crown Lands, cleared the bush and established cultivation. Since roads were non-existent or unbelievably bad in the rural areas, and since Trinidad had no effective police force, the government was quite incapable of preventing squatting or evicting squatters. By the 1860s many of these 'squatters' were established and even prosperous cultivators, some owning hundreds of cocoa trees in places like Montserrat and Tortuga. Others were simple peasants growing provisions, corn and vegetables on a few acres snatched away from the forest. Squatters or not, they contributed significantly to the opening-up of the island and to the development of its economy.

> *C'est la meme moen perdi gangan moen.*
> *C'est la meme yo blesse mun one moen.*
> *Ambas pons Marabella*
> *C'est la meme moen perdi gangan moen.*
>
> Under the Marabella bridge
> It's there I lost my grandmother
> It's there I lost my grandmother
> It's there they wounded my uncle.

These photographs show the descendants of the ex-slaves as they lived in the countryside. Picture above, Tobago; below, Trinidad. Pictures from Jackson's 'Book of Trinidad', 1904.

Tobit, the free African Porter. Photograph — U.W.I. Library.

LIBERATED AFRICANS

After Emancipation the planters were anxious to recruit labourers from virtually any part of the globe once they were available and not prohibitively expensive to import. Africans who had been captured by foreign slavers, were, at this time, often freed by British naval ships on anti-slave trade duty in West African waters. These 'liberated' Africans, who were not legally slaves but free people, might be persuaded or even compelled to emigrate to the British West Indies as labourers.

These 'liberated' Africans, once freed, were sent either to St. Helena, a small island in the South Atlantic, or Sierra Leone in West Africa. Conditions were not good in either place, so an organised emigration to the West Indies began just after 1838. They first arrived in Trinidad from Sierra Leone in 1841. Between 1841 and 1861, when this immigration ended, Trinidad had received a total of 3,383 from Sierra Leone and 3,198 from St. Helena; Tobago had also received a few, like the long-lived Panchoo Campbell. The immigrants were 'indentured' or bound to work for an estate for a year, after that they were free, but unlike the Indians they were not entitled to any return passage.

As estate labourers the 'liberated' Africans did not fulfil the planters' needs. For one thing their numbers were too small; for another, most of them left estate labour, mainly to squat and cultivate as small-holders, or to settle in or near towns as gardeners, artisans or general labourers. Despite their lack of numbers their contribution to Trinidad's culture was profound; they reinforced African cultural legacies that might otherwise have died out after the abolition of the slave trade (1807). Thus Shango was probably introduced by Yoruba immigrants in the 1840's and 1850's to become

the dominant African religious form in Trinidad. In Belmont, the Rada community, descended from Dahomey immigrants of this period, maintained its ancestral religion well into the 1950's. Because African immigrants spoke little or no English on arrival, and were unfamiliar with Western ways, they tended to settle with their own people in distinct settlements, often keeping up their own languages and cultural and religious practices, quite separate from the Creole and West Indian blacks. And this remained true at least to the turn of the 19th century.

A free African woman. Photograph — Maureen Hanton.

An African Rain Maker. Photograph — O. Mavrogordato.

Sources: D. Wood, *Trinidad in Transition.*
B. Brereton, *Race Relations in Colonial Trinidad.*
A. Carr, 'A Rada Community in Trinidad', *Caribbean Quarterly*, 3, 1953.

Name of Estate, or Domicile of Slaves.					

Pepper Hill

TOBAGO

RETURN

Of the **Number of Slaves** and **Estimated Value** thereof, in each Class, in possession of _Thomas Keene_

N.º 24

on the 1st day of August, 1834.

TOTAL NUMBER OF SLAVES ....

DIVISIONS.	No.	CLASSES.	Male.	Female.	Number.	Value in Sterling
Prædial attached	1	Head People				
	2	Tradesmen				
	3	Inferior Tradesmen				
	4	Field Labourers				
	5	Inferior Field Labourers				
Prædial unattached	1	Head People				
	2	Tradesmen				
	3	Inferior Tradesmen				
	4	Field Labourers				
	5	Inferior Field Labourers				
Non-Prædial	1	Head Tradesmen	3	"	3	330
	2	Inferior Tradesmen	3	"	3	24
	3	Head People employed on Wharfs, Shipping, or other Avocations	1	"	1	
	4	Inferior People of the same description .	2	"	2	
	5	Head Domestic Servants	"	1	1	
	6	Inferior Domestics	4	1	5	
Children under Six Years of Age on 1st of August, 1834.			2		2	
Aged, Diseased, or otherwise Non-effective						
			15	2	17	

WE, the undersigned, being two of the Valuers appointed to Classify and Value the Slaves in named Colony, do on our Oaths declare, after due examination and enquiry, that the above Return true, and accurate Classification and Valuation of the Slaves therein mentioned, on the 1st day of Augu. according to the best of our knowledge, information, and belief.

Dated this _22nd_ day of _October_   1834.   _Ja Chalmers appraiser_

Sworn this _5th_ day of _March 1835_   Signed _John Keens appraiser_

before me,
James A Jarvis
Chief Commiss

_A list of slaves on Pepper Hill estate, Tobago, giving
job descriptions, sex and value, for the purpose of remembering
the owner after the Emancipation. Tom Cambridge Collection_

SIXTEEN YEARS

IN THE

WEST INDIES

LIEUTENANT COLONEL CAPADOSE

IN TWO VOLUMES

VOL I.

LONDON

T. C. NEWBY. 72 MORTIMER St. CAVENDISH So.

1845.

Title page for, 'Sixteen Years in the West Indies', Lieutenant Colonel Capadose 1845.

On the fourteenth of May, 1839, I left Tobago, in H.M.S. Delight, (such is I believe the orthodox manner of commencing a tour), wishing to reach Port of Spain as speedily as possible. The sea was rough, the weather fine, though somewhat hazy, and as the packet kept away from the coast I could not enjoy so good a view of the scenery as is generally obtained. At an early hour of the evening we glided past the North Post, and a little before sunset entered, through the Grand Boca into the beautiful gulf of Paria. The wind then became adverse to our reaching Port of Spain, but as the mists dispersed, we had, so long as daylight lasted, an interesting, though transient view of that part of the South American coast, called Cumana — interesting from associations connected with the past; for, however opposed to the sentimental the traveller may be, such a spot must recall the memory of Columbus and his gallant crew, who first sailed into the gulf, visited, and bestowed its present appellation upon the Island to which we were hastening under such different auspices. And if Columbus could be forgotten when regarding Trinidad for the first time, the sight of the Caroni, as it dashes its billows to the ocean, would lead the beholder to the time, a few years later, when Sir Walter Raleigh made his successful attack upon San Joseph. That Columbus discovered Trinidad, is beyond all doubt; whether he resided there and explored a

The harbour at Port of Spain by Captain Wilson, 1825. The guns of Fort San Andrés can be seen on the right. Tom Cambridge Collection. What follows is an account by Lt. Col. Capadose of the British Army of a visit to Port of Spain and a trip to the east coast of the island. Lt. Col. Capadose acted as Governor on more than one occasion during the period.

considerable part of it, as many of its inhabitants believe, I leave others to decide; but his name, and that of Sir Walter Raleigh, give such an interest to the scene as I should be sorry to have taken from me. And the next morning when the sun rose, and, as the day advanced, shone brightly, on the shores on either side of the gulf, on its different islets, and gilded the town and shipping in the harbour of Port of Spain, I could not avoid thinking what a contrast all presented to the 31st of July 1498 — when first, as Washington Irvine so beautifully describes it, Columbus sent his boats on shore to obtain water. But a truce to all this sentiment and digression. Trinidad is no longer inhabited by Caribs; and the fishers' palm-leaved huts are now lost in the magnificent buildings of Port of Spain.

During our walk over a broad and then very hard road about a mile in length, I was surprised by the sight of a very large locust tree, which I think has never been mentioned by any writer. It is rather singular it should have been noticed, for, in addition to its being very unusual to see these trees in frequented places, it is not far distant from the lake, on the right of the pathway, and certainly forms one of the most attractive objects.

I saw one of these trees in Tobago, of considerable height, having forty or fifty feet of straight trunk, large in circumference, before the branches commence, and then apparently extending as many more to the topmost bough; it was profusely laden with fruit which consists of pods, in shape like a bean, the shell of which is extremely hard, and thick as a Spanish dollar. These pods

Breakfast was just finished on board the Packet when smoke rising from the Paria steam vessel denoted its immediate departure for Point La Brea. Near Point La Brea, lies the celebrated Pitch Lake – and I involuntarily expressed a wish not to lose such an opportunity of visiting it. The Captain kindly offering to send me on board the Paria, I hastily look leave of my fellow passengers, jumped into a boat and rowed briskly on towards the steam vessel, already on its way; in an hour I stood on its deck, and was proceeding with celerity past the quarter of S——, and so close in shore as to afford me a view of the estates on that coast, and the adjoining district of San Fernando, where we stopped a short time to land and receive passengers, goods, &c.

This ceremony completed, we proceeded on to Point La Brea, where we anchored about four o'clock p.m. I dined on board, for as the sun was intensely hot I resolved not to proceed on my projected excursion till the cool of evening.

As soon as the heat became less oppressive I went on shore accompanied by the captain of the steam-boat and one of the passengers, made a short visit to a gentleman in charge of an estate, to which, as he told me, a part, at least, if not the whole of the lake belongs, and then started eager for a sight of that wonderful phenomenon regarded as the greatest natural curiosity of Trinidad.

The Paria Steamer off the coast of La Brea, 1839, by Captain Wilson — Tom Cambridge Collection.

1845

SAVANNAH RE-NAMED QUEEN'S PARK
At a meeting of the Council of Government held on the 18th August, 1845, on the item '£100 for clearing and weeding the Savannah,' His Excellency stated that there were objections to the continued use of the term Savannah, which, at home was associated with swamps and fevers; and he suggested that as they were trying to make this as much as possible an English colony, they should give the Savannah an English name; and he suggested 'Queen's Park.' This was agreed to.

vary in size from three to eight inches in length and from one to four in thickness or depth, are of the colour of tanned leather, and rough like a shagreen case. When opened, which is not effected without some difficulty, the natives take out a sort of friable pith not unpleasant to the taste, having a slight resemblance to ginger-bread, but dry and husky; each pod contains three grains, or seeds, about the size of a large filbert, rather red in colour, when first taken out, but soon turning black as jet, which can easily be polished, and being very hard, capable of being converted into ornaments, &c. The pod itself is made into snuff boxes, powder flasks, &c.

Labat, a celebrated French author, tells of having made many small articles from the pod of the courbari or locust tree, but he was mistaken in asserting that it bears fruit twice in twelve months, like all other fruit trees in the West Indies. In Tobago, where I saw this magnificent tree, the inhabitants esteem it a fortuitous circumstance if they obtain a good crop once each year. It requires a growth of many years to bring these trees to perfection which accounts for their rarity and the comparatively few planted, whilst an infinite number have been cut down by Europeans for the sake of the wood, which is useful for axle-trees and wood-work for mills. The leaves are of a dark green colour, rather small in comparison to the size of the branches and fruit, forming a beautiful contrast to the flowers, which are of a yellowish white and of oval shape.

scorching of my feet, having taken off my shoes, to wade through the broad chasms of water, across which, at that time, there were no planks.' Probably Sir James visited it under midday heat, or that the effect of the sun is not always the same; certain it is, that this evening, the surface of the lake was quite cool though the sun was still above the horizon.

I was in hopes I should have found ships at La Brea laden with the matter dug from the lake, but the ardour, which for a time prevailed, in search of what was considered highly valuable, had abated. Cargos of it that had been shipped to England were not approved, the different trials made were declared failures, and though in some parts of France it was said to answer for improving foot paths, in the manner it is used for roads in the vicinity of the lake and the district of Naparima,

Point La Brea, 1839, by Captain Wilson — Tom Cambridge Collection.

The tree I now regarded was not of such large dimensions, but its beautiful branches were bending under the weight of fruit such as I have described.

It was sunset when we reached the lake and the air deliciously cool, thus enabling us to traverse its vast surface without difficulty, more particularly as planks were placed across the fissures or chasms, so accurately described by Doctor Nugent of Antigua, and inserted in the work of Mrs. Carmichael. To me the lake had the appearance of an immense level plain with here and there thickets of shrubs, grass and trees growing out of the bitumen, which was then of a very dark colour and generally quite hard; some few places yielded to the impression of the foot and were of the consistency of pitch.

The water flowing through the chasms was perfectly clear but lukewarm and of a disagreeable, acid taste. This warmth, no doubt, was owing to the heat of the sun, which, however, had no effect upon the solid part of the surface which was quite dry though the day had been one of the hottest ever known. Sir James Alexander, in his account of this extraordinary place, says 'The heat of the surface obliged me to dance up and down from the

few hopes were entertained of its becoming more useful. Still, though the prospect of its ever being a source of wealth appears closed, a time may come when some qualities more available may be discovered. A great deal of the bitumen is used for fuel in the distillation of rum, and partially in the sugar manufactories, as well as for steam navigation; and the question has arisen in my mind whether it could not be made of use in gas works. All this must be the result of experiment and time.

I was disappointed in seeing the bitumen taken from the lake, but I did not enjoy the beauties of its diversified margin the less; shrubs, trees, aloes, flowers and pineapples, all luxuriate around it, and during the day, birds and butterflies flying hither and thither, detract from the loneliness of the scene. We gathered a pineapple, the only one we found ripe, the captain pared and divided it with his cutlass, and we enjoyed its fine flavour.

We lingered till the calm stillness of night imparted an aspect of gloom, which, my curiosity satisfied, I gladly exchanged for hospitable refreshment at the house of the gentleman before named.

I felt no wish to prolong my stay at La Brea, which, though prettily situated, is only a small village consisting of poorly built cottages, the only one of neat appearance being that of our host. Ten o'clock found me on board the steam-boat, in which, next morning, we weighed anchor to return to Port of Spain, steering in the first instance for San Fernando, a distance of thirty miles, along a shore rich in luxuriant estates, cane fields sprinkled amongst noble forets, and conspicuous from their bright, green houses with their pleasure grounds stretching down to the water's edge, interspersed with cocoa-nut and palm trees. Whilst we stopped at San Fernando which is much superior to La Brea and pleasantly situated at the foot of the mountain, I paid a

I landed at Port of Spain, after four years absence, late at night–hastened to an hotel and betook myself to that rest the exertion of the previous two days demanded. Next morning my first care was to repair to the Packet Delight, to seek for the luggage I left on board when I so hurriedly transferred myself to the Paria–that duty performed, I returned to the Hotel to breakfast, then waited upon the acting governor, visited some friends, and passed the remainder of the day rambling about the town. Four years had witnessed great alterations and improvements, and as I walked through the long wide streets all running parallel to the sea, and shaded with trees, looked on its spendid buildings all of stone and uniform in appearance, and inhaled the

San Fernando, 1839, by Captain Wilson. On the hilltop may be seen the barracks occupied by the 74th Regiment — Tom Cambridge Collection.

hasty visit to the barracks, erected on a gentle eminence immediately above the town and then occupied by an officer and forty men beloning to the 74th Regiment. The meeting with a friend, and the sight of numerous pretty houses in the vicinity of this little town, made me enjoy this interruption in my voyage exceedingly, and I think had I known, that, from the boat having approached very near to the landing place for the convenience of the passengers, and the tide falling, we should have been detained an hour, San Fernando would have been my resting place for the night. But at length we got clear of the mud, and the continued loveliness of the shore soon made me forget the vexation I had felt at the delay.

Near Pointe à Pierre a magnificent estate called Plaisance was pointed out to me, and how much I wished to land and examine the warm springs situated on it; but there was no vessel near to convey me to them, so I could only promise myself that excursion another time.

delicious breeze from the ocean, I could but own the truth of the general assertion, that Port of Spain is the finest town in the West Indies; whilst its situation on the shore of the splendid Gulf of Paria, scarcely, I think, surpassed by that of Naples, the highly cultivated lands around producing all the luxuries of life, the entire freedom from hurricanes, which cause such devastation in many of the other colonies, and the exemption in a great degree from fatal sickness, combine to make it the most desirable as a residence.

I dined that day with my friend Dangaud, and made the first arrangement to commence my tour by borrowing his chaise to take me to San Joseph, the following morning after I had taken leave of the acting Governor and his family at the Government House, St. Ann's, and enjoyed a stroll through the beautiful grounds attached to that domain.

On my road to San Joseph, I saw, for the first time in the West Indies, a turnpike gate. This, and many other objects I had previously seen, recalled to mind the late Sir Ralph Woodford, who offered to make turnpike roads through the colony if the inhabitants would consent to pay toll. This proposition, had it been acceded to, would have proved a means of great prosperity, but the affluent inhabitants, from a feeling I cannot understand, declined the offer.

San Joseph, the ancient capital of the Island, is a quiet, healthy spot, frequently serving as a convalescent post for the troops at St. James, and certainly for such a purpose no place could be better chosen. The inhabitants one less skilful may choose a little to the right, where the depth varies from one to four feet, a spot to indulge in a similar pleasure. But let both the practised and unskilful swimmer beware of the shoals of small fish perceptible on both sides, for, on the slightest cessation of movement, he will be attacked by those biting creatures, and the enjoyment of his bath destroyed.

I had intended to go to Arima early the next morning, but the difficulty of procurring a horse detained me. To hire one was not practicable; the officers had none, or I should have been instantly supplied; and here let me observe that it would be advisable for the Government to allow every officer, in the West Indies,

The mission of Arima 1837, by Captain Wilson. In 1757 the Capuchins of the Aragon Province of Spain, founded an Indian mission in Arima, it was dedicated to the first of the New World saints Santa Rosa de Lima. The Tacarigua, Caura and Arouca missions were placed under the guidance of Padre Reyes Bravo, who later rose to the position of Vicar of Trinidad — Tom Cambridge Collection.

complain of its dullness, for their solitude is no longer enlivened by the band of the 1st W.I. Regt., to which they had been accustomed from 1825, till the chieftain, Donald Stewart, excited his African followers, then his fellow soldiers (all being alike, enlisted recruits of the 1st W.I. Regt.) to revolt. But the beauty of its situation renders it a most interesting spot, and of its dullness I saw nothing; many kind friends were there to give me a warm welcome, and I hastened to meet them, resolving San Joseph should be my head quarters for a few weeks, to enable me to enjoy their society in the intervals of coming and going. There were several estates in the neighbourhood I wished to see, and I should thus diversify my pleasures.

The barracks were now occupied by two officers and forty men of the 1st W.I. Regt., an officer and twenty men of the 74th Regt., and a staff assistant surgeon, whose office was nearly a sinecure, this year at least, although, he assured me, the previous one had been very unhealthy.

When at San Joseph, I never neglect to enjoy the luxury of a bath in the river, which in one part forms a natural basin never less than eight feet deep, with a fine sandy bottom. A shelving rock a few feet above the surface invites the practised swimmer to a dive, whilst forage for a horse, or the means of keeping one. However, the delay was not to be regretted as I was enabled to participate in the pleasure of a dinner given by the officer of the 74th Regt., to celebrate the christening of his child.

A horse, at last, was kindly lent to me, and much obliged I felt for the loan, but surely such an animal never before tried the patience of an impatient traveller. It had a sore back, and had lost a shoe, but the hope of getting another, or a mule to supply in place, from some friend on the road, induced me to proceed though it was but slowly.

Disappointment met me everywhere, so I was obliged to conquer my impatience, and stifle as well as I could my feelings of pity for the creature I bestrode, and jog on. As a proof of the extreme dryness of the season, I state, that on arriving at the fort of San Joseph, intersecting the river, I found it quite dry, and such had seldom if ever before been the case. The road was very dusty, the sun intensely hot, and even after its decline the air very sultry, but the beautiful scenery around compensated for these inconveniences. Lovely as ever looked the estates, Streatham Lodge, El Dorado, Orange Grove, Paradise, Laurel Hill, the Garden and various others to the right and left offering to view superb house, extensive pastures (many of which resemble the parks of noblemen or gentlemen in England), and luxuriant full grown sugar canes, with a variety of trees, shrubs, and flowers. All these beauties with the many coloured birds, fluttering in every direction tended to divert the tedium of a compulsory slow ride. Arima is estimated at only eleven miles distance from San Joseph, but the state of my horse and the calls I made on my way, though brief ones, prevented by reaching the house of Mr. S——, the corregidor, till past seven o'clock. Nothing can be more refreshing than hospitality such as I received from Mr. S——, who, though not able to accommodate me in his own house, directed the Casa Real to be opened, and everything provided for my comfort, that of the men who accompanied me, and for my poor horse.

To Mr. S——y, the Abbé, or Curate of the village, I was also indebted for much kind attention. Both he and the Corregidor opposed my determination to continue my tour to Band de L'Este the following morning, urging that the season was too far advanced, and heavy rain, such as would render the roads impassable from the overflow of the rivers, might be daily and hourly expected – particularly after the long drought of the present year–another reason they alleged for my stay was, that the horse would be better. These arguments were very good, but I knew I could get a mule at Touroure, and the weather was now fine.

Like the generality of mankind, as the present was propitious, I did not regard the future, so, on the twentieth of May, taking farewell of the Corregidor and the Curate–the former giving me a sketch of part of my route, and the latter a cup of delicious coffee, I set out for Touroure.

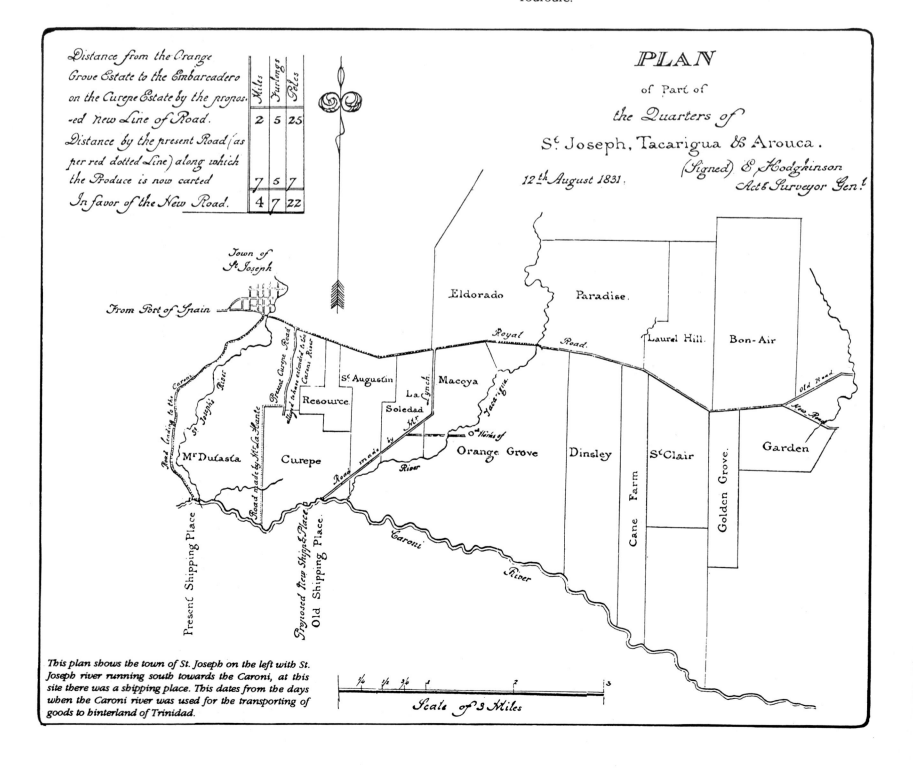

	Miles	Furlongs	Poles
Distance from the Orange Grove Estate to the Embarcadero on the Curepe Estate by the proposed New Line of Road.	2	5	25
Distance by the present Road (as per red dotted Line) along which the Produce is now carted	7	5	7
In favor of the New Road.	4	7	22

PLAN

of Part of

the Quarters of

St. Joseph, Tacarigua & Arouca.

12th August 1831.

(Signed) E. Hodghinson
Actg Surveyor Genl

This plan shows the town of St. Joseph on the left with St. Joseph river running south towards the Caroni, at this site there was a shipping place. This dates from the days when the Caroni river was used for the transporting of goods to hinterland of Trinidad.

Scale of 3 Miles

Hitherto, I had travelled what is considered in the West Indies a good carriage road, but Towards Touroure, the country assumed a wild aspect–the road becoming bad, then worse and worse, being intersected by the rivers, Arima, Maher, Guanapo, Aripo, Valentia, Quarro, &c., &c. Sugar canes are seen in great abundance the whole ride from Port of Spain to Arima, but no cocoa trees till after leaving the latter, then increasing in number to Guanapo at which place are estates of that produce to some extent, belonging to French and Spanish families. The cultivation of cocoa was formerly a source of great

A searcher after adventures or a lover of the picturesque would be delighted with a ride through such an almost impassable wilderness as it is from Touroure to Manzanilla, the road intersected by frightful ravines across which, in many places, were rough, slippery trunks of trees, scarcely wide enough for a footstep, whilst the wooden bridges over some of the streams or rivulets were no less difficult to cross. I encountered about forty of these rustic bridges, over which I walked, but the mule, who evidently did not wish to retrieve his bad character, was obliged to be hauled by ropes through the muddy water by two strong men.

Cocoa Nut Grove extending 7 miles on the Eastern Coast Trinidad

emolument; but the demand has so decreased that thousands and thousands of those trees, once so valuable, now obtain but a slender subsistence for the possessors. Gigantic trees of various kinds attracted my notice–the most conspicuous amongst which was the Balatas.

The only place of entertainment at Touroure, or indeed for many miles distance, is kept, or was at that time, by an old Sergeant of one of the West Indian Regiments,who has, with more of his discharged companions, located there for some years. His thatched cottage afforded no good 'entertainment for man and beast,' yet I was glad to rest beneath its roof for an hour, and to leave my horse in his care till my return, taking instead a small mule with a very bad character to carry me on to Manzanilla.

In the rainy season these rivulets rise to a great height and overflow the banks, but now, the water being shallow, the banks were high and the mud very deep. A great want of cultivation appeared all around me, but the trees were beautiful, and amongst them the balatas and silk mahot especially claimed my admiration, the latter from the peculiarity of its fruit (if I may so term it), which, with the exception of the toes, perfectly resembles the foot of a hare.

It was dark when I came to the beginning of the quarter called Manzanilla, and in the obscurity, crossing a small bridge that appeared to me formed of smooth planks but which was in reality a round, slippery trunk of a tree, the mule fell and I was precipitated with some little violence on to the hard wood, my face much bruised, my eye much cut. Judge then how glad I felt to reach 'The Place', and, though I found there but poor accommodation, having only a hammock to sleep in, how I enjoyed my rest. Those who love early rising and a walk on the sea shore can imagine why I, in spite of the pain in my face, was up with the birds and hastened to gaze on the sea for the first time on the eastern coast of Trinidad, and how I relished a breakfast after such a ramble.

Again I went along the seashore towards Mayaro, and at eleven came to Nariva; there crossing the river Mitan proceeded, still by the sea, to the river Ortoire, which I also forded, and leaving the shore took a path to the right leading through corn fields to an estate called Malgrétout, leaving which to the right, I again emerged on the beach. The gentleman I wished to see at Nariva was gone to Mayaro on magisterial business, and thither I followed, having made an appointment to call on him as I returned from Beau Séjour, the property of two gentlemen, one of whom, perceiving my approach, and recognizing by the aid of a lorgnette who it was, came forward with a cordial welcome.

We had not met for five years, and I own I was surprised at his discovering me, disguised as I was in a strange kind of travelling garb and a bruised face. In his wife, to whom he had been recently united, I recognised a niece of my old friend Monsieur Germon, who had resided many years at San Joseph, and whose hospitable doors were always open to the officers. I was especially a favoured guest, and when he left to return to France, and

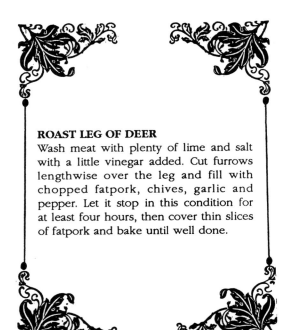

ROAST LEG OF DEER
Wash meat with plenty of lime and salt with a little vinegar added. Cut furrows lengthwise over the leg and fill with chopped fatpork, chives, garlic and pepper. Let it stop in this condition for at least four hours, then cover thin slices of fatpork and bake until well done.

The interior of the Estate house occupied by Mr. Samuel Carter at the Coconut Oil Factory at Manzanilla. By Captain Wilson 1837 — Tom Cambridge Collection.

TRINIDAD COCONUT ESTATES
Mayaro

Estates		Owners
*Bay Frank	. . . .	St. R. Guillaume
*Roget	. . . .	Panchoo
*Malgrétout	. . . .	Heirs P. Noel
Mon Plasir	. . . .	Joseph Gray
Esperance	. . . .	W.J.L. & O.J.
Pilgrim	. . . .	Huggins
*St. Helena	. . . .	Philip Jeanvier
*Belle Vue	. . . .	Pierre P. Noel
*Alphonsine	. . . .	Arthur Popwell
*Newcastly	. . . .	L.L. de Meillac
*Mon Repos	. . . .	G.E. Valentine
*Limit	. . . .	Hrs. Alex. Hobson
*Picton	. . . .	Randolph Ah Lit
*Lassean Venas	. . . .	Jane Arneau
*Belle Vue	. . . .	M. Thabourin
Hermitage	. . . .	E.J. Baker
Belle Vue	. . . .	Bernadine Brisson
*Sans Souci	. . . .	St. Rose Brisson
*Larafad	. . . .	Heirs, Eustache
*St. John	. . . .	Tourville Ferrier
*St. John	. . . .	Hrs. E. Lemessy
St. Catherine		
*Picton	. . . .	Lee Lum
*Santa Anna	. . . .	
*Sans Souci	. . . .	Marie F. Merrique
*Perseverance	. . . .	T. Merrique
*Leon	. . . .	Ignace Merrique
*Heritage	. . . .	Ignace Merrique
*Bannitier	. . . .	Heirs F. Sobion
*Esperanza	. . . .	Jas. Corbie
*Quizab	. . . .	Tim F.B. David
*Prosperity	. . . .	Hrs. Cath. Ferrier
*Sans Souci	. . . .	Marie Hughes
*La Fontaine	. . . .	Charles John
*Mòn Plaisir	. . . .	F.H. Popwell
*San Bernard	. . . .	Gustave Popwell
*L'Esperance	. . . .	Catherine Rust
*St. John	. . . .	John F. Vigilant
Nariva Cocal	. . . .	G. Huggins & Co.
*St. Bernard	. . . .	John Urich & Son
*Lagondoux	. . . .	John Urich & Son
La Cordonnière	. . . .	John Urich & Son
Geraldstein	. . . .	
*Beaumont	. . . .	W.G. Gordon
*Plaisance	. . . .	
St. Joseph	. . . .	Hrs. of Ganteaume
*Plaisance	. . . .	Hrs. Pierre
*St. Mary	. . . .	Schoener & Co.
Beausejour	. . . .	Hrs. of Popwell
St. Ann's	. . . .	G.A. de Pompignon
Beausejour	. . . .	G.A. de Pompignon
Tunbridge	. . . .	George T. Huggins
Providence	. . . .	O. Ligoure
*Britannia	. . . .	Hrs. E. Doyle
Salem Grove	. . . .	G.T. Brash
*St. Catherine	. . . .	Hrs. of Frontin
Fores	. . . .	Hrs. of Hughes
*St. Mary	. . . .	Leonce Thomas
*Limit	. . . .	Juan Bardales
*L'Esperance	. . . .	Gus. Valentine
*Santa Arima	. . . .	Randolph Rust
Breton	. . . .	Ros. Huggins
*Providence	. . . .	F.C. Prevatt
Cane Farm	. . . .	Wiltshire Eddy
Bocas	. . . .	Wiltshire Eddy

*And Cacao.

1845

CHARLES WARNER, — ATTORNEY

We learn with much pleasure that by letters received by this packet the confirmation of the appointment of the Hon'ble. Charles W. Warner as Attorney-General, though not officially announced, may be looked upon as finally determined. We sincerely congratulate the hon'ble. and learned gentleman on his promotion which he has well earned by his unwearied and most arduous labours in the reformation of our civil code, and the extensive aid he afforded his lamented predecessor in the introduction of the British criminal law and trial by jury.
(14th March, 1845).

Port of Spain Gazette. Special Centenary issue.

pressed me to accompany him, nothing but my duty as a soldier prevented me. I was in good health, and though certain of obtaining leave of absence, I refrained from asking. We parted full of hope in another meeting, but soon after his arrival at Toulouse, Monsieur Germon was taken ill, and died, *je vais retourner à vous mes quatre vingt dix enfants,* was his expression, in parting, to the ninety slaves on his estate; and when I lost a valued friend, they were deprived of the best of masters.

Soon after my arrival the associé came, and joined in hospitable attentions to the traveller–making a pleasant addition to our party, and assisting in inducing me to promise to stay and inspect the sugar works and other parts of the estate. The principal dwelling house of Beau Séjour is advantageously situated on a gentle eminence looking over a fine pasture, or rather lawn, and level lands filled with luxuriant sugar canes, extending to the sea shore; whilst in front, inclining a little to the right, in the distance, is Point Galeota: the whole well-watered, the lands rich, fertile, and extensive. The river Ortoire, flowing through a great part of the estate, is of good width, and navigable for boats to a considerable distance.

I have been all my life a soldier, and am, therefore, but little skilled in the technical terms proper to describe steam engines and sugar mills, but those at Beau Séjour appeared perfect; and such of my leaders as may regret the omission, I refer to a work by a clever English gentleman, published in London, and which contains a full description of the cultivation of the sugar cane, the mills and the whole process of distillation.

Had I read this valuable description, before viewing these mills, how much more interesting would everything have seemed.

The greatest drawback to agriculture in the West Indies is the idleness of the Negroes, who work only four hours in the day, and then, notwithstanding the high wages they obtain, very negligently. Three quarters of a dollar each per diem, or rather for four hours superficial work, besides other advantages equivalent to a dollar, four shillings and two-pence British, is what is usually paid to them, many will not work at all as long as they have any money, and, upon the slightest work of reproach, quit the estate for ever.

My friends were in great anxiety, lest, through the misconduct of these wilful labourers, the crops of this year should be lost, and as every month increases their insolence there was a worse prospect for the future.

The principal estates in the district of Mayaro are Malgrétout, Mayaro, Beau Séjour, Plaisance, Saint Margaret, Lagondoux, besides many rural farms where cocoa-nut trees, vegetables and roots, usually termed ground provisions, such as yams, sweet potatoes, cassava, tanniers, &c., are cultivated. Near the coast many of the inhabitants are chiefly supported by the manufacture of cocoa-nut oil.

The travellers in the islands must not be particular, they cannot roll along roads smooth as a bowling-green, reposing in their carriages; nay, like Tantalus, they must sometimes look at luxuries without enjoying them. Thus, nearly the whole way from Manzanilla to Point Galeota, a distance of twenty five or thirty miles, avenues of cocoa-nut trees seem to offer you a shelter from the scorching rays of the sun; but you only escape one dilemma to fall into another; on the beach you are in danger of being capsized by your horse stumbling against the heaps of broken shells thrown up by the sea on the stormy coast, but in the avenues 'tis impossible to get on at all, for the ground is covered by fallen nuts, and the husks of those which have been opened to obtain the pulp, to extract the oil. The conchologist would be equally tantalized for amongst the heaps of shells which he would be delighted to see, scarcely a whole one is to be found; repeatedly I alighted from my horse to seek for one but in vain.

At Point Galeota a discovery of a sort of fuel, resembling English coal, had just been made, and I witnessed the first experiment of using it. A small pile of English coal, one of bitumen, from the Pitch Lake, and one of the newly found fuel, were placed upon the ground in the open air close to each other, and all set light to at the same moment. The English coal and that (or its altitude) of Beau Séjour, blazed up and burnt perfectly clear, but the bitumen did not blaze, only smoked. The engineer gave the preference to the new fuel, which was better he said for a steam engine, as the flame was equally strong as that from the English coal, and left no cinders; he added that the Pitch Lake produce is not available for the steam engine or the manufacture of sugar, but for that of rum it answered well, and taking me to a furnace, he opened the door and shewed the bitumen burning with a bright flame. The proprietors had neither of them seen the spot where the fuel had been found, and were quite ignorant of its extent, but full of hope as to the result; they determined upon immediately examining the nature of and the importance to be attached to the discovery.

CALLALOO
This is best done in an earthenware canaree. Put everything in at one time. Use a small piece salt beef, a small piece salt pork cut up finely, one small melongene cut up, nine ochroes, cut up in two or three pieces each, one bundle dasheen leaves with strings removed, two crabs cleaned and with the members broken off and cracked, a green whole pepper, chives, thyme, garlic and onions. Pour over this enough water to fill the canaree, or put about three quarters full. Do not stir; only occasionally shake the pot. When half the water has boiled away remove green whole pepper and swizzle vigorously with a lala stick, serve with banane pilee, (pounded plantain).

The Ganteaume Family of Mayaro
Shown below are some members of the Ganteaume Family. Not every one has been identified positively but it has been ascertained, that the third lady on the left in the back row is Léonine Ganteaume and the fifth Elisa O'Connor née Ganteaume. The sixth, Isale O'Connor, a cousin, was married to Henri de La Bastide, the seventh is Henry Peter Ganteaume. In the middle row left, Henri de La Bastide and the third lady on the left is Mathilde O'Connor née Ganteaume. Photograph — Therese (Terry) Bedford née Ganteaume.

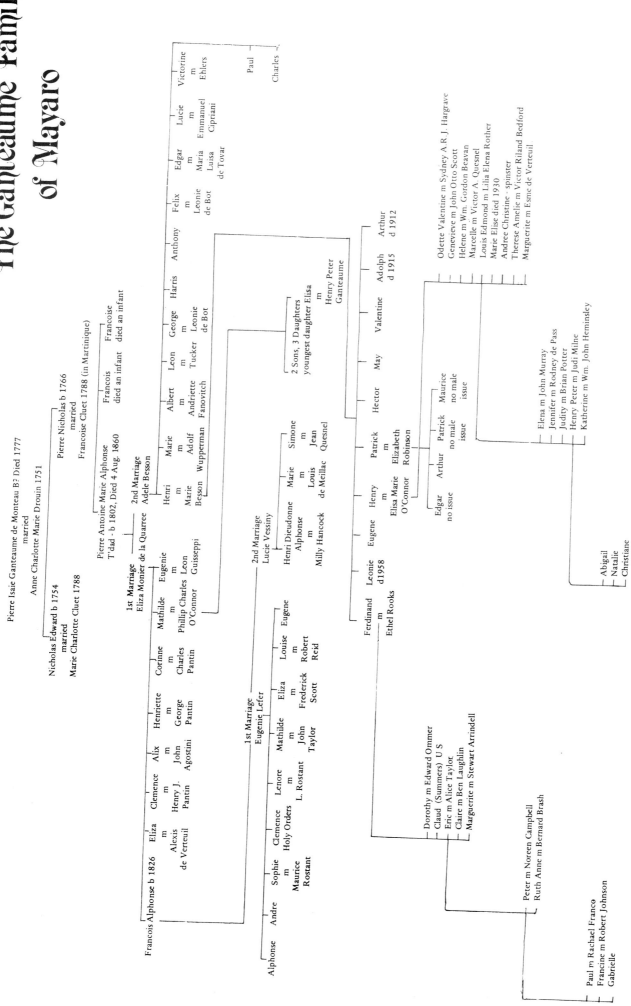

The Ganteaume Family
of Mayaro

Pierre Isaie Ganteaume de Monteau B? Died 1777
married
Anne Charlotte Marie Drouin 1751

Nicholas Edward b 1754
married
Marie Charlotte Cluet 1788

Pierre Nicholas b 1766
married
Francoise Cluet 1788 (in Martinique)

Pierre Antoine Marie Alphonse
T'dad - b 1802, Died 4 Aug. 1860

1st Marriage
Eliza Monier de la Quarree

2nd Marriage
Adele Besson

Francois
died an infant

Francoise
died an infant

Francois Alphonse b 1826

Eliza
m
Alexis
de Verteuil

Clemence
m
Henry J.
Pantin

Alix
m
John
Agostini

Henriette
m
George
Pantin

Corinne
m
Charles
Pantin

Mathilde
m
Phillip Charles Leon
O'Connor

Eugenie
m
Guisseppi

Henri
m
Marie
Besson

Marie
m
Adolf
Wupperman

Albert
m
Andriette
Fanovitch

Leon
m
Tucker

George
m
Leonie
de Bot

Harris

Anthony

Felix
m
Leonie
de Bot

Edgar
m
Maria
Luisa
de Tovar

Lucie
m
Emmanuel
Cipriani

Victorine
m
Ehlers

Paul

Charles

1st Marriage
Eugenie Lefer

2nd Marriage
Lucie Vessiny

Alphonse

Andre

Sophie
m
Maurice
Rostant

Clemence
Holy Orders

Lenore
m
L. Rostant

Mathilde
m
John
Taylor

Eliza
m
Frederick
Scott

Louise
m
Robert
Reid

Eugene

Henri Dieudonne
Alphonse
m
Milly Hancock

Marie
m
Louis
de Meillac

Simone
m
Jean
Quesnel

2 Sons, 3 Daughters
youngest daughter Elisa
m
Henry Peter
Ganteaume

Dorothy m Edward Ommer
Claud (Summers) U S
Eric m Alice Taylor
Claire m Ben Laughlin
Marguerite m Stewart Arrindell

Ferdinand
m
Ethel Rooks

Leonie
d1958

Eugene

Henry
m
Elisa Marie
O'Connor

Patrick
m
Elizabeth
Robinson

Hector

May

Valentine

Adolph
d 1915

Arthur
d 1912

Edgar
no issue

Arthur

Patrick
no male
issue

Maurice
no male
issue

Odette Valentine m Sydney A R J. Hargrave
Genevieve m John Otto Scott
Helene m Wm. Gordon Beavan
Marcelle m Victor A. Quesnel
Louis Edmond m Lilia Elena Rother
Marie Elise died 1930
Andree Christine - spinster
Therese Amelie m Victor Riland Bedford
Marguerite m Esme de Verteuil

Peter m Noreen Campbell
Ruth Anne m Bernard Brash

Elena m John Murray,
Jennifer m Rodney de Pass
Judith m Brian Potter
Henry Peter m Judi Milne
Katherine m Wm. John Heminsley

Abigail
Natalie
Christiane

Paul m Rachael Franco
Francine m Robert Johnson
Gabrielle

TO THE EAST COAST
(BANDE DE L'EST)

From Guide to Trinidad
J.H. Collens

For varied phases of tropical scenery in the most distant regions of the island you cannot do better than take a trip to the East Coast. You will require two desiderata at the outset, first, a pretty good animal, be it horse or mule, second, not a small modicum of endurance. The journey is long, sometimes trying, and the roads are—well, not exactly perfect.

Take the train to Arima, sending your beast in a horse-truck (cost five shillings). From Arima Station the journey will be *à cheval,* for I am afraid to say how many miles. If you have a good companion, so much the better and the more the merrier. You pass through the little town of Arima, which was been described in Chapter XIII,

and soon come into the land of cacao, with magnificent shady *Bois Immortel.* At first you will ha ford several rivers, which may be a little troubleso the wet season. Three miles beyond Arima, at Gua Village, you come to a fork in the road. Take the turning, for, as the old couplet has it,—

'If you go to the *left* you are *right,*
If you turn to the *right* you'll go *wrong.'*

I did the latter myself on one occasion, very muc my mortification, not discovering the error of my way I had reached Mr. John Agostini's house on the Co road, when of course I had to retrace my steps cons myself with the sorry reflection that there is no tea like experience. Three more miles through cacao Crown lands bring you to Valencia with its l

Philip Charles O'Connor, son of Dr. O'Connor who settled in Tri in 1820. The photograph was taken from a painting by an unk artist, and is reproduced here with the permission of Theresa (T Bedford née Ganteaume.

Portuguese shop and Registrar's Office in one. We call all shops of this kind 'Portuguese,' though the proprietor may be a Creole as in this case. He is a very obliging Creole too, for he lent me his horse and buggy once when I was in sore need. The road to the left leads to Toco, not your direction. You follow that to the right, which soon brings you to the 'long stretch,' a piece of road that goes due east as straight as the arrow flies for nearly four miles. Here you may ride for hours scarcely seeing a sign of human life except now and then a solitary bare-footed, shirt-sleeved pedestrian, (some of our black countrymen are tremendous walkers, and would give Weston himself a twister), briskly trudging townwards, cutlass in hand, coat and boots slung over his shoulder. Your genuine native would as soon think of flying as of travelling without his cutlass,

Henry Peter Ganteaume, was a much respected member of the Legal Profession. He married his cousin Elisa O'Connor. They are shown below with three of their nine children. On the left, Odette, the baby is Hélène, front, Geneviéve. Photograph — Therese (Terry) Bedford née Ganteaume.

(snakes!), and the boots betray the fact that he is bound for town. When he reaches Arima station, if not before, he will don coat, boots, etc., and play the swell till he returns. Here a marked difference is noticeable between the Creole labourer and the Coolie. When the former goes in for pedal coverings he usually prefers light dandy boots, and would rather undergo unutterable tortures from corns, bunions and such like ills, than let you imagine his feet are larger than they should be. Mr. Coolie on the other hand believes in quantity not in quality, and you may frequently see him stalking gravely along *sans* breeches, (*kapra* of course wrapped gracefully round the loins), with his inevitable whity-green umbrella, and shod in elephantine boots that would have worthily become a Brobdignagian.

Huge trees whose stems are crowded with parasites catch the eye continually, while the cries of birds unknown in more habited regions equally appeal to the ear. Now the air resounds with the discordant 'craw' of the crake, so loud as almost to startle you in your

Above: Frederick Ganteaume. Photograph — St. Mary's College Centenary.

The Ganteaume's home on the north-western corner of Abercromby and Oxford Streets. This was originally the site of the Royal Collegiate School the predecessor of the Queen's Royal College. This was before it was moved to the Prince's Building. Photograph – Lucille Quesnel.

The Ganteaumes were related by marriage to the Quesnel family. Below are the children of Alfred Quesnel and Phillipa Sorzano. They are, from the left, Louis, Rita, Robert and Alfredd Victor. Missing are, Ferdinand and Max. Photograph - Therese (Terry) Bedford née Ganteaume.

loneliness; or it may be the melancholy plaintive cooing of the wood-dove calling its mate, or the absurdly comic sounds emitted by the corn-bird, the inharmonious shrieks of parrots flying in pairs high above the tallest trees, and all the time the incessant but more familiar 'qu'-est-ce-qu'-il-dit.' The high woods abound with charms to the Botanist, rare Orchids, Filmy Ferns, etc.

About six miles from Valencia you pass the little wooden church of Turure, (Anglican), built in 1883, almost entirely by the exertions of the labouring classes of this quarter, who being too poor to give much in the way of hard cash, gave their labour *freely*. Turure Church too is a landmark, for it is nearly midway between Arima and the Atlantic, twelve miles more or less from either. Don't rely upon any information which the good country folk may tender you regarding distance. They mean well, but I emphatically deny that they have any conception of distance. The first time I did this journey alone, when about half way up the 'long-stretch' I enquired of an intelligent-looking road-labourer how much farther it was to Sangre Grande. 'About three miles' was the ready reply. My heart was gladdened, and I proceeded on my

A group of party goers aboard a wagon at the turn of the century. Photograph — Asché.

The Ganteaume's house at St. Joseph Estate Mayaro. Thatched roof and timbered, it housed the family for well over a century and it was typical of the rustic building in which the Creoles lived on their estates. Photograph — Lucille Quesnel.

journey. After another half hour, I repeated my enquiry, receiving the response, still with an air of authority that seemed to carry correction with it,—'Not too far, about a quarter of a mile.' This may have been correct, but if so, it was the longest quarter of a mile I have ever travelled, for it took another good thirty-five minutes to do it. Beyond Turure the cottages begin to dot the roadside with greater frequency, and there is more attempt at cultivation. Crossing the good Cunape bridge (the old one was a wretch!), you soon reach the Sangre Grande Rest-House, a boon to the dusty and way-worn. It would be advisable to stay here for the night, the Government provides the place on purpose; you will get a clean bed for yourself and stabling for the horse, while the

1848

PROTEST AGAINST WAKES

On Thursday last, the 29th September, one of those infamous admixtures of superstition, debauchery, profanity and riot, so peculiarly the disgrace of Trinidad, known as a 'wake' took place in the yard of a residence in Port of Spain. . . . . . . It occurred in consequence of the death of a negro who, in extremis (such is negroe sympathy for one another), was kicked out of the house by the woman with whom he cohabited, and was brought here expressly to die; which the poor wretch did in two days. . . . . . The relatives of the deceased were methodists. . . . . . . At 7 p.m. the riot began with psalm singing over the corpse, and by 9 o'clock at night the yard was literally crammed with women and girls of very doubtful character, a host of drunken sailors, and all the lawless ruffians of Port of Spain, —yelling in chorus, dancing in circles, and clapping their hands together. The uproar was fearful, the saturnalian orgies being further enlivened by every variety of swearing and profane language. To such a height at last were these revels carried that at last the police were sent for; but on arrival they were utterly powerless to quell the disturbance.
(3rd Oct., 1848.)

A statue of St. Joseph at St. Joseph Estate, Mayaro.
Photograph – Lucille Quesnel.

Members of the Ganteaume family on the front steps of
their home. Photograph – Lucille Quesnel.

Above: Mr. Urich at Radix Point. Photograph — Jackson's Book of Trinidad.
Below: The descendants of the slaves of St. Joseph estate. Photograph — Lucille Quesnel.

constable in charge, who is a civil obliging fellow, will do his best to find food for man and beast, at a fairly moderate cost. By the way, it is always a good plan in these country trips to have a few tins of provisions. You may be able to get crackers (small crisp flour biscuits) and sardines at the small shops, but you can be certain of

1848

OPENING OF NEW GOVERNMENT BUILDINGS

The new Government Buildings, of which the foundation stone was laid by Sir Henry MacLeod in 1845 have been so far completed as to enable the Government to take possession of them. The whole interior of the northern wing of the upper storey, with the exception of the Council Room is finished, and forms a very handsome suite of rooms, which contain the official chambers of the Governor and the Colonial Secretary with their two clerks and messenger. The ground floor is occupied by the chambers of the Attorney General, Colonial Treasurer, Surveyor General, and Superintendent of Public Works. The interior of the south wing, which is occupied by the courts and law officers, are conveniently arranged, with the exception of the large court-room, in which it is scarcely possible for Bench and Bar to hear each other without a great elevation of voice.
(20th Oct., 1848.)

1848

CEREMONIAL OPENING OF GOVERNMENT BUILDINGS

In accordance with a previous announcement, Divine Service was performed at Trinity Church yesterday morning preparatory to the first meeting of the Council of Government in the Council Chamber in the new Government Buildings. Prayers were read by the Rev. Henry Richards, Rector of St. Mary's, Tacarigua, and the lessons by the Rev. Joseph Peschier, Curate of the Parish of Holy Trinity, and the Ven. Archdeacon Cummins preached the sermon. The Rev. S.F.B. Richards, Rector of Holy Trinity read the prayers at the conclusion of morning service. Baron de Fleur presided at the organ, and the ordinary choir was ably assisted by several ladies and gentlemen of musical talent. At the conclusion of the service, His Excellency Lord Harris who wore his full dress uniform as Governor, proceeded from the Church to the Council Chamber, attended by the honourable members of the Council of Government, the heads of public departments, the Judges, the members of the Bar, the Military Officers of the line and star, the Worshipful Members of the Town Council of Port of Spain, with some of the members of the Town Council of San Fernando and their Town Clerk. The procession moved from the great western entrance door of the church through the west gate, and thence along the western side of

nothing beyond this, while with one of Silver's tins of soup, or Morton's Irish Stew, you have only to first 'heat' and then 'eat.'

Start early in the morning, for you have four or five miles of uncomfortable travelling before you. Even in the dry part of the year, the less said about it the better. I had the misfortune to pass along it a few weeks ago after one of the heaviest rainy seasons on record, and it was well-nigh impassable. Expecting the worst, just before starting I asked a road-officer, "How about those Manzanilla Roads?" "Oh," said he, "they are just what they ought to

After church one Sunday morning, the Leotauds on a visit to perhaps the Draggo family who lived on Marine Square North. Photograph — Asché.

Members of the Ganteaume family in a dug out canoe known as a coryal boating on the Ortoire River. Photograph – Lucille Quesnel.

Brunswick Square to the grand entrance to Government Buildings. The 88th Regiment, with the 1st West India Regiment kept the line clear for the procession, and saluted His Excellency as he passed along. On reaching the Council Chamber the members of the Council, with Lord Harris as President, took their seats at the table; and the national flag was then hoisted and a salute of 21 guns was fired by half a brigade of six-pounders planted in Brunswick Square; after which the Council entered upon the business of the day. *(3rd November, 1848.)*

1850

THE FIRST STONE PAVEMENT

We had much pleasure a few days ago in inspecting the stone pavement recently laid down by the church authorities on the south-eastern side of Trinity church, leading from Chacon Street to the vestry door. This pavement is entirely of local materials and local workmanship, having been quarried and dressed at the island of Monos, where similar material exists we understand equal to supply all of the wants of the entire colony. It gave us yet greater pleasure to learn that this pavement can be quarried, dressed and landed in Port of Spain, and furnished at one half of the cost at which similar pavements could be imported from England, while the quality is no way inferior to the best imported article. *(26th March, 1850.)*

COINAGE VALUES IN 1850

In connection with the proclamation of an Order in Council introducing the British sterling coinage into Trinidad, the following table of the legal values of the then existing local coinage, known as 'currency', is of interest, taken from the issue of the 18th June, 1850:-

The Dollar—100 petit sous.
The Half Dollar—50 petit sous.
The Two Bitts—20 petit sous.
The Bitt and Stampee—$12\frac{1}{4}$ petit sous.
The One Bitt—10 petit sous (also 'un escalia')
The Half Bitt—5 petit sous (also 'un cinq sous')
The Stampee—$2\frac{1}{2}$ petit sous.

There appears also to have been a coin known as the 'grand sou' which was equivalent to the modern penny, or a trifle more; and no doubt herein tios origin of the country name even to this day for pence and half pence, which are often heard referred to as 'large cents' and 'small cents', respectively.

be this time of the year."

My experience of them, however, convinced me that they were just what they ought *not* to have been, perhaps this is what Mr. Road-Officer meant. An amusing story is told that some travellers, floundering up to their knees in mud, came, in the worst part, upon a man who was probing the soft earth with a ten-foot pole. "What are you doing?" said they. "Well," replied the man, who was a contractor, "my cart and mules coming this way yesterday got stuck here and I am trying to find whereabouts they are." Unfortunately for the veracity of this story, it is repeated and vouched for in every locality that has bad roads, so the reader must take it for what it is worth. The fact is, the Government is somewhat shy of taking these roads in hand, on account of the expense in carting material, but the difficulty will have to be faced ere long, now that the country is being opened so rapidly. Money must be voted ungrudgingly, and expended judiciously. A few years ago these particular roads used to be impassable for want of traffic, now, it is the excess of it that makes them so.

There is compensation, however, for the difficult travelling, for every now and then the view is charming and it is always changing as you go up hill and down dale. A well-to-do Spanish Creole, Mr. Hernandez, has been doing wonders in the quarter during the last few years. His splendid Cacao Estates and flourishing well-planted provision grounds cannot fail to attract the eye. Some of the hills are pretty steep, one in particular, Mt. Calabash, is quite precipitous, though it is not so bad to ascend, which you are doing, as to descend. Manzanilla Roman Catholic Church, which you pass, was built in 1879, the Anglican one in 1880. The village is a large and straggling one, the inhabitants, or rather the majority of them, being descendants of the disbanded black soldiers, who received each man from the Government a grant of sixteen acres of Crown land (five carrées in the old Spanish measure, one carrée being $3^1/_5$ acres). Many also received grants of land at Turure, but they left the spot after a time, migrating further east, where the soil was more fertile.

Long before you get a sight of it you hear a muffled roar, the surging and beating of the waves of the mighty Atlantic ahead. A short distance from the beach you pass the Manzanilla Police Station, where Mr. F.A. Ganteaume, the Magistrate and Warden of Mayaro, holds his Court once a month.

At length the last steep descent brings you down to the beach, and the deliciously cool sea breeze and the pleasant beach will soon cause you to forget the first discomforts.

Off the Point to the left are the sunken rocks called the Carpenters, where a slaver was wrecked in 1802. The surf here sometimes is very heavy. All the coco-nuts within range of vision belong to the fine estate called the Cocal, a large property leased by Messrs. T.A. Finlayson & Co. from the Borough Council of Port of Spain. Just at the back of the Cocal is the Mitanor Nariva River, which meanders along more or less parallel with the beach till it discharges itself about ten miles below into the ocean. After riding along the sand about three or four miles you catch a glimpse on the right of what appears to be a lake. it is, however, a widening of the river, known as the Doubloon. A certain Jean Paul agreed to open out a passage here to the sea for the sum of one doubloon. He earned his money easily enough, for it is said that he simply drew his stick along the sand, and the water quickly following made such an outlet that for a long

time a ferry boat was required to enable travellers to cross it.

The origin of the Cocal is rather curious. Early in the eighteenth century, a vessel laden with coco-nuts was wrecked off the coast. The nuts in their husks floated ashore for miles, sprouted, took root, and in course of time became what you see it now, an apparently almost endless line of trees sixteen miles in length. The beach is the Queen's highway until you reach Mayaro, almost as far as you can see. If you are fortunate enough to have a letter of introduction to Mr. Legge you may call at his residence, which nestles among the coco-nut trees, nearly in the middle of the bay. A short rest, if only for a few minutes, will doubtless be acceptable to horse, if not to rider, probably to both. Mr. Legge has under him the largest oil-mills and fibre-factory in the colony. A look through the mill may not be uninteresting, and your horse will assuredly not object to the delay. On this estate there are more than 50,000 coco-nut trees, yielding a million and a half of nuts per annum. Here are manufactured 30,000 gallons of oil and 1,000 bales of fibre a year. I am told that accidents are exceedingly rare, though the fibre-making, like many other mill operations, seems dangerous, and the long sharp teeth have a cruel unrelenting appearance.

The beach makes a magnificent natural road at low tide, the only drawback to it being the trunks and branches of huge trees brought down by the Orinoco torrents from the South American mainland have drifted ashore, and dispute the way here and there. But this is a small matter. Look out on the smooth sand for the air-bladders of the Portuguese men-of-war, which abound at certain seasons. Should you bathe it is just as well not to tread barefooted on one of these little creatures, for they have a way of resenting it which will make you wish for a time that you had never felt one. An application of diluted ammonia, or failing that, eau-de-Cologne or Florida Water will relieve the pain. You may perhaps see the ridiculous chouf-chouf washed up by the tide. When scratched under the belly with a little sand or anything else of a rough nature, he inflates himself, (is it pride, pleasure or indignation?) till he looks for all the world like an animated Rugby foot-ball, indeed if pitched into the sea in this condition, he will be unable to sink till he has reduced himself to his original dimensions. Perhaps too, you may see a shark disporting himself in the shallow water, or a gigantic turtle solemnly creeping along. A Greenback recently caught here weighed 100lbs. You have to cross the Nariva and Ortoire rivers which empty themselves into this bay. A large punt will ferry you over easily enough, and you need not even take the trouble to dismount. Both of these are mighty streams in their way, for in the wet season, the fresh water rushes down with a current that defies the tide. They have abundance of fish which may be seen jumping about, not puny little things, such as we are accustomed to have on our dinner tables in town, but giant fellows, grupas, 7 to 8 feet long. An enormous female saw-fish $17^1/_2$ ft. in length was caught here a few weeks ago. An idea of its size will be gained when the reader learns that four strong men could not manage to carry one half of the liver without frequent haltings to rest. Among the thousands of smaller eggs, were picked out forty-eight of the largest, each about two-thirds the size of an ostrich egg. On the banks you may sometimes see huillias or water-boas *(anacondas)* from ten to nearly thirty feet in length. A huillia will seize upon a young pig or lamb with avidity, reduce it to a mash or pulp with his powerful contracting muscles, and gulp it down forthwith. This plan does away with the work of mastication, at any rate the teeth are brought very little into play. If one should come in your way, and you have not a good gun, you had better as our American cousins say 'skedaddle'. But more marvellous because more rare is the *Manati* or sea-cow. I have had the luck to see several in the Nariva river, though unfortunately these singular creatures are fast becoming extinct here as in other parts of the world. They are huge and clumsy, but otherwise timid and harmless enough. One fellow that was harpooned was 10 feet long and $7\frac{1}{2}$ ft. in girth. Alligators may be found lurking in the mangrove swamps, where are also swarms of iguanas. The high woods here, as elsewhere, abound in game. I have often met with the large-billed toucan, and there is another wood bird, probably the campanero, that I have heard but never seen. It makes a noise which sounds exactly like the beating of a smith upon his anvil.

About forty-five years ago Lord Harris and a party were crossing the Ortoire, when the conversation turned upon the large snakes found hereabout. One of the negro guides volunteered the information that he once saw a huillia so long that when its head reached the further side its tail was still 'on dis bank!' A small grain of salt must be taken with this. The natives are splendid at these yarns, and, with a little judicious drawing out, will give you anecdotes and experiences that put Baron Munchausen to the blush.

The Ortoire being crossed you have to ascend the steep Mayaro hill, from the top of which a magnificent view is obtained, overlooking the sea, the village, and the coco-nut estates of Messrs. F. Urich & Son, Mr. F.A. Ganteaume, Mr. Penco and a host of smaller proprietors. The nearest estate, Mr. Urich's *St. Bernard,* is very regularly planted, and the tall palms remind one forcibly of the pine forests of Europe. To avoid the steep ascent Mr. Urich offered the Government a right of way through his estate and this plan if adopted would give a carriage drive from Manzanilla to Guayaguayare, a splendid sweep. All along the beach extends the Village of Mayaro which boasts of the usual two churches. The Roman Catholic one, the larger of the two, has a fine altar of native wood, carved with much taste and skill by the Officiating Priest, Abbé Mailleux. The Anglican one, opened in 1880, is of cedar, and contains the Altar and Font originally in the Cathedral of the Holy Trinity, Port of Spain. It was built in 1879, close to the School House. The population of Mayaro is bout 600, nearly every man having his own little piece of land with a few coco-nut trees and cottage on it.

About three miles along this beach, you come to a straight road called Plaisance, branching off to the right; on the hill far down is the Police Station in a hamlet known as Ganteaumesville. Unless you have an introduction to some one, you had better steer for the Police Station and take there the, by this time, much-needed rest and refreshment. As yet hotels in these parts are things of the dim and, I fear, distant future, but the kindly Corporal will put you up for the night, and let you out again in the morning, provided you have not in the meantime disturbed the peace of Her Majesty's lieges. Five miles farther down the beach would have brought you to Messrs. Urich's coco-nut oil factory at Lagane Down, where about 30,000 nuts per week are converted into oil. Recently nuts have been shipped direct from this port to London, instead of sending them first to Port of Spain as formerly.

Having had a good night's rest, the next question is how to return. Probably you will prefer another route,—there is one across the island to Princes Town, known as the Mayaro Trace. Turning you back to the Police Station and your face westward ho!—you recross the Ortoire this time by a good bridge, and along a new road into the 'Trace.' Less than a mile and you are in high woods, primeval forest it might be termed so unfrequented is it, so lonely and so romantic. Here the sound of your horse's tread will send the startled game flying out of the cloistered recesses of this Cathedral of Nature, for it is a grand hunting country. The native sportsmen, who make quite a business of it, start on Friday evening, returning on Sunday laden with the sports of the chase. Here, too, even more than on the Manzanilla Road, caution will have to 'mark the guarded way,' for you are journeying along a 'Trace,' not a carriage road. Midway between Bande de l'Este and Savanna Grande you will be glad to dismount at the 'Queen's House,' where you will bless the thoughtful benevolence of a paternal Government, which shows such consideration for the weary. It is a rude sort of building, however, and you will have to be your own caterer, or you will fare badly, for there is no one to do it for you.

On one occasion Governor Keate, Judge Fitzgerald, Mr. Syl. Devenish, and his son Mr. Abel Devenish, paused here awhile to recruit the inner man. Each adapted himself to the circumstances, and I should have liked to have been there to see Her Majesty's representative collecting and bringing in the dry wood, the genial old Judge Fitz cleaning the plates and mugs, Syl. the humourist and *raconteur* for the nonce turned gastronomist, while the more youthful Abel performed the general duties of factotun.

A few more hours after this halt will bring you to Princes Town, where you may easily get to San Fernando, and so homewards, or you may stay and pay a visit to the neighbouring Mud Volcanoes.

Henry Peter Ganteaume. Photograph — St. Mary's College Centenary.

MAYARO IN HISTORY

Michael Anthony

Mayaro came into recorded history in 1690, when Capuchin priests from Spain, in an attempt to convert the Amerindians of Trinidad to Christianity, set up a Mission on this part of the south-eastern coast.

(The Capuchins, who had landed in the Naparimas in 1687, had set up several Missions prior to this one, including Purísima Concepción de Naparima, La Mision de Savenetta, La Mision de Savana Grande, and La Mision de San Francisco de las Arenales, more widely known as Arena).

The Mission at Mayaro appears to have been short-lived and was said to have been destroyed by marauding Caribs from across the Main, but at least the setting up of the mission was recorded, and the Arawak name of the site, 'Mayaro,' preserved. The word Mayaro is Arawak for 'The Place of the Maya plant,' but one is not certain as to what was the plant itself.

After the period of the setting up of the Mission not much is heard of Mayaro until the passage of nearly a hundred years — 1783. That was the year of the declaration of the famous Cedula of Population through which the King of Spain granted land and made other concessions to Catholics who would settle in Trinidad. This move was made in order to develop the country, give it a population, and generally make it strong to defend itself against nations who might otherwise prey upon it.

The Cedula of Population was proclaimed in November 1783 and the Spanish Governor who took up office here in 1784 — José María Chacon – decided to settle the immigrants not only around the capital, but in the most distant and far-flung places, and naturally a great attraction was the Mayaro coast.

Mayaro Beach in the 1880's. Photograph — Mrs. Héléen Farfan.

Trinidad was completely wild and untouched at that stage, with an interior covered with forests. It would have been exactly as Christopher Columbus had seen it when the island came into his path in 1498. There were certainly Arawak paths through the jungles but no roads. Therefore the most convenient place to settle the in-coming French planters and their slaves would have been along the coasts of the island, and Chacon proceeded to do just this.

The Mayaro coast appears to have been settled shortly after the Cedula but the details of what transpired there do not become available until the British conquest of Trinidad of 1797.

After the 18th February 1797, on which date the British captured Trinidad, the Commander of the British forces, General Sir Ralph Abercromby, asked his Captain of the Surveying Engineers, to survey the island, stating the people, crops, and everything that was contained in it. He wanted this in order to inform the British Secretary of State for the Colonies what comprised the island that he had captured.

The engineer, Frederick Mallet, left Port of Spain on the survey mission, and stopping at every point on the coast where there was a settlement, he made a most meticulous inventory of the crops he saw and took a census of the people he encountered.

A very old photograph of forest dwellers. — Photograph Mrs Hélène Farfan.

The Lady McLeod stamp reproduced here four times the actual size. This was the first stamp issued in a British Colony and it was done so by a Port of Spain businessman, David Bryce. He had imported a coastal wood burning paddle boat which he named the Lady McLeod in honour of the then Governors wife. (Sir Henry McLeod 1840-1845) This Port of Spain/San Fernando weekly service carried the mail. Mr. Bryce issued his own postage stamp, the five cents blue Lady McLeod. The Stamp was a wood cut and bears the picture of the vessel above the inscription L Mc L. Today the catalogue value for Lady McLeod is above £3,000.

1845

THE S.S. 'LADY MCLEOD'.
The new steamer *Lady Mcleod* arrived here on Thursday afternoon and we have been informed that her measurement is 66 tons. She has two engines of 30 horse-power each. It is in contemplation that once every week, namely on Saturdays, she should go as far as Cedros, starting from Port of Spain at 6 a.m. After landing her passengers at Couva and San Fernando she will reach La Brea at 11 a.m. so as to afford passengers going to see the Pitch Lake five hours clear. And it is expected that she will return to Port of Spain at half past seven in the evening.
(26th December, 1845).
Port of Spain Gazette.
Special Centenary issue.

1845

GULF SERVICE IN '45.

We are very glad to be able to state that a very fine steamer of 70 horse-power has been purchased for our coast communication, and that she is now on her way out to the colony. She is almost new, having been run only a few weeks prior to her purchase; is of iron build, and has accommodation for 100 passengers. She can do her 12 knots easily. We understand that Cedros planters are to be accommodated with at least a weekly service to the metropolis.

(12th Sept, 1845).
Port of Spain Gazette.
Special Centenary issue.

1846

DEMAND FOR POPULAR REPRESENTATION

We are requested to state that a petition to Her Most Gracious Majesty praying for "such an alteration in the present form of government as shall afford the inhabitants of this colony some voice in the making of the laws, and the levying and expenditure of the public revenues," the "mixed council" of Newfoundland being suggested as a suitable model, the additional members that would thereby be added to the present Board of Council to be elected by the people, is now in course of preparation, and will lie at the office of this paper from an after Monday next for signatures.

(3rd April, 1846).
Port of Spain Gazette. Special Centenary issue.

1850

SAN FERNANDO GAZETTE

Our advertising columns contain the prospectus of a newspaper to be established early in the ensuing month in the town of San Fernando and to be entitled the *'San Fernando Gazette'* and *'Naparima Agricultural and Commercial Advertiser.'* We gladly welcome the establishment of a third newspaper in Trinidad, and hope, notwithstanding the hardness of the times, that it may prove a source of profit to its proprietors. *(25th January, 1850.)*

As Mallet approached Mayaro he came to a long strip of coconut palms along a bay which he calls, on his survey map, 'Cocos Bay.' This was the shore the Spaniards called the 'cocal,' a word meaning an abundance of coconut trees. He may have been aware of the story that more than a century before, a ship laden with coconuts foundered on the Manzanilla Point. For in his 'Descriptive Account,' which accompanies the map, he writes: 'Along the shore of Cocos Bay to the distance of about fifty paces, are found a great quantity of palm or coco trees, whose species are not natural to the island. A launch coming from the River Orinoco laden with coconuts was wrecked in this bay, by which accident these trees were planted and continue to multiply.'

The next stop for Captain Mallet, as we see it, is at the mouth of the Ortoire, which he calls here 'Rio del Guatuaro.' Then he rounds the point, anchors, and lands.

Landing must have been a revelation for Captain Mallet. If he had expected that this coast was empty and barren he must have received a shock. He soon discovered that the entire coast was settled, and meticulous man that he was, he took note of everything.

The Ganteaumes are still very much around in Mayaro, so far as property is concerned. They also wielded a great deal of influence in this district and performed roles as wardens, etc. A grandson, Francis

The Nariva river ferry 1900. Photograph — Mrs. Hélène Farfan.

Alphonse was warden of Mayaro from 1866 to 1867. He it was who started growing coconuts in Mayaro, which, apart from providing good trade for well over a century has made the word 'Mayaro' almost synonymous with coconut trees.

After Mallet passed by in 1797 and did his survey, there was not much heard of Mayaro, but it continued to play its tremendous part so far as the economy was concerned. As is realized, there were no coconut plantations at that stage.

The principal crop was cotton, and there was a good deal of coffee, and the Spaniards had been trying sugar, which seemed to be beginning to hold sway. Plantains, too, had become a significant crop. A good picture of what was the position some years later could be seen from statistics sent in 1812 by Governor William Munro to the Secretary of State for the Colonies. From this we see that there were nearly 38,000 plantain trees in Mayaro. The area under sugar-cane was 196 acres, while 301 acres were under cotton. This showed that cotton had still retained its ascendancy. But sugar wasn't doing too badly for in the previous year, 1811, they had produced 800 gallons of rum.

The first thing was the name. He found out that the region was called Mayaro. The big headland he had just rounded was a grant made out to F. Radix, and he writes on the map: 'Radix F.' Then along the rest of the coast, he must have spent weeks doing this job – he writes down the names of everyone of the various planters and marks out their grants, and we find names like Guise, Thomasos, Mahan, Alatre, Duchatel, Huet, Mahau, Hugues, Duitron, Frontin, etc. There were twenty-six French planters who occupied grants along the coast, and a great many of those names are around today; for example, Hugues, which is almost certainly Hughes, and Frontin.

1852

OLD TIME MORTALITY RETURNS
Early in 1852 a committee was appointed to consider the question of the introduction of public heath reforms; and the question of improved sanitation in Port of Spain particularly. From the very lengthy report sent in by Dr. Garvin M.D., the Chairman, some interesting information as to the mortality rate in Trinidad in 1852 may be gathered. The population of Port of Spain in that year was estimated at 17,563; and the general death rate of the town was 4.38 per cent. But the chief interest lies in a special tubulated return of deaths of children in the four years ending December, 1852, appended to the report. From this table we find that 331 children under a year old died in Port of Spain; 505 under the age of five years; and 131 between the ages of 5 and 10 years; so that in the four years, 20 per cent of the deaths were children under 5 years of age; and 33 per cent were children under 10 years.

RED FISH PIE
Slice some boiled potatoes and put a layer of them in the bottom of a pie dish that is well buttered. Put a layer of sliced tomatoes on top of them. Then put a layer of boiled, filletted red fish. Then a layer of sliced potatoes. Covered with grated cheese bake until the cheese form a delicious crust.

1852

INTRODUCTION OF A DAILY POST
We call attention with much pleasure to the announcement made by the Postmaster General of this island of the introduction of a daily postal delivery in the town of Port of Spain and that of San Fernando. The attention of writers of letters to either of these town however is invited to the necessity of stating on the address the name of the street and the number of the house where the person to whom the letter is addressed resides, so that early delivery of the letters may be facilitated and ensured. *(10th August, 1852.)*

1853
COMING OF CHOLERA.
The painful rumour has been in circulation in this town since last Thursday that cholera had broken out in Nevis; and is now, alas! too fully confirmed by our exchanges from Antigua and St. Kitts. It is also painfully shewn, even to the most obstinate, that the disease is contagious, and consequently it should be guarded against by a strict enforcement of quarantine regulations. *(28th December, 1853.)*

WATER SUPPLY CHARGES
The following official notice, published in the Gazette of the 12th March, 1853, gives the charges for domestic water services to dwelling houses, under the original scheme by which for the first time, water was thanks to Lord Harris brought into Port of Spain from the Maraval River reservoir:

PORT OF SPAIN WATERWORKS
The following shall be the scale of charges applicable to the supply of water to private dwelling houses in Port of Spain:—
Where the rental does not exceed £25 per annum, at and after the rate of 8d per £ sterling of the value according to the valuation in the house rate book:
Where the rental exceed £25 per annum at and after the rate of 1s. per £ sterling of the value according to the valuation in the house rate book.
For every puncheon of water supplied to the shipping, 1s.

An important occasion at Mayaro in the 1890's, perhaps a visit by the Governor. This photograph was taken by Jacobson. Photograph — Mrs. Hélène Farfan.

Mrs. Ann Frontin lived at Mayaro for one hundred and thirty years. She died in 1939, and has left literally hundreds of descendants.

Mallet's census shows that in all there were 403 people in Mayaro. These comprised 48 whites, 44 people of colour, or mixed people, and 311 slaves. These people were responsible for a vast number of plantations, chiefly cotton, and Mallet counted no fewer than 65 cotton mills at work.

Mallet's map does not show a grant for the family name of Ganteaume but a few years before this – in 1793 – the Ganteaume family arrived in Mayaro in a most unusual and spectacular fashion. Because of troubles in all the French islands, caused by the French Revolution which broke out in 1789, a number of Royalists had to flee, and a family named Ganteaume fled Martinique in an open boat, and after drifting for some time could land nowhere else but on the Mayaro shore. Ganteaume stayed right here and naturally, owing to the fact that people were being settled along the Mayaro coast, Governor Chacon got to hear of the Ganteaumes and immediately granted him land to open an estate. So Ganteaume started what must be among the first – if not the first – estates in Mayaro. He called the first one 'Beau Séjour, which means 'happy sojourn,' and the second one was dedicated to St. Joseph, an estate we know by that name.

By 1825 we had a situation where the grants might have still been in the original names but there were a few new faces on the scene. One, St. Hilaire Begorrat, who had come to Trinidad under the Cedula of 1783, and was at one time a Member of the Council of Advice, under Picton, had drafted a rather repugnant Code Noir for Picton, and now in his declining years was showing up as one of the proprietors of land in Mayaro. For those who want to know what land he was proprietor of, there is Begorrat Road, going down towards Grand Lagoon.

Incidentally, at this time the number of white people in Mayaro had been reduced drastically, while there was an increase of slaves.

Another interesting feature due to the fact that Mayaro was so cut off, its people so thrown together, – the planters as well as the slaves — was that a close relationship between these two groups was becoming very evident. This could be seen in what was happening to some of the original grants. When the original grantee families died out the land seemed to be succeeded in ownership by other names, without a doubt names of former slaves.

Consequently it is not difficult to imagine that when Emancipation came in 1834 and Abolition in 1838 the relationship between the masters and the slaves in Mayaro could not have undergone the crisis which was widespread in other parts of Trinidad. In fact it is even doubtful that the masses in Mayaro had a clear picture of what was going on. However, the people who owned slaves had to make official claims for the people who were going to be released and what is revealed is of great interest.

The question of a close relationship between planter and labourer was mentioned, and this comes sharply into focus in 1851. 1851 was a very significant year for Mayaro, and indeed for the whole island. It was in 1849 that Governor Lord Harris divided the island into Counties and Wards, and this move was one to bring in

an era of development through local Government. Harris knew well that while planters in far-away districts like Mayaro would be moaning and pleading with the Government in Port of Spain to do something about roads, etc. it was quite unlikely that the Council of Government composed of people, some of whom had never even been outside of Port of Spain, would be mindful about Mayaro.

So in general Harris knew that the only thing to save the country districts would be the country districts themselves. He introduced the system of dividing the island into Counties and Wards, and let each Ward be headed by a Warden who would receive ward rates, especially from proprietors, that money to be used to do the things that were necessary for the development of the district.

The administrative division of the island into Counties and Wards took place in 1849 but it took sometime for the system to be properly set in motion and it was not until 1851 that proprietors were called upon to pay ward rates. As expected, the proprietors took this request very badly. They saw it as something wicked and diabolical and no doubt believed that this was some conspiracy to wheedle money out of them. So by and large they refused to pay. But Lord Harris was not to be trifled with and a great many properties were put up for

SAN COCHE
This is the all-filling midday meal of rich and poor alike on the plantations of Trinidad. It varies considerably as any kind of meat can be used; chicken, pork, beef or salted meats. Sometimes it has beans, sometimes not; but the general recipe run along these lines. Brown fatpork and add the meat used whatever it is. But if any kind of fresh meat is used you should still put a piece or two of salt beef. Stew for ten minutes and then fill the pot with water and add the beans or peas. When they are about to burst add the yams and dasheen. Then last of all put in the dumplings which have been cut up very small. Sometimes the dumplings are made of flour and cornmeal. Serve with the bottle of pepper sauce nearby.

A photograph of one of last remaining windmills on St. Joseph estate Mayaro. Photograph Maureen Hanton.

sale. Among the Mayaro estates advertised for sale in the Royal Gazette of 1851 we see estates like Beaumont, St. Margaret, St. Anns, and Grand Lagoon, and one sees well known names of small-holders like Popwell, Lemessy, etc. Many must have paid up in time, but during that year a number of Mayaro people lost their land.

That was not the only significant measure for Mayaro in the year 1851. Two other important things happened: Lord Harris started a system of public schools (schools for children of the public), and he established an inland postal service.

To deal with schools first. Of the very first seven ward schools he established Mayaro received one. The school were called 'ward schools' for they were to paid for out of ward rates, and controlled by the warden. The first schoolmaster was J.A. Miller.

The postal service was brought during August, and of the 20 places that were linked with Port of Spain to start the service, Mayaro was one. Those two events should give an idea of how important Mayaro had become.

Of course the reason for Mayaro becoming such a key district was because of the very estate mentioned. Mayaro could deliver the produce. On calling here the coastal steamers could hardly carry the produce from the various estates. There were several points along the coast where they anchored to receive produce, as well as passengers of course, for there was no other highway except the sea.

And this leads me to mention something of the distribution of population in the district. Since December of 1818 the coastal steamers had been plying on a regular basis, and it could be that they found that the anchorage was better off Radix Estate than elsewhere, and this was one of the places where they always anchored. Needless to say people always wanted to be where the steamer would anchor, for the steamer, like a lifeline, was the only means of commnication. Also, in 1819 when a Catholic Church was built, it was built there. There was even more reason for people to be nearby, as Radix became the centre of population for Mayaro, at first for the free blacks.

In 1881 when the coastal steamer brought the first mail it went naturally to Radix. The mail used to be handled by the police in those days – there being no Postal Department – and it would appear that it was just about this time that Mayaro got a Police Station, or, rather, a Police Post.

But the Police Post was not at Radix. What happened – and this would seem coincidental – was that Lord Harris, who had always felt, from the time he came as Governor, that there should be a road right across Trinidad from the Gulf Coast to the East Coast, asked one of the surveyors, St. Luce D'Abadie, to survey and cut a road from the Naparimas to Bande de l'Est, which was the name for Mayaro Beach. St. Luce surveyed and opened this road, which was a mere trace, then known

In 1909, Sir George Le Hunte visited the Oilfields being developed by Mr. Randolph Rust at Guayagayare. Photograph — Mrs. Hélène Farfan.

as the Mayaro Trace, and today as the Naparima-Mayaro Road. Of course there had existed that part of the road from San Fernando to the place then known as Mission, and since 1880 as Princes Town. When the Mayaro Trace was completed policemen were installed at the Mayaro end of it, for the obvious reason, that the trace would certainly be a temptation to people indulging in crime and contraband. The location of this post seems to have been exactly where the police station is today. The two policemen at this post were William Turville and Henry Thomas, according to the Royal Gazette of 1852.

Up to 1881 Mayaro was under cotton, coffee, and sugar cultivation, but somebody had plans for changing the crop on his estate. The Ganteaume family, which has been mentioned before, was always at the forefront of change. The early 1860's found one of the family, Francis Alphonse, as warden of North Naparima, but the seat of the Ganteaumes was at Mayaro and they would stay away from it only when better could not be done. Now that there existed the Mayaro Trace, Francis Alphonse Ganteaume used to ride from Mayaro to North Naparima first thing on Monday morning to get to his offce and when he shut it on Friday evening he would jump on his horse and ride through the trace to Mayaro.

During this time he had the idea of switching the crop from sugar to coconuts. So on his return home every weekend he would plant some coconut trees, and in time, instead of a sugar-cane field he had developed a coconut plantation. Afterwards, all the planters began to follow suit, and Mayaro became what it is, a coconut coast.

Apart from agriculture, there had always been fishing with the use of seines, because being a sandy coast, the seines could always be dragged up on the beach. But of course the fish would only be for the consumption of the folk of Mayaro.

All this while and throughout the years a number of other families played their part in the development of Mayaro. All along the coast estates continued to flourish, just as in the earliest days, and names from the earliest times became prominent in Mayaro's history. Two of those well-known families are the Frontins and the Richardsons. They have been land-owners since the early development of Mayaro, and have also taken part in every facet of Mayaro life. For example Pierre Gabriel Frontin is shown in Government statistics to have produced a great amount of cocoa at the turn of the century, and the Richardsons, among other things produced the first Mayaro-born schoolmaster to serve Mayaro, Clifford Richardosn. He was headteacher of the Mayaro Government School in the 1940's. There are also well-known families like the Sobions, the Prevatts, the Goulds, and the Pierres. This south-eastern village, founded after the Cedula of 1783, has made a fascinating contribution throughout the years.

CASSAVA FARINE
This native vegetable is at its best when served with stewed fish. The method of using it is to place a heap of it in your plate. Make a hollow in the centre of the heap into which you pour hot water. Then pour some of the fish sauce over it.

The coconut oil factory, the cocal, in the 1880's. Photograph — Mrs. Hélène Farfan.

1856

ORIGIN OF HART'S CUT

Those who have once experienced the pleasures of a long pull around Pointe Gourde from Chaguaramas Bay under a broiling sun, or those who my perhaps anticipate the journey, will be glad to learn that it is proposed to save the three or four hours now taken up by that portion of the voyage by cutting a canal through the narow isthmus which joins the promontory to the mainland. It has been found that the neck is not more than 1,800 feet in breadth, and presents no great difficulties to the work; and it is estimated that a channel navigable for boats may be made at a cost of only $2,400. The track is through a swamp of red mangrove wood, which has been valued at $400. The work is to be done under the supervision of the Superintendent of the gaol. *(15th March, 1856.)*

COMPLETION OF HART'S CUT

The work of cutting a canal inside Pointe Gourde, across the swampy isthmus which divides the two bays of Carenage and Chaguaramas was completed early this week, with the exception of a small strip on the eastern beach which was left until His Excellency the Governor should be present. On Thursday last, the 29th instant, His Excellency, accompanied by the Colonial Secretary and the Attorney General, embarked at Cocorite in the Government barge, and on their arrival off the eastern entrance to the canal just at the hour of high water, an opening was promptly effected by the labourers in attendance, and the barge, amidst hearty cheers of the pleased spectators, passed through, gliding easily and rapidly with the entering current; and having proceeded a few furlongs into Chaguaramas Bay, returned to the eastern entrance where His Excellency and suite landed. His Excellency expressed his entire satisfaction at the way in which the work had been done under the superintendence of Mr. Hart. *(31st May, 1856.)*

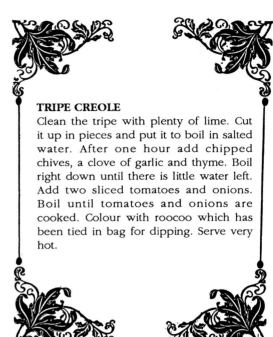

TRIPE CREOLE

Clean the tripe with plenty of lime. Cut it up in pieces and put it to boil in salted water. After one hour add chipped chives, a clove of garlic and thyme. Boil right down until there is little water left. Add two sliced tomatoes and onions. Boil until tomatoes and onions are cooked. Colour with roocoo which has been tied in bag for dipping. Serve very hot.

Mayaro Beach near to Radix Point in the 1880's.
Photograph — Mrs. Hélène Farfan.

DANIEL HART

Daniel Hart, respected Public Servant was also very active in masonic circles. Born 1806 died 1869. Assistant Clerk Commissariat Department, Trinidad, 1825; Ensign in the Royal Trinidad Battalion Militia Force, 4th October, 1831; Adjoint Commandant of the District of Santa Cruz, 1832; Commandant of the District of Las Cuevas and Maracas, 1833; Lieutenant of the St Joseph's Light Infantry Regiment of Militia, 20th November, 1833; Special Magistrate under the Imperial Act of Parliament for the Abolition of Slavery, 22nd July, 1834; Provost Marshal General Militia Force, 14th March, 1835; Captain in the St. Joseph's Light Infantry Regiment of Militia, 31st May, 1837; Sent by the Governor of the Island (Sir GEO. F. HILL, Bart.) Special Commissioner to Venezuela, to claim indemnification for a vessel belonging to the Island, that had been captured by a Venezuelan cruizer, as also to enforce the release of two British Subjects, 1837; Brevet Major in the Militia Force, 1838; Commissioner of Roads and Bridges, 1842; Sworn Interpreter of the Spanish Language, 1843; Governor of the Royal Gaol, 10th June, 1847; Sent to Antigua to Inspect and Report on the Prison of that Island, 10th April, 1857; Sent to Barbados to Confer with His Excellency the Governor-General of that Island under a Dispatch from the Secretary of State for the Colonies (H. Labouchere, Esq.) to Governor Hincks, in regard to the transfer of the Convicts from Barbados to Trinidad, 25th Octr., 1857; Superintendent of Prisons, 1st February, 1858; Acted as Inspector of Police and Inspector of Weights and Measures, from 22nd October, 1858, to 5th April, 1859; Superintending Inspector under the Ordinance for Promoting the Public Health and by Commission of His Excellency R. Keate, Esq., 26th May, 1862; again acted as Inspector of Police and Weights and Measures, in conjunction with his office of Superintendent of Prisons, from 8th February, 1862 to the 22nd August, 1863, when he resumed his duties of Superintendent of Prisons and Sanitary Inspector; Sanitary Inspector under the Local Board of Health (in conjunction with his office of Superintendent of Prisons) 9th November, 1865.

Daniel Hart Esq. He was a leading public figure and eminent mason during the 19th century.

Daniel Hart's Family Tree
John b. 1699 – d. 1830
m 1742 Rebecca Lyons

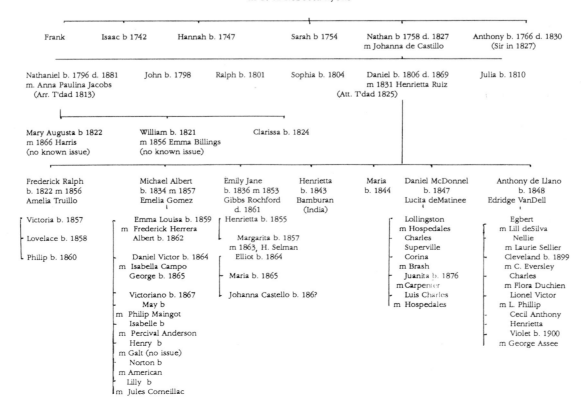

Some early Mayors of San Fernando

W.S. Robertson
1890–1892

W. Spencer Clerk
1892–1894

Dr. J.W. Eakin
1895–1902

A view of San Fernando taken in the 1880's. Photograph — The Dominican Sisters of St. Catherine of Sienna.

San Fernando

From Guide to Trinidad
J.H. Collens, 1886

San Fernando de Naparima, as it was originally named, is pleasantly situated at the foot of the Naparima hill about 32 miles by water, and 42 by road from Port of Spain. There are three trains to and from the capital on every week day, with two on Sundays. There is also frequent communication by Messrs. Turnbull's steamers, the passage taking two hours more or less.

Various ideas exist as to the derivation of the term Naparima. It is said that Sir Walter Raleigh, when on his trip from La Brea to St. Joseph, gave the hill the name of Annaparima, an Indian word signifying 'one mountain.' There is, however, another theory deserving of some consideration, namely, that Anap-Arima means the place lacking water, in contradistinction to Arima, or the land of abundant water.

The town of San Fernando was founded in 1792, a few years before the British occupation, by Governor Chacon. It soon had its Market in a Square called 'Plaza de San Carlos', its Cemetery, Church and Presbytery, and a kind of hostelry or rest-house for travellers and visitors

J.C. Lewis
1904–1906

The King's Wharf in the 1890's. Photograph — Hélène Farfan.

called 'Casa Real'. The principal thoroughfares were St. Vincent, Chacon, Penitence and Quenca Streets. In 1818 the old town was completely destroyed by a large fire, but it had been nearly restored by 1830, and building had extended beyond its former limits, especially in the direction of what was then Mon Chagrin Estate.

A Town Council, with President, appears to have been formed in 1846, and in 1853, during the Governorship of Lord Harris, the Council having become fully invested with the municipal rights and privileges, the town was converted into a borough, and Dr. Robert Johnstone, the last of the Presidents, was also the first of the Mayors. The Borough Council of San Fernando has always zealously watched over, and, if need be, protected the interests of the town, and under the several times renewed mayoralty of Mr. Guppy, an old esteemed colonist and Barrister-at-Law, this public-spirited policy has in noway diminished.

The Town Hall is situated in Harris's Promenade, an elevated piece of ground nearly parallel to and within a few yards of High Street. The last named is the chief business thoroughfare, and contains a number of well-arranged, amply stocked stores. Many of these are of new

and modern appearance, for in 1883 the town was unfortunately, or fortunately (who knows?), visited by a ravaging fire, which made a clean sweep of some of the mercantile houses. The San Fernandians, however, were not to be daunted by such a common-place occurrence, and ere long the the present structures arose Phoenix-like

Horse drawn vehicles make their way along San Fernando's hilly streets. These photographs taken in the 1920's or 30's show the old town very much as it was in the 1890's. Photograph — Dieffenthaller.

L.M. Hobson
1902–1903

High Street San Fernando in the 1880's, taken from a postcard.

Joga Grant
1903–1904

Edgell Johnstone
1906–1908

out of the ashes. It was this fire which led to the formation of the town Volunteer Fire Brigade, an organization now in a thoroughly efficient state, having an engine and hose, with the necessary fittings and appliances, to enable it at all times to turn out for immediate action. Since its establishment the Brigade has given several proofs of its usefulness; it musters 29 working and 9 honorary members, and is under the command of Mr. Corrie, the Captain. To mark their appreciation of its services, the leading firms and Insurance Agencies subscribed to give the members a room for meetings, which has been built over the engine-house, the whole presenting a smart, natty spick-and-span appearance.

Harris Promenade is the centre of a number of public institutions. Within a stone's throw are the Hospital, market, the Presbyterian, Anglican, Roman Catholic, Wesleyan and Baptist Churches, Police Barracks, Fire Brigade Station, Town Hall and Convent.

St. Paul's Church (Anglican) is a wooden structure built to replace a smaller one of stone, which after thirty years precarious tenure of treacherous foundation, had to be finally abandoned in 1873. The present Church, though at the time unfinished, was opened for Divine Service in 1875. It consists of nave with two aisles, and chancel, the total length being 114 feet, and width 28 feet. Both aisles and clerestory are lighted by double lancet windows. The interior presents a rather felicitous adaptation of material, the prevailing features being its roof, the many columns and light arches, and general airiness. The two stained windows, by Wailes of Newcastle, are of remarkable size for single lights, the subject being 'The Good Shepherd', and 'St. Paul.' The rebuilding of this Church was the first effort of the kind after the passing of the Act of Disestablishment. On the sudden and unforeseen withdrawal of Government aid, St. Paul's had to depend entirely upon the voluntary subscriptions of the parishioners. So far $10,000 have been expended, but the Church is still incomplete, sadly lacking a tower.

The Roman Catholic Church is a large cruciform shaped building, capable, like the Anglican one, of seating 800 people. The life-size figure of the Crucifixion

A painting, by an unknown artist, of the San Fernando Town Council during the term of office of the Hon. Charles Leotaud. Source — Port of Spain Gazette.

near the entrance, at once strikes the eye. The principal altar is a massive one of marble with granite steps, the front being adorned by a gilt plate representing the typical Lamb surrounded by aureole rays. The double marble slab to the left is in memory (1) of the late Father Christophe, 'Founder of the Catholic Church in San Fernando', and Hon. Vicar-General of the diocese, and (2) in memory of Father Griffin, for 26 years curate of the parish. On each side of the altar is a picture, one of Our Saviour, the other of the Virgin Mother. Of the two side Chapels, that to the left is dedicated to the Virgin Mary; it contains a handsome marble altar, above which are the figures of the Holy Mother and Son, with two Saints, surmounted by the inscription 'Ecce tua Mater.' There are various other figures, notably that of the Virgin Mary supporting the dead body of her Son. The organ in the gallery is a good one, but in bad condition, with two manuals and 16 stops.

The Presbyterian and Baptist Churches are good buildings, each with a residence near by for the Pastor. The Wesleyan Chapel is a comparatively new erection, with several coloured glass windows and a belfry.

The Police Barracks is a handsome stone edifice with some architectural pretensions, being much after the style of the one in Port of Spain. It cost £25,000, having been commenced in 1869 and finished in 1877. Here are stationed 1 Inspector, 1 Sergeant-major, 1 Superintending Sergeant, and 54 of subordinate rank. Here also are held the Magistrate's Court daily, and less frequently the Petty Debt, Criminal and Summary Jurisdiction Courts. The last named is held on the first Thursday in each month except September; the Criminal Sessions commence on the first Thursday in February, April, June, October, and December; the Petty Civil Court sits every Friday.

The San Fernando Hospital, though not on the Harris Promenade, is only separated from it by a ravine, so that it is almost within the stone-throw limit. It is a substantial, well-ordered structure, erected at a clost of £11,093 in 1859, by Mr. Samuel, the architect of the Port of Spain Hospital. It is 224 feet long and 56 feet broad with spacious galleries on each side, commanding a splendid view of the gulf and hill-side, and it is so situated as to catch the cool breeze from which ever direction it may

ORIGIN UNKNOWN is this old Spanish building with massive walls, on Carib Street, on the wooded slopes of Naparima Hill. Some say it was the home of the Le Cadres, one of whom was on the first Council in 1846.

J.D. Hobson
1908–1917, 1920–1921

blow. It is under the charge of a Resident Surgeon, who is assisted by a staff of 23 nurses and attendants. In 1885 there were 2,031 patients admitted, 1,656 were discharged, and 264 died. Three enormous iron tanks, each of a capacity of 16,000 gallons, are kept for storing water.

Apropos of wtaer, on occasions the supply of this necessary of life has, in San Fernando, run very short; in 1864 as much as 3/9 was paid for a puncheon of water. A few years ago, after long-drawn-out correspondence between the Government and Borough Council, a reservoir costing £15,755 was constructed at *La Coulée*. The water derived from this source was not at first at all favourably received, on account of it being strongly impregnated with bitumen and sulphur, thereby rendering it unpleasant for drinking and unsuitable for cooking purposes. It is generally admitted now that it has lost much of its objectionable flavour, though it is still not used for drinking, iron tanks having been almost universally adopted for the storage of rain water collected from the house-tops. The available capacity of these tanks has been estimated at nearly 100,000 gallons. At *La Coulée* is the largest Tennis ground in San Fernando; it is of gravel, not turfed like those in Port of Spain. Occasional tournaments take place between the champions of Naparima and those of the capital, but although the San Fernandians are vigorous and successful in most of their undertakings, they must as yet yield the palm for Tennis to the northern city. There has for many years existed a healthy spirit of emulation between the two towns, and whether the contest has been one of Cricket, Boat-racing, Fire Brigade Drill or what not, the honours have, on the whole, been fairly divided. From *La Coulée* to the top of the hill is a tough walk, but if your wind and legs are sound, you ought to go in for it, as the exquisite view at the summit will more than repay you for the exertion of mounting. You may almost rely upon the welcome of the courteous owner of Piedmont Cottage, Mr. Guppy, the Mayor, through whose grounds is the most agreeable path of ascent. The hill is not more than 600 feet high, but standing alone as it does, it towers high above the rest of Naparima, and is a conspicuous land-mark for miles round.

Public Schools were first opened in San Fernando in 1857. When the Borough Schools of Port of Spain were taken over by the Government, San Fernando determined to continue carrying on its own. But it has been for some time a veritable white elephant, and at length the city fathers have handed it over to the Government and relieved themselves of further responsibility in the matter by the annual payment of £500 into the Treasury of the colony. The large building erected on the hill to serve as the Borough School is now known as the Central School. Here of course the system of tuition is upon a secular basis, but there are other primary schools worked by the Roman Catholics, Anglicans and Presbyterians where denominational teaching is the practice.

The jetty of 100 feet length was erected by a company at a cost of £1,375, chiefly by the exertions of the late Mr. William Eccles. It has since been purchased by the Government. The wharf orginally of 300 feet length was constructed in 1842 by the Borough Council, but, like the jetty, it has been transferred to the Government, by whom it has been considerably extended. The principal Shipping Agencies are of course in the neighbourhood of the Gulf, as is also the Naparima terminus of the Railway.

There is a pretty little wooden place of worship in Coffee Street, quite near the Oriental Hall, connected with the Indian Mission of the Canadian Presbyterian Church. It is known as the Susumachar Church, and is under the charge of the Revd. K.J. Grant, a very worthy and zealous Missionary who has devoted many years to the Coolies of Naparima, with singular success. The handsome iron gate and columns at the entrance were the gift of one of his Indian protégés who, having been started in life by him, took this means of showing his gratitude to one to whom he owed so much. I have often read and heard what I used to consider exaggerated statements of the result of evangelizing work amongst the heathen, but I must confess that after having seen for myself the system as worked in Naparima, my eyes are opened. I do not hesitate to say that the Oriental, as he comes to Trinidad, ground down to the lowest depths of degradation by the slavish and tyrannical prejudices of caste, and the same man as he appears when guided by the Christianizing and humanizing influence such as the Revd. Mr. Grant and his hardworking colleagues bring to bear upon them, are as distinct and different as they can possibly be.

The Oriental Hall has been referred to above. It is a curious structure in Coffee Street, modelled, as its name indicates, upon the Eastern style, and indeed it was built by an Indian Doctor named Kelaart, who intended it as his residence. It is now in rather tumble-down condition, the lower part being let off in separate rooms to a colony of Chinese much devoted to opium and the whé-whé, while the large upper hall is occasionally utilized for entertainments.

The 'Poor House' or Alms House stands on the hill to the west of the Tram line. It is a municipal institution sheltering on an average about eight persons, who must be in a destitute condition, and have been resident in the town at least twelve months. There are several disused burial-grounds, one on the hill between Chacon and St. Vincent Streets, where are the remains of the celebrated Dr. John Baptiste Philip, author of 'The Free Mulatto', who died in 1829, and another to the westward of the hospital, where is a monument in memory of Mr. J.W. Begg, a former estate proprietor and prominent citizen.

The present Cemetery, a part of the old *Paradise* Estate, is pleasantly situated at the back of Harris Promenade. Some of the monuments and stones are in exceedingly good taste, many of them being of Aberdeen granite. One of the most curious is perhaps that in memory of Bhundoo and Koonjal, erected by their 'esteemed friend William Ramdeen.' These were father and son (Coolies), the latter of whom left the sum of $1,200 to pay for the monument. Graceful palmistes have been planted along the walks. The Mortuary Chapel was built by the late Abbé Christophe, who was the founder of the R.C. Church of the parish. In it is a fine mural tablet to the memory of Mr. Joseph Lambie, and there are also statues of Ste. Mary Magdalene and St. Jerome. Outside to the east of the Chapel is a life-size figure of our Saviour on the Cross.

The population of San Fernando, including the suburbs of the Coffee and Bushy Park, must be at least 7,000.

The Indians & Indentureship

1845 ~ 1917

Bridget Brereton

Established   1825
THE PORT OF SPAIN GAZETTE.

1845

FIRST LOT OF INDIAN IMMIGRANTS

We have much pleasure in announcing the arrival this afternoon of the long-looked-for coolie ship, the *Fatel Rozack*, 96 days from Calcutta and 41 days from the Cape of Good Hope, with 217 coolies on board, 'all in good condition' as the bills of lading have it. There were five deaths on board during the passage, but the general appearance of the people is very healthy. When our people are informed that there are countless thousands of these people, inured to a tropical climate, starving in their own country, and most willing to emigrate to the West Indies, it may be the means of opening their eyes a little to the necessity of working more steadily and giving greater satisfaction to their employers. The *Fatel Rozack* is a fine vessel of 445 tons, and is manned by a crew of lascars. *(30th May, 1845)*.

East Indian immigrant in the 1890's. Photograph — Mrs. Hélène Farfan.

After the emancipation of the slaves in 1838, many of the freed blacks gradually withdrew from full-time labour on the sugar plantations. This situation naturally caused severe difficulties for the planters, in Trinidad and elsewhere in the Caribbean, and they used their considerable influence on the government in London and on the local authorities to secure the adoption of a scheme to bring in immigrant labourers from many parts of the world. Eventually, after a period of experimentation, it was Indian immigration that proved to be the most important source of labour for the plantations, and it was people from India who came to comprise the great majority of the post-emancipation immigrants to the Caribbean.

The first ship-load of 217 Indians arrived in Trinidad in the 'Fatel Razack' on 10th May, 1845, and over the whole period of immigration (1845-1917) a total of 143,939 people came to the island from the subcontinent. The great majority came through Calcutta and had lived in the British Indian provinces along the Ganges river, especially the United Provinces, Bihar and Orissa, while a smaller group came from South India via Madras. Hindi, or a variant (especially Bhojpuri) was the majority language of the immigrants and Hinduism the majority faith, though a significant minority belonged to the Islamic faith. The Hindus represented, broadly, the caste spectrum found in North Indian society, with a sprinkling of high castes including Brahmins, a large group of people from the intermediate castes, and most belonging to the lower castes. The overwhelming majority of the immigrants were simple rural folk from the traditional communities of village India, accustomed to hard work and poverty and deeply attached to the land and all its routines. It was essential to tie them to the plantations and to extract a guaranteed minimum of labour from them by some legal restrictions.

Indian Ajoupa in central Trinidad, 1890's. Photograph — Mrs. Hélène Farfan.

Hence the indenture system. This was not slavery, yet the immigrant so long as he remained under indentureship was not free. He or she (for adult women were also indentured) had to work for the plantation to which he had been allocated, at the tasks prescribed by his employer and for the stipulated hours. He could neither change his employer, nor refuse to perform any lawful tasks, nor leave the plantation without written permission during working hours. Any breach by the immigrant of his contract (and indenture simply means contract) could be punished by criminal prosecution and jail sentences. This was no empty threat; at any point in time between 1845 and 1917, hundreds of indentured Indians were in jail, not for any criminal offence, but simply for breach of the Immigration laws. Even the Indian who had completed his indentureship still had to pay a special annual tax before becoming entitled to the 'free' return passage to India after living for ten years in Trinidad.

At first, the Indians were viewed as transients, as people brought to work for a few years and then sent back home. This is probably how the Indians themselves saw it, at least in the first phase of immigration (1845-70). But gradually, although attachment to Mother India remained strong, more and

1848

OPENING OF NEW GOVERNMENT BUILDINGS

The new Government Buildings, of which the foundation stone was laid by Sir Henry MacLeod in 1845 have been so far completed as to enable the Government to take possession of them. The whole interior of the northern wing of the upper storey, with the exception of the Council Room is finished, and forms a very handsome suite of rooms, which contain the official chambers of the Governor and the Colonial Secretary with their two clerks and messenger. The ground floor is occupied by the chambers of the Attorney-General, Colonial Treasurer, Surveyor General, and Superintendent of Public Works. The interior of the south wing, which is occupied by the courts and law officers, are conveniently arranged, with the exception of the large court-room, in which it is scarcely possible for Bench and Bar to hear each other without a great elevation of voice.
(20th Oct., 1848.)

East Indian immigrants in the 1890's. Photograph — Mrs. Hélène Farfan.

more Indians began to put down roots in the island. Of course, the growth of a locally born Indian population, people with no first-hand knowledge of India, reinforced this development. So did the movement of ex-indentured Indians off the plantations and the emergence of a large land-owning group. From 1869 it became possible for ex-indentured workers to obtain land, either through free grants from the Crown in lieu of a return passage to India, or through purchase of lots of Crown land, or through buying land on the private market. A large Indian peasantry soon developed, growing rice, cocoa, cane all kinds of food crops and raising livestock.

These Indian farmers and smallholders settled all over the island, helping to open it up after 1870 and creating new villages and settlements. By the time indentureship ended in 1917, the Indians were deeply rooted in the island, making a vital contribution to the economy especially as agriculturists and plantation workers.

As they were gradually transformed from immigrant labourers to settlers, the Indians contributed a great deal to their new society by practising their rich diversity of religious and cultural forms. Temples and mosques were built in villages, towns and estate settlements and Hindu and Moslem festivals were introduced. Indian dance, music and song enriched the already complex Trinidad culture. The island's cuisine was enlivened by the addition of roti and all kinds of curried dishes. Indian

jewellers and workers in gold and silver practised their traditional crafts. Thus the mosaic that was Trinidad and Tobago society and culture received new patterns, new colour and new beauty from the people from India, now true sons and daughters of the Caribbean soil.

INDIAN IMMIGRANTS
From Guide to Trinidad
J.H. Collens, 1886

As these people number in Trinidad probably not less than 60,000, comprising about one-third of the population of the island, it may be well to give a brief sketch of them, looking a little below the surface at the influences which control them and the social conditions under which they exist. This will be the more essential, since English people, and indeed, Europeans generally, unless they are brought into immediate contact with them, know next to nothing about them. They may be classed as Hindus, Mohammedans and Christians. The Hindus form by far the largest section, and for their religion they lay claim to a very high antiquity, their chronology running back to the remote ages of millions of years ago. Time with them is divided into four epochs—the Golden Silvern, Brazen and Iron epochs, each one 432,000 years longer than the preceding one. Thus—

	Years
The Iron or present Yug, of which 5,000 years have already passed, will be of duration	432,000
The preceding or Brazen Yug lasted ...	864,000
The Silvern Yug " ...	1,296,000
The Golden Yug " ...	1,728,000
Total number of years	4,320,000

Their oldest sacred writings are the four *Vedas,* which consist of two principal parts:–

I. Hymns and prayers written in poetry between 1500 and 1000 B.C. The Hindu race was then in its childhood and the form of worship very simple.

II. The *Brahmana,* or Directions to the Brahmans for sacrificing. These were prose writings of about 700 B.C., and mark the era of Brahmanical sacerdotalism.

The meaning of the term *Veda* is 'knowledge'; the four books were respectively the *Rig, Yajush, Sama* and *Atharva Vedas,* and they bore here and there some faint resemblance to the Holy Scriptures. In this sugar-growing colony it may be interesting to note that the *Rig Veda,* one of the oldest writings in the world, makes mention of the sugar-cane.

Brahmanism, with its elaborate system of priesthood, castes, and mystic rites, only attained its full sacerdotal force about 700 years before the Christian era. Of all the castes the *Brahman* is pre-eminent; the lower ones in their order are:–

Kshatriya—Principal families and military.

A prosperous Indian couple illustrated by Peter Shim, 1989 for A. de Verteuil, C.S.Sp., Eight East Indian Immigrants.

A Quarantine Station was established on Nelson Island to receive the immigrants. This photograph was taken in the 1890's. Photograph — Mrs. Hélène Farfan.

Vaisiya—Persons engaged in commercial and agricultural pursuits.

Sudra—*Servants*.

These classes are capable of an almost infinite number of sub-divisions or grades, as for example the *Chamars* or workers in leather, who are esteemed the lowest of the *Sudras,* since they mutilate the hide of the sacred ox. Some are thought so unworthy as not to be admitted into even the meanest of the above classes; such are called *Pariahs* or outcasts. The distinctions are not easily defined by the uninitiated, but they are none the less carefully observed, and the smallest infringement is a deadly sin. Different castes ought not to intermarry and should hold scarcely the slightest intercourse one with the other, a degree of exclusiveness which the haughty Brahmans carry to such excess, that the mere shadow of a *Sudra* cast upon their food will contaminate it. The three highest castes have special privileges. They may wear the Sacred Thread or Cord over the shoulder, with the bead made from the plant *Tulsi,* and may also be made acquainted with the Cabalistic name of the deity *Aum.* These rites separate the upper from the lower ranks of India much more than social position or the influence acquired from wealth could do. The *Sudra* is kept in as menial a condition as possible, being denied most of the rites pertaining to marriage, burial, &c., and while he is

graciously permitted to contribute from his hard-earned savings to the support of the temple, he may on no account enter it.

After the era of Brahmanical Sacerdotalism a reaction set in. About 600 B.C., Freethinkers arose, who questioned the authority of the Brahmans and the virtue of the blood of beasts. Buddhism was a manifestation of this feeling which developed a wonderful morality, but it was wanting in backbone, being built upon a foundation of Atheism. As its teachings were antagonistic to caste prejudices, and therefore threatening to the sway of the all-powerful Brahmans, the latter persecuted the Buddhists whenever and wherever they could, but nevertheless cunningly accommodated themselves to the new religion, by absorbing many of its most attractive tenets into their elastic creed. Buddhism in this way had a modifying influence upon the older faith. This was the age of Philosophy.

Upwards of a century after the reaction just alluded to, another series of sacred books appeared, known as the *Shastras*. These were six in number, and they regulated the Hindu laws as to property, caste, religion and customs. They were probably written between 500 and 400 B.C.

The Hindu had tried Nature worship and Sacrifice, which they called the way of *Works;* they had tested the

*The celebration of a Hindu religious festival in the 1890's. Photograph —
Mrs. Hélène Farfan.*

efficacy of Philosophy or the way of *Knowledge;* some
had tried *Atheistic Morality;* many hedged in life, duty
and dogma by *Laws,* but none of these brought rest, so a
new movement began, and here comes in for the first
time the doctrine of Incarnation.

The Supreme was regarded as taking form—coming
down to man. Hence gods with human attributes and
shape were multiplied, and it began to be taught that
faith in and devotion to, some of these was the road to
eternal bliss. This was called the way of *Faith.* The great
Epic Poems of India contributed to this movement, and
the eighteen Puranas were written to give it Divine
authority. None of them appeared previous to 800 A.D.
Throughout all the sacred books, but particularly in the
Puranas, there is the theory of a triple manifestation of
Deity, or a Trinity, thus:–

> *Brahma,* the Creator
> *Vishnu,* the Preserver } All evolved from BRAHM
> *Shiva,* the Destroyer   the Supreme.

The Philosophy of our Coolies in this colony is
substantially that which their forefathers adopted some
2,500 years ago in the Philosophic age; their Theology, or
rather Mythology, is that of the Puranas, of much more
modern date. It must be acknowledged that the Puranas

are a mass of contradiction, extravagance and idolatry,
though couched in highly poetical language. It is
nevertheless astonishing how familiar the Trinidadian
Coolies are with them; even amongst the humble
labourers who till our fields, there is a considerable
knowledge of them, and you may often in the evening,
work being done, see and hear a group of Coolies
crouching down in a semicircle or circle, chanting whole
stanzas of the Puranas which they have learnt by heart.

There is no doubt that Hindus coming to colonies
like Trinidad, far away from the land of their birth, would
like, if they could, to lessen the burden of Caste, but they
either dare not, or cannot do so. The mere fact of
crossing the ocean plunges any man, whether the
Brahman or Sudra, into depths of degradation, but the
relative distance between them *remains the same.* This is
an important point, for there is a general impression that
the Brahman and the Sudra (I merely take these by way
of example), sink to the same level, which is by no
means the case. They fall an equal distance, but the one
still continues to be immeasurably the superior of the
other. In the case of our agricultural labourer 'the sceptre
of the maharaja Brahmin', as a writer cleverly puts it,
'dwindles to the insignificance of a hoe-handle', but all
the same, he has a certain dignity to keep up, and he

A sugar cane estate in central Trinidad, 1890's. Photograph — Mrs. Hélène Farfan.

looks, poor as he may be, with haughty disdain upon his inferiors in caste.

The Brahmanical priests or Babagees, who are wise in their generation, foster and encourage this feeling. Many a heathen Coolie here, having served his term of indenture, works as a free labourer, saves a little cash, buys a small property, or starts shop-keeping, and in time becomes a rich man, socially raised above his former fellows. Such a man naturally aspires to a higher caste, to which he thinks his improved worldly position fairly entitles him, and he becomes at once the prey of the lazy impostor who sets himself up as a Babagee or *Sadhu*, (holy one). Although the wealthy Sudra may not as such partake of the mystic rites, nor can he be admitted to the higher caste, the Brahman is crafty enough to flatter him with a spurious sort of initiation in which he is invested with the fragment of Tulsi, and is told the Sacred Word. I

Every year the (Islamic) festival of Hosay is celebrated on the 10th day of Muharram, the first month of the Islamic calendar, in order to coincide with the anniversary date on which Imam Hussein, the grandson of the prophet Mohammed, was slain at Kerbal, Iraq, about 1365 years ago. A Shiah festival, Hosay was first celebrated at the Phillipine estate just south of San Fernando in 1850, and was recognized by the Government in 1863. Queen Victoria had granted permission for Hosay to be celebrated in Trinidad so long as there were residents who were willing to do so.

1884

THE COOLIE HOSEIN RIOTS

It was known on Monday, in town, that the Government, in view of the feeling believed to exist amongst the coolies, and their opposition to the new Hosein regulations, had deemed it desirable to strengthen the police force in the country districts. A special train left town at 1.30 p.m., taking detachments of police as well as some of the military from St. James' Barracks, and a party of marines from H.M.S. 'Dido'. No news of any trouble was received until Thursday evening, when it was reported that the police had fired on the coolies at San Fernando. The particulars to hand are not as full as might be wished, but we understand that the coolies assembled as usual in large numbers, and marched as they have been accustomed to do towards San Fernando, it being usual for the procession to pass through the streets and then return to the country after the throwing of their temples into the Gulf. The military were kept in reserve, while the police kept the entrances to the town with strict orders not to allow the procession to enter. Major Bowles commanded the men at Bushy Park entrance to San Fernando, and Captain Baker commanded the men at Mon Repos entrance. Communication with the Government was kept up by telegraph, as the situation became every hour more grave, and every persuasion to get the coolies to go back proved of no avail. One or two wealthy coolies are said to have interposed and done all in their power to get the rest to desist; but they refused. The crowd came on . . . . the police remained across the passage with fixed bayonets; the riot act was read and explained to them, and they were told to disperse . . . . . . The position of the police became so critical every moment that at last the order was given to fire. . . . Much the same scene was enacted at both entrances. . . . The result is deplorable. When the roads were cleared 10 were found dead and 83 wounded. In other districts the Hosein passed off without any fatality.
(1st November, 1884).

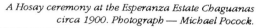
Sword stick formerly very much a part of the Hosay festival. Photograph – Ruby Finlayson.

need hardly say that the victim pays for this through the nose. The genuine *Sadhu* in India either leads an anchorite life in woods and caves, or he joins a community of similar men. This being out of the question in Trinidad, often when a labourer becomes a Sadhu he takes to Gunja, spends his time in idleness, and lives at the expense of his deluded countrymen, whom he does not forget to fleece. A few years ago, in this very island, one of these false priests, having taught his misguided people that caste could be recovered by payment, except when the fatal error of turning Christian had been committed, actually made thousands of dollars by investing with the 'Cord'. He got as much as he could out of the unfortunate people, and—'skedaddled'.

Amongst other rites there is an annual one affected by the Madras people, viz., 'passing through the fire'. The oldest priests, with their most fervent disciples, all nearly naked, pass repeatedly to and fro over smouldering ashes, shouting and gesticulating vehemently meanwhile. This they do quite publicly, even preferring spectators to privacy. All the same, they bitterly resent anything approaching to ridicule or interference; and being worked up at such times to an almost incredible pitch of frenzied excitement, a collision would be fraught with the most unpleasant consequences. The feasts, which are very common, are generally in honour of some god, and all who attend them and partake of the things sacrificed are supposed to do honour to some deity in whose name the feast is held. One of the South India gods, named Madrivele, had the marvellous faculty of entering houses through the smallest crevice; he used to display an inordinate fondness for fowls and rum, and he would help himself freely to these at all times. Hence, in the

A Hosay ceremony at the Esperanza Estate Chaguanas circa 1900. Photograph — Michael Pocock.

sacrificing to Madrivele, the eating of chickens and the drinking of copious libations of rum play an important part.

One of the Hindu doctrines is the 'transmigration of souls'. The Hindu lives, has lived, and will live through all time in some animal form or other. This partly accounts for his horror of mutilation, as the loss of a limb during one life may involve the same misfortune in the succeeding one.

The Mussulman's religion is one of Faith and Practice. Their creed may be embodied in the one great precept kept ever before them, 'There is but one God and Mohammed is Prophet'. Their religion of Practice comprises several duties, of which the most important is Prayer. Five times a day, with his face turned towards Mecca, he must bow down to ALLAH (God), uttering the words *'Allah Ackbar'* (God is good). Morning, noon, afternoon, evening and night, no excuse can be admitted for the neglect of it; time, place, business, pleasure, are as nothing in comparison with God's unalterable command, 'pray'. Other duties are cleanliness, frequent ablutions, the giving of alms to the poor and rigid abstention from wine and all strong drink. In Trinidad, as in India, many of these people become renegades to their creed, solely for the sake of being able to drink and sell rum, and it must be borne in mind that, with the Coolie, who will not partake of proper nourishing food when he has to pay for it himself, to drink rum is to become a drunken besotted beast. With regard to the first duty of Prayer, and in fact all the duties, Mussulmans in Trinidad soon grow lax and careless, but I have nevertheless frequently seen on an estate, a devout follower of the Prophet leave his work to face the rising sun, profoundly salaam, utter his formula, and then proceed with his labour as though no interruption had occurred.

The two chief Mussulman sects are the *Shiahs* and the *Sunnis*. The former especially reverence Hassan and Hosein, the two sons of Ali, in whose honour are their greatest festivals, and to celebrate the events of whose lives they even perform Mysteries or Passion plays in Persia. The Sunnis, for their part, do not reverence them, but merely recognize them as holy men. Both sects anticipate the coming of a great 'Mahdi', who will set right all wrongs, and restore peace and happiness to the universe, but the Sunnis expect him more as a Conquerer than a peacemaker. Knowing this it is easy to understand the infatuation' and adoration of the Mussulmans the other day in the Soudan for their 'Mahdi'. No wonder poor Gordon was so anxious to 'smash' him.

Much importance is attached by the Coolies to the yearly festival of the 'Mohurran', or, as it is better known here, the 'Hosein'. The 'Ashura', or last day of the Mohurran, is above all held in the greatest respect by the Shiahs, as it is intended to commemorate the death of Hosein, the son of Fatima and Ali. The Sunnis do not believe in the 'Hosein', and five or six years ago the chief of the sect in Trinidad petitioned the Government to put down the *Taziya* procession on the ground that it was an insult to their religion, having on several occasions led to riot and murder, and that at the best it was but a foolish ceremony. By way of explanation I may here remark that the Coolies make *Taziya* houses of cardboard ornamented with tinsel and coloured paper modelled to represent the tomb of Hosein, and, placing these in carts or on the heads of men, march about with them, beating tom-toms and shouting 'Hosein'. Each estate has its *Taziya* jealously guarded by the labourers who have

Palmiste Estate house, the home of Sir Norman Lamont.
Photograph — M. Pocock.

helped, either by subscription or otherwise, to construct it. All the estates in the same locality join together, and form up in procession; sometimes serious quarrels and fights taking place at this stage of the proceedings. Having paraded for some time with dancing, cries of 'Hosein, Hassan', &c., they at length repair to the sea if practicable, if not, to the nearest body of water, and, throwing their *Taziyas* into it, the ceremony is ended.

The Government did not accede to the petition of the Sunnis referred to above, but placed certain restrictions upon the festival. These new regulations being highly unpalatable, and looked upon by the Orientals as an infringement of their privileges, riots ensued, which were promptly suppressed, though unfortunately not without loss of life. For some time the relations between the Indian immigrants and the authorities were of a very strained nature, but happily things have righted themselves, and for the last few years the 'Hosein' has passed off in a most orderly manner. It will be seen that this is essentially a Mohammedan festival, that it is confined to a very small section of the faithful, and that the Hindus have nothing in the world to do with it. Nevertheless, either because it affords them an excuse for a holiday, and therefore for unlimited rum-drinking, or perhaps from sheer ignorance, they join in it with as much zest and earnestness as if it bore a religious significance to them.

Physically, the Coolie is well shaped, with regular features, wiry, though not over muscular, and possessing considerable powers of endurance. He is frugal and saving to a fault, living on the plainest and coarsest of diet, often denying himself sufficient even of this fare to gratify his love of hoarding. The Coolies, though mostly labourers and small shopkeepers, yet managed to deposit in the Government Savings Bank the sum of £44,774 during the year 1885. But even this by no means fully represents the wealth of this section of the population. Many of them look upon Banks with the greatest suspicion, and prefer to conceal their hard-earned gains in hollow trees or in holes in the ground, keeping at times the secret of their hiding place so closely, that it is often buried with its owner. Now and then an Oriental will withdraw all or a great part of his deposit from the Treasury without in the least requiring it, but simply to satisfy his uneasy mind that it is safe. In spite of this, however, they place much more confidence in the

'Queen's Bank' as they term it, than in any other. In their simple manner they reason—'He good da Queen's side, spose any man go tief um money, God sabby help um,—Queen *must* gi um.' Every year some take their departure for the land of their birth with the view of enjoying their savings among their relatives, but frequently finding no trace of either family or friends, or perhaps being coldly received, they re-emigrate to Trinidad, and start a little shop, or buy a patch of land. In 1885 upwards of six hundred returned to India, taking with them the sum of £11,000 in bills and specie, besides gold and silver ornaments to the value of another £1,000. Fancy the wife of an English peasant having a dozen silver bangles, or a beautiful and valuable necklace of gold coins! The thing is incongruous, and as difficult to imagine, as it is unlikely, and yet it is a common occurrence with these people. As a friend of mine smartly puts it in an unpublished essay, 'Coolies have three gods, *L, S* and *D,* which they worship in a variety of forms. One method they have of amassing wealth is by usury; 10 per cent *for a month,* or in reality 120 per cent per annum is the moderate rate of interest asked where the security is faulty'. In 1885, there arrived from India 2,162 immigrants, of whom 104 had originally emigrated to this or other sugar-producing colonies, saved a little money, gone back to their own country, and had now once more returned to the West. Six of these even paid their own passage money! As another instance of their thrift I may mention that in 1853 a coolie named Moolchan was indentured as a labourer on the St. Madeleine Estate; in 1878 he died a respectable and respected merchant of Port of Spain, leaving effects to the value of $60,000. This is no exceptional case, I know at this moment, two Coolies who, commencing some years ago as indentured labourers, are now worth fully *double* the sum just named. Within the last decade, and for two or three years in succession, the principal events in the annual races were taken by horses belonging to two well-to-do Indians.

The Immigration system was started in Trinidad about forty years ago. With it is closely connected the name of one of our oldest, ablest veterans, Mr. Charles Warner, C.B., who, in conjunction with W.H. Burnley and Mr. Losh, both long since gone over to the majority, by earnest and eloquent advocacy, overcame the opposition to a step which has doubtless saved this colony from irretrievable ruin.

The ship 'Fatel Rosack', which brought the first instalment of Coolies, arrived on the 30th of May, 1845. During the earliest three years of the system, 5,162 immigrants were introduced. As the importation of these Coolies (some of them were Chinese), was found to be a costly undertaking, a few years later, in 1850 and 1853, the colony, taking advantage of an Imperial Act guaranteeing certain loans to the West Indian Colonies, borrowed £125,000 from the Consolidated Fund for the purpose of promoting the introduction into this colony of free labourers.

The Coolies are bound for five years, receiving meanwhile free lodgings, medicines and medical attendance, with twenty-five cents per day wages. Stringent regulations are issued and insisted upon by the Government as to the accommodation provided for them whether sick or well, and if either houses or hospitals are found to be in any way deficient, the planter is mulcted in heavy penalties. The Immigration Offices are situated near those of the Public Works in Edward Street, on the site once occupied by the Commissariat. The present

The '45ers

These are the names of the Indians who arrived on board the Fatel Rozack on the 30th May, 1845. The list is taken from the 'Indian Centenary Review, 1845-1945'.

NAME	MALES	AGE	NAME	MALES	AGE
Bhuruth	"	20	Aunon	"	17
Sookra	"	15	Seedam	"	16
Dookhee	"	22	Aunand	"	25
Halladhur	"	18	Nunkoo	"	19
Anhatch	"	24	Beharee	"	18
Chowdry	"	18	Sookur	"	36
Bundhoo	"	19	Saroock	"	22
Panchoo	"	16	Ruttoo	"	32
Potem	"	23	Fatur	"	21
Gopaul	"	30	Ghunsem	"	30
Curmun	"	27	Maghoowa	"	20
Sunbir	"	21	Meetoo	"	25
Munee	"	27	Ramdihal	"	24
Mohun	"	18	Teeluckdharry	"	20
Buznauth	"	27	Greedharry	"	19
Anhach	"	20	Seedayal	"	16
Sooniah	"	25	Gunja	"	23
Neerown	"	28	Anjaeb	"	30
Nobin	"	21	Lullet	"	28
Bhaden	"	—	Podaruth	"	24
Minia	"	30	Bhowaney	"	27
Munsaran	"	28	Boodhun	"	24
Purmessur	"	24	Gopaul	"	35
Gungaram	"	22	Choin	"	20
Siloram	"	18	Doolar	"	20
Pithoe	"	16	Comul	"	17
Dahee Singh	"	28	Mungur	"	32
Sukroo	"	33	Ubhoun	"	25
Roopehand	"	30	Poorah	"	27
Dhumaram	"	25	Bundhoo	"	27
Jeebun	"	25	Dookhun	"	32
Lodhan	"	24	Rughoo	"	38
Unhora	"	18	Soomar	"	38
Denma	"	25	Nunkoo	"	26
Bolakee	"	26	Bhola	"	20
Auheeluch	"	31	Doolee	"	24
Khadoo	"	—	Jurum Singh	"	27
Julloo	"	18	Cundroo	"	27
Bheekarry	"	22	Ramsingh	"	25
Toolaram	"	18	Goorah	"	20
Tulokee	"	36	Bhoyreeh	"	23
Bajoonath	"	32	Deepoo	"	23
Foolchand	"	18	Nundo	"	19
Lakhoo	"	17	Mohun Singh	"	20
Neemy	"	21	Gopaul	"	26
Takoordayal	"	24	Soma	"	25
Boodhay	"	28	Bhanggee	"	25
Bahadoor	"	25	Busurma	"	26
Sookum	"	22	Sohyra	"	18
Bhowanipersad	"	20	Asson	"	19
Kawal	"	25	Omruddee	"	32
Rampal	"	23	Beersingh	"	18

NAME	MALES	AGE			
Ramdayal	"	27	Bhooseya	FEMALES	20
Greeharee	"	25	Guranes	"	18
Untram	"	26	Gungeeya	"	26
Bhoyram	"	26	Gowree	"	19
Nemchand	"	30	Aublokheeya	"	25
Gooroodayal	"	38	Deepa	"	20
Bahadoor	"	14	Mohoorun	"	–
Nadhon	"	14	Bulleeya	"	16
Buttoo	"	30	Mandoo	"	33
Lofur	"	30	Sookooanroo	"	16
Gooroocharm	"	19	Bhookhu	"	18
Boodhoo	"	31	Etwareeya	"	20
Mohun	"	19	Radum	"	32
Khadun	"	24	Toya	"	30
Ramcharam	"	28	Samareeya	"	20
Chabooree	"	30	Sookooawaroo	"	20
Nundoo	"	19	Ghowlee	"	20
Abeeluck	"	16	Seeklia	"	40
Lattoo	"	24	Maunkee	"	25
Gunnes	"	28	Dossy	"	22
Doorjun	"	30			
Neemy	"	28	Bhadoor (Children)	MALES	9
Kistoe	"	28	Muma	"	8
Causmollee Khan	"	32	Goonoo	"	5
Gondoury	"	18	Bolakee	"	9
Lantoo	"	25	Hardutt	"	9
Sonatun	"	36	Bhandoo	"	9
Furreed	"	32	Rajnauth	"	9
Sobrooghun	"	20	Bodeel	"	9
Jahul	"	28	Chotooya	"	9
Motee	"	25	Jaipaul	"	7
Emambocus	"	36	Jhurry	"	9
Faize Buxo	"	30	Gunnes	"	7
Madar Buxo	"	28	Golamina	"	6
Nemchand	"	30	Samodha	"	9
Jagoo	"	14	Maighun	"	9
Tacoor Singh	"	14	Amree (Children)	FEMALES	6
Nanhoo	"	16	Faizan	"	4
Deersun	"	18	Mungree	"	8
Bundhoo	"	20	Acklee	"	6
Ramnath	"	23	Jhalowa	"	5
Caleecharan	"	20	Dhonee	"	6
Sonatun	"	30			
Seeodeen	"	25			
Nyak	"	30			
Golab	"	27			
Nundoo	"	17			
Aliar	"	–			
Jaunkee	"	24			
Bhekharry	"	30			
Ruchparr	"	40			
Ramsaran	"	21			
Ramdhun	"	18			
Rughoobungss	"	31			
Dookhoo	"	30			
Chumroo	"	28			
Baharry	"	25			
Taka	"	32			
Bhola	"	30			
Bhoyroo	"	28			
Rutheeya	"	25			
Gopaul	"	24			
Numdoo	"	18			
Ropun	"	21			
Ramjeehun	"	30			
Ajoodhia	"	30			
Aunatch	"	24			

head of the Department is the Hon'ble C. Mitchell, son of Dr. Mitchell, C.M.G., who for many years filled the post, and whom the Coolies still lovingly term 'Papa' Mitchell. At first Immigrants who served ten years were granted ten acres of Crown land, then this was changed to a grant of five acres with a bonus of £5, now they receive nothing.

Certainly these people live a happier and more prosperous life here than they could possibly do in their own country. Mark the difference between a new arrival and an old stager, the former timid, cringing, almost servile in manner; the latter erect, keen with an air semi-respectful, semi-defiant viewing with an amused look the profound salaam of the newcomer.

I have stated that by the Koran the Mussulman is prohibited from indulging in strong drink. It is not unlikely that many in Trinidad forsake the religion of their forefathers from no better motive than to gratify their craving for alcohol. Years ago, when a youngster, I remember seeing a pictorial sketch in Punch entitled 'Accommodating'. An officer is seated in his bungalow, enjoying the *dolce far niente* of military life in India. Addressing his native body-servant who stands near,—"What caste are you Ramsammee?" *Native:* "Same church like Sahib; me eat beef and drink brandy, sar!" To him Christianity and grog-drinking were unfortunately synonymous terms.

After all Coolies are much like other people; treat them properly and they will serve you well, always however with an eye to main chance, but is not human nature the same all the world over?

When the Indian takes to Ganja and Opium smoking, as he too often does, his faculties become dulled, his constitution enervated, he is unfitted for work, and not being willing or able to take nourishing food, he becomes an easy prey to disease.

The preponderance of males over the opposite sex leads not seldom to unpleasant complications. The Coolie husband is of a frantically jealous disposition, and any real or fancied unfaithfulness on the part of his spouse he visits with condign punishment. Three-fourths of the murders in this colony may be traced to this cause. The women are rather below the average height, and from having to undertake the onerous duties of wifehood and maternity at a tender age, when most English girls would be wearing short frocks, and withal being perpetually treated as the 'worse' half, they become prematurely old, so that at thirty they are often absolutely haggard and aged in appearance. As a rule they dress becomingly and decently, generally exhibiting taste in the arrangement

GROUPER
Cut the fish in slices and season with chives, salt, pepper and cloves. Put a couple of tablespoons of butter in the pot and stew some onions, tomato and a bit of garlic. When brown put in some flour until the sauce thickens adding a little water gradually. Then put the fish in, cover the pot and simmer slowly. Just before it is done if you add a little red wine the flavour will be considerably improved.

A Hindu temple of the 1920's. Photograph — Monica Johnstone.

and harmony of colours. A favourite ornament with them is a gold ring passed through the nostrils. They wear too any amount of silver bangles on their arms, toes and ankles, with necklets of gold round their necks, and a gold band across the forehead.

A Babagee or priest in easy circumstances may be recognised by the conspicuous whiteness and amplitude of the embroidery trimming about his costume. His voluminous *kapra* takes more the form of paejamas, reaching nearly to his feet, while that of the low class Indian is much more contracted.

If you ask a Trinidad Immigrant where he hails from, his reply will be either Calcutta or Madras. This, however, merely implies that he has embarked from one or other of these ports; he may in reality be from the Punjaub, Nepaul or elsewhere.

These people dearly love litigation in any form, and you may always see a number of them hanging round the Courts and lawyers' offices as though they had some great interest at stake. Even if not in the slightest degree concerned in a case, they will spend hours listening to the evidence, perhaps not understanding a single word of it.

The evangelising missions among them have done much to raise them from their degrading superstitions and prejudices—in fact, it is hardly possible to over-estimate the amount of good done, more especially by the missionaries of the Canadian Presbyterian Church. In this they have been very greatly assisted by the leading proprietors, Messrs. C. Tennant & Sons, John Cumming, W.H. Burnley, Gregor Turnbull, Lamont and the Colonial Company, who, being all large employers of labour, contribute annually liberal sums towards the up-keep of these missions.

Before closing this Chapter it may be well to give one or two marks by which a Hindoo is to be distinguished from a Mohammedan. The former almost invariably shaves under the chin and buttons his upper garment or *chapkan* on the *left* side; the latter fastens it on the *right* side, and abjuring the razor, delights in a flowing beard such as the great Prophet had. At dinner parties too, while the Hindus sit in rows, the Mussulmans arrange themselves in circles.

Hindu man and wife, note chillum for smoking ganga.
Photograph — Jackson.

CHRONOLOGICAL LIST OF EVENTS
compiled by Jose M. Bodu

1850

On the 16th April, 1850, the town of Port of Spain was witness of an event without a parellel in the history of the island, and, we believe, of the British West Indies. Allusion is made to the celebration by the Right Rev. Dr. Parry, Lord Bishop of Barbados, of the nuptials of His Excellency the Right Honourable George Francis Robert, Lord Harris, Governor and Commander-in-Chief of the colony of Trinidad, and Sarah, second and youngest dauther of the Venerable George Cummings, A.M. Archdeacon of Trinidad. The marriage of the representatives of Her Majesty the Queen with a daughter of theisland excited universal enthusiasm and the popular rejoicings were great.

This photograph of crowds at Esperanza Estate looking on at the Muslim festival of Hosay was taken by Sir Norman Lamont. Photograph — M. Pocock.

1851

On the 20th of the month, a moment before the Cross was placed on Mount Calvary, it was struck by a flash of lighting which opened it in twain.

The first Annual Race Meeting at Queen's Park was held in the month of December this year under the patronage of His Excellency the Governor, Lord Harris. Since then the races have been a constant feature of the holiday season, and many celebrated horses have competed for the laurels of the Trinidad turf. The neighbouring colonies have frequently participated in the sport, and not a few prizes have been won by our friends. But Trinidad, has, on the whole maintained her reputation, and recently Wyanoke, an American filly belonging to the Messrs. Borde, was the acknowledged Queen of West Indian racers.

CURRIED MUTTON
Brown the mutton, cut in small pieces, in butter and a little oil. Add some seasoning chopped very fine, some salt and black pepper. simmer a few minutes. Mix a teaspoon of flour with some water and add to pot in which enough water to cover the meat has been placed. Cook for fifteen minutes and add a tablespoon of curry paste or powder. This can be improved by adding some of those little cucumbers to it. They should be put in at the same time as the water.

This taj of the 1880's is remarkable because of its unique design. Photograph — Hélène Farfan.

Established 1825

THE PORT OF SPAIN GAZETTE.

Special Centenary Number

NO. 13,911 VOL. XLVIII.   TRINIDAD :   MONDAY,   SEPTEMBER   21,   1925.   THIRTY-TWO PAGES.   PRICE : SIXPENCE.

1885

INQUIRY INTO THE HOSEIN RIOTS

General Sir Henry W. Norman, K.C.B., C.G.E., arrived by the packet late last Wednesday evening as Royal Commisioner into the circumstances of the Coolie Hosein Riots last year, and began his inquiry on New Year's Day when, we understand, the statements of Mr. Mitchell, the Protector of Immigrants, and Captain Baker, Inspector-Commandant of Police, were taken. On Friday morning a Gazette Extraaordinary was issued containing the following notice which was also placarded about the streets:–

Government House,

1st January, 1885.

His Excellency Sir Henry W. Norman, K.C.B., C.I.E. has arrived in Trinidad under instructions from Her Majesty's government to inquire into the conflict which took place in San Fernando on the 30th October last between the police and certain Indian immigrants, and which resulted in the death of a considerable number of the latter.

His Excellency will at once commence to take the statements of such persons in the public service as may be summoned by him, and arrangements will be made through the Protector of Immigrants for his receiving the statements of certain coolies.

Any persons not in the government service who may be able to furnish information with respect to the conflict or the causes which led to it, are invited at once to address Captain Coxhead, private secretary to Sir Norman at Government House, stating the particular point on which they can furnish information, and whether they would wish to wait upon His Excellency at Port of Spain or at San Fernando.

By Command
R.W. PAYNE.

Above: Muslim workers parade with quarter staff beneath the watchful gaze of their negroe overseers, on the Esperanza Estate, Chaguanas.

Below: A photograph of an Indian and Negroe batoniére on the Perseverance Estate, Chaguanas. It is interesting to note that they are both dressed in the traditional costume of stick fighters of the 19th century. These photographs were taken in the 1900's by Sir Norman Lamont and are reproduced by kind permission of M. Pocock.

CURRIED SHRIMPS

Melt a little piece of salt pork. Add some butter and oil and simmer cleaned shrimps for a few minutes. Add chipped seasoning and marsala or powdered curry to taste. Cook until sauce is smooth. Serve with rice boiled very dry.

1885

REPORT ON THE HOSEIN RIOTS

In report of General Sir Henry Norman, in connection with the unfortunate events connected with the late coolie Hosein riots in this island, is published in another column of this issue. It clearly acquits the local authorities of all blame in the matter. . . . . . The three chief points in the inquiry were:—First, were the local authorities justified in interfering to regulate the annual procession? Secondly, were the regulations when issued fully made known to the coolies? Thirdly, were the police justified in firing?. . . . In answer to the first of the questions, the Commissioner, after pointing out that these processions are regulated in India by the police, concludes by saying:— "in fact I think the error has rather been in delaying to issue regulations too long." On the second point, the Commissioner says:— "It is no doubt possible, but not probable, that some few individuals may have joined the procession who were ignorant that it was prohibited,. . . . but making every allowance for that possiblity, I have no doubt that the great bulk of the coolies perfectly understood the regulations and that, with possibly few exceptions, all who persisted in going forward, were determined to disobey them." On the third point the Commissioner says:— "I am of opinion that under the circumstances shewn, it was justified to fire, and that the police shewed steadiness:. . . . Speaking of the action of the magistrates, the Commissioner says,—"I am of opinion that no blame attaches to these gentlemen." As to the causes which led to the occurrence, the Commissioner expresses the opinion that it was no wages or labour question, or in fact any grievance, real or supposed, which led the coolies to infringe the law with regard to processions; and he continues,— "I am led to believe that the coolies have been induced to oppose authority by being at times too much indulged by an amount of consideration which could not permanently be extended to them. . . I think that the circumstances of bodies of coolies being allowed to come up to the Immigration Office to prefer complaints in an overbearing way, carrying their cutlasses and other agricultural implements, has encouraged in them an idea that they are powerful and can do what they like.' As to the course to be pursued in future, the Commissioner lays it down in the most clear and unmistakeable terms:— "I think it would be unwise to cancel the regulations and I see no way of modifying them so as to make them more acceptable to the coolies without rendering them useless. *(4th April, 1885).*

A Visit To Peru Village, St James In 1880.

by Lafcadio Hearn

Marine Square in the late nineteenth century. Photograph — Mrs. O. Mavrogordato.

ASHORE, through a black swarming and a great hum of creole chatter . . . .Warm yellow narrow streets under a burning blue day; — a confused impression of long vistas, of low pretty houses and cottages, more or less quaint, bathed in sun and yellow-wash, — and avenues of shade-trees, — and low garden-walls overtopped by waving banana leaves and fronds of palms . . . . A general sensation of drowsy warmth and vast light and exotic vegetation, — coupled with some vague disappointment at the absence of that picturesque humanity that delighted us in the streets of St. Pierre, Martinique. The bright costumes of the French colonies are not visible here: there is nothing like them in any of the English islands. Nevertheless, this wonderful Trinidad is as unique ethnologically as it is otherwise remarkable among all the other Antilles.

TWO YEARS

IN THE

FRENCH WEST INDIES

By LAFCADIO HEARN
AUTHOR OF ''CHITA'' ETC.

ILLUSTRATED

*Title page from 'Two Years in the French West Indies', Lafcadio Hearn ,
1890. At right is an extract taken from that book.*

It has three distinct creole populations, — English, Spanish, and French, — besides its German and Madeiran settlers. There is also a special black or half-breed element, corresponding to each creole race, and speaking the language of each; there are fifty thousand Hindoo coolies, and a numerous body of Chinese. Still, this extraordinary diversity of race elements does not make itself at once apparent to the stranger. Your first impressions, as you pass through the black crowd upon the wharf, is that of being among a population as nearly African as that of Barbados; and indeed the black element dominates to such an extent that when upon the streets a white face does appear, it is usually under the shadow of an Indian helmet, and heavily bearded, and austere: the physiognomy of one used to command.

. . . I hire a carriage to take me to the nearest coolie village; — a delightful drive . . . Sometimes the smooth white road curves round the slope of a forest-covered mountain; — sometimes overlooks a valley shining with twenty different shades of surface green; — sometimes traverses marvellous natural arcades formed by the interweaving and inter-crossing of bamboos fifty feet high. Rising in vast clumps, and spreading out sheafwise from the soil towards the sky, the curves of their beautiful jointed stems meet at such perfect angles above

A visitor to Trinidad in the 1890's. Photograph — Mrs. Hélène Farfan.

the way, and on either side of it, as to imitate almost exactly the elaborate Gothic arch-work of old abbey cloisters. Above the road, shadowing the slopes of lofty hills, forests beetle in dizzy precipices of verdure. They are green — burning, flashing green — covered with parasitic green creepers and vines; they show enormous forms, or rather dreams of form, fetishistic and startling. Banana leaves flicker and flutter along the wayside; palms shoot up to vast altitudes, like pillars of white metal; and there is a perpetual shifting of foliage colour, from yellow-green to orange, from reddish-green to purple, from emerald-green to black-green. But the background colour, the dominant tone, is like the plumage of a green parrot.

. . . We drive into the coolie village, along a narrower way, lined with plantain-trees, bananas, flamboyants, and unfamiliar shrubs with large broad leaves. Beyond the little ditches on either side, occupying openings in the natural hedge, are the dwellings — wooden cabins, widely separated from each other. The narrow lanes that enter the road are also lined with habitations, half hidden by banana-trees. There is a prodigious glare, an intense heat. Around, above the trees and the roofs, rise the far hill shapes, some brightly verdant, some cloudy blue, some gray. The road and the lanes are almost deserted; there is little shade; only at intervals some slender brown girl or naked baby appears at a doorway. The carriage halts before a shed built against a wall — a simple roof of palm thatch supported upon jointed posts of bamboo.

Above: Port of Spain street scene of the 1930's showing Indian pedlars selling lace on Frederick Street. Photograph — Sr. Marie Thérèse Retout. Below: A Hindu holy man. Photograph — O. Mavrogordato.

1855

THE PORTRAITS OF THE CITY COUNCIL

At a meeting of the Council of Government held on Monday last, His Excellency the Governor stated that he had forgotten to mention previously that some months ago the Town Council had sent in a letter claiming the pictures of the late governors of the colony, then at St. Ann's as their property; but it appeared at the time that there was not a room fit to put them in. Since then, the drawing room at St. Ann's had fallen into such a dilapidated condition that it became necessary to remove the pictures; and last week he had them put up for the time in the Council Room,—Sir Ralph Woodford, Sir Thomas Picton, General Munroe, Sir Ralph Abercrombie, and Sir Areas W. Young. (4th July, 1855.)

TONGUE A LA GRENADE

Trim the tongue, soak it in cold water for one hour. Make a broth with a small piece of salted pork and some pieces of salted beef, three onions, three carrots, three turnips, a clove of garlic and some celery tops and thyme. Put salt and pepper and simmer the tongue in it for three hours. Take the tongue out and scrape off the skin and slice the tongue in slices half an inch thick. Strain the broth and thicken with flour. Add a large wine glass of rum flavoured with Angostura to it. Pour this sauce over the tongue that has been sliced half an inch thick. Leave it in the pan thus until wanted. Place over fire and warm over slow fire. When serving garnish with small boiled onions.

It is a little coolie temple. A few weary Indian labourers slumber in its shadow; pretty naked children, with silver rings round their ankles, are playing their with a white dog. Painted over the wall surface, in red, yellow, brown, blue, and green designs upon a white ground, are extraordinary figures of gods and goddesses. They have several pairs of arms, brandishing mysterious things, — they seem to dance, gesticulate, threaten; but they are all very naif, — remind one of the first efforts of a child with the first box of paints. While I am looking at these things, one coolie after another wakes up (these men sleep lightly) and begins to observe me almost as curiously, and I fear much less kindly, than I have been observing the gods. "Where is your babagee?" I inquire. No one seems to comprehend my question; the gravity of each dark face remains unrelaxed. Yet I would have liked to make an offering unto Siva.

. . . Outside the Indian goldsmith's cabin, palm shadows are crawling slowly to and fro in the white glare, likes shapes of tarantulas. Inside, the heat is augmented by the tiny charcoal furnace which glows beside a ridiculous little anvil set into a wooden block buried level with the soil. Through a rear door came odours of unknown flowers and the cool brilliant green of banana leaves. . . . A minute of waiting in the hot silence; — then, noiselessly as a phantom, the nude-limbed smith enters by a rear door, — squats down, without a word, on his little mat beside his little anvil, — and turns towards me, inquiringly, face half-veiled by a black beard, — a turbaned Indian face, sharp, severe, and slightly unpleasant in expression. '*Vlé béras!*' explains my creole driver, pointing to his client. The smith opens his lips to utter in the tone of a call the single syllable '*Ra!*' then folds his arms.

Almost immediately a young Hindoo woman enters, squats down on the earthen floor at the end of the bench which forms the only furniture of the shop, and turns upon me a pair of the finest black eyes I have ever seen, — like the eyes of a fawn. she is very simply clad, in a coolie robe leaving arms and ankles bare, and clinging about the figure in gracious folds; her colour is a clear bright brown — new bronze; her face a fine oval, and charmingly aquiline. I perceive a little silver ring, in the form of a twisted snake, upon the slender second toe of each bare foot; upon each arm she has at least ten heavy silver rings; there are also large silver rings about her ankles; a gold flower is fixed by a little hook in one nostril, and two immense silver circles, shaped like new moons, shimmer in her ears. The smith mutters something to her in his Indian tongue. She rises, and seating herself on the bench beside me, in an attitude of perfect grace, holds out one beautiful brown arm to me that I may choose a ring.

The arm is much more worthy of attention that the rings: it has the tint, the smoothness, the symmetry, of a fine statuary's work in metal; — the upper arm, tatooed with a bluish circle of arabesques, is otherwise unadorned; all the bracelets are on the forearm. Very clumsy and coarse they prove to be on closer examination: it was the fine dark skin which by colour contrast made them look so pretty. I choose the outer one, a round ring with terminations shaped like viper heads; — the smith inserts a pair of tongs between these ends, presses outward slowly and strongly, and the ring is off. It has a faint musky odour, not unpleasant, the perfume of the tropical flesh it clung to. I would have taken it thus; but the smith snatches it from me, heats it red in his little furnace, hammers it into a nearly perfect circle again, shakes it, and burnishes it.

Then I ask for children's *béras,* or bracelets; and the young mother brings in her own baby girl, — a little darling just able to walk. She has extraordinary eyes; — the mother's eyes magnified (the father's are small and fierce). I bargain for the single pair of thin rings on her little wrists; — while the smith is taking them off, the child keeps her wonderful gaze fixed on my face. Then I observe that the peculiarity of the eye is the size of the iris rather than the size of the ball. These eyes are not

A view of Peru Village, St. James, in the 1900's. Photograph — Port of Spain City Council.

Pretty Indian girl. Photograph – Hélène Farfan.

soft like the mother's, after all; they are ungentle, beautiful as they are; they have the dark and splendid flame of the eyes of a great bird of prey.

. . . She will grow up, this little maid, into a slender, graceful woman, very beautiful, no doubt; perhaps a little dangerous. She will marry, of course: probably she is betrothed even now, according to Indian custom, — pledged to some brown boy, the son of a friend. It will not be so many years before the day of their noisy wedding: girls shoot up under this sun with as swift a growth as those broad-leaved beautiful shapes which fill the open doorway with quivering emerald. And she will know the witchcraft of those eyes, will feel the temptation to use them, — perhaps to smile one of those smiles which have power over life and death.

And then the old coolie story! One day, the yellowing cane-fields, among the swarm of veiled and turbaned workers, a word is overheard, a side glance intercepted; — there is the swirling flash of a cutlass blade; a shrieking gathering of women about a headless corpse in the sun; and passing cityward, between armed and helmeted men, the vision of an Indian prisoner, blood-crimsoned, walking very steadily, very erect, with the solemnity of a judge, the dry bright gaze of an idol . . .

A milk vendor. In days gone by cow's milk was sold almost exclusively by Indians. Photograph — Hélène Farfan.

THE INTEGRATION OF INDIAN SETTLERS IN TRINIDAD AFTER INDENTURE, 1921 – 1946

Marianne D. Ramesar

In his book *Race and Nationalism in Trinidad and Tobago,* Selwyn Ryan notes that the 'ending of Indentured Immigration in 1917 had forced the Indians ... to come to terms with the society which they had chosen to adopt'. This paper analyses some of the factors in this adjustment. The development of Indian group consciousness during this period was to contribute to friction with other groups which were developing similar nationalisms.

In general, aspiring Indians aimed at rising above the original status of members of their ethnic group as a bonded agricultural labour force. Entry into the public service and the professions was strongly desired. For this the attainment of competence in English and a western education were necessary. But because these tools were acquired mainly through the agencies of Christian schools and churches, Indians – especially the non-Christian majority – were faced with the prospect of losing religion, language and valued cultural remains, while gaining these new benefits.

The process of westernization often involved the adoption of European dress and life style, and some intermixing with non-Indians. This aroused expressions of antipathy towards miscegenation which orthodox Indians protested would result in the loss of ethnic identity. Indeed Indian settlement implied integration rather than absorption, that is, an adjustment similar to the scond alternative proposed by John Rex in his *Race Relations in Sociological Theory:*

> There are circumstances in which a minority seeks its own disappearance through assimilation within the cultural and social system of the group which dominates the state. There are also circumstances in which the group seeks simply to coexist, maintaining its own culture and social system with that of the dominant group.

The Indians were an evident minority, distinguished from others in Trinidad by physical and cultural characteristics, and by their peculiar historical role in the society. But the fact that they had already lost many original social and cultural features did not lead them to seek 'disappearance through assimilation'. Ambitious Indians sought the mastery of useful elements from the culture and social system of the dominant European group. In addition they aimed at coexistence with other groups, and at the revival of traditional practices.

Indians did not advocate any wholesale repatriation to India except during periods of general unemployment, and it became increasingly apparent that the majority of Indians and their descendants were in Trinidad to stay. The 8,000 repatriates to India during the 1921–1931 decade were less than 6% of the Indian population which numbered 138, 667 in 1931.

Potential repatriates were no doubt influenced by accounts in the Trinidad newspapers making unfavourable comparisons between conditions in India and the advantages of life in Trinidad and the West Indies. For instance a report was quoted from the British Guiana *Daily Argosy* concerning one Gayadeen, a 'well-

F.E. Hosein

known cow-minder and farmer of Kitty in Demerara'. Leaving Guiana where he had achieved a certain affluence in the ownership of a cottage, cows, rice and provision farms, plus about $2,000 in savings, he returned to the village of Tamaria in Lucknow *Zillah* (District), United Provinces. His unfortunate experiences included being robbed in Calcutta, having to spend $500 in a few short weeks, drought and suffering in his native village, the low rate of wages and high cost of living. He therefore returned to British Guiana, the land which had given him 'wealth, comfort and equality of rights with neighbours of all races', along with 19 other disillusioned repatriates from Guiana and Trinidad.

A similar but formal report was sent by the Secretary of State for the Colonies concerning a paty of 50 repatriates in Calcutta with their children and dependents, who wished to return to Trinidad on the ship *Sutlej*. The Government of Indian had decided to allow this, once they paid their own passages or could return (in special cases) at the expense of the Government of the Colony. Two years later the Immigration Department in Trinidad questioned the advisability of repatriates taking their Trinidad-born children to India where an uncertain fate awaited them in the event of their parent's death, as had been the case of two orphans 'mercifully' returned to Trinidad by the shipping firm of James Nourse.

Employers' representatives and others with similar interests no doubt magnified these instances in order to influence potential labourers to remain in Trinidad – and with some sucess. In 1928 the Indian National Party of San Fernando recommended that the sum of $144 should be given to Indians in lieu of a return passage to India. James Mungal, the Party spokesman, a successful India-born businessman, claimed that the majority of repatriates were not well received in India, but considered as outcastes. Others had grown accustomed to life in the West Indies, to which they could not afford to return.

By 1921, a minority of Indians had gained respectable status according to the generally accepted criteria of educational attainment, occupational level and material acquisitions. This gave them a stake in Trinidad, and a lever for demanding further opportunities in the society.

Articulate Indians proudly acclaimed the achievements of their fellows. For instance, in 1921, Hon. C.D. Lalla, Member of the Legislative Council and a Presbyterian clergyman, declared that although the Immigration System had aimed at making the Indians 'hewers of wood and drawers of water', they had been raised to the 'highest pedestal of British citizenship', mainly through the educational institutions provided by the Canadian (Presbyterian) Mission and supported by His Majesty's Government and by the planting community. This was especially true in San Fernando, and in the southern half of the Colony which boasted the first East Indian solicitor in Trinidad, as well as the first Barrister, Medical Doctor, Minister of the Gospel, Mayor and Member of the Legislative Council.

Indians of substance included A.A. Sobrian, cocoa estate owner and a pioneer manufacturer of chocolate at his Alta Gracia Factory; Ben Roodal, C.W. Samlalsingh and Boodoosingh were owners of race horses; while sportsmen included Dr. Frank Mahabir who was honoured by the West Indies Cricket Club in London in 1923.

The activities of Christians as well as leading Hindus and Muslims were reported in the Trinidad newspapers. Indians had their own secular associations – The East

Augustus Gobin

Above: Quarantine station on Nelson Island showing newly arrived Indian immigrants. Photograph — G. MacLean.

Indian National Association and the East Indian National Congress – but were also active in wider colonial institutions like the Trinidad Agricultural Society and the Child Welfare Association.

Informed Indians based their claims to greater representation largely on the numerical strength of their group, which formed the majority in some counties and rural villages. In relation to their numbers they were greatly under-represented, especially in Government positions: A.H. Hosein was only one complainant who charged that Indians were not being given 'fair and equal consideration' with members of other races with regard to appointments.

This imbalance was compared not with the whites who were the accepted ruling group, but with groups introduced under similar conditions into Trinidad, especially the slave-descended Africans. Thus in 1928 F.E.M. Hosein, Barrister and Member of the Legislative Council noted that the 'coloured population' that is, those of mixed African-European parentage 'have risen in point of education, culture and refinement'. A later Report noted that like other 'elements in the population', originally introduced to supply estate labour, there were Indians who wanted to improve their position, and that these should have the same facilities as members of other communities to contribute according to their abilities to the life of the Colony, in the Government Service, professions, commerce and industry.

The unfavourable position of the Indians with regard to occupations in Trinidad was documented in this 1938-39 Report by J.D. Tyson who had been sent by the Government of India to meet Indian communities in the West Indies, following the labour disturbances of the 1930's, and to prepare evidence for an investigating Royal Commission.

The reality of a lowly position for most Indians was revealed to be quite different from the official picture which in fact described the fortunate few. Protectors of Immigrants in their Annual Reports had repeatedly stressed the upward mobility of Indians as measured by occupation. In 1921 Protector Arneaud de Boissiere noted that Indian occupations 'are the same as those of the rest of the community, that is, in Government and the Mercantile Services; they include many large and wealthy proprietors and numerous small ones'. In 1931 de Boissiere's successor G.E. Lechmere Guppy reported that 'many (Indians) had sons in the professions, or were in the Government Service'. During this post-Indenture period of the 1920's and 1930's Indians too acclaimed the success of their fellows in pursuing further education, in entering the professions, and in securing Government appointments.

In fact, the number of Indian 'professionals' was relatively small (See Table). These 637 represented only 12% of the Trinidad total, and only teachers were relatively numerous, as the result of recruitment and training by Christian missionaries. Most glaring was the very small number of Indians in the Public Service – a mere 119, or only 5% of the total number of Trinidad Public Servants – and nearly half of them were messengers in Government offices. On the other hand Indians comprised a substantial proportion – one-quarter

Lalmathura Pundit

OCCUPATIONS OF INDIANS IN TRINIDAD AGED 15 YEARS AND OVER IN 1931

Occupations	Males	Females	Total	Indians as Percentage of Work Force
Government Service				
Public Officers	68	1		
Messengers etc. in Government Office	44	1	119	5.56
Police	5	—		
Professions				
Legal	9	—		
Medical	7	—	637	12.41
Ministers of Religion	181	—		
Teachers	368	72		
Commercial				
Merchants	123	4		
Clerks and Shopmen	1,246	104		
Shopkeepers and Hucksters	1,237	837	3,574	22.51
Hotel Keepers	9	—		
Spirit Dealers	14	—		
Industrial				
Mechanics (Artisans)	2,556	—		
Boatmen and Fishermen	130	—		
Mariners	23	—	3,015	6.86
Laundress and Seamstresses	—	306		
Domestic Servants	304	949	1,253	5.21
Agricultural				
Managers and Overseers	270	—		
Peasant Proprietors	3,303	755		
Metayers and Farmers	362	25	40,679	51.75
Agricultural Labourers	24,638	11,326		

Source: Derived from Tyson, Report, 1938-39.

– of those engaged in commerce. But as before, the large majority of Indians remained in agriculture where their numbers exceeded those of all the other races put together. One-tenth of Indian agriculturists were peasant proprietors and there were a number of Indian cane farmers; but Indians, male and female, still provided the bulk of the labourers on the sugar and cocoa estates.

The disadvantageous conditions obtaining for these labourers in Trinidad had been catalogued in 1929. These included seasonal unemployment, resulting in restricted output and limited earnings. (Increases of 33⅓% to 50% in money wages following the strikes of 1919 to 1920, had hardly compensated for wartime Cost of Living increases of about 140%). The estate labourer appeared to be involved in a vicious circle of defective diet, low stamina, disease, indifference to work, small output and low wages. Nearly ten years later the West India Royal Commission Report was to observe the persistence of most of these problems for the entire British West Indies. By this time even landholding for peasant farming and the growing of cash crops – which had been urged as policies by earlier authorities, and which had been so promising during the 1890 to 1921 period – had become unprofitable. This Report painted a gloomy prospect for agricultural export crops, especially cocoa and coconuts, whether produced by large planters or small proprietors. Agricultural activity had become a trap for most of those involved in it, including a large proportion of the Indians in Trinidad. Yet alternative openings were not easily available for those who were willing to change. Tyson reported that the presence of Indians as 'industrial' labourers was resented. Since indenture, this tendency had been shown by the African-descended who were the traditional work-force in this sector.

Non-Indians were somewhat apprehensive of the large numbers of Indians and their potential influence as a group. Tyson was told that in certain circumtances Indians would 'rule this Colony and every race in it'. He saw no apparent danger in this. On the contrary he stressed the need for Indians to have the opportunity and the education to enable them to be more adequately represented at higher levels. From the figures compiled and the evidence with respect to the Civil Service, Tyson found 'considerable force' in the constant complaint about 'differentiation against the Indian as such'. He deplored a situation in which there were only nine Indian Justices of the Peace out of a total of 230 in Trinidad, and none in areas where Indians were concentrated such as San Fernando, Chaguanas, Penal, Siparia and La Brea. There were few Indians in the Colony's medical services, none in the San Fernando General Hospital, and no Indian nurses. Tyson recommended that this situation should be remedied urgently on grounds of merit since results in the secondary schools suggested that there was no lack of suitable Indians for Government employment. He suggested that Indians should be encouraged to overcome diffidence in making applications, by the appointment of an Indian to the Colonial Administration's Appointments Board.

The consensus was that the main thrust was to be through education. Both Indian and other observers blamed the unfavourable position of their group on illiteracy (as well as on discrimination) and despite some improvement, they continued to lag behind the rest of the population in levels of literacy and school attendance.

According to the 1931 Census Indians comprised 33% of the Trinidad and Tobago population, but 60% of the total illiterates. These persistently high rates were related to their residential location and activities as a rural population. In the countryside there was no system of compulsory school attendance as was the case for Port of Spain after 1935. Irregular school attendance was affected by the seasonal work needs of agriculture – and by the general difficulties of estate labourers – low wages, poverty and the inability of parents to provide books, clothes and meals.

For this reason the work and results of the Canadian Mission schools were vitally important since they operated mainly in the rural areas, with the direct intention of serving the Indians. For the most part, education remained the province of the Christian Churches which had a tremendous advantage from the receipt of regular Government grants which were not given to non-Christian denominations until the 1940's.

Education was seen as the ladder to the superior advancement of groups whom Indians wished to emulate. In 1942 Dennis Mahabir, Associate Editor of the *Observer* wrote that:

> The Negroes were distinguishing themselves in all phases of activity ... the short period of half a century had worked a great change in the patient, plodding, ambitious and resolute black man .... His parents saw that he got an educational training, and today as a whole the Negroes are comfortable .... It is regrettable that such indifference was displayed by the Indians for improving themselves.

The Indians apparently found the work of the Christian agencies effective for education and advancement. The rates of literacy among Christian Indians were much higher than among non-Christians, being 50% and 17% respectively in 1931. The attention of the missionaaries to the education of women was particularly significant. Rev. K.J. Grant, the pioneer of secondary education for Indians, rejoiced that his mission had been a liberating agent for Indian women, 'raising their value in the society'. In practice this meant release from the legacy of indenture, that is, the tendency to remain as uneducated estate labourers, and the opportunity for some women to become teachers, and other professionals, as well as wives and mothers with some education. The number of Christian Indians grew by more than 60% between 1921-31 although the Indian population increased by only 14%. Even non-Christians who retained their traditional religions were influenced by the Mission schools, with effects which were generally considered to be beneficial. In 1945 more than 60% of the Indians regarded as prominent persons in the community had been educated at Canadian Mission Schools or Colleagues.

The influence of Nationalist activities in India, reported regularly in the Trinidad newspapers, inspired Trinidad Indians, especially non-Christian leaders, to aim at the maintenance and revival of at least some religious and cultural features, and to perpetuate them through influence on the young, especially through education. The effects of the Christian school were to be resisted and the young saved from total cultural loss. This Trinidad resurgence sprang from the important cultural Renaissance in India, and many of the Trinidad programmes followed similar ones in India. For instance in 1928, following moves to organize an All Indian Hindu Mahasabha 'to promote, encourage and preserve religions

Clarence Hamilton Gopaul

Rampartab Pundit

of Indian origin against foreign domination', a movement was announced in Trinidad to establish night and day schools 'for the teaching of our National language. As soon as this takes place there would be a natural tendency to everything Indian'. In the following month a meeting was held at the Palladium Theatre in Tunapuna, attended by a number of prominent Hindu and Muslim leaderss, to raise money for an Indian school. In his address on this occasion the Chairman, Sahadeo Pundit (probably Pundit Tiwary) urged the necessity for a school where:

> Hindi and Urdu will be taught, more so especially as our boys and girls in this Colony are fast losing their identity, and it behoves every Indian to do something to put a stop to this scandalous state of affairs....

Other speeches stressed the aim for young men and women at least to speak Hindi, and considered it disgraceful that '92% of young men and women of today cannot speak the Mother Tongue'. The Muslim school building achievements were noted, especially those of Haji Gokul Meah who established a Mosque and *Maktab* (school) in St. James near Port of Spain where young children could have lessons in Arabic and Urdu.

But ambitious Indians, proud of their advancement from a history of indentured labour, still aspired like other Trinidad colonials to public appointments and the professions – the path to which lay through western education. This was the basis of the dilemma: they were caught between gratitude to the Christian missionaries who had made this possible, and the realization that the missionary influence helped to erode traditional religious and cultural vestiges. These conflicting tendencies were voiced in a succession of newspaper accounts during 1928-31. In an editorial dated 11 August 1928, C.B. Mathura, Hindu Editor of the *East Indian Weekly,* paid tribute to the 'tremendous work' – social, religious and educational – done by the Canadian Mission under Reverend J.B. Cropper and J.A. Scrimgeour, Head of Naparima College, but suggested that Hindi should be introduced into the school curriculum as was done in the Canadian Mission Schools in British Guiana, since it was essential to preserve the 'language of a race' among coming generations. On another occasion the Presbyterians were acknowledged for their work on behalf of the Indians, and it was stated that only through their Mission could such educational progress – 'the Mecca of every other progressive outlook' – have been achieved in so short a period. Yet one point detracted from this record – the fact that no Indian could get a job in an 'Indian' school or College unless he was a Christian.

In 1931 a solution to the problem was suggested. In reply to a question from Hon. Sarran Teelucksingh, Member of the Legislative Council, the Colonial Secretary had stated that the qualifications for Civil Service appointments included a Higher School Certificate and a good general character. An editorial advised that since Indians wanted their sons and daughters to be employed in the Government Service, their first duty was to educate them for this goal. As most Indians in the professions, and the few in the Service, had been educated in Canadian Mission Schools, it seemed doubtful wisdom to send them to schools where they could only get a sprinkling of knowledge of their ancestral religion and language, yet where they would not become qualified for positions in the Service (a reference to the non-Christian schools). Religion and language could be taught at home and in night schools. The potent conclusion which

summed up the dilemma of aspiring Indians during that period declared that:

> this is the land that we have made our home; let us therefore put Hindi and Urdu aside just a little....

The pursuit of Christian education persisted effectively. The *Indian Centenary Review,* celebrating 'One Hundred Years of Progress' noted that Indian graduates of secondary schools, especially of Naparima, the Canadian Mission College in San Fernando, held important positions in the professions and the Civil Service. Others were attending Colleges in Port of Spain as well as the 'first and only seconday institution conducted by a purely Indian organization', the St. Joseph High School in Curepe established by the Arya Pratinidhi Sabha. The numbers of Indian professionals had grown to include 29 Barristers and Solicitors, and 24 law studentss; 19 Medical Practitioners and 20 medical students; as well as dentists and druggists, University graduates in Education, and Engineering; opticians, qualified agriculturists and others.

In the process of integration, Indians were also caught between the tendencies to westernization on the one hand and the traditional bias against intermixing. Some Indians adopted western life styles, including the contemporary fashion of establishing literary and debating clubs and sporting groups. These included the East Indian Literary and Debating Association; Star of India Debating Club in Tunapuna; southern Indian Debating Association; Fyzabad Indian Literary and Debating Association; the Oriental Club; and the East Indian Cricket Board of Control. Most of these had exclusively Indian members, which was not an uncommon practice in Trinidad, as the activities of the Portuguese Association and the Chinese National Club showed. Indians also participated in non-exclusive bodies like the Trinidad Workingmen's Association, the Trinidad Labour Party, and the Trinidad Agricultural Society; and they took an interest in West Indian Federation and West Indies Cricket.

Intermixing with non-Indians was one aspect of integration which proceeded slowly and continued to draw objection from the orthodox. The India-born component of the Indian population declined steadily as the entry of new-coming immigrants ceased. Yet despite the increasing tendency for most Indians to be Trinidad-born, there was no notable increase in the rate of intermixing with non-Indians. According to a formula which attempted to measure these rates, the proportion of 'Indian Creoles', or persons with one Indian parent, was 1.47 per 100 Indians of unmixed descent in the year 1911; 1.87 in 1921 and 4.29 in 1946, indicating that 'the process of mixing, at least as far as revealed by the Census has not gone very far'. On the other hand there were 65.11 'Chinese Creoles' for every 100 Chinese 'indicating a high degree of mixing'. Harewood notes that this is a very crude measure as there must be little mixing in areas where there is a large concentration of the particular group, and in the case of the Indians this was true of areas like Caroni, Victoria and St. Patrick Counties.

Conversely, intermixing was more common in urban areas where Indians were least important numerically, as in Port of Spain where there was a rate of 21.37 'Indian Creoles' per 100 unmixed Indians. Here westernization and education had their effect as Indian purists recognized in their calls for increased education for Indian women. Changed social relationships had also affected the lower levels in the society. Thus the tendency to intermarriage on the coconut estates in Cedros where Indians had grown accustomed to giving respect to black and coloured overseers and had lost 'their traditional contempt and aloofness' towards these groups, was contrasted with the the 'tight-knit exclusively Indian groups' on the sugar estates.

No doubt there was a mutual reluctance to intermixing between different ethnic groups. Non-Indians in Colonial Trinidad would have been slow to mix with non-Christian descendants of indentured servants who were still frequently portrayed in local newspaper accounts as a lowly, litigious, quarrelsome and often violent group. Also there was steadily less imbalance between the sexes among Indians than among other groups like the Syrians and the Chinese, so there was less need for intermarriage. Again as Indians became more nationalistic and articulate, traditional prejudices were openly expressed. F.E.M. Hosein in 1928 deplored:

> the growing tendency of cultured Indian gentlemen whom the impact of western influence has captivated to such an extent that they consider it the highest piece of wisdom to seek as a suitable life partners ladies of a lighter hue and of a different race .... Intermarriage in this Colony between Indians and others is becoming a social evil which must react on the race.

In his view the problem stemmed from the failure to educate and uplift Indian women as suitable partners for educated men. The awful prospect was the loss of the separate identity of the Indian 'race'. This was a theme which recurred during the 1940's.

Similarly, Supersad Naipaul attacked the twin evils, intermarriage and 'Bobism', that is, the adoption of western styles of dress, as two of the 'many symptoms of demoralization among westernised Indians'. Attacking the anti-Indian marriage craze as 'that perversity responsible for race-dissolution', he warned that, as a result, the whole Indian population would 'waste its identity in the universal throng of an alien population'. One of the few Indians to refute his views was A.C. Rienzi (Krishna Deonarine), the Trade Union Leader and politician who argued that mixtures of Easterners and Westerners might produce a better race, and who welcomed modernity as a sign of progress.

The hope of maintaining a special identity and cultural survival was only possible because Indian numbers were sufficiently large and concentrated in Trinidad, compared for instance to Jamaica, and Indian religious leaders and organizations were sufficiently active to make this feasible.

The viewpoints expressed by Indians in Trinidad were far from unanimous or static even on a limited number of issues. The East Indian National Association (E.I.N.A.) and the East Indian National Congress (E.I.N.C.) may not have differed fundamentally, but they defied efforts to unite them and made differing proposals on the question of representative institutions for Trinidad.

On the question of the Nationalist movement in India there was growing interest among Trinidad Indians, including a congratulatory telegram from the E.I.N.C. to the new Viceroy, Lord Willingdon, in 1931; acclaim for Gandhi's success; and open identification with the 'Motherland'. Yet on occasion Trinidad Indians showed

Below: A photograph of the last group to arrive in Trinidad. Photograph – G. Durity.

C.C. Sooden

differing responses to events in India. For instance at a meeting of the Indian National Party held at the Union Diamond Hall in San Fernando in July 1923, the Chairman James Mungal, and George Adhar a leading photographer, opposed a resolution by N.E. Ramcharan that greetings should be sent to the relatives of C.R. Das, Indian Nationalist, who had died in prison. The two objectors argued that as Das had been considered by the Government of India to be the leader of an extremist organization, it was unwise for the Indian National Party of Trinidad to support him. Ramcharan's resolution was carried with only the two dissenting votes.

As already noted, A.C. Rienzi disagreed openly with Naipaul on the question of intermarriage. Also, there was occasional friction between Christian and non-Christian Indians, despite generally good group relations. At a joint meeting of associations under the auspices of the Debe East Indian Friendly Society in December 1928, James Sukdeosingh expressed satisfaction that the Debe Society welcomed Christians, unlike a 'certain (unspecified) Indian Society'.

There was open controversy between Indians over the passing of a Divorce Bill for Trinidad (as there was also between non-Indian supporters of divorce like Lennox O'Reilly and its Catholic opponents). C.B. Mathura, a Hindu pundit, warned Hindus who supported divorce that they ran the risk of falling 'into the arms of Reverend C.D. Lalla and his Church which welcomes divorce', that is, the Presbyterians. As the debate grew more heated, leading pundits replied to the criticisms of Hon. Sarran Teelucksingh and Andrew Bahadoorsingh. Pundit Sahadeo Tiwary of Tunapuna objected that since Teelucksingh and Singh were not Hindus nor Muslims, they were not qualified to decide on a question of Hindu law and customs.

By the 1940's Indians, like other colonials, had been exposed to the activities of organized labour overseas, the War, as well as Nationalism. They had participated in Caribbean labour disturbances, heard the official revelations of abysmal conditions on the estates, and struggled over the question of an English Language Test

for voters in Trinidad. Under these influences some young educated Indians had changed the preoccupation with aspiring to middle class occupations – to a concern with reforms on behalf of the underprivileged Indian labourers.

This emerging younger generation of Indians in Trinidad was no longer begging to be included in the socio-economic system. They were demanding changes in that system. New attitudes were evident in the issues which the editors of the *Observer* championed during the 1940's. (S.M. Rameshwar, graduate in Education was Editor; Martin Sampath, graduate in Agriculture and Dennis Mahabir, Law student, were Associate Editors). These 'progressives' were no doubt influenced by the socialist ideas of A.C. Rienzi, and above all by the exhortations of visiting Indian Nationalists like Dr. D.P. Pandia and Pandit H.N. Kunzru, President of the Servants of India Society and member of the Council of State in Delhi. Their concern was with social issues: for instance, the abuses of the barrack system of housing on the estates, the poor health conditions and illiteracy among Indians, and the need for education for Indian women.

This group insisted that Indians had a right to a place in colonial Trinidad, without sacrificing traditional religion or identity. They appeared less dependent on, and more critical of, the Christian missionaries than earlier educated Indians had been. There was pride in the legacy of Hinduism, for example in H.P. Singh's article on 'The World's Oldest Bible – The Rig Veda'. One columnist even suggested State control of all the existing means of education in the Colony, with universal free education being given up to the secondary level.

These Young Turks were critical also of prominent elders like M.J. Kirpalani, a Sindhi businessman and philanthropist. An article entitled 'Weak, Silent Men', chided Kirpalani and the Committee which he headed on behalf of the newly-informed Indian Welfare Association for their failure to organize a programme of social welfare for Indians. Letters supporting their criticisms were published, one declaring that 'if older leaders have failed, get new ones.'

A militant tone, reminiscent of F.E.M. Hosein's in 1913, was apparent in an editorial replying to one 'Ubiquitous' who had accused Indians of segregation in establishing the Welfare Association:

> The Indian today is in no mood either to be cajoled or to be threatened. To progressive Indians the mission is clear and they will brook no interference. Illiteracy needs eradication and it will be eradicated; horrible housing conditions exist among the labouring classes and an attempt will be made to improve them; the aged, the destitutes, the orphans are in urgent need of succour and every effort will be made to help relieve their distress. . . .

In contemporary wartime language it continued:

> . . . our blitzkreig is not against the Government or the forces of law and order. We are out to break the chains that hold our people to the earth and make them menials in a land of plenty.

Similarly the proposal that a Language Test in English should be included as a condition for the Franchise was assertively opposed as disadvantageous to Indians. Public meetings were held and letters were written to the *Port of Spain Gazette* denouncing the stand taken on the question by the Legislative Council and the Chamber of

Commerce, and also answering critics like the Barrister, H. Hudson Phillips. The news that the Secretary of State had disallowed this section of the Bill was hailed as a 'signal victory for Indians.'

Inspired by Nationalism in India, as well as more confident in their position in Trinidad, Indian leaders had developed an adequate sense of security under the British umbrella to demand a better deal, as Trinidadians of other origins were doing, but to demand it on behalf of their community. The attempts of Indians to seek integration as a group would bring them into conflict with these other groups which were developing their own self-consciousness. As Trinidad approached Independence during the following decade, however, Indians would face the need to make yet further adjustments to the problem of settlement in the land of their birth.

Sources:

1. Ryan, Selwyn: *Race and Nationalism in Trinidad and Tobago*, Toronto, *1972, p. 30.*
2. Rex, John: *Race Relations in Sociological Theory*, London, pp. 26-27.
3. 1931 Census Report for Trinidad and Tobago, p. 31.
4. *Trinidad Guardian*, 5 April and 4 May, 1921.
5. *Weekly Trinidad Guardian*, 25 August, 1923.
6. *East Indian Weekly*, (E.I.W.), 18 August, 1928.
7. *Trinidad Guardian*, 19 May, 1921.
8. *Weekly Trinidad Guardian*, 21 July and 6 October, 1923; Trinidad Guardian, 2 April, 1921.
9. E.I.W., 7 March, 1931.
10. E.I.W. 20 October, 1928, Paper read to the East Indian Literary and Debating Association on 5 October, 1928.
11. Memorandum of Evidence for the Royal Commission to the West Indies presented by J.D. Tyson, Esq., C.B.E., on behalf of the Government of India, 1938-39, Section III, p. 68.
12. Annual Report of the Protector of Immigrants for 1920, Council Paper No. 55 of 1921; for 1930, Council Paper No. 36 of 1931.
13. Shephard, C.Y.: 'An Analysis of the Present Shortage of Agricultural Labour in Trinidad'. St. Augustine, 1929; Report of the West India Royal Commission 1938-39, p. 35.
14. 1946 Census, p. xiii: Location of Assisted Primary Schools by Religious Denominations.
15. *Observer*, Vol. 1, No. 12, December, 1942.
16. Grant, K.J.: *My Missionary Memories*. Halifax, N.S., 1923, pp. 87, 149.
17. *Indian Centenary Review*, Port of Spain 1945, pp. 131-169.
18. E.I.W., 28 July and 11 August, 1928.
19. E.I.W., 9 September, 1928.
20. E.I.W., 2 May, 1931.
21. 1946 Census, Part G. p. 19.
22. Harewood, Jack: *The Population of Trinidad and Tobago*, 1975, p. 105.
23. 1946 Census, p. XXV.
24. E.I.W., 17 November, 1928.
25. See above footnote 10.
26. E.I.W., 24 November and 8 December, 1928.
27. Jha, J.C.: 'Pressure Groups in Trinidad, 1897-1921'. *Fifth Conference of Caribbean Historians*, Trinidad 1973, p. 12; Tikasingh, Gerard: 'The Representation of Indian Opinion in Trinidad, 1900-1921. *Conference on East Indians in the Caribbean*, Trinidad 1975, pp. 29-31.
28. E.I.W., 21 July, 1928 and 1 December, 1928.
29. E.I.W., 21 March, 1928, and 4 April, 1931.
30. *Observer*, Vol. 2, No. 5, May, 1943.
31. *Ibid.*, Vol. 2, No. 12, December, 1943.
32. *Ibid.*, Vol. 3, Nos. 7 and 8, June, 1944.
33. *Ibid.*, Vol. 3, No. 5, May, 1944.

Census taken from 'Voices in the Street'
Olga J. Mavrogordato
1977.

	Indians	Spaniards	Slaves	Total Persons
1498	18,000	—	—	
1530		70	—	
1593	6,000	85	—	
1595		46	—	
1606	4,000	40	470	4,510
1687				
1712	1,768*	500	100	2,368
1725		200		
1733/39		162		
1741/50				
1776				
1777	1,440*	1,113	222	2,775
		Spaniards & Others		
1783/84	1,491*	1,000	2,462	4,953
1797	1,078*	6,625	10,009	17,712
1803	1,127*	8,400	18,473	28,000
1815	1,147	12,314	25,817	39,332
1825	727	18,217	23,230	42,174
1834	—	22,356	22,359	44,715

* Total population of encomiendas (Indian settlements protected by Spaniards in return for labour), and missions. Those outside not included.

	Trinidad	Tobago	Total Persons
1844	59,815	13,208	73,023
1851	68,600	14,378	82,978
1871	109,638	17,054	126,692
1901	255,148	18,751	273,899

East Indian Immigration

1845 to 1892	—	93,569
1893 to 1900	—	14,483
1901 to 1905	—	12,792
1906 to 1917	—	20,771
Total in 72 years	—	141,615

A Visit to PORT OF SPAIN in 1847 by C. W. Day

The water was bright green in the Gulf of Paria; the sea was dark green; although the description of some traveller, quoted in Osborn's guide-book, speaks of purest ultramarine, a colour which previously I had always imagined to be blue. "Is the water always this colour?" I inquired of our Grenadian pilot. "Always Sir; it never changes," was the response. As we neared the city, the sea resembled in colour that of the Isle of Wight Channel, and off Port of Spain it was of a dull milky-green or drab, and extremely turbid, as well as shallow.

Of the four bocas, the one nearest the city (del Monos) being exceedingly narrow, is only for very small craft, which in case of accident can use their sweeps. The second, Boca de Huevos, through which we came, is for brigs and small vessels. Then comes the Boca de Navios; and lastly the Boca Grande, five miles wide for men-of-war, or other heavy ships.

The wharfs of Port of Spain are good, although the water is not above three feet deep. There is a wooden jetty, and hard by a small lighthouse, doing all honour and glory to the powers that be, as the former inscription, whatever it might have been, has been erased, and [V] [R] MDCCXLII, 1842, carefully inserted in its place.

Standing at the extremity of the jetty, the view is not a particularly interesting one. The mountains at the back of the town are not from this distance very picturesque in their forms, whilst seaward, to the east, there stretches out towards San Fernando a long line of coast as flat as the fens of Lincolnshire. Westward are the bocas, at this distance by no means fine, whilst the Spanish Main looks like a cloud, and from its height (five thousand feet) is often obscured altogether. Seldom indeed have I been more disappointed than in this scenery, after the exaggerated descriptions.

Port of Spain has a very foreign air; feluccas, canoes, and other odd-looking craft skim about; whilst Indians, Spanish Americans, French, English, Bengal coolies, Scotch, and Negroes, from all sorts of places speaking all sorts of tongues, are good materials for making one feel far afield. Even to a somewhat experienced traveller like myself, South America, so close, began to savour of the Pacific, and I almost felt inclined to go over to Otaheite. One has only to cross the Isthmus of Darien, and then — only to go a little further.

To the right of the lighthouse are the commercial rooms, and Harbour Master's Offices; left, Fort San Andrés. This photograph was taken in 1873. — Tom Cambridge Collection.

Above: Boats are moored in an area where there now exists a car park opposite the Treasury Building on Independence Square This photograph of the 1880's shows on the left the Commissary Building and opposite the premises of the Colonial Bank, which were both situated at the foot of St. Vincent Street. Photograph — O. Mavrogordato.
Below: The fountain at the foot of Frederick Street depicted a boy and a swan. This photo looks westward showing cabs at the cab stand which was once situated there. Photograph — G. Mc Lean.

For this rude part of the world, Port of Spain might, by straining a point, be called a fine, as it certainly is, regular city. The streets are broad, and at right angles with each other, following the leading points of the compass. In the centre of two of them, King's Wharf Street and Marine Square, are long avenues planted with trees, under which, however, no one seems to walk. The houses, which are ugly enough, are long and low, having latticed wooden galleries in front, and are often entered through a large, heavy, wooden gate, daubed brick-dust colour, leading into a shabby courtyard, usually redolent of every sort of filth, sweltering and fermenting, and emitting a sickening combination of foul smells, which often has the effect of making people ill.

The leading character of Port of Spain is decidedly Spanish. The greater part of the community are Roman Catholic, and, for a colonial building, the unfinished Catholic cathedral may be called a good edifice. It is built of yellow brick, partially stuccoed, but will not bear the most remote comparison with the Catholic Cathedrals of Europe. In these colonies, architecture is in a very low state, and all sorts of preposterous arrangements in building astonish the stranger; uncomfortableness predominates, and the most palpable want of judgement makes him wonder whether the skull of the contriver was not filled with mortar instead of brains.

There is an Episcopal church here of some pretensions. From the jetty to the extremity of the city,

north, may be a mile; and the city is less than half that distance in breadth. The streets are kept very clean, and a species of buzzard, or carrion vulture, erroneously called Corbeau, or crow, are the authorized scavengers. These birds, which are black, and as large as young turkeys, have long gawky legs, keen eyes and an iron-grey cowl covering their necks, which gives them a ludicrous resemblance to barristers in costume. They are knowing fellows too, and fight as keenly for their offal as any gentleman of the bar can do for his fee. It is very droll to see them in the morning, after a night's dew or rain, sitting in rows on the house tops, spreading out their wings to dry.

French and Spanish mulattoes abound here, and almost every white native of Great Britain will turnout to be a Scotchman, vulgar, coarse, ignorant and dogmatical. The horrible twang of 'Glaskie' and Ayr, and of Dunfrieshire predominates, and the refuse of all Scotland seems to have its way to the West Indies, cottars in rank, and shopmen in mind. Indeed, excepting always the military, a gentleman is a *rara avis* in these colonies.

Port of Spain is an extremely expensive place to live in. There is no sufficient reason for this, as it is but one night's sail from Barbadoes; yet that which can be had for fifty cents in Barbadoes, costs a dollar in Trinidad, notwithstanding that the soil is more productive in the latter island. House rent, too, is extravagantly high. For the upper part of a house in Port of Spain, consisting of

The old Eastern Market which was erected by the Illustrious Cabildo.
Photograph — G. Mc Lean

"
Belle ti beke epi dez ye si ble
Belle ti Zindien epi de nat chevez
Belle ti Negresse epi bondai mate
P'is bondai mate ca fqir dondon bave
Glo, Glo, Gloria, Glo Gor Gloria
Glo, Glo, Gloria, Gloria c'est pou ou
Gloria pas pou moen.

A beautiful white girl with two eyes of blue
A beautiful little Carib Indian with two plaits of hair
A beautiful Negress with well-developed posterior
Because she had a well developed posterior it made Dondon dribble.
Glo, Glo, gloria, Glo, Glo, Gloria
Glo, Glo, Gloria, Gloria is for you
Gloria not for me. "

Below: Almond Walk came into existence as a result of the reclaimation of the foreshore and was named for the two rows of almond trees which were planted along its length. A delightful promenade where passersby could hear music played from the various upper storey rooms as they strolled by. Photograph G. Mc Lean.
Right: People making their way home after church along Independence Square. Photograph — Aché.

two good rooms, partitioned into four mere closets, and unfurnished, sixty pounds a year was demanded, and considered reasonable. An iced punch that costs six pence in Barbadoes, is priced at a shilling in Trinidad. English copper coins will be refused by the negroes, a silver stampee (penny farthing) being the lowest coin that will be taken. Indeed, for a British colony, the monetary system of Trinidad is most disgraceful. An English sixpence will only pass for a bit (fivepence here), and a shilling for a franc. This leads to all sorts of frauds upon strangers. Surely the money should be made exclusively British. If any coin at all depreciates in an English colony, it ought surely to be foreign, and not British.

The most curious members of this mixed population, are, perhaps, the hill coolies from Madras and Calcutta. They walk about the streets, accompanied by their women and wretched little progeny, who look more like attenuated monkeys than children. The dress, what there is of it, is extremely picturesque; but, in truth, some of them are costumed in as free and easy a style as the Comanche Indian, who, in the streets of Washington, finding the heat too great for him, coolly took off the unmentionable, which civilization had compelled him to adopt, and paraded the streets pretty nearly in nudibus, much to the affected horror of that most decorous but indelicate community. These coolies are quite as picturesque as any North American Indians. To these Easterns, living is so easy here, that many of them will not work, but saunter about, catching game and feeding on plantains.

City as it would wish to seem, Port of Spain, until lately, had no barber. At present there are two, both Portuguese immigrants. A regular ladies hair-dresser, with all the implements of his craft — wigs, false hair, &c. — is still wanting, and a good one would make a fortune. In truth, with all the attempts at style, Port of Spain is a beggarly place. Omitting the item of convicts, society here reminds me of what I have read of Sydney, in New South Wales. The French shopkeepers, however, seem to be of rather a higher class than the British.

At night, Port of Spain is a miserably dark, dull place. The stores close at five o'clock in the afternoon, and an hour after, the streets are comparatively deserted. The few merchants and shopkeepers go to dinner, and so night closes in. The streets are not lighted, so that all is as dark as Erebus; nor is there any place of public amusement — no theatres, concerts, or cafés, none of the diversified modes of spending an hour open to a stranger in Europe. the Ice-house is a sort of exception, a superior sort of liqueur-shop, where iced punch is retailed at a shilling a glass. One stationer's shop, as a circulating library, boasts of a small stock of trashy, sentimental Leadenhall novels, but not one work that can improve the mind, or increase our knowledge, whilst in the day, all is flour-barrels, staves, salt-fish, and butter-firkins. Either through ignorance of what is customary elsewhere, or from overwhelming selfishness, the inhabitants are not attentive to strangers, however well introduced.

An iron steamer, the Lady McLeod, plies five times a week between Port of Spain, San Fernando, and La Brea. she is a pretty little craft, but her lower half is painted bright scarlet, whilst the upper part rejoices in bright green, so that literally she is as spruce as a scraped carrot. So much for colonial taste.

The foundation stone of the Roman Catholic Cathedral was laid on the 24 March 1816. Its plans were drawn by the secretary of the then Governor Sir Ralph Woodford Philip Reinagle who was also an architect. Both photographs shown on this page are from the Tom Cambridge Collection.

The Tropics can only be seen by strangers at a great amount of personal discomfort. Everything is coarse, clumsy, and inconvenient, arising from the inhabitants being either ignorant creoles or low-caste Europeans — the British of all three kingdoms in particular — backed by a semi-barbarous negro population. There is a vast amount of outside show, but pride and vulgarity go together amongst all classes. Even in Trinidad, warm as it is, there is not such a thing as a warm bath to be had, and indeed the very mention by me of such a want was met with a shout of ridicule, "A warm bath in the West Indies! why we want to keep cool therefore we take the cold bath," — this is a fair specimen of the sort of knowledge which these people possess, and their mode of reasoning.

West Indian towns are most disagreeable places, and the only way that the delightful climate (for in spite of the heat, it is delightful) or the exquisite tropical scenery can be enjoyed is in the country, where one is free from filth, bad smells, and wrangling. If the owner of an estate

the houses of those to whom they bring letters; if a stranger 'do business' to the amount of four or five hundred dollars with a merchant, he will most likely be invited to take a glass of sangaree at the counting-house, but, however respectable, will never be introduced to the private circles of the man of business unless perchance he be a Scotsman! There is no liberality of feeling whatsoever. All come to scrape money together in order to go away, and meantime all the socialities are lost sight of."

1857

THE QUEEN'S COLLEGIATE SCHOOL
At a meeting of the Legislative Council held on the 1st September, 1857, the following resolutions were passed, on the motion of the Colonial Secretary:—

1.— That in order to place within the reach of the youth of the colony the opportunity of obtaining a classical education at a moderate charge, there be established in the town of Port of Spain a Collegiate School;

be originally habituated to the decencies of life (which few of them are), he can surround himself with almost all the comforts of civilization, or at least can neutralize most of the annoyances resulting from African barbarism.

I do not think the Trinidadians an unkind people, though they are overwhelmingly selfish, and neglect to proffer to a stranger those attentions usual in civilized communities. Out of four letters of introduction to civilians — considered here persons perfectly respectable — only one of them invited me to his house, or introduced me to its mistress, with whom I sat an hour, and there it ended. The military alone (the 19th regiment) did what was usual, and in their society I spent the few agreeable hours that I passed in Trinidad. I think that the current idea in England of West Indian hospitality should be corrected as soon as possible, as the truth will prevent great disappointment. On discussing this subject with a French gentleman, who had spent a considerable time in Port of Spain, he said: "No! strangers are never invited to

2.— That such Collegiate School be open to students of any religious denomination, and that there be no direct religious teaching, but that attendance at some place of worship be a condition of admittance and of continuance at such Collegiate School;

3.— That for the purpose of encouraging emulation among the students there be annual public examinations, and that the two successful candidates for honours at such examination be entitled to exhibitions of £150 each for three years to assist them in pursuing their studies in Great Britain;

4.— That for the purpose of maintaining such Collegiate School there be paid from the public funds the sum of £3,000 annually the income from fees to be paid into the Treasury.

QUEEN'S COLLEGIATE SCHOOL
The petition to Her Majesty in favour of the establishment of the proposed collegiate school in Port of Spain has not only been most graciously received, but our beloved Sovereign has vouchsafed to denote her approbation of the proposed institution by directing that the school shall be honoured with the designation of the 'Queen's Collegiate School.' *(9th December, 1857.)*

REMINISCENCES OF OLD TRINIDAD

Writing of the 1930's about the 1850's and 80's
L.O. Inniss

In these days of 1,000 Candle Electric Lights it is difficult to imagine that in most of the houses of the people in those days, the lighting problem was solved by a tumbler half filled with water then, a couple of inches of coconut oil floating upon the water and in place of a wick, a piece of twisted cotton wool, kept floating upon the oil, by a contrivance made of two bits of coconut straws tied crossways, with four bits of cork on the points of the straws as floats. Better off folk used sperm candles, shielded from the wind by a

full of Mandingo sugar, unloaded them on to the wharf, then went round to the Cooper yard, for empty ones, to take back in the afternoon, along with other estate supplies. Nowadays we have changed all that.

The Usine Sugar is put into bags which come down to town in railway trucks, and the poor cooper is a back number.

As regards City Lighting, the Moon and the Stars did that for us. In the Mayoralty of Cipriani, Kerosene Lamps were erected and very proud we were of them. The advent of Electricity is comparatively recent. What Posterity will use in the lap of the Gods!

I never took much stock in Politics but there were always folks talking and writing about Reform, ever since I can remember and stigmatising Crown Colony Government as being the bane of the Island, but my readers can see for themselves that we have decidedly progressed since those days, Crown Colony Government to the contrary notwithstanding, and let us hope that now

A panoramic view of Marine Square looking west showing the foot of Frederick Street on the right, and Almond Walk on the left. Photograph — O. Mavrogordato.

tall circular glass shade resting on the table, in the hall and smaller candlesticks and shades for locomotion in the bed rooms. In the remote country parts half a coconut shell took the place of the tumbler.

There was a trade which flourished greatly in those old days, which has apparently quite died out, that is 'Coopering.' There used to be three large Cooperages in Marine Square: One run by Farr Brothers in the vicinity of the present Cathedral Presbytery; one belonging to J. Cumming & Co., where the Union Club now is and one belonging to Campbell Bros., where Gordon Grant & Co.'s Warehouse is on St. Vincent Wharf, where hundreds of hogsheads for shipping sugar were made; and the rattle of the Coopers' hammers as they drove the hoops could be heard all day–a not at all disagreeable sound. Strings of Estate wagons drawn by 5 mules (2 in the shafts and 3 tandem) driven by an expert wagoner, who could drop his lash with precision, on any mule who was inclined to be a malingerer, came into town every morning, during the Crop Season, loaded with hogsheads

we have got to the brink of a change, that we will progress still more. It has been my lot to see lots of Red-Hot politicians who when they had succeeded in getting into power and had responsibility placed upon them, have become quite different persons and I venture to bet the Labour Party now that they have been put into responsibility, will cool down considerably and I am reminded of an incident in Captain Marryat's 'Midshipman Easy' when Easy had taken home Mesty, the black cook from on board the man-o'-war and made him Major Domo over his estate, he ruled the other servants with a rod of iron and when East twitted him with his former sentiments, when he was preaching 'the equality of man,' his answer was "Ah Massah Easy, that time I was cook, but now I Major-Domo, damn equality!" I hope my readers will excuse my shortcomings as an historian and have derived some instruction and entertainment from my reminiscences of long ago.

FIVE YEARS' RESIDENCE

IN

THE WEST INDIES.

BY CHARLES WILLIAM DAY, ESQ.
AUTHOR OF "HINTS ON ETIQUETTE."

IN TWO VOLUMES.
VOL. II.

LONDON:
COLBURN AND CO., PUBLISHERS,
GREAT MARLBOROUGH STREET.
1852.

Title page of the book, 'Five Years' Residence in the West Indies', C.W. Day, 1852. The extract beginning at right is taken from that book.

A VISIT TO PORT OF SPAIN IN 1847 BY C.W. DAY

As we roamed about, I observed that the Gulf of Paria is gradually filling up, so that what was deep water forty years ago, is at present scarcely up to one's knees. We climbed the mountains which are exceedingly picturesque, and one peculiar-looking tree, the poui, which grows on the sides, is sure to arrest the attention. It looks like one mass of bright yellow, and may be considered characteristic of Trinidad. Altogether we had a very pleasant day; but with one thing I could not but be struck, that is, the vast superiority of all the foreigners out here over the English of the same rank, our countrymen, whether English or Scotch, being uneducated and vulgar. The British Trinidadians are cold, selfish, and full of ridiculous pretension, without qualifications of any sort to justify it. There are very few Irish in Trinidad, and those very low ones. There is an utter want of principle amongst all classes, and great peculation is known to be going on in many of the official departments, but no one likes to interfere.

Chacon Street looking north towards the Holy Trinity Cathedral in the 1880's. It once formed part of the bed for the Rio de Santa Anna which was diverted from its course by Governor Chacon. Photograph — O. Mavrogordato.

1856

SELF-DENYING MUNICIPAL PROPOSAL

At a meeting of the Legislative Council held on Tuesday last, the Colonial Secretary laid before the Board a letter from the Town Clerk covering a resolution passed by the Borough Council of Port-of-Spain that no money vote above £100 should take effect unless there should be a majority of two-thirds of the members present voting for the same; and requesting that the Municipal Ordinance might be amended accordingly. The application was not favourably received by the Board!!
(2nd July, 1856.)

1857

OPENING OF THE ORPHAN HOME

The buildings erected as an orphan asylum and industrial school for coolie orphans in the Tacarigua district having been completed the ceremony of formally opening it was appointed to take place last Thursday the 2nd instant. Favoured by an exceedingly delightful state of the weather, a tolerably large party from Port of Spain responded to the invitations issued to be present on the interesting occasion. Amongst those present, we noticed His Excellency the Governor and Lieut. Keate, the Attorney General and his lady, the Inspector of Schools, the Agent General of Immigrants, the Hon'ble R.S. Darling, and his lady, the Very Rev. the Rural Dean and Mrs. Richards, and others. . . . . Shortly after 2 p.m. the proceedings were opened by the singing of Bishop Heber's missionary hymn, after which appropriate prayers from the liturgy were offered by the Rev. S.F. Richards, Rural Dean. The Rev. Henry Richards, Rector of the Parish then gave a brief report of the building of the orphanage, in the course of which he stated that the island had to thank the personal generosity and munificence of Mr. Burnley and Mr. Eccles for the scheme being carried out, as well as for the maintenance of an East Indian missionary to the coolies of the district. *(4th July, 1857.)*

Right: The old toll gate to the city which was erected in 1878. It now stands on the grounds of the National Museum. Photograph — O. Mavrogordato.
Below: A view of Broadway in the 1900's, it was previously called Almond Walk. These trees were removed for the tram lines. Photograph — Jackson.

Above: Port of Spain street scene with gas lamps. Photograph — O. Mavrogordato.
Below: A view of Marine Square from Eugene Boissiere and Company which occupied the corner of Almond Walk and Marine Square south. Photograph — Muriel Boissiere.

I breakfasted one morning *à la fourchette* with Signor Gioanetti, of Bologna, of a noble family, a doctor of laws, and a nephew of the late Cardinal Gioanetti, Archbishop of Bologna. Like the rest of the people here, Signor Gioanetti is a merchant, and keeps a shop. I merely mention this, to show the great difference there is in rank between the foreign settlers in Trinidad and the British following the same pursuits. Signor Gioanetti was educated at the University of Lucca, studied Greek with the present Cardinal Mezzofanti, and is a most accomplished amateur of music, playing the piano-forte and singing in a masterly manner, speaking also, in addition to this native tongue, English, French, and Spanish; yet he makes not the least pretension, which, as I have already observed, all the British shopkeepers display. There is also a French Viscount, a shopkeeper, who, of course, has dropped his title. However little the title may go for, these *ci-devant* noblemen are all educated, well-bred gentlemen; whilst the English, on the contrary, are proverbial for their coarseness, with a predominance of the importance of a vestryman, a churchwarden, or of a Mister Bumble, the master of a parish poorhouse.

The novelty once over, I began to find the West Indies a very tiresome place; the ignorance of the majority of all ranks of that knowledge common to the educated in every country, precludes anything like profitable social intercourse, so that the greater part of those one meets become bores of the first magnitude. The knowledge of the planters is confined to sugar-making; of the tradesman to his dry goods, boots, or provisions; whilst the clergy are vulgar and presuming. Nothing remains but the military, and a few (not all) of the official people, for the majority of those even are very second-rate — too worthless for England, but considered good enough for these critically situated colonies!

The dislike of the negroes in Trinidad to the introduction of the emigrants from either India or Madeira is very great, and they take every opportunity to insult and deride the newcomers. The way in which the Portuguese work compared with themselves, shames the negroes; and they fear the consequences, foreseeing that they will have to work as they never yet did; and it shows them also that the country is not so exclusively their own as they fondly hoped it would be; there is no doubt of the policy of the coloured demagogues, by whom blackee is led, in desiring to oust the whites altogether, and make the West Indies their own.

I attempted to get acquainted with a coloured family of the highest respectability, but found it impossible to continue the intimacy. The family consisted of three young ladies, almost white, and two brothers, one of whom was qualifying for the Church. All were very kind, and the female part sufficiently intelligent, so that as far as they themselves went, they were perfectly unexceptionable. But coloured families like these labour under great disadvantages, as they are generally so glad to get white people of any rank to visit them, that one is apt to meet very inferior whites in such houses, and some by no means reputable.

We were consequently formally introduced to shopmen of the town, and people whose acquaintance we would, from their indifferent characters, willingly have avoided. So after some ineffectual remonstrances against the practice of introductions in so heterogeneous a set, we were fairly compelled to give up the acquaintance, and leave them to their connections previously formed. The objection there must ever be to meet the class of whites who visit coloured people, will effectually prevent these aspirants from rising in the scale of society. In this case, the female part were more intelligent and refined than the men; but all seemed to retain the laughing propensities of their negro progenitors.

The Custom house and the Harbour Master's Offices. These handsome buildings were erected in 1880 and have since been destroyed by fire . They however marked an important stage in the development of the borough facilities of Port of Spain which began in the 1800's with a series of reclamation projects, the first of which took place in 1803. Sea Lots, which were really mud flats were laid out between King Street (Independence Sq. North) and the sea. During the next 20 years reclamation of these lots continued, in this was Marine Square and South Quay came into being. By 1845 the area from the Battery to St. Vincent Street Jetty now called the Whaft Extenstion was filled. In 1872 Chacon, Frederick, Henry and Charlotte Streets were extended across Marine Square. Photograph — Gregor Duruty. Historical Notes: O. Mavrogordato.

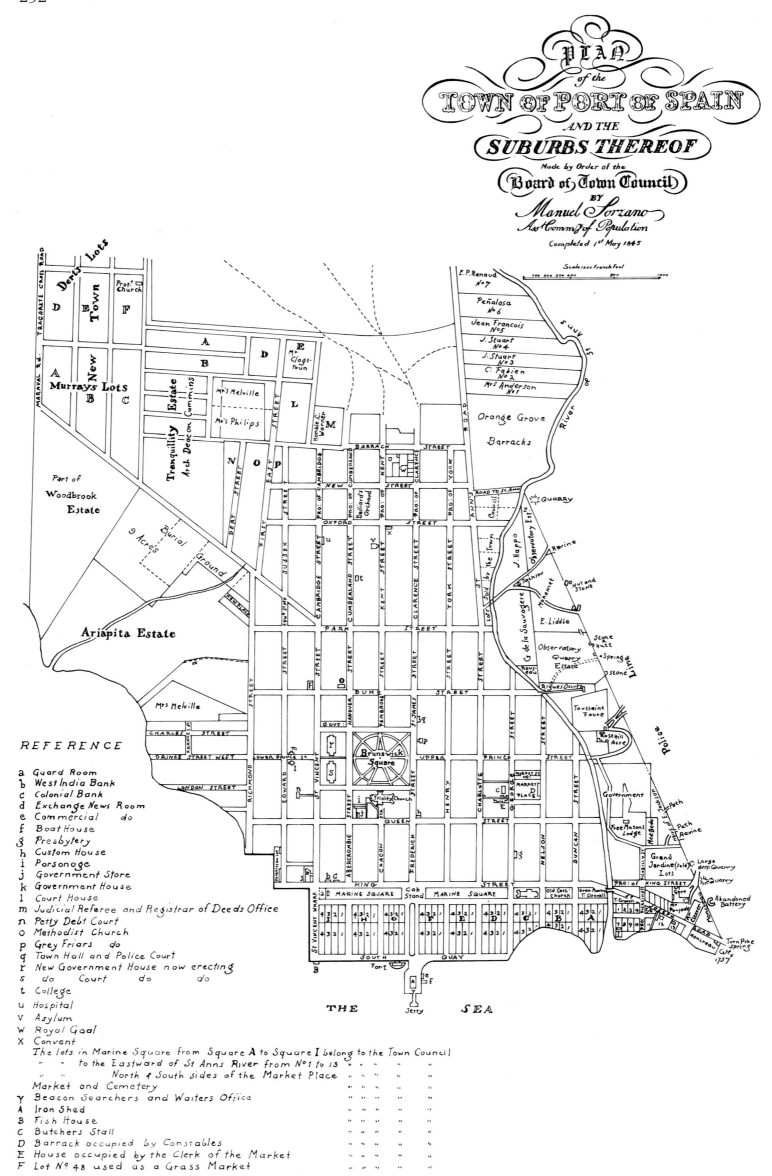

REFERENCE

a   Guard Room
b   West India Bank
c   Colonial Bank
d   Exchange News Room
e   Commercial   do
f   Boat House
g   Presbytery
h   Custom House
i   Parsonage
j   Government Store
k   Government House
l   Court House
m   Judicial Referee and Registrar of Deeds Office
n   Petty Debt Court
o   Methodist Church
p   Grey Friars   do
q   Town Hall and Police Court
r   New Government House now erecting
s   do   Court   do   do
t   College
u   Hospital
v   Asylum
w   Royal Gaol
x   Convent
     The lots in Marine Square from Square A to Square I belong to the Town Council
       "   to the Eastward of St Anns River from No 1 to 13   "   "   "   "   "
       "   North & South sides of the Market Place   "   "   "   "   "
     Market and Cemetery
Y   Beacon Searchers and Waiters Office
A   Iron Shed
B   Fish House
C   Butchers Stall
D   Barrack occupied by Constables
E   House occupied by the Clerk of the Market
F   Lot No 48 used as a Grass Market

North Post Signal Station. Photograph — G. Mc Lean.

NORTH POST

From A History of Diego Martin 1784 – 1884
Anthony de Verteuil, C.S.Sp.

North Post was used by the Spaniards as an observation post but was set up as a signal station at the same period that Fort George was established, that is around 1804, since it communicated by 'telegraph' with that Fort and then to the Harbour Master's Office at Port of Spain. The Signal Station was (and is) situated on the ridge forming the northern watershed of the Diego Martin Valley. There is a relatively easy climb from the valley floor at 250 feet to the site of the station at 747 feet. On the north there is an extremely steep descent by a narrow path to the sea, where from a shelf of rocks, in the early nineteenth century, fishermen would cast lines for the kingfish which were very numerous in those days.

Major Cappadose describes a visit to the Post made in 1840. 'Before ascending to the Post, we breakfasted at the Estate called the Cascade, and thus were the better enabled to encounter the somewhat steep though not long ascent. The North Signal Staff is immediately over the seashore, and commands a view on a clear day, of the islands of Tobago and Grenada, and of vessels sailing outside the Bocas. Its situation renders the air much cooler than it is within the Gulf, which is in a great degree deprived of the sea breezes by lofty mountains . . . Communication of the appearance of vessels is made (from North Post) by telegraph to Fort George, where it is repeated'. (Looking south a beautiful view is obtained of the whole of the Diego Martin valley). The telegraphing or signalling was done by the use of balls and flags during the day. A full description of the system used is given in Franklin's Diary for 1891.

The signal man at North Post in 1810, and continuing on to 1814, was Sergeant Birchnought, who lived there with his wife and family and was great friends with the Le Cadres at La Cascade Estate, who had cared for his children when they were ill. On the 1st of November 1814, Samuel Jennings was appointed Superintendant, and held that post for very many years.

After a short illness, he died in October 1828. He left a number of descendants in Diego Martin and in Trinidad. Later, two Fuller brothers from the south of England, succeeded to the post. Around 1850, however, one brother fishing in Fuller Bay (named after the family) fell off the rocks to a ledge below where he was picked up unconscious and died later. His descendants are prominent in Trinidad today and were at one time owners of Beau Sejour Estate near Blue Basin.

Directly north of North Post is the aptly named Point-a-Diable (Devil Point) where the cliffs are steep and the waves smash in with ferocity, the spray flung high into the air. A quarter mile to the east in the shelter of Point Contrelle (probably a corruption of 'Contrôle' – Checkpoint – where the boats were checked by the signalman) boats could on occasion land passengers with difficulty, and this was the reputed landing spot for the slaves that Begorrat was supposed to have smuggled into his cave.

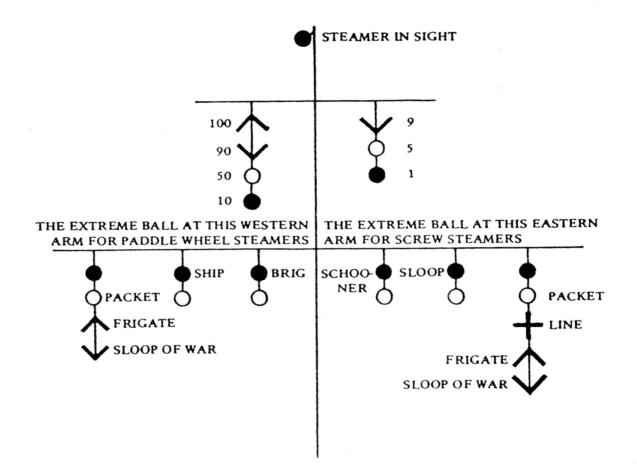

SIGNALS AT FORT GEORGE

When a black ball is hoisted on the lower yard it denotes a ship, Brig, Topsail Schooner, or sloop –
A ring denotes, a Barque, Brigantine, Ballahou Schooner or cutter. The signals for Her Majesty's ships are made on the lower year at the extreme ends.
+ In a Brig's place, a three-masted Topsail Schooner, and in a schooner's place, a three-masted Ballahou Schooner.
When a vessel has entered the Bocas, a small pennant is hoisted under the ball.
When the English Mail Packet is signalled outside, a black ball is hoisted at the masthead, with a red flag underneath. When it has entered the Gulf of Paria, a red flag only is hoisted.
When the French Mail Packet is signalled, the French flag is hoisted with a ball over it, and when inside the Gulf, the flag is hoisted without the ball.
In the case of all steamers showing a private or house flag outside the Bocas, a Black Ball will be hoisted at the masthead above such flag; and when inside, the flag only will be hoisted.

Numerical Signals

There were 115 such signals which may be summarised as follows:
1-9 Various e.g. Has mails on board; has immigrants on board.
10-24 Nationality e.g. French, Dutch.
25-68 Position or course or doubtful e.g. Has entered the Bocas; Has drifted out again; appears to have stock on deck.
69-78 Anchored e.g. Anchored off Maracas; Anchored off N. Post.
79-87 Weather e.g. Blows hard outside; Clear, can see Grenada.
88-100 Distress e.g. Mainmast gone; Requires steam tug.
101-115 Name of Owner e.g. J.N. Harriman & Co.; F. Zurcher & Co.

The Grand Savannah

Photograph — O. Mavrogordato.

An excerpt from Mrs. Olga Mavrogordato's 'Voices in the Street', published 1977:
For many years the Queen's Park was not heard of, and the only use to which it was devoted was the
pasturage of cattle of the residents of Port of Spain. In 1828, however, a visitor to Trinidad mentions
that horse races were held in the Grand Savannah, as the Queen's Park was then called. In 1854 the
Grand Stand was erected and horse-races were held annually.

AT LAST A CHRISTMAS IN
THE WEST INDIES

PORT OF SPAIN
Charles Kingsley, 1879

The first thing notable, on landing in Port of Spain at the low quay which has been just reclaimed from the mud of the gulf, is the multitude of people who are doing nothing. It is not that they have taken an hour's holiday to see the packet come in. You will find them, or their brown duplicates, in the same places to-morrow and next day. They stand idle in the market-place, not because they have not been hired, but because they do not want to be hired; being able to live like the Lazzaroni of Naples, on

'Midshipmans half-pay—nothing a day, and find yourself'. You are told that there are 8,000 human beings in Port of Spain alone without visible means of subsistence, and you congratulate Port of Spain on being such an Elysium that people can live there—not without eating, for every child and most women you pass are eating something or other all day long—but without working. The fact is, that though they will eat as much and more than a European, if they can get it, they can do well without food; and feed, as do the Lazzaroni, on

Photograph — Hélène Farfan.

In 1887 a Pavilion, built in the Moorish style, was erected in the Savannah, midway between Government House and the Queen's Park Hotel, being completed in time for the visit of the American Cricket Team in December of that year. The last cricket match was played in the Savannah in 1896, when the Club moved to the Oval. The Pavilion was demolished due to public protest made against it.

mere heat and light. The best substitute for a dinner is a sleep under a south wall in the blazing sun; and there are plenty of south walls in Port of Spain. In the French islands, I am told, such Lazzaroni are caught up and set to Government work, as 'strong rogues and masterless men', after the ancient English fashion. But is such a course fair? If a poor man neither steals, begs, nor rebels (and these people do not do the two latter), has he not as much right to be idle as a rich man? To say that neither has a right to be idle is, of course, sheer socialism, and a heresy not to be tolerated.

Next, the stranger will remark, here as at Grenada, that every one he passes looks strong, healthy and well-fed. One meets few or none of those figures and faces, small, scrofulous, squinny, and haggard, which disgrace the so-called civilisation of a British city. Nowhere in Port of Spain will you see such human beings as in certain streets of London, Liverpool, or Glasgow. Every one,

plainly, can live and thrive if they choose; and very pleasant it is to know that.

The road leads on past the Custom-house; and past, I am sorry to say, evil smells, which are too common still in Port of Spain, though fresh water is laid on from the mountains. I have no wish to complain, especially on first landing, of these kind and hospitable citizens. But as long as Port of Spain—the suburbs especially—smells as it does after sundown every evening, so long will an occasional outbreak of cholera or yellow fever hint that there are laws of cleanliness and decency which are both able and ready to avenge themselves. You cross the pretty 'Marine Square', with its fountain and flowering trees, and beyond them on the right the Roman Catholic Cathedral, a stately building, with Palmistes standing as tall sentries round; soon you go up a straight street, with a glimpse of a large English church, which must have been still more handsome than now before its tall steeple

the Members

The members of the Queen's Park Savannah Cricket Club in 1890.   Photograph — O. Mavrogordato.

Besides being a pasture and an open playground for local as well as intercolonial cricket, horse-racing, polo, football, hockey and all forms of athletic sports, the Savannah provided the residents with their first golf course, and the game was played with cows browsing at will. In 1834 the 5th Regiment encamped in the Savannah during February as a result of a number of deaths and cases of fever occurring at the Garrison Headquarters at St. James Barracks.

was shaken down by an earthquake. The then authorities, I have been told, applied to the Colonial Office for money to rebuild it: but the request was refused; on the ground, it may be presumed, that whatever ills Downing Street might have inflicted on the West Indies, it had not, as yet, gone so far as to play the part of Poseidon Ennosigæus.

Next comes a glimpse, too, of large—even too large —Government buildings, brick-built, pretentious, without beauty of form. But, however ugly in itself a building may be in Trinidad, it is certain, at least after a few years, to look beautiful, because embowered among noble flowering timber trees, like those that fill 'Brunswick Square', and surround the great church on its south side.

Under cool porticoes and through tall doorways are seen dark 'stores', filled with all manner of good things from Britain or from the United States. These older-fashioned houses, built, I presume, on the Spanish

model, are not without a certain stateliness, from the depth and breadth of their chiaroscuro. Their doors and windows reach almost to the ceiling, and ought to be plain proofs, in the eyes of certain discoverers of the 'giant cities of Bashan', that the old Spanish and French colonists were nine or ten feet high apiece. On the doorsteps sit Negresses in gaudy print dresses, with stiff turbans (which are, according to this year's fashion, of chocolate and yellow silk plaid, painted with thick yellow paint, and cost in all some four dollars), all aiding in the general work of doing nothing: save where here and there a hugely fat Negress, possibly with her 'head tied across' in a white turban (sign of mourning), sells, or tries to sell, abominable sweetmeats, strange fruits, and junks of sugar-cane, to be gnawed by the dawdlers in mid-street, while they carry on their heads everything and anything, from half a barrow-load of yams to a saucer or a beer-bottle. We never, however, saw, as Tom Cringle

the Polo Club

Among the many sports played in the Queen's Park Savannah was Polo. Shown below is the Trinidad team which played against Barbados. They are, back row: Hazeltyne, Hayes, Wright, Rogers, Street.
Front row: de Verteuil, French, A. de Boissiere (Capt.), Edwars, Lanel.
Photograph — M. Pocock.

In 1819 the Hollandais land lying north of the Paradise Estate was bought by the Cabildo. This parcel of land appears to be that on which the front part of the Botanic Gardens now stand, and includes the site of the President's residence and the pasture in front of it. All these lands were cleared and a fence erected around them. From the lands originally forming the Paradise and Hollandais estates, the Queen's Park was laid out at a cost of £10,363. Later on, the land for the Pitch walk was added to the entire circumference.

did, a Negro carrying a burden on his chin.

When you have ceased looking—even staring—at the black women and their ways, you become aware of the strange variety of races which people the city. Here passes an old Coolie Hindoo, with nothing on but his lungee round his loins, and a scarf over his head; a white-bearded, delicate-featured old gentleman, with probably some caste-mark of red paint on his forehead; his thin limbs, and small hands and feet, contrasting strangely with the brawny Negroes round. There comes a bright-eyed young lady, probably his daughter-in-law, hung all over with bangles, in a white muslim petticoat, crimson cotton-velvet jacket, and green gauze veil, with her naked brown baby astride on her hip; a clever, smiling, delicate little woman, who is quite aware of the brightness of her own eyes. And who are these three

boys in dark blue coatees and trousers, one of whom carries, hanging at one end of a long bamboo, a couple of sweet potatoes; at the other, possibly, a pebble to balance them? As they approach, their doleful visage betrays them. Chinese they are, without a doubt: but whether old or young, men or women, you cannot tell, till the initiated point out that the women have chignons and no hats, the men hats with their pigtails coiled up under them. Beyond this distinction, I know none visible. Certainly none in those sad visages—'Offas, non facies', as old Ammianus Marcellinus has it.

But why do Chinese never smile? Why do they look as if some one had sat upon their noses as soon as they were born, and they had been weeping bitterly over the calamity ever since? They, too, must have their moments of relaxation: but when? Once, and once only, in Port of

Lavendar and Swiss lace, the ladies look on, the sun sets and a cool breeze stirs the trees. In the distance, the band is playing. 'The Monkey Wrapped his tail around the Flagpole'. Photograph — Colin Agostini.

In 1902 the Electric Tramway started a pleasure car running around inside the railings on the Savannah, from four to ten p.m., a distance of two and a quarter miles, at two cents a round. This was a very popular outing for children and nurses, especially on Sunday afternoons when the Police Band played in the Governor's Gardens. This tram was scrapped in 1950. On January 23, 1913, the first aeroplane flight took place in the Savannah, when pilot Frank Boland crashed and was killed.

Spain, we saw a Chinese woman, nursing her baby, burst into an audible laugh: and we looked at each other, as much astonished as if our horses had begun to talk.

There again is a group of coloured men of all ranks, talking eagerly, business, or even politics; some of them as well dressed as if they were fresh from Europe; some of them, too, six feet high, and broad in proportion; as fine a race, physically, as one would wish to look upon; and with no want of shrewdness either, or determination, in their faces: a race who ought, if they will be wise and virtuous, to have before them a great future. Here come home from the convent school two coloured young ladies, probably pretty, possibly lovely, certainly gentle, modest, and well-dressed according to the fashions of Paris or New York; and here comes the unmistakable Englishman, tall, fair, close-shaven, arm-in-arm with

another man, whose more delicate features, more sallow complexion, and little moustache mark him as some Frenchman or Spaniard of old family. Both are dressed as if they were going to walk up Pall Mall or the Rue de Rivoli; for 'go-to-meeting clothes' are somewhat too much *de rigueur* here; a shooting-jacket and wide-awake betrays the newly-landed Englishman. Both take off their hats with a grand air to a lady in a carriage; for they are very fine gentlemen indeed, and intend to remain such; and well that is for the civilisation of the island; for it is from such men as these, and from their families, that the good manners for which West Indians are, or ought to be, famous, have permeated down, slowly but surely, through all classes of society save the very lowest.

The straight and level street, swarming with dogs, vultures, chickens, and goats, passes now out of the old

Photograph — O. Mavrogordato.

In July 1876, the foundation stone was laid for the new Government House at St. Ann's on the present site.
It was designed by Mr. Ferguson, on the Indian model, and was built of native limestone.
In 1876, more than one hundred years ago, the building was occupied by
Sir Turner Irving, having cost £44,630.

into the newer part of the city; and the type of the houses changes at once. Some are mere wooden sheds of one or two rooms, comfortable enough in that climate, where a sleeping-place is all that is needed—if the occupiers would but keep them clean. Other houses, wooden too, belong to well-to-do-folk. Over high walls you catch sight of jalousies and verandahs, inside which must be most delightful darkness and coolness. Indeed, one cannot fancy more pleasant nests than some of the little gaily-painted wooden houses, standing on stilts to let the air under the floors, and all embowered in trees and flowers, which line the roads in the suburbs; and which are inhabited, we are told, by people engaged in business.

But what would—or at least ought to—strike the newcomer's eye with most pleasurable surprise and make

him realise into what a new world he has been suddenly translated—even more than the Negroes, and the black vultures sitting on roof-ridges, or stalking about in mid-street—are the flowers which show over the walls on each side of the street. In that little garden, not thirty feet broad, what treasures there are! A tall palm—whether Palmiste or Oil-palm—has its smooth trunk hung all over with orchids, tied on with wire. Close to it stands a purple Dracæna, such as are put on English dinner-tables in pots: but this one is twenty feet high; and next to it is that strange tree the Clavija, of which the Creoles are justly fond.. A single straight stem, fifteen feet high, carries huge oblong leaves atop, and beneath them, growing out of the stem itself, delicate panicles of little white flowers, fragrant exceedingly. A double blue pea and a purple Bignonia are scrambling over shrubs and

Photograph — G. Mac Lean.

Over a period of nine years 1867-1876, a building known as 'The Cottage' was used as the Governor's residence.
This was a rambling building of one storey, formerly the house of the estate manager, and also painted
by Cazabon. It was here, in 1870, that the celebrated writer, Charles Kingsley, wrote his famous
'At Last – A Christmas in the West Indies', dedicated to the then Governor, Sir Arthur Gordon.

walls. And what is this which hangs over into the road, some fifteen feet in height—long, bare, curving sticks, carrying each at its end a flat blaze of scarlet? What but the Poinsettia, paltry scions of which, like the Dracæna, adorn our hothouses and dinner-tables. The street is on fire with it all the way up, now in mid-winter; while at the street end opens out a green park, fringed with noble trees all in full leaf; underneath them more pleasant little suburban villas; and behind all, again, a background of steep wooded mountain a thousand feet in height. That is the Savannah, the public park and race-ground; such as neither London nor Paris can boast.

One may be allowed to regret that the exuberant loyalty of the citizens of Port of Spain has somewhat defaced one end at least of their Savannah; for in expectation of a visit from the Duke of Edinburgh, they erected for his reception a pile of brick, of which the best that can be said is that it holds a really large and stately ballroom, and the best that can be hoped is that the authorities will hide it as quickly as possible with a ring of Palmistes, Casuarinas, Sandboxes, and every quick-growing tree. Meanwhile, as His Royal Highness did not come, the citizens wisely thought that they might as well enjoy their new building themselves. So there, on set high days, the Governor and the Lady of the Governor hold their court. There, when the squadron comes in, officers in uniform dance at desperate sailors' pace with delicate Creoles; some of them, coloured as well as white, so beautiful in face and figure that one could almost pardon the jolly tars if they enacted a second Mutiny of the *Bounty,* and refused one and all to leave the island and the fair dames thereof. And all the while

The Botanic Gardens was laid out by Sir Ralph Woodford and David Lockhart, the first curator. Many exotic trees were imported from countries around the world to create the lush and beautiful Botanic Gardens. Illustration from 'At Last', Charles Kingsley.

the warm night wind rushes in through the high open windows; and the fire-flies flicker up and down, in and out, and you slip away on to the balcony to enjoy—for after all it is very hot—the purple star-spangled night; and see aloft the saw of the mountain ridges against the black-blue sky; and below—what a contrast!—the crowd of white eyeballs and white teeth—Negroes, Coolies, Chinese—all grinning and peeping upward against the railings, in the hope of seeing—through the walls—the 'buccra quality' enjoy themselves.

An even pleasanter sight we saw once in that large room, a sort of agricultural and horticultural show, which augured well for the future of the colony. The flowers were not remarkable, save for the taste shown in their arrangement, till one recollected that they were not brought from hothouses, but grown in mid-winter in the open air. The roses, of which West Indians are very fond, as they are of all 'home', *i.e.* European, flowers, were not as good as those of Europe. The rose in Trinidad, though it flowers three times a year, yet, from the great heat and moisture, runs too much to wood. But the roots, especially the different varieties of yam, were very curious; and their size proved the wonderful food-producing powers of the land when properly cultivated. The poultry, too, were worthy of an English show. Indeed, the fowl seems to take to tropical America as the horse has to Australia, as to a second native land; and Trinidad alone might send an endless supply to the fowl-market of the Northern States, even if that should not be quite true which some one said, that you might turn an old cock loose in the bush, and he, without further help, would lay more eggs, and bring up more chickens, than you could either eat or sell.

But the most interesting element of that exhibition was the coco-nut fibre products of Messrs. Uhrich and Gerold, of which more in another place. In them lies a source of further wealth to the colony, which may stand her in good stead when Port of Spain becomes, as it must become, one of the great emporiums of the West.

Since our visit the great ballroom has seen—even now is seeing—strange vicissitudes. For the new Royal College, having as yet no buildings of its own, now keeps school, it is said, therein—alas for the ink stains on that beautiful floor! And by last advices, a 'troupe of artistes' from Martinique, there being no theatre in Port of

Spain, have been doing their play-acting in it; and Terpsichore and Thalia (Melpomene, I fear, haunts not the stage of Martinique) have been hustling all the other Muses downstairs at sunset, and joining their jinglings to the chorus of tom-toms and chac-chacs which resounds across the Savannah, at least till 10 P.M., from all the suburbs.

The road—and all the roads round Port of Spain, thanks to Sir Ralph Woodford, are as good as English roads—runs between the Savannah and the mountain spurs, and past the Botanic Gardens, which are a credit, in more senses than one, to the Governors of the island. For in them, amid trees from every quarter of the globe, and gardens kept up in the English fashion, with fountains, too, so necessary in this tropical clime, stood a large 'Government House'. This house was some years ago destroyed; and the then Governor took refuge in a cottage just outside the garden. A sum of money was voted to rebuild the big house: but the Governors, to their honour, have preferred living in the cottage, adding to it from time to time what was necessary for more comfort; and have given the old garden to the city, as a public pleasure-ground, kept up at Government expense.

This Paradise—for such it is—is somewhat too far from the city; and one passes in it few people, save an occasional brown nurse. But when Port of Spain becomes, as it surely will, a great commercial city, and the slopes of Laventille, Belmont, and St. Ann's, just above the gardens, are studded, as they surely will be, with the villas of rich merchants, then will the generous gift of English Governors be appreciated and used; and the Botanic Gardens will become a Tropic Garden of the Tuileries, alive, at five o'clock every evening, with human flowers of every hue.

archipelago situated off the west coast of Morocco. Madeirans or *Madeirenses,* who originally came to work on the cocoa and sugar estates under the scheme of indentureship, constituted the main body of ancestors of Trinidad's small Portuguese community.

In 1834, the year of the abolition of slavery (some four years prior to the full emancipation of the slaves), the first Portuguese entered Trinidad, not from Madeira, but from the Azores. At that time, planters were approaching a crisis situation as the need to locate other sources of regular labour was becoming more and more pressing since slavery was about to come to an end. Aware of the profits to be made at the expense of the increasingly desperate planters, a group of men who manned slave ships illegally solicited twenty-five Portuguese labourers from the island of Faial (or Fayal) in the Azores. Within less than two years, these labourers either died due to extreme weakness and illness or returned to the Azores because of difficult living and working conditions, leaving no trace behind.

Legitimate measures were put into place to facilitate immigration by 1838. Planters first commissioned free black labour from the United States, several Eastern Caribbean islands and later West Africa but after these attempts failed, they turned to European labour. Labourers from France and Germany, among other European countries, were attracted by the purportedly high wages on the sugar estates, but this bid too met with little success.

In the early nineteenth century, Madeira found itself in great economic and social upheaval. The Madeiran wine industry, the anchor of the island's economy, began to experience a decline. Natural disasters led to famine, neglected vineyards and widespread unemployment. These factors as well as overcrowding led to a reduced standard of living and for many, emigration was a matter of survival. The troubled situation was further intensified by religious tension that arose due to the emergence of a group of recent Presbyterian converts in traditionally Roman Catholic Madeira.

Two waves of Madeirans, therefore, came to Trinidad in 1846 and onwards for very different reasons. In a sense, both groups were refugees – one made up of mainly rural folk fleeing severe economic disaster, and the other comprising largely educated urban dwellers fleeing violent religious persecution.

In the 1830's, Madeirans had already begun to emigrate in droves to Demerara (or British Guiana) and planters and estate labourers alike found this venture successful and mutually beneficial. When Trinidadian cocoa planters requested urgent help from the Governor for their estates, the governments of England and Portugal agreed to allow Madeiran immigration to Trinidad as they recognized the relative success of the British Guianese experiment (despite an initially high mortality rate) and the probability that Madeiran peasants, who were used to viticulture and sugar cane cultivation, would prove to be suitable for the cocoa plantations.

Sugar planters, however, privately chartered the *Senator,* the first barque with 219 Madeiran immigrant labourers. They arrived in Trinidad on 9th of May 1846, eleven years after the arrival of the Faial Portuguese, and were put to work on the more rigorous but better-paying sugar estates, contrary to original government stipulations. The harsh conditions of tropical sugar plantations proved to be too much for the Portuguese. Deaths were not infrequent and some left for the cocoa estates while others abandoned plantation labour

The Portuguese of Trinidad

Jo-Anne S. Ferreira

The Portuguese immigrants to Trinidad were the first to come to the West Indies and were drawn from the Portuguese Atlantic provinces of the Azores, Madeira and the Cape Verde Islands during the nineteenth century. There was also a group of Portuguese in the island as early as 1630 and Sephardim (Portuguese and Spanish Jews) were in Trinidad in the eighteenth century and some may have been numbered among the nineteenth century immigrants. By far the largest group of Portuguese, however, hailed from the Madeira Islands, a small

Robert Reid Kalley, M.D.

Members of the Pereira Family who arrived in Trinidad in the 1850's. The photograph on the right shows the three brothers. The one on the left stayed in Portugal, the one in the middle went on to Brazil, the one on the right came to Trinidad.

altogether and turned to petty shopkeeping. Other ships arrived later in 1846 and in 1847. The Portuguese were not compelled by law to indenture themselves and Madeira did not prove to be a viable source of labour. After 1847, Portuguese immigration was no longer considered a solution to the planters' predicament and the Madeirans were followed by two groups of Asian indentured labourers: the Chinese and the Indians.

The Protestant converts, led by Dr. Robert Reid Kalley, a medical missionary of the Free Church of Scotland encountered a great deal of hostility and intolerance in Roman Catholic Madeira and were eventually forced to seek asylum abroad. The first group of 197 refugees sailed on the barque *William* in Trinidad on 16th of September 1846, just four months after the arrival of the first Madeiran immigrants. In Trinidad, where freedom of worship and religious tolerance were decreed in the final year of the reign of George III, they were welcomed by the already established but small Church of Scotland, but were again brought face to face with their countrymen who harboured the very same prejudices that the refugees had sought to escape in their flight from Madeira.

Like their impoverished Catholic compatriots who came to better their fortunes, many of the Presbyterian refugees arrived in Trinidad destitute. After some initial difficulty in finding employment, some being forced to indenture themselves to the estates, they too managed to

embark on small scale entrepreneurship. The first Portuguese shop (the ownership of which is uncertain) opened in 1846, the year of arrival of both Catholic immigrants and Protestant refugees. In general, it seems that the Protestants opened the better dry goods stores, mainly in Port of Spain and Arouca (where there was another Scottish Presbyterian community), while the Catholics found work on the estates as shop managers and opened the typical rum shops and adjoining 'shops' or groceries, dispersed all over the island. Established Portuguese shop owners readily hired newly arrived Madeirans, who could speak no English and therefore could not easily secure jobs elsewhere, as shop clerks, and joint Portuguese ownership of rum shops was not uncommon. Several Portuguese were also employed as gardeners and housekeepers and the community gained a reputation for being industrious and enterprising.

After being accommodated by the Scottish community of Greyfriars Church on Frederick Street in Port of Spain, the refugees built their own church in 1854 under the leadership of Reverend Henrique Vieira. It was named the St. Ann's Church of Scotland (because of its location on the corner of St. Ann's Road, now Charlotte Street, and Oxford Street) but was once more commonly identified as 'the Portuguese Church'. The Portuguese language and Portuguese Bibles and hymnals were in regular use up to twenty-seven years after the arrival of the first refugees and Scottish ministers even

Reverend Henrique Vieira

endeavoured to learn Portuguese before taking up a term of office at St. Ann's in order to effectively minister to the largely Lusophone congregation. The very religious Catholic Portuguese, with their love of and strong adherence to their *festas* (feast days), especially that of their patron saint *Nossa Senhora do Monte* (Our Lady of the Mount), jeeringly referred to the Presbyterian Portuguese as *'Kalleyistas'* or *'Calvinistas'*. Relations between these two denominations were so strained at the outset that inter-marriage as well as business relationships were not only frowned upon but often strictly forbidden by both factions.

After the first two waves of Madeiran Portuguese in 1846, Catholic Madeirans continued to emigrate in trickles well after the end of the nineteenth century and by the turn of the twentieth, it was estimated that the entire Portuguese community was some two thousand strong. Although emigration was no longer necessitated by economic woes and misfortunes, Madeirans continued to migrate voluntarily to Trinidad to seek improved living conditions and stories are told of immigrants who travelled as stowaways on the long journey from Madeira to Trinidad. Family emigration was not usual and Madeirans often emigrated to join family members who had settled in Trinidad before them, sometimes accompanied by cherished family servants.

At this point, it is worth mentioning that emigration from the Cape Verde Islands was allowed by the local authorities, because of a critical food shortage there in 1856, and was welcomed by West Indian planters. Less than a hundred immigrants reached Trinidad, immigration having ceased by 1858, and the emigrants seem to have been of Negroid origin rather than Caucasian.

By the last decade of the nineteenth century, the Presbyterian Portuguese community, which had once numbered well over one thousand, had dwindled greatly as close to two-thirds of them chose to emigrate to Brazil and the United States, where other Portuguese Protestant communities were thriving, leaving behind just a few hundred who opted to remain in Trinidad. With the passage of time and a weakened Presbyterian community, a breakdown of religious barriers through contact in the social, business and educational arenas resulted in several mixed marriages. The two groups eventually merged, so undeniably strong were their ancestral, cultural and linguistic bonds, and the outnumbered Presbyterians became absorbed by the wider Roman Catholic community, comprising not just Portuguese but French, Spanish, Irish and English settlers.

Now, no longer distinct as an ethnic group, the Portuguese Creoles have been completely assimilated into the wider society. Their forebears must have formed a curious sight on disembarking in Port of Spain, some of the men bedecked in their workman's woolly caps with pompoms and earflaps and their traditional island footwear of plain knee-high boots worn rolled down to the ankle. They became well-known for their rum shops and retail groceries, which later gave way to larger scale commercial enterprises, for their predilection for salted cod, soups, their liberal use of olive oil and for the garlic pork (*carne de vinho e de alhos* or *'calvinadage'*, to give it its evolved local pronunciation) prepared at Christmas time, which has become virtually the only lasting symbol of Trinidadian Portuguese ethnicity. Their love of music and dancing is as much Trinidadian as it is Portuguese and their two clubs in Port-of-Spain, A Associação Portuguesa Primeiro de Dezembro and The Portuguese Club, stand as silent testimony to a formerly vibrant and close-knit Portuguese community.

Little else is left to recall the presence of the Portuguese in Trinidad, with the exception of a preponderance of surnames which continue to adorn business places, dot the pages of the nation's history and

As there is no Register of Members of the Old Portuguese Church extant, the following list of members of that Church who subscribed in 1855 towards the Patriotic Fund, during the Crimean War (a year after the founding of the said Church), gives an idea, at least who were some of its earliest members and is here-incorporated to assist in amplifying their records. The extract was taken from the *'Trinidad Royal Gazette.'*

PATRIOTIC FUND

Collections made by the Revd. Mr. Vieira from his congregation (Portuguese), viz:—

Henrique Vieira	$ 2.00
João Baptista	0.50
Joaquim dos Santas	0.50
Marcial da Costa	0.50
Lucia Baptista	0.50
Marcellino de Freitas	1.00
Antonio de Souza	0.50
Antonio da Silva	0.90
Margarida de Esperança	0.50
Vicente Telles	0.50
Manoel Correa	1.00
Manoel Ferreira	1.02
Jezuina da Silva	0.90
João Martins	0.50
Jose Gomes	0.50
Joaquin Mendes	0.50
Antonio Pires	2.00
João Martins	1.00
Maria Carvalha	0.60
Manoel Mendes	0.50
Francisco Marques Pereira	0.90
Maria Ferreira	0.48
No Name	0.25
Antonio Gomes Nogueira	0.50
Jose Fernandes	0.50
Anna Ferrera	0.15
João	0.25
Antonio de Freitas	0.50
Faustino	0.20
Joaquim de Freitas	0.60
Manoel Marques	0.25
Manoel Jardim	1.00
Antonia Jacinta	0.25
Maria Gomes	0.25
Anna Marques	1.00
Augusta de Esperança	0.50
Antonio Correa	0.50
Antonio Franco	1.00
Claudino Alexandra	0.90
Francico M	0.60
Maria Francica	0.50
Manoel Fernandes Neves	0.50
Francisco de Costa	0.50
No Name	2.00
Querino Baptista	0.90
Jetudes de Freitas	1.00
No Name	2.00
Antonio M. de Freitas	0.60
Antonio de Freitas	0.65
Manoel Jose de Souza	0.50

Sebastiano de Freitas	0.48
João de Mendonça	1.00
Vincente Silviera	1.00
Fernando Joaquim	1.00
No Name	0.10
Francisca Correa	0.30
Martinho Jose de Souza	0.30
Maria d'Andrade	0.30
Julia de Souza	0.20
Maria Vieira	1.60
Anna d'Andrade	0.30
Beneiacio Gomes	1.00
Manoel Vieira	0.48
Luiza Marques	0.24
Joaquim Correa	0.50
Antonio d'Andrade	0.25
Jose da Castra	0.50
Francisca dos Santos	0.96
Thereza de Souza	0.30
Jose Fernandes	0.25
Jeznina Ferreira	0.20
Ludevina Ferreira	0.30
Maria de Abreo	0.49
Antonia dos Santos	0.50
From Various Individuals	2.93
Maria da Costa	0.50
João Cabral	1.00
Carolina Roza	0.25
Antonio Jose Souza	1.00
Margarita de Souza	0.20
João Baptista	0.40
No Name	0.20
Domingos de Mendonça	0.48
Joaquina Baptista	0.25
Antonio Mendes	0.60
Francisco d'Andrade	0.12
Manoel Gonzales	0.48
No Name	0.39
Joaquim Correa	0.10
Johny Baptista	0.10
Anna d'Andrade	0.20
Francisco Souza	0.26
Jose Anto. da Esperança	0.50
João Christina	0.60
No Name	0.60
Joaquim Ferreira	0.20
	————
Total	$ 59.50

Trinidad Royal Gazette,
2nd May, 1855.

EARLIEST MARRIAGES OF THE PORTUGUESE

In the Marriage Register of Greyfriars Presbyterian Church, Port of Spain are the following entries:

On 2nd December, 1846:

Joseph Ferreira
Maria Nunes
Witnesses: Joauim da Santos Dias
Manoel de Vasconcellos

On 3rd December, 1846:

John Vieira
Maria de Freitas
Witnesses: Joaquim da Santos Dias
Manuel Freitas Reiz
Officiant: Rev. Alex. Kennedy (2)

On 12th December, 1846:

Joseph De Souza
Antonio De Souza
(of Sta. Cruz)
Witnesses: Manoel de Vasconcelles
Joaquim da Santos Dias
Officiant: Rev. George Brodie (1)

CARNE VINHO E ALHOS
Dice the pork in squares about an inch thick. Place in a jar filled with vinegar and two whole heads of garlic and some seasoning crushed. Leave to soak for three days. When ready to use take out of jar and fry in their own fat until crisp. Serve on pieces of dry bread done in the same fat. This is a delicious dish that is traditionally eaten by the Portuguese in Trinidad on Christmas morning.

Members of the D'Abreu-Gomes Family. The second youngman on the left is the father of politician Alber Gomes, who is pictured here with his mother, seate l and father and older brother and sister. Photograph -- Sonya Moze.

On 12th April, 1847:

	Manoel De Corea
	Leonarda De Nobriga
Witnesses:	Arsenio Nicós de Silva
	Jose Marques Pereira

On 13th April, 1847:

	João Ferreira
	Carlota Corea
Witnesses:	Joaquim da Santos Dias
	Antonio Corea

On 19th April, 1847:

	Candido D'Abreu
	Maria Vieyra
	(at Sao. Jose, Orange Grove)
Witnesses:	Jose d'Ornellas Vasconcellos
	João Rodriguez Figueria

On 23rd April, 1847:

	Luiz De Crastus
	Caralota de Corea
Witnesses:	Arsenio Nicós da Silva
	Francisco de Freitas
Officiant:	Rev. W.H. Hewitson (4)

which are borne by their descendants whether they are full-blooded Portuguese or not. Names like Camacho, Coelho, Correia, Fernandes, Pereira, Querino, Ribeiro and Sá Gomes are not only among the more notable in the business sector past and present, but speak of the Portuguese community's bewilderingly rapid yet unheralded rise to prominence out of the bosom of an impoverished immigrant group, no doubt harking back to an unerring combination of ambition, diligence and perseverance.

The lasting economic transformation of the Portuguese more or less coincides with their influential though fleeting political and literary ascendancy. The names of Cabral, Dos Santos, Gomes, Mendes and Netto once figured regularly in the nation's dailies. Two of these, Albert Maria Gomes and Alfred Hubert Mendes, were among the literary pioneers of the Caribbean and flourished in the 1930's, a crucial decade in Trinidad's recent political history. As a Portuguese Creole who began as a radical, left-wing champion of the social, economic, political, religious and cultural underdog, Gomes loomed large on the political scene. He made his mark in politics to the extent that that political era was referred to as 'Gomesocracy' and he was undoubtedly one of Trinidad's more colourful and controversial

*The Gomes Family in Trinidad in about 1915. They are
Leone Francis D'Abreu Gomes, his wife, Clara, née
Roque Albert and Hilda. Photograph — Sonya Moze.*

Albert Gomes, late Chief Minister of Trinidad, in his book 'Through a Maze of Colour', describes his ancestry and tells of how the family acquired the name Gomes.

I often think that it must be a very comforting experience to own a genealogical tree with main trunk firmly planted and branches well defined. This nostalgia, perhaps, is only natural in one whose genealogy is shrouded in doubt and ambiguity and lends itself to such riotous speculation. My maternal grand-father having been a founding, a main branch of the tree has been abruptly cut off at that point, leaving me free to speculate, as vanity or convenience might determine, whether prince, rogue or ordinary seducer set in motion the dramatic incidents that must have preceded the abandonment of my poor, hapless grand-parent on the doorstep of an orphanage in Madeira many years ago, resulting in the curious patronymic 'De Cambra' being bestowed upon him, which, so I was informed by my mother, translated means 'of the orphanage'.

But the other main branch, the paternal, is also afflicted by complication, albeit of a lesser kind. This latter requires somewhat more elaborate explanation. My paternal grandmother was previously married to gentleman named Gomes; and when he died she met and married my paternal grandfather whose name was D'Abreau. Antonio Gomes, son of the previous marriage and my father's half-brother, having

federalist politicians. The magniloquent editor of *The Beacon,* the monthly magazine which acted as a forum for multifarious political views and literary expression, Gomes was a close associate of another outstanding product of the Portuguese community, Alfred Mendes, who was the leader of the pluridisciplinary and multiracial liberal socialist group of early Trinidadian writers known as the *Beacon* group and was also a successful civil servant.

In a remarkably short space of time, the Portuguese community has quietly spawned a number of eminent sons and daughters of the soil, far out of proportion to its relatively small size and against all odds, and has contributed more than its fair share to the progress of its adopted land. They remain small in numbers but great in influence and occupational status and the vast majority of Portuguese descendants have become inseparably interwoven with other ethnic groups, to form the total picture that is unmistakably and irrevocably Trinidadian.

emigrated from Madeira to Trinidad and achieved some success in business, sent for my father, who, when he took up employment in his half-brother's provision shop, discovered to his mortification that having a half-brother with a different name left him open to suspicion of illegitimacy. When this anomaly became the subject of vulgar taunts hurled at him across the counter of the shop by customers, he decided that the solution was to adopt his half-brother's name, which he did. And it is thus that D'Abreau, our proper name, was abandoned and we got stuck with the name Gomes.

Members of the Gregorio, Pereira and Ferreira Families.

Albert Gomes and his wife Zilla on their honeymoon.
Photograph — Sonya Moze.

SCAPULAR

Alfred H. Mendes

As a boy, I lived in Sangre Grande, a village about thirty miles to the east of Port-of-Spain. My father managed a small dry-goods store in the village; but our house was a little outside the village, on the Manzanilla road. The river Cunapo flowed past at a distance of not more than a hundred yards from our house; and when the Cunapo was in flood, in the rainy season, we boys had great fun. About twelve miles up the river Mr. Francois, a creole of French extraction, owned a tidy acreage of forest land: balata and crapeau and purple-heart and cedar and so forth. As soon as the rains came Mr. Francois, in order to save time and expense, employed a few men to launch his innumerable logs into the swirling waters of the Cunapo. At the Manzanilla road bridge their further downward passage was impeded by a huge wire-net stretched from bank to bank; then the logs were dragged up to the road, loaded into lorries and taken down to Port-of-Spain for local sale and shipment abroad. We boys, unknown to our mothers, used to tramp the twelve miles to Mr. Francois' plantation, watch the launching operations and, no sooner was Mr. Francois' back turned,

board the logs and sail down the river on their precarious surfaces. Usually, with a good current, the twelve miles were covered in four hours, and four hours of such excitement as I have, in no other activity, since known. It was a dangerous game, as you may well imagine, but only once did we ever have an accident that looked for a moment like being fatal; and it is that story I shall now relate.

Anthony was a school friend of mine. At the time, we were both about fourteen years old. Although so many years have slipped by, I can still picture Anthony as he was then: tall and gawky, his face yellow almost, the cheek bones sticking up from under the tightly drawn skin. There was, really, nothing remarkable in his appearance: but his behaviour, his character was so religious (unusual for a growing boy) that he came to be known in the village as Saint Anthony. Every morning you could see him, if you were so minded, walking to early mass, his chaplet dangling from his hand, his prayer book bulging out his pocket. Once a week he went to confession and as often took communion: and this was everybody's wonder: what did Anthony find sinful in himself to confess? I need hardly tell you that we chaffed him at every favourable opportunity, but he took it all kindly, smiling his saintly smile and sometimes saying, quite seriously, that he would pray for us. In spite of his complete difference to me —to be frank, I was a little pagan—I liked Anthony. We were not often together: once or twice he came to our house, and my mother, good Catholic that she was, was never tired of holding Anthony up to me as an example after which I should be striving. But I could not be often with Anthony because the things of which I was fond he took no interest in. I loved cricket, I loved football, I loved mischief of all kinds: whereas Anthony was seldom seen on a cricket field, never on a football field (it was a savage's game, he said), and any play that smacked of adventure and risk he refused with a pious smile. And yet I like him and felt, also, that he like me; so that when, that morning so many many years ago, Peter came up to our little group and suggested that someone should ask Anthony to accompany us to Mr. Francois' plantation, everybody looked to me as being the only one who stood any chance of success with the proposal.

"You can't do it, Auguste," Peter said to me. "You'll never get him."

"It would be fun having him," Joe said. "Can you picture him on one of those logs?"

Everybody laughed.

"Auguste'll never get him."

"I bet you I do," I said, in the manner of a boy accepting a challenge: and I walked off.

Arrived at Anthony's house, I called him out into the yard and persuaded him into joining us. Of course, at first he refused. Then he said he would have to ask his mother, at which my eyes opened wide with fear; but, a brilliant idea jumping into my mind, I said:

"And supposing your mother was dead, who would you ask then?"

"All right, all right," he said, shuddering. "But let me put on my scapular first."

Anthony went into the house and returned in a moment with the scapular in his hand. I was curious and asked him to show it me. Attached to a braid was a small woollen disc, the size of a penny, and into this disc the pattern of a head was knitted.

"Is this you?" I asked, pointing to the head.

His eyes turned up in horror. "No, no," he said. "That's Saint Anthony." He took it away from me and adjusted it around his neck, inside his clothes. "My patron saint," he added, smiling his saintly smile.

"But why do you wear it?" I asked, moving into the street beside him.

"It keeps me from harm. It was given me by father O'Brien when I took my first communion."

I remember wondering why my mother did not get one for me so that I, too, might be kept from harm.

When we arrived at Mr. Francois' clearing on the river bank, all was hustle and bustle. Dressed in a khaki suit, an old white helmet on his head, Mr. Francois himself was there superintending the work. A dozen or so burly black men, their naked torsos perspiring and shining in the sun, moved to and fro. Now and again Mr. Francois raised his voice angrily, giving orders. For a while he took no notice of us, but suddenly he strode up to where we were standing and addressed Anthony in a stern tone:

"Now look here, you little vagabonds, it has come to my hearing that you are in the habit of riding down the river on my logs. I cannot prevent you from doing that, but I can tell you this: if any of you gets drowned, that's not my business." saying which he turned right about turn, stamped down to his men and gave his attention to the labour once again.

Anthony stood open-mouthed, blushing up to his eyebrows. We all looked at him, poked each other in the ribs and laughed. Mr. Francois' mule, tethered to a nearby tree, knocked the turf with his forefeet and neighed,

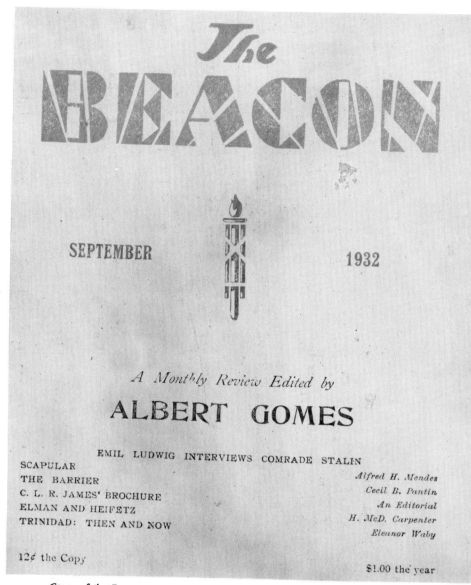

Cover of the Beacon September 1932. The short story depicted here is from this issue.

1851

CENSUS OF 1851:

We are at length in possession of the results of the general census of the colony taken on the 1st day of July last. The total population of the colony appears according to the returns sent in to be 68,600; that is 33,631 males and 32,969 females. We feel sure this is considerably short of the mark; the real total must be upwards of 70,000. The total number of the native population is retuned as 29,913:— Africans 8,000. The creole population of Port-of-Spain is 10,929; and thus there are 20,000 creoles in the country districts,—persons whom one might expect to find employed in the production of the exportable produce of the island. From what we learn, however, there are not 5,000 creole labourers employed on all the sugar estates of the colony. Thus out of the larger half of the population of the island, we have only one eighth employed in the cultivation of the principle staple; and yet there are persons who see no need for further immigration. The different religious denominations are put down as follows:—

Church of England	16,264
Church of Rome	43,605
Wesleyans	2,508
Presbyterians	1,017
Independents	133
Baptists	448
All other Christians	98
Mahommedans	1,016
Gentoos	2,694
Heathens	880
	68,600

(24th Oct., 1851.)

where-at we all laughed the more.

"Don't laugh," Anthony said. "When a mule neighs like that, it means bad luck."

"Saints can't get drowned," Peter said.

"Especially saints who wear scapulars," I put in. As young as I was, I regretted the remark immediately I had made it: Anthony's face clouded over with a most painful expression: I though he was going to cry. I said nothing, however; but the others took the cue and continued taunting him. Anthony didn't seem to mind them for his expression changed into a saintly smile, and he remained smiling like that until they were done taunting him.

At last the logs were all launched. Mr. Francois wiped the perspiration off his sunburnt face with a huge coloured handkerchief, gave us a last menacing look, threw himself astride his impatient mule, flicked his whip and disappeared down the bridle path at a quick canter.

In a moment we all woke up. Running down the bank to the waters' boisterous edge, I cried, trying to make amends for my ugly behaviour of a minute before:

"Anthony, there's a fine log for you. Jump!"

"It's too far out," he said, gazing helplessly at the retreating log. With a spring, I landed on to it and nearly lost my balance. I shouted out to Anthony, drawing his attention to another sailing past within his reach. Awkwardly he clambered aboard it and in a short while we were side by side, slowly gliding down. All the other boys had already found berths and there was a hullabaloo echoing and re-echoing about the thickly wooded banks. Keskidees, darting from high green sanctuaries, sang shrilly, and wood doves cooed in lofty excitement. On each side of the river, not more than fifty fee across, the trees rose tall and stately, their overhanging branches intertwining to make a majestic arch through which sunlight fitfully slanted. The current of the river was here strong and noisily bubbled about the jostling logs. Great clumps of bamboos, creaking like hundreds of cicadas when the wind shook them, here and there bordered the river; and a solitary deer, no doubt recognising us for what we were, with one leap disappeared into the forest.

Meanwhile, we shouted across to each other, a regular fusillade of tease and counter-tease. The buoyant waters played ducks and drakes with our logs, but all of us, by dint of long practice, had become adept at the game. Not so Anthony: by this time he was kneeling on his log, grimly holding on to its sides. His face betrayed his inward panic. His scapular had somehow or the other escaped from under his clothes and was now swinging from his neck. Our logs had, earlier, sheared apart, and I was screaming out frantic instructions to him, but he did not seem to hear me for he took no notice of me. He simply held on, his log swerving this way and that, every now and again rising on the crest of a dashing current.

"Can you swim?" Peter called out to him. He did not answer.

"Can you swim?" I screamed.

Without looking at me, he nodded—and with that nod lost his balance. His log rolled over and the next moment he was in the water. I saw one hand lifted high, like the hand that gripped Excalibur, then it splashed the water and he sank. By a miracle of luck I sprang from log to log without mishap, until I landed on his. The others looked on, their voices for once silenced. My heart beating very fast, I ran to the stern-end of the log. Gasping for breath, Anthony rose, one hand beating the water. I threw myself flat along the log, leaned over and grasped him by the collar. After a long and difficult time,

the other boys and I managed to navigate the log to the bank and we helped Anthony on to dry land.

As soon as he recovered, he pulled the scapular from around his neck and threw it into the river. Dumbfounded, we stood gaping at him. All that he sputtered, however, was:

"That damn thing nearly made me drown. My hand caught in it. The damn. . . ."

What follows is a list of names of prominent Trinidadians who in 1843 presented a sword to the Governor Sir Henry McLeod.

Continued on page 286.

THE PORT OF SPAIN GAZETTE.

01. NEW SERIES.]	TRINIDAD: SATURDAY, AUGUST 17, 1872.	[VOL. II.

NOTICE.

THE STEAMER
"ALICE"
WILL PLY AS FOLLOWS:—

FROM PORT-OF-SPAIN.		FROM SAN FERNANDO.
MONDAY	2 P.M.	
TUESDAY	3 P.M.	7 A.M.
THURSDAY	4 P.M.	4 P.M.
FRIDAY	11 A.M.	3 P.M.
SATURDAY	4 P.M.	4 P.M.

On THURSDAYS and SATURDAYS the Steamer will call at OROPOUCHE, LA BREA, IROIS FOREST and CEDROS.

FARES:

Children in arms, free; under 12 years of age, half price. The same fares returning.

Excursion Tickets

Will be issued to persons going and returning on the same day as follows:—

From Port-of-Spain to La Brea & Cedros ...$3
From San Fernando to ditto do ...$2

Parcels and Light Goods will be conveyed according to the following Regulations:—

Parcels	10 Cents
Hampers	15 "
Boxes (2 Cubic Feet)	20 "
Trunks, Chests, Baskets, Clothing, &c.,	24 "
Barrels	24 "
½ Barrels	15 "

(Non Enumerated Packages in proportion.)

Passengers' Luggage not exceeding 4 Cubic feet in measurement, free; all in excess, and Articles of Furniture, &c., liable to being Charged as per Tariff. Freights according to the above will be payable on the Goods or Packages being put on board the Steamer.

All Goods, Parcels, or Packages to be taken from on board immediately on the Steamers arrival at any point of debarcation and if not so taken will be landed on the Jetties or landing places at the risk of the Shippers.

TURNBULL, STEWART & CO.
1st Aug., 1871.

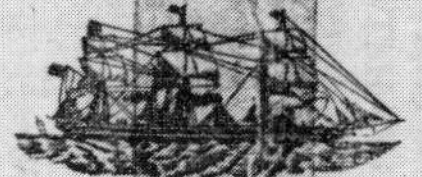

Hamburg - American Packet Company.

Only direct Line from Trinidad to Europe.

THE DAY OF DEPARTURES FROM THIS PORT DIRECT TO EUROPE IS NOW FIXED ON THE

17TH OF EACH MONTH.

OUTWARD ROUTE.		HOMEWARD ROUTE.	
From HAMBURG	the 23rd of each month	From COLON	the 4th—5th of each month.
... GRIMSBY	the 26th	... CURACAO	the 9th
... HAVRE	the 29th	... PUERTO CABELLO	11th
... ST. THOMAS	the 15th	... LAGUAYRA	the 13th
... LAGUAYRA	the 18th	... TRINIDAD	the 17th
... PUERTO CABELLO	19th	In PLYMOUTH	the 1st—2nd
... CURACAO	the 20th	And from there via HAVRE back to HAMBURG.	
in COLON	the 24th		
... COLON	the 26th		
... SANTA MARTA	the 29th		
... SABANILLA	the 31st—1st		
And back to COLON	the 2nd—3rd		

For further particulars apply to

GEROLD & URICH.

South Quay, No. 2,
October 30th, 1871.

CARSONS' PAINT,

PATRONISED BY THE QUEEN,

The British Government, 7,000 of the Nobility & Gentry, The Indian Government, Railway & Canal Companies, The Colonial Governments, Collieries, Iron Masters, &c., For all kinds of

OUT-DOOR WORK,

And is proved, after a test of upwards of 70 years, to surpass any other Paint.

Is especially applicable to Iron Roofing, Park Fencing, Farm and other Buildings, Bridges, Hurdling, Farm Implements, Carts and Wagons, Gates, &c. &c., and all exposed Work, effecting a

Saving of more than 50 per cent.,

as not only is it cheaper in the first place when purchasing, but lasts twice as long as Genuine White Lead, or any other paint, and

CAN BE-LAID ON BY UNSKILLED LABOUR.

It is sold in a fine dry powder, with keep any length of time, and requires neither grinding or staining, but simply to be mixed as per Directions for Use.

COLOURS.

Bright Red	Dark Red
Chocolate	
Purple Brown	
Black	
Bronze Green	
Bright Green	
Deep Green	
Blue	

Prepared Oil Mixture for the Anti Corrosion.
Oils, Turpentine, Varnishes, Brushes, &c.

CARSONS' PAINT,

For Public Edifices, Mansions, Villas, and every kind of Brick, Stone, Compo, &c., is unrivalled, and is the only Paint that will effectually resist the rays of the sun upon Conservatories, Greenhouses, Frames, &c.

Patterns and Testimonials sent Post Free. No Agents

Walter Carson & Sons,
LA BELLE SAUVAGE YARD,
Ludgate Hill, London, E.C.;
AND 21, BACHELOR'S WALK, DUBLIN.

CARSONS' PAINT.

DR. ROBERTS'S CELEBRATED OINTMENT,

CALLED THE
POOR MAN'S FRIEND,

is confidently recommended to the Public as an unfailing remedy for wounds of every description; a certain cure for Ulcerated Sore Legs, even of twenty years' standing; Cuts, Burns, Scalds, Bruises, Chilblains, Scorbutic Eruptions, and Pimples on the Face, Sore and Inflamed Eyes, Sore Heads, Sore Breasts, Piles, Fistula, and Cancerous Humours, and is a Specific for those afflicting Eruptions that sometimes follow vaccination.

DR. ROBERTS'S PILULE ANTISCROPHULÆ, OR ALTERATIVE PILLS, confirmed by sixty years' experience to be one of the best medicines ever compounded for purifying the blood, and assisting Nature in her operations. They are useful in Scrofula, Scorbutic Complaints, Glandular Swellings, particularly those of the Neck, &c. They form a mild and superior Family Aperient, which may be taken at all times without confinement or change of diet.

SOLD BY THE PROPRIETORS,
BEACH & BARNICOTT,
AT THEIR
DISPENSARY, BRIDPORT,
and by all respectable Medicine Vendors.

J. & A. BLYTH,
ENGINEERS,
LONDON.

THE Undersigned, Agents for the above firm, are prepared to receive orders for all kinds of Machinery for Sugar Estates, and are authorized to arrange liberal terms of payment. References, if required, can be given to owners of Estates whose Machinery has been supplied.

HOLLOWAY'S PILLS

HOW TO ENJOY LIFE.

It is only known when the blood is pure, its circulation perfect, and the nerves in good order. The only safe and certain method of expelling all impurities is to take Holloway's Pills, which have the power of cleansing the blood from all noxious matter, expelling all humours which taint or impoverishing it, and thereby purify and invigorate and give general tone to the system. Young or old, robust or delicate, may alike experience their beneficial effects. Myriads affirm that these Pills possess a marvellous power in securing these great secrets of health by purifying and regulating the fluids, and strengthening the solids.

OUR MOTHERS AND DAUGHTERS

The functional irregularities peculiar to the weaker sex are invariably corrected without pain or inconvenience by the use of Holloway's Pills. They are the safest and surest medicine for all diseases incidental to females of all ages, and most precious at the turn of life, or when entering into womanhood.

DEBILITATED CONSTITUTION—BAD HEALTH

In general debility, mental depression, and nervous irritability, there is no medicine which operates so like a charm as these famous Pills. They soothe and strengthen the nerves and system generally, give tone to the stomach, elevate the spirits, and in fact render the patient sensible of a total and most delightful revolution in his whole system. Thousands of persons have testified, that by their use alone, they have been restored to health after all other means had proved unsuccessful.

INDIGESTION AND ITS CURE.

Indigestion with torpidity of the liver is the bane of thousands, who pass away their lives with accumulated sufferings, all of which may be avoided by taking these Pills according to the accompanying directions. They strengthen and invigorate every organ subservient to digestion, and effect a cure without debilitating or exhausting the system; on the contrary they support and conserve the vital principle by a complete purification of the blood.

COUGHS AND COLDS.

This purifying and regulating medicine should be had recourse to during cold, changeable, and wet weather. It is the best cure for hoarseness, sore throats, diphtheria, pleurisy, and asthma; and an infallible remedy for congestion, bronchitis, and inflammation, indeed as a family medicine, they are invaluable for subduing all ailments of young and old of both sexes.

Holloway's Pills are the best remedy known in the world for the following diseases:—

Ague	Female Irregularities	Lumbago	Secondary Symptoms
Asthma	Fevers of all kinds	Piles	Tic-Doloreux
Bilious Complaints	Gout	Rheumatism	Venereal Affections
Blotches on the Skin	Headaches	Retention of Urine	Worms of all kinds
Bowel complaints	Indigestion	Scrofula, or King's Evil	Weakness from whatever cause &c.
	Liver complaints	Sore Throats	
		Stone & Gravel	

The Pills and Ointment are sold at Professor Holloway's Establishment, 533, Oxford-st., London; also by nearly every respectable Vendor of Medicine throughout the Civilized World, in Boxes and Pots, at 1s. 1½d., 2s. 9d., 4s. 6d., 11s., 22s., and 33s. each. The 2s. 9d. size contains three, the 4s. 6d. size six, the 11s. size sixteen, the 22s. size...

YARROW AND HEDLEY'S

Small Steamers and Steam Launches,

BUILT OF WOOD, IRON OR STEEL,

30 feet long	seats for 14 persons	complete from £145.
37 feet long	seats for 20 persons	complete from £195.
43 feet long	seats for 30 persons	complete from £360.
50 feet long	seats for 60 persons	complete from £650.

&c., &c., &c.

Steamers up to 45 feet in length can be transported on a ships deck complete, and ready for immediate use on arrival.

The above may be used for conveying passengers, carrying cargo or as tugs.

The total working expenses of a steamer 45 feet long, amount to 15s. a-day in England; the consumption of fuel being about 6 cwt., and a man and a boy the crew required. Paddle and Screw Steamers specially designated for river navigation, having a very shallow draught of water.

MACHINERY SUPPLIED FOR BOATS BUILT ABROAD.

YARROW AND HEDLEY,
ENGINEERS AND BUILDERS, ISLE OF DOGS, POPLAR, LONDON.

ORDERS WILL BE RECEIVED BY
SCOTT & CO.
Agents.

RIGAUD & Co's PERFUMERY

45, RUE DE RICHELIEU, PARIS.

Patronised by the French Court and extensively used in all Fashionable Circles.

GENUINE YLANGYLANG PREPARATIONS

Offered genuine and characterised with any other sold under the same name, Messrs. RIGAUD and Co., being the only original importers.

YLANGYLANG

SOAP	POMADE
OIL	COLD CREAM
POWDER	COSMETIC
TOILET WATER	

EXTRACT OF YLANGYLANG
MANILLA BOUQUET

The two favorite perfumes for the handkerchief.

KANANGA

The fashionable Perfume, just imported by Messrs. Rigaud and Co.

Sole Agents for the Island of Trinidad:
C. DESINAIS & CO.

GRIMAULT and Co's

Chemists to the Court,
45, RUE DE RICHELIEU, PARIS.

FRENCH MEDECINES

WOMEN'S AND CHILDREN'S DISEASES
GRIMAULT AND Co's

SYRUP of IODIZED HORSE RADISH

Patronised for more than twenty years by the Paris Physicians. Cures lymphatism, rachitism, scrofula, congestion of the glands of the neck, paleness and dabbiness of the flesh, loss of appetite, weakness of constitution, the various eruptions on the face, boils, pimples, and itchings.—It is the best remedy against consumption, and it is the most powerful depurative known.

Dr. LERAS'
SOLUBLE PHOSPHATE of IRON

Clear as spring water and tasteless; has the advantage over all ferruginous preparations of containing Iron and Phosphorus, which are the elements of blood. It cures chlorosis, pains in the stomach, difficult digestions, dismenorrhea, anemia, general debility and poorness of the blood, and agrees especially with the most delicate stomachs.

LUNG DISEASES
GRIMAULT and Co's

SYRUP of HYPOPHOSPHITE of LIME

It is the best and the most rational of all remedies against consumption. Under its influence the cough abates, the night sweats cease, and the patient rapidly recovers health. It gives the same results in cases of coughs, catarrhs, hooping-coughs and influenza. In comparing this syrup with the other and under the same name, it will be easy to recognise the superiority of this preparation.

Therefore, to avoid any substitution, please to require on the bottle the signature: Grimault and Co.

NERVOUS HEAD-ACHE & NEURALGIA
GRIMAULT AND Co's

GUARANA

A single powder of this natural vegetable production is sufficient to cure instantly the most violent sick headache. It is the most valuable remedy against diarrhea.

GRIMAULT AND Co's
DIGESTIVE POWDERS, PILLS & ELIXIR
of **PEPSINE**

Of certain effect against nausea, pituita, heart-burn, gastritis, gastralgia, children's diarrhea, inflammation of the mucous coats of the stomach and bowels, vomiting during pregnancy, pyrosis, jaundice, etc.

Sole Agents for the Island of Trinidad:
J. POLLONAIS & CO.

For Sale.

THE HOUSE situated at the Corner of Queen and Fre...

LUMBER AND WINE.

THE Subscriber offers for sale, at very moderate rates, a Cargo of Choice WHITE PINE BOARDS, now landing, and 2-inch WHITE PINE PLANKS, of unusual width, suitable for Sugar Coolers and good carpenters' work.

Also: 3-inch SPRUCE SCANTLING; 1-inch SPRUCE BOARDS and 3-inch SPRUCE PLANKS, well adapted for Bridges, etc.

He is also prepared to supply, at cheap rates, to his good Customers, some of the best FRENCH WINES, from the well-known House of Messrs. JULES HUE TH. LAMARQUE & Co., of Bordeaux.

N.B.—The best prices always paid for the Good Qualities of SPANISH MAIN COCOA.

EUGENE ESTAVARD.

South Quay, July 26.

NOTICE.

Consulado General de los E.E. UU. de Venezuela en las Antillas Británicas.

Puerto España, Julio 19 de 1872.

SE hace saber á los Venezolanos y al comercio en general que las facturas, sobordos y conocimientos que se traigan á este Consulado para ser certificados, deben llevar todos los requisitos que demarcan las leyes de Hacienda de Venezuela, según el sistema métrico decimal adoptado; y que al efecto de ser bien examinados aquellos documentos deberán quedar hasta dos horas en el Consulado, antes de ser entregados al Capitan del respectivo buque, único empleado á quien se entregaran los citados documentos.

Á la llegada todo buque Venezolano á este puerto debera su capitan ó patron presentar al Consul ó su Secretario los papeles del buque con una declaracion de su cargamento y pasajeros.

Horas de oficina de las 11 á las 4 de la tarde.

Dr. D. MONTBRUN,
Consul General de Venezuela en las Antillas Británicas.

RECEIVED

Per Royal Mail Steamer.

CHAMBERS' STANDARD READING BOOKS, 2nd, 3rd and 4th;
Sullivan's English Grammar, &c.;
Currie's do. do.
United Presbyterian Hymn Books with Psalms, various sizes; and other Books too numerous to detail.

STATIONERY:

Note Paper and Envelopes, fine and thick;
Mourning Note Paper and Envelopes;
Pott Paper; Foolscap at different prices;
Ledgers; Journals; Cash and Day Books;
Quire Books; Ink Erasers;
Steel Pens, all makers; Elastic Bands;
Antoine's Celebrated Copying and Writing Inks;

HABITS AND PECULIARITIES OF THE LOWER CLASSES

From Guide to Trinidad
J.H. Collens

The term 'lower classes' might, of course, include all of humble origin, whether Creoles, Coolies, Chinese, or what not. It is intended in the present instance to let it apply, unless otherwise stated, to the native portion of the community.

It must often strike visitors as being a remarkable feature, that with a large labouring class of black people, West Indian planters are still compelled to import labourers all the way from the East Indies. I will, in a few words, endeavour to give the reason.

The black population may be roughly divided as regards estate work into three classes:—

No. 1. Those who will not work.
"   2. Those who do little or no work.
"   3. Those who work regularly.

No. 1. Those who will not condescend to estate labour generally find some good soil where water is handy, and build there a little shanty of timber with roseau partition laths, thatching it with palm leaves. Here if the spirit moves them they now and then dig an hour or two, planting maize, tanias, bananas,—anything that gives no trouble. In the early morning or on a bright moonlight night they go out with an old fowling-piece and a lean, mangy, half-starved cur, to pick up a stray deer, quenck or lap, or it may be a 'wild-tame' (a neighbour's fowl). If they are lucky enough to get more than they can eat, they smoke the remainder and sell it to the nearest planter.

No. 2 class also go in for a 'squatting' life, but in the dry season they emerge from their obscurity to take part in some well-paid work which they like, such as driving cane carts, etc.

No. 3 or the drones are generally hard-working, but otherwise of primitive habits. Of the older men very few can read and still less write. No man ever makes a mistake as to the amount of pay he should receive: rough notches on a stick, or an accumulation of pebbles in the corner of the one room he calls his house, being his perfectly infallible system of computation.

On one occasion on pay-day an old black woman threw down her money with a highly indignant air, exclaiming "No! me wuk 24 day, de Lord see me mark ebbery day behind de do (door) wid de coal-tick!"

The creole labourer, especially in the country districts, drinks rum to a frightful extent, with the result that at holiday seasons, broken heads are knocking about as freely as if the scene were Donnybrook Fair or Limerick Races rather than Trinidad.

In my capacity as Dominie I have continually had to check the disposition of my pupils in Trinidad to use long-winded words and high-flown phrases. Boys and young men spend hours poring over dictionaries, simply to try and master the meanings of words which for length might be measured by the yard. They positively do not believe in the sweet simplicity of the Saxon tongue. Only today in the street one man talking to another in the usual loud tone, said while passing me "I estimate it to be my particular and elementary duty." I should like to have discovered what duty combined those two essentials, but the speaker was out of hearing. I have heard, too, a woodcutter gravely tell his employer, "it was with the utmost difficulty that I managed to disintegrate those logs, sir."

The lower classes are very impressionable with regard to religion, and to outward appearance become earnest and attached members of their church. Whether their devotion is real or feigned I do not pretend to say, probably they are neither better nor worse than their superiors in social position. There is one thing that I am quite sure of, that is, their liberality to their church. Whether their donation be in labour or in coin of the realm, they give ungrudgingly.

They are superstitious almost beyond conception, combining in the country districts, a mixture of shrewdness and credulity, that is as absurd as it is

Trinidad Folklore

Harry Pitts and Alfred Cadallo

Folklore has been described as 'the legendary traditions that prevail among a people respecting themselves or their original beliefs and practices'. The students of local folklore must therefore ask the question; just who are the 'people' of Trinidad? The answer is, of course, rather disturbing; there are representatives of many different racial groups who consider themselves, with good reason, to be true Trinidadians yet who had little or nothing in common 150 years ago.

Is the folklore of the Island, then, comprised of a number of traditions peculiar to the different elements—Indians, African, French, Spanish and so on—or have the original beliefs and practices of the various groups become welded together over the years to produce folklore which is common to all, or the majority, of the population? The many interesting points which arise from this question have never been seriously explored or debated, but it is generally accepted that whatever traditions may remain with individual

Papa Bois.   *Illustration— Avril Turner.*

The old story tellers, The Raconteurs were the ones who kept alive the Oral Tradition of the Patois speaking Creole Culture. Photograph — Mrs. Hélène Farfan.

race groups, there has emerged a distinct pattern which can be described as truly Trinidadian.

Like the Trinidad folk-song—the calypso—the Island's folklore is predominantly of African origin, flavoured with French and to a lesser degree, Spanish and English influences. In keeping with well-recognised African traits, the picture is full of colour and decorated with a wealth of detail. Closely enmeshed with this is a vast amount of material which might be said to belong more strictly to a study of religious practices, and Shango, Rada and other religious or semi-religious cults of African origin have undoubtedly contributed much to the Island's folklore; many of the supernatural folklore figures possess characteristics which are identical with those of African deities. Indeed, it is extremely difficult to draw a dividing line between the strictly religious elements and what may be described as "legendary traditions".

Whatever the source, the old beliefs are still taken very seriously by a great number of Trinidadians.

inconsistent. Smart and quick enough in business matters, they can drive a good bargain as well as any Yorkshireman or Scotchman, but if they once form the impression that occult influences are working insidiously against them, any argument which you may adduce to the contrary will have about as much effect as the boring of an iron target with a wooden skewer. A jet or black bead bracelet for instance must be placed round the wrist of an infant to keep off the 'evil eye,' which might cause it to pine away. If your rooster being of a sociable turn of mind, steps upon your threshold and gives vent to his feelings by a lusty crow, all will be well provided he faces the house during his exclamation, but if he turns his back to the interior while crowing, it is a sure sign that somebody in the house will be shortly carried to his last resting place. If your babe suffers, as young children always do, from hiccough, two little strips of wet paper placed in the form of a cross on its forehead will bring speedy relief. Should a child in the course of its play stumble across that spiteful little animal the centipede, the mere repetition of the formula 'St. Peter, St. Paul,' several times, will render the creature powerless to do any harm. If while you are going on important business you should have the misfortune to strike the left foot,— 'stump' is the Trinidad way of putting it—against an unperceived obstacle, (*coiné le mauvais pied*, in Patois), it is all up as regards the success of the business, and you may as well right-about-turn and wend your way home. On the other hand, if it is your right foot that 'stumps,' it is a capital portent, and things look promising ahead.

On no account step over a coffin if you happen to meet one lying across the road. It has never fallen to my lot to see anything of this description in such an unusual place, and if I did, I do not think I should feel at all disposed to step over it, if there were any alternative, who would? It is impossible, however, to over-estimate the evil results which might ensue if such an indiscretion were committed. Of course, it must be clearly understood the coffin is not a reality, it is placed there by the jumbies, and if you deal with it respectfully, and with becoming reverence, by gently putting it on one side, it will at once vanish into space, which I think is about the wisest thing it could do.

I ought to stop, but I have one more example, this one so ridiculous and preposterous that, like the perplexed Dragoons in 'Patience,' I must fain leave you

A fashionable young lady of the 1880's. Photograph — Mrs. Hélène Farfan.

PAPA BOIS

Perhaps the most lovable, and at the same time feared, character of Trinidad folklore, Papa Bois is the protector of the forest animals. He is known by many names — including 'Maître Bois' and 'Daddy Bouchon' ('hairy man') — and very serious belief in his existence extends throughout the entire island. Indeed, he can lay strong claims to being the most popular and 'real' figure of our legends.

Physically, however, Papa Bois is a creature of many descriptions; so much so that the artist was forced to compromise, and

explains that 'Papa Bois appears in so many different forms and fashions that in the painting, while I gave him Negroid features and a Spanish nose, I had to remember that he sometimes appeared as a deer, that he wore ragged clothes, was hairy, and though very old, was extremely strong and muscular'. The portrayal is therefore a composite of many descriptions.

The popular concept of Papa Bois' origin is that he is an old, retired hunter who repented of his past and disappeared into the forest to make amends by looking after the creatures which he had previously pursued. He lives in a secret cave where he tends the to 'explain it if you can.' You will be told that certain malevolent individuals in league with the Evil One, and called *Soucouyans,* have an unnatural and indelicate propensity for casting off their skin, which they usually conceal in or under a Chocolate Mortar. Divested of epidermis they have the marvellous faculty of flying through the air, resembling at the time balls of fire. They then, vampire-like, suck the blood of those against whom they have any animosity. I am sure you will be glad to know of a way of overcoming or counteracting the machinations of such a dire and uncanny enemy. There are two plans, one is to sprinkle salt upon the cast-off skin, should you meet with it, (there's the rub!); or when you are expecting a visit from the 'thing,' strew the floor around your bed with rice. This the *Soucouyan,* by some mysterious law, will be compelled to pick up grain by grain, thus affording you an opportunity for slaying or otherwise disposing of the monstrosity.

These are not a hundredth part of the many queer notions that prevail in sunny Trinidad among certain classes in the latter part of the nineteenth century. I could with ease fill a book with them, but I refrain, and simply give two or three that have occurred to me while writing, in order to convey a suitable idea of the credulity of the people. It is a waste of time to attempt to reason with them about the improbability and inconsistency of some of their beliefs. They meet you with proofs indubitable and incontrovertible. After some story that sounds like an old legend, only much more unlikely, you say, "Oh, that is absurd." "But sir, I saw it myself," is the reply, and you are doubled up.

They are firm believers in 'Obeah', a kind of Fetishism very much in vogue amongst the African Radas, and introduced into Trinidad probably by Rada slaves. The obeah-man, or priest as he is generally called, makes a fetish or image of wood, with a moulded clay head, glass eyes, human hair and teeth. These priests are dreaded beyond every thing by the common people on account of their assumed mystic power. When a peasant contractor, stepping out of his hut one morning, finds a sealed bottle lying at the entrance, containing abominations as horrid as those of Macbeth's witches, his heart sinks within him, for he feels that calamities dire and untold are looming ahead. Somebody, one of his enemies, is working 'obeah' on him. His children will get 'yaws', his cow dry up, his crops will fail, goodness

A fashionable young lady of the 1880's. Photograph — Mrs. Hélène Farfan.

wounded animals, but is sometimes seen in the villages as an old man, dressed in rags, purchasing medicines (for his veterinary practice) from the drug stores.

In the forests he blows a cow's horn to warn his friends of the approach of hunters, although he does not usually object to a reasonable 'bag'. But beware of Papa Bois if you try to make a business out of hunting or shoot animals indiscriminately! If you are lucky he will appear to you and issue a warning which, if unheeded, is followed by more serious action.

This may take the form of his turning into a deer and luring you into the depths of the forest where he finally disappears, leaving you hopelessly lost. Several days later, you will be found, half-dead with hunger and exhaustion, wandering in circles only a stone's throw from a well-beaten track which somehow or the other you were unable to find. On other occasions he may lecture the hunter severely and order a 'fine' of several pounds of fish (Papa Bois never eats meat) to be brought back to him. So awe-inspiring is Papa Bois that few, if any, hunters have ever returned to the forest after such an experience, either to pay the 'fine' or to hunt! It is also told that for serious offences Papa Bois may, by hideous threats, extract from the

The Belmont Playhouse. It would be interesting to know where in Belmont this building was situated. Photograph — O. Mavrogordato.

Ligahoo. Illustration — Alfred Cadallo.

hunter a promise to marry 'Mama Dlo' ('Mama de l'Eau') — a horrible female supernatural creature — on his next visit to the forest. Such a return trip has, of course, never, never been known to happen!

One thing is quite certain: there are hundreds of ex-hunters in Trinidad who have been scared away from the forests by 'Papa Bois'. This helps considerably to preserve supplies of 'wild meat' for the wise and conscientious hunter.

LIGAHOO

The 'Ligahoo' (or 'Loup Garou') is the Trinidad werewolf. He is usually associated with an old magic-dealing man of the district who is both respected and feared, not only for his ability to change his form to that of a vicious animal, but also for his power over nature. If his wrath is aroused he will lay potent curses on crops and persons but if treated with consideration he can extend effective protection.

The English Pharmacy owned by Alex Shaing and Co. on the Corner of Prince and Frederick Street, Port of Spain. Photograph — O. Mavrogordato.

In Codallo's paintings the 'Ligahoo' is shown surrounded by the tools of his trade — animals' heads, bones and impressive volumes — while outside his window a frightening procession passes by. To the would-be-curious, the sight of a coffin being carried to the clank of chains and in the protection of a gigantic 'Phantome' is sufficient to send them scurrying back to their beds with prayers.

If by any chance the coffin and its gruesome attendants were designed to facilitate the uninterrupted transportation of 'bush rum', however, the effect would be equally successful. Actually, one such technique is recorded as having been regularly used in the vicinity of St. James for several years until discovered and stopped by unbelieving policemen.

A large and important part played by the 'Ligahoo' is often his role as chief 'Obeah Man' (witch doctor) of his village. He does a nice trade in charms and advice which he dispenses with an air of wisdom and secrecy

Two good-looking Creole ladies pose in this Felix Morin photograph taken in the late 1890's. Felix Morin was a noted photographer in his day and operated a studio on the corner of Frederick and Hart Streets. Photograph — Hélène Farfan.

which seldom fails to impress, while the mere mention of his name is sufficient to quiet the most badly behaved child.

DUENNES

Like the elves of other countries, the Duennes of Trinidad are responsible for a great deal of mischief. Traditionally, they are the "spirits of children who died before being 'christened' " (baptized) and as such they are fated to roam the forests of the island practising their wide repertoire of pranks which they chiefly aim at the more fortunate living children.

Duennes are said to have their feet turned backward and no faces. They wear large mushroom-shaped straw hats, and have no sex, and their hair is worn in the form of 'pig-tails' or 'dada' hair. By a majority opinion the Duennes wear no clothes although they have been described in some districts as sporting transparent, red, nightgown-like dresses.

By the use of several tricks, they try to

Frederick Street looking North, from the premises of Felix Morin the Photographer. An old photograph Brunswick Square (Woodford) still has its old railings. In the distance is a mule tram. Photograph — O.J. Mavrogordato.

entice the children from across the river by sounding convincing cries of 'whoop' as commonly employed by Trinidadian children in their games of hide and seek. The common employment of these imps is to lure children into the heart of the forest and there abandon them, leaving them to their own resources. This is, of course, the logical explanation for the number of children who disappear from country homes and are discovered many hours later deep in the woods and in a state of near collapse.

For some unexplained reason, the Duennes also exhibit a marked dislike of dogs, and hunters will relate how their dogs have been misled by the calls of the Duennes and lured far away from their master never to be recovered. Smart hunters, realising the false call in time, will summon their dogs back and break the spell by saying a Spanish prayer over them.

MAMA DLO

Mama Dlo' or 'Mama Dglo' whose name is derived from the French 'maman de l' eau' which means 'mother of the water' is one of the lesser known personalities of Trinidad and Tobago folklore.

knows what may not befall him. One thing is certain, all will go wrong with him, unless he can counteract or overcome the evil. So he goes to some wretched old humbug who professes to have the mysterious power, and fees him heavily to prepare a charm which shall have the desired effect. I need hardly say that the Police authorities and the law come down 'hot' on these obeah quacks, but such is the hold that the superstition has on the minds of the ignorant, that nothing will shake their faith in it, and it will take years, if not generations, to eradicate it. I have been told that one of these obeah men has made quite a considerable sum of money by practising his art; he has his little harem, and lives *en prince*.

A Doctor in a remote district had one day assembled a number of children for vaccination. In the course of his operations he came to a little girl, and the following conversation ensued with the person bringing her:

Doctor: "Are you the child's mother?"

Woman: "Yes, sir,—is me darter."

Doctor: "And what is your name?"

Woman: "Is me name?"

Doctor (rather impatiently for he is many miles from home, and is getting hungry): "Yes, I asked you what is your name?"

Woman: (hesitatingly): "Dey does caal me Sal."

Doctor: "Well, Sal what?"

Woman (assuringly, but with a suspicious side-glance at a neighbour who is intently taking all in): "Dey does allus' caal me Sal."

Doctor (getting desperate): "Oh! botheration, will you tell me your proper name or not?"

Woman (with much reluctance approaching Doctor, whispers in the lowest possible tone of voice): "Delphine Segard."

Doctor (with intense disgust): "Then why couldn't you say so?"

However, my medical friend now bears these little passages with more equanimity, for he has gained experience, and knows that the reason why the unwilling woman was so reluctant to utter her name aloud, was that she believed she had an enemy in the room who would take advantage of the circumstance if she got hold of her true name, and would work her all manner of harm. It is a fact that these people sometimes actually forget the names of their near relations from hearing and using them so little.

This reminds me of another little incident. A man selling fowls, brought some to a planter of my acquaintance. A bargain was struck, and my friend liking the man's appearance asked him his name.

Fowl Vendor: "Bully, dey does caal me, but I is name Ralph Woodford Jones."

Planter: "Ah! I have a man working for me of that name, Samuel Jones, is he any relation to you?"

Fowl Vendor (shaking his head with no sign of intelligence): "No, 'Bouge.' "

Planter: "His nickname is Manicou, is he anything to you?"

Fowl Vendor (beaming): "Eh! Eh! He me brudder's son!"

Perhaps one reason why the lowest class of peasantry make so little use of proper names, is that, in reality, they are not entitled to them. The rites of marriage and baptism are so frequently ignored, and the sexes intermingle so indiscriminately, that it is small wonder if the offspring grow up nameless.

It is natural that a people so simple in their minds. should believe in spirits. I do not mean the alcoholic, though they certainly do not reject these, but the ethereal. Nothing would induce them to pass through a burial ground at midnight for fear of meeting with 'Jumbies', the ghosts of the departed. However, this repugnance is not confined to Trinidad only, nor to the lower classes.

Your West Indian working man has an inordinate love of public ceremonies. A Baptism, Wedding and Funeral rank with them as good, better, best. When your groom marries the lady who does the woman in the next street the honour of cooking for her, he must have his

A hideous creature, her lower half takes the form of a 'houilla' (wheel-a) or anaconda. She is sometimes thought to be the lover of Papa Bois, and old hunters tell stories of coming upon them in the 'High Woods'. They also tell of hearing a loud, cracking sound which is said to be the sound made by her tail as she snaps it on the surface of a mountain pool or a still lagoon.

Mortal men who commit crimes against the forest, like burning down trees or indiscriminately putting animals to death or fouling the rivers could find themselves married to her for life, both this one and the one to follow.

Sometimes she takes the form of a beautiful woman 'singing silent songs on still afternoons, sitting at the water's edge in the sunlight, lingering for a golden moment, a flash of green - gone. Nothing but a big Morte Bleu, rising in the sun beams. - "Did you see a fish jump?"

"Yes, but it did not go back in again!"

If you were to meet Mamma Dlo in the forest and wish to escape her, take off your left shoe, turn it upside down and immediately leave the scene, walking backwards until you reach home.

SOUCOUYANT

The Soucouyant - 'A ball of flame, along she came flying without a wind' was how the Soucouyant of Saint D'eau Island was described. She is the old woman who lives alone at the end of the village road, seldom seen, her

carriage and pair (and not one only but several); he puts on his topper, swell frock coat, and light lavender gloves, and leads his blushing bride to the altar with the airs and graces of a lord. However, they may well be pardoned this little bit of vanity, since in the majority of cases they dispense with the church's rites and simply consort. Immorality is unhappily gross, flagrant and shameful—or rather shameless. You will scarcely find· a domestic servant who has not had two or three children, and yet she has no lawful husband. You expostulate, perhaps, with your cook about her mode of life. She excuses herself by saying that she and her 'keeper' cannot afford the marriage ceremony. "Oh, but," say you, "you can surely walk to church, and the parson will then marry you for nothing." With a deeply injured look she replies, "Oh, madam, how you want me to walk to de church door?" It must be either the whole hog or none with them. The men, however, have another and perhaps better reason for not binding themselves by any civil or religious form. They candidly assert that a paramour behaves much better than a wife would, because she knows if she didn't she would soon get her ticket!

I have spoken of funerals as being a source of pleasure to them. It is a custom here amongst all classes when any individual dies, to send a circular round inviting the presence of all and everybody to assist in the obsequies. This seems odd to our English notions, but one soon gets accustomed to it. No matter how humble was the station in life of the departed, you will probably see a hundred or so of his neighbours and acquaintances soberly following him to the Cemetery in all their sombre bravery. Wakes and sometimes the anniversaries of wakes are kept up, either by Psalm-singing of a very dismal character, or in a more objectionable manner. Occasionally, the singing is of a decidedly secular, not to say profane, turn. Games are indulged in, and—when the rum-bottle has been circulating pretty often—a fight or two varies the monotony. I have known an individual of straitened circumstances go scrupulously into mourning six or seven months after the decease of a friend, not

having been able to afford it earlier; this is showing respect with a vengeance.

The majority of the domestic servants, male and female are Barbadians, natives of 'Bimshir', attracted hither by the higher wages that Trinidad offers. They are an exceedingly cute and smart race, and as not a few of them may have left their country for their country's good, it is as well to be wide awake in all your dealings with them. I am convinced they must be devout believers in the philosophy of the celebrated Tichborne Claimant, Arthur Orton, who pencilled in his pocket-book:–

> 'Some men has money and no brains,
> Some men has brains and no money,
> Them as has money and no brains
> Were made for them as has brains and no money.'

It must be admitted, however, that they are willing enough, and when properly looked after, make excellent servants. *Apropos* of this, on one occasion, during an Amateur Dramatic Performance at the Prince's Building in this town, a comical episode took place. All the actors were on the stage playing, save one who was waiting his turn in the wings. This individual, who was capitally made up as a feeble old man, suddenly disappeared, and we heard a slight scuffle, which terminated very soon, and our decrepit friend appeared again just in time to take up his part, but with his hoary locks rather dishevelled and his cuffs blood-stained. He had observed, through a chink in the scenery that a Barbadian servant of one of the performers was quietly improving the shining hour by rifling the pockets of the clothes left in the dressing-room. When interrupted in this interesting occupation by a miserable-looking old party, he showed fight; but much to his surprise and discomfiture, he received two or three powerful arguments in the nose and eyes, and before he received his presence of mind, he was in the hands of the Police. Next day our nimble and wiry little son of Thespis being, like 'Richard', himself again, gave evidence in the Court which led to the prisoner's conviction. The funniest part of it is that the defendant did not recognize in the chief witness the

house always closed up as she sleeps away the day.

As evening draws near and the bats replace the birds in the ancient trees that seem to lean over her miserable shack, she stirs and sheds her old and wrinkled skin, which she deposits into a mortar that she hides carefully away. Now, as a glowing ball of flame, she rises up through the roof and with a shrill cry that sets the village dogs to howling, she flies through the night in search of a victim and she would suck his 'life-blood' from him clean.

As the blessed day dawns, she makes a beeline through the forest for her home, finds the mortar with her wretched skin and proceeds to put it on, - but something's wrong, it burns like fire, it seems to shrink and slide away, "skin, kin, kin, you na no

me, you na no me", she sings, crooning softly, pleading to the wrinkled, dreadful thing. "You na no me, old skin." Then, with horror, she realizes the dreadful thing that has been done: The village boys and men have filled her skin with coarse salt and pepper and will soon come and get her, with a drum of boiling tar, the Priest and his silver Cross, the church bells - and then, the end.

If you wish to discover who the Soucouyant in your village is, empty 100 lbs of rice at the village crossroads where she will be compelled to pick them up, one grain at a time - that is how you'll know the Soucouyant.

venerable gentleman of the previous night, and begged earnestly to be allowed to bring a counter-charge of assault against a wicked old man who 'beat him too bad.'

The Trinidadians are very quick at learning, whether it be in the school or in the workshop. In fact they are ready and sharp enough at most things to which they give their minds, though their natural adroitness has a tendency to make them smatterers: A young fellow will sometimes essay quite a variety of trades and employments before settling himself finally. A country schoolmaster came under my notice, whom I knew to have been recently a tailor; he confided to me that his proper trade (profession he called it), was that of shoemaker. Such a readiness to adapt oneself to circumstances must be a convenience. 'Jack of all trades and master of none', is rather applicable in these cases. At the same time they often make first-rate workmen, and have any amount of physical endurance.

This roving disposition is even more manifested in domestic servants: Of course, a housemaid may easily become a nurse or butler, but when she essays to try her 'prentice hand at the culinary art, it is very far from being a certainty that her attempts will be crowned with success.

A bachelor acquaintance had a cook of this calibre. He had impressed upon her that he had an affection (plebeian but English) for onions, especially in conjunction with beef-steak. A nod is as good as a wink to a blind horse. One day a friend was invited to share the frugal board. Here was a golden opportunity. Cook made a superlative effort, and as far as the soup and meat portion of the fare was concerned, out-did herself. Then with a triumphant air, she brought in the *chef-d'œuvre*—a custard! The guest partook and swallowed one mouthful, with laudable presence of mind, but with mental pain and anguish only too clearly betrayed by the spasm passing over his face. My friend the host had not such Spartan fortitude; at the first and only mouthful, he rushed spluttering to the window, and—. The prevailing flavour of the custard was ONIONS; the guest, who is by

La Diablesse. Illustration — Stuart Habn.

LA DIABLESSE

La Diablesse, the devil woman of Trinidad and Tobago folklore, is sometimes personified as an old crone - 'the sound of chains mingling with the rustle of her petticoat' - who steps forth with her cloven hoof from behind a tree on a lonely road at dusk to lure some unsuspecting passerby to his death or perhaps to madness.

Sometimes she appears as a tall, handsome Creole woman who with swinging gait and erect stature, passes through a cane or cocoa field at noon and catches the eye of a man who then proceeds to follow her, and, never being able to catch up with her - her feet, they hardly touch the ground -, finds himself lost, bewildered, far from home and is never himself again.

She may have a bag of bones, grave yard dirt and shells, she may cast a spell and be perceived as young and desirable, her rich perfume blending with the smell of damp and decaying things. Although she may appear young, she will be dressed in the ancient costume of these islands: A brilliant madras turban, chemise with half sleeves and much embroidery and lace, zepingue tremblant (trembling pins of gold), and all the finery of the by-gone days. But do not be deceived my friend, or ever be misled, for an encounter with Madam La Diablesse will be sure to leave you dead.

If you feel you may encounter a La Diablesse on your way home from a party - take off all your clothes, turn them inside out

A fashionable young lady of the 1880's. Photograph — Mrs. Hélène Farfan.

out and put them on again, and this will surely protect you from a La Diablesse.

THE STORY OF THE GIANTS

Once upon a time there were two giants, Zolee and Kalpet, whose tremendous appetites were devastating the whole countryside. After eating all the cattle, goats, sheep and vegetables from a village they would retire to the deep forest to sleep.

The king of the land was very worried about this situation, especially as his soldiers were terrified of the giants, until one day his beautiful daughter, Fiffin, came up with an idea.

The very next day the king announced that anyone producing the heads of Zolee and Kalpet would win the hand of the Princess and half of his kingdom. For quite some time no one brave enough came forward and the people got poorer and hungrier until one day a young man declared that he would attempt it.

The whole population turned out to see the hero, and was shocked to see this young man armed with a small bag of heavy stones. They laughed him to scorn and gave him up for dead. But Basil, which was the young man's name, had his plan and soon located the sleeping place of the giants by their loud snores.

Climbing a large tree whose branches

way of being a wag afterwards relating the story to me, irreverently and with unbecoming levity told me that mine host 'cussed hard'. Probably he did.

Various fêtes and holidays are observed. All classes of course celebrate Christmas with rejoicings, and let off any amount of gunpowder and superfluous steam in the form of fireworks. On Christmas Eve, from sunset to midnight it is a continual succession of bangs, pops, and fizzes. The French element, like many of the Scotch make more of a holiday of New Year's Day, *le jour de l'an*. Corpus Christi is a great Roman Catholic fête, processions and services being the order of the day. Trinity Sunday ought to be a specially important festival in both Roman and Anglican Churches in this island, but little is made of it. The Africans even pay more attention to it, as they hold high jinks on this day and Trinity Monday. Good Friday is, of course, marked by solemn services, the 'Tenebres' of the Roman Catholics being particularly impressive. A wretched custom exists here among the street *gamins* of parading the streets with 'ra-ras', rattles of the old Greenwich Fair type, making a hideous noise which they say is to drive away the Devil. The Portuguese on this day too make an effigy of Judas Iscariot, the betrayer, and stone it. During the days of Carnival the lower classes and even the sedate Spaniards have a high old time of it, but we will revert to this later. The Coolies have their chief fun at 'Hosein'. At whatever season of the year the visitor comes to Trinidad he will generally find something novel and unusual in this line, unless he is as travelled as one of Quida's heroes.

To the ignorant Asiatic the word Christmas conveys, as might be expected, simply the notion of 'holiday-time.' At the hearing of a case in Court one day, when a Coolie was asked if a certain event happened at Christmiss. "Kissmiss?" he replied, "Who man Kissmiss? White man Kissmiss? Coolie man Kissmiss? Chinee man Kissmiss?" ("Whose Christmas? White Man's, Coolie's, or Chinese?") The last named Christmas refers to the Feast of Lanterns, a great time with the Celestials.

The Race days of Port of Spain are alluded to elsewhere as being practically a public holiday for all classes; even the stolid, money-grubbing Coolies come from all parts clad in their best, to see the fun.

We have one or two characters, one in particular 'General Dan', a harmless, half-witted fellow who dresses himself as a soldier, sometimes a Hussar, sometimes a subaltern of the Rifle Brigade, and occasionally a felicitous combination of both. He attends all weddings and funerals of any consequences, stationing himself at the front door or gate, and assuming an air of authority, he performs constabulary or military duty. Goodness knows how he hears of everything, but there is not a Fête or Ceremony in the vicinity of Port of Spain at which the 'General' does not lend his assistance.

Patois,—a compound of bad French and English, with a flavour of Spanish—is spoken not only in Trinidad, but even in Grenada and St. Lucia. Some years ago Mr. J.J. Thomas, a native, with considerable ability, wrote and published his 'Creole Grammar', in which he endeavoured to elevate the Patois to the dignity of a language. Certainly, this *lingua* is an expressive one. It is sparkling with humour, masterly for sarcasm and ridicule, magnificent for abuse, but I am afraid it is wanting in elegance of diction. Some of the Creole proverbs are very witty and pregnant with meaning. Thus, quoting from Mr. Thomas's book:—

'You doègt pas sa pouend pices.'
(A single finger cannot catch fleas.)
'Dèièr chein, cé 'chein,' douvant chein, cé 'missier chien.' '
(Behind dog's back, it is 'dog,' but before dog, it is 'Mister dog.')

Coolie English, too, is in itself a sort of patois of another kind, and it needs a little apprenticeship for you to understand when your newly-engaged Oriental servant tells you, 'Gi um pitty mangy, massa, me sabby do um all something dis side,' that he intends to convey to you that if you give him his food he can undertake any work you may require.

The French, Spanish and Portuguese classes usually speak their own tongue in their home circles, but nearly all understand English, and converse tolerably fluently in it. In this respect the French particularly beat us hollow, and as I have a pretty strong conviction that a

stretched over the giants, he hid among its leaves. He then took out a large stone and let it fall on the forehead of Zolee, who at once jumped up and accused Kalpet of hitting him. Both got angry and argued for a while, but fell asleep again.

But Basil took another large stone from his bag and dropped it this time on Kalpet's forehead, and again a heated argument started. After the fourth stone had been dropped the giants were so mad at each other that they picked up their clubs and the real battle started. The fight, which lasted a whole day, was so terrible that people for miles around could hear the snapping of large trees and the thud of heavy blows, not to mention the snarling and grunting of the great antagonists as they struck at each other. At last, after an interminable struggle silence fell on the field

of battle—both the giants were dead.

Only then did Basil descend from the tree, and with his cutlass, severed the heads of Zolee and Kalpet which he presented to the King and claimed both the beautiful Princess and his share of the kingdom. This herculean deed was applauded by all and was followed by a week of carnival and rejoicing.

Blue bottles: They are more remarkable in Southern Trinidad than in, say, the Santa Cruz peasant area. They are generally Milk of Magnesia bottles, and on a trip through Moruga, every garden and holding seemed to abound in these blue glass flowers.
Blue is used in rural districts to avert the evil eye or "malyeux". Blue bottles are placed in gardens to encourage a fortuitous crop, and the blue that is used in washing is also used on doors and windows to ensure the spiritual safety of the inhabitants of that home.
A note on "Malyeux":- If a person contracts "malyeux" the leaves of the sweet broom plant is quite an effectual remedy.

— Ursula Raymond

DUENDES' MEAD

Nightfall on the Seashore

When the sun has sunk to rest,
Somewhere—who knows—in the west,
O'er yon fairy dome that marks the crest
Of the towering Spanish Main;
And skies erewhile in crimson drest
Doff their mantle, and in plain
Hodden-grey are clad again;
When the darkness 'gins to thicken,
(Ah, that hour of doom,
Then it is sweet babes do sicken,
By curst necromancers stricken,
To their early tomb),
And lifeless things beseem to quicken
'Mid the growing gloom;
See, along the shelving strand,
Over shingle, over sand,
Over cruel rocks, unmeet
For little toddling feet,
One by one, or hand in hand
Tiny figures steal along
In a shadowy band.
Without father, without mother,
Without God to bless,
Close they cling to one another
In their helplessness.

— "Legends of the Bocas Trinidad", A.D. Russell, 1922.

The St. Clair tram makes its way south along Frederick Street crossing Hart Street. The picture above, from the Tom Cambridge Collection and the one opposite, courtesy Michael Pocock constitute the buildings between Queen and Hart Streets on the westernside of Frederick Street.

Below: Belmont tram crosses Marine Square in the distance can be seen the old Railway building at the foot of Charlotte Street.

The French umbrella mender. Photograph — U.W.I. Library

Frenchman's English is infinitely better than an Englishman's French, I wisely refrain from airing my little Gallic knowledge.

The lower classes do not discriminate well between 'meum' and 'tuum.' Not so much in grave matters as in small ones, they have hazy and grave notions of the propriety of honesty, which does not always strike them as being the best policy. Of course, they are not peculiar in this—the labouring classes of other nations are more or less the same, be they English, Yankee or Indian. Was it not a Scotchman who gave his son when starting out in life the doubtful advice? 'Mak siller laddie, honestly if ye can, but at ony reet mak siller!' Recently it has been found necessary to pass an Ordinance prohibiting the sale of cacao except by licensed persons, on account of the depredations of rascals who used to steal the cacao pods or nibs, and sell them.

But by far the most universal failing of the Creole lower class is the absence of thrift. A *laissez-faire,* live for the day feeling, is the grand motive of existence. Perhaps they are not altogether to blame for it, this is a Crown Colony in which the public works and institutions are mainly supported by Government, and people are only just beginning to learn to rely upon themselves. This is the reason why we have no Building Societies, no strictly Co-operative Stores, no Doctors' Clubs, and scarcely any Provident Societies, those we have being little known and still less supported.

The creoles are born with a love of music. They have a marvellously correct ear, and pick up a tune in no time. The artisan class acquire the rudiments of music, and you will often hear the sol-faing of humns and part-songs in a little hut. This love of one of the most refining of all the Arts is probably hereditary, and may be traced back to the old slavery period, when the negroes amused themselves in their leisure time by singing impromptu songs, while their Spanish masters in their turn, serenaded the ladies to the accompaniment of the melodious guitar. The Coolies in this respect are far

GANG GANG SARA
A Tobago Folk Legend

The legend of Gang Gang Sara, the African witch of Golden Lane, has its origins in the latter half of the 18th century. Of the stories told of old "Sarie" there is the one that tells how one very stormy night she was blown from her home in Africa across the sea to Tobago and landed quite safely at the village of Les Coteaux. From there she journeyed to Golden Lane in search of her family who had long ago been transported there. She became the trusted house keeper of 'Grandfather Peter' who owned plantations at Franklyn's, Les Coteaux and Golden Lane. She became the loving wife of Tom whom legend says she had known as a child in her native Africa. She lived to a great

age and is remembered for her wisdom and kindness. After her Tom had died, wishing to return to her native land, she climbed a great silk cotton tree and tried to fly, not knowing that she had lost the art of flight as a result of having eaten salt. To this day the names of Tom and Sara can be seen inscribed upon the head stones of their graves where they have lain side by side for close upon two hundred years.

Soucouyant: is not a French or patois version of the English word 'suck' which is the main activity of this legendary character. It is supposed to be derived from the French 'soupcon', 'soupconner', 'soupconnant', that is, the suspecting of a person to be a witch.

These legends are still very strong in everyday life. In Moruga recently, I was introduced in all seriousness, to an East Indian old woman, called Ma Balgobin, who was suspected of being a soucouyant, and was aware of these accusations, since before we had a chance, she sneered at us for not wanting to shake her hand.

— Ursula Raymond

behind them for they seldom sing, and when they do, their music is of a melancholy, lugubrious and depressing character. I once tried the experiment of getting together four hundred and fifty Creole children from all the Government schools within easy distance, for a Concert, after the style of the Crystal Palace School Concerts, at home. They had all been practised in their several schools, and when they were brought together the effect was very pleasing.

The two days immediately preceding Ash Wednesday are, as in most Roman Catholic countries, devoted to King Carnival. Business is partially, if not altogether, suspended; masquerading and tomfoolery generally being the order of the day. The better class of Spaniards dress themselves in fantastic costumes and ride or drive about visiting their friends, showering small confitures upon them. The custom is gradually dying out, and of late years it has degenerated into the lowest form of buffoonery, vulgarity and thinly-disguised obscenity, being rather the rule than the exception. The roughs, rowdies and *diametres* take advantage of the privilege of masking, and indulge in coarse ribaldry, till the police finally take them temporarily under their wing. These orgies used to begin with 'Canboulay'. Bands of ruffians armed with staves calling themselves Bakers, Freegrammars, etc., each set having their leader, paraded the town of Port of Spain at midnight on the Sunday and fought each other, annoyed the peaceably disposed, and even defied the Police on occasions, if the latter presumed to interfere with them. Things got to such a pitch at last that the Government was compelled in the interests of Law and Order to put this down with a high-hand. This caused some trouble at first, and not a little bitterness of feeling, but eventually Might which for once was also Right, prevailed, and the 'Canboulay' as such has become a thing of the past. Peace be to its ashes!

I must give the Trinidadian lower classes credit for one more virtue at least—that of politeness. In the course of nine years' residence here, during which I have often knocked against the roughest element, I have rarely if ever been treated with rudeness. I have interfered in fights, I have even been soft enough to step between a man and his wife (brevet-rank, probably), when the fists and finger-nails have been having a lively time of it,—and have come off scot-free, which was, perhaps, more than I deserved. Be that as it may, the bearing of any man of humble position towards one whom he considers socially his superior, is almost invariably that of respect. This is, however, more noticeable in the men than the women. The latter are too given to discussing audibly the good or bad points in your physiognomy or dress—even though you are an utter stranger. This is not an intentional rudeness, but it is nevertheless somewhat embarrassing. Another of their characteristics is their affectionate mode of addressing one another. One buxom matron on her way to or from market meets a friend:

"Marnin' darlin'! how you is?"

"Too sick, ma chère, me tink me go dead just now!"

"Ah! poor darlin', I too sarry fo' you. I go come see you to marrow, *please God.*"

The last two words are *de rigeur,* and being always used in season and out of season, must not be looked upon as an evidence of piety.

It would be an omission not to notice the street cries which are some of them unique. In place of the clean apron, bright cans and incisive if odd cry of the English milk-man, a Coolie man with several vinegar or beer bottles full of milk will deposit one at your house,

A beautiful mestisse wearing 'trembling pins' of gold (zépingue trémblant) to attach the folds of her brilliant madras turban; a great necklace of three or four strings of gold beads bigger than peas (collier-choux) immense earrings as light as egg shells were all considered to be very fashionable. Photograph — G. Mac Lean.

meekly ejaculating 'mil-lik' as if he were not quite sure if the article were really milk or water, or a Simpsonian compound of both. We make up for this short-coming, in our knife-grinder, who comes out very strong with '*O, filez les couteaux, les cisseaux, les rasoirs,*' his strong baritone giving a long 'O' on the note mi, and finishing in a recitative on do. All our 'scissors to grind' artists are Frenchmen, many of them from the neighbouring province of Cayenne, and they couple the art of sharpening cutlery with that of repairing umbrellas, so that the '*O filez*' cry is occasionally varied by '*Arrangez les parasols,*' chanted similarly on *mi* and *do*. If during any evening you hear a long Soprano recitative with the words *noyau* or *vanille* recurring at intervals, it is the marchande of ice creams.

One word more and I must bring this overgrown chapter to a close. If you want to annoy a native beyond measure, make the slightest allusion in disparagment of his maternal parent. Of course, filial affection is a thing to be admired and upheld, the oddity lies in this. Suppose a man or youth to be' on terms of bitterness or enmity with one or both of his parents; he will bear an unkind remark about his father without flinching, but for him to hear the words 'your mother,' offensively uttered, is sufficient to send him at once into frenzy of rage. This must be a relic of African customs, for Mungo Park in his travels, fully eighty years ago, found the natives of Africa exceedingly sensitive on this point,—'strike me, but do not curse my mother,' was their cry.

Queen's Park Hotel.

EDGAR TRIPP & CO.,
Trinidad, B.W.I.

Commission and Shipping Merchants, Consulate of Sweden and Norway, Commercial Agency for the Government of Canada for Trinidad and Tobago.

All descriptions of Commission Business for Produce or Manufactures, import or export promptly attended to.	Exporters of Trinidad Asphalt and Manjak, Cocoa, Coconuts and other Produce.

Special Attention to Chartering of Vessels.

Steam Coal always in Stock.

AGENCIES.

Commercial Union Assurance Co., Ltd., London (Fire, Marine, and Accident).
Dunville & Co., Royal Distilleries, Belfast and Glasgow.
Lochrin Iron Works, Wm. Bain & Co., Coatbridge, Scotland.
Pulsometer Engineering Co., Ltd., Reading, England.
The Trinidad Match Manufacturing Company.
    „   „   Soap   „   „
    „   „   Brewery Company, Ltd.
Marabella Manjak Company, Ltd.

Cable Address : **"TRIPP,"** PORT-OF-SPAIN.

CODES.

NOTE.—For directions to Captains of Vessels proceeding to Trinidad, see Special Code Words :—
WATKIN'S—**Zucconal. Zucconanno. Zucconando.**
SCOTT'S—**Behoof. Bendlet. Besom. Betel. Bery.**

BANKERS : Armstrong & Co., London ; Colonial Bank, and Union Bank of Halifax, Trinidad.
LONDON AGENTS : Musgrave & Co., 7, Great St. Helen's.
NEW YORK AGENTS : G. F. Lough & Co., 118, Produce Exchange Building.
MONTREAL : Robert Crookes & Co., Stock Exchange Building.

Edgar Tripp was one of the foremost businessmen in Trinidad at the end of the 19th century an innovator and entrepreneur he was joined by Ernest Canning and other like minded businessmen in opening the Queen's Park Hotel. Photograph — O. Mavrogordato.

REMINISCENCES OF OLD TRINIDAD

Writing of the 1930's about the 1850's and 80's
L.O. Inniss

When we get into the sere and yellow leaf of life, we are prone to speak of 'the Good old days of long ago' and it takes some argument to prove to us that the present day is better. It has been suggested to me by some friends, that as I have passed my 'three score years and ten,' I ought to jot down my reminiscences for the benefit of future generations; and seeing that 'Old things' are in vogue now-a-days, I have consented to jot down those which might interest 'collectors.' My first recollections are in connection with the epidemic of Asiatic Cholera, which visited Trinidad in 1854 and swept away thousands of its inhabitants. I was six years of age and distinctly remember rows of carts driving past our house at New Town, piled up with empty coffins, being carried out to Maraval and Diego Martin, and the queer, rumbling sound which they made.

I still have a cut glass decanter in my possession which has a story attached to it. It is this. In order to render 'first aid,' as soon as possible, the Government Medical Department gave free to every householder who wished, a supply of two mixtures, with directions for their use and the decanter in question contained one mixture, which, along with the other, was kept on the side-board at our house. I was the youngest of three brothers; and imbued with the usual curiosity of small boys, we wondered what those mixtures tasted like. As soon as we had broken the Tenth Commandment, by coveting 'forbidden fruit' it was not long before we set to work to break some more Commandments, in order to accomplish our end. The directions on the decanters for the household were:- 'For pains in the stomach' and 'For pains in the bowels.' We held a consultation and I, being the youngest, was told to go and tell mother that I had a pain in the stomach, whereupon the dear anxious dame administered a dose of No. 1 Mixture. As soon as she turned away, the other conspirators enquired in whispers: "What does it taste like?" "Oh beastly" I reported, and it was decided to leave No. 1 severely alone. But what about No. 2? So the next in age was deputed later on, to

La Peyrouse Cemetery photograph 1880's. Photograph — G. Mc Lean.

complain of a 'pain in the bowels', when poor frightened mother administered a dose of No. 2, which he reported as "not bad." It tasted of Peppermint and made you "feel warm inside." So mother was worried during the next two days, by one or other of the conspirators complaining of pains in the bowels, which were promptly cured by a dose of No. 2. Until she grew suspicious; and by means of a few pertinent questions, assisted by our guilty consciences soon discovered the conspiracy. And oh how mean we felt! when she almost tearfully pointed out to us the sinfulness of deceit and the utter thoughtlessness of our conduct, in giving her so much anxiety without cause. Not to speak of the sin against God, by making a mock of his dread visitation. Though I was young at the time, I have never forgotten the remorse I felt, when a couple of weeks after, the awful reality visited our house and took away our patient, loving mother. The Cut-glass Decanter has remained a sad memento of that time. I remember that during the Cholera, we boys recommended the eating of mangoes, as we thought that they were laxative, and as Cholera usually took the form of a severe Diarrhoea,

anything which loosened the bowels, would induce it. I was told afterwards that this opinion was erroneous, because in Martinique the Doctors used to recommend the eating of Mangoes as a preventative of Cholera. Our Doctors disagreed, and we boys were deprived of our Mangoes. I also remember that the "forbidden fruit" was very plentiful that year, as we could get a dozen large mango verts for a penny. One day when we had made a surreptitious purchase and were about to enjoy ourselves, retribution, in the form of our Pater, overtook us, when the contraband goods were promptly confiscated and a good lot of strap medicine was shared round to the young delinquents as a warning—not to do it again. "Sic Transit! !"

Speaking of Cholera, naturally brings the Sanitation of the Town in those early days to my mind. The theory of the connection of Mosquitoes with Malaria and Yellow fever had not yet been discovered and Anopheles and Stygomias had a high old time, breeding in millions in our gutters, which were paved with round stones, with mud between them, while many were simply earth drains which could never be cleaned and it is a wonder that any

View looking north along Abercromby Street. The Government Building on the left later became known as the Red House. Lower Prince Street passed between the buildings, the two columns visible indicate the top of that street

of us survived the attacks of the numerous microbes to tell the tale. It is the fashion in these days to say that 'Millions' are a product of Little England, but I can testify that in my boyhood days they abounded in our earth gutters. We did not call them Millions, but 'Big belly fishes,' they were the same fishes nevertheless. The streets were swept and the drains flushed (those down town) once a week by a gang of short-time Prisoners and the Corbeaux saw after them in the intervals. It was simply disgusting to see flocks of those filthy birds, fighting over the carcass of a dead fowl, or a dog, or cat, raising meanwhile clouds of microbe-laden dust, which would have given our present-day Public Health Officers the fits, had they happened to be there! ! The theory about infectious diseases, such as Cholera, Small Pox *et hoc,* was, that it was something in the air, which no amount of dodging could avoid, so it was much better to assume a devil-may-care attitude towards it. Keep your courage up and take your chance, rather than run away.

Frederick Street looking south the electrification of the city has commenced. The Tramway divides itself to allow two trams to pass abreast at this point. Photograph — G. Mc Lean.

1862

ABOLITION OF IMPRISONMENT FOR DEBT

The long pending discussion upon the partial abolition of imprisonment for debt has at length terminated in a compromise. While the principle contended for by the Committee has been accepted by the government, the minimum amount, £20, which they proposed has been reduced to one half, £10. For debts under £10 after the passing of the ordinance, there will be no recourse against the person of the debtor unless in the case of the fraudulent obtaining of goods. *(1st Oct., 1862.)*

1863

TRINIDAD FLOWER SHOP

A novel and we should think very attractive and useful store has just been opened in Queen Street for the sale of a large assortment of European flowers and fruit trees. Messrs. M.M. Pilforce and Co. have on hand a collection of choice plants to delight the floral amateur, and we have little doubt that, at the moderate prices at which these beauties are offered, they will soon effect a clearance. *(28th March, 1863)*

I remember an epidemic of Small Pox, when no precaution of any kind was taken to isolate cases to prevent infection, but the popular idea was that if you were brave and visited all your acquaintances who had it, you were safe but if you tried to run away from it, you would inevitably catch it or rather, it would catch you, which sounds like a Paradox. As was to be expected, that kind of philosophy resulted in the disease soon spreading all over the City and several thousands died of it, while many were greatly disfigured by its marks. Fortunately for the present generation, we have changed all that; and by prompt isolation and compulsory vaccination that disease has practically disappeared. In order to combat the 'disease in the air pitch was kept burning at the corners

1864

INTRODUCTION OF CABS

The public of Trinidad are indebted to our enterprising townsmen Messrs. P. and H. Creteau, for introducing to the streets of Port of Spain some two years ago, the cab system of Europe, which has since expanded, from the two hansoms then imported to the dimensions of an institution which may now rank amongst the fixed establishments of the colony. Ten or a dozen cabs now make their appearance daily in King Street and Marine Square, of which the greater number would do no discredit to the streets of London itself. They are decidedly superior to the general run of the metropolitan cabs, which are rarely characterised by ordinary cleanliness to say nothing of the usually worn out hack in the shafts. Our vehicles are decent to look at; they are clean, and well horsed, and the drivers are tolerably civil. *(19th Oct., 1864.)*

The Town Hall

The Cabildo Hall, known now as the Town hall, occupied many rented premises in Port of Spain over the years until 1899 when Nos. 11– 12 – 13 Brunswick Square, (now 2 – 4 – 6 Knox Street) became the first permanent offices of the City Council. On 27th December, 1789 the Borough Council bought the premises from Joseph Leon Agostini for $38,000. In 1899 the Council moved into No. 2 Knox Street and by 1907 it became necessary to occupy the three buildings as the municipal offices. Until then, parts of the building had been used for various purposes: residences, barristers' chambers, club rooms and the offices of the government departments. There is good reason to believe that the former Town Hall was really three buildings built in the same style and adjoining one another, as there were thick party walls dividing the three buildings, and the archways in the walls connecting the buildings were probably made after the building had been originally constructed. Most convincing, however, is the fact that it was assessed in the House Rate Books of the City as Nos. 2, 4 & 6 Knox Street. It is generally accepted that the building was erected by the Spaniards, and its graceful architecture is characteristic of that time. Someone writing under the name of 'Historian' in the Trinidad Guardian of 17th April 1948, states:

The unusual massiveness of the outer walls of the structure, the unique architecture of the Woodford Street frontage with its balcony over the street supported by a long row of massively built columns connected by a series of stone arches – the characteristic ground plan of the three buildings, namely, a square stone-paved central courtyard surrounded on all sides by balconied buildings - these all point unquestionably to the days of Spanish occupation, and strongly suggest some public rather than private purpose as that to which the building was devoted.' Photograph — Gregor Duruty.

of the streets, covering the City with a cloud of Black Pungent Smoke and giving the pernicious microbes a bad time. In the country parts, no one thought that Mosquitoes carried fever; but everybody objected to their blood-sucking habits and in order to drive them out of the houses, a piece of Wood-ants nest was burnt in a coal pot. This produced an acrid smoke, before which the Anopheles and Stygomias fled in disgust, when the house was hermetically shut up and the inmates slept in peace, in defiance of Dr. Masson and all his Tubercular theories about Fresh Air.

Speaking of the City streets brings to my mind the country roads which were all formed of natural earth, raising clouds of dust in the dry season and forming into oceans of mud in the wet season. The manner of keeping them in repair was, to fill up the ruts and holes with quantities of megass, during the dry season, over which the cane carts ran merrily to the mill yard; but when the rains began, these megass-filled holes became dangerous quagmires, into which mules, horses and even carts sometimes disappeared. There was a good joke told of a rider who was carefully picking his way along a country road, when he saw a good looking hat lying in the mud, which he thought was worth while retrieving, so he leaned over and lifted it with the crook of his hunter when, what was his astonishment to see the head of a man, who abjured him in mournful tones: "For the Lord's sake, go and get assistance, there is a mule under me." I remember my first acquaintance with one of these roads at Chaguanas, for a couple of miles, in the wet season, which resulted disastrously to me, from slips and falls, and when I got home my father made me stop on the step outside and poured a bucket of water over me, before he could let me in, because I was entirely covered with mud. The rivers along the Eastern Main Road were all unbridged and pedestrians had to wade through or get over on stepping stones during the dry season, and in the wet season, when the rivers 'came down', they were

Abercromby Street looking south towards towards Marine Square. The large building on the right is the Union Club. Photograph — U.W.I. Library.

simply impassable for a day or two afterwards, and even
horses or vehicles had to wait for hours, until the water
had subsided sufficiently, to make it safe to attempt to
cross. Fatal accidents from drowning at the Crossings
were frequent. In these days of cheap Railway and Bus
communication it is hard to conceive how difficult it was
in those days and a journey from Port of Spain to Band
L'Est as Mayaro was called, in those days, almost entitled
the intrepid traveller to the distinction of F.R.G.S.

Anyone wishing to go to Arima would have to hire a
carriage and pair for Six Dollars for the day or a saddle
horse for Three Dollars and be responsible for any
damage or injury which might occur to it during the
journey. In addition there had to be paid the Tolls,
charged in going and coming, at the 'Toll Gate' which
was situated at the boundary of the Town, at the foot of
the hill on which the Powder Magazine stands. When the
Railways was extended to Arima, the Toll Gate was
abolished. Communication Southward was by sailing

1864

THE EARLIEST PITCH LAKE COMPANY

The pitch lake of La Brea is about to be rescued from its
stereotyped reputation of an extraordinary spectacle embodied from time
immemorial in a remote corner of this island. . . . .The capital, skill and
enterprise of an influential English company are at length in the field to
convert this subterranean Tartarus into a burning and a shining light. The
Trinidad Petroleum Company, backed by a capital of £150,000 are about
to make the Pitch Lake through its latent treasures into the lap of
commerce, and shed its luminous properties abroad for he benefit of
humanity. . . . *(14th September, 1864.)*

COURT-BOUILLION FO TAZA SALE
Soak the salted Kingfish (taza sale) for
some hours. Put in a pot a little oil, a
little butter, and onion cut up, chive,
thyme and tomato. When this begins to
brown add a desert spoonful of flour
and add water to the required thickness
of the sauce, put in the taza sale and
cook slowly in the covered pot.

*Marine Square North, looking East. The Ice Establishment where ice
imported from the United States was stocked and sold. Iced drinks were
also available. From the tower there was a view of the harbour. An elderly
resident remarked that the owner and his friends gathered there to
gamble at cards. Photograph O.J. Mavrogordato.*

This photograph was taken in the 1890's and shows cabs and carts outside the Ice House grocery. This building was later acquired by Cannings. Photograph — O. Mavrogordato.

boats, which plied from Port of Spain to Chaguanas, Couva, Claxton Bay and San Fernando and Sloops, which sailed occasionally to La Brea, Cedros, Icacos and round to Band L'Est, the times of their arrival being as uncertain as the Greek Kalends, and ranging from anything between three days and two weeks. It was bad enough being cramped up in these boats during the journey to the places between Port and San Fernando, but what was worse, was to find that when you reached the mouth of

the river, the tide was too low to allow the boat to cross the bar. Then you had to await high tide, while being devoured by swarms of mosquitoes and sand flies, and when a steamer began to ply in the Gulf, it was almost as bad, rowing out to the mouth of the river, to meet it at all hours, in the sun and rain. Locomotion along the Eastern Main Road, after a while, was facilitated by a Van capable of seating a dozen persons, which made one trip a day, between Port and Arima, the fare being ten cents per

A view of the British fleet in the harbour taken from the tower of the Police Headquarters, showing the western end of the city. Photograph — U.W.I. Library.

Croney & Co. were the proprietors of The Carlisle, a hotel that offered single rooms to gentlemen. There was a Billiard Room a bar and a restaurant. Photograph — O. Mavrogordato.

mile. This was patronised by the Aristocracy, and those of the hoi polloi, who wanted to save their legs, negotiated, at the Cart Market–at the spot which is now Columbus Square–for a lift on one of the numerous Estate Carts or Wagons which plied daily, bringing down produce and taking up supplies; the fare being generally Eight cents for the journey. Between Port and Arouca there were Twelve Sugar Estates worked by Steam, water or animal

power and during crop season the air along the road was beautifully perfumed with the smell of Hot Liquor, the Sugar was produced by Common Process and was called Mundongo. In these days Usines were unknown. The main road ran through the Villages of St. Juan and St. Joseph. It was only when the railway was laid that the Main Road was carried straight on as it is now.

When I was twelve years of age, I walked from Port

of Spain to Mayaro. After leaving Arima the track, (I won't call it a road) led through Primeval forest until it terminated on to the beach at Manzanilla, from which spot we had to negotiate about twenty miles of sea-beach. We had to wade through all the rivers on the way, with the exception of the Ortoire, where there was a boat to ferry travellers over. I took two days to do the journey, sleeping at a place then called Morne Calbasse (in the vicinity of the present village of Sangre Grande) but some "Mayaronians," who left Port at the same time as I did, slept in Mayaro the same night, carrying something on their heads besides! This was good going you will admit! When I got to Mayaro, on the evening of the second day,

it took me some time to convince the Police Corporal, in charge of the Station, that I had really travelled by land. The Nariva Cocal which was then the property of the Town Council, was leased by a person named Carter, who had a mill there, for the purpose of making coconut oil. Mayaro was an out-of-the-world place in those days and I heard an anecdote of a Governor who visited it and had the oldest inhabitant presented to him by the Warden-Magistrate. The inhabitant in question, when asked his age, told the Big Man that he had lived "30 years in Trinidad and 50 years in Band l'Est."

A building that is now referred to as the old Cabildo building was one of several similar buildings erected in a Spanish style. Built on lower Prince Street, now called Sackville Street, it was marked out as a government building on a map of 1834. It was referred to on Soranzo's map of 1845 as Judicial Reference and Registrar of Deeds Office.

GOVERNMENT BUILDINGS

THE RED HOUSE

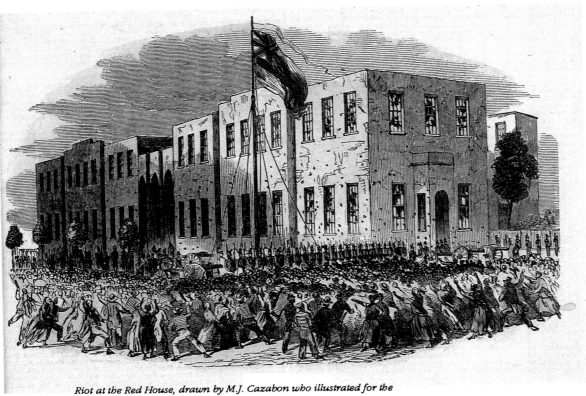

Riot at the Red House, drawn by M.J. Cazabon who illustrated for the London Illustrated News.

THE RED HOUSE

Olga Mavrogordato

O n the 15th February 1844 the Governor, Sir Henry McLeod, laid the foundation stone for a new block of government buildings, on a site on the west side of Brunswick Square (Woodford Square). The land belonged to a group of eight persons. The architect was Mr. Richard Bridgens, Superintendent of Public Works, while the builders were Messrs G. de la Sauvagère and A.A. Pierre. The buildings comprising two main blocks, north and south, were to be connected by a double archway, much as the Red House of today, but on a smaller scale. The double archway was a feature required by the City Council to keep Prince Street open, as the building was built over it, with the stipulation that it should never be closed to the public, and through which pedestrians and wheeled traffic passed freely. Though incomplete, the southern wing, containing the law courts, was opened in 1848 and a month later the Council Chamber was formerly inaugurated with much ceremony by Lord Harris, after an impressive ceremony in Trinity Cathedral.

To quote from the *Port of Spain Gazette* of 1892:

'Nothing further had been done to complete the buildings since their erection some fifty years ago. The only attempt to relieve the monotony of the whole is to be seen in the arching of the carriageway through the courtyard which is a perfect skeleton and, like the ruins of Pompeii, is more suggestive of what the buildings must have been than of what they were intended to be.'

The urgent need for a proper record office arose, and the plans proposed by the Director of Public Works, Mr. J.E. Tanner, showed that two new buildings of two storeys each, were to be erected at the southern corners of the northern building, and two similar structures on the other side of the carriageway, abutting the Court House or southern building. One of these was to become the office of the Registrar and the other, the Record Office. These and many other additions and alterations and ornamentations were carried out at a cost of £15,000.

In 1897, as Trinidad was preparing to celebrate the Diamond Jubilee of Queen Victoria, the buildings were given a coat of red paint, and the public promptly referred to them thereafter as the Red House.

The Riot of 1849

London Illustrated News

A summary of the intelligence received by the West India and Pacific mails on Friday last appeared in our late edition of last week.

Among the occurrences, we regret to have to record a serious riot which took place at Trinidad on the 1st October, which led to loss of life, and subsequent outrage on person and property. It is stated in the *Trinidadian* and *Port of Spain Gazette* newspapers, that on the above day a considerable crowd of Trinidadians, comprising people of the lowest order, assembled in front of the Government-House to protest against an obnoxious clause in the gaol regulations recently introduced, which had been passed by the Council; and which, among other things, provided that debtors committed under the petty civil courts ordinance should have their hair cropped close, and wear a prison dress, and assist in gaol work.

Trial of the Rioters October 1st in the Court House at Trinidad
illustrated by M.J. Cazabon for London Illustrated News.

The first manifestation of public feeling on the subject was a meeting at which certain resolutions, condemnatory of the gaol regulations, were passed, and six deputies appointed to present them to the Governor in Council. The deputation proceeded to the Government-House, accompanied by a great concourse of people (nearly 3,000), and having been admitted to the presence of the Governor, His Excellency informed the members of the deputation that it was his intention to have these clauses reconsidered and modified.

This determination was well received by the mob outside. Immediately after, a young man was arrested in the Council Chamber by the police, which becoming known to the people outside, they imagined that the Council was not attending to the Gaol Clause as promised by the Governor; and instantly, a shower of stones came through the windows of the Council-room: the Council broke up, the members and spectators seeking safety where they best could. The military were sent for, and on their arrival some degree of order was restored, and the Council resumed business. The obnoxious clause in the gaol regulations was abrogated, and the deputation hastened and informed the people outside of the fact, advising all to proceed to their homes; when a large number of those, chiefly Trinidadians, who had peaceably assembled in the morning to remonstrate and protest against a partial and degrading law, retired from Government-house. A crowd of mischievous persons, however, remained, and soon began to annoy the police, and pelt them with stones, The Riot Act was read, the order to fire was given, four or five muskets were discharged, and four persons fell wounded, three women and a lad; the latter and one of the former subsequently died. This did not stay the fury of the mob.

They continued to assail the soldiers and police with large stones torn up from the causeway, and, we understand, there would have been more firing and more bloodshed but for the intervention of the Governor. The mob then vowed vengeance against the Attorney-General, but he escaped their rage, escorted by soldiers with fixed bayonets.

During the night the houses of the Attorney-General and the stipendiary magistrate were attacked, the inmates forced to fly, and much damage was done. The residence of the keeper of the gaol was likewise attacked. The conduct of Colonel Shirly, and the temper, firmness and ability he displayed throughout the affair, were much extolled; the officers and men of the 88th Regiment, and of the 2nd West India Regiment, were highly praised, as well as the brave tars of the *Scorpion,* for their eagerness to be put on active service in dispersing the insurgents. Captain Todd, of the armed Venezuelan steamer *Libertador,* was warmly thanked for having placed at the disposal of the Government his services, with those of his officers and crew, as well as the arms and ammunition of his vessel.

Next day much damage was done to sugar estates in the neighbourhood. On the night of the 4th the house of the clerk to the warden at Oropouche was attacked and burned, and outrages to property were increasing.

At the time of the departure of the packet the island was in a state of much disquiet, and further troubles were apprehended. Lord Harris had sent a vessel to Barbados for more troops. The Government buildings were converted into a temporary barracks, and were occupied by the 88th Regiment, a company of the 2nd West India Regiment, and by the men of her Majesty's sloop *Scorpion,* who landed with a six-pounder when the disturbances first broke out. Upwards of 300 special constables had been sworn in, and a volunteer horse patrol formed, at least 70 strong.

Several of those most conspicuous had been arrested and committed to prison, and it was hoped that the firm measures of the Government would prove sufficient to repress any further efforts of the disaffected to create an insurrection.

Our Correspondent's Sketch represents the Government buildings during the riot, when the companies of the 88th Regiment were drawn up by the side of the flat-staff, with two guns in their rear; as also two other guns opposite one of the entrances to the buildings, and which is represented on the right of the picture. The soldiers patrolling from the main entrance to the buildings down the street are those of the 2nd West India Regiment, the remainder of the company being inside the archway.

TRIAL OF THE RIOTERS AT TRINIDAD

In our Journal of November 10, 1849, we gave an account (with an Illustration) of the destructive riots which took place at Trinidad on the 1st of October, which led to loss of life, and outrage on person and property. Before the dispatch of this intelligence from the island, several persons who were most conspicuous in the riot had been arrested, and committed to prison.

These and other prisoners have since been brought to trial; and when the mail received on the 20th inst. left Trinidad, there was some excitement prevailing in the island relative to these trials, which were proceeding. The evidence against the prisoners did not make it appear that there was any preconcert or plot to break the peace on the occasion of the disturbance; and the Jury, after two days' confinement, not being able to agree upon a verdict, were discharged. On the 21st of December, the Attorney-General summoned another Jury, which, it was expected, would convict the prisoners, who consisted of ten men (ignorant labourers) and four women, all Negroes. It was the general opinion in the island that if these helpless persons should be condemned, the year 1850 will not elapse without serious disturbances.

The accompanying Illustration is from a Sketch by Mr. Cazabon, a native artist of Trinidad. It shows the interior of the Court-House, on the 17th of December, during the trial. Upon the bench are seated Chief Justice Knox and Justice Bowen; below them are the Registrar and the Marshall of the Court; in the witness-box is Mr. Guiseppi: the barrister standing is Mr. Anderson, counsel for the defence; and to his right are the Hon. Henry Fuller, Advocate and member of Council; and next to him, Mr. Celestine Surrera, the chief prisoner.

Continued from page 272

The Governor's New Year Dinner

Port of Spain Gazette Special Centenary Issue.

On Wednesday last, the 2nd instant, His Excellency the Governor gave his annual New Year's Day dinner to the public officers. The assembled guests, ninety in number, comprised the heads of the public departments, military, ecclesistical and legal, the members of Council, the Stipendiary Magistrate, Wardens, etc., etc. At half past seven o'clock the doors of the banqueting hall at St. Ann's were thrown open, and the band of the 72nd Regiment playing 'The Roast Beef of Old England', the guests proceeded to take their respective places, arrangement previously made was accomplished without the slightest disorder of confusion. After the cloth had been removed His Excellency the Governor proposed the health of 'Her Most Gracious Majesty' which was drunk with every demonstration of loyalty; and His Excellency then proposed the 'prosperity of the different nations represented at that board by their several consuls', which was replied to in a net speech by Mr. J. Scheult, consul for France, and also acknowledged by E.B. Marache, Esq., consul for the United States. His Excellency then retired from the table, with one of two of the more distinguished of his guests; and the health of 'Lord Harris' was then proposed by the Hon'ble. Joseph Peschier, and drunk most enthusiastically, with Highland honours, each guest standing on his chair, with one foot on the table. The guests then retired to the drawing room, where they were entertained with a Highland fling and a reel, danced by the pipers of the 72nd, after which they returned to their respective homes.

For the gratification of the curious we reproduce the 'carte' of this splendid banquet:—

Soups
Turtle
Potage de la Pate Italie
Potage à la Jerusalem

Fish
Boiled; Stewed, à la Mâitre d'hotel; Fried.
Hors d'Oeuvres
Petits Croutades de Burre à la Duke of York
Petit Pate à la Patissiere
Rissolettes de Volant
Petit Bouches de Macqueraeu.

Removes.
Baron of Beef à l'Angleterre
Dinde aux Truffles à la Bechamel
Saddle of Mutton au Laver
Calif's Head au Nature!
Roast Turkey with Chestnuts
Fillet of Veal à la princesse
Gigot de Moutton aux Capres
Haunch of Vensiona à la Belmont.

Flancs.
Neck of Lamb aux Petit Pois
Westphalian Ham
Petit Paussines à la Moskovites
Carbonade de Moutton à la Bourgenotte
Langue de Boeuf à la Prima Donna
Casserole de Riz Pollaise.

Entrées.
Filets de Poulardes à la Pierre le Grand
Pieds D'Anneau farcies
Escalopes de filet Boeuf à la Nemours
Lamb's Brains à la Innocent
Quenelles de Volaile à la York Minister
Cotelettes de Pore à la Voulle Angleterre
Filets de Canetons en Salami
Grenadines de Veau Pique aux racines nouvelles
Cotelettes de Veau à l'Anglaise
Pigones aux Pois verts
Rognons en caisses
Curry of Fowl à la Inite
Poulardes à la Provencial
Lambs & Fry.

Rots.
Wild Ducks
Capons
Guinea Birds
Ramières
Water Fowls, etc., etc., etc.

Savoury Dishes
Gelatine de Dinde à la Voliere
Moule d'Aspic à la Royal
Poulettes Printamier à la Santa Cruz
Loin of Beef au Jambon à la Dame Blanche.

Extrementes.
Plum Pudding
Calf's Foot Jelly
Mince Pies
Blanc Mange
Greengage Tarts
Cherry Tart
Plum Tart
Currant Tart

Macaroni; Scalloped Oysters; Diablotins au Permessan; Green Peas; Artichokes au Blancs; Comcombres Farcies;

Macaroni; Scalloped Oysters; Diablotins au Permessan; Green Peas; Artichokes au Blancs; Comcombres Farcies;

Relevées de Rots
Jambonneau Glace en Surprise
Marveau de Champignon en Surprise
Pyramid de Meringue Glace à la Harlequin
Cortellettes de Moutton Glace en Surprise Reforme
Turban de Coude
Glaci aux Fraises

Dinde Nouveau aux Truffles Glace en Surprise.
(8th January, 1850).

AN EXTRACT FROM DANIEL HART'S HISTORICAL AND STATISTICAL VIEWS OF TRINIDAD

PRODUCE OF TRINIDAD EXPORTED FROM 1799 TO 1820:—

Years.	Lbs. Sugar.	Lbs. Cocoa.	Lbs. Coffee.	Lbs. Cotton.	Gallons Rum.	Gallons Syrup.
1799..	8,419,859	258,390	335,913	323,415	170,671	142,636
1800..	9,895,634	284,170	449,614	317,395	194,488	128,507
1801..	15,461,912	324,720	328,666	262,997	343,113	173,369
1802..	14,164,984	138,669	278,274	190,210	350,049	143,237
1803..	16,014,056	361,070	185,658	478,046	344,292	214,120
1804..	18,595,416	503,210	304,138	164,069	371,544	355,877
1805..	29,438,276	527,690	286,379	256,792	426,469	564,558
1806..	29,045,439	588,805	418,049	167,700	399,122	649,432
1807..	..	..	..	..	..	..
1808..	25,950,928	668,993	387,028	139,200	940,584	606,100
1809..	24,856,973	719,230	264,350	134,190	539,081	477,262
1810..	21,746,775	726,173	295,443	114,980	463,870	82,163
1811..	18,513,302	640,732	276,243	159,136	426,691	324,942
1812..	20,971,580	1,375,539	282,460	130,390	548,014	366,070
1813..	22,288,145	1,029,512	540,716	184,490	666,761	301,795
1814..	21,604,038	1,158,163	382,888	148,505	487,142	262,098
1815..	25,075,281	1,065,808	262,289	115,150	523,632	682,718
1816..	24,122,415	1,056,662	119,974	303,045	449,067	373,873
1817..	22,784,767	1,341,461	215,190	65,951	371,422	351,234
1818..	23,200,326	1,232,685	224,972	109,070	439,663	415,251
1819	30,205,731	1,506,445	258,220	131,990	534,626	545,406
1820	30,714,363	1,744,465	211,555	96,545	524,316	471,001

PRODUCE OF TRINIDAD EXPORTED FROM 1821 TO 1865:—

	Sugar.			Molasses.		Rum	Cocoa.	Coffee.	Cotton.		Indgo
	Hhd.	Trcs.	Brls.	Puns.	Trs.	Puns	Pounds.	Pounds	Bales.	Sers.	Sers.
1821	20,412	576	7,999	2,730	...	1,208	1,214,093	192,555	268	...	...
1822	20,051	714	7,908	2,932	...	761	1,780,379	347,399	222	...	...
1823	23,362	510	7,038	6,245	...	566	2,424,703	299,408	460	...	...
1824	23,362	882	6,856	7,409	...	471	2,661,628	264,637	352	...	...
1825	22,512	1,370	7,890	7,896	...	68	2,760,603	177,348	492	567	...
1826	25,541	1,358	8,075	8,672	...	353	2,951,171	321,254	107	2,811	...
1827	26,075	1,320	7,618	9,694	..	589	3,696,144	273,424	201	2,368	...
1828	29,605	1,067	6,634	11,320	306	285	2,582,323	266,754	148	2,915	50
1829	30,629	877	5,184	10,686	596	559	2,756,603	199,015	123	1,234	10
1830	19,812	480	3,781	4,846	163	258	1,646,531	197,860	50	1,010	7
1831	28,756	449	5,500	8,297	94	853	1,888,852	19,994	31	250	12
1832	25,912	774	6,895	10,977	504	65	1,530,990	150,966	40	498	11
1833	22,761	583	5,165	9,964	590	13	3,090,526	276,959	47	817	31
1834	26,280	1,098	5,535	11,958	592	59	3,363,630	170,825	33	1,165	...
1835	22,434	1,125	4,768	9,458	577	115	2,744,643	102,707	102	585	59
1836	23,956	1,367	4,928	9,562	782	59	3,488,870	219,994	45	815	...
1837	22,925	1,078	3,622	8,842	666	11	2,507,483	194,740	38	1,243	...
1838	20,721	1,280	2,679	7,939	596	130	2,571,915	451,437	370	2,585	6
1839	20,046	1,310	3,538	7,715	444	112	2,914,068	212,982	2	1,785	6
1840	16,942	1,290	3,795	6,647	419	191	3,237,005	358,892	100	1,321	5
1841	18,031	1,251	2,713	6,772	371	22	1,122,220	144,930	...	1,190	...
1842	19,176	1,401	3,783	6,650	439	123	3,141,505	178,673	...	861	..
1843	22,615	1,327	4,863	9,557	339	43	2,803,295	394,583	4	2,390	...
1844	20,370	1,628	2,700	9,080	337	32	3,305,715	327,550	1	2,537	1
1845	23,900	1,620	3,538	10,185	402	22	4,021,198	168,836		777	6
1846	23,730	1,466	2,904	11,510	300	2	2,628,562	309,759	2	354	...
1847	27,728	2,068	6,068	11,288	357	1,076	3,738,376	134,026	237	41	34
1848	26,316	2,331	5,584	8,165	149	1,135	2,956,354	119,912	25	280	3
1849	28,080	2,374	6,422	12,932	329	718	4,728,186	28,405	729	235	7
1850	23,892	2,303	4,545	9,789	142	272	3,816,728	136,835	...	98	19
1851	28,001	3,157	7,561	10,709	121	528	5,008,920	74,416	4	30	8
1852	31,408	4,058	7,774	14,919	193	817	4,246,851	103,162	386	513	10
1853	30,555	3,505	6,601	13,162	216	1,213	4,842,875	61,115	224	557	1
1854	33,930	4,742	10,116	11,604	216	3,267	3,761,057	56,391	703	191	2
1855	28,783	3,820	5,990	6,256	88	3,735	5,427,351	48,056	81	164	268
1856	31,362	4,375	5,353	10,168	141	2,926	4,905,796	5,588	12	214	4
1857	31,691	6,120	5,609	11,811	358	1,038	4,690,166	22,876	141	342	9
1858	35,368	5,908	3,695	10,696	278	2,781	5,292,800	112,260	56	...	3
1859	38,366	6,079	3,466	12,371	271	2,238	4,758,350	54,180	295	22	9
1860	32,857	5,173	3,052	8,038	183	1,446	4,882,230	6,660	...	26	1
1861	31,593	6,709	2,501	7,580	418	2,422	8,472,392	5,760	216	44	...
1862	41,232	7,935	3,460	7,954	228	2,481	4,319,453	56,070	91	...	1
1863	37,394	6,549	4,867	8,926	187	2,547	7,014,337	89,3.0	7	...	2
1864	39,634	6,738	5,383	15,227	408	611	5,039,006	7,110	381	30	...
1865	30,837	6,143	5,215	9,324	293	933	6,611,160	46,902	920	..	3

The average weight of the hogshead is 20 cwt.; tierce, 1,000 lb; barrel, 220 lb.
The average number of gallons of rum and molasses to the puncheon is, the former, 120 gallons; the latter, 110 gallons.
The average return of sugar of the whole island is taken at 1¼ hhds. per acre.

VALUE OF IMPORTS AND EXPORTS FROM 1809 TO 1865.

	Imports. £	Exports. £
1809	328,512	579,719
1810	300,990	357,073
•	•	•
1850	476,910	319,394
1851	548,471	390,009
1852	493,274	458,851
1853	504,380	446,076
1854	559,067	380,873
1855	554,434	387,999
1856	666,474	574,767
1857	800,820	1,073,878
1858	825,969	785,863
1859	734,902	820,606
1860	829,304	714,603
1861	856,726	645,561
1862	733,598	739,507
1863	710,972	796,497
1864	883,940	1,101,510
1865	810,347	820,109

REVENUE & EXPENDITURE OF THE COLONY FROM 1850 TO 1865.

	Revenue. £	Expenditure. £
1850	88,084	77,362
1851	95,733	106,316
1852	107,310	110,944
1853	142,782	118,827
1854	101,408	101,016
1855	72,323	80,657
1856	93,213	80,304
1857	131,285	102,247
1858	145,391	174,022
1859	167,385	187,016
1860	184,861	187,220
1861	171,729	188,841
1862	199,372	196,058
1863	184,377	188,981
1864	207,473	193,156
1865	194,087	195,991

ACCOUNT OF THE POPULATION OF THE ISLAND OF TRINIDAD IN THE YEAR 1811:—

	White.				Free Coloured.				Slaves.						Indians.				Total Persons.
			Children.				Children.				Children.						Children.		
	Men.	Women.	Males.	Females.	Men.	Women.	Males.	Females.	Men.	Women.	Males.	Females.	Runaways.	Births.	Men.	Women.	Males.	Females.	
British	506	255	284	235	516	804	1031	1024	...	...	...	...	...	...	...	...	...	...	4655
Spanish	227	183	80	69	570	577	241	239	...	...	...	...	...	...	...	...	...	...	2186
French	347	275	25	34	621	940	184	154	...	...	...	...	...	...	...	...	...	...	2580
Maltese	10	...	...	...	...	...	...	...	...	...	...	...	...	...	...	...	...	...	10
Corsicans	20	...	...	...	...	...	...	...	...	...	...	...	...	...	...	...	...	...	20
Italians	17	1	...	...	...	...	...	...	...	...	...	...	...	...	...	...	...	...	18
Portuguese	...	4	...	...	...	...	...	...	...	...	...	...	...	...	...	...	...	...	4
Dutch	...	...	...	...	12	1	...	...	...	...	...	...	...	...	...	...	...	...	13
Germans	22	3	...	...	...	...	...	...	...	...	...	...	...	...	...	...	...	...	25
Americans	16	4	...	...	...	...	...	...	...	...	...	...	...	...	...	...	...	...	20
Chinese	...	...	...	...	17	...	...	...	...	...	...	...	...	...	...	...	...	...	17
Danish	...	...	...	...	1	...	...	...	...	...	...	...	...	...	...	...	...	...	1
Indians	...	...	...	...	...	...	...	...	...	...	...	...	...	...	442	476	415	403	1736
Africans	...	...	...	...	...	...	...	...	9321	7019	2506	2297	142	553	...	...	...	...	21842
Ditto	...	...	...	...	53	58	...	...	...	...	...	...	...	...	...	...	...	...	111
	1165	725	389	328	1790	2380	1456	1417	9321	7019	2506	2297	145	553	442	476	415	403	33273

Port-of-Spain. Trinidad, January 31, 1812.

WILLIAM MONRO,
Major-General.

J. E. MAINGOT,
Commissary of Population, and Acting Surveyor-General.

RETURN OF THE POPULATION OF THE ISLAND FROM 1797 TO 1861.

	Whites.	Coloured.	Indians.	Chinese.	Slaves.	Aliens and strangers	Apprentices.	Total.
1797	2,151	4,474	1,078	...	10,000	...	...	17,712
1798	...	...	...	...	...	...	...	...
1799	2,128	4,594	1,143	...	14,110	...	...	21,975
1800	2,359	4,408	1,071	...	15,012	...	...	22,850
1801	2,153	4,900	1,212	...	15,964	...	...	24,229
1802	2,222	5,275	1,166	...	19,709	...	...	28,372
1803	2,423	4,812	1,154	...	20,138	...	...	28,527
1804	2,561	6,102	1,416	...	20,925	...	...	31,004
1805	2,434	5,801	1,733	...	20,108	...	...	30,076
1806	2,274	5,401	1,697	...	21,761	...	...	31,043
1807	...	...	...	...	...	...	...	...
1808	2,470	6,478	1,635	...	21,895	...	...	32,478
1809	2,589	6,384	1,647	...	21,475	...	...	32,095
1810	2,487	6,269	1,659	...	20,728	...	...	31,143
1811	2,617	7,004	1,736	...	21,841	...	...	33,277
1812	2,765	7,066	1,804	...	21,900	...	...	33,535
1813	3,896	8,102	1,265	...	25,717	...	...	57,988
1814	3,127	8,714	1,236	...	25,409	...	...	38,482
1815	3,219	9,653	1,147	...	24,329	...	...	38,348
1816	3,512	10,655	1,141	24	25,871	...	...	41,203
1817	3,793	11,856	1,157	33	23,828	...	...	40,667
1818	3,221	11,337	939	28	22,380	...	...	37,905
1819	3,716	12,485	850	30	23,691	...	...	40,772
1820	3,707	13,965	910	28	22,738	...	...	41,348
1821	3,440	13,388	956	28	21,719	...	...	39,526
1822	3,341	13,392	893	20	23,227	...	...	40,873
1823	3,386	13,347	872	16	23,110	...	...	40,731
1824	2,313	13,995	783	12	23,117	...	...	41,220
1825	3,310	14,983	727	12	23,230	...	...	42,262
1826	3,113	10,352	...	...	23,123	6,195	...	42,790
1827	...	...	...	...	...	...	...	...
1828	4,326	16,412	...	...	22,436	5,820	...	48,994
1829	3,841	16,180	...	...	21,847	5,600	...	47,468
1830	...	...	...	...	...	...	...	...
1831	3,319	16,285	762	...	21,302	...	...	41,668
1832	3,683	16,302	...	...	20,265	4,615	...	44,865
1833	...	...	...	...	...	...	...	...
1834	3,632	18,724	...	...	...	...	16,569	38,945
1835	...	...	...	...	...	...	...	...
1836	...	...	571	...	...	...	40,854	15,759
1844	...	...	...	...	...	...	...	59,815
1851	...	...	...	...	...	...	...	68,600
1861	...	...	...	...	...	...	...	84,438

RETURN OF IMMIGRANTS FROM 1845 TO 1865.

Year	COOLIES.					CHINESE.		AFRICANS.			WEST INDIA ISLANDS, FAYAL, &c.			
	M.	F.	B.	G.	Tot'l.	M.	F.	M.	F.	Tot'l	M.	F.	Chiln	Tot'l.
1845	182	22	15	6	225	...	...	...	...	590	...	...	...	...
1846	1142	222	145	46	1556	...	...	...	...	...	3334	1673	461	5468
1847	685	97	20	19	821	...	...	...	...	...	2258	830	674	3762
1848	538	62	16	8	624	...	...	...	...	...	995	350	205	1550
1849	...	...	...	...	...	...	...	...	...	...	1479	550	233	2262
1850	...	...	...	...	...	...	...	...	...	762	868	407	100	1375
1851	159	11	2	3	175	...	...	...	...	...	...	...	...	...
1852	1065	166	47	28	1306	...	...	...	...	...	...	...	...	...
1853	1508	318	94	61	1981	988	...	...	...	...	...	...	...	...
1854	605	49	9	7	670	...	...	...	...	...	...	...	...	...
1855	230	36	14	4	284	...	...	...	...	...	...	...	...	...
1856	428	138	20	22	608	...	...	...	...	...	...	...	...	...
1857	912	852	82	41	1887	...	...	...	...	...	...	...	...	...
1858	647	393	142	93	1275	...	...	29	8	82	...	...	...	...
1859	1907	887	293	281	3368	...	...	...	...	...	...	...	...	...
1860	1736	682	243	193	2854	...	...	561	126	687	...	...	...	...
1861	1495	460	115	111	2181	...	...	...	...	...	...	...	...	...
1862	1497	331	90	49	1967	341	125	...	...	...	...	...	...	...
1863	1390	299	64	45	1798	...	...	...	...	...	...	...	...	2850
1864	683	179	51	36	949	...	...	...	...	...	...	...	...	2590
1865	1538	417	145	103	2203	412	179	...	...	...	...	...	...	2339
	18347	5121	1607	1156	26231	1741	305	590	129	2071	8934	3810	1673	22205

RETURNED TO INDIA.

Year	COOLIES.					CHINESE.		AFRICANS.		
	M.	F.	B.	G.	Total.	M.	F.	M.	F.	Total.
1851	265	37	19	9	330	..	..	..	..	..
1852	159	40	6	8	213	..	..	..	..	..
1853	497	41	16	14	568	..	..	..	..	..
1855	105	24	18	22	169	..	..	..	..	..
1856	167	38	41	28	274	..	..	..	..	..
1857	266	33	18	19	336	..	..	..	..	..
1858	246	54	36	26	362	1	..	..	..	..
1859	...	...	...	...	...	3	..	..	..	..
1861	236	34	13	20	303	..	..	..	..	..
1864	..	..	..	..	..	5	..	..	..	..
1865	354	87	35	32	508	..	..	..	..	..
	2295	388	202	178	3063	9	..	..	..	..

A TABLE SHOWING THE COMPONENT PARTS OF THE POPULATION OF
TRINIDAD by the Census Returns of 1851 and 1861, and the Comparative
Increase and Decrease.

Where Born.	Census of 1851.	Census of 1861.	Increase.	Decrease.	Total Increase.
Trinidad	40627	46936	6309		
British Colonies	10812	11716	904		
United Kingdom	729	1040	311		
Foreign	4915	4301		614	
China	.	461	461		
India	4169	13488	9319		
Africa	8097	6035		2062	
Not Described	260	461	201		
	69609	84438	17505	2676	14829

RETURN OF IMMIGRANTS AND LIBERATED AFRICANS introduced into Trinidad
from 1843 to the end of 1856, and in each year since 1st January, 1857,
to the end of 1861, as shown by the Twenty-second Report of the Immigration Commissioners, 1862.

	1843 to 1856.	1857.	1858.	1859.	1860.	1861.	Total.
Madeira	725	...	...	...	...	...	725
Cape de Verdes	..	172	..	...	...	...	172
Sierra Leone	2,474	..	...	...	226	...	2,700
St. Helena	2,292	...	30	4	270	...	2,796
East Indies	10,569	1,414	2,083	3,363	2,169	2,544	22,142
China	988	...	..	...	...	...	988
United States	47	...	...	...	...	...	47
British West Indies	4,773	..	...	...	...	...	4,773
Rio de Janeiro	879	...	...	...	...	...	879
	22,747	1,586	2,113	3,367	2,865	2,544	35,222

BRITISH WEST INDIAN IMMIGRANTS

Bridget Brereton

The people who came to Trinidad, after 1838, from the British colonies in the Eastern Caribbean soon constituted a very important element in the island's black population. For a start, they came in large numbers; over 10,000 arrived between 1839 and 1849, and about 65,000 came in between 1871 and 1911; the majority settled permanently. In 1897 it was estimated that at least 14,000 immigrants from Barbados alone were living in Trinidad.

Even more important was their social and cultural contribution. It is important to realize that they were differentiated from the Trinidad Creoles in three major respects: they were Protestants (Anglicans, Methodists etc.) they spoke English as their first language and they were the products of slave societies established for well over one hundred years, as opposed to Trinidad's fifty years approximately. These attributes, and especially their familiarity with English, gave the immigrants more confidence in their social relations than the mainly patois-speaking Creoles could muster. Many of the immigrants especially the Barbadians, were quite well-educated and could write as well as speak the language. As immigrants they tended to have more drive, more ambition, than many of the rural Creoles.

A Barbadian immigrant of the 19th century. Photograph — Mrs. Hélène Farfan.

As a result of these factors, the British West Indian immigrants tended to be an upwardly-mobile element in the society. Often the men were skilled artisans and practised their trades in Port of Spain and the other towns, or took jobs as mechanics on sugar estates. Some became headmen and overseers on the estates. Their skills in English and their literacy enabled some of them to move into 'lower-middle class' occupations and become policemen, clerks, teachers or minor civil servants. From this base they could educate their children and see them become solidly 'middle class'.

Even in the case of these West Indian immigrants who remained clearly working-class, there was a self-assertion, an independence of mind, which often distinguished them from the rural Creoles. Barbadian workers in particular became famous for their aggressive independence – or, as the planters called, 'insolence'. In other words they did not share those habits of deference so often found among the Creole country folk in the 19th century. Coming from an island with an elected Assembly and therefore familiar with electoral politics, the Barbadians were also quite politically conscious, and were often accused of 'agitating' the simple Creole folk who would otherwise never dream of entertaining political ideas. This, of course, was the prejudiced view of the guardians of the status quo, but it does seem true that Barbadian artisans and teachers in the towns and villages of 19th century Trinidad were 'natural' politicians and leaders of opinion.

Sources: B. Brereton, *Race Relations in Colonial Trinidad.*
H. Johnson, '*Barbadian Immigrants in Trinidad, 1870-97' Caribbean Studies,* Vol. 13, No. 3, 1973.

CHOLERA EPIDEMIC IN TRINIDAD

It is our painful duty to announce the existence in the town and its vicinity of an epidemic which there is but too much reason to fear is the same disease which has afflicted several of the other West Indian Islands. The cases are as yet few, and their number is increasing with no great rapidity, and it is still hoped the disease may be kept under, seeing that the districts into which the town has been divided in anticipation of such a visitation, are each in charge of a medical man, and a system of daily house to house visitation is being enforced. It is in this latter measure we must confess we place our principal trust. It is not cholera that has to be combatted as yet, so much as diarrhoea and dysentery,—the precursors of the more terrible disease. Serious apprehensions are also entertained with regard to the sufficiency of food in our present emergency. There is only enough flour for two days consumption in Port of Spain at present; and the propriety of the government importing from Barbados where there is an ample stock and to spare ought to engage serious attention.
(30th August, 1854.)

Various measures of relief have now been taken with reference to the prevailing epidemic. A committee comprising five members of the Borough Council, and five gentlemen appointed by His Excellency the Governor, have established a house of refuge in each of the several sanitary sections of the town, where indigent persons, taken ill of cholera in the streets, are received, and to which all people taken with the premonitory symptoms of the disease may resort as a matter of precaution, so that, should they grow worse they may be on the spot where immediate medical attention is to be had, and if not, after preliminary treatment they may be sent home, with necessary supplies of medicines, and some advice and a little nourishing food. The committee originally appointed have associated themselves with divers each of the eight divisions of the town. They are gentlemen, so that there are now 32 members formed into eight sub-committees, one of which employed themselves in soliciting subscriptions for the relief of the needy, and for the establishment of soup kitchens where those suffering from sickness as well as from want of food may get nourishment. The subscriptions already obtained amount to upwards of $2,000.

The burials at Lapeyrouse Cemetery of cholera victims from Port of Spain since our last issue have been as follows:

Thursday–27

Friday–40

Saturday–20 (up to noon only)

the epidemic is now, we trust, approaching, if it has not already reached its culminating point; for it is upwards of three weeks since it made its appearance, and as far as the experience of the neighbouring colonies

can prove a guide to us, we may reasonably hope soon for a material reduction of the number of deaths, and an early cessation of the dreadful malady. The burials since the 26th August at Lapeyrouse from Port of Spain have been as follows:-

August 26th—7
August 27th—5
August 28th—9
August 29th—3
August 30th—6
August 31st—8
September 1st—12
September 2nd—15
September 3rd—19
September 4th—19
September 5th—24
September 6th—26
September 7th—27
September 8th—40
September 9th—40
September 10th—53
September 11th—52
September 12th—55
September 13th—61
September 14th—55
September 15th—48
September 16th—61
September 17th—55
September 18th—51
September 19th—80
September 20th—75

This gives a total of 911 burials to date; if we take off 70 as a fair proportion from other causes for the period, it leaves 841 cases of cholera that have terminated fatally; but as there have been many interments of residents of Port of Spain in burial grounds to the east and north east of the town, the total number of deaths in Port of Spain may safely be said to have already exceeded 1,000. The disease has in the past few days also extended itself amongst the class of inhabitants who are of better condition in life, and of an European or mixed parentage. In these victims, however, it is found in most instances to yield to the application of timely remedies. here and there, however, a case occurs which baffles every effort and treatment to arrest its speedy and fatal termination.
(20th September 1854.)

NOTE:— The epidemic seems to have continued, however, for some time longer; and did not finally cease, as such, until the 27th October, which appears to have been regarded officially as the end. From the subsequent issue of the Gazette the following details and statistics are taken from an official report on the epidemic by Dr. Clarke, senior military medical officer of the colony on the request of the Government:

The total population of Port of Spain in 1854 was estimated by Dr. Clarke at 18,501; which he states includes in addition to ordinary inhabitants, the gaol, the hospital, the asylums, the convent, and the other institutions. The total number of cases reported was 4,200 or 25 percent of the total population,—one in every four inhabitants. the deaths were 2,112, in the space of nine weeks, from the 13th August to the 27th of October. That is 57 percent of the victims died; and the deaths numbered more than a tenth of the entire population of Port of Spain. The weekly interments from cholera in the Lapeyrouse Cemetery were: 49, 170, 364, 455, 495, 256, 144, 43 and 36. Dr. Clarke compares the statistics of death here with some other places as follows; Port of Spain 10.6 percent of the population; Barbados, 19.2 percent; Jamaica, 26 percent; San Fernando, 14.3 pecent. The Gazette, commenting upon the results of the tabular statements of results, points out whimsically that 'apparently the districts of the town which were generally regarded as the healthiest, had the greatest number of deaths; while other districts notoriously sickly and insanitary, escaped with comparitively unexpected immunity'!

Port of Spain Gazette.
Special Centenary Issue.

THE CHINESE OF TRINIDAD

Bridget Brereton

Immigrants from India were not the only people to enter the society in the decades after emancipation, though they were by far the most numerous. From Asia also came a small but important stream of Chinese immigrants. As early as 1806, a small number of men from China had been settled in the island, but significant Chinese immigration really began after emancipation. Between 1853 and 1866, about 2,500 Chinese, mostly men, arrived to work on the estates as indentured labourers under the same terms as the Indians. 1866 marks the end of indentured Chinese immigration because in that year the Chinese government insisted on a free return passage, which would have been prohibitively costly; but it does not, of course, mark the end of Chinese immigration to Trinidad. After 1866 they arrived in small numbers as voluntary, 'free' immigrants; some came via British Guiana where a larger Chinese community had been established.

The Lee Lum dynasty, for example, was established here when John Lee Lum arrived in 1912 at the age of 20. After the Chinese revolution in 1911, immigration picked up and was quite high between the 1920's and the late 1940's, a turbulent era of China's modern history. Thus Trinidad's Chinese population had increased from 1,334 in 1921 to 8,361 in 1960. Many of the post-1911 immigrants came via Hong Kong or even the United States and arrived knowing some English and familar to some extent with Western ways.

Few of the early Chinese immigrants remained on the estates for long. Most of them became shopkeepers, market gardeners or butchers. Many married Creole women and adopted Christianity. The post-1911 immigrants, coming in larger numbers, were probably better able to hold on to some of their cultural and family traits as a sizable Chinese community was gradually established. Above all the Chinese established themselves as rural and village shopkeepers, along with their Portuguese rivals. By the 1940's important trading terms had been established by Chinese families, such as the Lee Lums and the Scotts.

Culturally, the Chinese language (in its two major forms, Hakka from North China and Cantonese from the South) survived among the Trinidad Chinese community and in fact the 1940's saw an effort to revive the langugage and the culture. But the Communist takeover in 1949 severed virtually all links between China and the Caribbean Chinese, so that the language dwindled until, today, few of the young Chinese in Trinidad can speak it. the demise of Chinese religions in Trinidad was even swifter: by 1960 virtually no Chinese-Trinidadian practised their Buddhism or Confucianism. The vast majority were fully integrated into the Christian Churches, especially the Roman Catholic Church. Traditional Chinese culture is rapidly disappearing among the community, and it is perhaps only in the field of food preparation that it has made a profound impact on the wider society.

Yet Trinidad's Chinese Community has produced outstanding figures such as Eugene Chen who served as Foreign Minister in Sun-Yat-Sen's Government in China, Solomon Hochoy, first local Governor and first Governor-General of the nation, the artist Carlisle Chang, and Carnival bandleaders Stephen and Elsie Lee Heung. Prominent especially as businessmen and professionals, the Chinese community seems to exercise an influence out of all proportion to its numerical strength.

Sources: D. Wood, *Trinidad in Transition.*
T. Millette, *The Chinese in Trinidad*

S. Hochoy

V.I.T. Hochoy

S. Atteck

S. Lee Lum

A Chinese oyster vendor of the 1800's.
Photograph — U.W.I. Library

The date of the introduction of Chinese immigrants into the island is given by Joseph as 12 October, 1806, that being the day on which the ship 'Fortitude' anchored in our harbour. He gives the information that the men were Tartars and not accustomes to working in the fields, and that only one woman was among the number the total being 193. He accounts for the absence of women from the fact that they would be unsuitable as field workers from the restricted size of their feet. He further stated that with the exception of about 23 the whole number returned by the same ship 'Fortitude'.

The Chinese Association
of Trinidad

OFFICIALS AND MEMBERS OF THE EXECUTIVE COMMITTEE, 1929

Missing: Dr. S.E. Ammon, Dr. M. Chu-Cheong, and J. Ling.
Standing from left to right: J.E. Lai Fook, F. Yip Young, C. Lee Ghin, Miss C. Hosang, G.L. Francis-Lau, Lee Chee, L.R. Lum Yan.
Sitting from left to right: C. Tan Yuk, H. Chinasing, Dr. T.P. Achong, J.R. Hingking, E. Lee Lum, J. Leung, Marfoe.
Photograph — Moyin Chinasing

H. Lu Affatt   D.R. Huggins   C.D. Fung-a-Fatt   R.L. Low

U.L. Look Yan   G.M.C. Ling   P.A.S. Ling   K.M. Lee

C.E. Huggins   C.M. Fung

R. Austin

C.H. George

The Chinese Council, Queens Park West. Originally the
home of Packer Hutchinson. It was acquired by several
members of the Chinese community in Trinidad to serve
as a cultural centre and Council after the collapse of the
Chang Kai-Shek Government in China. It fell into disuse
and was eventually demolished. It is now a vacant lot.
Photograph — I.P. George.

MEMBERS OF THE MADAME CHANG KAI-SHEK CLUB, an American
Organization composed of Chinese girls, march past in the chorus in
'Strike Up the Band' which formed part of the celebrations for American
Independence Day. Left to right are: Vida Wong, Ulrica Lee Kai, Adrie
Archer and Madge Chin. (U.S. Army Signal Corps Photograph —
courtesy of Trinidad News Tips.)

Miss Thora Thomas dancer and choreographer, whose contribution to
dance to the young in Trinidad cannot be exaggerated. Photograph —
I.P. George.

CHINESE IN TRINIDAD

Based on a lecture by Dr. Robert K. Lee

The first documentary evidence of the Chinese community in Trinidad is contained in the census of 1810 which mentions 'a colony of 22 Chinese males who lived in misery in Cocorite, making their living selling charcoal, oysters and crabs'. Prior to Emancipation the small number of Chinese immigrants can be accounted for by a general indifference to the outside world in China and the fact that the legal penalty for emigration was death (this law was not repealed until 1894); there was also a strong tradition that ancestral spirits should only be cared for by descendants. Towards the end of the 19th century however, various factors in China prompted a move towards emigration: the collapse of the feudal system; the doubling of the population from 120 million in the 1790's to 300 million and the burden of increased taxation imposed by the corrupt Empire.

The Chinese immigrants came from 2 groups: the Punti and the Hakka. The Cantonese speaking Punti, originally from the North of China had intermarried with the ethnic Chinese Miao. The Hakka, who spoke their own language, had settled on land cleared of Punti, who were suspected of disloyalty to the Empire. Following the Civil War between Hakka and Punti 1854-68, the Hakka who were already accustomed to the maritime life began to look across the sea, especially after hearing the news of the discovery of gold in California in 1848.

Chinese immigrants came to Trinidad in different ways: some came under contract as indentured labourers; many were 'shanghaied' – abducted into virtual slavery by European traders either in the West Indies or South America. Hakka prisoners were also sought by Punti traders for the infamous 'Pig Trade' whereby Hakka described as pigs on bills of lading were shipped off to the New World. Older Trinidadian Chinese still refer to mainland Chinese or recently arrived immigrants as 'mee chee chai' – young pigs or fresh pork. By 1874 the Governor of Canton had banned the 'Pig Trade' and the Chinese were replaced with the more tractable East Indians as indentured labourers.

During the early years of immigration Chinese Merchant Houses acted as facilitating agencies for new arrivals; they provided temporary accommodation, job placements and community centres; they also imported brides and shipped back bones for village interment.

Although the Chinese community has apparently been assimilated in Trinidad to a greater extent than anywhere else in the world it has left indelible marks on contemporary Trinidadian culture: it was the Chinese who originally introduced 'whe-whe' or 'Pakka Piu'. Today's game still bears a strong resemblance to the original Chinese game – the marks are largely derived from the Chinese zodiac and still retain much of their original symbolism. Trinidadian cuisine also owes a debt to the original Chinese immigrants who brought various plants and vegetables with them; the East Indians later supplemented these and consequently the fruits and vegetables in Trinidad are the best in the Caribbean in terms of freshness and variety (Chinese cooks insist on using only young, tender and nutritious produce). Cantonese cooks set up shops and over the years have educated the Trinidadian palate. Thus it was that ghingee, carailee, christophene, snow peas, Narchoi, Pakchoi, mustard bush, white radish and white melon entered local markets.

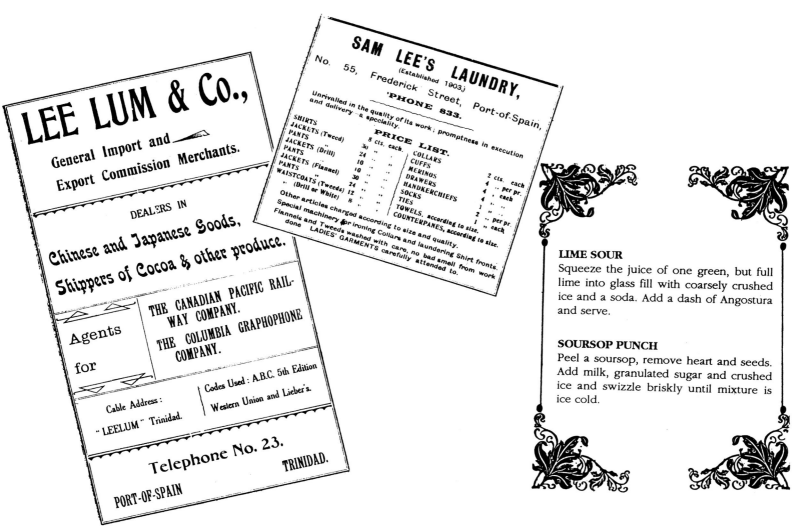

LIME SOUR
Squeeze the juice of one green, but full lime into glass fill with coarsely crushed ice and a soda. Add a dash of Angostura and serve.

SOURSOP PUNCH
Peel a soursop, remove heart and seeds. Add milk, granulated sugar and crushed ice and swizzle briskly until mixture is ice cold.

HISTORICAL AND STATISTICAL VIEW OF THE ISLAND OF TRINIDAD

Daniel Hart

COCOA

The principal articles of produce exported are sugar, cocoa, coffee, rum, molasses, and cotton. Indigo is also exported, but not raised in the island; it is brought from Venezuela for exportation; but in 1783 there were plantations and manufacturers of the article established in the island. The number of sugar estates does not exceed from 152 to 155, and those of cocoa and coffee 700. The total extent of land under cultivation is as follows:– In canes, 36,739 acres; cocoa and coffee, 14,238 acres; provisions, 9,914 acres; pasture, 7,356 acres. Total, 67,247 acres.

The correct name of the cocoa is 'cacao'. The cultivation of cocoa, with the exception of a small quantity grown in the island of Grenada, is peculiar as an article of British production to Trinidad. With the exception just mentioned, Trinidad is the only colony throughout the wide extent of the British Colonial Empire producing the materials for this wholesome and palatable beverage. In 1827 the number of cocoa trees amounted to 3,091,945, and the quantity exported that year was 3,696,144, valued according to official returns at £57,851. The value of each tree being then taken at two dollars, or eight shillings and four-pence. After 1827, a sudden depression in the price of the article reduced the cocoa proprietors at once and without warning, from a state of affluence to one of comparative–nay, in many cases real–destitution. For the last ten years, however, the article has maintained a fair and remunerative price. The culture of cocoa is the only one of our Tropical productions at all adapted to the constitution of Europeans. The cocoa tree itself of some 20 feet in height, and affording a grateful shade from the blaze of the sun, is again shaded in its turn by the *bois immortel,* whose protecting services have justly obtained for it among the South Americans the appellation of *La Madre del Cacao.* The weeding of the soil, picking of the pods, husking them, and carrying the produce to the drying house; in short, the whole of the agricultural operations and all but the last stage of the manufacturing process, is carried on under this impervious and ever verdant canopy; the air gently agitated and refreshed by the river or mountain stream, upon whose *vegas* or banks these plantations are invariably established. Here, and here only, the European may measure his strength with the descendants of the Africans, and derive direct from the soil without the intervention of the latter, the subsistence which in every other kind of agricultural pursuits seems denied him by his own physical exertions. Under the double shade of the cocoa tree and the *Madre del Cacao,* the European feels himself as in his native climate. By official returns made in 1842, there were 182 small plantations having from 100 to 500 trees; 147 having from 500 to 1000 trees, and 268 having from 1000 to 5000 trees; 55 having from 5,000 to 10,000 trees; 29 having from 10,000 to 20,000 trees; 28 having from 20,000 to 50,000 trees, and 1 above 50,000: making a total of 710. Upon a general average, each cocoa tree ought to yield annually two and a half pounds nett of cocoa. The distance at which cocoa is planted in this island differs from four to five *varas.* I have taken the latter as the basis of my calculations. At that distance there are about 800 trees in a *quarree,* which is the old Spanish measurement of 3.1-5 English acres. Consequently, 40,000 trees occupy fifty quarrees, and the average yield bring something near 2½ lbs. per tree, 22 fanegas per 1000 trees, and $12 (with few exceptions) as the highest price obtained in the market in 1865. Pruning is an essential operation. Five years would be sufficient to intervene between the pruning; and on an Estate of 40,000 trees, I would do it by using the knife to 8000 trees only in one year, and continue at such rate until the whole shall have been pruned–to re-commence again by the first 8000 trees. Forty-eight dollars is put down to be expended in that operation, not that the whole of that amount would be expended (for the pruning should be light), but because in that sum is included the cleaning of trees from moss, parasites, ants, and guatepajaro,–a work which, though strongly recommended to both men and women (for on many Estates picking is performed by women) employed in picking pods, it is, nevertheless, very imperfectly done, or not done at all. Hence, at the proper season, which is immediately after the December crop, say, in March and April, a skilful gang should be employed to trim and clean the 8000 trees apportioned for the season. The expenses and net revenue of Cocoa Estates are subject to variation, according to extent and locality: an Estate of 30,000 trees requiring almost the same establishment as one of 40 or 50,000,–hence the increase or decrease of the net revenue and cost per bag of cocoa on different Estates. The amount paid for cutlassing 100 trees varies from 30 to 60 cents. Some Estates in the quarter of Maracas, not having labourers located on the property, are in the habit of cutlassing their Estates by 'gallapa', a system much preferred by small proprietors, though it raises the expense to the ruinous amount of $1 20 per 100 trees. The 2½ lbs. which I have put down as the yield per tree, in the present imperfect state of cultivation can produce; but I am quite certain that with increased care and attention, a cocoa tree at 13 feet apart can be made to yield double that quantity. As a proof: on the Estate of Mr. Victoriano Gomez, in the Ward of Maracas, there are 200 trees planted at 22 feet apart that yielded 6 lbs. per tree. A quarree planted at that distance holds 288 trees, giving a total of 2128 lbs. At 13 feet a quarree as already stated contains 800 trees, at 2½ lbs. per tree gives 2000 lbs.—a difference of 128 lbs. in favour of wide planting. But is wide planting more profitable? The following particulars will show. Cocoa planted at 22 feet apart require 139 quarrees for 40,000 trees, at 6 lbs. per tree would give 24,000 lbs.; 139 quarrees planted at 13 feet apart would contain 111,400 trees, which, at 2½ lbs. per tree is 278,000 lbs.; planted at 22 feet in 50 quarrees there are 14,400 at 6 lbs. is 86,400,; at 13 feet, there are 40,000 trees, which, at 2½ lbs. will give 100,000 lbs. Difference in favour of narrow planting in 50 quarrees, 13,000 lbs. or 123½ fanegas, which, at $12, would give a total profit of $1480. In addition to the foregoing remarks, it is necessary to state, that on every well-regulated Cocoa Estate, there should be a nursery of cocoa trees of the best quality, in order to supply 'fallos' or missing trees. The following is a statement of the expenses of a Cocoa Estate of 40,000 trees, and cost per fanega (110 lbs.) or bag:–

It is worthy of remark that a Cocoa Estate by the planting of provisions and the raising of Stock ought to considerably tend to decrease the expenses above given, because the labourers are only required to pick—twice in the year—June and December. Each estate of the size herein given should also be provided with 8 or 10 good donkeys for crooking, and 25 good steady labourers would be sufficient to carry on the working of an estate of 40,000 trees. It is necessary, however, to state that for the last 3 or 4 years cocoa has been disposed of in the London Market from 65s., 70s., 80s., 90s. and as high as 110s. per cwt., nor has it been under nine dollars in the Trinidad Market. Indeed as much as 13 dollars the fanega (110lbs.) has been paid, hence the nett annual income should be much more than is herein given. There is however, a want of energy on the part of the Cocoa planters in regard to planting provisions and the rear of stock. It is, at the same time, just to remark that they labour under great difficulties in the way of procuring labourers. A negro can live for 24 hours on a sugar cane. Hence, he would rather work on a sugar estate for one shilling a day than for two shillings on a cocoa estate. In former years when the price of cocoa was low, little or no attention was paid to the cultivation; the increase of price has, however, acted as a real stimulus to the planters of the article, and greater attention is now paid both to the cultivation and to the curing and preparing of the article. The largest cocoa estate in the island is the 'La Pastora', situate in the Ward of Santa Cruz, and belonging to Mr. H. Borde. On this estate there are 50,000 trees, but this estate, like others, in 1837 (a year also that the cocoa planter laboured under very great disadvantages for the want of labour) only yielded a crop of 70,200 lbs. In the year 1727 the cocoa trees were greatly injured by the severity of the North Wind—a disaster which the Priests represented as a judgement upon the inhabitants for their enormity in refusing the payment of tithes. Alcedo relates this ridiculous story—'The production of the greatest value in this island', says he 'is the cocoa which from its fine quality, is everywhere in request, in preference to that of Caracas; and the crops were even bought up before they were gathered, so that the person to whom they belonged refused to pay their tenths to the clergy, and strange to say, that, as it should seem, Heaven in chastisement of their covetousness had entirely deprived them of this means of emolument in as much as, since the year 1727, the whole of their crop have turned out fruitless and barren, with the exception of one that belonged to a certain man named Robles, who had continued to pay his tithes, and whose estate is the only one in which that production is now furnished.' Unfortunately for the theory of the Monks, and the faith of Alcedo, the crops of cocoa have been, and I hope they ever will be, exuberant since Trinidad has been cultivated, as the Tables of Exports herein given fully proves. It is worthy of remark that the 'Robles' mentioned by Alcedo was the father of Christoval de Robles, who inherited from his father the San Antonio and Santa Catalina Estates in the Ward of Santa Cruz.

San Juan Estate Grand Couva, Trinidad was owned by Francois Agostini. This great house was destroyed by fire a few years ago.
Photograph — Mrs. Hélène Farfan.

Cocoa, The Golden Bean.

Cocoa and the Second Frontier (1870-1920).

Bridget Brereton

Trinidad was first opened up for plantation development and large-scale settlement in the 1780's with the influx of French immigrants after the Cedula of Population. The first phase of rapid development–the first frontier–was dominated by the expansion of sugar production and could be said to have lasted from the 1780's to the 1820's. Yet, even by the 1830's, Trinidad was still an undeveloped country. Vast amounts of potentially fertile land were still untouched by human enterprise. In 1838, only some 43,000 acres were cultivated out of a total acreage of 1.25 million. Much of the island was still in the hands of the Crown and under its original forest cover. Only a fairly narrow band of territory stretching west to east from Chaguaramas to Arima, and north to south from Port of Spain to San Fernando, was extensively settled and cultivated. The southern half of the island, the north coast and its hills and valleys, the whole of the east coast and much of Central Trinidad were virtually untouched and unpopulated. Trinidad was still a frontier colony by the middle decades of the nineteenth century.

The second phase of internal colonization of the island began around 1870 and was associated above all with the expansion of cocoa, though later on (after 1910) the development of the oil industry was also important especially for the southern half of the island. But it was cocoa which dominated the second frontier: settlement and population followed the cocoa trees into the newly opened up districts.

Cocoa is indigenous to the New World–it was the Aztecs' chocolate, Montezuma's favourite drink–and it had always been cultivated in Spanish Trinidad. But around 1850 it was quite insignificant as an export crop. Its take-off into a period of rapid expansion can be dated to around 1870. As eating chocolate, and cocoa as a beverage became items of mass consumption in the industrialised countries; demand for cocoa in Europe and North America expanded tremendously, and this was the most important single reason for the expansion of cocoa in Trinidad.

Locally, the opening up of Crown lands through a change of government policy in the late 1860's and the gradual improvement of internal communications after 1870 (roads, railways, bridges) had the effect of removing serious obstacles to the progress of settlement and cultivation. Capital, labour, and some land became available in the years between 1884 and 1903 because of the sugar depression in that period: for instance, workers retrenched by the sugar estates might enter cocoa as wage labourers or as peasant growers, money received through sale of small, marginal sugar estates to big firms could be invested in the establishment of cocoa plantations, and in some cases abandoned sugar land could be switched to cocoa. Since the establishment of a modest cocoa estate did not require a massive outlay of capital (unlike sugar), many local families could mobilize their personal resources and finance the gradual building-up of a cocoa property.

While the market situation remained favourable, therefore, and it did right up to 1920–all the ingredients for a rapid expansion of production were present. Exports had averaged 8 million lbs a year in 1871-80; by the decade 1911-20 they averaged 56.3 million, a seven-fold increase. By the turn of the century cocoa had overtaken sugar as Trinidad's most valuable export: King Sugar had been dethroned.

The new King Cocoa, during his short ascendancy, profoundly influenced many aspects of Trinidad's social and economic development. Previously inaccessible areas which had been barely populated at all were opened up

Heaping Cocoa. After the beans were picked they would be brought in baskets from the surrounding fields, heaped and sorted.
A photograph of the 1880's. Photograph — Mrs. Hélène Farfan.

to cultivation and settlement, especially the valleys of the northern range, the country between Sangre Grande and the east coast, and parts of central Trinidad and the deep south. New villages sprang into life, with their churches and chapels, schools, lodges and friendly societies, post offices and warden's offices, markets and shops. Old towns like Arima took on a new lease of life, as cocoa marketing centres. The population spread out from the original centres of settlement along the eastern main road to Arima and from Port of Spain to San Fernando. People of all races were involved in this movement: the Creole blacks, the peons who had been the first pioneers of cocoa, the African and West Indian immigrants, the ex-indentured after 1870.

The expansion of cocoa had a significant impact on Trinidad's social development. The industry came to be dominated by French Creoles, who pioneered the second frontier movement in the last third of the nineteenth century and who reaped the greatest rewards. As estate owners and as cocoa dealers and financiers (marketing the cocoa, supplying the estates and extending the necessary credit), the French Creoles established a firm grip on the industry as a whole.

The profits from successful cocoa estates, especially between the 1880's and 1920's, enabled many French Creoles to live like lords, building splendid estate houses and town mansions in Port of Spain, entertaining lavishly, employing small armies of servants, educating their

children in Europe and paying frequent visits back to the old continent. Cocoa gave the French Creoles the economic base to stage a social and political come-back after some decades of relative powerlessness between the 1830's and the 1880's. Even after the cocoa market collapsed in the 1920s, many French Creole families were able to diversify their economic activities by shifting into the commercial and financial fields. But cocoa had been the secure base of their prosperity.

Cocoa however was never exclusively an estate crop. Thousands of peasants of all races cultivated the cocoa trees as contractors (raising trees on land belonging to estates) and as small producers on their own land. Cocoa contributed very significantly to the growth and prosperity of Trinidad's peasantry, and these small farmers created new settlements and new social and cultural institutions all over the country. To take just one example: parang and the culture associated with it are inseparable from the cocoa peasantry. As cocoa prospered, some of the profits filtered down to the labourers and small producers, and many of them were able to educate their children, contributing to the growth of the middle class and the general spread of literacy and modernization.

King Cocoa fell, in his turn, in the 1920's and 1930's; but not before he had played a key role in opening up the island, strengthening its economy and enriching its social and cultural development.

*Cocoa Pañols at the Ortinola Estate 1890.
Photograph — Hélène Farfan.*

*List of Trinidad Cocoa Estates are from Franklyn's Year
Book 1916.*

Tacarigua & Blanchisseuse Ward Union

Estates	Owners	Estates	Owners	Estates	Owners	Estates	Owners
	Mohammed			Caurita, Guamal		St. Anns	Rev. Dr. Maingot
La Gloria	"	Santa Basilio	Manoel Alonzo	Hope Well	Heirs C. Leotaud	El Choro	Victor Adrien
Oriol	G.R. Alston& Co.	La Soledad	"	San Pedro		St. Helena	
Santa Rita	Cecil Awang	Mundo Nuevo	Max Reimer	Destin		G. de Silva	Laurel Hill
Pleasant Vale	Celestine Davis	Valencia	"	W. Bowring			
La Clarita	F. de Boehmler	La Pastora	Gordon Grant & Co. Ltd	San Domingo	Josefita de León	La Belle Vue	Juliana Bonair
Santa Eleanora	Fleming Rios & Co.			La Soledad	Hrs. of De la Rose	La Soledad	A.A. De Matas
Stella	Mrs. M. Gransaull	Algarabo	Heirs of L. Philip	Gonzales		St. Catherine	
Colonden	D.A. Laurie	La Soledad	E. Lezama	San Isidro	Alan Mc D. Horne	La Florida	F. De Matas
Laventura	Geo. Liddlelow	Montserrat	J.P. Zepro	Trafford	Marie Holler	El Broyo	
Grand Hall	Hrs. D. Marcelin	San Francisco	"	Redemption	Edward Mohipath	Santa Margarita	"
La Belle Vue	"	La Deseada	"	Santa Rita	Jos. Reyes	La Merced	
St. Charles	"	La Realista	Mrs. M.E. Olivieri	La Soledad	Heirs Reyes	San Pedro	Cadbury brothers
		Des Consue		Maracas Valley	Cadbury Brothers	San Miguel	A.T. Eligon
TACARIGUA & BLANCHISSEUSE		La Florida	Wilsons, Ltd.	San Pedro	"	La Soledad	Fred Herrera
				Santa Barbara	V.L. Wehekind	Williams Field	"

Polishing cocoa to give a lustre to the beans as a fine appearance was very important.

La Sombadoura	"	Lorete	A.V.C. Gomez	Arima Ward Union		San Antonio	Heirs of Garcia
San Pedro del Valle	J.B. Garner	La Belle Vue	M.M. Castillo	Mon Repos	Hrs. L. Centeno	Santa Maria	F.A. Neubauer
Ortinola	Tennants Est. Ltd.	Intricacy		La Reunion	"	Glencora	"
Santa Rita	D. Betancourt	Mon Repos	Heirs L. Centeno	L'Espérance	"	Perseverance	"
La Provindencia		La Chaguaramas		Verdant Vale	"	Piedmonte	Paul Caracciolo
La Fortuna	A.A. De Matas	Shaldon	A. J. & A. G. Hamlyn	Willow Vale	Trinidad Cocoa	La Fertilite	"
Bickham	Heirs of Wharf	La Grande Source	Ragoonanan	S. Patrick, La Razón	and Coffee Co.,	Monte Cristo	"
San Lorenzo	Fred. Herrera	El Recobro	Est. C. Schoener	San Mateo and	Limited	El Carmen	"
La Victoria	Caroline Borberg	San Miguel	Lucy Langton	Cedar Hill		Jouvence	Hrs of Hospedales
La Carola	"	Providence	A.C. Poyer	Mount Pleasant	Hrs. de Lapeyrouse	Santa Barbara	"
Belle Vue	Dhanoolall	Caledonia	W. Archibald	El Retiro	Hrs. De Martini	El Combata	H.J. Delisle
Guiria	Hrs. J. V. de León	La Fortune	Joaq. Ribeiro	Mon Plaisir	F.J. Le Blanc	La Conception	"
La Soledad	E. Gonzales	Caroni Farm	"	La Compensación	S. De Gannes	La Horqueta	Hrs. Joa. Ribeiro
El Retiro	Heirs T.B. Meja	St. Helena	"	San Jose	"	Belle Vue	J.R. Metivier
Buena Vista	M.J. de Silva	Mon Jaloux	"	Buena Vista	Hrs. Jules Cipriani	Jouvence	P. Stevens
San Miguel	"	El Carmen	A.H. Burt	La Victoria	Wm. E. Foster	San Rafael	A. Angeron
San Juan	Simon B. Pierre	Buen Esperanza	"	Belle Vue	"	Los Armadillos	C. Faustino
Santa Barbara		Caroni (Cacao)	E.R. Clarke	Prospect	J.S. McDavid	Sta. Catalina	Thos. Lacon
Calcutta	Cadamee	La Florida	Jane Cossila	Oropuna	H. Machado	Santa Rosalia	Manuel Luces
El Reposo	Hrs. S. Castillo	Hermitage	Hector Court	San Antonio	A.M. Tinoco	San Gregorio	"
Esperanza	"	La Preferencia	B.T. Coryat	San José	A. Harry	San Rafael	"
El Discurso	G.T. Brash	Woodland	De la Rosa & Smith	Torrecilla	M.S. Strickland	Prosperite	Hrs. C. de Verteuil
La Lucia	E. Gabaira	Providence	C.J. Decle	Santa Rosa	Hrs. C.G. Seheult	Havering	W. Carpenter
St. Jena	Xavier Hardy	La Solitude	"	Sin Verquenza	F.A. Nuebauer	Laventille	Heirs of Llanos
Providence	Margaret Hunter	Union	O. Kelly	Hermitage	"	Monte Cristo	Paul Caracciolo
San Juan	Edm. Kelly	Trafalgar	Nazarat Ali	La Ressource	Robt. J. Miller	San Jose	M.J. Roach
Rosalia	"	Santa Rita	M.J. Nanco	Mausica & Trianon	Hrs. C. Cleaver	L'Agnesia	Dr. R.C. Bennet
El Guamo	C.A. Morrison	La Soledad	S.F. Proctor	Valley Vale	F.W. Meyer	New Providence	G. de Verteuil
Santa Lucia	Hrs. José Votor	Santa Isabella	E.W. Savary	San Francisco	C. Leotaud	La Cruz	P.R. Pierre
	Bennysingh and	La Soledad	"	Orange Hill	"	La Soledad	Carmona
Canaan	Rampersadsingh	Perseverance	L.W. Snagg	El Ricon, San Felipe	"	El Regalo	A. Giuseppi
La Belle Vue	Hrs. Chinibas	St. Charles	A.V. Stollmeyer	Mon Repos	C.O. & L. Robertson	La Corona	"
WARD UNION				La Retraite	L. Hamel-Smith	La India	M.A. Vignale
Glenside	Commdr. W.H.	La Victoria	"	S. Carlos de Caigual	West Indian	La Esmeralda	George F. Huggins
	Coombs, R.N.	San Francisco	Geo. B. Geoffroy	St. Patience	Trustees	Arizona	H. Monceaux
Charles Vale	S. Augustin	Santa Ignes	Heirs Nakid	Agua Santa	C. Blasini	San Bartolo	H.J. Vieira
Redemption	Hrs. B. de Lamarre	San Joachim	"	St. Adelaide	L.A. Riley	Providence	"
St. Michael	Resal Maharaj	Tierra Nueva	Heirs C. Léotaud	Spring Bank	Gordon Grant & Co.		

El Socorro   "
La Solidad   "
Prosperidad   "
Sta. Isabella   "
La Soledad   "
Santa Cruz   S. Bercon
Felipe
San Carlos   C. Stollmeyer
Candelaria   L.A. Sellier
Esperanza   A.D. Brown
Santa Cruz   Jos. N. Maingot
Murray's Vale   Henry E. Murray
Santa Maria   Hy. Court
New Providence   Alb. H. Cipriani
Val de Cacao   "
La Romancia   Dr. A.H. Burt
La Marouna   Heirs of J. Payne
C. Stollmeyer   San Juan J.A. Aquie
Paradise   C. Luces
Santa Marta   W.S.E. Barnardo
Spring   "
Sios Me Ayudes   A. de Matas

Couva & Chaguanas Ward Union

Estates	Owners
St. Charles	
Esperanza Brown	Heirs Hoadley
Verdant Vale	Heirs Penco
Philippine	Hrs. L. Preau
Balmain	J.P. Bain
La Rosalia	J.A. Ortiz
Belle Vue	Boodhin
Peking	Numa Nathaniel
Williams	Naseban
Good Luck	Satuarine
Enaree	Beddoo Bhagat
Sitar-i-Hind	E.M. Madoo
Hope	E.V. Downey
Carolina	Agostini and Mc Lelland

Diego Martin & St. Ann's Ward Union

Estates	Owners
Mt. Carmel	Pitman & de Suze
San Diego & Victoria	George G.
La Ressource	Catherine R. Rust
La Ressource	Jean Isidore
San Carlos	W.T. Campbell
Perseverance	L.S. Disney
St. Emelia	L.D. Alcazar
Mon Repos	Edgar Borde
Covigne	E. Hamel-Smith
St. John	Madeleine Joseph
Grand Fond	"
Jamson	J.A. Brown
La Fromage	Mrs. C. Fitzwilliam
Mount Catherine	Louis Julien
La Oferta	André de Verteuil

Prospect	F. Isaac	La Sagesse, Zig Zag	Hrs. J.E. Coryat
Perseverance	J.E. Bonneterre	Santa Barbara	"
Don José	F.A. Gómez	Prosperidad	"
The Hope		Santa Carolina	"
St. Luke	Dyett & Grant	La Madeleine	"
Bon Aventure	Heirs W.C. Dyett	La Pastora	J. Ribeiro
Mon Plaisir		Tranquilidad	"
St. Vale, Lee Vale	C.P. Lee	Maracas Bay	Hrs. de Lapeyrouse
L'Argenville	Dr. A.B. Duprey	Paradis Terrestre	J. Penco

Dancing cocoa. This was done to put a shine on the beans.
Photograph upper left, Hélène Farfan, right, Elspeth Brierly.

Venezuelan peons were to a considerable degree responsible for the revival of cocoa. From the 1870's they were encouraged to settle on lands suitable for its development. Cocoa Pañols, as they were called were people of mixed Amerindian and Spanish descent. Photograph — Mrs. Hélène Farfan.

DIEGO MARTIN & ST. ANN'S WARD UNION

La Chaguaramas	Chaguaramas
Mt. Hazard	Estates, Limited
Crystal Stream	Heirs of J. Dickson
Fond Palmiste	
St. Sophie	J.C. Benlisa
St. Lucien	Croney & Co.
Richplain	Erroll & A. Artfield
Les Fontaines	Michael P. Maillard
La Ressource	"
Bagatelle	"
Cedar Hill	F. & J.A. Jones
Hermitage	Anna Lange
Esperanza	"
La Puerta	Dr. J.I. Denior
Tucker Valley	T'dad Ltd. & Finance
Haleland Park	Co., "
Moka	W.G. Gordon

Tacarigua & Blanchisseuse Ward Union

Estates	Owners
La Fortuna	Marie Watson
La Pastora	Thos. Wilson
Las Cuevas	Lord Rendelshan
Leslie Vale	B. de Nobriga
Paria Valley	C. Dookram
Marianne	Mrs. J. Drago
Northcote	I.B. Phillipps
Tayrico	S. Wilson
Paria	Hrs. Etienne
San Antonio	V.J. Philip
Belle Vue	V.J. Philip
Fournillier	Wilsons Ltd.
St. Marie	S. Leequay

Mon Repos   "

Perd Mon Temps	"
San Antonio	Sir J. Needham
Soconusco	Wilsons, Limited
San Patricio	Francois Tomasi
El Carmen	Henrietta Kavanagh
La Soledad (Guanal)	J.S. de Bermudez
Concordia	Marie Duprey
Brasso Toco	J.C. Poyer
North Laventille	Gordon Grant &
Morvant	Co., Ltd.
South Laventille	Earl of Dundonald
Beau Séjour	J.A. Antoni
San Miguel	Emma Dreyfus
San Antonio	
El Corosal	Joaquin Webster
Providence	Louis de Gannes
San Carlos	Mrs. Jul. Borde

Toco Ward Union

Estates	Owners
La Soledad	G.R. Alston & Co.
Buenos Ayres	F.G. Scott
St. Antonio	
St. Laurent	
La Soledad	Samuel Hosang
La Ardita	
La Anicetta	
San Antonio	L.J. Gransaull
Belle Vue	"
San Isidore	
La Palmiste	L.J. Gransaull
La Juanita	E. Paisley
Malgretout	Mrs. M. Gransaull

SIEGES AND FORTUNES OF A TRINIDADIAN IN SEARCH OF A DOCTOR'S DIPLOMA

Pedro Valerio

MY BIRTH AND EARLY CHILDHOOD

I was born in a miserable little thatched hut, on the outskirts of the small village of Tortuga, in the island of Trinidad, British West Indies. To the villagers, my father and mother were known respectively as José Tiburcio Valerio, and Eleonore Valerio; both being natives of the island. From them I have inherited a natural legacy, which it is perhaps the privilege of comparatively few people to fall heir to, and the possession of which I dare say the majority of them would be only too willing to ignore. This legacy consists of a mixture of three strains in my blood: the Caucasian, the Indian and the Negro. My father, a man of small stature, was born of white and Indian parents, and, in color and other external characteristics, would have had no difficulty in passing for a white man. My mother, a dark-skinned woman, also of small size, and very kindly disposition, is descended from the Negro and the Carib Indian; the latter being now almost extinct on the island.

Breakfast time in a cocoa field. This photograph was taken in the 1880's. Photograph — Mrs. Hélène Farfan.

It was the custom in the country villages of the island at the time of my birth, to greet the advent of a newcomer into the world with peculiar ceremonies. There was much firing of guns, eating, drinking and dancing, terminating occasionally in a free-for-all fight. Should the child be of the male sex, its birth was signalled by three successive shots from the barrel of an old-fashioned musket, mounted on a block in the yard several weeks before, to await the glorious event. The birth of a girl was made known in the same way, except that instead of firing three shots, they only fired two.

I have been told that upon the occasion of my birth, there was great feasting, drinking and merry-making. This unfortunately gave rise to some contention among the participants, and terminated in one of the aforementioned occasional disturbances. The scuffle which followed would seem to have been little short of epoch-making in its intensity, and only ceased when the hut had been nearly demolished. Although indirectly the cause of it, my part was necessarily a passive one, and I do not seem to have suffered any great damage. Its effect upon my mother, however, was pernicious; and ever since she has suffered from severe attacks of headache; which she ascribes to that memorable struggle, which rather ominously celebrated my birth.

The section of the country in which we lived at that time was newly settled; and the young plantations, sown with such vegetables as corn, cassava, tania, beans, pumpkins and yams, were not yet sufficiently advanced to enable us to beat the lean spectre of hunger; an unwelcome guest who came in the train of that awful period of hard times.

Food in those days was scarce, and the further scarcity of odd jobs around the settlement, made it still harder for my father to provide food and clothing for his small family.

The small hut in which we lived was not nearly as substantial nor cosy as those you may have seen in the lumbering districts of the United States. It was a small, four-sided, shifty concern, built of wood and palm leaves. The roof was thatched with the leaves of a variety of palm, known in the island as the carrat palm. About three-quarters of the interior was converted into a sleeping room, by hanging carrat leaves loosely around on cross pieces of wood nailed to the posts. The remaining space was utilized for various purposes. A square piece cut out of the leaves at the back of the hut constituted a window, while an opening in the front, with a piece of sacking for a curtain, served as a door.

The bedroom furniture consisted of the most

Cocoa being bagged and weighed to be sent to the great warehouses at Port of Spain. Photograph — Mrs. Hélène Farfan.

Belle Vue	Ed Leequay		Adventure	Elizabeth A. Hosang
Pointe Yara	V. Ducharne		Diamond Field	
San Antonio	Mrs. Tinoco		Orphan	
El Carmen	E. Dolabaille		La Victoria	Thomas Hosang
La Mascota	Hy. Siung		Nola Fana	
Mancharia	L. O'Connor		California	
San Pablo	A.G. Agostini		Esperanza	
Briley Park			Aragua	
Paradise	Louisa George		La Prosperite	A. Besson
Mundo Nuevo			Belle Vue	
Diamond Field			Poor Man's Progress	McBurnie
Montpelier	Benny George			
Dreamland	Henry Siung			

Arima Ward Union — Continued   **Cedros Ward Union — Continued**

Estates	Owners		Estates	Owners
Spring Hill	F.W. Meyer		Sta. Maria	A.S. Kernahan
La Prospérité	N. Cowlessar		Denmark	Chs. Ker (Trustee)
San Antonio	"		Enterprise	Geo. Grant
San Antonio	T. de Soublette		S. John	A. Attin
Melton	R. Hamlyn Nott			The Industry Est.
Brothers	F. Léotaud		Industry	Corporation of N.Y.
El Cedro	M. Quesnel		Monte Christo	L. Tanwing & Sons
Naranjo	Hrs. J.A. Rapsey		Penbury	E.C. Skinner
San Federico	"		El Puerto	P. Collington
	C.O. & L.N.		COUVA & CHAGUANAS WARD UNION	
La Violeta	Robertson		Cocoloco	J.B. Todd
La Trinidad	S. Thannoo		Montrose	Dr. A.P. Lange
Mon Bonheur	G.R. Alston & Co.		Rich Ville	A.B. Richards
Providence	"		Ednavale	Geo. Bancroft
San Expedito	A. Albert		Edinburgh	Hrs. S. Henderson
My Hope	H. Josse Delisle		Esmeralda	Gordon, Grant & Co.
San Salvador	A.C. de Verteuil		Sta. Emilia	Hrs. of Joyce Ltd.
	C. de Verteuil & J		La Providencia	Fritz L. Boos
Perseverance	D'Abadie		Henksdale	Hrs. Hendrickson
La Conformidad	A. Gómez		Félicité	Smith Bros. & Co.

primitive sort of home-made couch, on which the family slept; an old Carib basket containing the scanty supply of clothes for the family, and a soap box in which salt provisions were kept, to protect them from the ravages of rats and mice.

The meals, consisting usually of plantain, buc-buc (which is also a species of plantain), sweet or bitter cassava in various forms, and salt fish were prepared in that part of the hut which was left open. As each one received his share, either in a soup plate or calabash, he would simply sit down on a bench or on the bare ground, with his dish beside him, and eat his meal. The only table implements used were a tin soup spoon or a fork, and it sometimes happened that the family supply of silver consisted of but one spoon or fork, in which case my father would be given the preference.

Except for the few rose bushes standing a little distance apart in front of the house, the yard was left bare purposely, that we might detect more easily the approach of snakes and other unwelcome visitors from the surrounding woods. But we occasionally received a visit from a very welcome guest, the opossum. His visits were apparently directed to the chickens; but, as they roosted on the cabin roof, the opossum hardly ever escaped, even on the darkest night.

Besides tilling the ground, my parents devoted much

Estates	Owners	Estates	Owners
Buena Vista	M. Martínez	St. Marie	Hrs. de Boissière
La Gloria	Jos. de Verteuil	Roupell Park	Dan Mc D. Hart
St. Ann	P. Pampellonne	Bon Aventure	Hrs. C. Robertson
Prosperidad	A. de Verteuil	St. Jules	Jas. Stewart
Talparo	T.H. Warner	Murrayvale	Onnarey &
Spring	W.E.S. Barnardo		Robertson
Santa Ignalia	C.A. Pollonais	Eva's Hope	Heirs Langton
Santa Barbara	"	Waterloo	Kleinworth, Sons & Co.
Spring & Armonica	Hrs. Edgard Borde	Pays Perdu	J.R. Tom
		S. Madeleine	"

CEDROS WARD UNION

Estates	Owners	Estates	Owners
		Málaga	Heirs H. Stone
Annandale	L.F. Ambard	St. Margaret	J.W. Fletcher
Buenos Ayres	"	Sta. Philippa	W. Mills
St. Michael	"	Hillandale	"
La Ressource	W. Ind. Estate Co.	Orange Field	Beatrix A. Lange
Providence	"	La Soledad	
Sta. Barbara	"	Sta. Isabella	E.W. Savary
El Pilar	"	Uquire, Las Lomas	E.L. Agostini
Bon Aventure	"	and Elibox	
Santa Isabella	"	Palmiste	Miss Léotaud
El Guamal	"	tcarridonum	Carr Brothers
La Deseada	C.C. Stollmeyer	St. Mary	Pierre Bartlett
Mon Valmont	A.V. Stollmeyer	Paradise	"
La Fortunée	"	La Virgin y Tierra	
Clydesdale	"	Linda	Albert Mendes
El Ordo & Sta. Anna	"	Eureka and Cura	E.D. Clarke
St. Luce	Mrs. C. de Verteuil	Otaheite	Hrs. Clem. Lange
Mon Desir	"	Boa Ventura	Hrs. Joaq. Ribeiro
La Soledad	Smith Bros. & Co.	La Fortunée	Un. Brit Oilfields
El Socorro	F. Herrera	Clifton Hill	"
Concord		St. Valentine	Harold Fahey
Barataria			

MANZANILLA WARD UNION

Estates	Owners	Estates	Owners
Aranjuez	Hrs. J.A. Rapsey	La Josephina	F.A. Neubauer
Coblentz	Carlos Rovedas	Sta. Estella	General Pacheco
La Trinidad	Solomon Dreyfus	Windermere	Croney & Co.
Belle Fleur	Ed. Manuel	St. Joseph	Mrs. O. de Gannes
Ste. Marie	H.F. Figeroux	La Concordia	C. Allard
La Ultima	Jos. J. Ribeiro	San Antonio	"
Champs Fleurs	M.M. Gransaull	La Union	E. Hernandez
Brothersvale	Hones Bros.	Brooklyn	Percival Stevens
		Barcelona	J.B. Robinson
		Non Pareil	E.A. Robinson
		St. Marie	
		Santa Rita	

LA BREA & OROPOUCHE WARD UNION

Estates	Owners	Estates	Owners
		Concord	A.P. Maingot
Alta Gracia	Albert A. Sobrion	El Reposo	Hrs. C.F. Sellier
Patna	Boodhoosing	St. Privat	Dr. de Gannes
Nelson	J.J. McLeod	Santa Rita	Geo. Johnson
La India	Partap	Errolvale	Thomas Lyder
S. Martin & S. Philip	Hrs. of Allum	Perseverance	George McLean
Santa Maria	T. Geddes Grant	St. Elizabeth	Henry A. Reid
Perseverance	C.C. Stollmeyer	El Palmito	A. Protheroe
El Socorro	W.C. Robertson &		
	Others	St. Joseph	J. Riley
El Kola	"	Mt. Taldon	B. Romney
Canton	Geo. F. Huggins	La Mascotte	R. Vignales
Santa Cecilia	"	St. John	John F. Wallen
Esperanza	Mrs. Felix Smith	Sta. Clara	J. Jacelon
San Francisco	A.M. & R.A. Low	Santa Anne	Mrs. C. Kirton
Good Intent	"	St. Patrick	Heirs of Logan
Adventure	J.B. & S. Waith	Montrose	E. Damian
La Fortunée	De Wolf & Mathison	Williamsville	George Williams
El Campo	Beatrice Huggins	El Recuerdo	Murray and Wake
Pluck	Tennant's Est. Ltd.	May Vega	Dr. C.F. Lassalle
Common & Kingsland	Shadrach Medford	La Brea & Oropouche Ward Union — Contd.	

Diego Martin & St. Ann's Ward Union — Contd.

Estates	Owners	Estates	Owners
Union	F. D'Heureux	La Siparia	T'dad Properties Ltd.
Belle Aire	Heirs of B. Mussio	La Tranquilidad	"
Hermitage	Arthur Cipriani	Kimberley	Geo. Blake
La Regalada	C.P. Stollmeyer	Cura	John Bleasdell
San Rafael	"	La Pastora	Smith Bros & Co.

TOCO WARD UNION

Estates	Owners
El Carmen	
El Calvario	
La Soledad	
La Maravilla	
Santa Barbara	
St. John	
El Toco	
Mon Plaisir	
Belle Vue	W.G. Gordon
Susannah	
Santa Teresa	
St. Luke	

The Town House of Francoise Agostini, Henry Street, Port of Spain. Photograph — Mrs. Hélène Farfan.

of their time to the preparing of cassava bread, both for home use and the market. The making of cassava bread is a somewhat complicated process, accompanied by much hard work; and one which necessitates an unusual amount of patience on the part of those engaged in its preparation.

I remember very well the time when my mother and father used to get up at four o'clock in the morning, and begin what might be considered the first step in the preparation of cassava bread—scraping the roots clean. This is done with a large-sized knife or spoon. My little sister and myself were often called out of bed to assist in this work. At about seven o'clock, when the scraping was finished, the family would have breakfast, then we would start with the grating of the roots, which had been thoroughly washed and cleansed after the scraping.

People who worked with large quantities of cassava generally hired men to grate the roots for them; but my father could not do this, so he and my mother were compelled to grate the roots themselves. The grating reduces the roots to a pulp, from which all the moisture must be strained, as the cassava juice is poisonous.

The grating and straining finished, the pulp, which is now free from liquid, is in small cylindrical pieces, which form it assumed under pressure in the strainer. These bars are broken up into fine particles, and passed through a sieve of very small meshes. The flour thus formed is nice, white and coarsely granular, and ready to be spread on a hot circular piece of iron, and baked into bread. This part of the work requires a great deal of skill; for easy as the process may appear from the description, it requires a skilled hand to turn out good cassava bread.

But that is not all. These discs of cassava bread, as they leave the hands of the baker, must be put out in the sun and dried. Here again we little ones took an active part. The large, flat, circular loaves are laid on carrat leaves in the sun, and the child is entrusted with the care of them. He is given a whip and told that he must keep the chickens away from the cassava bread; and at the same time watch and give notice of any change in the clouds, which might threaten the drying of the precious loaves. Should the weather be stormy the bread must be returned to the hot baking iron, and kept there for at least ten minutes, to make it dry and cripsy. This is imperative, because if the bread is allowed to remain moist over night, it becomes so tough and difficult to swallow, that it is almost impossible to eat it. My mother has often spent almost the whole night drying cassava bread.

My father's death was caused by a severe form of measles, prevailing in the district at that time. My sister and myself were also stricken with the disease. My mother, though suffering from a severe spell of headache, was the only one able to go out and gather the different herbs and roots, from which were prepared the various infusions and decoctions used in quelling the disease.

My father's death overwhelmed us with sorrow and gloom, and threw a responsibility upon my mother's shoulders, which only a woman of unusual courage and fortitude could support. There was no money, and as we had only recently left the plantation which my father had cultivated under contract, we did not know what to do. The body had to be buried. My mother's efforts to borrow money for the purpose were only met with rebuffs and disappointments. The poor woman was helpless. Finally a kind-hearted East Indian volunteered to lend her a few dollars, and thus the money was obtained for his burial.

After the remains had been buried in the church cemetery, on the road between Tortuga and Besessa's Village, and those friends who had spent a night or two with us had all returned to their homes, we were left desolate and in a most pitiful condition. There we were in a cabin, sick and penniless, and almost starving. My poor, sick, heart-broken mother was willing to work, but she could find nothing to do.

It seemed to us a special provision of Providence that a sand-pit in the neighbourhood, which for many years past had been lying idle, was now again to be operated. My mother, though feeble from the effects of her passing illness, was among the first to apply for work. She was successful, and obtained a job as carrier. She worked all day carrying sand from the pit to a given point, getting as wages one dollar and eighty cents per week. It often happened that when the week was up, and she had paid the debts which she was forced to contract during the week, she would have only a few cents left, by no means enough to take us through the following week. Often times the only thing we had to eat was rice boiled in water and salt, or a roasted plantain or buc-buc, which we would eat with a grain of coarse salt.

The impression made upon my youthful mind by these early sufferings was such that I decided that when I became a man I would aim to choose an occupation that would bring me in contact with better conditions, that I might be able in some degree to make up for what I did not get in my childhood. But, more than this, I also felt deeply that I would like to do something to recompense my mother for the many hardships and trials which she suffered in trying to provide for me when I could not provide for myself.

Previous to my father's illness he had bought about six acres of land in the ward of Savanna Grande. The attention of farmers had only recently been attracted to this section of the country and most of the country was undeveloped and was still covered with dense forests, teeming with snakes and monkeys and other wild animals. We might have migrated to that place very soon after my father's death, had we been able to cut down trees and perform the other labors incident to the establishing of a cocoa plantation. Not being able to do this, we, in our straightened condition, simply wondered as the days went by whether or not we would ever be able to have a home on those lands.

About this time one John, a former policeman, seemed to be imbued with a great deal of agricultural ambition, and became very much interested in our welfare. He offered to till the grounds for us, for which he was to receive payment when the cocoa trees had begun to bear. This offer we accepted. A three-cornered hut was built, and by dint of much hard work we managed to move our few belongings to our new home in the virgin forest. After a portion of the woods had been cut down and burnt, the land thus cleared was planted with corn, cassava, tania, beans, pumpkins, yams, sugar-cane, plantains, bananas, buc-buc and cacao; the cacao being the main crop, and planted in rows twelve feet apart. Rice and baji, which was made by stewing the leaves of various varieties of spinach with cocoanut oil, butter or pork fat, formed our principal diet during the early part of our life on the new plantation. Later, as the different crops matured, food-stuffs became plentiful. We also received occasionally a few dollars from the sale of provisions.

As the cocoa trees gradually grew up, and expanded their branches and threw out their leaves, the low plants were smothered out of existence, which cut down our principal source of food. The few chickens we had were gradually eaten by the family.

My sister and I now began to attend school again. The school was located in Hard Bargain, a small settlement about two miles from home. With the increasing hard times at home, it was necessary for Clemancia and me to stay at home one or two days during the week, to assist in preparing cassava bread. The bread was usually taken by my mother and myself to the people in the village who kept small groceries, or to the Saturday market at Williamsville. We exchanged it for other articles of food, such as rice, hogshead, salt codfish, pork, and the like. In those days my lunch basket was very scantily furnished, and being sensitive about it I would usually go off into the woods near the school to eat my lunch in order that my schoolmates might not notice the poverty and scarcity of my food. My sister,however, was not troubled much in this manner; indeed, she usually managed to fraternize with somebody whose lunch basket was particularly well furnished.

About this time my mother decided to send me to my grandfather in Port of Spain, believing that in the city there would be a better prospect for a good education, and some chance for a start in life.

It was only about forty-six miles to Port of Spain, but it was considered a very important event and a serious journey by the country people of the neighbourhood. So the day before I started they came around with a good supply of food to see me through. They brought plantains, buc-buc, sweet cassava, cassava bread, sweet potatoes, tanias, beans, bread-fruit, yams, bananas, sugar-cane and chickens. Being used to the country, they feared the city atmosphere might be hard on me at first.

Soon after my arrival in Port of Spain, Mr. Eriché, an intimate friend of my grandfather, and teacher of a private school, expressed a desire to take me as his valet, he being elderly and an invalid. My grandfather consented, and I was placed with Mr. Eriché. For the short time Mr. Eriché lived my position was very much like that of a son in his house. I endeavored to discharge such duties as were allotted to me with thoroughness and care. As remuneration for my serviced I received, besides my board and lodging, the same training as the rest of his pupils, who paid five dollars a month. In addition to this I also received two cents each morning as spending money.

Notwithstanding the fact that I now had a comfortable home, my boyish mind still harbored the ambition and determination to go forward and try to reach a position where I might be of some use to my country and to humanity. My people were not in a position to send me to college and give me the education necessary to the successful execution of my plan, and I realized that in Trinidad the field of opportunity was too limited for me to hope to accomplish my purpose if I stayed there; so it seemed to me that the only practical method was to run away from home and hide in some vessel bound to a foreign port. Then, if I escaped being thrown overboard, I might land in some country where I could obtain the training I desired by working my way through school.

Accordingly I began to work toward this end, and when Mr. Eriché died I felt free to follow out my own plans.

J.J. THOMAS
Michael Anthony

John Jacob Thomas was perhaps the most learned and erudite black Trinidadian of the last century. Born in or around San Fernando in 1841, he struggled against the adversities and squalor that surrounded him, and while still a young man he stood out from the crowd by his accomplishments.

Beginning his education in the first primary schools inaugurated in 1851, John Jacob Thomas was selected in 1858 for special training as one of the first qualified teachers and in 1859 he was awarded one of the six places at what was called the Model School, or school where model teachers were trained. In 1860 he was sent to his first appointment as Schoolmaster at Savonetta, and since this was a completely Patois-speaking village, the 19 year-old Thomas taught himself Patois, the better to teach his pupils. He learned the dialect so well that he published the book 'The Theory and Practise of Creole Grammar'. It is still the only book of its kind. Following is an extract from J.J. Thomas' Creole Grammar.

"In the course of the linguistic studies with which I occupied my leisure hours, when a Ward-school teacher, at a distant out-station, I turned my attention to our popular patois, for the purpose of ascertaining its exact relation to real French; and of tracing what analogies of modification, literal or otherwise, existed between it and other derived dialects. These investigations, though prosecuted under the disadvantage of a want of suitable books (which as regards Creole was absolute, and as regards French nearly so), were not altogether fruitless. For I managed to discover, at least in part, the true nature and status of the Creole, in its quality of a spoken idiom. Moreover, finding that the Creole, considered in its relation to correct French, exhibits the whole derivative process in actual operation, (and not in fixed results, as is

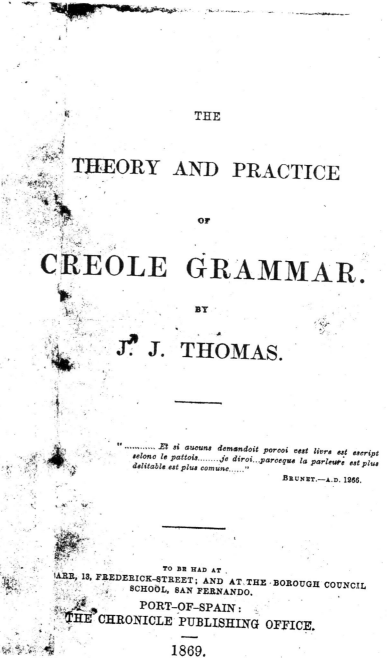

This is the title page from the book 'The Theory and Practice of Creole Grammar' by John Jacob Thomas, 1869.

the case in older and more settled dialects,) I thought that a grammar embodying these facts would be useful, as a basis of induction and comparison, to Creole-speaking natives who may desire to study other languages etymologically. Still, it must be confessed that these opinions would not, of themselves alone, have induced me to publish this book — a result brought about by considerations having a wider and more urgent importance, and bearing upon two cardinal agencies in our social system; namely, Law and Religion. I might have added Education; but as I mean to treat separately of the nullifying effects of the patois on English instruction among us, I shall say no more on the matter here."

In 1866 Thomas was appointed from the teaching service to the office of the Receiver-General, and in 1869 he was sent to Cedros as a Clerk of the Peace. When the English writer Charles Kingsley came here during the Christmastide of 1869/1870 Governor Arthur Gordon, who much admired Thomas, introduced Kingsley to him. Kingsley was extremely impressed with Thomas, and shortly afterwards the Governor appointed Thomas as

Children of the poor on the streets of Port of Spain during the early 1900's. Photograph —

1867

WONDERFUL CELESTIAL PHENOMENON

Mr. T.W. Carr, who was evidently an observer of some repute, records the following wonderful celestial phenomenon as having been seen by him on the evening of the 13th August, 1867.

At 9.15 p.m. today a singular apparition was observed by myself and Mr. Pashley against the southern sky. It had the form of a vast candelabrum of light, with two pairs of branching arms curved upwards, and inwards at the upper ends towards the main stem: covering almost 90 degrees in width, it reached from the horizon almost to zenith; and was brighter far than any cloud at night, and without any scintillation. It kept the same relative position and size for about three hours, appearing only to move more towards the west. It was pointed out to and seen by Mr. Pashley, Mr. W. Main, and the head warder at the Asylum. Meteorological apparitions of somewhat analogous character sometimes accompanying the greater meteor swarms, but their nature is not ascertained with any precision. At 10 to 11 p.m. several persons in Port of Spain, on Laventille Road and in Belmont heard a sudden, short, sharp crash on the hillside in the still night towards the north; each thought the sound was only about one or two hundred yards distant; it was as the sound of a small wooden cottage crashing to the ground by a single coup, or a great dry tree suddenly broken down. This is noticed here as it was probably a meteor bursting over Cascade or Santa Cruz valley.

Secretary both to the Education Board and to the Council of Queen's Royal College, which was inaugurated that year.

The pinnacle of Thomas' accomplishments came in 1876 when an Englishman, James Anthony Froude, published a scathing attack of the blacks in the West Indies, through the book, 'The Bow of Ulysses'. Thomas replied with a spirited attack on Froude and his opinions in a book called 'Froudacity'. The book attracted international attention and set out John Jacob Thomas as an author of exceptional scholarship and ability.

In 1879 illness forced this brilliant man to retire from the civil service. Yet although he was bed-ridden and half-blind he translated – from the French – Gustave Borde's 'History of Trinidad Under the Spanish Government'. In 1883 he recovered sufficiently to assume

A page taken from J.J. Thomas' book on Creole Grammar.

the headmastership of San Fernando's Borough High School. Relations were bad, however, and Thomas did not stay there long. In 1888, racked by illness, he went to England, hoping not only to look after his health, but to see if he could bring out new editions of Froudacity and 'Creole Grammar'. While in England, although his health worsened, he is said to have lectured and to have delivered many learned papers on West Indian affairs. But what with his poor eye condition and his fast-failing health, the storm-clouds were piling up for this exceptional man. He died in England on September 20, 1889.

PROVERBS.   121

...cess of the extreme difficulty of fixing the birth-place of a saying, especially when we find its parallel in so many different languages. Nevertheless, after deducting from our proverbs those of whose foreign extraction the acute reader is certain, enough will yet remain to prove that the Africans are not, after all, the dolts and intellectual sucklings that some would have the world believe them. The predominant characteristic of our proverbs is their figurativeness. Everything in Nature symbolises to the Negro something in man or man's affairs; and these applications are usually so truthful and ingenious that they are worth volumes of comments and laboured definitions. Not seldom a jingle of rhyme or a rhythmical arrangement adds to their piquancy. But the unlaboured proverb is, generally, the truest and most significant. In the ensuing selection, there are some sayings which are not current here: these are marked with asterisks.

Creole.	English.
Bêf pas jamain ca dîe savane, "mêci."	Ox never tells the pasture, "thank you."

This proverb alludes to the scant gratitude commonly shown to benefactors by those most indebted to them. It means also that men have little claim to acknowledgment when their good deeds have been the result of pure accident, and not of spontaneous liberality.

Pas fôte langue qui fair bêf pas sa pâler.	It is not for want of tongue that an ox cannot speak.

Men with great advantages are not always gifted with ability to improve them.

* *Toute bois cé bois;*	All wood is wood,
Main mapou	Yet mapou (a worthless wood)
Pas cajou.	Is not cedar.
Bon-temps pas bosco.	Ease is not hunch-backed.
Boudin pas tini zoreies.	The belly has no ears.

No train of reasoning, however exquisite, can appease the cravings of hunger.

1870

RETIREMENT OF THE HON'BLE CHAS. WARNER

The retirement of the Hon'ble Charles Warner C.B. from the important and responsible position of Attorney General of this island is an event that has evoked the strongest expressions of regret from a large and influential portion of his fellow colonists. For more than 30 years, Mr. Warner has been the leading spirit of the colony, the chief framer of of its laws, the principal adviser of the Crown, the brightest ornament of the local Bar, the most able and accomplished debater that ever sat in our Legislature, the guide philosopher and friend of all appellants from the pressure of misfortune or the grip of injustice. . . . .

Like most men of distinguished position and ability, Mr. Warner has had a good deal to contend with in his day . . . . . . but though enjoying the distinction of being the best abused man of his time, Mr. Warner lays aside the silk gown with fewer enemies than most public men after serving the Crown as long and with such fidelity.
(9th April, 1870.)

INAUGURATION OF QUEEN'S ROYAL COLLEGE

On the 11th July, 1870 the *'Gazette'* reproduces from the columns of the *'Trinidad Chronicle'* of the 3rd June in that year, the speech of the Governor, Mr. Arthur Gordon on the occasion of the inauguration of the new Queen's Royal College; from which the following extracts are taken:

His Excellency said:— We are met here to day to inaugurate the new Queen's Royal College, an institution by which the benefits of education will I trust be secured to Protestants and Roman Catholics alike, without the slightest compromise of the religious principles of either, The Queen's Collegiate School, of which this College is in some sort an out growth, and development, was founded with the same object; but, successful as it has been in other respects, it cannot be said to have altogether attained this. St. Mary's College was founded by private enterprise with a different view, and to meet the wants of those who objected to the Collegiate School. . . . I determined to endeavour to effect the establishment of a college where combined study might be carried on in those branches of education with respect to which no objection to such a course was felt, and to support with government aid and bring under the government's supervision those establishments where such branches of education in which a separate training was deemed necessary were taught. . . . I had, when last in England some anxious conferences with the highest ecclesiastical authority of the Roman Catholic Church in England on the subject, and came to a complete understanding with him on the subject. . . . He expressed a strong preference for a totally separate education, but candidly admitted the objections to such a course in a small and not very wealthy island; and he drew a wide distinction between combination for all purposes, and for some only . . . . On this understanding the plan now carried into effect is based; but the Legislature have gone far beyond what was then agreed upon; and while Archbishop Manning would have assented to an arrangment which would have excluded certain branches only from the common course of education, the law as now in force allows exemption from all, provided competent instruction is given to the pupils in the same branches elsewhere: till, in fact, all that remains obligatory is attendance at the examinations and at the course of instruction in one or more of the four given branches of education if it should so happen that no adequate teaching in that particular branch is given in the pupils' own school.
(11th June, 1870.)

> *C'Est vrai. C'est vrai*
> *La jolle dangereux*
> *C'est vrai*
> *La jolle dangereux*
> *A force la jolle dangereux*
> *Johnny Zee Zee le semantay*
> *Greasy Pole sorti la jolle*
> *E gros con Lolotte Brode*
>
> It is true, it is true
> The jail dangerous
> It is true, it is true
> The jail dangerous
> The jail so very dangerous
> Johnny Zee Zee has taken an oath
> Greasy Pole come out the jail
> And he big like Lolotte Borde.

(Anon.)

A crowd of people follow a Carnival band up Broadway past Royal Bank during the 1919 Victory Carnival Celebrations. Note the dress of the time, the popular use of hats and long white dresses. Photograph — G. Duruty.

This building once stood on Park Street, the second on the left after the Henry Street corner where the National Commercial Bank now stands. It once housed the Y.M.C.A. which had been relocated there in the 1890's. In the 1910's it became the residence of the Anglican Bishop of the time, when Hayes Court was rented out to the French Government. Photograph — P. Stone.

1871

MR. MAXWELL PHILIP, SOLICITOR GENERAL

The Hon'ble M. Maxwell Philip has been confirmed in the post of Solicitor General for this colony. Mr. Philip has filled the acting post on two or three occasions, and his confirmation is but the just rewards of past services. As a son of the soil, Mr. Philip's appointment has given general satisfaction, but by a large section of the community it will be regarded with feelings of pride and rejoicing as another triumph over a narrow minded policy which was wont to create and maintain invidious distinctions of birth and race. Mr. Philip is a representative man, and as such his appointment is memorable. *(Port of Spain Gazette, 1st April, 1871.)*

1872

THE ORIGINAL Y.M.C.A. VENTURE

On Tuesday evening the 27th February last, a large and respectable company assembled at the invitation of the Trinidad Young Men's Christian Association at No. 4 Marine Square on the occasion of the opening of a reading room and library which has been established by the Association. The chair was occupied by Charles W. Warner, Esq., C.B. *(2nd March, 1872.)*

1872

CABLE COMMUNICATION WITH TRINIDAD

We have much pleasure in announcing the complettion of the West India & Panama Cable, which event places this island in direct telegraphic communication with the United States, England, and we might almost say, the world. The subsidy payable by this colony has now commenced; and so has the obligation of the company to furnish us with a daily bulletin of European news. . . . . . . *(9th March, 1872.)*

TRINIDAD'S FIRST ANGLICAN BISHOP

The Right Revd. Dr. R. Rawle, Bishop of Trinidad, arrived in the packet on Friday morning. A programme for his reception had been prepared, and a programme of the proceedings issued: but his lordship telegraphed from St. Vincent requesting that he might be allowed to land quietly, and his wishes were complied with. Immediately after his arrival, the bells of Trinity Church rang out for the mornig service, and a large congregation attended. After the service, the Rector introduced the Bishop to the congregation, who addressed them *(sic)*. The installation will take place on Tuesday at noon.
(3rd August, 1872.)

This photograph of the 1880's shows a party of people at the corner of Sackville and St. Vincent Streets. The chimney missing from the lamp-post may give a clue to the year, perhaps the Carnival disturbances of 1891. Photograph — M. Pocock.

THE HONOURABLE MICHEL MAXWELL PHILIP Q.C. 1829-1888

Based on an essay by C.L.R. James and L.O. Inniss' 'Reminisences of old Trinidad'.

Michel Maxwell Philip was a remarkably talented Creole whose life impacted on many Trinidadians. He was distinguished both by his superior intellect and his commanding voice and presence; over 6 feet tall, he was handsome with an unsurpassed elegance of style and eloquence of speech.

After being educated abroad Maxwell returned to Trinidad and worked in a solicitor's office, where his love of law was kindled. He saved money in order to read for the Bar in England and supposedly during the course of his studies wrote asking for his father's assistance which was refused, a slight he was never to forgive. Undaunted he published the successful 'Emmanuel Appadoca' the earnings from which paid for his tour of Europe. Returning to England, C.L.R. James notes that he married a Miss Engleheart, an English girl from a middle class family.

The circumstances of his birth are shrouded in mystery. He carried the names of both his ancestor Michel Philip and of Frederic Maxwell, a highly regarded manumitted slave who became manager of the family's Philippine estate; some speculation holds that Frederic Maxwell could have been his father. Another school of speculation holds that his father may have been a Scottish engineer on the estate, especially in light of the fact that he was educated at a Jesuit College in Scotland. At school he excelled in languages including Latin, Greek, Spanish, French and Italian; many years later he would add Hindi to the list.

After being called to the Bar, Maxwell returned to Trinidad in 1855 and commenced his brilliant career. He was soon to give a demonstration of his extraordinary rhetorical skill and power in the dispute between the Attorney-General Charles W. Warner and the Roman Catholic Church. Warner was refusing to pay Archbishop Spaccapietra's salary on the grounds he was not British. The public rose in opposition and Maxwell gave a moving speech in support of the Archbishop which resulted in his position being regularized.

Maxwell was extremely active in the public service: he was appointed an unofficial member of the Legislative Council; in 1867 he was made Mayor of Port of Spain and appointed Solicitor General in 1871, a post he held until his death in 1888. Additionally he served on several boards, including the Boards of Education and Health; he acted as Chairman of the Road Commission, was a member of the Trade & Taxes Commission and served as Counsel for Venezuela. His ambition led him to aspire to the post of Attorney-General and when C. Warner died in 1881 the question of filling the position seemed a foregone conclusion. However, heartbreakingly for Maxwell his ambition was not to be realized, as one of his speeches in 1886 records:

'I am not a Chief Justice, I am not a Puisine Judge. I do not aspire either to be one or the other. I am not even an Attorney-General. It will suffice me in the afternoon of my life when, broken with the conflicts of the Forum I should seek ease in retirement, I shall be able to express my contentment in the language of the Roman wanderer to Sextilius, "Tell him you have seen Caius Marius, though not a fugitive, sitting on the Ruins of Carthage."

The Honourable Maxwell Philip Q.C. Photograph — Fr. A. de Verteuil.

Despite the obstacles placed in his path Maxwell dedicated much of his time and talent to the island he so loved.

Maxwell the private individual was equally fascinating. He was a known spendthrift but never indulged in drinking or smoking, although he was susceptible to women's charms. He was full of eccentricities ranging from a dislike of china (which ensured his guests ate off silver plates) to a complete disregard for his appearance when caught up with the spirit of the moment. (He was often to be found miles from his Maraval home enraptured with the beauty of nature and totally oblivous to his gardener's attire.) Reputedly he was also an excellent impersonator and mimic.

Although he died of Brights Disease on 30 June 1888 without realizing his life long ambition of being named Attorney-General, he left a legacy of attainment in the practice of law which has rarely been matched since. Continuing the tradition of his ancestor Jean-Baptiste Philip, Maxwell exemplified the best of the collective West Indian and specifically Trinidadian spirit – a born Creole who dedicated his genius to the evolution of Trinidad society.

1873

VOLUNTEER FIRE BRIGADE

The members of the newly-formed volunteer fire brigade turned out for their first practice last Saturday, and the movement may therefore be considered as fairly inaugurated. We have no wish to say anything either in favour or against the brigade. . . . . .but it is only just to add that the great doubt publicly expressed is not as to their willingness or capability to deal efficiently and quickly with any fire that may occur, but as to the probability of their being able to keep the brigade together for any length of time. . . . . . This doubt is greatly strengthened by the fact that a similar movement commenced in 1859, and had but a short experience.
(12th April, 1873.)

Excerpt from 'Reminiscenes of Old Trinidad' by L.O. Innis

Maxwell was a great chap in criminal cases and the one who secured his services generally considered himself safe, even if it was murder. He was a very good advocate, but the dunning clerks did not love him. It was almost as easy to "take the breeks off a Highlander" as to collect a bill from him. There was a good story current of a man who tried to see if he could *do* him over a leg of mutton, which his dog had stolen. having to deal with a lawyer he thought it best to use a little guile, so he approached him thus:

"Mistah Maxwell, I come to ax you opinion 'bout a case, sah. Suppose a pussun have a dog an it do something aint he risponsible for it?"

"Yes," said the legal one, "an action for damages will lie against the owner."

"Well, sah, a dog come an tek a leg ah mutton out ah me shop, aint he master have to pay me for it?"

"Certainly," said Max.

"Well, den, is your dog, Mistah Maxwell !" said the man of guile triumphantly.

"Is that so?" says the lawyer, "and what may be the price of that mutton?"

"It wort three dollar, sah, but I will tek two," says our smart friend, with pleasant anticipations of coins of the realm tinkling in his hand.

"So it seems that I owe you two dollars," said Maxwell blandly. "Well, my fee for consultation is five dollars, so if you give me three we can cry quits."

"Good Lord! Mr. Maxwell," said the crestfallen one, "I aint got no money, leh de dog go wid he mutton, and I beg you pardon, besides!" and he departed pondering sorrowfully that it was as easy to catch Maxwell with guile as to pluck a nettle without getting stung.

Extract from C.L.R. James' Essay Michel Maxwell Philip: 1829-1888

Whenever the Hon. Michel Maxwell Philip, Q.C., was engaged in a case it was always an exciting adventure to go into the Court. To begin with, there was the man himself, 6ft. 2 ins. in height, and broad in proportion; handsome as few creoles have been, with that prominent nose and fire in the eye which warned you at first glance that here was one marked out from birth to lead his fellows; carrying easily a dignity which in a lesser man might have been pomposity.

Most often, it was his mastery of the grand style, coupled with his unrivalled fluency.

"Exactly, Your Honour," said Mr. Philip, holding someone else's

papers, and seeing a chance to make a psychological point he swung round to the Jury, "And how then, gentlemen of the Jury, can you expect that a man like my client, could under these circumstances. . .?"

Thrilled as by some great actor, thrilled indeed by a great actor, the Court burst into involuntary applause.

"Mr. Philip," said the Judge, justifiably angry, and showing his anger. "You have turned my Court into a theatre."

Down to his seat crumpled the rebuked, the picture of dignified humility. The Judge looked at him for a minute and then struck as was the whole Court by the change of demeanour, he relented.

"Mr. Philip," he said more kindly, "you seem hurt."

No man could use such an opportunity better.

"May it please Your Honour," said the Hon. Michel Maxwell Philip, rising gravely to his feet, "censure, coming from a veneration such as yours, must always be accepted."

Nor was His Honour unworthy of the occasion, "Gentlemen," said he delightedly, "Where are we? In Trinidad or in the Court of the Lord Chancellor of England?"

Sometimes it was his wit.

"Fools rush in where angels fear to tread," he said to a Judge who had declared his mind made up on a certain point.

"Come, come, Mr. Philip," ventured the Judge (for it was always a perilous adventure to cross swords with him), "I never said you were a fool."

"Neither, Your Honour," and Mr. Philip bowed to the Bench, "was I so imprudent as in any way to intimate that Your Honour was an angel."

Sometimes it was his learning.

Mr. Justice Needham quoted Virgil from the bench, and there was Mr. Philip on the feet finishing the quotation for him.

When a Spanish interpreter interpreted badly, Mr. Philip called him to order, exposed his ignorance (or wickedness) and set the matter right so as to earn the plaudits of the Bench.

"Where did you learn your Spanish, Mr. Philip?" asked His Honour.

And here is perhaps as good an example of his style as one can wish.

"I learnt Spanish, on the banks of the Dee in Scotland, when I was fourteen years old."

A simple answer to a simple question and yet the sentence somehow sticks in the mind. A man who heard that reply over half a century ago has not forgotten it to this day.

Always there was this unfailing flow of dignified language, set off by his magnificent presence and the ringing silver of his voice.

Standing from Left to Right. —E. E. S. POLLARD, K.C., L. A. WHARTON, K.C., His Hon. C. P. DAVID, K.C., A. V. DEMONTBRUN, K.C.
Sitting from Left to Right. —A. E. HENDRICKSON, Hon. H. A. ALCAZAR, K.C., H. P. GANTEAUME, Hon. VINCENT BROWN, K.C., E. AGOSTINI, K.C., E. A. ROBINSON.

At the turn of the century, Trinidad saw a grand procession of the finest legal minds that this nation has ever produced.
Men who set the tone for the interpretation of Justice for generations to come.

Formerly known as the Bolivar College, it was here that the Dominican Order of St. Catherine of Sienna established a Convent in March 1890. To the right of the photograph can be seen the converted outbuildings that was used as a chapel. Photograph — The Dominican Sisters of St. Catherine of Sienna.

EDUCATION AND SOCIAL MOBILITY IN TRINIDAD 1834 – 1902

Carl C. Campbell

Before emancipation the core of the middle class in the island consisted of the scores of wealthy and respectable free coloureds whose economic base was in the ownership of plantations, town houses and to a lesser extent merchant businesses. Most of these coloured families were of French extraction; but some had English or Spanish blood. Their status as a middle class had not come about as a result of personal achievement in education; but from their participation with whites in the development of the plantation system.[1] Indeed before 1838 no social group owed its standing to its education. Race and wealth were the predominant determinants of class.

These determinants continued to be of great importance after emancipation. But a new factor of incalculable importance after emancipation entered the scene: the establishment of schools for the masses, however inadequately, brought into existence a new mechanism of upward social mobility. Even if nothing but inefficient primary schools had been started after 1838, these schools constituted a base from which a few ambitious blacks and coloureds, by private study would have advanced socially. In fact teaching became such a new career even before training for teachers became general. These poorly educated black and coloured teachers of the 1830's and 1840's were the vanguard of a new black and coloured middle class who, unlike the pre-emancipation free coloureds and their descendants, owed their social position to personal achievement in education. They were self-made people.

For black and coloured children of the ex-slaves the road out of the cane fields passed through the primary schoolhouse. Those who had access to land for commercial farming or those who became skilled craftsmen in the towns had indeed found ways of

Some of the young ladies who were in the charge of the Dominican Sisters of St. Catherine of Sienna. The Dominican Sisters established the Belmont Orphanage and ran the Leper Asylum at Cocorite. In addition to the Holy Name Convent School for girls on Charlotte Street.

improving their economic base and their social standing. But for every black or coloured who could become a successful farmer or a comfortable artisan there were a thousand who had no land, no capital or any desire to exchange one form of manual work for another. As Bridget Brereton has argued white collar occupations became the hallmark of the black and coloured middle class of the later 19th century. To achieve these occupations the children of the ex-slaves had to go beyond primary schooling to post-primary education locally or abroad. For this reason any discussion about upward social mobility via education has to be a discussion about post-primary schools and colleges, in other words essentially about secondary and university education.

It took time naturally for some children of the ex-slaves to become the beneficiaries, even to a limited extent, of such secondary educational opportunities as existed on the island. For at least the first thirty years after emancipation it was the children of the older French free coloured families, and of course the whites, and not the children of the ex-slaves, who were able to capitalise on the two or three institutions of secondary education. The black and coloured children of the ex-slaves, in the denominational or government primary schools of the 1830's to 1860's, were still just proving that they could be educated. Significant also was the fact that in the first thirty years after emancipation it was the descendants of the free coloured families, not the descendants of the ex-slaves, who provided the few spokesmen for the non-white class interest. It was not until the latter 19th century that some black and coloured descendants of the ex-slaves had received enough education and achieved middle class status enabling them to begin to take leadership roles; and when this happened it changed significantly the character of public opinion. It is not without reason that a liberal press, edited by coloureds sometimes, arose in the later 19th century, and not in the 1830's; it is not without reason that black and even coloured promoters of black race consciousness were more in evidence from the 1860's and then in the 1840's. It took some time for the discerning people to realise that

The Police Station at St. Joseph, in the distance can be seen a church. It's construction began in 1815 it was completed and consecrated by The Most Rev. John Pius Dowling, O.P. Archbishop of Port of Spain in 1913. Photograph — Mrs. O. Mavrogordato.

though the economy and politics of the colony were still controlled by whites the contours of the society were changing under the impact of black and coloured teachers, medical practitioners, lawyers, solicitors, surveyors, pharmacists, journalists, minor civil servants and clerks.

The first schools after emancipation to offer education above the primary school level to ex-slaves were the teacher training schools, first the Mico Charity training school established in 1836, but soon closed, and more particularly the government training school established at Woodbrook. Associated with the training of teachers were two practising schools, the Boys 'Model' school and the Girls 'Model' school. These latter institutions, later removed and renamed Tranquillity Boys school and Tranquillity Girls school stood at the centre of the primary school system for nearly a century, and their importance cannot be overstated. Because they were the practising schools they were allowed to set themselves more advanced curriculum than the ordinary primary schools; this was more true of the Boys 'Model' school than the Girls 'Model' school. These schools usually had white expatriate Headteachers and Headmistresses who doubled as heads of the training schools. Under pressure

from the middle class of Port of Spain for cheap secondary education, these schools became superior primary schools, not quite intermediate schools in the 19th century; in the higher classes, students could be asked to do work similar to that in the non-classical lower forms of St. Joseph's Convent or St. Georges College, without external certification. It must not be forgotten that the secondary schools also did primary school work, having in fact preparatory departments to obviate the necessity of better class children mixing with lower class children in the ordinary primary schools.

Ironically the Boys 'Model' school and the Girls 'Model' school even attracted a few white children who sat in the same classes with blacks and coloureds whose parents were capable of paying the fee of 5/– per week. Within ten years of its establishment the Boys 'Model' school could boast that some of its ex-pupils had become planters, managers, estate overseers, clerks and others had gone overseas for university education. We can be quite certain that white and coloured students rather than black students had embarked on these careers. About 20 years after its foundation a retiring superintendent, Mr. L.B. Tronchin, its first non-white Headmaster, proudly proclaimed it to be one of the most important

A fashionable young lady of the 1880's. Photograph — Mrs. Hélène Farfan.

SOME PATOIS SAYINGS

Collected by Otto Massiah

Bush doo ka ashtay shuval ah crayde
Sweet mouth buys horses on credit

Kan ou vueh barb canarad ou puis defay wousay cella ou
When you see your friend's beard on fire, sprinkle yours

Malair pah kah charjay con laplee
Accidents don't threaten like rain

Ravett pah jammay tinne raison duvan poule
The cockroach never has any right to the eyes of a fowl

Say souleah sel ke connet se shoson tinni too
The shoe alone knows if the socks have holes

Say coute ke connoit sah ke nan bouden jermu
Only the knife knows what is in the inside of the pumpkin

Say mezeh qui fair macaque manger piman
Trouble made the monkey eat pepper

Sa zeah pah kah vueh, cheh kah teh mal
What the eye does not see the heart does not grieve at

Se crab pah mashay le pah grah, le mashay trap le
tombay dan showdeah
*If the crab doesn't walk he don't get fat. If he walks too
much he falls into the pot.*

Se zandolee tay bon vian le passay ka dreevay
*If lizards were eatable they would not be so common
about*

Se crapeaud di ou caiman tini mal zieu queh le
*If the frog tells you that the crocodile has sore eyes believe
him*

You dwett pa sah pwan peice
One finger can't catch flies

Tampay ka ashtay maleh, gaude passah paveh
A penny will buy trouble which pounds cannot pay

educational institution in the West Indies. No such importance or achievement was credited to the Girls 'Model' school, one obvious reason being that women were expected to be only good wives and mothers. The 'Model' schools however offered some black and coloured children, boys more than girls, the chance to improve their social status through an education superior to that of the ordinary primary schools. To a lesser extent than the 'Model' schools, the Port of Spain Borough Council schools, and the San Fernando Borough Council school also provided a better base for social advance than the rural schools. The same point can be made about a handful of above average Port of Spain primary schools run by the Roman Catholic Church, the Church of England and the Methodist Church.

Although ironically the 'Model' schools over-shadowed the training schools whose students helped to teach them, the government training school for teachers (males) is not to be underrated as a lever of upward social mobility, most obviously within the non-white community. The fact that Keenan scoffed at it does not mean that this institution did not have any social importance. Significantly he noticed that the teacher trainees were pretentious, reflecting perhaps their appreciation of their own importance in the teaching hierarchy. It was not a good training school, but it was all the island had between the 1850's and the 1890's. Its graduates established themselves as Headteachers of many primary schools; they were the best examples of successful products of the school system for black and coloured working class people. They were self-made men on meagre salaries. Their efficiency as teachers

A house in St. Joseph. Photograph — U.W.I. Library.

might be doubted in several instances but they held key positions among the descendants of the slaves. Some of these teachers themselves were the immediate descendants of the ex-slaves; others were probably related to the pre-emancipation free coloureds and free blacks of little means. To these persons teaching offered an improved life style compared to the life of hard manual work which was the usual fate of others of their own social origin. Unlike the early decades of the 20th century no one thought seriously that secondary school education was necessary for primary school teachers, hence the 19th century graduates of the government training school were without the prestige which flowed magically from attendance at St. Joseph's Convent, or later CIC or QRC. It must distinctly be understood that graduates of secondary schools down to 1870's belonged by birth and education to a different class from the trained primary school teachers. So enormous was the prestige of secondary education to which the children of the ex-slaves had no access before the last quarter of the 19th century that no secondary school graduate would condescend to teach in a primary school unless forced by an absolute absence of other opportunities. Something like this began to happen on a very small scale in 1880 when two or three College exhibitioners, having spent three years in QRC, resorted to teaching in primary schools. These boys had not done very well at the college.

Perhaps the best known black schoolteacher of the 19th century was J.J. Thomas, author of *Creole Grammar* and *Froudacity*. Thomas was exceptionally talented, but his career still illustrates how the black son possibly of an ex-slave could rise to middle class status through education. Born about 1840, Thomas went to an ordinary primary school, then on to the government training school where he distinguished himself, and then to various teaching posts. Several of his black and coloured contemporaries took the same route to a poorly rewarded, but respectable career in teaching. Thomas also distinguished himself by self-education, for he gave himself a secondary education. Several other teachers did the same though with less conspicuous results. The point

A crowd gathers to see the arrival of Sir William Robertson K.C.M.G., Governor of Trinidad from 1885 to 1891. A scene of sail and horsepower, 19th century costume and the colony's cosmopolitan population. Photograph — G. Mac Lean.

is that black and coloured teachers, especially the Headteachers were among the most ambitious and enterprising of the descendants of slaves. Their business was education, and the acquisition of European culture through reading and study. Real promotion for these men meant leaving the teaching service, possibly for a job in the junior ranks of the civil service, which was the white collar job to which literate and ambitious black and coloured men aspired.

Thomas was born too early for the Queen's Collegiate school which opened in 1859. But even if he was not too old he would not have been able to afford the fees. As shown previously the advent of this college, later to become the famous QRC, marked a new chapter in the history of education in Trinidad. In 1863 the Roman Catholic Church leaders started CIC and QRC. These two colleges were not racially exclusive, but they were attended mostly by the sons of the white upper class, French or English, and secondly by the sons of the older and respectable coloured families. But because apartheid did not exist in the colony, it proved impossible in the long run to keep out black children, however undesirable an addition to the secondary school population they were thought to be by illiberal white and coloured people.

With the advent of the Queen's Collegiate school in 1859 the range of schools supported by public funds was brought in line with the social assumptious of a class and colour conscious community. The denominational schools unassisted by government and the ward schools were intended for the labouring class who were to remain labourers. Most of them were black; some coloureds. The schools in San Fernando and Port of Spain, particularly the 'Model' schools, were expected to be above the standard of the ward schools because they provided partly for the middle class, largely coloureds, some blacks and some whites. There is evidence of social class tension in the above average urban schools because of the greater gradations of class and colour among the pupils. In the Port of Spain Borough Council school in 1857 there were the boys who wore shoes and the boys who did not. There were early difficulties at the Boys 'Model' school in 1852 which led to suggestions that the pupils should be separated along class lines, but this was apparently not done although some boys left the school in 1859 to attend Queens Collegiate school. Queen's Collegiate school would maintain the distinctions which appeared threatened at the Boys 'Model' school. It would prevent the 'toe of the peasant coming too near to the heel of the courtier as to gall his kibe'. The Queen's Collegiate school would give a classical education to the

1873

HIS OWN OBITUARY

"Died,—on the 27th instant, Mr. William Herbert, Editor of the "*Telegraph*", aged 42 years."
(5th May, 1873.)
(*Note:*—The above was written by the deceased about one month
before his death, the date being left blank, and was handed to his
wife, with a request that it might be the only obituary notice to
appear for him.— *Editor, P.O.S. Gazette).*

CHANGE OF PUBLISHERS

On and after Saturday next, the 1st prox., this paper will be
published by George H. Clark, at his office, No. 9 Chacon Street. . . . . .
It would be both presumptious and ridiculous for us, who have been
but a few days in the colony, and are totally ignorant of its wants, to
attempt to conduct a newspaper almost entirely devoted to the
discussion of subjects of local interest. We think it well, therefore, to tell
our readers at once, quite frankly, that many of the aticles which may
from time to time appear in our columns will be from the pen of a
gentleman well versed in local politics, who has, during a long
residence, gained that experience of the ways and wants of the colony
which is necessary to the successful editing of a newspaper like this.
(25th October, 1873.

FOUNDATION STONE OF GOVERNMENT HOUSE, ST. ANN'S

On Thursday the 24 July, 1873, according to the "Gazette" of the
previous Saturday, the Governor was to lay the foundation stone of the
new official residence of the Governors of this Colony of St. Ann's; and
though no report of the event subsequently appeared, the following
comments on the occasion are made by the paper:— "Events of this
kind in Trinidad do not appear to have been surrounded by even the
semblance of those grand displays and elaborte ceremonials which are
considered so indispensable on similar occasions in the Mother Country.
. . . . . Yet the laying of this foundation stone marks an epoch in the
history of the colony. It speaks of a Present, when the colony is willing
and more thankable to spend £20,000 on building a residence for its
Governors' and that, too, at a time when it is engaged on other public
works entailing an expenditure of over a quarter of a million sterling:. .
. . . . and it reminds uf of a Past,—a dar Past,—when hope had al but
deserted our most sanguine leaders, and when it was even necessary
for public officers to submit to a reduction of their salaries, the revenue
being unable to meet the expenditure." *(19th July, 1873.)*

A fashionable young lady of the 1880's. Photograph — Mrs. Hélène Farfan.

boys of the upper class and upper middle class, and
nothing the Boys 'Model' school offered could compare
to the majesty of an education along the lines of an
English Grammar school.

The resistance to the education of non-whites by the
whites took the form of not wanting education to be a
lever of upward social mobility. Inspector Anderson
explicitly denied any intention to promote pupils above
their 'station in life'; he defined the purpose of the
ward schools as giving the common people an
education in the elements of learning to make them
'industrious, contented and happy'. At least however
there were no sustained attempts to turn the schools into
instruments of habituating children to the routine of
agricultural toil, as in Jamaica, under the euphemism
of industrial education. There were not even estate
schools until the Indians arrived. The presence of
Indian immigrant labourers rendered it unnecessary for
the planter class to attempt to control the curriculum in
the interest of the preservation of the plantation labour
force.

Colour and class played some part in the reaction of
the ex-slaves to educational opportunities. Black and
Indian estate workers gave the schools least support;

Inspector Anderson estimated that most of the children in
the rural ward schools were children of peasant farmers.
But demography also was a factor because in rural areas
when the population was not dense, and peasant farmers
lived near subsistence level, free from the competitive
pressures of towns, suburbs or estates, attendance at
school was very poor. Of course the middle class
coloureds and whites of Port of Spain and San Fernando
ensured that attendance at schools in these towns,
especially the 'Model' schools, was unsurpassed in the
colony. Schools had more meaning for aspiring urban
parents. This is well illustrated by the new opportunities
in the later 19th century in secondary education which
was an urban phenomenon.

The single most important mechanism for the
penetration of QRC and CIC by black and coloured boys
was the system of scholarships called the College
Exhibitions which started in 1872. The College
Exhibitions, the prestigious forerunner of the nerve-
racking Common Entrance examination of today, took
only a handful of bright boys, about four per annum first
to QRC and then to CIC as well; but it was a
development of the greatest social importance because it
was not long before a few of these boys began winning

In 1890 the Boy's Reformatory was established in Diego Martin by the Anglican Church of J.T. Hayes O.P. Bishop of Trinidad 1889 to 1904. Photograph — G. Mac Lean.

the University Scholarships (Island Scholarships) which took winners abroad to study for professional careers, usually in law or medicine. the idea of bright black and coloured boys from the primary schools moving on to secondary schools can be traced as far back as Governor Lord Harris in the early 1850's. However when the Queen's Collegiate School (later QRC) was opened in 1859, the governors, down to 1871 only nominated to free places the sons of deceased senior civil servants and clergymen of the Church of England. All these boys were white and did not have to face a competitive examination for entry.

The idea of free places for bright boys was revived by Governor Gordon as part of the reorganisation of QRC to which CIC was affiliated. The number mentioned was two per year, but by the following year, when Governor Longden moved to implement the idea, the figure had climbed surprisingly to six per annum, provided that no more than 24 such exhibitioners were at any time in the college (QRC). To allow six exhibitioners per year from 1872 was perhaps not ungenerous to start the programme, but unfortunately it never worked in this manner. The original quota was soon seen to be dangerously high; by 1875 the limit of 24 exhibitioners would have been reached; then the College exhibitioners would have been about 40% of QRC's enrolment. Inspector Guppy and the Board of Education reduced the number to three per annum, raised the standard and

lowered the age limit. By 1878 a pattern of winners which was to last a long time was emerging. The leading schools which won were in Port of Spain, and the winners were mostly black or coloured boys, not Indians, especially from the fee-paying extraordinarily well staffed Boys 'Model' school, and the parents of these boys were from the middle class: teachers, small businessmen, skilled artisans and junior civil servants.

Between 1872 and 1903 there were four University Scholarships to be won annually. These prestigious awards, the 'educational blue ribbon of the island', taking winners overseas to an English university, were based on the Cambridge School Certificate Examinations. All the winners prior to 1872 were white youths. The Principal of QRC, Mr. William Miles, (1872-1894) took a prejudiced view of 'free place boys'; he felt that they lowered the tone of the college. Miles and the white supporters of QRC were faced with a difficult situation; since the college's enrolment was small the advent of even a handful of black and coloured 'free place boys' threatened to change the composition of the student body. Miles allegedly chose to make progress difficult for these exhibitioners. There were reports that bright boys did not advance beyond form III (Junior Cambridge examination form), and that it was difficult for them to get into Miles' own class which was the only one from which the University Scholarship could be attempted.

On the 3rd June 1870, the Queen's Royal College then known as the Queen's Collegiate School was inaugurated at the Prince's Building. A part of the building was used as a classroom for thirty-four years until the college established its own building in 1904. Later on it existed as a Government Girls High School for some years. This was eventually closed after the establishment of Bishops Anstey High School in 1922. Photograph — M. Pocock.

Discrimination probably contributed to low performance by some exhibitioners. Nevertheless the historic and all important link between College exhibitioners and University Scholarship winners began while Miles was at the college. By the 1880's at least four exhibitioners, including Stephen Laurence (coloured), and C.P. David (black) had won University Scholarships.

In 1890 the College exhibitions were discontinued; whether they were abolished or lapsed is not clear; in the heated religious discussions surrounding the Education Ordinance of 1890 the provisions supporting the exhibitions were omitted. From this point of view the death of the exhibitions seemed more accidental than premeditated; however the discussions about their revival suggest that perhaps murder had been silently committed; it was revealed that apart from Miles there were other important enemies (for example the French Creole legislator Eugene Lange) of the exhibitions among the white elite. A motion in the Legislative Council in January 1893 to block funds for the exhibitions was defeated, but it elicited from the French Creole editor of the *Port of Gazette* the following:

'. . . . to make the upper and middle classes pay for the higher education of the children of the poorer class is to make them pay three times for education – first for the higher education of their own children, secondly for the elementary education of the children of the poor, and thirdly for the higher education also of the poor.

The social disadvantage it would have would be to artificially foster ambitions for which the natural walk of life would provide no place except in the case of real geniuses.

Educated or non-educated, the people of the colony must split up into the various classes marked out for them by their means or the means of their parents, and the place they can find in the race of life.

It is therefore right that the line should be drawn in the matter of free education at elementary level'.

Another way in which the same sort of sentiment was put came from the pen of the editor of the Catholic News in July 1901. In opposing a new building for QRC he propounded the view that '. . . . the bottom has been touched in the social strata of the colony whence College students are recruited and that no brand new College will add to the number of such students'.

Independently of the College exhibitions, CIC

A small island immigrant of the 1890's posing as a fruit vendor for a photographer's postcard. Photograph — Hélène Farfan.

organised its own exhibitions, and this was a trend followed by new secondary schools, private or public, in the early 20th century. Eventually non-government exhibitions to secondary schools outnumbered the government exhibitions, thus opening up a new era in education opportunities for black and coloured children. In turn the existence of these exhibitions led to a partly healthy competition of no ordinary proportion among the Headteachers of the leading primary schools for the coveted prizes of producing College exhibitioners. The College exhibition system grew from an uncertain indulgence to an expected privilege by the start of the 20th century, and finally to a political right in the 1930's.

Concurrent with the increased penetration of the secondary schools for boys in the last quarter of the 19th century was the opening of new opportunities for advancement in the junior civil service and the field of law. A most important development was the arrangement whereby locals could study to become solicitors without leaving the island or going to a university. From the late 1820s when the first coloured youths began to become clerks in the judicial departments, a supreme career objective of ambitious, non-whites was to become lawyers, which like the study of medicine, gave independence, privilege, and an adequate income. At a time when there were only 10 solicitors in practice Ordinance 7 of 1871 permitted locals to be articled in Trinidad, and after passing the examinations of the Incorporated Law Society of London to practice as solicitors. Although they could not become lawyers without expensive study abroad, those black and coloured youths who succeeded in becoming solicitors in the late 19th century had raised their social standing enormously, and some of these youths had already gone through CIC and QRC as exhibitioners but without winning University Scholarships. Others had gone to secondary schools at their parents' expense. French Creole youths, for example F.J. Maingot and J.D. Sellier whose families already had status grasped the opportunities of studying locally to become solicitors, articling themselves to other French Creole solicitors. The opportunity to qualify locally greatly altered the racial composition of the solicitors, breaching the wall of white occupational privilege in one of the traditional high status professions. It could not be allowed to continue. In 1894 when there were 30 solicitors and 18 articled clerks some barristers, solicitors and merchants successfully petitioned the government to restrict the admission of new locally trained solicitors. The public objection however was not of course related to race, but to the alleged overcrowded nature of the profession and the alleged low standard of education and training of the locally produced solicitors. A new law in 1894 made it necessary to study in England to become a solicitor.

There was one Trinidad youth of Chinese extraction, whose academic career in the late 19th century was the foundation for a remarkable life in China. Eugene Chen, born in 1875, of Chinese shopkeeping parents, went to CIC where he failed to win an University Scholarship, despite herculean efforts. He took the opportunity of studying locally to be a solicitor by being the articled clerk of J. Maresse-Smith. He had a longing for education in England which led him to study the 10th edition of the Encyclopedia Britannica at nights in the hope of winning a certain overseas scholarship based on its contents. These nocturnal labours of Chen were not unlike those of scores of other ambitious young men who studied one thing or another outside the school system, often with the help of correspondence courses. Chen became a solicitor; had a practice in San Fernando, but sometime in 1911 he suddenly disappeared from the island. He was always interested in politics. Trinidadians were astonished to hear later that he had made his way to China and had taken part in the Chinese revolution, rising to the rank of Foreign Minister of the Republic of China.

A very narrow channel to improved social status was opened with the advent of competitive examination for the civil service. One of the first blacks to benefit was J.J. Thomas who topped the examination one year, and subsequently got employment in the junior ranks of the civil service, becoming the most senior black man in the civil service. But there were obstacles; passing the examination did not give a right to employment, though failing it was a bar. Competitive examination for entry into the civil service soon looked like such a dangerous experiment that it was suspended. The whites who monopolised most of the senior posts preferred the governor to have absolute discretion in appointment, unhindered by blacks and coloureds waving certificates.

In the last quarter of the 19th century competition in education waged through examinations, reached proportions hitherto unknown in the island. There are two ways in which we can explain this, and these ways are not mutually exclusive. One can simply say that Trinidad followed the English metropolitan model, and moved from non-competition to competition in the 19th century. Additionally there was a local dynamic at work determining the colony's willingness to follow the metropolitan model. In the first generation after emancipation (1838/1868) competition in education was substantially absent from all schools largely because the social system was unresponsive to intellectual talent. This unresponsiveness was a legacy of slavery and the plantation system where muscle power was more important than ideas, and business success more vital than formal education. It has been argued recently that a new plantation system established itself in the later 19th century. Some whites were not convinced that substantially more education was needed to run post-emancipation Trinidad than a slave plantation society. Nevertheless educational opportunity grew after emancipation until it had to be systematised by competitive examinations. Concurrently with competitive College exhibition, primary schools were put on a system of payment by results. Teachers competed to improve results fees; pupils had to pass examinations to move to higher grades; as for the pupil teachers, they faced a long series of examinations; uncertificated teachers were obliged to present themselves for examinations, and indeed even for the certificated teachers there were higher certificates to be obtained. In other words the clearest path to upward social mobility for non-whites was to study and to pass examinations which were very competitive. If this seems normal today it was a new phenomenon for the sons and daughters of slaves, poor free coloureds and free blacks.

The supreme examination in the 19th century was the Cambridge School Certificate Examination. It derived its importance from being an external examination set by a prestigious examination authority in the metropole. It set a definite standard for secondary schools. It was also the examination in which the University Scholarships were based; only the senior students at QRC and CIC could take it until Naparima College joined the select club; it was though too strenuous or otherwise inappropriate for girls at St. Joseph's Convent. Private candidates were not yet allowed. It took some time before even CIC or QRC mastered the curriculum. It might be surprising to learn that between 1870 and 1893 as few as 5% of the Island Scholars (winners of University Scholarships) achieved first class certificates; but there was a great improvement at the turn of the century; between 1894 and 1903 as many as 60% of the winners got first class certificates. The rise in the level of mastery of the Cambridge Examinations, plus the greater social acceptability of black and coloured exhibitioners in the colleges, created the conditions for the triumph of intelligence and industry at QRC and CIC. By the early 20th century, before World War I, the College exhibitioners, black and coloured, had come completely into an inheritance of University Scholarships which led to overseas training in the professions.

Of course it should not be forgotten that only a very tiny minority of black and coloured working class youths managed to raise themselves through education to middle class status. Most of those who attended primary school fell back into the ranks of the illiterate or semi-literate working class, despite the fears of illiberal whites that primary school education would unfit them for

A well loved nanny of the Fahay family sitting with her young charge. Photograph — E. Fahay.

agricultural labour. Many of the better graduates of the primary schools did study for pupil teacher examinations, and a few went to teacher training schools. And there were a number of youths, for example the coloured Michael Maxwell Philip (Solicitor General from 1870) who had returned after education in colleges in England or Europe. The route to the U.S.A. to work one's way through College existed, but the migrant might not return. By a process of gradual accumulation one could find by the end of the 19th century, among the blacks and coloureds, about three hundred trained teachers, the most numerous of the educated non-white middle class; scores of clerks, tens of minor civil servants, pharmacists, surveyors and solicitors, and a handful of lawyers and doctors, plus the odd newspaper editor. Other occupations were represented, but it would serve no purpose to attempt an exhaustive list. Men outnumbered women, despite female teachers whose attraction for the authorities was their relative cheapness; and at least we know of one fearless coloured female, Emile Marese Paul, who must be reckoned among the intelligensia of San Fernando.

Some examples of individuals who benefitted from the schools will make the point. It would be an error to believe that whites were left behind in the race for academic honours. If they tend to be under-mentioned it is because some were secure in their social positions without the need for competitive academic success. R.S.A. Aucher Warner, born the son of Charles Warner in 1859 would most likely have had university education even if he had not won University Scholarship (Island

Scholarship) from QRC in 1876. He studied law at Oxford University, and later became Attorney-General in Trinidad and Tobago. The same point, perhaps with less certainty, could be made about the three sons of Rev. John Morton, who all won University Scholarships from QRC in 1887, 1890 and 1892. The point about upward social mobility through education has to be made with greater force for non-whites. Two great examples were Henry Alcazar and Stephen Laurence, both coloureds who won University Scholarships respectively in 1877 and 1883. Alcazar had a brilliant career as a lawyer, being with Edgar Agostini the earliest Queen's Councils in the island; Alcazar was appointed to the Legislative Council. Laurence became a medical practitioner and indefatigable member of many Boards. Alcazar was born four years earlier (1860) than E. M'Lazare (1864) who became a black lawyer. As a boy Lazare went to two of the leading Port of Spain schools, the Boys 'Model' school and De Suze's St. Thomas Roman Catholic school, and apparently QRC or CIC; and became articled to Andre Maingot. he became the first person to pass the local examinations of the Law Society of England – without going abroad. He joined the volunteer militia and was part of Trinidad's delegation to the 1898 Diamond Jubilee of Queen Victoria. He reportedly caught the eye of the Queen and dined with royalty some of whom took a liking to him. Lazare what might be called a colourful personality.

Because the Indians were late in getting even primary education, the rise of an Indian middle class through education lagged behind that of the black and coloureds, although the Canadian Presbyterian Mission was remarkably swift in commencing a secondary school. For instance the Indians missed the opportunity, because of lack of secondary education, to become solicitors via local study in the last third of the 19th century, as blacks, coloureds and French Creoles were doing. In 1919 there was only one Indian solicitor at a time when they already had a long tradition of purchase of Crown land. At the end of the century Naparima College ran a very poor third behind CIC and QRC; but a fruitful link between it and the Presbyterian Mission's Theological school unobtrusively gave a few Indians greater opportunities than in the case of members of other churches to study locally for the priesthood. Failing to enter and adequately into the education stream which led from primary schools to the College exhibitions, to QRC or CIC, and perhaps University Scholarships, the Indians were fortunate to find in the white leadership of the Canadian Presbyterian Church clerics who had contacts with Canadian colleges and universities, and this later opened a peculiar side door to the better products of the Mission in a less prestigious part of the British empire.

As Bridget Brereton has clearly seen the black and coloured educated middle class of the late 19th century paraded their education and culture because it was the only thing they had to boast about. Some of them gave lectures, slide demonstrations (lantern demonstrations); a few became amateur naturalists proud of their small collection of insects or stones. We might begin to see in the later 19th century the early foundations of the literary and debating societies which blossomed into a craze in the early 20th century. The lowly paid teacher, bossed by a white inspector of schools, and sometimes harassed by white clerical managers, was the base of the new unrecognised intelligensia in the country. The black and coloured middle class had begun the long march to overtake the French and English Creoles as the intellectual leaders of the colony. They had of course

neither economic power nor political influence to match the revolution in educational achievement which was in progress.

> " Ja Ja Romey Eh   }
>   Ja Ja Romey Shango   }   *(Repeat twice)*
>
>   Ja Ja Romey Eh Mete Beni }
>   Ja Ja Romey shango   }   *(Repeat twice)* "
>   (Anon.)

MUSIC IN TRINIDAD'S POPULAR CULTURE
Andrew Pearse

The idea of 'popular culture' is used here to refer to the cultural manifestations of non-élite strata in class societies insofar as these are distinct from those cultural forms maintained by the élites, which may be out of reach for economic reasons or guarded jealously as a badge of élite membership. Popular culture is associated with peasants and urban workers, with artisans, petty traders and underworld fringes. It frequently contains features of the culture of an absorbed or conquered ethnic group retained after their incorporation in the lower strata of a society. In this paper, the popular culture discussed is that of a group of Caribbean islands, namely Trinidad, Tobago, Grenada and Cariacou, in the period following emancipation from slavery, up to the time when commercial mechanically reproduced music began to have an overwhelming influence, i.e. from the 1830's to the 1950's. During this period, all four islands were under British colonial rule.

The formation of these island societies was a by-product of the predatory recruitment of a labour-force to work in field gangs and in manufacturing and related artisan operations in the production of tropical crops and commodities, especially of sugar. The capture and forcible removal from Africa of this labour force meant the separation of individuals of varied cultures and social situations from the worlds in which they had been brought up and the cultures they had learned and known. It meant their forcible fitting into a coercive apparatus whose task was agricultural production, – the plantation – which was designed to ensure their custody and the full exploitation of their labour and their persons. And within the plantation framework there was little that offered human support to the individual worker whose place in it was that of chattel slave. Moreover continuity with cultural background within the regions of origin, and the deliberate policy of the colonial and plantation authorities tended to keep any such solidarity derived from ancestral cultures to a minimum. However, there are signs that behavioural forms developed to defend and preserve areas of interstitial liberty, and to preserve certain elements of the African cultures, as, for instance, many of the basic West African patterns of thought and feeling, and the syntax of expression which made possible the creating of African-type languages out of the vocabulary of the colonizers, i.e. the various creole tongues. And of course, a vast substratum of cultural forms and penchants simply escaped the attention of the colonial culture-strippers as being of no apparent threat to their imposed order or their concealment in the mind.

Bongo Dancers by Alfred Cadallo, artist, storyteller and folklorist. Bongo is danced, to placate the spirits of the dead, in sexual burlesque and mime. A competitive male oriented dance seen at wakes. Reproduced with the permission of Hand Arnold & Co., The Trinidad Guardian and the R.V.I.

This would be true of somatic style, of tales, myths, melodic and rhythmic motifs, of religious beliefs and attitudes and other propensities which were to be realised and given body in the new environment, where their economic requirements were slight and where they were easily passed on from mother to infant.

It seems a reasonable hypothesis that with the withdrawal of much of the coercive regulations and especially of forced labour towards the end of the 1830's, a period of exceptional social creativity opened.

Major changes took place in the economy of the islands and especially in the position of labour. Patterns of settlement altered as new villages were formed, and as houses appeared along the roadsides and adjacent to existing towns. Peasantries emerged in places. new judicial rights were exercised, new institutions and organisations sought members. And around these major currents social life began to take on new elements, and to acquire novel permanent forms. Co-operative work in agriculture, neighbourhood organisation, life-cycle observances within the family, organisation for mutual aid, self-improvement, insurance against illness, commercial enterprises, the practice of religions and the performance of magic, recreation, competitive games and battles between individuals and organised bands were among the social activities which began to acquire new and characteristic form.

The emergence of the new society redefined the lines of social division and conflict, and generated a freer popular or 'creole' culture from several distinct sources. From above and outside legal codes, direct rule, and ecclesiastic and school systems were imposed with their own language, music ideology and symbols, and colonial upper class comportment was fostered. Many cultural forms were implanted in this way and those which proved viable in many cases underwent a certain créolisation. But a possibly stronger creativeness was that which transformed and developed existing cultural elements, at the same time adding to them from other components of the environment including the newly arriving Africans, Europeans and Orientals, and the neighbours of the Spanish Main. And men and women created and adapted institutions to meet their needs in much greater freedom than before.

Music and Social Institutions

Music was an important component of creole culture, not in any diffuse way but because it had a central role in the emergent social institutions. Though there was some input from the colonists, e.g. fiddle tunes at the plantation dances, hymns from the missionaries and sea shanties from the sailors, etc., the musical style was predominantly of African source, though it was always undergoing a process of creolisation.

Kalinda music to accompany quarter staff duels or stick fights, by Alfred Cadallo 1957. Reproduced with the permission of Hand Arnold & Co., The Trinidad Guardian and the R.V.I.

What we may call a typical musical item consisted, with few exceptions, of several separable elements: melodic pattern, percussion, stylised movement and words (when the melody was sung). The occasions for musical activity were the ceremonies or performances which were central to some of these social institutions, for instance, parades and representations, games, story-telling, religion and magic, social gatherings, the critical junctures of the life-cycle in the family, and the performance of work by teams of co-workers. Within a particular category or kind of music, types came to be distinguished by variation in rhythmic patterns coupled with the dance movement. Each type has a common rhythmic base, and is probably referred to by the name of a particular dance fitting that rhythm. The diverse *items* within the type are distinguished by melody and words.

The association of music with particular social institutions is crucial to the understanding of differences in musical character and also to the understanding of the process of musical change under conditions of cultural pluralism. Moreover the attachment of items of music to the ceremonious aspect of social institutions is the basis of classification of musical items or *kinds*. Indeed, popular nomenclature recognises the different kinds of music, and the musical character of the items of a kind is not primarily due to common origins of melodic motif

(and rhythmic motif)—which are usually most diverse, but rather to the conditions of execution which are shared by personnel who participate in the institution.

An appraisal of the total system of behaviour of the particular social institution yields a variety of determinants of the conditions of transmission and execution of the music, and of the career of the musical form. The music may have to effect certain immediate ends—to synchronise group efforts in a song for hauling timber, to accompany the symmetrical movements of a dance, to produce psycho-physical tensions leading to dissociation or 'possession', to act as a vehicle for amusing comments on abnormal conduct, etc.; roles of musicians and dancers may be ascribed to them on non-musical grounds, i.e. a certain dance may belong to people of a certain tribal origin, a certain song to a particular initiate; a certain type of music may be appropriated to a rare festival only, or to an especially expensive one; some ceremonies may have to be kept up all night, yet appropriate musical material may not be available, thus leading to the introduction of extraneous material—or a minimum number of personnel may be needed to execute ceremonies; a social institution in decline is likely to evince the weakening of authority or consensus in its structure, which can show itself in the failure of the correct transmission and reproduction of norms; execution of music may be legal or illegal, may require a certain administrative nucleus; the interaction of components such as the relative importance of dancing as compared with musical variation, the relationship of audience to performers; these are but a few of these determinants.

For example we are taking the group of islands Trinidad, Tobago, Grenada and Cariacou, whose populations, though culturally differentiated, are in frequent interaction. Excluding East Indian, and purely superstructural music, we have listed below the different kinds of music in the area, calling each by its local name.

Kinds of Music	Institutions Containing It
1. "CONGO". Tr. – 'Congo', Patois. Songs dances with 3 drums acc. Chantwell and Ch.	Music for wedding and christening dances held by groups of persons of Congo descent, and financed by contributions of group.
2. 'RADA'. Tr.–'African' Hymns, chants, drums and sticks, 1 iron and chac chac. Chantwell and Ch.	Music for ceremonies of Rada (Dahomey) Cult groups; vehicle for invocation of saints, induction of spirit possession and pleasure dancing.
3. 'SHANGO'. Tr.–'African' Patois. 3-4 drums and sticks, chac-chacs. Chantwell and Ch.	Music for the rites of the cult groups of Yoruba origin, including hymns, litanies and invocations, items associated with the immanence of particular deities. The music helps to induce possession and to support possession dances.
4. 'YARRABA'. Tr.–'African' Patois. 3-4 drums, sticks, chac-chac. Chantwell and Ch.	Music for pleasure dances held by descendants of Yorubas and their friends co-operatively.
5. 'KALENDA'. Tr., Gr.–Patois English. Songs with 3 drum acc. or Tambou Bamboo (Stamping Tubes). Chantwell and Ch.	Music to accompany quarter-staff duellings, between regional champions backed by followers at Carnival. Eccentric drum-beats act as lead in foot work, feint attacks, etc. Words boast prowess of champions and bands, throw challenging insults, etc.
6. 'BELE'. Tr.–Patois. Dance songs of 5 or 6 types with 3-5 drums and chac-chacs. Chantwell and Ch.	Music for formal secular festival organised by neighbourhood group and presided over by elected King and Queen, women wearing old fashioned dress, held on Public Holidays, etc., for pleasure dancing and occasional social commentary.
7. 'BELE'. Gr.–Patois. Dance songs of 8-10 types with 3 drums and chac-chacs. Chantwell and Ch.	Music for festival as above, or for crisis, etc., in association with Saraka or sacrifice to to ancestors. Carries derisive comment on behaviour.
8. 'BELE'. T.–English. Bass drum and stick, keg drum Tambourines chac-chacs Chantwell and Ch.	Music for a pleasure dance, and for 'working' by magicians involving possession. It has appropriated as a type a formerly independent kind, namely Congo music of
9. 'BIG DRUM DANCE'. C–'African' Patios, English. 3 drums and chac-chac. Chantwell and Ch.	nineteenth century immigrants to Tobago. Verbal context largely about magical power and dead magicians. Music of family or neighbourhood ceremony for ensuring favour of ancestors, accompanied by offering of food. For weddings, raising tombstones, boat-launching, etc., and in other critical situations, usually as the mandate of a dream. Also as a pleasure dance.
10. 'BONGO'. T–English. Songs, dances, games and mimes, hand-clapping. Chantwell and Ch.	Music for a Wake traditionally to placate spirits of dead and the spirit of a culture hero. Sexual burlesque in word and mime and verbal parody of hymns predominates.
11. 'BONGO'. Tr.–Patois, English. Qua-Qua or pieces of bamboo beaten together or in South Trinidad, 'Tambou bamboo', i.e. African stamping tubes. Chantwell and Ch.	Music for competitive male dance and games in the yard at a Wake whilst hymns are singing in the House. Nine or forty nights Wake, carrying social commentary.
12. 'SINGS'. Tr., T., Gr., C.–Patois, English, Nonsense Chantwell (Tale Teller) and Ch.	Music to punctuate tales told to pass the time at Wakes, and to maintain participation of audience.
13. 'PASS-PLAY'. Tr., Gr., C., T. English, Patois. Unison songs, many traditional English children's games, or similar in musical style with slight off beat flavour.	Music (a) for the games of children's playgroups but usually discouraged in school, (b) for pleasure and passing the time by adults at Wake.
14. 'WORK-SONGS', Tr., Gr., C., T. English, Patois. Chantwell and Ch.	Music for formal co-operative work-days, with common meal, called Marroon (Gr.), Lend Hand (T.), Gayap (Tr.). Occasionally still used for informal group labour.
15. 'CHANTIES'. C., Gr., T. English. Chantwell and Ch.	Music for (1) synchronising effort in hauling at the launching of a schooner. (2) The Wake of a skipper, along with the ceremonial breaking of a barrel.
16. 'REEL DANCE'. T.–English. 3 Tambourines, Triangle, chac-chac and singer.	Music for pleasure dancing and invocation of spirits of ancestors and spirits of dead magicians for divination, etc. Held before weddings, in cases of sickness, etc.
17. 'QUESH'. T.–French. Choral singing with harmony of French and folk traditional Cantiques de Noel.	Music for house-to-house visiting at Christmas season. The words are printed in a

18. 'SANKEYS AND TRUMPETS'. Tr., T., C., Gr.—English. Choral singing with harmony. From Hymnody of Churches or of local formation—sung as dirge, or highly rhythmic, modified with hand-clapping.

Music (a) for Wakes and (b) for the rites of the Shouters, Shakers, etc., where the 'trumpets' may be associated with certain modes of psychophysical experience known as doptions, and also inducing possession.

19. 'VEIQUOIX'. Tr.—Spanish. Competitive, recititive-style singing accompanied by Tiple, cuatro, bandol, guitar and chac-chac.

Music for Cross-Wake or Velorio de Cruz, a family anniversary kept in accordance with a vow, and consisting of ballads of the Spanish Main, traditional folk-Catholic hymns sung before an ornate altar, quizzing on Biblical and schoolbook knowledge and 'piccong' or ribbing.

20. 'FANDANG'. Tr.—Spanish. As above with addition of bass. 7-8 types. Song-dances such as Manzanare, Joropo, Galleron, etc.

A pleasure dance following the end of a Veiquoix.

21. 'ROAD MARCH'. Tr., Gr.,—English. Played by an ensemble. Short incessant reiterated chorus sung or played, usually a fragment of Calypso chorus, a kalenda chorus.

Music for street to lead dancing by carnival bands. Used for integration of group for hostile action.

22. 'CALYPSO'. Verse and Chorus in modern song form, accompanied by string band or dance band ensemble.

Music sung in 'tent's erected prior to Carnival by singers competing for fame, money, love of women, in humour and social comment set suitably in a traditional style, to music.

23. 'REEL ENGAGE'. C—Patois, English. Fiddle, Bass Drum, Tambourine, Triangle and occasionally singer.

Music for dancing Reels, Quadrilles, etc., held either as a family dance for pleasure accompanied by an offering to ancestors, or as a 'bouquet' or subscription pleasure dance organised by a small society.

24. 'PARANG'. Tr.—Spanish. Acc. as above. Songs are serenades, aguinaldos (Carols).

Music for going from place place visiting friends in their homes day and night throughout the Christmas season.

25. WILD INDIANS.

26. BLACK INDIANS.

27. DAME LORINE.

Music for particular masquerades in Annual Carnival.

28. SEBUCAN.

29. BURAQUITE.

30. SPEECH BAND.

31. STEEL BAND. Combination of marimbas tuned from 40 gallon oil drums.

Music (1) for Road Bands in Carnival, (2) for modern dances at all social levels.

Ch. — Chorus.   C. — Carriacou.   Gr. — Grenada.
Tr. — Trinidad.   T. — Tobago.

Scrutiny of the kinds listed above and their relation to one another in time and space, leads to the conclusion that the most important type of change is that which can be summarised as the movement of items from kind to kind, that is, from one social institution to another. This includes the movement of persons bearing musical norms from one culture to another, from one island sub-culture to another, from one social institution to another at the same level in the same society, from one institution to another up or down the social scale, from a rural to an urban institution inside the same society.

A common phenomenon has been the arrival of the immigrant, bearing norms of musical forms and techniques, who in the process of adapting himself to the society he finds in the New World, become a participant in a social institution already in existence there. The institution may or may not permit him to reproduce his own music. From the start it is probable that he will have to execute the norm on instruments different from those to which he is accustomed, and conform in general ways to the conditions of the institution, so that the process of modification begins immediately, and the norm, reformed, becomes an item of the kind already in existence, largely taking on its musical characteristics. Should he fail to lodge his norm in an institution during his lifetime (or to transmit it individually to someone who will) then it ceases to exist in that territory.

Immigrants have in certain cases been able to recreate a social institution in the New World, and thus to introduce a new kind of music, although in most cases the supporting social structure soon imparts new functions to the transplanted institution, so that its internal system changes, and with it the musical form. In the case of African immigrants arriving as slaves, the possibilities of maintaining an old ceremonial were slender owing to the variety of tribal backgrounds and the rigid regulation of slave life by the planter. However, Africans who arrived shortly before or in the period following emancipation have in some cases maintained in changing form cults and ceremonies to the present day. Rada exemplifies this situation. Whatever modifications may have taken place, there is little sign of Creole influence in this music, and there is reason to believe that the music we hear today is close to that of the ancestral Africans who were performing it in the 1840's in Dahomey. The music belongs to the religious rites of a group of immigrants who were able to establish their cult on a solid footing in Port of Spain, Trinidad, soon after their arrival. The controlling factors were (1) the leader had already lived through maturity in Dahomey before he reached the new world at the age of approximately 55, and was thoroughly versed in the practices of the cult; (2) he was accompanied by other mature practitioners; (3) he was able to establish himself on his own lot of land and build a cult house there within thirteen years of arrival; (4) he lived from 1868 to 1899, i.e. from the age of approximately 69 to 100 as undisputed head of the household of the cult, raising twelve children who lived with him at the compound, and to some of whom he transmitted the cult practices including the music. After his death his daughter and son established their respective homes on a larger plot of land, which became a compound with the houses of other kin, cult houses and a private cemetery; (5) the area, Belmont, in which both properties were established, was one in which many

Limbo, a dance for weddings and also for wakes has its origins in fertility rites, by Alfred Cadallo 1957. Reproduced with the permission of Hand Arnold & Co., The Trinidad Guardian and the R.V.I.

Africans settled, particularly Dahomeans, Ibos, Congos and Madingos; (6) the head of the cult at the time it was studied is the son of the founder and leader drummer (i.e. the chief musician).

In contrast, the following is an example of the failure of a set of imported norms to find lodgement in a social institution. An old Trinidadian, son of a Congolese, remembers a group of old Africans who would sit in the house of the dead person at wakes, playing the 'banja' (sanza) and singing about the dead while the younger people danced the Bongo outside. Neither songs nor instrument became a part of the ceremonies connected with the dead. Bongo in the yard, and the singing of 'Sankeys' in the house was still the firmly established form in 1955. But the Banja re-appeared made by the boys of Belmont out of a kerosene tin with bamboo tongues attached. This they used for hide-and-seek, the hider playing the banja and singing 'Allez toujours! C'est là même i'est, cherchez pou'l'i, c'est là i'est.' They had 'refabbed' the instrument in local material, given it a temporary standing as one of a regular set of children's games, and maintained a vestige of a belief about the banja that it spoke with a 'spirit voice' and that you could not tell where this voice came from. The instrument was still extant in 1955 as the 'basse-en-boîte', large enough to stand on the floor and be played with the thumbs as a cheap substitute for the plucked three stringed 'cello, used for a bass in the traditional String Band (with bandol, cuatro, guitar, etc.)

The amount of movement of items 'from kind to kind' is related to the tendency of institutions to maintain exclusively their traditional content, to take in exotic material, or to sanction the invention of novelties. Thus, when the Rada cult uses oleographs of Christian saints graphically to represent its African deities, in respect of music it is exclusive, as far as the evidence shows. In contrast, the Shouters find justification for the introduction of new musical material in dreams, e.g. 'I saw Abraham and he gave me this song to sing' or 'As I journeyed up Mount Sion this trumpet came to me'. The institution of Calypso demands 'composition' of novelties each year. Yet in these two kinds of music it is virtually impossible to identify true melodic or rhythmic novelties except a few Calypsoes composed by middle-class sophisticates, and the growth of items comes from the introduction of items from other institutions or kinds (or often from superstructural sources) and the stretching and minor alteration of existing items to fit new words. From our point of view, therefore, no special consideration need be given to institutions sanctioning invention, and they can be subsumed under accretive institutions.

The Big Drum Dance of Carriacou provides a very

A Wake in the Country, by Alfred Cadallo, this event included hymn singing, storytelling, Bongo and Limbo dancing. Christian and African beliefs overlap with French Patois as the common language. Reproduced with the permission of Hand Arnold & Co., The Trinidad Guardian and the R.V.I.

good example of the accretive process. We must take it that at some stage before 1830 a 'Cromanti' (predominantly Ashanti) group of African slaves started to practice in the West Indies ritual observances connected with belief in the power of ancestors, and those were accompanied by music and dancing known commonly to several members of the group from African experience. At a number of subsequent stages other slaves (and later freemen) either African or Creole, but with different tribal backgrounds, participated in the ceremony, finding it acceptable, and performed different dances to different music, which was learnt by the original groups and played and sung by them in inevitably modified form. These other dances came to carry the names of 'nations' (Cromanti, Ibo, Scotch-Ibo, Temné, Manding, Congo, Rada, Moko Bangé, Moko Yégé-yégé, Banda). Colaterally it became customary in the island for each individual to identify himself with his 'nation', traced patrilineally, and collectively this principle of classification became in some way a regulative factor in the selection of mates and associates in enterprises. But whatever discriminatory or competitive overtones the system may have had, a deliberate and conscious catholicism developed in the sense that, in addition to its role as an ancestral cult, the institution of the Big Drum Dance came to have social role giving recognition to the 'multi-national' nature of the community, and affording a recognised place to various culturally differentiated groups which entered the

island from time to time. Thus it came to have a generally accretive character, absorbing the songs and dances of the Old Creole group, and then, as Cariacouans travelled abroad for work, and sailed their schooners and sloops, they brought back and added to the latter part of the dance the Piké from Grenada, Ladderis, Quelbé and Lora from Union, and from Trinidad the Kalenda, Cariso, and Man Bongo.

The music of the Big Drum Dance and the Rada Cult provides examples of the social basis of the tendencies towards exclusiveness and accretiveness as regards musical items. The adding of new items to a *kind* by accretion can be seen in *Bongo 11* from 5, 22 and 13 in *Bongo 10* from 13, 14 and 18. Whilst the sacred *Veiquoix 19* remains exclusive, and is supported by the intermittent arrival of singers from Venezuela, its participants appropriate to *Fandang 20* popular music similar to its own kind but broadcast by radio from Venezuela, and also Calypsoes which are rhythmically closely related to a dance of the Spanish Tradition – Paseo –; and *Parang 24* has added to its traditional Spanish language serenades 'Stille Nacht' and 'I'm dreaming of a White Christmas'. As Calypso 22 became established in connection with the Port of Spain Carnival, first as the nightly pre-Carnival rehearsal of the masquerades of individual bands with their Chantwells, and later as a public performance on a commercial basis, it drew upon the musical content of a variety of rural

The Serenaders, in days gone by before radio and television the music of the island played a greater role in our home life. Few homes were without a piano or some musical instrument, by Alfred Cadallo, 1965. Reproduced with the permission of Hand Arnold & Co., The Trinidad Guardian and the R.V.I.

social institutions (5, 7, 11, 13, 16, 18, 20 and 23) setting the melodic schemes of these items in its own basic rhythm. The choral element gave way to elaborate verbal virtuosity and wit, giving to these items quite a new character.

The most interesting recent emergence of a new kind, is the growth of the Steel Band; yard-gang percussion bands, used for road marches, developed well-tuned steel marimbas out of oil drums during the 1940's each with up to twenty-eight notes; (1) being thus capable of providing music for modern dancing they become permanent dance-bands, as well as Carnival Road-bands. (2) Their musical norms were gathered in from traditional and current popular music. (3) Because of the technological limitations of the instruments and the folk-traditional skills of the musicians, these norms were radically transformed, and (4) for technological and other reasons, singing ceased to be a component. Thus they have come to provide a new kind of music and a new and important institution in the society.

Desuetude is apparent in those kinds belonging to displaced social institutions. *Congo 1* – Descendants of mid nineteenth-century Congo immigrants have almost completely lost identity and intermarried. *Work Songs 14* are seldom sung with the disappearance of co-operative labour on peasant holdings, and *Chanties 15,* which were important in the nineteenth century under the

technological conditions of sailing, are remembered by but a few, who lead the singing at the infrequent launchings. *Quesh 11* belongs to a small cultural minority subject to assimilation and living near the town. *Black Indians 26, Buraquite 29* and *Dame Lorine 27* are merely 'plays' and have not withstood competition with other traditional and original possibilities for Carnival Masquerading.

The instances of change referred to, and the numerous others which we have no space to mention, could be subjected to explanatory treatment in terms of the wider system of patterned behaviour in the setting of which they take place, with special attention to (a) the movement of items from one kind to another; (b) the participation in a particular kind by executants who have received their musical technique in another kind; (c) the changing social function of a particular institution, and the consequent changing of the conditions determining its kind of music; and (d) the influence of technological changes. Whilst it is true that in the area under discussions, cultural interpenetration has been intense throughout several centuries, we see no reason why the same approach should not provide some explanations in areas of greater cultural unity, where change has come more slowly.

1874

CHANGE OF COINAGE

After the 15th day of December next, the old copper coinage will not be a legal tender in this colony. These coins representing the penny, halfpenny and farthing, respectively, will be taken at the Treasury at their full face value until that date, but not after. In place of these coins, the corresponding Imperial bronze coinage has been substituted. *(16th September, 1874.)*

RE-COMMENCEMENT OF THE SAN FERNANDO GAZETTE

The San Fernando Gazette, publication of which had been suspended for a few weeks on account of the death of its proprietor, Mr. Alexander Murray, has re-appeared in a new series, under the auspices of Mr. Samuel Cartar.
(12th September, 1874.)

1876

OPENING OF THE ARIMA LINE

The opening of the railway from Port-of-Spain to Arima, 16 miles, on Thursday last, the 1st September, is the one event of the week. That day was also the Feast of Santa Rosa, the patron saint of the town of Arima, and the annual holiday of the surrounding districts. Excursion trains ran to and from the ancient capital at reduced fares and quite a crowd of townsfolk availed themselves of the opportunity. The merchants of Port-of-Spain generously closed their stores, and although no official holiday was proclaimed many of the public offices were closed. Ten trains were run up and and down with the greatest regularity. The three last return trains were somewhat late, but that was to be expected. There were no accidents, and not the slightest breakdown. The government and the railway officials are to be congratulated on the success of the opening.
(7th September, 1876.)

Columbus Square in Port of Spain full of trees and lit by glass lanterns. In those days it was an elegant part of town. Photograph — 'Starks Guide to Trinidad', 1890.

> " *igon pas tini habilment (repeat thrice)*
> *.ormi en had stevedore*
>
> Joe Dragon don't have good clothes
> He sleeping in his stevedore clothes. "
>
> (Anon.)

1874

BUILDING AND LOAN ASSOCIATION ADVOCATED

Commenting upon suggested remedies for the above state of affairs, the 'Gazette' continues:— 'We would be wrong to say that the Government has been inattentive to these results. They first attracted the attention of Governor Gordon, and the remedy was the Port of Spain Improvement Ordinance, and the Loans Ordinance, to enable poor people to procure the means of effecting improvements to their homes. The former did too much, and put a stop to building; the other did not carry out what it professed to do with sufficient clearness. . . . . . Private effort is now, we are glad to learn, being aroused to do what government has failed to accomplish. We understand that it is being agitated to set on foot a society on the basis of the English Loan and Building Institutions, the sucess of which combinations have surpassed the most ardent expectations.
(19th September, 1874.)

1875

CLOSING OF THE BOROUGH SCHOOLS

It must be assumed that the Borough Council is the best judge of its own affairs, and especially in its determination to hand over its schools to the Government. Recent meetings of the Council have not been characterised by any discussions as to the wisdom of the step; nor does it appear that the popular clamour which has been excited out of doors has influenced their sympathies to any great extent. Worshipful councillors have one and all voted for the suppression with the calm assurance that denotes a foregone conclusion. . . . . And the Borough Council is simply conforming to the necessities of the case in delcaring its inability to maintain schools without money. *(7th September, 1875.)*

1876

OPENING OF WILSONS STORES

The handsome store recently erected by Messrs. Wilson & Co. at the corner of Frederick and King Streets will, we understand, be opened for business on Monday next, when we have no doubt the enterprising proprietors will have a run upon them. . . . . . The building itself is well worth a visit. If not the handsomest, it is certainly one of the handsomest stores in the West Indies. Built of tooled blue limestone, the facings are of polished freestone imported from Scotland, it is two stories high, and is lighted by a skylight rising from the main roof, the semi-elliptical copula spaces of which are filled in with stained glass, the subjects illustrated being science, commerce and the arts and industries. The whole internal fittings are of pitch pine and mahogany, while three very large plate glass windows add very much to the style as well as to the utility of the lower floor. The upper floor is surrounded by a splendid iron gallery running round both sides of the building. . . . .
(14th March, 1876.)

1876

MR. CIPRIANI ON A DRAINAGE SCHEME

We owe Mr. Cipriani many thanks for his bold scheme for raising a loan of £10,000 for the improvement of our streets and drains. The poverty of the Borough Council has up to now crippled its energy. . . . No more economical administration of the funds of the Council could be suggested than that of setting aside every year for the next 12 years a certain lump sum to meet the expenditure on a present outlay which is to secure solid and durable work once and for all. . . . . .
(4th April, 1876.)

The old fish market on South Quay was situated on reclaimed land just west of the lighthouse. This photograph is of the 1890's.
Photograph — G. Mac Lean.

1877

THREE TIMES MAYOR

The election, for the third time in succession, of Mr. J.E. Cipriani as Mayor of this city cannot but be matter of congratulation to all all well wishers of the Municipality. The devotion that Mr. Cipriani has shown in the discharge of his duties, and the numerous and great improvements which he has carried out, are too well known to require any notice from us. It is, however, with much pleasure that we publish the following letter, proving, as it does, not only the amicable relations existing between the government and the municipality, but also the very high opinion which is entertained by the government of the chief Municipal officer:

Government House,
13th November, 1877

Sir,

I am directed to acknowledge the receipt of your letter of the 5th instant reporting the re-election of Mr. J.E. Cipriani as Mayor of Port-of-Spain, and the Lieut. Governor thinks the Corporation is to be congratulated in again having for its chief officer one who has shewn himself so devoted to its interests.

(Sgd.) J. SCOTT-BUSHE
Colonial Secretary.

The Town Clerk
Port-of-Spain

UNIFORM FOR THE CUSTOMS

It is intended to provide all the customs employees with suitable uniforms. This has been long needed. There are many things to recommend such a step, not the least is the respect and fear which our visitors from Venezuela have for the orthodox gold lace. (*3rd March, 1877.*)

1877

RAILWAY EXTENSIONS

A proposal to extend the railway to Couva and Montserrat has met with the approval of the Secretary of State, and the work will be begun at once.
(*10th March, 1877.*)

1878

SALARY BY FEES

The office of Marshalll has been offered to and refused by several local officers. The salary has, we hear, been withdrawn, and the new holder of the office will have to depend entirely upon fees. This attempt to return to a most pernicious system of paying public officers meets with general condemnation throughout the island.
(*19th January, 1878.*)

PLANTERS PUNCH
Put a liquer glass of lime juice in tumbler. Add two liquer glasses of syrup and a full cocktail glass of rum. Fill to the brim with ice and stir. Put a piece of green lime peel, grate some nutmeg over it and add a dash of Angostura and serve with straw.

PASSION COCKTAIL
Strain the juice of a granadilla into a jug and add four cocktail glasses of rum, two teaspoons of sugar and plenty of crushed ice. Swizzle well until very very cold and strain into glasses. Grate a little nutmeg into each and put a dash of Angostura on top.

PINEAPPLE BEER
Take peel of two pineapples and place in four quarts fresh water with six cloves leave soaking for three days, strain, sweeten to taste and bottle.

SORREL COCKTAIL
To make six cocktails put into a jug three cocktail glasses of rum, two cocktail glasses of strong sorrel drink, some crushed ice and six good dashes of Angostura. Swizzle well and strain into glasses.

1878

FIRST LIGHTING ON THE STREETS
The inauguration of the lighting of the lamps placed by the Municipality in Marine Square and from the square northwards to the gaol, took place, as announced on Christmas Eve. The first lamp was lit by His Excellency the Governor; and among those present we notice the Hon. the Attorney-General, The Hon. T.A. Finlayson, The Hon. L. Guiseppi, John Agostini Esq., L. Mathieu Esq. Oliver Warner Esq., R.D. Mayne Esq., Joyhn Fanning Esq., J.F. Rat Esq., (Town Clerk). We also noticed that, His Worship the Mayor's published programme notwithstanding the Borough Councillors were conspicuous by their absence. We were ourselves unable to be present at the display of fireworks offered to the population, (at the cost of the population), by His Worship the Mayor. *(28th Dec., 1878.)*

1879

CHAMBER OF COMMERCE FORMED
The long talked of Chamber of Commerce has at length been formed. It begins with 41 members. The Hon'ble Leon Agostini has been elected its first President, the Hon'ble T.A. Finlayson, Vice-President, and Wm. Norman Esq. Hon. Secretary. The managing committee for general business consists of these gentlemen, with the Hon'ble Andre Bernard and Messrs. Kavanagh, Murray, Archer and Howatson. *(29th March, 1879.)*

ORIGIN OF THE POLICE BAND CONCERTS
A notice in the *Royal Gazette* announces that the Police Band will play at the stand in the Queen's Park onthe second Wednesday in each month, on which day the polo club plays, and at the Botanic Gardens on the Monday of the same week. *(18th April, 1879.)*

1880

INAUGURATION OF THE ISLANDS SERVICE
The steamer *'Ant'* will ply three times a week, as may be seen from an advertisement in another column of this issue, between Port-of-Spain and the island of Gasparillo, calling at Five Islands, Carenage and the Carreras each way. This arrangement represents an enormous reduction of expenditure and increase of accommodation to families and paties taking trips down the islands in future. . . . The public will not fail to appreciate this great boon, for which we are indebted to the foresight and enterprise of Messrs. Turnbull Steward and Co. *(7th April, 1880.)*

The corner of Knox and Frederick Streets, Port of Spain, in the 1880's. The house was the property of Don Ramon Garcia and it later became the Town Hall. Photograph — The Dominican Sisters of St. Catherine of Sienna.

• BEHIND THE BRIDGE •

Gerard Besson

In the evening light, the city of Port of Spain, encircled by an embrace of hills north, east and west, nestles closest to the eastern arm and as night falls with all the lights a-twinkle, seems to have flowed down from the eastern hillsides and to have settled into the flat lands that stretch south and west to the sea.

In the hard light of day this illusion vanishes, for the hills of Laventille, as this eastern area is known, are of a different world. The very old houses, the shacks, the noisy yards, the disused quarries, the winding lanes, the hills — steep and carved with flights of concrete steps, represent another side of life very different from the lifestyles lived by those who inhabit the hills to the north and the west.

Dividing the city and its northern and western suburbs from this teeming hillside, is the River, the East Dry River of which someone remarked that it was neither eastward, dry, nor a river, nor did it always exist. It was in fact, the creation of the last Spanish Governor.

In those days the Dry River was known as the Río Tragerete or Río Santa Ana, the source of which lies to the north in the hills of St. Ann. It ran along its course as far as Observatory Street, as far as L'Hospice, and then turned westward, across Park Street, down Frederick Street, across Woodford Square and down Chacon Street, to the sea.

During the rainy season, the St. Ann's River often overflowed its banks, flooding the town, causing much damage and great loss of property. It was therefore decided in 1787 to avoid further damage and remove the danger caused by the river altogether and Governor Chacon had the course diverted at Observatory Street to run along the foothills of Laventille to the sea, a distance of just over one and a half miles. In 1817, under Governor Woodford, the river was widened and altered at several points.

The hills east of the river were covered in those days by thick forests, in which a few free Black people lived — hunting and collecting fire wood. Don Cosmo Churuca had caused a road to be built to the ridge, now called Observatory Street, and there in 1783 constructed an observatory where in the same year he established the first meridian of longtitude in the western world. This building, now called Fort Chacon and presently used by the Police, probably stands on the site of the observatory. A few years later, another Fort, called St. David's Tower or Fort Picton, was built a quarter of a mile to the west of it.

In 1804 the Masonic Lodge, Les Frères Unis, was established at Mount Moriah over the river, opposite to

The Old Queen St. Bridge looking east. Photograph — P.O.S. City Council.

Upper Duke Street looking west, until very recently this part of town had not changed much for more than 150 years. Photograph — G. Mac Lean.

Queen Street. By the 1820's, Edward Jackson had created Rose Hill Estate in the area opposite to Park Street, and with emancipation, many of the freed slaves found refuge in the forested hillsides. By the 1840's, these were joined by large numbers of Africans who had been liberated as a result of the action taken by Britain to suppress the slave trade north of the equator. Free Africans from many tribes settled in this area, among them were Mandingos, Ibos, Yorubas and Krumen, the entire area was called for many years Free Town, after the liberated Africans.

The land over the Dry River known as Piccadilly, was called Grand Jardin, further north was Mango Rose and even further north, Belle Eau Road was known as Shapotie. The large central area stretching from Argyle Street to St. Paul Street, was called Sorzanoville, parts of it being covered with sugar cane. Later, as the cane was abandoned, it was known as Gros Rouge.

For many years the Dry River was crossed by only one bridge — a foot bridge made of a few planks at the Crossing at Cadiz Road, and the boys who had built it would extract a penny from any pedestrian who would use it at his own risk. The first real bridge was built at this spot and it was called McCarthy's Bridge.

The inhabitants of this area retained, to a considerable degree, many African customs and usages. Being comprised of several yards divided along tribal or religious lines, there were many gangs or bands, some perhaps organized along the lines of the secret societies of West Africa. There were 'malongues', special groupings of people who had shared the experience of the slave ship or the British Man-O-War that had brought them here.

These bands or societies, were devoted to singing and dancing and their rivalries often led to feuding and open fights. There were wakes, dances and religious ceremonies accompanied by big drums, chac chac and banjoes. The English traveller, C.W. Day, describes one such scene in 1852:

'One night, hearing a horrible drumming on the tum-tums, I followed the sounds, and in the suburbs of the town, came to a very characteristic scene — a negro ladies' ball. A narrow entry led to spacious shed, rudely thatched with palm branches, from the joints of which hung a clumsy wooden chandelier and at intervals, stuck upon high poles, serving as candelabras, were large tallow candles, casting a fitful glare over the place. At the

'Carting Sugar' on Rose Hill Estate by Richard Bridgens. This was painted in the 1820's it shows an estate house facing west and overlooking what is now Park Street. The bridge on the left is the Park Street Dry River Bridge. Rose Hill Estate was the property and residence of Edward Jackson Esq. Photograph — Tom Cambridge Collection.

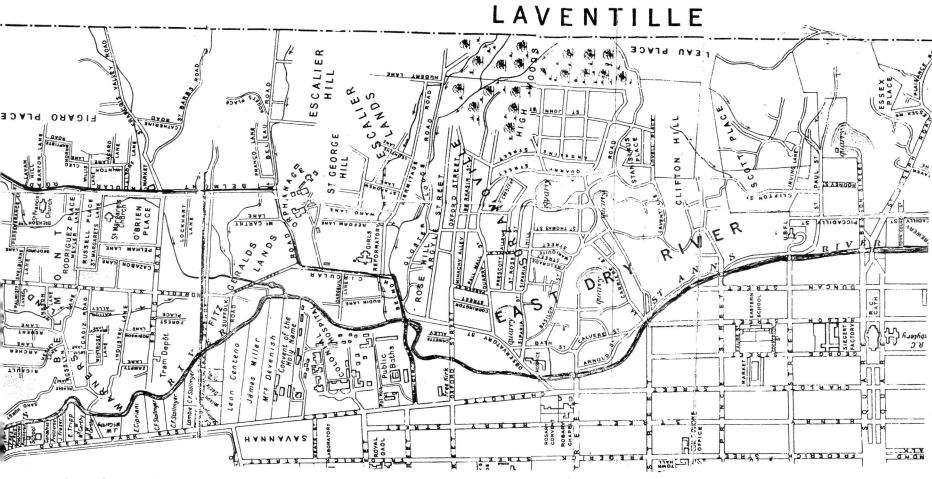

A map of east Port of Spain by Girod in 1900's.

A photograph taken in the 1880's from approximately where Rose Hill once stood. The building on the right partially shown is still in existence. The bridge pictured here has since been replaced by the one that joins Park to Picadilly Streets.

head of this dingy salon de danse were five huge negroes, thumping might and main on casks, the tops of which were covered with parchment. Ranged on one side were twenty negresses roaring a chorus, each being in motion, turning half round alternately without moving from the spot. These dingy damsels, of whose features nothing but their rolling eye-balls and brilliant teeth were visible, raised their voices to a pitch that would have satisfied the King of Ashantee. In front of the choristers were about a dozen other ladies, having their woolly hair inclosed by a Madras handkerchief, an Indian imitation of a Scottish tartan, green and red, with white checks which was preposterously elongated over the back of the head, and stuck over with gold shirt pins, and a profusion of showy Martinique gold ornaments of the filmiest texture. Enormous bunches of earrings hung from their ears, and their necks were adorned with a perfect gorget of gold chains and beads, as large as gooseberries, of the same material. These reposed on a large handkerchief, as still as buckram, worn ruff fashion, and projecting very far behind. The waists of the Trinidad negresses are absurdly short, so that a skirt, or jupe, always of a different colour, bags out when the wearer is at rest, in one unbroken line, from nearly under the arms quite to the feet, or rather as a train. Nothing can be more grotesque than the whole costume. Each of the ladies was performing a set of ludicrous evolutions, turning quite independently of her neighbour; and such jerkings, and courtesies, such

genu-flections and whirls as I beheld, baffle description! All danced with bare feet, for the dancing sake, as men rarely join the festive throng, and each performer had to pay a small sum for the pleasure. The place was surrounded by a crowd of dark men and women, quietly looking on, and smoking. the Terpischoreans were chiefly servants and laundresses, who, for such displays, make use of their customers' cambric handkerchiefs. Many ladies, indeed, lend their ornaments to favourite servants for these occasions, but no negress would wear anything but gold. The presence of a white person at these balls, though on the whole considered complimentary, is only half relished, as negroes have a great dread of being quizzed. The whole scene was truly African, and showed how little the negroes are advanced in civilization. If left to themselves, they would in fifty years relapse into their pristine barbarism.

I afterwards attended several of these balls, some of which were held in demi-toilette, each of the characters holding in her hand a 'shock-shock', a little calabash, filled with peas, by shaking which a rattling is produced in cadence with the tambours,which keep admirable time. So fond of dancing are negroes, of all ages, that I traced two tum-tums to a private yard, where the chorus was composed of young negro females, and the dancers of old women, while the ball was lighted by two tallow candles, held by boys.'

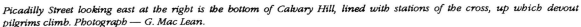

Picadilly Street looking east at the right is the bottom of Calvary Hill, lined with stations of the cross, up which devout pilgrims climb. Photograph — G. Mac Lean.

CREOLE EGG PUNCH
Beat two eggs in a jug. Add a half tin of
condensed milk and plenty of crushed
ice. Swizzle well and add a pint of rum
slowly. Strain off into sherry glass with
rims frosted by dipping them first in
water, then in granulated sugar. Place a
small piece of green lime rind in each
glass, then sprinkle them with grated
nutmeg and finish off with a couple
dashes of Angostura to each punch. This
is served before West Indian breakfasts
particularly on Sundays.

The Old Duke St. Bridge in the 1930's. Photograph — Port of Spain City Council.

The Dry River unpaved. Photograph — P.O.S. City Council.

A Barrack Yard East Port of Spain in the 1930's. Photograph — Port of Spain City Council.

" Hand me the Port-of-Spain
I want to read the nonsense once more again

Ziggilee Ziggilee Marble Stone
What an awful Shame
To use a schoolboy quotation
To a man of education Poynter is his name. "
(Executor)

Over the river, or behind the bridge, on the eastern boundary of the town, a large and somewhat insanitary and very crowded slum began to take shape. The district gained an unsavoury name for crime, it was the kind of place where no constable would venture alone.

In 1865 it was reported that a serious street battle took place between two factions of women – the *Mousselins* and the *Don't Care Damns*. Other bands were called after the *'Immaculate Conception'* and there were the terrible *'Beka Boys'* who had the awful habit of tossing foul smelling bits of cloth inot the faces of respectable women and using obscene language in the streets. The streets were called the French Shores or French Streets and those who inhabited them were known as Jamettes or Diamètres, or those beyond the diameter of polite society.

The Jamette society of east Port of Spain was in the eyes of the Colonial Government, outrageous, obscene and very vulgar. There were famous whores, badmen, panders, touts, chantwells, stickfighters, thieves and murderers; and it was from this social matrix that the basis for such present day institutions like the steelband and many aspects of Carnival and Calypso, as we know them, would spring.

Arnim 'Mitto' Sampson, known as Strongman, recounts in an article by Andrew Pearse and published in the Caribbean Quarterly, Volume 4, Nos. 3 and 4, something of the people, the Jamettes of the period just prior to the close of the century: 'There were Petite Belle Lily, Alice Sugar, Mossie Millie, Ocean Lizzie, Sybil Steele, Darling Dan and Ling Mama. Hannibal the calypsonian and Cutaway Rimbeau the stickfighter and Gumbo Glisier the greasy pole climber and his son, Gumbo Lili. Thunderstone and chantwell to the Congo Jackos. Another famous chantwell was Ojuba the slave and Surisima the Carib, the old calypsonian.

'The drums would beat and Canboulay stickmen sing Djab se yo neg, mé Die se nom-la bla Bam bou la Bam bou la so as to feel nothing. And it is described that when Roucou John fought the invincible Tiny Satan at Laku Pebwa (Bread Fruit Tree Yard) in 1875, Tiny Satan caught him six consecutive blows and smashed his skull in. Yet, Roucou stood up. When he fell finally to the ground shortly before he died, he was still mumbling Djab se yo neg Die nom-la bla Bam boula.

'The use of this theme was condemned by the famous mulatto Barrister, Mr. Maxwell Phillip. In his opinion it stigmatised the negro race atrociously, the words meaning:

The Devil is a Negro
But God is a White Man
Bamboula Bamboula
Bamboula Bamboula

'Some co-operated but the majority of the leading batonniers of the period refused, saying that when they sang 'Djab se yo neg' they were possessed by satanic spirits which made them feel nothing; they could walk into battle and meet sticks, stones, conch shells and even daggers.'

The entire area was full of bacchanal, as this incident recorded by Andrew Pearse tells how 'Petite Belle Lily became so notorious in spite of her great beauty, even Congo Jack from the Jamette world aspired to win her. Hannibal her man was jealous and attacked her in song, he refers to an incident that took place one Canboulay night. Petite Belle was assaulted by Congo Jack who threw some inflammable liquid on her dress and tried to set her ablaze, but Pappy Mammy put it out.' Pappy Mammy was a notorious homosexual of the period, and an outstanding member of the Jamette class of behind the bridge.

Behind the bridge in those days produced, just as it does now, some of this country's most colourful characters and bizarre incidents.

When Hannibal the Mulatto died in jail, his last words were directed at his great rival Zandoli. "Zandoli" he murmured, "why you ain't find your hole?".

His death in 1873 was just as stormy as his life. Annie Coals and Myrtle the Turtle, fought over his grave, later his body was dug up and ghouls carried away his head and shroud, leaving the rotten carcass at the side of the grave. A vast crowd gathered in Lapeyrouse Cemetery led by Bodicea, the female chantwell and famous Jamette who had taken off her dress and waving it like a flag, sang:

'Congo Jack vole tet la Hannibal
U vole la mo, gade bakanal
(Congo Jack steal Hannibal's head
You steal from the dead, look bacchanal)'
Cedric la Blanc, the white calypsonian sang of them:
'Bodicea first and then Petite Belle,
The Devil waiting for them in Hell.'

Right: The Moko Jumbie, a stilt dancer, was a mas played only by men on stilts that were sometimes 15 or 20 feet high. The stilts were usually brightly painted and the masquerader wore long trousers, a jacket or 'eton' of brightly coloured satin or velvet. His hat was made of tosho, the dried up pulp of the wild cucumber, which was fashioned into an admiral's hat decorated with feathers. They were sometimes accompanied by a dwarf in a similar costume.

Below right: The Jab Molassi or Molasses Devil has not disappeared off the scene and is, in fact, one of the oldest surviving 'mas'. He may wear horns or a wreath of weeds or one stolen from a grave, and would be covered in tar, stale molasses grease, creosote or mud and is followed by one or more little boys carrying cooking pots, biscuit tins or dust bins on which they beat a fast tatoo with bolts as drum sticks. They would also carry an extra bucket of grease or mud so as to repaint the costume.

Below left: The Rosary Chapel was completed in 1867 and blessed by Archbishop Gonin O.P. It was built by Pere Forestier with much help from the parishioners. Photograph — J. Sabga.

Above: A view of the roof tops of the city, at left is the Roman Catholic Cathedral and at right is the Trinity Cathedral.
Below: Old St. Joseph Road enters Port of Spain. Columbus Square is in the foreground, the spires of the Catholic Cathedral
can be seen over the tops of the trees. Photographs — G. Mac Lean.

OLD TIME CARNIVAL
Andrew Carr

Carnival in Trinidad has had a long and interesting tradition going back well nigh two hundred years. For although it has been difficult to trace this definitely, it has been thought by some that there might well have been a modest form of the festival in Spanish times prior to 1783.

However, for fifty years during the pre-Emancipation period, from 1783 to the Abolition of Slavery in 1833, it was the French who stimulated the growth and development of the Carnival into a fête of national significance.

The French were never in possession of the Island by virtue of discovery or conquest, but they migrated to the island in such numbers that they exercised a cultural dominance in the society. For example, in 1783, the Spaniards in the population numbered 126 Whites and 245 Free Coloured, and when the British captured the Island in 1797, their total was still merely 150 whites and 200 Free Coloured. At that time the French, on the other hand, numbered 2250 Whites and 4700 Coloured.

Although many of the French people, both white and free coloured, had subsequently emigrated to the Spanish Main, their number in the population was, nevertheless, sufficient to maintain their cultural dominance.

It was they, therefore, who set the patterns of gaiety for the Carnival season which lasted from Christmas to Ash Wednesday, and as one writer has put it, they held their 'concerts, balls, dinners, hunting parties and fêtes champêtres', which occurred with greater frequency during this festive season.

During this French period, in addition to the gay balls and parties, bands of individuals indulged in much frolic for some weeks before the Carnival Monday and Tuesday. Disguised and masked, and accompanied by musicians playing such instruments as the violin, guitar, quatro, bandol, mandolin and chac-chac or maracas, they went on foot or in carriages to the homes of friends or on parade in the streets. This form of merriment, with continuous modifications, was to last through the post-Emancipation period and well into the present century.

In the Carnival itself before the Abolition, it is said that the Amerindian people kept entirely aloof, and while the African slaves were interested onlookers, they were prohibited by law from taking part except by special favour or permission. Free persons of Colour, however, could participate, but under restricted conditions.

At that time, among the elite in the society, apart from the elegant disguises like the French marquis and marquise, English noblemen and noblewomen, Swiss damsels and the like, there were grooms and postillions, priests and friars, whilst some women wore the graceful 'mulatresse' of the time, and many of the men disguised as 'negres jardin' or garden labourers.

These pretended 'negres jardin' formed themselves into bands, and with torches and drums indulged in an elite form of Cannes Brulées or Canboulay in their fêtes, a forerunner of the riotous form subsequently adopted by the emancipated populace and which led to the famous Canboulay Riot of 1881. Cannes Brulées or 'burning of the canes' was the name given to the custom of sending

Long time carnival wire masks and white faces a string band in accompaniment. Photograph — G. Duruty.

gangs of slaves to put out bush fires which somewhat frequently occurred on sugar-cane estates.

When slavery was abolished in 1833 the exclusively aristocratic character of the Carnival naturally disappeared. Thus, Fraser, in his paper on the 'History of the Origin of the Carnival' was moved to say, 'After the Emancipation of the Slaves things were materially altered, the ancient lines of demarcation between the classes were obliterated and as a natural consequence the Carnival degenerated into a noisy and disorderly amusement for the lower classes.'

A record of the Carnival of 1847 gives us an interesting picture of the masquerade wherein there appeared bands of ten to twenty persons. In one of them, the men were disguised as 'Pulichinello' and the women were dressed in bodices of the same colour. All wore white flesh-coloured masks, which the writer said 'contrasted with the bosom and arms', and 'was droll in the extreme'. Incidentally, it was remarked that where a black mask was worn, it was sure to be a white person.

In this Carnival, there were Pirates and Turks, and Wild Indians of South America realistically portrayed by Spanish peons from the Main, 'themselves half-Indian', and there was the personation of Death, with his tight-fitting black costume with white skeleton painted thereon, and a ludicrous Highlander.

There was a band of 'primitives' comprising half-naked men of African descent, one of whom 'had a long chain and padlock attached to his leg, which chain the others pulled'. Occasionally, the man was thrown to the ground and mock-beaten. The chronicler, Day, thought that this may have portrayed the inhumanness of slavery, and Andrew Pearse was of opinion that this character may well be the forerunner of the Dragon or Beast in later day bands of Devils and Demons. This may not be so, however, for the Beast here may have instead a biblical connotation.

Year after year the Carnival was heavily criticised in the press as being eminently undesirable, degenerate and disgraceful, and an attempt at least at partial suppression was made in 1858 when Governor Keate tried to prohibit the wearing of masks.

By 1870 stick-fighting bands were playing 'Canboulay', which was described as 'an unremitting uproar, yelling, drumming and blowing of horns'. By this time the critics were calling the festival 'Jamette Carnival'

The Argos Grand Stand for the 1919 Victory Carnival. Inset: Some robbers. Photograph — G. Duruty.

because of the 'low character and social level of the street participants', the women being adjudged as 'below the diameter of respectability', or of the 'underworld'.

Whilst Inspector of Police Fraser did his best to bring about better control over the Carnival and establish public order generally, he could not apparently be won over to support suppression of the festival. Eventually, he was accused of 'masterly inactivity', dismissed in 1877 as being too weak, and replaced by the 'redoubtable and famous Capt. Baker', in whose time the masqueraders were being referred to as 'savage and ferocious hordes'.

Capt. Baker was subsequently to carve for himself an unforgettable niche in the history of the Carnival when he led the police in a pitched battle against the masqueraders in what is known as the Canboulay Riot of 1881.

The Canboulay bands, comprising the stick-fighting men of the day and their women supporters, used to come out on the streets just after the stroke of midnight on the Sunday night, armed with sticks, carrying flambeaux or lighted torches and singing war-like songs to the accompaniment of goatskin drums. They were fierce. Fights were fast and furious. And on the whole, they posed a danger from possible fires to the numerous wooden buildings in the town.

Capt. Baker was determined to stamp out the Canboulay, to seize the sticks, drums and torches. Mounted on horseback, he charged into the bands, followed by his policemen with riot batons. The masqueraders retaliated with their expertly wielded fighting sticks, the supporters hurling bottles and stones.

Many were injured on both sides, and among the many heroic tales of the day is that of a leading Belmont stickman, with the Dahomean (formerly French West African) name of Hodonu, who had the crown of his beaver or top-hat completely cut off by a sword-swipe from Capt. Baker. The family is said to have kept it for many years as an hierloom and precious memento of that great day. By 1884 this type of masquerade was abolished.

By the 1890's the Carnival began slowly to improve. Merchants began to appreciate the economic value of stimulating improvement in the Carnival, quite apart from the genuine desire of many to see the festival freed of unsavoury influence.

Ignacio Bodu, Town Councillor and Merchant, is credited with holding the first competition about 1900 for Best Dressed Bands and Individuals. The Councillor,

popularly known as 'Papa Bodi', had offered a cup for the winning band. The competition began at 2 o'clock on the Tuesday afternoon, and bands had to pass in front of Metivier's Store – La Favourite – on 42 King Street on Marine Square, now Independence Square.

The Carnival of that year was recorded as being 'one of the most respectable, most orderly, least obscene, and yet most thoroughly and generally enjoyed carnival and a credit to its numerous supporters'. At the time some bands boasted a membership of some 30 to 40 men and women, and all the better bands had their Kings and Queens. There were also a goodly number of Wild Indians, Robbers, Clowns, Devils and other traditional masqueraders.

" Gal, who you voting for? Cipriani.
We doh want Major Rust to make bassa-bassa here. Cipriani.
We do want no Englishman, we is Trinidadian. Cipriani.

War, I had to tell this ex-soldier,
Was the work of politicians, I fear
Then I went on to describe 1914
And the horrible thing I had seen
When the flower of the manhood of the nation
With music, songs, and jubilation
Went to the Front all bright, brave and game
But knowing millions would not come back again. "

(Atilla the Hun)

1881

THE ORIGIN OF CANNES BRULEES
The attempt made by the police to transform the carnival by forcibly suppressing the most distinguishing of its features, the cannes brulees having resulted in a serious fray, people are being led to inquire into its origin and signification. . . . We think it opportune to state what we know of the matter,—in fact what every son of Trinidad knows:—

Cannes brulees,—and not canboulay, which is a joint English and creole phoneticism of the original words,—existed when the present generation of old men and women were in their teens. In those days the elite of our society took an active part in the carnival. The favourite costume of our mothers and grandmothers was the graceful and costly one of the 'mulatresse' of the time; whilst gentlemen adopted that of the 'negres de jardin,' or in creole, 'negue jardin,' or field labourer. In that costume, the gentlemen often figured in the 'bamboola,' in the 'giouba' and the 'calinda.' It is traditional in our old families that General P. aide-de-camp to Governor Woodford, and Commander in Chief of the militia, with Mr. P.G. who, though then 70 years of age, was still strong and robust, both excelled in the above mentioned dances. These pretended negres de jardin were wont to unite in bands, representing the camps of different estates, and with torches and drums to represent what did actually take place on the estates when a fire occurred in a plantation. In such cases the gangs of the neighbouring estates proceeded alternately accompanied with torches at night to the estate which had suffered to assist in the grinding of the burnt canes before they become sour. . . . After emancipation, the emancipated slaves entered heart and soul into the carnival, which as a natural consequence became more boisterous and less distinguished. But that which mostly contributed to give the boisterous character which it still preserves, is the retrenchment of the Sunday as a masquerading day. The people having only two instead of three days to amuse themselves, did not wish to lose a moment of the 48 hours allowed to them. Hence on their coming out as the clocks struck 12 of Sunday night, they naturally started with the cannes brulees, as it chimed in with their humour and former habits. If in their hands it became more boisterous and noisy than heretofore, if it has degenerated, and become the occasion of hostile collisions between the different bands, we are indebted for all this to the administrative measures which curtailed one of the three days allowed for the carnival. . . . We have no wish that the Sabbath should be desecrated; and it might perhaps be sufficient to add the Saturday to the two days now allowed for the carnival. But that under pretext of suppressing an abuse the police should give battle to the people; that their annual festival should be violently interfered with; that they should be called 'canaille' by the defenders of the police; all this constitutes an abuse much more intolerable and much more dangerous to the public than is the cannes brulees.
(26th March, 1881.)

Carnival continued to improve, and in 1910, for example, there was a keenly contested competition for Best Dressed Bands and Individuals organised by Messrs. Smith Bros. of 'The Bonanza', a store on Frederick Street which stood where the present-day Woolworth establishment is located. Another was held by the proprietors of the 'La India' Hotel, which was at the corner of Frederick and Duke Streets situated in downtown Port of Spain.

Stores in those days were replete with a variety of goods for Carnival. One was offering costumes made by a reputable Continental Court Costumier portraying Armenians, Jesters, Arabs, Officers, Clowns, Assyrians, Chinamen, Japanese,, Pierrots and Pierrettes at attractive prices varying from $2.40 to $25.00. There, one could have obtained a 'painted clown suit' for as little as $2.40.

Others were offering Silk-Finish Velvet at 15 cents per yard; Gold Braid; Bright coloured Satins and Lawns; Coloured Cotton Velvets in all shades at 8 cents per yard; Gold and Silver Laces and Stars and Spangles; Tinsel; Fringes and Feathers; Foulards; Coloured Stockings and Gloves; Beads and Mustaches; Heads and Wigs; Wire Masks for Men, Women and Children at 9 cents; Gauze and linen ware Masks; Dominoes; Paper Masks in Clowns, Devils, Animals, Ghosts and Negroes; Confetti, Serpentine and Serpentine Pistols, among other things.

The competitions that year brought out some good bands among them being Red Dragons, Sangschaw, (named after a famous race-horse of the day), Navy Dock, Khaki and Slate, Newtown Cavalry, Esperanza, Fighting Cock, All Trinidad Cricketers, Belmont Wild Indians, Dry River Red Indians, Juveniles, Bonanza, Siberians, Tourists and Barbadians (domestic servants).

At the 'Bonanza Competition' held on Marine Square, the top prize — a 'Loving Cup' — went to the Red Dragons Band, and the judges thought that the 'Fighting Cock Band' was deserving of a special prize. The 'Sangschaw Syndicate' parading with their refrain:

'come down with you Sangschaw maneema',
did not seem to have impressed the judges at either of the competitions, for they received no award nor commendations. According to a press report, 'the decision of the judges did not meet with popular approbation, it being the consensus that 'Navy Dock Syndicate' had outclassed all other competitors'. In those days most bands styled themselves as 'such and such' Syndicate.

At the 'La India Competition' the first prize — A Cup — was won by the 'Belmont Wild Indians' comprising about 20 members. Second prize of ten shillings went to 'Dry River Red Indians'. 'Fighting Cock Syndicate' again came in for some commendation as deserving a prize. The judges said that although they hardly contained ten persons 'they were well costumed and carried a fine banner'.

Parading the streets, also, were some half-a-dozen 'beautifully and originally decorated cars', some cabs and carriages with disguised people, all indulging in the custom of throwing at each other Confetti and Serpentine paper rolls, but not as much as in previous years. A damper on the spirit of this amusement may have been occasioned by the clamping down by the police of the throwing of any other substance with the Confetti, such as powder, flour, rice, peas, etc.

Some enlightened control techniques seemed to have motivated the police, also, in that year's Carnival, for apart from being addressed by the Commissioner of the day on desirable psychological attitudes, for the first time

Robbers in town challenge and attack with a volly of words. Photograph — G. Duruty.

in years the police, a report commented, 'did not appear at street corners in large numbers with their batons'. Rather, they were dispersed less conspicuously, and I am sure that herein lies a lesson of value for those in charge of such matters, when it was noted that it was a comparatively peaceful Carnival, and that the much reduced fighting spirit was expressed by one of the band in this refrain:—

'I don't want to fight,
Cause I 'fraid Mr. Blackwood Wright.'

Mr. Blackwood Wright was known as a magistrate of stern attitude and heavy hand against anti-social behaviour.

In the Jour Ouvert (Monday morning) celebrations of 1910 there was also a 'Band of Prisoners' dressed in the 'shabbiest and most grotesque costumes possible', capering along to the refrain:—

'Hold you cup for you ginger tea,
Hold you cup.
The matron behind you, etc.'

And, among the disguises on the streets were the usual Indians, both blue and red and some purple ones, Yankee minstrels, Bats, Clowns, Devils (those with the long fork and the long snapping rope tail which have almost disappeared from the scene), Sailors, animals, including bears and monkeys, a few Chinese and Japanese and Policemen, and Ghosts.

It is well to remember, also, that these were times when there was Carnival on the streets, with music accompaniment much of it amateur and voluntary, at least two weeks before the Carnival, on every night except Sunday. There were the disguise dances and balls and impromptu parties. And, provided they were alerted in time, hosts were lavish with their hospitality to visiting bands of friends. Some were always prepared for such eventualities.

Carnival was dull during the World War I years of 1914 to 1918, and perhaps it is not inappropriate in dealing with a subject like Old Time Carnival to end with some comments on the Victory Carnival of 1919 which occurred fifty years ago.

" *Wrightson pas vlai bo nous g'leau*
Maloney pas vlai nous entrer
Vincent Brown fair un l'ordinance
Pour tax nous, sans humanity.

Wrightson wouldn't give us water
Maloney don't want us to enter
Vincent Brown make an ordinance
To tax us without humanity. "

(Anon.)

A large crowd in downtown Port of Spain Carnival. Photograph — G. Duruty.

Taking place on March 3rd and 4th in that year, one of the highlights of the occasion was the intense competitive spirit between *The Trinidad Guardian* and its contemporary evening newspaper, *The Argos*. A Carnival competition was being sponsored for the first time in the Queen's Park Savannah by *The Guardian* and the traditional one at Marine Square (now Independence Square) was being organised by *The Argos*.

The other existing newspaper *The Port of Spain Gazette* reported that the 'Up Town idea fell flat', whilst the 'Down Town' competition was a great success. There was much advertising of the respective events and it is said that the organisers regarded the affair as 'direct rivalry between them' as to 'whether King Carnival should hold sway on the Grand Savannah or 'downtown'. The 'down town' adherents were accused of saying that going to the Savannah was a Government trick to get the masqueraders at the Savannah, and further, that they were not animals to go to the Savannah.

The reference to animals in the Savannah could be best appreciated when it is recalled that at that time numerous cattle were being pastured there by private owners. This must have irked the 'Savannah' promoters considerably, for it is reported that on the Carnival Monday their advertising van 'took up a position of prominence within the Marine Square premises and created a fairly strongly worded combat', until the police was called in to 'eject the intruder'.

Savannah prizes for Best Dressed Band were $60.00; $40.00 and $20.00 in cash respectively, whilst 'Down Town' they were $75.00, $50.00 and $30.00 respectively. There were cash prizes also for Most Original Band, Best Carnival Song, Best Patriotic Song, Best Creole Song (in Patois or English), Best Paseo by Band, etc. There were plate prizes for best decorated motor cars, whilst cash prizes of $10.00 and $5.00 were given for Best Decorated Lorries, Vans and Cabs. Smaller prizes went to Donkey Carts, Dray Carts and Bicycles. And lo and behold, 'The Savannah' organisers came up with the novel idea of awarding a prize (plate) for the Best Queen of any Band. That was fifty years ago, and some of us had thought it was quite an original and thoughtful idea when awards were made for Queen of the Bands in the Carnival of 1958.

The Victory Carnival of 1919 was rich and varied and more than made up for the poor and restricted merriment of the War years. There were numerous bands, traditional masqueraders and decorated vehicles of various kinds. At the conclusion of the competitions on the Tuesday evening, competitors were addressed at the respective venues, by two leading barristers of the day, the late Mr. Charles Henry Pierre at Marine Square, and the late Sir Lennox O'Reilly (then Mr. L.A.P. O'Reilly) and the late Major Randolph Rust at the Savannah. This quaint procedure would be impossible today with the tens of thousands of people .

In the evening, Queen's Park West, from Charlotte Street to Cipriani Boulevard, (the southern section of the Grand Savannah) was brilliantly illuminated with strings of electric lights hung over the roadway and a parade of decorated and other motor vehicles proceeded around the Savannah to culminate these outstanding Carnival festival of 1919.

1881

THE CARNIVAL RIOTS

It is strange that no actual description appears in the *'Gazette'* of the carnival riots of 1881; but the following extracts from an editorial on the subject, and another from the report of the proceedings at a meeting of the Legislative Council at which the riot was the subject of a series of questions of a remarkable charcter, are of interest:—

QUESTIONS IN COUNCIL

The following questions were put by the Hon'ble A.P. Marryat, and the appended replies given by the Colonial Secretary:—

1.—Whether it was the avowed intention of the police authorities to put down carnival by force, and whether a number of heavy staves were ordered from the Public Works Department for the special use of the police?

The Colonial Secretary replied:—That the Inspector Commandant states there was no intention on the part of the police to put down the carnival; but the orders were given by him to the police to put out all torches, (as was done in 1880), and to arrest all parties engaged in street fighting, singing obscene songs or otherwise behaving in an indecent manner. The staves used by the police are stated to have been the ordinary 'night duty' staves, and were requisitioned for through the proper channel. Captain Baker observes that he was not even aware that the new staves had been supplied by the Public Works Department until Monday afternoon, when he was parading the men for duty.

2.—Whether the Inspector Commandant had a bet that he would put down the carnival?

This Captain Baker states he is prepared to deny on oath.

3.—Whether the Inspector Commandant during the disturbances drew his sword and wounded severely one or more persons?

This also Captain Baker states he is prepared to deny on oath.

4.—Whether the police commenced the disturbance by extinguishing torches, and by general overbearing behaviour?

The Inspector Commandant states that prior to the attack on the police one torch only had been extinguished by them; that there was no general overbearing behaviour on the pat of the police, but that, on the contrary, they, in his opinion, shewed the greatest forbearance under the most trying circumstances during the whole night.

5.—Whether bands of men came to Port of Spain from outlying districts such as Diego Martin, St. Joseph, Arouca, Arima, Chaguanas, and from San Fernando for the express purpose of creating a disturbance and of beating the police?

The Inspector Commandant says he can only speak as to Diego Martin and Chaguanas from whence bands undoubtedly came; but he is led to believe that bands came from other districts for the express purpose of attacking the police should their torches be interered with.

6.—Whether the lamps of the town were broken on Monday night after the police had been confined to barracks?

The Town Clerk, of whom inquiry has been made, states that he has made strict inquiries as to whether other lamps were broken on Monday night after the police force had been confined to barracks, from the street overseers, and also from Mr. St. Mark, the contractor for the lighting; and all unite in saying that after daylight on the 28th February no other lamps were broken.

7.—Whether houses of the Attorney-General and of Mr. George Garcia were stoned on Monday night while the police were confined to barracks?

8.—Whether the persons creating the disturbance were being urged on by a white man in a helmet, stated by some to be a government official?

Captain Baker states that such is his belief, but that at present is not prepared to prove it.

9.—Whether there are any, and if so what grounds for the belief that the town would have been set on fire by the mob on Monday night supposing the police had not been confined to barracks during that night?

The Governor is not aware of the grounds for such a belief or the extent to which such belief prevailed in the community; but the Mayor and Borough Council informed him on the 28th February that not only a disturbance, but also fire and rapine were to be feared.

10.—Whether the number of singers of filthy and indecent songs had not been greater at this carnival than on any previous occasion?

The Inspector Commandant believes this to be a fact that can be substantiated by many.

11.—Whether it is the intention of the government to issue a commission to inquire into the late disturbances with a view of taking measures for the prevention of similar disturbances in future years?

The Governor is in correspondence with the Secretary of State on the subject.

(2nd April, 1881.)

1881

COMMISSIONER'S REPORT ON THE CARNIVAL RIOTS

The Gazette of the 29th October, 1881, publishes at full length the text of the report sent in by Mr. Commissioner Hamilton on the Carnival Riots of that year,—the report occupying nearly six columns of the paper and 23 paragraphs being devoted to the summary of the evidence. In his findings, the Commissioner stated,—

'Summing up the evidence as to the causes which led to the disturbances, I attribute them to a belief on the part of the mob that the police were going to put a stop to all masquerading. . . . . and to the action of certain unprincipled persons having the command of the local press, who for personal and private ends inflamed the minds of the people against the police. . . . . .and in a lesser degree, but appreciably by the want of tact and judgement of certain subordinates of the police force in their dealings with the people, and by the feeling on the part of the lower population that many of the store-keeping and shop-keeping community sympathised with them, or at least would not take any active part against them in any conflict which might take place between the police and themselves. . . . . . A good deal has been made of the issue of a certain number of balata sticks to the police force as evidence of a determination on their part to fight the maskers; but a reference to the official demand for these sticks will show that it was made simply in the ordinary course of business. . . . . . I do not for a moment think there was anything like a general and widespread feeling of disaffection amongst the population or that the police, with the aid of the troops, if need be, could not easily have quelled any disturbance which might have arisen. Yet bloodshed might have occurred, and houses might have been set on fire, and these were contingencies which it was well worth having recourse to conciliatory measures to avoid. . . . . . The immediate effect of the measures taken by the Governor were, as regards the police, that 58 sent in their resignations in writing,though these were withdrawn at the request of Captain Baker who brought the circumstances to the notice of His Excellency and obtained from him the following expression of opinion respecting the force:—'It having been represented to the Government that the police force imagine that the order issued for their remaining in barracks on the evening of the 28th February last arose from some presumed misconduct on their part, His Excellency hastens to assure Captain Baker and the officers and men of the force who were employed in a hazardous and dangerous service, that he is not aware of any of the force having misconducted themselves; and his reasons for keeping them in barracks were neither for tht cause nor for any doubt as to their loyalty or courage. No one can regret more than His Excellency the numerous injuries sustained by the force in the performance of their duties. The Inspector Commandant is at liberty to publish the above in general orders'. . . . . . The immediate effect was that when the police were sent out on duty after the Carnival they were jeered at, and for some time had to be posted in couples instead of singly. Moreover, Captain Baker's family were insulted in the street. But Captain Baker is sanguine that with patience and firmness on the part of the police this will eventually be removed. . . . . . It was stated to me by several witnesses that there has been a remarkable difference in the attitude of the black and coloured people towards the whites, in that they are not nearly so civil as formerly; but unless this state of things should unfortunately be fostered by unwise and pernicious agitation, it may be hoped that the previous satisfactory relations between the various races will be restored. . . . . . In my view the Carnival should be allowed to be held, but its proceedings should be carefully regulated, and this is the view of the bulk of intelligent opinion in the island. . . . . . It is urged by many that the hours during which the Carnival is permitted should, as in the French islands, be restricted to daylight, say from 6 a.m. to 6 p.m. on the Monday before Ash Wednesday. This would get rid of all the difficulty as to the carrying of torches. . . . . . and would save the town from the rioting and confusion which takes place during the night. . . . . . It is urged in support of this that in 1849, the Carnival had previously extended over several days, was in that year restricted to two without any opposition on the part of the people; and that therefore it might now be further restricted to twelve hours without any real difficulty arising. And I have little doubt that this course might have been carried out this year if due and timely notice had been given and the people had been approved by the supreme authority and would be rigidly enforced and carried out if need arose. But in my opinion circumstances have greatly altered since then, and to adopt such a course now would be to run the risk of raising a spirit of disaffection in the colony amongst the working classes, a spirit from which, hitherto, this island, unlike some others, has been entirely free. . . . . . As regards Captain Baker, he is personally popular, as well as thoroughly efficient, and will no doubt, if properly supported, be able to do good work. . . . . . I had no time, nor was it any part of my business, to inquire into the Coolie Festival or "Hosea" as it is called. But I think it most desirable that their festival also should be most carefully regulated so as to prevent them from developing another species of Carnival which might eventually cause a good deal of trouble."

1882

NEWSPAPERS OF TRINIDAD

The following list of the newspapers then in existence in Trinidad with their characteristics and avowed circulation, is reproduced in the issue of the *Gazette* for the 1st July, 1882 from *"Hubbard's Newspaper and Bank Directory:—*

The Advertiser, issued gratis, 250, weekly.
Fair Play, general news, 150 weekly.
New Era, general news, 250, weekly.
Palladium, Roman Catholic news, but edited by a
    Protestant Clergyman, 60 weekly.
Port-of-Spain Gazette, general news, 400, weekly.
Royal Gazette, Government advertising sheet, weekly
Chronicle, general news, bi-weekly, 260.
Guppy's Almanac, yearly.
San Fernando Gazette, general news, 110, weekly.

(1 July, 1882.)

Captain Cipriani and party make their way up Frederick Street after declaring the start of Carnival 1919. Photograph — G. Duruty.

A Shango ceremony illustrated by a 19th century artist depicting the ritual as carried out in the French islands.

SHANGO WORSHIP IN TRINIDAD

Naomi Laird

The Yoruba religious cult Shango, is one of the few African cultural institutions which survived the Middle Passage to Trinidad. According to William Bascom, in his book 'Shango in the New World'; the reason the Yoruba cult reached the new world at all was due to the wars of the Dahomy and Yoruba, when captives were sold as slaves, ultimately arriving in the Caribbean. In addition to this some of the Yoruba came to Trinidad as immigrants as well. It is this latter fact that is largely responsible for the survival of the Shango cult.

Bearing in mind the fact that Shango was brought to the new world in stages by both slaves and immigrants, it was inevitable that the interpretation of the religion would have varied a great deal over time. This has resulted in a slightly altered version of Shango being handed down to present day. The reason the cult lost some of its ritual in the Middle Passage was due to the misinterpretation and misunderstanding of the cult's mythology. The elaborate mythology which underlies and explains the religious worship of the Yoruba was not allowed to be maintained by the slave population. Therefore, only the few priests who knew the myth, and who survived the Middle Passage possessed this knowledge. Further, on arrival in the new world, the myth was adapted to the slavery conditions under which the worshippers found themselves. With the migration of the Yoruba later in the century however, a great many came to Trinidad to establish themselves in a new land. This arrival injected new life into the fast fading cult and contributed greatly to the fact that Shango worship has persisted till today. The religion however has maintained a strong community of worshippers throughout its evolution in Trinidad. Furthermore, not only did Shango experience changes in structure due to internal elements, but external pressures from the middle-class laws also tested the strength of the Shango unity as well.

Shango is one of the Yoruba gods of thunder. The word Shango is English, in the Yoruba language the correct spelling is Sango. The God Shango has many wives, three of whom are Oya, Oshun and Oba, all named after rivers. These three wives hold a superior position over all the other wives of Shango. Shango, according to the myth, was known to fight with trouble-makers and people who used bad medicine to harm others, as well as worshippers who neglected their sacrifices.

During the Shango ceremony, the possessed worshipper is called a 'mount' or 'horse'. This member is entitled to don particular garments, such as: a red coat, cowry shells, charms, appliqued cotton panels on his waist, knee length cotton trousers reddened with camwood and trimmed with cowries, and sometimes a large red cape. The 'horse' performs magical tricks just like the god he is a 'mount' for. These tricks consist of carrying hot coals and passing an iron rod through his tongue. The shrine of Shango, where all the ceremonial rituals of the feast take place contains certain symbols, such as: the plate of thunderstones, hollow gourds, carved dance wands and leather shoulder bags which are appliqued. The worshippers wear strings of imported beads which alternate in colours of red and white as their insignia.

The necessity of Shango as a religion for either the slave or the immigrant in the new world was important as it offered a form of identification and security from a cultural as well as a religious perspective.

This identity and security was found in the commonality of the worship. Since Shango in Africa originally provided reassurance about life after death, certain illnesses, major crisis and certain mystic experiences, the worshipper in the new world strove to maintain similar circumstances to which he or she was accustomed back home, in order to cope with the new lifestyle. For the believers in Shango who were deprived either politically or economically, the practice of the religion substituted for the denial of their accustomed way of life.

Shango Worshippers shared a common need for the ritual and therefore maintained an identity which became a means of perpetuating the group. Having begun in Trinidad as a small group who were originally from Africa, Shango worship passed down to other generations. With the passage of time, some rituals were maintained, and some forgotten. Through an inter-marriage of nations, and the eventual modification of the structure, a form of religious syncretization came about. The Rada community is an example of this. It is a religious cult of the Dahomy, which syncretized in the new world with the Shango cult.

An example of the establishment of a Shango/Rada compound for sacred worship came about shortly after Emancipation. The founder of the compound, Robert Antoine acquired land and proceeded to build a house, chapel and tent. There, shrines were erected, and the compound flourished. The community of worshippers grew, keeping the original compound as sacred land. One of the biggest feasts to occur on the compound is the annual feast. This event occurs after an immense amount of time is spent on the preparation. The leader and his helpers collect candles, bottles of olive oil, animals to be sacrificed and food which will be served to participants. The ceremony is four days long, and all the preparation of food and drink is done beforehand. Along with the preparation the leader may ask for a mass to be said in the Catholic Church on the morning of the beginning of the ceremony, (usually a Tuesday evening). The rhythm of drums being tuned sets the worshippers dancing and singing about half an hour before the official opening of the feast.

While the drums are tuning and the worshippers dancing, an assistant to the leader walks around the shrine (Palais) swinging incense, making sure all four corners are covered. A lighted candle is placed in each corner after the incense has been waved over the area.

A prayer meeting begins the ritual, with members of the cult saying original or authentic prayers, followed by several repetitions of the Lord's Prayer. The leader goes through the prayers of particular saints with the group of worshippers following. The purpose of the repetitious prayers is to dismiss the evil spirit of Eshu, who is compared with the devil. The ritual for dismissal takes the form of a food offering in a calabash (gourd) for Eshu. The food is placed on the ground and a song sung for Eshu. After the song, the calabash is carried outside the shrine and emptied. Having dismissed Eshu, the summoner of Ogun (St. Michael) proceeds with the playing of a rhythm particular to this God, and the singing of songs in his honour.

The types and numbers of drums depend on the feast or ceremony. In this particular ceremony, there are three consecrated drums which have sponsors and special names.

The group of worshippers consists mostly of women who stand around singing and moving in time with the rhythm. In the words of Frances Mischel:

> Generally a woman dancing in the circle begins violently swaying back and forth. Her eyes become glazed and dilated, her face undergoes a radical transformation, becoming quite masculine with lips and chin protruding. She falls back, is supported by bystanders thereby breaking the circle of dancers. Singing and drumming stop for the moment. One bystander ties a red (Ogun's colour) headband about the possessed woman's head, another ties a sash underneath her stomach, and her jewelry and shoes are removed.

Having been possessed, the woman will then require the weapons of the God she holds power for. In the case of Ogun, the weapon will be a cutlass. Olive oil is rubbed into the heads of the audience, who may also be required to drink the olive oil. Once Ogun has arrived several other powers begin to 'manifest' themselves on other individuals in the audience. When general fatigue comes upon the group, at around five in the morning, they may find somewhere to sleep. Other members, who have regular jobs will leave the compound and return later that day. Meanwhile, the animals that were sacrificed during spirit possession to the God, are cooked with the other food. Some of the meat is salted, some is not. The meat without the salt is placed on large leaves in front of the tombs of the Gods, the rest of the meat is eaten later.

Among the sub-divisions of Shango are the folklore characters and healing rituals which provide a base for the middle-class to associate Shango with evil and criminal actions. The characters from the Trinidad folklore scenario are the 'Soucouyant' or female vampires. The 'Lagahou' is a the male equivalent to the 'Soucouyant'. These characters live a normal life as human-beings during the day. However, they are said to possess certain marks of identification easily recognisable to a Shango worshipper. The main character of the folklore scenario which the Shango worshippers have a great respect and fear of, is the 'Jumbie' which is the spirit of the dead. Whereas, the 'Soucouyant' and 'Lagahou' fall into the practice of interpretation, in that, often a worshipper may have an unexplainable mark, or pain. These mysteries are explained by the belief in the 'Soucouyant' and 'Lagahou'. The 'jumbie' is an evil spirit which haunts certain people, whether they are worshippers or not. The Shangoists communicate with the 'Jumbie' in order to rid the person who is haunted of the evil spirit. On the other hand, the Shangoist may use the evil spirit to perform deeds. As a result of these beliefs, prayers are said and offerings are made to the dead during the annual Shango ceremony.

Although the structure and ritual of the traditional Shango may have changed, the cohesiveness that is still present in Shango is due to the fact that Shango provides a meaningful world view for its devotees. The meaningful view includes explanations of the spirits, the rites of life, life after death, and other basic questions. On their return to the faith, or being born into it, the youth of today may realise the necessity of maintaining the rituals. John D. Elder observed in his study of the village of Gasparillo, that the strength of Shango among the villagers is what held the community together. He saw Shango as a force which aided the slaves through periods of social and political deprivation. He felt that belief in the cult assisted the people in dealing with the distress and trauma common to people in a stage of transition between cultures and allowed them to come together as a community to exert a collective force and make a place for themselves in their new homeland, while at the same time making a valuable contribution to the cultural and spiritual life of the island of Trinidad.

Trinidad has the distinction of being the world's forerunner in oil exploration. This is so because in 1857 the Merrimac Oil Company of the U.S.A. drilled the first successful well in the world at La Brea. Oil being struck at 280ft. As there was no real need for large amounts, oil production was abandoned a year later.

It was some ten years later that because of the endeavour of a young man, Walter Darwent, who was born in Plymouth England and who had served as a captain in the Union army during the American Civil War, that oil was drilled for again in Trinidad. He formed a company called the Paria Petroleum Company Limited. His endeavours did not flourish however as he died just a year or two later at the early age of forty-seven.

Once again the pumps stood still and the forest closed in to reclaim the land and oil would not be sought after in Trinidad for another forty years. This time the world had changed. The industrial revolution was creating demands for other types of fuel. Coal could not carry the technology of the day any further and the opportunity presented itself for two young entrepreneurs Mr. Randolf Rust and Mr. John Lee Lum.

John Lee Lum had left his ancestral home at Kwangtung China to seek his fortune in the California gold fields. Years later he arrived in Trinidad possibly about 1885. He made money in the provision trade and owned cocoa estates. As a result he was in a sound position when a young Englishman already well established in business by the name of Rust approached him with the view to develop Trinidad's oil resources. This they proceeded to do with remarkable results.

Walter Darwent

John Lee Lum

THE PIONEERS OF TRINIDAD'S OIL INDUSTRY

Randolf Rust

A mule tram in Port of Spain in the 1880's. Photograph — G. Duruty.

1883

TRAMWAY CONSTRUCTION

On the 29th ultimo, the work of laying down the tramway was begun opposite the railway station. The telephone to enable one to transact business without moving from one's chair; the tramway, to enable those who must move about to do so quickly, and with comfort and cheapness,—these two great boons will remove the only drawback to our town,—its great area compared to its population. *(2nd June, 1883).*

THE TRAMWAY

On Thursday last the tramway made its trial trip and, we understand, gave complete satisfaction to the Directors. *(15th December, 1883).*

ICE FACTORY STARTED

We are glad to state that owing to the persevering energy of Dr. Ford. . . . an ice-making factory on a large scale is now in operation in Port of Spain. We visited the place and were informed that the machine is equal to giving 5 tons of ice per day. *(4th August, 1883).*

1884

THE PALMS SCHOOL

We have much pleasure in announcing that the Misses Margaret and E.M. Buncle are about to open a seminary for young ladies at *'The Palms',* Tranquillity. The Misses Buncle are certificated by the University of Oxford and it is intended that the curriculum shall be that of a high school course for girls, so as to be the centre for the University of Edinburgh examinations. . . . The assistant teachers will be Miss Reid, Misses Archibald and Miss McFarlane. The subjects will include English, arithmetic, natural science, literature, needle-work, mathematics, drawing, water colour and oil painting, piano and singing, Scripture, French, German and Latin. *(23rd August, 1884).*

CONFEDERATION WITH CANADA

The proposal to admit the West Indian Colonies into the Dominion of Canada is now being seriously discussed at the request of and with the entire approval.of, Lord Derby, Her Majesty's Secretary of State. Though it seems to be the general opinion that complete federation is for many reasons impossible, yet it is to be hoped that some mutual arrangement will be secured by which West Indian sugars will be admitted into Canada free of duty. *(25th October, 1884).*

1885

PLAGUE OF LOCUSTS

From different parts of the island reports are being received of the presence of locusts, but the most serious news is from Icacos, where they are said to be in thousands. The Warden, Mr. Newsam has reported the matter to the government and is doing his utmost to have the insects exterminated. *(1st August, 1885).*

1885

THE ST. JOSEPH RAILWAY COLLISION

The following account of the memorable railway collision near St. Joseph Junction, in which three persons were killed on the spot and many more injured, is summarised from the report in the *'Gazette'* of the 31st January, 1885:—

The midday passenger train for San Fernando left town at 11.10 and was followed by a special goods train sent up with empty trucks to bring down sugar. According to the system in vogue, the driver of the goods train carried the staff, which was to have been handed to the station master at St. Joseph to indicate that the line to Port of Spain was clear. The train for San Fernando passed the train from Arima at St. Joseph and the Arima train should have been detained in that station until the goods train from town had arrived, when the station master should have taken the staff from the driver of the goods train and given it to the driver of the Arima train. An alternative system appears however to have been in practice of giving a written 'pass' occasionally in lieu of the staff; and in this instance the station master appears to have given a pass to the driver of the Arima train, who started to Port of Spain without being aware that a goods train was approaching. When about half a mile from St. Joseph station, proceeding to town at the usual rate of 20 miles an hour, rounding the curve opposite La Viviere estate, where some high bush hides approaching objects, and where there is a slight downward gradient, the driver (Roberts) of the Arima train sighted the goods train approaching at the ordinary rate of speed at the other end of the curve. He immediately reversed his engine, and so imminent was the collision that he instinctively shouted to his assistant to jump. This the assistant could not do or had not the time to do Freddie, the driver of the goods train appears to have taken the similar step of trying to stop his engine; but it was too late. The impact of the two trains was such that a terrible collision resulted. Roberts, the driver of the Arima train was pitched a considerable distance, but was only slightly hurt; and on returning to his engine he found his assistant injured in the chest. Freddie, the driver of the goods train was also injured in the chest; but his assistant escaped unhurt. . . . . . . Mrs. Louis Gomez, and a man named Lord, employed in the government telegraph department, were killed on the spot; while Mr. Armstrong, builder and contractor, sustained fractures of both legs and one arm and died next day in the Colonial Hospital. Amongst the wounded are Mrs. Francis Gransaull (fracture of the thigh), and the two Misses Fraser, daughters of the magistrate of St. Joseph,,one of whom Miss Minnie Fraser, sustained fractures of both thighs, while her sister suffered a severe contusion of the chest . . . . No less than eight others were seriously injured.

STATION MASTER CHARGED

The station master of St. Joseph was subsequently arrested and charged with the manslaughter of Mr. Armstrong. The case aroused great public feeling, it being regarded that he was the victim of a terrible consequence of a bad system allowed by the government. He was tried the following April sessions, and was defended by Mr. George Garcia; and was unanimously acquitted by the jury, the verdict being received with loud applause in court.

INFANCY OF THE LONG DISTANCE TELEPHONE

By the simple connection of the telegraph wire to a telephone instrument in the Newsroom it was found possible on Sunday last to get telephonic communication with San Fernando, a distance of 45 miles by wire; and conversation could be carried on with as much ease and and precision as between any two places in the city. . . . The day may perhaps not be far off when telephone subscribers may be able to talk with the other towns and to the police service such an acquisition would be an immense boon. *(25th April, 1885).*

LIGHTING THE TOWN WITH GAS

A committee of the Borough Council appointed to consider the tender for the lighting of Port of Spain with gas held a meeting on Wednesday. . . and resolved to accept the tender of Mr. Christopher Danbys of Gravesend, England, who wants a concession for 50 years; but the Committee recommended that Mr. Danbys be offered a concession for 30 years, the Council reserving to itself the right to purchase the works from the contractors at the end of 15 years should they be in a position to do so. *(19th September, 1885).*

Above: Champaigne, an attendant at the Belmont Orphanage.
Photograph — The Dominican Sisters of St. Catherine of Sienna.
Right: The old gas lantern that once stood in front of the Catholic
Cathedral. Photograph — Jackson's Book of Trinidad.

1885

BELMONT ORPHANAGE

The consecration of the new buildings of the Belmont Orphanage, which are to be the future home of the younger children and infants at the institution, took place on Sunday last. *(26th September, 1885).*

1886

ANNEXATION OF TOBAGO

On the 8th December, 1886, there appeared in the *'Gazette'* the text of a proclamation published officially in the Royal Gazettes of both Trinidad and Tobago, stating that the question of the annexation of the colony of Tobago to Trinidad was under consideration, and might take one of the two following forms:—

(a) The colony of Tobago to be wholly and completely incorporated with the colony of Trinidad; or

(b) The colony of Tobago to be annexed to the colony of Trinidad as a dependency, with a separate treasury and subordinate legislature, holding to Trinidad the same relation that the colony of Turk's Island does to Jamaica.

The former appeared to Her Majesty's Government to be preferable; but her Majesty's Government was desirous of ascertaining the opinions and wishes of both colonies; and after a sufficient time had been allowed to elapse for full consideration and discussion of the matter, resolutions would be introduced into the respective legislatures for incorporation or annexation as the case might be.

1887

ORIGIN OF THE VICTORIA INSTITUTE

An appeal issued by His Excellency Sir William Robinson shortly after the jubilee, and published in the *'Gazette'* of the 2nd July, 1887 shows how the idea of the erection of the Royal Victoria Institute was originated. After setting forth the idea that there should be some permanent memorial of the jubilee, His Excellency wrote:-

'The amusements and festivities of the celebration were secured at the really trifling cost of $2,000. . . . . . I shall require about $25,000 for my idea; but what is that amongst our population of 180,000 persons? Let us say that 100,000 out of that number cannot afford to give anything at all;—what is $25,000 amongst the remaining 80,000? I venture to believe that there are more than 2,000 persons in this island who are well able to give $10 each to such a cause, and another 2,000 at least who are able to give $5 each, without missing it. And no credit is due to those who give to such a cause that which they do not miss. For the furtherance of such a cause as I am advocating, everyone should be prepared to make a sacrifice. . . . . .Two methods of securing a permanent memorial of the jubilee occur to me: the one, the erection of a maternity ward and a chapel for the Colonial Hospital; the other the erection of an institute to be called the 'Victoria Institute'. I am of opinion that the first suggestion is one the charge for carrying out which should fall upon general revenue; and the cost of the second should certainly be met by public subscription. . . . . . . I cordially trust my appeal will be liberally and worthily responded to, and that ere long I may be called upon by the united voice of the people to lay the foundation stone of an institution which, if established and properly managed, cannot fail to be of great permanent benefit to present and future generations in Her Majesty's colony of Trinidad.'

(Sgd.) W.M. ROBINSON

Government House,
Trinidad,
25th June, 1887.

THE VICTORIA INSTITUTE

Messrs. Barber and Greig, who are at present on a visit to the island in connection with the lease of the Pitch Lake, have presented a cheque for $500 as a contribution towards the building of the Victoria Institute. The cheque was received by the Attorney-General, and forwarded to the Secretary, Mr. E. Cipriani. His Excellency the Governor has contributed £50 towards the fund. *(7th September, 1887).*

Group taken at the residence of Sir John Gorrie, (Chief Justice) at Diego Martin on the occasion of a Garden Party in honour of the third visit of Prince now our Gracious Majesty King Goerge V during February 1891.
From left to right: Mr. Bro. Collins (Secty. to Sir John Gorrie) Mr. Justice Lumb, His Excellency, Sir William Robinson; Flag Lieutenant Trowbridge; H.R.H. Prince George; Charles Philip; Sir John Gorrie; Vice-Admiral Watson of H.M.S. 'Bellerophon'.

1888

THE STRUGGLE WITH THE CHIEF JUSTICE

The long struggle with the judges of the Supreme Court, Sir John Gorrie, and Justices Lumb and Cook, which ended in the Royal Commission which purged the bench of all three, commenced early in 1888. One of the earliest stages of it was entered upon when the *'Gazette'* remonstrated editorially upon the action of the Chief Justice in practically trying actions in private in Chambers instead of in open Court. This was soon followed up by the first famous article, *'Results of Uncertain Justice'* which appeared on the 17th March, 1888. This article stated in part,—

'We had hoped to have done with His Honour the Chief Justice, in Chambers interfering with and setting aside the ordinary and safe course of law by advising and helping possible litigants and deciding cases their objectionable practice is still being pursued. Of this fact, the most painful evidence has been given by the publication yesterday in the columns of our contemporary the 'New Era' of a letter from the pen of Mr. Scipio-Pollard, barrister-at-law, enclosing a report of a scene in the Chambers of the Chief Justice, where Mr. Pollard has been summoned to attend to have a case against him heard and decided out of the due and proper course of. . . . . . In our own, columns, under the heading of 'The Courts', another instance is afforded of the irregular and capricious administration of justice, in the case of Marie G. Brown v Mr. Howatson, trustee in bankruptcy of A. Ambard and Sons. It came out that the plaintiff, being disappointed in getting some money, complained that 'capitalists did not care to lend money to persons like her, because they said, the Judges were much too lenient with persons like her, and so they did not like to risk lending money to her', as a result of which she was unable to profit by a decree of the Court in her favour.'

CHARGED WITH CONTEMPT

At the sitting of the Full Court immediately following, 'by direction of the Chief Justice, the Registrar, Mr. C.H. Philips, called the matter of 'Applewhaite v. Pollard', and proceeded to read the affidavit of two persons, one of them, the plaintiff in the matter, setting forth that the letter signed by Mr. E.S. Pollard in the 'New Era' was a 'false and malicious report of what occurred in the Chambers of the Chief Justice.'

The Chief Justice:—Upon the reading of these affidavits and exhibits let a rule of this Court issue calling upon T.R.N. Laughlin, Joseph Lewis and E. Scipio-Pollard to show cause why they should not be dealt with and punished for the contempt set forth in these affidavits. . . . . . There is one little matter, Mr. Registrar: I see that they style Mr. Pollard a barrister of this Court; you will see that they call him here not as a barrister of this Court, but as a litigant.

The rule was made returnable peremptorily on the following Friday morning at 11 o'clock. *(21st March, 1888).*

FINED FOR CONTEMPT

The Chief Justice, Sir John Gorrie, with Justices Lumb and Cook, took their seats on the Bench punctually at 11 o'clock on Friday the 23rd March, 1888. The Court was densely crowded long before the hour appointed for the hearing. Mr. L.M. Power appeared with Mr. Frederick Warner for the persons against whom the rule had been issued. The Registrar read the affidavits of Benjamin Applewhite, a cab-owner and Mr. F.A. Collins, Clerk in the Registry, both asserting that over Mr. Pollard's signature in the 'New Era' and in the form of an article in the 'Gazette' there appeared 'libellous and scandalous words reflecting on the administration of justice, tending to the great obstruction of the course of justice, and in contempt of this honourable Court.'

Mr. Power as counsel for the accused took the preliminary objection that His Honour the Chief Justice, being really the accuser and the person attacked in the letter and the article, should not sit to try the matter.

After lengthy argument between counsel and the judges,—

The Chief Justice:—I need not say that I had carefully considered this point before I came here today. . . . . . You tell me that my predecessor, on a similar occasion to this, retired from the Bench. I do not know the circumstances under which he did so: but I have taken many a course in this colony which has differed from the courses taken by my predecessor, and I intend to take a different course today. I intend to preside here and to take the responsibility for this trial. *(Sensation).*

Lengthy arguments, both Mr. Justice Lumb and the Chief Justice proceeded to comment on the case at length. The former called upon the Registrar to produce the records of the previous trial of Mr. Laughlin some years before for libel and contempt in publishing an article in which he accused Sergt. J. Brierly of perjury, but afterwards apologised, and was fined £5.

Each of the defendants Laughlin and Lewis was then fined by the Chief Justice, Laughlin £150 and Lewis £50.

The case of Mr. Pollard was then called on.

Mr. Pollard appeared without his robes, and was proceeding to take an objection upon a legal authority when the word 'stupid' was heard to escape the lips of the Chief Justice.

Mr. Pollard insisted on this expression being withdrawn, and refused to proceed until it was: he stated that he knew he was at His Honour's mercy in that Court, but that His Honour could do whatever he liked.

The Chief Justice thereupon closed the matter by ordering Mr. Pollard to enter into his own bond to come up for judgement if called upon. The greatest excitement prevailed as the Court rose. The two fines were at once paid. *(24th March, 1888).*

1888

RESIGNATION OF BISHOP RAWLE

On Friday last, to the great regret of all classes of the community it became known that His Lordship Bishop Rawle had placed his resignation in the hands of the Primate of the West Indies, and that he had only returned to settle up some private affairs and arrange certain matters connected with the diocese. Bishop Rawle desires to place the diocese in younger hands; and there can be no doubt that his recent sad bereavement, in the death of his wife in England, the faithful partner of his joys and sorrows for many years, and the infirmities of advancing age, have induced His Lordship to take a step which we feel sure he has taken with the deepest regret, and only under the strongest convictions of duty. To the Anglican Church in this community his loss will be almost irreparable. He arrived here in 1872 to undertake the arduous duties of first Bishop of the new diocese at a promised salary of one thousand a year: but finding that, with the many pressing needs of the diocese, the payment of such a stipend would be too great a strain upon the funds of the Church, which were then in accordance with a resolution of the Legislature of the 1st August, 1871, being reduced whenever a vacancy occurred through death,—Bishop Rawle declined to receive more than £600 per annum: and even that sum, having some private means of his own, he has devoted entirely to supplying the needs of his diocese. Afterwards, when the rectory of Holy Trinity became vacant, His Lordship undertook the duties of rector, declining, however, to receive any portion of the emoluments attaching to that post. New and enlarged churches, parsonages and school houses attest everywhere throughout the island to his active interest and zeal in the welfare of his flock: while the lighting of Trinity Cathedral, and the gift of its peal of bells, are both due to his exertions and liberality. Of his real and large-hearted charity it is not for us to speak. No real tale of distress ever fell on his ears unheeded. His Lordship leaves for England on the 4th of June next. *(9th May, 1888).*

ATTEMPT TO POISON THE BISHOP

A most diabolical attempt at poisoning the Bishop was made on last Saturday morning, the 26th instant, at the rectory, the residence of the Right Revd. Bishop Rawle. On the morning of that day, soon after partaking respectively of beef tea and coffee, the Bishop, as well as the Revd. Mr. Moor, Mrs. Smith, and the cook and her two children, were all of them taken ill with violent vomiting. Dr. Pasley was sent for, and was able to afford relief and rescue his patients after they had undergone considerable suffering. The Bishop, from his age and feeble health, was so utterly prostrated by the violence of the attack, that he was for a time in a critical state. . . . . . The poison used has been verified by Mr. McCarthy, Government Analyst, as having been arsenic, which had, it would seem, been put into the kettle wherein the water was boiled from which beef tea was made for the Bishop and tea and coffee was drawn for the others in the house. Suspicion fell upon Miriam Moore, a servant who had been dismissed that very morning for misconduct, and she was arrested on the evening of the 30th. *(2nd June, 1888).*

DEPARTURE OF BISHOP RAWLE

The departure for England on Saturday last of His Lordship Bishop Rawle finally severed his connection with this diocese. . . . . . It is an open secret that during his stay in the colony he has spent over £5,000 out of his own private pocket on the repair and rebuilding of churches and on other church work. . . . In accordance with his own strongly-expressed desire, no address or testimonial of any kind was presented to him prior to his departure. . . . After attending the Synod of Bishops to be held in England shortly, he will return to Barbados where he hopes to spend his remaining years, having accepted, without salary, the position of theological Lecturer at Codrington College, where we trust he may be spared to many years of quiet usefulness. *(13th June, 1888).*

1889

DEPARTURE OF TROOPS

For the first time in the history of Trinidad since the date of the British occupation, the departure of the first packet of June has left the colony entirely denuded of British troops. . . . and the spacious barracks at St. James, erected at a cost of £80,000, will be left to the charge of a few caretakers.

BARRISTER vs MAGISTRATE

On Friday the 6th September, 1889, at the Port of Spain Police Court, before Mr. H.J. Harragin, S.J.P., of Couva, but then acting as S.J.P. of Port of Spain, a man was being prosecuted by Mr. E. Scipio-Pollard, Barrister, on a charge of malicious damage to property. After the magistrate had questioned a certain witness, he suddenly intimated his intention to dismiss the case. Mr. Pollard asked to be allowed to cross-examine the witness. The magistrate replied that he did not wish to hear anything more. Counsel insisting on his rights, the magistrate slammed his book and rose to leave the Court; and upon counsel protesting, the magistrate stated that he adjourned the Court, and then, as he descended the steps from the Bench to enter his private office, called back to counsel,—"You had better hold back your tongue, man," adding some further remarks to the effect that Mr. Pollard "called himself a lawyer." Counsel replied "Do you dare to address counsel in that way, Sir?"; whereupon the magistrate returned into Court and ordered the sergeant who chanced to be still there, to hold counsel and forcibly eject him from the Court. An action for assault was then filed by Mr. Pollard against the magistrate: The magistrate entered the statutory plea of not guilty; and Justice Lumb then made an order shortening the date of hearing of the issue. Plaintiff, finding himself unable to comply in time, filed a notice of discontinuance. This Justice Lumb ignored; and instead of striking it out as provided by the rules, he called the defendant, took his evidence, and gave judgement for the defendant with costs. Against this order Mr. Pollard appealed. This was in November, 1889.

In the *'Gazette'* of the 17th December, 1889, we find the report of the appeal before the Chief Justice, Sir John Gorrie, and Justices Cook and Lumb. Mr. H.A. Alcazar appeared for the appellant barrister; Mr. Vincent-Brown for the defendant magistrate. 'The Chief Justice said the objections taken by Mr. Alcazar were perfectly frivolous; and he thoroughly agreed with the manner in which his brother Lumb had dealt with the case.' Justice Cook concurred.

Against this decision of the Court of Appeal, Mr. Pollard petitioned the Queen in Council, going to England personally to conduct his case before the Privy Council.

In the judgement of the Privy Council, reproduced from the *'Times'* in full in the issue of the *'Gazette'* of the 21st July, 1891, their Lordships declare that the order made by Mr. Justice Lumb and confirmed by the Trinidad Appeal Court 'went very far, if not entirely to prevent the real merits of the case from being tried'; that 'it did not appear that the learned judge had before him any grounds upon which to make such an order'; that 'no reason appeared for the very extraordinary and quite irregular course taken by the Court'; and that, so far from the judge being justified in dismissing the case, 'Their Lordships would venture to advise Her Majesty that the evidence taken by the Court *(that of the defendant magistrate himself),* appeared to them to be such as it would be proper to submit to a jury, and that the plaintiff had been seriously prejudiced by not having a trial by a judge and jury.' The order was accordingly made, setting aside the judgement of the Trinidad Appeal Court, and ordering the magistrate to pay the costs.

By a resolution of the Legislative Council taken on the 2nd November, 1891, a vote was taken to pay Mr. Pollard's costs out of the Treasury and also to recoup Mr. Harragin the sum of ¢411 7. 3. spent by him on his own defence.

In 1892, the judicial commission having in the meantime made a clean sweep of the old Bench of Trinidad judges, Mr. Pollard's action came on, in compliance with the directions of the Privy Council, for a fresh trial before a judge and jury. It was tried by His Honour Mr. S.H. Gatty, the new acting Chief Justice, and a special jury. Mr. Pollard conducted his case in person; Mr. Vincent-Brown again appeared for the magistrate. The jury, after a long hearing and a careful summing up by the judge, returned a verdict for Mr. Pollard for £150 damages, and full costs of the trial.

Subsequently the costs were taxed, and a resolution of the Legislative Council was taken to the tune of £277 8. 10 to meet the bill.

“From a scandal and hideous bacchanal   }
Today we got a glorious carnival   }   *(repeat)*
We used to sing long ago
Moen tini youn seine pour seiner yo
But today you can hear our kaiso
On the American Radio.

Long ago you used to see
Half-naked woman call *pissen-li*
With chac-chac and vera held in the hand
Twisting their body like electric fan
You were not even safe in your own home
With *negre jardin* and bottle and stone
But today you can hear our kaiso
On the American Radio.

A prophet hath no honour in his own land
The truth of the proverb I now understand
When you sing kaiso in Trinidad
You are a vagabond and everything that's bad
In your native land you are a hooligan
In New York you are an artiste and a gentleman
For instance take the Lion and me
Having dinner with Rudy Vallee. ”

(Attila the Hun)

BLACK SOCIETY & CULTURE 1900
Bridget Brereton

At the turn of the 19th century, Trinidad possessed a growing coloured and black middle class which would play an increasingly important role in the island's social and political life. Most of these people were distinguished from the masses not so much by wealth (for often they were quite poor) but rather by literacy in English, command of British culture and occupations which involved no manual labour. In other words they constituted for the most part a salariat of 'white-collar' workers: professional men, teachers, civil servants, clerks or assistants in firms and stores, druggists, journalists and printers. Very few coloured or black people in this period owned estates or large businesses, although several did own small enterprises like pharmacies, newspaper presses, or shops of one kind or another. For most members of this middle class, education was the key to upward mobility.

1889

The Order in Council uniting the colonies of Trinidad and Tobago came into effect on 1st January.

The Government was authorised to enter into a contract with Messrs. Turnbull, Stewart and Co., for steam communication between Trinidad and New York, also around Trinidad and calling at Tobago, after a long discussion in the Legislative Council on 1st March.

Above: Interior of St. Crispin Church, Woodbrook in the 1900's.
Below: A photograph of the Mother's Union in the 1930's. Organisations such as this underscored the social mobility of the black and coloured middle classes. Photographs — Paria.

These men and women were proud of their command of British culture and were generally admirers of things European. Today they might be dismissed as Afro-Saxons. Yet they saw their success in mastering British culture as important for their race: every literate and cultivated black man was a living vindication of the African race against its detractors. And many of them had developed a conscious ideology of black nationlism, black pride, at a time when such an ideology was far more difficult to maintain than it is now. These people were certainly not ashamed of their race even if they believed western civilization was the only one which counted and the one to which they, as British blacks, should naturally aspire. A man like J.J. Thomas, who died in 1889, admired British culture yet also recognised the merits of his own Creole tradition. He wrote a scholarly book on the despised patois of his countrymen and he urged Trinidadians to remember their slave ancestors by celebrating August 1st as the anniversary of freedom.

The great majority of Trinidad blacks at this time belonged to the labouring masses. Leaving aside the immigrants from Asia, there were several distinct groups: the descendants of the creole ex-slaves, patois-speaking and Roman Catholic; the British West Indian immigrants, English-speaking and mainly Protestant; the natives of Africa, now quite a small group; the 'peons' or people of Venezuelan origins, Spanish-speaking. Most of these people lived in the countryside and were estate labourers, small farmers, cocoa contractors and cane-

These three young men all won scholarships from St. Mary's College in 1918. They are from left standing Roderick Marcano and Aldwin Francis. The one seated is Montgomery Forester. Photograph — St. Mary's College.

Below: The junior division of St. Mary's College, 1913, from a College Annual.

THE FIRST SCOUT TROOP IN TRINIDAD & TOBAGO

Farm House, Q.R.C., Hayes Street, Port of Spain, 1912

From left to right:— Back Row: C.R. Farrell, G.A. Busby, A.C. Farrell, K.L. Grant, C.E. Horne, F. Vincenti,.R.Wade.
Middle Row: A.L. Potter, Rev. C.S. Doorly (Scout Master), C.R. Massy (Asst. Scout Master, V.L. Burton.)
Front Row: O. Nothnagel, J. Worsfold, H.L. Knaggs, H.C. Rooks, W. Robinson, C. Siung, G. Horsford.

farmers, artisans, hucksters and shopkeepers. A growing minority lived in the towns, especially Port of Spain which grew rapidly in the later 19th century, gaining an often precarious livelihood as stevedores, porters, messengers, shop assistants, cabmen or carters, artisans and general labourers. They lived in the slums of the city which, just as at this time, were the centre of a Creole cultural complex involving Carnival, stick-fighting, calypso and (later) steelbands.

It was the descendants of the Creole ex-slaves who formed the nucleus, the core group, in the cultural complex of the folk. The medium of this cultural complex was patois and it was Afro-French in character. This nuclear culture had much in common with that of the 19th century French Antilles. Folklore and folksongs, early forms of Calypso, dances like the Belair, African and Creole musical instruments, Carnival and Camboulay, stick-fighting and tamboo-bamboo, were all part of the culture core. Other groups within the Creole masses added their special contributions. The 'peons' brought parang, the Velorio de Cruz, Spanish-Venezuelan musical instruments and tunes, special Spanish-Amerindian methods of preparing foods. Liberated Africans contributed religious beliefs and practices (Shango from Yoruba especially), British West Indians helped to spread knowledge of the English language and brought with them their own customs and traditions from their home lands. Black culture in Trinidad at the time of the 19th century was far from static: it was dynamic, fascinating, constantly shifting and growing, highly absorbent of new influences.

1889

His Grace Archbishop Gonin died on 13th March and was buried with high honours the next day, His Excellency the Governor and other notables attending the funeral.

The final meeting of the Franchise Commission was held on 30th March when the report of the Chairman, the Hon. S.H. Gatty, was read. A large section of the public viewed the report with regret as it was decidedly antagonistic to the cause of the would-be reformers.

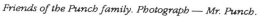

Friends of the Punch family. Photograph — Mr. Punch.

Lionel Belasco as a boy, he was already an excellent pianist.

LIONEL BELASCO

Sue-Anne Gomes

Lionel Belasco was certainly the great man of music in Trinidad at the close of the 19th Century. Born in Duke St. in 1881, he was a member of a musical family his mother had been a concert pianist. He began composing at the age of 12 and by the time he was 16 he had written four hundred ballards, pastiches, waltzes, calypsoes, sambas and rumbas and was also the leader of his own band. Lionel toured all the islands of the West Indies and visited the greater part of the South American countries. He saw Europe and the United States and was recorded by The Victor Company who in 1914 sent technicians to Trinidad to record his music; incidentally this was the first recording ever made in Trinidad. 'Lanky' as he was known to his friends appeared at Carnegie Hall and Grand Central Palace on national broadcasting chains, as well as in several motion pictures made by Paramount Pictures Corp., and Columbia Pictures. He had a great influence on music and musicians in Trinidad; men like Cyril Montrose, James Minerve, Lovey and The Donawa Brothers, to name a few, were influenced by the magic of Belasco's music.

Lionel Belasco led a remarkable life, and this was further illustrated by an incident that occurred when he was in his seventies. It involved a law suit brought against an American by the name of Morey Amsterdam. It was alledged that he had stolen the melody of Belasco's song — 'L'Année Passeé'. This song had been written in 1906 and it related the tragedy surrounding a young Trinidadian girl who had came from a very respectable family. She left her home to live with a common man. One year later her lover had put her out and she became a streetwalker. Just as the situation, the music line had been written with great pathos. More than 30 years later during the early 1940's a local calypsonian, the Lord Invader received permission from Belasco to use his melody to which he composed other lyrics, that song was entitled 'Rum and Coca Cola'. In 1943 Morey Amsterdam an American comedian claimed ownership of both lyrics and music. One year later The Andrew Sisters recorded it and it became a smash hit, over two hundred thousand records were sold. The composers were listed as Morey Amsterdam, Jeri Sullivan and Paul Baron. This patent infringement of copyright led to swift action against the perpetrators and Lionel's publisher Maurice Baron (not related to Paul Baron) filed a law suit. Lionel by then about seventy years old was brought to New York to testify in the case. A handsome man, very distinguished looking who appeared younger than his years, was put onto the witness stand. Under examination the court heard from Belasco that the original material had been written in patois and he proceeded to sing in patois the words and music of his song. The music had been constructed with dramatic harmonization adding an unessential discord to the chromatic chord, which reflected the awfulness of the situation related in the original lyrics. This was a dead give away for it had been copied exactly and used with the gay words of 'Rum and Coca Cola' — a musical

Lionel as a man; this photograph was taken in New York and appeared on his concert programme. Photograph — The Belasco Family.

misnomer. Through astute and rigorous examination the prosecuting lawyer proved the outrage and the defendants were made to pay. Lionel Belasco's publisher emerged victorious and most importantly his musical integrity was maintained. Lionel Belasco a remarkable musician, a gentleman of the old school he is of revered memory.

Sources:
Trinidad Guardian
The Belasco Family
Notes from the 'Rum & Coca Cola' court case.

Hon. Dr. Laurence, M.D., M.L.C.
Champion Emigration Oppositionist.

Charles Secundyne Assee, Barrister-at-Law.

1889

Ice was unobtainable in Trinidad for some time due to the non-arrival at the expected time of the usual vessel of C.L. Haley & Co.

News of the death, in Barbados, of His Lordship Bishop Rawle reached Trinidad on 11th May. The successor to the Anglican Bishopric, His Lordship Bishop Hayes, arrived on 17th May.

Frederick Warner and Dr. de Verteuil were appointed Companions of the Order of St. Michael and St. George on 1st June.

The detachment of the York and Lancashire Regiment stationed in Trinidad sailed for Barbados on 8th June leaving the colony without any Imperial troops for the first time since 1797.

The Dry Goods trade gained direct representation in the Legislature when W.M. Murray was appointed an unofficial member of this body, and shortly after this was announced John Bell-Smyth was similarly honoured.

It was learned during the month of July that Captain Baker, Chief of the Trinidad Police Force, was to switch appointments with Captain fortescue, Inspector of Prisons in British Guiana.

A month later advance proofs of J.T. Thomas' 'Froudacity', written in answer to 'The Bow of Ulysses', were received with high praise by the inhabitants of all the West Indian colonies.

Sir John Gorrie, Chief Justice, received a warm welcome from a crowd of some 8,000 persons on the wharf on his return from leave on 4th October.

Port of Spain's Borough Council abolished the practice of illuminating the cemetery on All Saints' night.

Cocoa from Las Cuevas as well as produce from other bay plantations and Tobago were shipped to London on the 'Bel Air' which commenced her round-the-colony trip on 5th October.

News of the death of J.J. Thomas, author of 'Froudacity' and the Hon. Frederick Warner, C.M.G., senior member of the Legislative Council, both in London, was received on 18th October.

First aeronautical experiments made in Trinidad were witnessed at Shine's Pasture during November when a member of Donavan's Circus, then visiting the island, sailed upwards, on one occasion to a height of 500 feet, in a balloon.

Sir William and Lady Robinson returned from holiday on the Quebec Line Steamer 'Trinidad' on 5th December and were greeted by public and official demonstrations of welcome.

The Gordon Ward of the Colonial Hospital was opened during December while Grenada and Barbados gained major honours at the Queen's Park Races on 30th and 31st.

General Navarro, Venezuelan millionaire, died in Trinidad on 18th March.

1890

The prospectus of a company to convert the residence of the late Hon. Frederick Warner into the Queen's Park Hotel was published during January.

It was announced on June 4th that a new body of 50 armed Police or Constabulary was to be added to the Police Force and stationed permanently at St. James Barracks under the command of Sergeant Superintendent Shelston.

October 28th was declared a public holiday to celebrate the opening of the colony's first great Industrial Exhibition. Thousands crowded the vicinity of the Prince's Building where His Excellency the Governor performed the ceremony and opened to public view a wide range of agricultural and other industrial exhibits.

1891

Twelve lives were lost in a fire at the Guiria Hotel on Marine Square on February 15th. The Press clamoured for the reorganisation and modernisation of the Fire Brigade, while one witness at the subsequent enquiry stated that all the lives could have been saved if two ladders had been available.

Four British warships, including the gunboat 'Thrush', commanded by H.R.H. Prince George of Wales, put into Port of Spain harbour on February 19th. On arrival His Royal Highness was made the guest of His Excellency the Governor and Lady Robinson at Government House and from then until the departure of the fleet at the end of the month a number of entertainments were arranged for the distinguished visitors. There was a rifle match at St. Clair between the officers of the fleet and the local Volunteers on the 26th, which the latter won, and on the same day the Prince was taken to Blue Basin and from there to a Garden Party given by Sir John Gorrie. For about nine miles the streets along which the party passed were luxuriously decorated with flags, streamers and triumphal arches. On the afternoon of the 27th the fleet beat Trinidad at cricket and this was followed at night by a Grand Ball at Government House. The illumination of this residence was elaborately conceived and executed and the night was brightened by hundreds of coconut flambeaux tracing the extent of the lawns and gardens. In the ballroom blocks of ice were used to 'cool the atmosphere'.

The female prison at St. James was opened on May 2nd.

Several persons were injured when rioting broke out at Arouca on March 31st after the police had interrupted a 'bamboula' or drum dance at Arouca. The police authorities were severely criticised for attempting, in the first instance, to quell the disturbances with a handful of unarmed men.

Dr. Comins, Commissioner sent by the Indian Government to enquire into the condition of Indian immigrants in Trinidad, arrived in the island on June 1st.

The Norwegian brig 'Gunvor' was wrecked off Mayaro on July 6th.

Sir William Robinson left for Europe on July 30th prior to his taking over the administration of Hong Kong. The Hon. Henry Fowler was sworn in as Administrator.

Sir F. Napier Broome arrived as Governor on August 19th.

The 'Erne' left Trinidad with 684 East Indians on September 2nd.

Mr. Algernon Albert Burkett,
Drummer in his Majesty's 2nd West India
Regiment (of foot). He wrote the book
'Jewel of the West', 1900.

Arthur Hutton Mc Shine, M.D., C.M.
Prominent Oculist.

1891

The Church of Our Lady of Laventille was blessed by His Grace the Archbishop on December 13th.

1892

The Dutch Mail steamer 'Orange Nassau' collided with the small British ship 'Pirata' outside the Grand Boca on March 13th. The 'Pirata' sunk with the loss of two lives.

His Honour Sir John Gorrie was interdicted from performing his duties by a Judicial Commission's decision given on June 20th.

The Victoria Institute, erected at the cost of $6,500, was opened on September 17th by S. Devenish instead of His Excellency the Governor who was indisposed. For the first time the Trinidad public were given the opportunity of seeing microscopic exhibits while the Police Band rendered several musical items.

A 'Reform Meeting' was held at the Town Hall on October 22nd under the chairmanship of the Hon. Robert Guppy.

News that His Honour the Chief Justice, J.T. Goldney, had been knighted reached Trinidad on December 30th.

1893

Eight British warships, under the command of Vice-Admiral Sir John O. Hopkins, K.C.B., arrived on February 7th. The flagship, H.M.S. 'Blake', a twin-screw cruiser, was the largest British warship that has ever entered the gulf.

The 'Port of Spain Gazette' of April 13th noted that on the previous day 4,323 pounds of beef had been exposed for sale at the Eastern Market at prices ranging, in the morning, from six to ten cents per pound.

Celebrations were held at the Cocorite Leper Asylum on April 12th to honour the 25th anniversary of the advent of the Dominican Sisters of the congregation of St. Catherine of Sienne to Trinidad to undertake the care of the island's lepers. The sole survivor of the original group of Sisters was presented with a Purse and an Address.

1894

C.C. Knollys, Colonial Secretary of Barbados, was appointed Colonial Secretary of Trinidad on January 4th.

A grouper seven feel long, five feet in girth and weighing 360 pounds was caught in the gulf by Leon Centeno on April 27th. This fish was exhibited at 'Coblentz'.

Sewing machines were advertised by Messrs. James Todd & Sons at prices ranging from six to ten dollars each, with special discounts for cash.

The Hon. Count de Verteuil and his wife celebrated their 50th wedding anniversary on July 16th. Special Mass was celebrated in their honour at the Rosary Church by His Grace the Archbishop and this was followed by a reception and lunch. H.E. the Governor called on Count de Verteuil in the afternoon, bringing the congratulations of himself and his wife.

The corner stone of the new Roman Catholic chapel at Teteron Bay was blessed on August 15th.

Twelve gentlemen enrolled in 'The Trinidad Light Horse' when the troop was inaugurated at a meeting at the Victoria Institute on the evening of October 22nd. A.S. Bowen presided over the meeting.

TERRIFIC FIRE IN MARINE SQUARE

The ink had scarcely dried upon the paper on which we chronicled the fire of Thursday last, when we are called upon to relate the story of another conflagration, perhaps the greatest catastrophe since the great fire of 1808 which had destroyed many lives and much valuable property.....

It was near 3.45 on Sunday morning when the alarm bell and the bells of the Catholic Cathedral rang out the announcement that a fire was raging............

The breeze of the time was strong, blowing from the northeast, and fanned by it immense volumes of flame shot athwart the sky, whilst countless sparks scattered in every direction. Arriving at the scene of the fire, a horrible scene met the eye. On the greensward in Marine Square in front of the Hotel Guiria lay the roasted remains of a woman and her child........Beside them lay the remains of an infant of perhaps a year old, who had just been vaccinated, we were told, and had the linen bandage still around his arm. Something similar was to be noted in a cart utilised by the police, for the ambulance being out of repair could not be used, and arrived at about 3.30 a.m. Lying in the vehicle were forms writhing in agony; low groanings reached the ear and the eye rests upon a scene which the pen cannot faithfully depict. Half charred were some, while others were washed in blood from the haemorrhages consequent upon their injuries. But was this all? Unfortunately not: opposite the upper floor of the Phoenix pharmacy was a whole family of burnt out persons gathered around the bedside of a girl child of perhaps ten years, who was groaning in agony with the injuries which she had received and from which she was dying. She had been thrown from one of the windows of the Hotel Guiria and had suffered a dislocation of the hip and of her ankle. But before proceeding to give a detailed account of the casualties we will refer to the destruction of property that resulted.

Originating in the Hotel Guiria, the fire spread rapidly to the next house, used as an annex to the hotel..........and the brigade was wholly unable to cope with the devouring element. From building to building went the flames until by five o'clock the entire frontage on Marine Square from Henry Street to Almond Walk was a mass of smouldering ruins.

Certainly for all that goes to make up the lack of an efficient fire brigade, Trinidad stands in the front rank. We have no hesitation in saying that nowhere within the four corners of the civilised world is there to be found such an utter want of means to extinguish a fire as was to be seen here.

But to return to the appalling loss of life that attended this cruel conflagration. In order to arrive at a proper understanding of the matter it is necessary to state that the Hotel Guiria, kept by Mr. Joaquin Pildain, had on Saturday night 50 passengers, all, with but a single exception, being Venezuelans ...

Light is thrown on the occurrence by the statement made to us by a Mr. Tucker, a lodger at the hotel. This gentleman says that there is no doubt that the fire originated in one of two ways: either by the lamp in the W.C. exploding or by a lighted cigarette setting fire to the paper with which the place was strewn..... It seems according to the accounts we have received that when

*The crowd outside the Hotel Guiria, which was situated on the corner of Almond Walk (Broadway) and Marine Sq. (Independence Sw.).
Photograph — Gregor Duruty.*

the guests upstairs discovered that the place was on fire beneath them, Mrs. de Osio rushed down the staircase to ascertain the nature of the danger and the means of escape. A coolie servant who saw her on the top of the stairs told her to come down at once if she wished to be saved ...

But the mother's instinct was there; it rose above the danger of the situation and she hurried back to her children. When she got there again it was too late for anyone to come down by that one staircase which the flames had seized in that extraordinary rapidity which consumed the building. And then was seen that heartrending spectacle of the mothers throwing their children and then endeavouring to throw themselves from the attic windows into the street.

No doubt in the agony of the moment all presence of mind was lost by the unfortunate persons. Mrs. de Osio threw her four children on to the roof below, whence they rolled to the ground; Mrs. Escheveria threw her three, and tried to follow them; the nurse with the fourth and fifth remained and perished in the flames. Others were overpowered by the flames before they could jump. Mr. Heromino Fagasin threw himself out of his window and broke his neck, in the fall. Mr. Kramer, a lodger in the hotel, attempted to get some of the ladies in the attic to follow him over the roof on to an adjoining building.

Only one of them, a Miss Escheveria, aged 12 years, had the courage to follow the plucky young man. They crept along the ridge of the roof until they reached the last house in Almond Walk where, with the aid of a brigadesman, they got in through a window. Both Mrs. Escheveria and Mrs de Osio with her children were terribly burnt about the body as well as injured by the fall from the roof; the former in an almost nude state lay dying on the ground near the palm tree in Marine Square, asking the police to help her, that the stones were hurting her broken back, that they would be paid as she and her people had money; but nothing was done by the unfeeling guardians of the peace near by. The Rev. Father Emmanuel, O.P., passing from one to another of the injured, came near her and proceeded to administer the last sacraments, at which she folded her arms across her breast and joined in heroic faith in the last prayers ...

Her three children were also being looked after, a policeman was trying to get one of them aged about 10 and all burnt and with limbs broken by her fall, to walk to hospital, and the little thing was crying and complaining that she could not.

Mr. Alonzo and another who came up asked the constable why he did not lift the child and carry her, and the inhuman brute answered that he could not dirty himself by taking her up in that burnt and wounded condition! The names of the dead as afterwards ascertained were as follows:-

Rose E. Escheveria – 12 years

Aurora Escheveria – 12 years

Claudia Escheveria – 4 years

1894

The new temple of the Royal Prince of Wales Lodge was dedicated on November 27th by the Hon. C.C. Knollys, C.M.G., of Barbados, assisted by the Bishop of Trinidad with S. Henderson, J.M. Laing, E. Tripp, C.O. Bock, S. Wood, J.A. Harragin, J.H. Hart and T.C. Pile.

The yacht 'Lusitania' arrived from England on February 5th with 100 tourists including the famous writer W.S. Gilbert and his wife. Journeys to Blue Basin and the sugar and cocoa estates were arranged. The next evening the 'Lusitania' left Port of Spain for La Brea where the Pitch Lake was visited.

The much-debated 'Reform Motion' was lost in the Legislative Council by 12 votes to 6 on February 12th.

'All Trinidad' scored a first innings total of 180 runs against the total of 94 made by a visiting English cricket team on the first day of the match – March 4th — at the Queen's Park Savannah. L. Constantine (father of the famous Learie) figured as one of Trinidad's opening batsmen.

The Victoria Institute, built as an Art and Science Museum, was founded to commemorate the Jubilee of H.M. Queen Victoria. It was opened on the 17th September 1892 and was built at the cost of $6.500.00 and was expanded over the next two or three years. It housed among other rarities microscopic exhibits, a collection of stuffed birds which had been presented by Dr. A. Leotaud, a valuable collection of shells from R.W. Keate, a former Governor. Unfortunately the building and its contents were destroyed by fire on the 1st April 1920. Photograph — G. Duruty.

1894

The Hon. Count de Verteuil introduced the following motion in the Legislative Council on December 3rd:-

'That in the opinion of this Council the time has arrived for granting to the people of this island a voice in the management of their affairs and for amending the existing political constitution of the said island by providing that a fair proportion of the members of the Legislative Council be elected by the people, instead of being appointed by the Governor, as at present.'

This motion was seconded by Mr. Howatson and a change to the Jamaica constitution was advocated. The Acting Solicitor-General (Aucher Warner) in opposing the motion said in part that 'to grant the franchise to this community would be like feeding a three months old baby on beef and brandy', and that 'the result of inflicting such a medicine on this country would probably be disastrous'.

Given strong prominence in the Press the Reform Debate was adjourned several times and was still undecided at the end of the year. For more information of the reform movement see 'The Years of Revolt' by Fr. A. de Verteuil published by Paria.

1895

While literally the whole town was watching cricket the 'Great Fire' of Port of Spain was in the making. At about 4.30 p.m. large volumes of smoke were seen to be issuing from the premises of Messrs. James Todd & Sons between Henry and Frederick Streets. The Fire Brigade was slow to arrive and when they did some time elapsed before water could be obtained. The flames soon crossed both streets and the heart of the town began to be consumed by fire. So enormous was the fire that 300 sailors and Marines were landed from H.M.S. 'Buzzard' and the U.S. cruisers 'New York', 'Cincinnati' and 'Raleigh' then in port. Strong measures were necessary to clear the streets of thousands of excited citizens. When water and other usual means were found ineffectual the men from the ships blew up several buildings with explosives and so managed eventually to check the devastation. A count on the morning of the 5th revealed that 57 business houses and residences in Frederick, King, Queen, Henry and Chacon Streets had been burnt. Damage was estimated at £750,000 and the origin of the fire is still a mystery. Official and public tribute was paid to the men of both navies and the actions of several members of the visiting English cricket team who assisted at the fire were loudly applauded.

Dr. Pierre Ange Rostant, a prominent San Fernando physician. Photograph – Trinidad Guardian, San Fernando Centenary Issue

1895

On the afternoon of the 5th the cricket match ended in an eight-wicket victory for the Trinidad side who scored 78 for two wickets in reply to the visitors' second innings' total of 162.

At 8.30 p.m. the same day the streets of Port of Spain were lit by electric light for the first time.

The retirement of the Hon. Count de Verteuil, member of the Legislative Council for over 30 years, was announced by H.E. the Governor on March 11th. E. Cipriani was appointed to the vacant seat.

A message conveying the sympathy of Her Majesty the Queen to the sufferers from the recent fire was received on March 12th.

The next day the English cricketers left for Demerara.

An address was presented to Count de Verteuil by the members of the Legislative Council on April 9th.

The new electric trams were tried at midnight on may 18th and Lady Broome formally opened the Belmont Tramway Line on June 26th. The three cars of the company were gaily be-decked for the occasion and the Press remarked that 'the rate of speed was very high, fully 15 miles an hour'.

Dr. de Verteuil, C.M.G., was knighted on November 18th.

1896

Rev. Canon Doorly was inducted as Rector of St. Paul's Church, San Fernando, on February 12th.

1896

The Ladies Golf Club presented Mrs. Gordon-Gordon, their honorary secretary, with a gold bracelet in appreciation of her service on May 27th, the eve of the departure for England.

Protests against the government decision to introduce the meter system for water supplies were handed to H.E. the Governor by a deputation on August 21st. It was requested that the protests be forwarded to the Secretary of State for the Colonies.

The Queen's Park Cricket Club opened their new grounds (the 'Oval'), purchased at the cost of £500, on September 5th. Nearly $3,000 had been spent in resodding the ground.

The railway line to Guanapo was opened on October 1st.

1897

Lord Hawke's cricket team arrived on 27th January. Celebrations in honour of the 100th anniversary of the occupation of Trinidad by the British commenced with a municipal dinner for the poor, a banquet at the Prince's Building and a review of the Local Forces by the Acting Governor and General Butler on 13th February. Special services were held throughout the island's churches on the next day and on the 16th the Victoria Institute Historical Exhibition was opened, a municipal sports meeting was held and there was an official Ball at Government House. Two days later Centenary Races were held at the Queen's Park Savannah while Port of Spain was illuminated and a 'Celebration Fete' was held at St. Joseph.

The Royal West India Commission arrived in Trinidad by H.M.S. 'Talbot' on 24th February.

The Clydesdale Cricket Club came into being, with Jas. Neilson as its first secretary, and played their first matches during April.

Trinidad's Diamond Jubilee Contingent of Local Forces left for England on 13th May.

Governor Sir Hubert Jerningham arrived on 2nd June and on the 22nd the Diamond Jubilee of Her Majesty Queen Victoria was celebrated. The Jubilee Contingent returned on 29th July.

The Sangre Grande railway extension was opened on 1st September.

> " De brave, de brave
> De brave, de brave
> Many were sent to eternity
> In the riots of 1903.
> (Fijornel) "

The Water Riots of 1903

A large crowd gathers outside the Red House in Port of Spain, in protest to the Proposed Bill. Photograph — Mr & Mrs. Peter Stone.

Square and Abercromby Street, as well as the grounds to the west and along St. Vincent Street; and headed by the Committee of the Ratepayers' Association, they proceeded to the main entrance to the building and demanded admission. The doors which had been closed against them were all guarded by strong bodies of police. Lieut-Col. Blake refused to allow anyone to pass.

THE DAY OF THE RIOT

The adjourned meeting of the Legislative Council was held at noon on Monday the 23rd March, 1903, His Excellency the Governor, Sir Alfred C. Maloney, K.C.M.G., presiding... Admission to the Council Chamber was from an early hour refused the general public, strong guards of police, armed with sticks being posted at all entrances. In addition to the usually provided accommodation, 150 chairs had been hired and ranged all round the room. As noon approached, some 50 to 60 of these began to be occupied, the large proportion being Government officers. In the meantime an immense crowd of the general public filled Brunswick

Ticket holders will be admitted to the Government Buildings by the northern door, Knox-Street. This ticket must be presented at the door of the Council Chamber.

A ticket to the Public Gallery of the Legislative Council.

The Southern Wing of the Red House, prior to the Water Riots. Photograph — Mrs. Hélène Farfan.

MASS MEETING IN BRUNSWICK SQUARE

In the same Friday morning there appeared in the 'Gazette' an official notice in the following terms, with regard to the admission of the public to the Council Chamber on the following Monday:-

'Public notice is given that, on accont of the limited accommodation in the Council Chamber, and the great inconvenience caused when the members of the public are anxious to attend the debates, admission to those parts of the Chamber not appropriated to the use of the members will in future be given by tickets only, in accordance with the practice of the Imperial Parliament ...

Tickets will be issued.....in the order of application, at the office of the Clerk to the Legislative Council ...

Special arrangements will be made for the Press.

(Sgd.) Harry L. Knaggs,
for the Clerk of the
Legislative Council.

On the next day, Saturday the 21st March, a mass meeting was convened by the Ratepayers' Association in Brunswick Square, for the purpose of discussing this 'ticket regulation,' which was declared on high legal authority to be illegal ...

(22nd March, 1903).

The advanced members of the Association then asked for permission to enter the Council Chamber, and were met by Col. Blake, standing one pace in front of the constables, who informed them that he was instructed by the Governor to oppose any attempt to forcibly enter the building. Admission would be, as had been announced, by ticket only. He was backed by an armed squad of police and would oppose force by force; and the degree of violence of the one would be measured by that of the other.....The challenge was accepted by one or two members who, partly pressed forward by the surging but orderly crowd, partly advancing with hands and arms raised high above their heads to show that no violence was intended, came into contact with the Colonel and were forced back....Mr. Lazare then from the top of the steps informed the crowd what had taken place, and begged them to let their protest take a quiet and peaceable form most likely to recommend itself to the English people whom they might depend upon to see that they got ample justice for the wrongs and outrages that were being heaped upon them....He begged them to refrain from any further acts and merely remain about the grounds of the building while the debate proceeded ... The crowd then drew off to the square, where speeches were delivered urging that strict order be observed.... In the meantime the rising temper of the people was not lessened by the discovery that orders had actually been issued to the fire brigade to turn three fire-hoses upon them should they assemble outside the Council Chamber ... Shortly after, the order was given to Lieut. Whiteman to turn on the hose, but this he refused to do, saying he was appointed to put out fires, not to drench crowds; and

The Hon. Sir Henry Alcazar, the leading coloured Barrister and Legislator of the period. Photograph — Mrs. Hélène Farfan.

presently the cheering, the singing of the National Anthem, and the lessening of the crowd gave a clear demonstration of the resolution of the public protest ... Shortly before noon, all the stores and business places in the town closed, as a further mark of protest against the action of the Legislative Council.

Immediately after 12, the Governor, accompanied by his Private Secretary, drove down to Government House, closely guarded by police, and protected by a similar guard, proceeded to his office where there had been stationed another 35 armed constables, and accompanied by the Colonial Secretary, with Captain Dutton, A.D.C., His Excellency entered the Council Chamber and took his seat: at the same moment 10 more armed constables entered the room and took up positions with the rest. Amidst every mark of public demonstration against the proceedings and a momentarily growing scene of popular excitement, the Legislature came to order, and the Clerk rose to read the minutes of the proceedings of the previous Monday's meeting.

MR. ALCAZAR PROTESTS

As the clerk began to read,

Mr. Alcazar rose to a point of order....as to whether it was in pursuance of any standing orders of the Legislative Council, requiring all meetings of the Council to be in public, that this day's meeting was held. He referred to the 'ticket regulation', and without a present going into the question as to whether it was not, as many persons considered, ultra vires for the President to make such a regulation, he stood on the point that standing order 4 required all meetings to be held in public; and he understood that a number of members of the public had been excluded today from this meeting.

Some discussion arose, and the Colonial Secretary having inquired what exactly was before the house, Mr. Alcazar formally moved the adjournment of the house.

Mr. Goodwill seconded.

Lt. Emmanuel Lazare

The motion was lost by a vote of 14 against 6, Messrs Fenwick, R.S. Aucher Warner, Marryat and McLelland voting with the officials.

Mr. Alcazar:- I rose to move the adjournment as a protest and to discuss a public grievance, and upon such a motion it was most inappropriate and improper that the officials should have voted. I now give notice of protest against the vote; I beg to notify Your Excellency that I leave this Council and decline to take any further part in its proceedings.

Mr. Alcazar then left the Chamber.

Messrs. Goodwill, Gordon and Leotaud also gave notice of protest against the vote.

His Excellency then read his formal ruling on the question of order as to the 'ticket regulation,' that he maintained his right to act as he had done.

Mr. Gordon then rose and said, that after what had fallen from His Excellency, he felt it incumbent upon him, with great respect, to follow the course taken by Mr. Alcazar. He could not consent to remain at a Council

The Red House in flames. Photograph — O.J. Mavrogordato.

The Southern Wing gutted by fire. This photograph was taken by Mr. H. Stone Acting Registrar, who with the help of firemen, saved the records in the Registrar General's Office. Photograph — Mr. & Mrs. Peter Stone.

whose standing orders and regulations could be varied at the irresponsible whim of the Governor.

Mr. Gordon then left the Chamber.

After a pause,

The order of the day was proceeded with the Clerk reading the minutes of the previous Monday's meeting.

....

The debate on the second reading of the waterworks ordinance was resumed ... His Excellency rose and proceeded to read a lengthy address to the Council on the history of the bill. During the reading the crowds around the building outside had been growing more and more noisy and turbulent, - the singing of the National Anthem, Rule Britannia, the beating of drums, the blowing of whistles and the cries of women carrying flags, were on the increase. Almost all the windows in the lower storey had been broken; and after a while, an accident occurred which acted like a spark upon a train of powder. And in a moment a most regrettable riot had broken out. For some offence, a woman on the Red House lawn was arrested by a constable, who was immediately struck by a couple of stones flung by some small boys. Thereupon the constable released the woman, and was at once attacked by her, too. Members of the crowd closed on her and dragged her and the boys away; but the evil was done. In a moment, stone-throwing was widely taken up by the crowd. Stones were pelted in a terrific shower into the Council Chamber through the glass doors and windows. People and police alike fled from the eastern galleries into the Chamber, and the Council came to a standstill. So hot became the 'shelling' that in a few minutes the whole of the unofficials had to rise and seek shelter, as did the reporting staff also, behind pillars, bookcases, etc. Presently the crowd to the west of the building got wind of the proceedings on the east; and at once without question, started to pelt stones too. Then the entire Council rose and moved for shelter to the inner galleries around the fountain courtyard in the interior of the building. For fully ten minutes was the fusilade kept up, several people in the building being hit. After a while the crowd broke in through the east and west iron gates into the inner courtyard, overpowering and driving back the squads of constables who had been hastily summoned to oppose them; and the whole crowd proceeded to stone the Council and the other fugitives from the Council Chamber who crowded the inner balconies. A suggestion was made to His Excellency to stand forward and state to the crowd that he withdrew the ordinance; but this he

Edgar Agostini V.C.

The Hon. Mr. Louis Wharton, K.C

The arrival of the troops. Photograph — Hélène Farfan.

declined to do. The Governor, his A.D.C., Major Collens, the Press representatives and others then took shelter in the small vacant office behind the Education Department on the upper floor, the whole party seeking what shelter they could behind presses and bookcases with which they barricaded the doors from the showers of stones and broken glass which assailed the room. It was the Director of Public Works and Mr. Fenwick who were the two members of Council for whom, judging by the occasional cries heard, the most apprehension was to be felt. What became of the latter is not clear; but Mr. Wrightson was with much difficulty smuggled out of the room by a strong guard of police, disguising himself in a police tunic and helmet. In a similar way was the Attorney-General got safely over, and both remained at the police barracks. For the Governor, however, and those with him, for a good while there seemed no way of escape, it being impossible to venture out of the room. Presently, the news came, — and was immediately after confirmed by the penetration of the pungent smell of smoke into the room, — that the Red House had been fired. The discovery was made from the brigade station opposite that fire was set in the Registrar-General's Office (under which the Governor and party were imprisoned), the Survey Office and the Hall of Justice simultaneously. And fanned by a gentle breeze, the flames spread so rapidly that in a few moments it was decided by the whole part, including the Governor, to risk the blows from the showers of stones which were still flying, rather than risk the fire. The door into the Council Chamber was

opened; and the rush of dense black smoke into the room where the party was imprisoned, at once justified the wisdom of the decision to move on. At the same moment a sound of firing from the police immediately followed the reading of the riot act by Mr. A.S. Bowen, in the presence of Colonel Brake, caused a sudden cessation of the stone-throwing. The whole party then ran down the Colonial Secretary's main staircase into the crowded streets, and the Governor was rushed under a strong police guard right across into the police barracks and kept there till he could be sent privately up Edward Street to St. Ann's; while Mr. Wrightson, also under a strong police guard and surrounded by a guard of armed

Mr. Lamy, Barrister-at-Law, (Town Clerk) Secretary for the New Water & Sewerage Board.

Mr. A.D. O'Connor, Crown Solicitor

The H.M.S. Pallus of the South Atlantic squadron brought the British troops to Trinidad. Photograph — G. Duruty.

The Hon. Vincent Brown, K.C.

sailors who had been fetched from the warship in the harbour, was rushed to the wharf and sent off in a small boat and kept on board H.M.S. Pallas.....Although the riot was checked by the first volley fired and the crowd at once began to disperse, it was noticed that volley after volley was fired, and that, too, quite indiscriminately in all directions....The killed were afterwards found to have numbered 16; while 42 at least were wounded, some of them at quite a distance from the scene of the riot.
(25th March, 1903).

ARRIVAL OF THE REGULARS

A couple of men of the Lancashire Fusiliers, sent for by the Governor, from Barbados, arrived on Wednesday evening by the three-masted schooner Sunbeam, having been towed up from the Bocas by the Iere and Paria. An immense crowd gathered to witness the landing, and was at first driven back by the police:

But on the advice of Supt. Sergt. Peake and a naval guard of 12 men from H.M.S. Pallas the crowd was allowed to reform, and in a most peaceful and orderly manner watched the landing, easily controlled by the sailors ...
(27th March, 1903).

ARRIVAL OF THE ROYAL COMMISSION

The Special Commissioners appointed by the Secretary of State to inquire into the recent riots in Port of Spain, arrived on the R.M.S. Trent on Tuesday morning the 28th April, 1903....accompanied by Mr. H.M. Vernon as Secretary, and Mr. W. Walpole shorthand writer.....The first sitting was held on Wednesday the 29th at the Prince's Building, which had been specially fitted up for the purpose. The grounds around the building and to the north on the Queen's Park Savannah, presented a very pretty, if unusual scene of military activity: a double row of white conical tents were ranged right across marking the encampment of the Lancshire Fusiliers,who, to the number of 21, exclusive of another 210, in barracks at St.

James, came over from Barbados. In the centre was mounted one maxim gun..
The appearances of counsel were:-

For the Government: The Hon'ble Vincent Brown (Attorney-General), Mr. R.S. Aucher Warner, Mr. L. A. Wharton.

For the Ratepayers' Association, the Chamber of Commerce, and the United Committee, and relatives of the killed:- The Hon'ble H.A. Alcazar, Messrs E. Scipio-Pollard, E.A. Robinson and C.J. McLeod.

THE REPORT OF THE COMMISSION

The report of the Commission was dated 2nd July, and was at once sent out by the Colonial Office: it was a lengthy document, and was published in extenso in the Gazette; its findings were:-

1. That the riot is to be attributed to public opposition to the proposed waterworks ordinance, stimulated by falsehoods and incitements to violence of certain speakers and the *'Mirror'* newspaper.

3. That there was excessive and unnecessary firing by some individual members of the police force ...

4. That two, if not three, persons were brutally bayonetted and killed by the police without any justification whatever.

5. That the Executive Government failed to take adequate measures to correct misrepresentations about the draft ordinace.

6. That there is a regrettable and serious division between a large and influential portion of the community of Port of Spain and the Executive Government regarding public affairs.

7. That there has been most deplorable delay in prosecuting the rioters ... and the taking of steps to enable the police who committed outrages to be also prosecuted; but most significantly, they also recommended the reference of the draft ordinance to a select committee.
(July 1903)

FIRST TRIAL OF RIOTERS

Punctually at half-past ten yesterday morning, the special sessions of the Supreme Criminal Court, ordered by the Governor to be held for the trial of 22 persons indicted for riot on the 23rd March last, were opened by His Honour Mr. Justice Routledge in Greyfriars Hall, Frederick Street. In addition to the usual strong guard of police sent down to every sitting of the sessions, a feature which excited considerable remark was the presence of 26 rank and file of the Lancashire Fusiliers, under rifles and fixed bayonets, a somewhat unusual show of military ferocity in the precincts of Greyfriars Hall ...

The Hon'ble V. Brown, with the Hon'ble L.E. Agostini and Mr. L.A. Wharton, prosecuted, instructed by Mr. A.D. O'Connor; and Messrs E. Scipio-Pollard and G. Johnson, instructed by Messrs. E. Maresse-smith and J.A. Lassalle, appeared for the defence ...

The trial lasted for a week, and it was on the afternoon of the 30th July that the jury retired at 4.30 after a most emphatic charge by the judge. Ten minutes afterward they returned into court; and in the meantime the square opposite the Hall, and the length of the pavement on either side of the street as well as Knox Street had filled with a dense crowd, composed of all classes of the community... A strong guard of police appeared and took up positions at various points of the Hall; while a detachment of fusiliers with loaded rifles and fixed bayonets were posted about the yard and outside the judge's chambers. The jury again retired after further directions ... Close upon three hours passed and no verdict had been returned. The closely-packed Court House, which was fortunately lit by electricity, grew more and more filled; and all waited anxiously for what seemed likely to be an abortive verdict. At 7.15 the Acting Chief Justice returned into Court, and the jury came back. After the usual questions, 9 prisoners were unanimously declared not guilty; one prisoner was found not guilty by 7 to 2; and one not guilty by 8 to 1; the jury was not unanimous as to any one prisoner's guilt. By a majority of 8 to 1 they convicted another; as regards the other three, they were divided 6 to 3. The judge refused to accept the verdicts, to the fact that after three hours a majority verdict either way could be taken. The judge held he was only empowered, not compelled, to do so. The jury retired, His Honour intimating that he would take the verdicts or discharge the jury at 9 p.m. He then formally discharged those who had been acquitted, and as each reached the street he or she was received with round after round of cheering. Punctually at 9 p.m. the judge returned to Court; and to the surprise of all, the jury returned a verdict in two more cases, one guilty by 7 to 2 and one not guilty by 7 to 2. In the remaining case that of Lolotte Borde, they remained 6 to 3 .... The following sentences were passed:-

Joseph James and Lilla Assing, 5 years each,

Abraham James, 4 years,

Octave Romain and Johnnie Blades, 5 years each.

(21st-30th July 1903)

THE TRIAL OF THE FOUR

It was not until the December sessions that the trial of Messrs. J.C. Maresse-Smith, H.N. Hall, E.M. Lazare and r.R. Mole, on the charge of inciting to riot, was held. Mr. Vincent Brown, with Messrs. Edgar Agostini and L.A. Wharton prosecuted, for the Crown: Mr. Alcazar and Mr. A.E. Hendrickson, instructed by Mr. H.M. Iles, defended Maresse-Smith; Mr. E. Scipio-Pollard, instructed by Mr.

Sir Evans James K.C.S.E., Sir Clements Smith G.C.M.G., Mr. Stuart Macaskie K.C. Their Honours the Commissioners. Photograph — A. Burket, Trinidad, A Jewel of the West.

L.J.A. Lassalle, defended Hall; and Messrs. A.E. Robinson and W. Blanche-Wilson, instructed by Mr. T.M. Kelshall, defended Lazare. The instructions of the Secretary of State to the prosecution of Mr. Mole were not given effect to, it was understood on the strong advice of the local law officers. The trial ended on the 18th December in a unanimous verdict of acquittal for all three accused. *(19th December, 1903).*

The Hon. W. Wrightson   *Alfredo G. Siegert Esq.*

THE NEW WATER AND SEWERAGE BOARD

One of the earliest victories of the riot was the transfer of the management of the water-works and sewerage system to a Board of mixed official and unofficial personnel; and the 'Gazette' of the 30th September, 1904, records the holding of the first meeting of the new authority, composed as follows:-

Hon. R.G. Bushe (Auditor-General) Chairman

Hon. W. Wrightson (Director of Public Works)

Hon. D. slyne (Receiver-General)

Dr. C.F. Knox (Acting Surgeon-General)

Dr. G.H. Masson

Mr. Alfred G. Siegert

Mr. L.A. Wharton

Mr. B.H. Stephens

Mr. H.Y. Vieira

with Mr. J.A. Lamy, barrister-at-law (Town Clerk) as Secretary.

(30th Sept. 1904).

PROMINENT TRINIDADIANS

St. Mary's College.

The Archbishop of Port of Spain Monsignor Ferdinand English was the main motivator behind establishing a Catholic College in Port of Spain. A man of great verve he undertook this cause relentlessly, but as fate would have it he died before his dream could be realised. Upon the news of his death, several of the priests in Paris, whose help he had previously enlisted, took up the challenge of his quest. In 1863 one year after Archbishop English's death Fathers Guilloux and Sundhauser embarked at Cherbourg in the month of May and landed at Trinidad two months later.

'From a letter of the Very Rev. Father Guilloux, we are able to glean some particulars about this first day spent by the Holy Ghost Fathers on the soil of Trinidad. The first kind service was rendered them by an Irish merchant, whose name unfortunately is not given in the letter, who drove them in his own carriage to the presbytery, where the Administrator of the archdiocese received them most cordially. The two Fathers were soon conducted to the house destined for them by Mgr. English, namely the old St. George's College. Arrived there, thanks to the kindness of the Sisters of St. Joseph, whose convent bordered on the college grounds, they were soon made to feel at home in their new country of adoption. Preparations were immediately started for the opening of the college. It was resolved to name the new institution, St. Mary's College of the Immaculate Conception; a prospectus was published, and on the 1st of August, 1863, the classes began with 14 pupils of whom eight were boarders, and six day pupils.'

From St. Mary's College Centenary publication.

Mr. F.E. Scott

Mr. J.B.D. Sellier
Solicitor

The Hon. D.S. de Freitas

Dr. F.A. de Verteuil

PROMINENT TRINIDADIANS

Mr. Ernest Sellier

Rev. Father Julien, C.S.Sp.

Mr. Louis Devenish

The Hon. Carl de Verteuil

Monsignor Allgeyer, C.S.Sp.
Vicar-Apostolic of Zanzibar

The Hon. Dr. E. Prada

Dr. A.P. Lange

Dr. G.A. Vincent

Mr. A. Monteil
Chief Clerk of the Treasury

Mr. J.A. Orsini
Consul for Mexico

Monsignor C.B. de Martini
P.P. of Arima

Mr. F.J. Maingot
Solicitor

PROMINENT TRINIDADIANS

Mr. A.V.M. Thavenot
Solicitor

Mr. M. Hamel-Smith
Solicitor

Dr. C.F. Lasalle
Port Health Officer

Mr. A. Pollonais
Assistant Receiver-General

Mr. C.G. Pantin
Chief Clerk Audit Office

Dr. D. de Montbrun
Consul for Portugal

Dr. C.G. Savary

Dr. R. Scheult
Resident Surgeon Colonial Hospital

ST. MARY'S COLLEGE FOOTBALL TEAM, 1912

Which won the Junior League Shield and the Wilson's Challenge Cup.

J. Alonzo,   G. Clarke,   B. Warner,   H. Knox,
W. Knox,   M. Fraser (Captain),   G. Lange,   B. Warner,
P. Walke,   P. Ganteaume,   E. Pollonais,   M. de Verteuil

SECOND FOOTBALL ELEVEN
Winners of Junior League Cup, 1918
Standing:—Xavier J., Russian A., Stewart A., Podmore E., Capecchi L.,
Ganteaume C., Rafalli G. Sitting:—Benlisa E., Williams E. (Captain),
Achong H., Maingot E. Photograph — C.I.C. Annual 1919.

PROMINENT TRINIDADIANS

James Joseph Hobson   Oliver Talbot Cazabon   T.I. Potter   Henry Alphonse Nurse, F.E.S. Lond.

D.F.E. Bass, M.D.   Chas Decle   Domingo Maria Navarro   Edward Gransaull

Alfred Mendez   H.I. Jeffers

Lt. Col. J.M. Collens, V.D.

CAPTAIN CIPRIANI AND THE
LABOUR MOVEMENT

C.L.R. JAMES

Captain Cipriani was back in Trinidad in 1919. Before the end of the year he had started his post-war public career by accepting the post of President of the Trinidad Workingmen's Association.

This Association had been founded in the last decade of the nineteenth century, the leading spirit being Mr. Alfred Richards, now an Alderman of the City of Port of Spain. It led a chequered existence, and in 1906 had but 223 members. By 1914 it had fizzled out. But 1919 was a time when new things were being born, and old things were being re-born. The Workingmen's Association was resuscitated, chiefly through the efforts of Mr. W. Howard Bishop, now dead, who became in time Editor of the 'Labour Leader', the organ of the Association. With him were Fred Adams, Julian Braithwaite, R. Braithwaite, D. Headley and W. Samuel, most of them merchants in a small way or men in business, but all coloured men and interested in their own people.

Captain Cipriani was not one of the original group, but early in the life of the new Association he was asked to become President, and accepted.

If there is anything which can prove the fitness of the people of Trinidad for self-government it is the progress of this resuscitated Association during the thirteen years since it has been restarted.

When Captain Cipriani became President in 1919, the Association functioned only in the City of Port of Spain. By 1928 there were forty-two affiliated sections in other parts of the island, besides six others distributed among the various classes of workers in Port of Spain. In January, 1930, replying to a call from Tobago, Captain Cipriani and half-a-dozen other colleagues proceeded to the island-ward and there established thirteen sections. Today the Association has ninety-eight sections comprising thousands of members. Each section manages its own affairs, appoints it own officers, and keeps its own funds. Delegates meet once a quarter to discuss matters of general policy. Today, as in 1919, the public meetings of the Association are assisted by plain clothes officers busy taking notes, and doubtless the Government would rejoice to get hold of something seditious. But though Captain Cipriani gives these amateur reporters a lot to take down, they get little to

Lest We Forget!

Trinidad Workingmen's Association, Inc., 1906

Representative: Thomas Summerbell, M.P., *(Sunderland)*
Affiliated to Parliamentary Labour Party *(England.)*

Men who fought to Secure Political Reform for the People

Back Row: J. L. Blondel, Leon Fuentes, Urbain Lewis, J. Sydney de Bourg.

Sitting: Montgomery E. Corbie *(Hon. Secretary)*, Alfred Richards *(President)*, Adrien Hilarion *(Vice-President)*, Walter H. Mills *(Treasurer.)*.

carry away. Meanwhile, the frequent rallies of different sections, the questions which they discuss, Captain Cipriani's visits to section after section explaining to them matters of policy, the circulation of the 'Labour Leader' until Mr. Bishop died a year or two ago, all this has made the agricultural labourers and the artisans, the masses of the people, alive to politics as at no other time in the history of Trinidad. Where formerly those who wished no change in the constitution urged the apathy of the labouring classes and their lack of interest in politics, today they use other arguments. The Association has been responsible directly or indirectly for shorter hours of employment in many branches of labour, particularly in wine and provision shops; for preventing employers paying wages to employees in liquor establishments; for the establishment of an Agricultural Bank; and for the introduction of Workmen's Compensation Laws. This, the introduction of a limited Workmen's Compensation Law, has on the whole been the most stimulating achievement of the Association so far. Since the introduction of this piece of legislation the working-people have received as compensation for injuries and deaths many thousands of pounds. Of the seven elected members of Council, four are supporters of the Association. At present the Association has as its chief aim the right to form Trade Unions, and, of far more importance, self-government. Perhaps the story of the eight-hour day and Trade Union agitation will show why this is so, besides at the same time revealing local labour conditions and the typical methods of a Crown Colony Government.

THE SYRIANS AND THE LEBANESE OF TRINIDAD

Gerard Besson

As the end of the 19th century approached, the world order seemed fixed as it were by Pax Britannica. The other great powers of Europe had drawn for themselves borders that crossed mountains and indeed continents, cleaving apart whole peoples and in the process creating new territories for themselves in most of the world's southern hemisphere. Without a doubt, it was fashionable to be an empire.

It was during this time that people of an even older empire came to settle in Great Britain's crown jewel Trinidad; a people who had their roots in the very antique origins of mankind's earliest civilisations. These new settlers were elements of the Ottoman empire, and they hailed mainly from the mountain villages and coastal towns of greater Syria. From the seashores of the eastern Mediterranean to the islands in the furthest west journeyed young men and women in search of their fortune. The sentiments of their desert homelands and a high sense of adventure is expressed in the words of Alfred Galy son of Elias Ibrahim Galy one of the earliest immigrants, who wrote:

Peter Aboud

Elias Galy one of the first immigrants who came to Trinidad at the turn of the century. The Galy family originated out of the Lebanon town of Macheta Azar.

Go Forth from the land of your kinsfolk and from your Father's House; to a land that I will show you'– 'Genesis'.

And so it was, with these thoughts; Elias Galy, born Elias Ibrahim GHALI, in the town of Macheta Azar, Telkeleh, Syria in 1889, decided to leave his native land, and the Country of his many ancestors, in the year one thousand nine hundred and ten of the Christian era at the tender age of 21. He left behind his elder brother, his 3 sisters, his estates, and his birthright; fired with a burning desire to find a new home in Trinidad & Tobago; a British Colony.

The land of his birth Greater Syria, which today comprises the countries of Iraq, Syria, Palestine and Lebanon, had for centuries been the crossroads of the known world. Trade and commerce had flourished here from the earliest times and from this cradle have come some of the world's first religions. The peoples of the book, Jews, Christians and Muslims all have their origins in these ancient sands.

Abdullah Gabriel was among the earliest Lebanese settlers in Trinidad. He was instrumental in assisting many of the other Lebanese families to come to this blessed isle. Among them Abdullahs, Chami, Hadad and Matouk families.

Mr. & Mrs. Joseph Sabga and family.

1. Abdou
2. Asad
3. Ayoub
4. Naim – (nephew)
5. Linda
6. Venus
7. Mariam
8. Jessimin
9. Polina
10. Odette
11. Emelyn
12. Joseph
13. Josephine
14. Evelyn
15. Minerva
16. Rahme
17. Issa
18. Norma
19. Gaby
20. Fred
21. Albert

'Among the early arrivals was Joseph Sabga who came here in 1909 in search of his wife whom he had sent ahead of him with his younger cousin to Pennsylvania. He himself had previously lived in Pennsylvania for a few years before returning to Syria to collect his wife. His cousin was denied easy admission into America because he had trachoma, so Mrs. Sabga landed in Trinidad, hoping to cross the bridge to Pennsylvania. Her husband came a few months later to collect her, found a small but supportive Syrian/Lebanese community, he also found the people here very friendly, began to peddle holy pictures while waiting for the next boat to America, fell in love with the people and the place and just never left.

Before World War I there were perhaps less than 100 Syrian Lebanese in Trinidad. Some had already established businesses, stores in the city and even an hotel. By 1916 the store 'Joseph Sabga and Sons' had been established at 12 Marine Square. Administered by Joseph Sabga and his eldest son Abdo, this store there and at its subsequent locations, Queen and Henry Streets 1926, Henry Street and Marine Square South 1927, 18 Henry Street 1930, became a focal point for the peddling immigrants. The Sabga family would establish £50 bonds for a two-year period to cover each arrival, many of whom came from the same area as the Sabgas – Syria's Valley of the Christians which houses the famous Castle des Chevaliers.'

From A. Rahael's lecture on the History of the Syrian Lebanese Community in Trinidad and Tobago.

Nasiff Abrahim and his brother Amin Nasiff married Evangeline Rodriguez in 1908 their children were Valtrude, Felicitie, Laurencia and Nicholas.

David Gillmore in his authoritative book *Lebanon a Fractured Country* writes:

> In the fifth century, the Christian world was bitterly divided over the question of whether or not Christ had both a divine and a human nature, and it was from this quarrel that the sects originated. The Monophysite group, which had most of its support in Egypt, denied that Christ had a double nature and managed to impose this view on the Eastern Church at the Second Council of Ephesus. In 451 AD the Byzantine Emperor reversed this decision at the Council of Chalcedon, and most of the Syrian Church accepted the new decrees. They formed the Melchite Church, accepted the Byzantine rite, and later followed the Patriarch of Constantinople into schism with Rome (1054). Partly owing to the zeal of the Jesuit missionaries, however, the Melchite Church split at the end of the seventeenth century and a group of them formed a Uniate Church with Rome in 1727. They became Greek Catholics and the non-Uniate Melchites became known as Greek Orthodox.
>
> The Monophysites, however, refused to accept the decisions of the Council of Chalcedon and by the seventh century the controversy had engulfed the whole of the Byzantine Empire. Since it then began to threaten the safety of the Empire itself, a compromise was attempted. This was the Monothelite doctrine, which affirmed that Christ had two natures but only a single divine will. Unfortunately, both the Eastern Church and the Monophysite heretics rejected the solution and at the Sixth General Council of the Church in 680 it was officially banned. However, it was enthusiastically accepted by one solitary group of Syrian Christians who became known as the Maronites.
>
> The term 'Maronite' was first used by John the Damascene in the eighth century, and it may have originated either from a Syrian hermit, St. Maron, or from John Maroun, the first Maronite patriarch. It referred to a Syrian group of Aramaic origin who had embraced the Monothelite heresy and were later persecuted on that account by Emperor Justinian II. A large number of Maronite monks were executed on the

Orontes river by Justinian, their principal monastery near Antioch was destroyed, and a part of the Maronite community shipped off to Thrace in the seventh century. As a reaction to these events, and also perhaps to the encroachments of the Muslim Arabs, most of the Maronite population retreated to the northern mountains of Lebanon where they settled, and where many of them have lived ever since. According to the medieval bishop, William of Tyre, they formed a Uniate Church with Rome in 1182, although the union was not consolidated until much later, but they retained their Patriarch and their own liturgy in the Syriac language.

Over the years the Maronites emerged as the largest of the Lebanese sects and the most influential and privileged group in the country. During the crusades they were the staunch allies of the Knights. In fact several families who made their way here including the Sabga family originated in Syria's Valley of the Christians where is situated the famous crusader Fortress Castle de Chevaliers.

The majority of these first middle eastern emigrants to Trinidad were in fact part of a movement of people that had commenced in the 1860's. As a result of expanding population on the one hand and pressure from Muslims groups on the other, there had arisen in the hearts and minds of young people the desire to travel to the Americas, to the U.S.A., Brazil and the Argentine. Sometimes taken advantage of by unscrupulous ships' captains these travellers would often find themselves stranded thinking that they had arrived on the outskirts of some great city in the west.

Standing: Elias Abraham one of the earliest arrivals to Trinidad. His entrepreneurial spirit founded the business K.S. Abraham and Sons. Sitting: Peter Aboud.

Aziz Joseph Hadeed,
the former Honorary Consul for Syria.

Right: Mr. & Mrs. Peter Aboud and family, at left is his son Jimmy, and on his right is Waheby, in front of her Salwa and in her mother's arm s the baby Magdelaine.

Often their fare would only take them as far as the Caribbean and sometimes they were simply put off at the port where their money had run out. As Annette Rahael notes in her paper on the *History of the Syrian-Lebanese Community in Trinidad*

> 'No one knows for sure, which if any of these reasons caused the first influx into Trinidad and Tobago but somewhere around the turn of the present century they came to Trinidad as a small population of families from the Lebanese village of Buhandoun among them were the Habib family. There were other arrivals such as Joseph Sabga, Elias Galy, Francis Gabriel, Elias Akat and Elias Abraham and later on Nagib Elias from the Lebanon village of Amyoun'.

Joseph Razouk Sabga came here in 1909 in search of his wife who had been sent ahead of him with his younger cousin on their way to Pennsylvania. He eventually found his young bride and because of the friendliness of the people, he settled. In the case of the Galy family their account is given in the words of Alfred Galy.

> 'Despite the fact, that Elias was born into a comfortable home, and grew up with a well distinguished, and respected family, that was financially independent; he left Syria in 1910, and migrated to Trinidad, driven by a deep ambition, and the spirit of enterprise; to succeed in a new found land. At that time, cocoa, coffee and sugar dominated the world scene, and the agricultural economy was thriving under a Colonial Governor, as the absolute representative of Great Britain.
>
> After some three years of struggle; peddling his wares across the Country districts, Elias soon was able to accumulate an adequate trading capital, upon which he was able to start a retail import business at Marine Square (now Independence Square). The Sabga family who had in the meantime arrived in Trinidad as well; soon recognised his diligence, honesty, and ability and accepted him into a business partnership, which went pretty well for a short time. He subsequently retired from the partnership and re-established his own business operations; achieving a great

Norman Sabga who arrived in Trinidad circa 1925.

Members of the Habib, Charles and Abraham families.

degree of financial success, and independence. In 1928, after an absence of some 18 years from his homeland; he returned to Syria, where he met his wife Nasema Gelish, a very vibrant and elegant woman; daughter of a well known and distinguished family in the village of Ein Deybish, Safita; the Gelish family.'

Life in Trinidad at the turn of the century offered many opportunities. The cocoa economy was booming and this made for a reasonable, comfortable middle class and for an exceptionally well off upper echelon. Further, the cocoa economy was not the only source of wealth. Sugar was the other power house behind the colonies' fortunes at the time. Trinidad was wealthy both in the town and in the countryside.

Annette Rahael notes in her paper:

'This peddling and hawking of goods became a pattern for the original immigrants. We are all familiar with the tales and images of the Syrian peddlars carrying bundles on their backs travelling through the countryside in search of the markets. And then failing to off load all their merchandise on market day they would peddle their goods from door to door, sleeping wherever night would fall, eating as cheaply as they could. Separated from their families they were usually made welcome by the village folk to whom they extended credit. Undaunted by the taunts of the school children or their own lack of fluency in the language, they persevered and sold their wares before returning to the city.'

It is of interest that these, the last of the immigrants lived in the old inner city which the first immigrants had built and lived in. They made their first homes in the boarding houses along Marine Square and the old and delapidated mansions of George, Duke, Duncan and Charlotte Streets.

1. Gloria Habib m Jean Khouri
2. Amin Habib m Antoinette Yhagi
3. Shirky Habib
4. George Habib
5. Adib Habib, a cousin
6. Khalil Charles
7. Karim S. Abraham
8. Mrs. Amelia Habib née Charles Habib
9. Nicholas Habib
10. Nadwa Habib
11. Edward Habib
12. Mrs. Rose Abraham

Essa Azar   *Afifi Azar*

These old French buildings built upon even older Spanish ones were in fact to serve as the economic base from which the community would eventually grow.

Life was made especially difficult for apart from having to live in poverty in the city's slums the newcomers often had to deal with loneliness as Miss Rahael further points out:

> Very many of the men came without their wives and families, they landed in a strange country which spoke a whole new language and worse yet, had literally cents in their pockets. We have learnt that some of us carry names and spellings of names which were assigned to us by immigration officers who would transcribe the difficult sounding Arabic words as best they could. Many of us have fathers and grandfathers who have far more intimate knowledge of this country's landscape than we could ever hope to gain in our leisurely Sunday drives. They collected their merchandise from Joseph Sabga and Sons and literally trekked through the countryside for 3 or 4 days, dreaming of saving enough money to bring their wives and children and owning their own business.
>
> A select few were taught to read and write English by Law Clerks, but the majority picked up enough of the spoken languages, including Patois, to get by in their work. Their monies went first to pay off their credit at the business places, maintenance of their families back home, their own meagre living expenses and then of course, savings for growth.

John Aboud and Kathrine Fakoory, on their wedding day. John was one of the founders of the Trinidad and Tobago Businessman's Association and served as President for many years.

Abraham and Wahid Hadeed.

The latter was a compelling force in their lives. They sought to obtain security by establishing their own businesses even though it was a modest one-door operation. At the same time they would sacrifice their weekends and free time to continue servicing their countryside clientele, leaving wives and very young children to mind the store. Their contact with the past was limited to playing Arabic music in their homes, the letters from Syria and Lebanon and the group gatherings on occasion. Recreational relief took the form then, as it often does now, of a card game with the boys.

In the period between the First and Second World War as the old Ottoman Empire collapsed and the French and British mandate took hold, Great Syria was divided into what is now Syria and Lebanon with Lebanon having a large Christian population.

During this time another wave of immigrants arrived in Trinidad. Amongst them were the Fakoory, Matouk, and the Naim Sabga families and also Norman Sabga and his son Anthony.

In a very real sense Anthony Sabga was to epitomize the strong entrepreneural spirit of his people and to demonstrate what hard work dedicated sacrifice and the fearless taking of the calculated risks could achieve. From very humble beginnings, he arrived as a boy with his father from Syria, and helped him in his business, learning all the while. Later inspired by his own keen business sense he branched out on his own, creating enterprise and employment. It is not without irony that as this present century comes to a close that Anthony, Tony as he is known to his friends should have acquired one of the foremost conglomerates not merely in Trinidad and Tobago but in fact the Caribbean.

The work ethic firmly in place and the support of family as expressed by Alfred Galy who wrote that the fact that his father Elias attained no small measure of success was attributable to the support of his 'wife Nasema who quite literally stood by his side during his trials and his triumphs. She was a bright light in a scene of darkness and the stabilizing force in time of turbulence.'

Sources:
Oral Traditions — Joe Sabga and Albert Hadeed.
Albert Galy's paper on his father
Annette Rahael's paper, 'The History of the Syrians Lebanese Community in Trinidad'.
David Gillmor, 'Lebanon a Fractured Country'.
All photographs were made available by the members of the families shown and are reproduced here with their permission.

TAMARIND
Boil a pound of granulated sugar to a thin syrup. Pour over shelled tamarind and allow to soak for twenty-four hours. To make a delicious drink place a cocktail glass of syrup in a tumbler fill with crushed ice and soda and stir.

Annette Rahael to whom we are in deed indebted for the information contained in her most informative paper in fact puts into perspective the basis both moral and social for the dynamic growth when she writes:

By this time the children of the earlier immigrants were growing up and a second generation was arriving upon the scene, born with the help of midwives, in rooms above and at the back of stores. They were often given Western names by their black, Indian and mixed neighbours and became alumni of Nelson Street Boys R.C., Rosary School, Belmont Intermediate. Like other peoples of peasant stock, the Syrian Lebanese valued education; so much so that in their short presence here they have nurtured island schol winners — Michael Mansoor, George Nadur, Jeanette Zakour, Jerningham Gold Medal winner Anthony Hadeed and Eddie Koury.

Because of their experience in their homeland they valued their new found religious freedom and defined religion in the broad terms of Christian versus non-Christian. So when the earlier settlers moved into Marine Square and saw the Cathedral of the Immaculate Conception they immediately claimed it as the House of God and adopted Catholicism as their religious affiliation. This was of course a sensible and practical approach since there were no churches in Trinidad celebrating the liturgy of the Antiochan Orthodox – the religion that they practised in the mother country. Faith in God and involvement in religious activities have remained a hallmark of the community, with most youngsters attending Catholic schools and a fair percentage of the youth and adults being very actively involved in Church organisations.

It seems ideal that in a country so cosmopolitan so diverse in its mixture of race, religion, class and station that there should be people of the Levant amongst us, that the sounds of Arabic music could have been heard coming from an upstairs balcony on George Street to mix and mingle with the Patois of the street cries and the smells of accra and float being prepared for sale by a Chinese man while in the distance the ubiquitous drum summons and the church bells in the old Catholic Cathedral peeled a solemn note.

Wahid and Saide Matouk on the occasion of their 50th Anniversary. The Matouk family first arrived in Trinidad during the 1920's.

Parties down the islands were very popular among the young people of the day. This one was on Pelican island and the people here are from the back left: Overton, Marge Darwent, Letia Darwent, Mrs. Walter Darwent, Mable Fahay, unidentified, Joan Darwent, May Hawthorn and Lillian Nock. In the foreground, seated to the two coastal officers, who were visiting from the steamer Belize, is Dorothy Darwent. Photograph — Gregor Duruty.

Sunny Memories

Sunny Memories of the turn of the century depicts the innocence and beauty of the young people of Trinidad as they entered the twentieth century. The first decade had hardly passed when the winds of war howled out of Europe and challenged the sovereignty of the Empire a challenge that was taken up by our very own boys and girls.

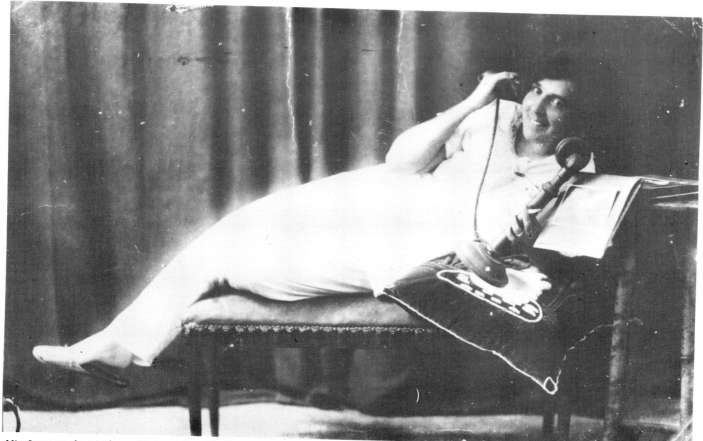

Miss Lamy on the telephone. Photograph — Phyllis Lastique.

The Boys, as they were on the 17th November 1915 just before they left Trinidad to join the war. They are, from the back left:
Eric Duruty, Willie Miller and George Stally. Front: Horace Darwent, Gregor Duruty and Toby Crighton.
Photograph — Gregor Duruty.

Captain Patrick Maingot   Flight Commander Horace Bowen   Private Alloy H. Pantin   Private Harold Duprés
Lancashire Regt., Military Cross   *Royal Air Force*   *Devonshire Regiment*   *Devonshire Regiment*

George Stally and Eric Duruty on a 9h.p. motorbike and side car. This photograph was taken in 1913.   Photograph — Gregor Duruty.

Gunner Joseph Peschier
Royal Garrison Artillery

Lieutenant Pierre Lange
King Edward's Horse

The American aviator Frank Boland landed his Biplane in the Savannah in January 1913. This was truly an amazing event for the people of Trinidad to behold. Photograph — Stella Duruty.

Captain Arthur Pantin
North Fusiliers

Captain Pierre Rostant
R.A.M.C.

Trooper Edwin L. Ferreira
King Edward's Horse

Seaman Ludwig Ache
Wireless Section, R.N.

Gregor Duruty's first motorcar. Photograph — Gregor Duruty.

The Foregoing is a List of Names of some of the Men from Trinidad and Tobago who served in the First World War

Taken from a publication which gave the 'List of the Public Contingents from Trinidad'. This material was made available to us by Gregor Duruty.

Dear Boys of Ours

'They would not have us weep,

    Dear boys of ours whom we have lost awhile.

Rather they'd have us keep

    Brave looks, and lips that tremble to a smile.

They would not have us grieve,

    Dear boys of ours whose valiant hearts are stilled;

Nor would they have us leave

    OUR task undone; OUR service unfulfilled.'

—Selected

LIST OF YOUNG WOMEN DOING WAR WORK ABROAD

The following are but a few of the many representing Trinidad who are thus employed in the Great War.

ALSTON, MILDRED—Refreshment Branch, War Work (Now Mrs. Martin).

ALSTON, WINIFRED—Red Cross Nurse.

ATKINSON, HAZEL—Ambulance Work, France.

ATKINSON, MAUD.

AUSTIN, MARIE ESTELLE BRUCE—Admiralty Office.

BRODIE, ALICE MAY—Red Cross Nurse.

GOODEN-CHISHOLM, MAIRI—Associate of the Baronness de T'serclases in the work of rendering First Aid to the wounded at Pervyse, and succouring Belgian soldiers in the trenches under shell fire.*

CLARKE, MAY RADCLIFFE.

CLEMENS, Miss.

CORDER, GRACE—Acting Matron, Q.A.I.M.N.S.R. Awarded the Royal Red Cross Decoration, 1st Class. (Assistant Matron Colonial Hospital, Trinidad).

DAVIDSON, GRACE—Red Cross Nurse, Edinburgh.

DICKSON, ISABEL RAEBURN—V.A.D., Darrel Hospital (Now Mrs. Taperell).

DOYLE, KATHLEEN—V.A.D., hospital near Regent's Park.

ECCLES, WINIFRED.

FENWICK, STELLA—V.A.D. Hospital, Margate. Owing to frequency of bombs in that locality, this hospital was closed. She is now at Michie Hospital, Queensgate.

GREIG, DOROTHY—C.P.O. Women's Royal Naval Service. Was 6 months at R.F.C., and 6 months at Tank Station. In charge of 22 cars and girls.

HARRAGIN, MAVIS—V.A.D., 3rd London General Hospital.

HAMEL-SMITH, MAY—V.A.D., London Hospital.

HAVELOCK, Mrs. E.W.—Red Cross Nurse.

HATT, EDNA—Steno-typist, Air Board, London.

HENDY, MAY EULALIE—V.A.D. Serving in St. John's Red Cross Hospital, Great Malvern, Worcestershire, (England).

JEFFERS, AUDREY.

KNAGGS, RUTH—V.A.D., Cheltenham.

KNAGGS, BARBARA—Munition Worker, Newcastle.

KNAGGS, PHYLLIS—V.A.D., Cheltenham.

KNAGGS, HILDA—V.A.D., Cheltenham.

LAMBIE, DORIS—Red Cross Nurse.

MARWOOD, FLORA.

MILLEE, ETHEL—V.A.D., Hospital, Aberdeen.

MUNN, MAUD A.—Red Cross Nurse. Died 1st December, 1918, U.S.A.

RAPSEY, GERTRUDE—Red Cross Nurse, London Hospital. (Now Mrs. Hird).

RUSSELL, Mrs. LEILA—One of three Adjudicators on Objectors to Active Service. (Other two being men).

SCOTT, SYBIL—Driver of Automobile at Naval Base.

SOLIS, MARLA—Red Cross Nurse, U.S.A.

TAYLOR, ELSIE—Red Cross Nurse.

THOMSON, GRETA—Red Cross Nurse, London.

THOMSON, MINNIE—Red Cross Nurse, London.

TOMLINSON, MAY.

WHARTON, MURIEL—Munition factory.

WHARTON, VIOLET—Red Cross Nurse.

WILSON, Mrs. TERTIUS—Refreshment Branch— refreshments to Returned Soldiers at Victoria Station.

*Note—For further information regarding their noble and self-sacrificing work, read 'The Cellar House of Pervyse', published under their joint authorship.

LIST OF FRENCH SOLDIERS WHO HAVE ANSWERED THE COUNTRY'S CALL FROM TRINIDAD

Roll of Honour

AGOSTINI, HENRI—Brigadier to the 31st Regiment of Artillery, DIED in Hospital, 28th January, 1915. (War Cross).

DUBANTON, MAXIME-ALBERT—Pte. to the 7th Regt. of Colonial Infantry. DIED in Hospital, 19th May, 1915.

DECORI, DOMINIQUE—Private to the 8th Regiment of Colonial Infantry. KILLED in action at Manastir, 9th May, 1917.

LIMONGI, JOSEPH-JEAN—Pte. to the 144th Regt. of Cavalry. KILLED in action at Craonne, 13th May, 1917.

DRANGUET, GEORGES-LOUIS—Sub-Lieut. to the 92nd Regt. of Infantry. KILLED in action at Verdun, 23rd August, 1917.

NOUAIS, HENRI-MARIE—Interpreter in the British Army. KILLED on the 4th February, 1918. Awarded War Cross Posthumously.

BARIOU, ANTOINE-CLAUDIUS—Pupil Officer to the 358th Regt., of Infantry. KILLED in action 21st July, 1918, at Sept-Saulx. (War Cross.)

LOTA, ANTOINE-JEAN-BAPTISTE—Sub-Lieut, to the 59th Battn., of the Alpine Chasseurs. KILLED in action at Bois la Tournelle (Fére en Tardenois) 28th July, 1918. (War Cross.)

FORTIER, JEAN ROGER—Auxiliary Doctor to the 152nd Regt. of Infantry. KILLED in action at Ostniewkerke (Belgium) on the 30th September, 1918. (War Cross).

————

ON SERVICE

AGOSTINI, LOUIS-ANDRÉ—Quarter Master to the 31st Dragoons.

AGOSTINI, MARIE-JOSEPH-FRANCOIS (alias 'Frank')—Sergt. Postman to the 4th Regt. of Zouaves.

AGUIRRE, JEAN-BAPTISTE—Pte. to the 142nd Regt. of Infantry.

ALBERT, PIERRE-CHARLES—Corpl. to the 11th Regt. of Foot Artillery. Trans. to 75th Regiment, and was in many battles on the Western front. In action at Verdun, and Fleury. Was GASSED once. Honoured as Marechal de Logis. Returned to Trinidad 28th February, 1919.

ALBERT, VICTOR-HUGHES—Pte. to the 166th Regt. of Infantry.

CARLIN, DURAND—Pte. to the 144th Regt. of Infanry.

COLONNA, JEAN-MARIE—Pte. to the 7th Regt. of Artillery.

CRÉMONE, ISRAEL—Pte. to a Regiment of Infantry.

DICANOT, JULES—Pte. to the 129th Regt. of Infantry.

DUMAR, TÉLESPHORE—Pte. to a Regiment of Infantry.

FORTIER, ROGER—Auxiliary Doctor to the 152nd Regiment of Infantry. (War Cross.)

JOAS, JUSTIN—Pte. to a Regiment of Infantry.

LOTA, VICTOR—Auxiliary Doctor to the 4th Engineer Corps. (Was taken prisoner in Belgium and released).

MAJANI, DOMINIQUE-ANDRÉ—Chauffeur, Section of Tractors of Heavy Artillery.

MAJANI, JEAN—Pay-Sergt. to the 44th Regt. of Infantry.

OLIVIERI, ANTOINE—Pte. to the 44th Regt. of Infantry.

PALAZZI, JEAN-PIERRE-FÉLICIEN—Sergt. to the 69th Regt. of Infantry. (War Cross.)

PERRIN, ALPHONSE—Sailor in the Mediterranean Sea Fleet. Returned to Trinidad, 28th February, 1919.

PHELAN, JOSEPH-GREGORY—Sergt. to the 123rd Regt. of Infantry. Now Sub-Lieutenant. (War Cross). Left Trinidad 3rd August, 1914.

PIERI, CHARLES-PHILIPPE—Pte. to the Corsican Regt. of Infantry.

QUESNEL, ANDRÉ-ROBERT-MARIE-ALFRED—Quarter Master Interpreter in the British Army.—Awarded British Military Medal.

QUESNEL, MAURICE-ROBERT-HENRI-GEORGES— Interpreter in the British Army.

ROLLIN, PIERRE—Pte. to the 99th Regt. of Infantry. (War Cross).

SAULNY, EUGENE—Pte. 23rd section of the Medical Corps.

SOTER, CELIEN-FLORIUS—Pte. to the 129th Regiment of Infantry.

THE MILITARY TRADITION IN TRINIDAD

Taken from C.M. Kelshall: The Evolution of Civil Military Relations in Trinidad & Tobago. U.W.I. West Indian Section.

Trinidad's military traditions are predominantly volunteer in so far as the volunteers have a history that carries them back to 1791. Apart from the involvement of small detachments in both World War I and II, the local military tradition has been carried by the various volunteer units established since 1797 when the first military force was founded in Trinidad. Shortly after Sir Ralph Abercromby became governor, the 1st West India Regiment was established and recorded in the London Gazette of May 1797. The foreign Regular Garrison troops were constantly sick, plagued as they were by yellow fever, hence the reason for establishing this permanent Trinidad Militia. The principal role of these militia was to help defend the island from the constant attacks by the French and Spanish regular forces, and from privateer attacks.

The first regular (not volunteer) unit of soldiers in Trinidad was left under the command of Thomas Picton who had a garrison of one thousand and forty-seven men, within which were Colonel De Soter's Black Corps, the first regular Trinidad military unit. The unit numbered only forty men and came to be known eventually as the Royal Trinidad Rangers who formed the nucleus of the

SILVER WAR BADGES

Presented to the following Returned N.C.O.'s and Men of the British West Indies Regiment, at the Queen's Park Savannah, on Saturday 19th October, 1918, by the Commandant of the Local Forces, the Hon. Colonel G.H. May; V.D. (in the unavoidable absence of His Excellency, the Governor and Commander-in-Chief).

Returned to Trinidad, 3/11/1915.

Ex. R.M.S. 'Magdalena'

COLLINS, V.

Returned to Trinidad, 5/5/1916.

Ex. S.S. 'Siena'

MAUGE, O.
CLEMENTS, W.J.

Returned to Trinidad, 26/8/1916.

Ex S.S. 'Europa'

BOUCAUD, J.
CALLAN, SILENCE,
CASIMIR, P.
COZIER, R.T.H.
DONAWA, R.
GABRIEL, L.J.
HENLEY, H.A.—Sergt.
MARK, W.A.
MARQUES, L.
MOORE, J.B.
RICHARDOSN, J.
TOTA.

Returned to Trinidad, 22/9/1916.

Ex. R.M.S. 'Chaudiere'

BARTHOLOMEW, W.
BLENMAN, H.
CARTER, D.
DARMANIE, E.
HENRY, R.N.
HUSBANDS, H.
JOHNSON, S.
PAUL, W.
PAYNE, J.
PERKINS, M.B.
PHILLIP, N.
PROVIDENCE, J.
ROBERTSON, F.W.
ST. CLAIR, McKAY
STANFORD, R.A.
TORAILLE, F.C.
WEEKES, D.

Returned to Trinidad, 8/12/1916.

Ex. R.M.S. 'Magdalena'

AKIE, H.
CLARKE, J.—Corporal
CUFFIE, J.A.
DE SILVA, R.
DOTTIN, A. MCD.
LING, P.—Lance-Corporal

The police contingent on parade at the opening ceremony of the Queen's Collegiate School   Photograph — G. Mc Lean.

10th West Indies Regiment. In response to a series of threats by French and Spanish privateers Picton commissioned his own Coast Guard, whose only unit was a launch by the name of Barbara, which was armed and manned by the Trinidad Rangers. The Barbara was 60 feet long, had two masts and eight guns. The crew were predominantly black ex-slaves loyal to Britain. The whole crew in fact were totally local and they were the forerunners to the Sea Fencibles, a volunteer naval unit begun in 1803. The local naval tradition thus originated with Colonel de Soter and his Black corps the first Coast Guardsmen.

During 1831-1834 there were over twenty-five (25) units of volunteer troops divided into five divisions, some of these were The Trinidad Light Dragoons, The St. Anns Hussars, The Royal Trinidad Artillery, The St. Joseph Light Cavalry, Savannah Rangers, The Royal Trinidad Light Infantry, Mayaro District Battalion, The Cedros District Company, Royal Trinidad Battalion, Arima Pioneer Corps, Diego Martin Chasseurs and the Couva and Carenage Battalions. Training for the battalions and companies was once a month for drill and musketry practice. Parade grounds in Port of Spain were Brunswick (now Woodford) Square, Fort George and the bottom of St. Vincent Street. The barracks on Nelson Street was destroyed by fire in 1808 and the Fort George Barracks was destroyed in 1846. Fort Picton was located on Laventille Hill and was also known as St. David's Tower (having been named after the patron Saint of the Welsh

MATHEW, T.
OXLEY, J.*
PARKER, J.B.
PHILLIPS, O.
STEWART, A.
WATSON, C.L.—Lance-Corporal

Returned to Trinidad, 3/7/1917.

Ex. R.M.S. 'Magdalena'

ALEXANDER, H.C.
CALLENDER, C.
COLLYMORE, R.
LYNCH, R.
MILLINGTRON, J.
VANDERPOOL, A.

Returned to Trinidad, 4/12/1917.

Ex. R.M.S. 'Magdalena'

BENN, J.
CLARKE, C.
LA CAILLE, J.
LEWIS, H.
STIRLING, P.
GUMBS, J.

Port of Spain Light Artillery performing exercises.
Photograph — G. Mc Lean.

FIRST TRINIDAD CONTINGENT

BRITISH WEST INDIES REGIMENT

OFFICERS

Major ALLASTAIR MURRAY MCCULLOCH,—now Captain.
Capt. ALFRED ERNEST ALBERT HARRAGIN,—now Major (M.C.)
Capt. ERNEST BOVELL CONNELL,—now 2nd Leut.
Capt. HERBERT JAMES LAWRENCE CAVENAUGH.
2nd Lieut. UALLEAN HAMISH MCU. GOODEN-CHISHOLM, now Lt.
   R.A.F.
2nd Lieut. ALEXANDER STURROCK LOWSON,—now Capt. and Adjt.
2nd Lieut. LEONARD RICHMOND WHEELER,—now Lieut
2nd Lieut. ROBERT PHILIP JOHNSTON,—now Captain.
2nd Lieut. EDWARD VIVIAN BYNOE,—now Lieut.
2nd Lieut. JOHN PATRICK THOMPSON,—now Lt. (Ag. Capt. and
   Adjt.)
2nd Lieut. EDMUND RICHARD LICKFOLD,—now Lt. (attached R.A.F.)
   Surg.-Capt. Albert James Clarke.
ABDULA—Returned unfit.
ABRAHAM, HUBERT BERTIE. . . . . .DIED 23rd October, 1918.
ACHE, LOUIS FELIX.
ADAMS, AUBREY—Sergeant. Wounded in thigh.
ADAMS, NORMAN A.—Lance-Corporal, Egypt.
AKIE, HENRY—Returned Medically unfit.
ALEXANDER, LUCIEN. . . . . . .Addicentally killed, 19th June, 1917.
ALEXANDER, HENRY CLAUDE—Returned Medically unfit.
ALEXANDER, WILFRED—Lance Corporal.
ALLEN, JOSEPH.
ALLI, SIRDAR—Returned unfit.
ALLICK, JAMES.

governor Sir Thomas Picton). The troops based in St. David's tower actually wore St. David's star as part of their uniform to help identify which unit of volunteers they belonged to. This is actually the origin of the six pointed star which was eventually adopted by many of the volunteer units and used by the present day Regiment. The corner stone of the St. James Barracks was laid in 1823; uniforms were differentiated according to whether the units were infantry or artillery: The infantry wore scarlet uniforms with green facings and the artillery, blue uniforms with scarlet facings.

In 1854 the regular foreign garrison troops were withdrawn from Tobago and by an act of government a corps of volunteers was begun there in the same year to see about the defence of the island.

In 1879 a royal commission of defence was appointed and construction of a drill hall on Tragarete Road begun.

By 1898 the Trinidad Rifle Volunteers of Artillery was formed and comprised nine companies of infantry with four in Port of Spain and one each in San Fernando, Arima, Princes Town, Couva and Tunapuna. By 1902 the strength was six troops of Cavalry, a Battery of Artillery and six companies infantry, headquartered in Port of Spain at the St. James Barracks.

The Zouaves saw active service in wars fought in many parts of the British Empire. In the Zulu and Ashanti Wars in the Gambia and later in the Boer War in South Africa. Above are the non-commissioned officers of the second W.I.R. then stationed in Barbados 1878. Photograph — Maureen Hanton.

Early in 1914 the unit's name was changed from the Trinidad Rifle Volunteers to the Trinidad Light Infantry Volunteers and in addition to Mounted and Infantry units a bicycle company and a Motor Cycle platoon came into existence. (Volunteers had to supply their own bicycles and motor bikes). One of the members of the Trinidad Light Infantry Volunteer Motor Cycle platoon was a Trinidadian who became one of the highest ranking officers of the Royal Air Force, Air Vice Marshall Claude Vincent, C.B., C.B.E., D.F.C., A.F.C., Silver Star of Serbia.

At the outbreak of war in 1914 the volunteers were mobilized and those who did not join the merchant contingent or the West India Regiment instead carried out Defence duties for the duration of the war as a type of National Guard. The Merchant Contingents of 1914-1917 were so called because merchant firms in Trinidad put together to defray the cost of transporting troops overseas.

During World War I seventeen (17) contingents of volunteers were sent to England to fight for Britain and twenty-two (22) Military Crosses were won by the members of those contingents.

ALLUM, CHARLES RAMSEY.
ANDERSON, CHARLES—sent back from England.
ANDREWS, JAMES.
ANDREWS, STEDMAN.
ANTOINE, CANA.
ANTOINE, FORTUNE.
ANTOINE, PETER.
ANTOINE, SAMUEL.
ARNEAUD, EMANUEL—C. Co., 1st Batt. B.M.E.F.
ASH, JAMES.
ASHBY, FITZ CLARENCE—Corpl. Mesopotamia, Acting Quarter-Master.
ASHBY, LAWRENCE.
ASSAI, JAMES ALBERT.
AUSTIN, FRANK. . . . . .DIED 12th October, 1918.
AUSTIN, HENRY AUGUSTUS.
AUSTIN, JAMES
BABB, EDWARD—Machine Gunner.
BAGWANSINGH—Returned from England.
BATWANT,—Returned unfit.
BAPTISTE, ANDREW DE VIRE.
BAPTISTE, EVANS.
BAPTISTE, FREDERICK MOSES.
BAPTISTE, JERRY A.—Lance Corporal, Egypt.
BARNETT, GEORGE.
BARNWELL, ADOLPHUS ERNEST—Sergeant, Egypt.
BARROW, HEADLEY.
BARTHOLOMEW, WESLEY—Returned Medically unfit.

The Police Band. Photograph — Mrs. Hélène Farfan.

BASTIEN, JOHN.
BEHARRY, LAL—Returned unfit.
BENJAMIN, REZY.
BERNARD, NORMAN.
BERTETE, HENRY—Private, Egypt.
BHOLAH—Returned unfit.
BHOORISINGH—Returned unfit.
BISHOP, DELSON.
BLENMAN, GEORGE WILBERT.
BLENMAN, HUBERT—Returned Medically unfit.
BOBB, ARTHUR.
BOMARSINGH—Returned unfit.
BONNETT, AARON. . . . . .DIED 27th April, 1916.
BOUCAUD, JOHN—Returned Medically unfit.
BOYD, HENRY. . . . . .DIED October (?) 1918.
BRACKENREED, JAMES—Sergeant, E.E.F. Egypt.
BRATHWAITE, MALCOLM ATHELSTAIN. . . . . .DIED October (?) 1918.
BRATHWAITE, NATHANIEL.
BRATHWAITE, THEODORE.
BRIDGEWATER, URIAS—Drummer, O. Co., 1st Serv. Battalion.
BRIGGS, GEORGE HUBERT AUGUSTUS.
BROWNE, LEONARD FITZ GERALD. . . . .DIED 19th August, 1918, Italy.
BRUCE, JAMES DOLLY—Signalling Sergt. B. Co., 1st Bat. M.E.F. Egypt.
BRYAN, CHARLES ISIDORE—Lce-Cpl. Served Ger. E.A.F. Invalided Egypt
BUDALOOSINGH—Returned unfit.
BUNTIN, ALFRED WASHINGTON. . . . . .DIED 13th January, 1919.
BURKE, FRANCIS ALBERT.
BURNETT, JOSEPH NATHANIEL HERBERT
BYNOE, FRANCIS.
CAESAR, WALTER.
CAINS, FITZ HERBERT. . . . . .DIED 4th January, 1916
CALLAN, SILENCE—Returned unfit.
CALLENDER, CAMPBELL NEWTON—Gr. No. 3, Armd Trn. E.E.T. Egypt.

After 1918 most of the units were disbanded except for one company of Light Infantry in Port of Spain and a troop of Light Horse in San Fernando. In 1920 yet another battalion was formed as a reserve unit.

During the civil disturbances of 1937 the Trinidad Light Infantry Volunteers and the Light Horse Troop were called out to quell the disturbances and to maintain law and order. At the end of the year for unrelated reasons the Light Horse was disbanded and a machine gun company implemented in its stead; it still carried the name Light Horse unofficially for tradition rather than descriptive reasons. In 1938 the 2nd Battalion Trinidad Volunteers was formed with three companies and the Trinidad Light Infantry Volunteers changed its name to 1st Battalion Trinidad Volunteers of which Brigadier Joffe Serrette COV, MBE, ADC, was a member.

At the outbreak of World War II the 1st Battalion Trinidad Volunteers was mobilized into full time service while the 2nd Battalion maintained its part time status. Once again as in World War I the volunteers served with distinction in the British Armed Forces overseas. The 2nd Battalion was disbanded after the war in December of 1943 and the 1st Battalion followed suit in 1948.

After this point the most significant military happening was the formation of the West India Regiment which began recruiting in September 1961 to form the Federal Defence Force. Recruiting for the force was carried out on a percentage basis according to the

The Police Hospital was established in 1895 on the grounds, to the South of the Old Colonial Hospital which was once the Orange Grove Barracks. British troops were stationed there before the building of the St. James Barracks which was completed on the 11th June 1827. Photograph — Marshal, Stark's Guide to Trinidad.

population of each of the ten islands of the federation. By 20th September (the death knell of the Federation) two hundred Trinidadian and Tobagonian nationals were serving in the West India Regiment. When the Federation ended serving members of the West India Regiment were given a choice of options:-

(a) Nationals of Jamaica and Trinidad could either join the Jamaica Defence Force or the Trinidad Defence Force or opt for a discharge.

(b) Nationals of the Leeward/Windward Islands could either join the Trinidad or Jamaica Defence Forces or the British Army or take a discharge.

One hundred and fifty of the Trinidadian nationals serving in the West India Regiment opted to join the Trinidad and Tobago Regiment in addition to fifty nationals of the other territories. Approximately two hundred soldiers who were already trained therefore were made available to the newly formed Trinidad and Tobago Regiment.

CALLENDER, LUTHER JAMES.
CALLENDER, SCIPIO AUGUSTUS—Corporal, fought German E. Africa.
CALLISTE, JONIAS—Returned Medically unfit.
CAMPBELL, LEONARD JAMES—Accidentally Wounded 17th April, 1918.
CAMPBELL, WALTER.
CARRIDGE, NATHANIEL CHARLES.
CARTER, DOUGLAS—Returned Medically unfit.
CASIMIR, PHILIP—Returned Medically unfit.
CASSIDY, PATRICK JOHN—Sergeant, E.E.F., Egypt.
CATO, JOHN LOUIS—Private E.E.F.
CHAPMAN, ARTHUR MALCOLM.
CHARLES, JAMES NATHANIEL.
CHARLES ROBERT.
CLARKE, MILTON—No. 1 Platoon.
CLARKE, RUFUS ADOLPHUS.
CLEMENTS, JAMES WILLIAM—Returned Medically unfit.
CUFFIE, JOSEPH ALEXANDER—Returned Medically unfit.
COLLINS, VINCENT—Returned Medically unfit.
COURTENAY, CORNELIUS WILLIAM.
CROOKS, JAMES EGBERT YEATES.
CROUCHE, ALEXANDER CYRIL.
DADAM CHRISTOPHER.
DALLOO—Returned unfit.
DALRYMPLE, GEORGE SAMUEL
DALY, CHARLES.
DANIEL, GEORGE ALEXANDER.
DANIEL, HORATIO.
DARLINGTON, ALBERT PRINCE.
DARMANIE, EMANUEL—RETURNED MEDICALLY UNFIT.
DEARE, SAMUEL.
DEDIER, RICHARD.

This photograph, taken at St. James Barracks just prior to their departure, shows part of Trinidad's Jubilee Contingent. At left are the Trinidad Volunteers, and on the right are the members of the Trinidad Light Artillery. The Officers seated are, from the left, Lt. Robert Prizgar, Capt. A.C. Rooks and Lt. M.E. Lazare.

DEFOE, BINU.
DELANEY, REGINALD.
DERRELL, EGBERT.
DERRICK, ALFRED.
DE CRAY, MCFIELD.
DE GANNES, ALBERT HUGH—Corporal, E.A.E.F.
DE PAIVA, ANTONIO.
DE SILVA, RAYMOND—Returned Medically unfit.
DES VIGNES, JAMES ARTHUR—Lce.-Cpl. . . . . . .DIED 29th October, 1918.
DES VIGNES, JAMES RAYMOND—Corporal, Egypt.
DICK, GEORGE ALEXANDER—Pt. Awarded MILITARY MEDAL, 1918.
DICKSON, ERNEST.
DILLON, JOSEPHUS THOMAS—Sgt. Dispenser 3rd Ser. Batt., B.E.F. France.
DILLON, LEOPOLD.
DONALDSON, THOMAS ARMSTRONG.
DOOKAL—Returned unfit.
DORSET, HENRY JOHN.
DORSETT, JOHN EDWARD.
DOS SANTOS, ALAN PERCY CARLYLE—Sergt. Egypt, now Mesopotamia.
DOS SANTOS, JOSEPH—Pte. B. Co., 6th Platoon, 1st Serv. Bat., E.E.F.
DOUGLAS, WALTER.
DRAYTON, PHILIP WILLIAM.
DUKE, NATHAN.
DUNCAN, LAWRENCE.
DURIEUX, HUGH.
DYALL, VICTOR LEOPOLD—Private I. Co., E.E.F., Egypt.
EASTMAN, EDWIN.
EDGAR, EVANS.
EVANS, EDWARD—Capt. 6th Battn., B.W.I.R., Flanders.
EVERSLEY, DIAMOND.

FELIX, SYLVESTRE.
FENWICK, ALDFRED—Lance-Corpl. C. Co., 1st Serv. Batt., Egypt.
FERNANDEZ, JOSEPH.
FLEMMING, WILFRED.
FLYNN, PETER PAUL.
FORTUNE, JOSIAH.
FOX, MATHEW WALTER.
FRANCIS ARTHUR.
FRANCIS EMANUEL
FRANCIS WILSON.
FRANCOIS, PERCY DILLON—Lance Corporal.
FRANCOIS, ST. HILL.
FRANCOIS, THEODORE AUGUSTUS—Sergt. B. co., 1st Serv. Batt., Egypt.
FRASER, AUGUSTUS.
GAJADHAR, PAUL OLIVER—Returned Medically unfit.
GEORGE, BENTLEY.
GEORGE, PHILLIP.
GEORGE, SEIFORT—Returned Medically unfit.
GIBARO, ALEXANDER.
GILKES, ROBERT.
GITTENS, JOSHUA.
GLAUDE, CLEOPHUS MATHEW.
GONSALVES, ARTHUR (or GAFFOOR)—Returned unfit.
GONZALES, BERTIE ANTHONY ETHELBERT.
GONZALES, FREDERICK,—Corporal, Egypt.
GOULD, GEORGE ANTHONY.
GRAINGER, URIAS PHILLIP.
GRANT, DANIEL
GRAVES, FITZ STEPHEN MAURICE.
GREENIDGE, JOSEPH BENJAMIN.
GRIFFITH, ALONZO.
GRIFFITH, BANFIELD BERNARD CECIL—Corpl. B. Co., Egypt.

"Run you run, Kaiser William, run you run (repeat)
Hear what Kitchener say, cheer boys cheer
With surety and sincerity, we goin' conquer Germany.
(Inventor)"

Officers of the 8th W.I. Regiment stationed in Italy.
Lt.-Col. A. de Boissiere, Major Smith, Capt. Mc Lelland, Capt. Arrindell, Capt. Mac Minn,
Capt. Niblock, Lieut. Pittam, Lieut. Massy, Lieut. Morton, Lieut. Ince, Hon. Lt. & Q.M. Wilshere,
2/Lieut. Smith, 2.Lieut. Smith, 2/Lieut. Cooper, 2 Lieut. Skeete, 2/Lieut. Kirton, 2/Lieut. Manning,
2/Lieut. Walcott, 2/Lieut Eldridge, 2/Lieut. Mc Donald, Capt. Hendy, Capt. O'Brien, Surg-Capt. Deane.

GRIFFITH, FRANCIS SAMUEL—Sergeant Farrier, Egypt.
GUDGRAJ, JOHN—Returned Medically unfit.
HAMILTON, MORRIS DONALD IFIL.
HARLEY, AUGUSTUS CHAPMAN—Corpl. B. Co., 1st Serv. Batt., Egypt.
HARPER, CLAUDE WALLACE—Sergeant, Egypt.
HARRINGTON, LLOYD GUSTON.
HARRIS, CHARLES HENRY.
HARRIS, REYNOLD SYLVESTRE.
HARRISON, LESLIE.
HARRY, THEOPHILUS.
HENDY, HAYNES O'CONNELL—Sergt. E.E.F., Palestine.
HENLEY, HENRY AOLPHUS—Returned Medically unfit.
HENRY, RENE NORMAN—Returned Medically unfit.
HERBERT, ALDFRED.
HERISSON, MELVILLE—Sergeant, Egypt.
HILLS, CALVERT.
HINDS, ROBERT.
HOLDER, CECIL FREDERICK.
HOLDER, THEOPHILUS DUDLEY.
HOOSAMBOCUS—Returned unfit.
JOOSEIN, JAFFUR—Returned unfit.
HOYTE, GEORGE—Sent back for Misconduct.
HUMPHREY, BERKELEY.
HYNDMAN, CHRISTOPHER ADLOPHUS—Military Medal, 7/11/17.
HYPOLITE, PATRICK FLEMMING.
ISAAC, RANDOLPH.
ISON, GILBY.
ISURA—Returned unfit.
JACKSON, MICHAEL—Private, Egypt.
JACOB, ADOLPHUS WILLIAM.
JACOBS, GEORGE HAMILTON. . . . . .DIED January, 1916.
JACOB, SAMUEL.
JAMES, CHARLES MONTGOMERY.
JAMES, LUCIEN.
JAMES, THOMAS.
JAMES, WILLIAM.
HEREMIAH, LEO. . . . . . .DIED 12th October, 1918.
JOACHIM, ALFRED JAMES—Sergeant, Egypt.
JOAQUIN, ARTHUR ALFRED—R.E. Mtd. Linesman Southern Canal Div.
JOEFIELD, O'CONNELL.
JOHN, CHARLES.
JOHN, ENOCH.
JOHNSTON, SYLVESTRE—Returned Medically unfit.
JONES, PERCY.
JOSEPH, ADOLPHUS ALISTER.
JOSEPH, ADOLPHUS THOMAS.
JOSEPH AUGUSTUS.
JOSEPH, MILFORD.
KARIM, ABDOOL—Returned unfit.
KHAN OMEER—Returned unfit.
KHAN, NAGIR—Returned unfit.
KNIGHT, EDMUND.
KNIGHTS, JAMES NATHANIEL.
KUNDANSINGH—Returned unfit.
LAGUERRE, EDWARD.
LAKE, LIONEL WHARTON—Sergeant, Egypt.
LAMOREL, HUBERT.
LANG, EVANS SAMUEL. . . . . .DIED 4th June, 1918.
LA ROSA, FRANCIS DE SALES.
LAWRENCE, OSCAR ADOLPHUS.
LAYNE, ALBERT.
LAYNE, CHARLES LETCHMERE.
LEDEE, DONALD.
LEEKHAM, THEODORE MCCOLLIN—Ag. Corpl. Military Medal.
LE GENDRE, LAWRENCE.
LENARD, HUGH.
LEWIS, HERBERT.
LEWIS, RICHARD.
LIGERTWOOD, JAMES.
LINDSAY, DANIEL.
LING, PHILIP—Returned Medically unfit.
LOGAN, THOMAS ALEXANDER.
LONDEA, HYPOLITE.
LORD, NORMAN ST. CLAIR.
LOWDIN—Returned unfit.
LUCAS, FELIX ALEXIS.
LUCES, MARIANO EGNACIO—Private Egypt.
LYNCH, ALBERT AUGUSTUS.
MACINTOSH ANDREW ('Toby')—Sergeant, German East Africa.
MAHASTE, JOHN.
MAHOMED, JOHN—Returned unfit.
MAHOMED, OMEER—Returned unfit.
MAHOMMED, DIN—Returned unfit.
MAINGOT, FELIX.
MALONEY, SAMUEL.

MARCELLINE, LUCOVIC.
MARQUES, LOUIS—Returned Medically unfit.
MARSHALL, ALLAN ALEXANDER—Gnr. 1st Serv. Bat., B. Co., Palestine.
MARTIN, CHARLES.
MARTIN, MARTIN WILLIAM.
MATHEW, THOMAS—Returned Medically unfit.
MAUGE, JOHN CECIL—Returned Medically unfit.
MAUGHN, JOSEPH.
MAXWELL, STEADY—Private Signaller E.E.F.
MAYERS, LAURIE PHILIP ARGON.
MEOSA, CELESTINO.
MERCER, HERMANS.
MILLER, SAMUEL
MITCHELL, HEZEKIAH.
MITCHELL, ROBINSON FRANCIS—Pte. 1st Battn. E.A.E.F., East Africa.
MODESTE, SHULE.
MOOLEA—Returned unfit.
MOORE, BLANCHFIELD DAVID—Private, Egypt.
MOORE, JACOB BENJAMIN—Returned Medically unfit.
MORALDO, JAMES ANTONIO. . . . . . .DIED 18th February, 1916.
MORGAN, JOHN. . . . . . .DIED December, 1917.
MORRIS, NATHANIEL FITZROY—Pte. E.E.F., Palestine.
MOSES, MANUEL.
MOSES, THOMAS.
MOTTLEY, JAMES GEORGE.
McCOY, FITZ GERALD.
McDONALD, JOHN McINTOSH
McINTOSH, CEDRIC.
McINTOSH, JAMES
McINTOSH, MARTIN ADOLPHUS.
McKENZIE, EDGAR.
McKIE, EDWARD.
McLEOD, JAMES.
NATHAN, WELLINGTON.
NATHANIEL, JAMES.
NELSON, EDWARD.
NELSON, JOSEPH.
NEVISON, HENRY.
NEWALLO, CLIFFORD.
NIMBLETT, NORMAN.
NOREIGA, LOUIS.
O'KEIFFE, HUGH FORESTER.
OMETTA, ARCHIE.
OXLEY, JOSEPH—Returned Medically unfit.
PANTIN, JOEL.
PARKER, JOHN BADCOCK—Returned Medically unfit.
PARKS, JAMES.
PARRIS, BERESFORD GILBANKS.
PARRIS, CHARLES CYRIL ST. CLAIR.
PARRIS, JACOB.
PARRIS, THEOPHILUS.
PARRIS, THEOPHILUS JOSHUA.
PAUL, WHITFIELD—Returned Medically unfit.
PAYNE, EBENEZER WILFRED.
PAYNE, JONATHAN—Returned Medically unfit.
PENA, CHARLES OSWALD—Sergt. B. Co., 1st. Serv. Batt., Egypt.
PENA, NIAM.
PERRY, SAMUEL.
PETERS, ARCHIBALD. . . . . . . .DIED 17th February, 1916.
PETERS, CADMAN.
PHILLIPS, NATHANIEL. . . . . .DIED 9th November, 1915.
PHILLIPS, NATHANIEL—Returned Medically unfit.
PHILLIPS, OLIVER—Returned Medically unfit.
PIERRE, ALBERT FREDERICK ERNEST—Sergeant, Egypt.
PIERRE, ALSTON.
PIERRE, LAWRENCE.
PILLAY, NADARAJAH—Returned unfit.
PINDER, EDMUND. . . . . . .DIED 23rd March, 1917.
PINTO, JOHN BAPTISTE.
POLLONAIS, ALBERT LIONEL—Company Sergeant-Major.
PROVIDENCE, JAMES—Returned Medically unfit.
PRENTICE, MOSES. . . . . . . .DIED 28th November, 1916.
PURCELL, ALEXANDER CRESS.
RAHAMAN, ABDOOL—Returned unfit.
RAM, OUDA—Returned unfit.
RAMNATH—Returned unfit.
RAMSAY, RUFUS ADOLPHUS.
RATMAH—Returned unfit.
RAWLINS, RONALD ROWLAND RODERICK—Sergt. E.E.F., Egypt.
REID, LOUIS—Corpl. . . . . .DIED 26th December, 1918.
REGIS, EGBERT.
RENNES, EDWARD.
RICHARDS, FITZ HERBERT.
RILEY, BENJAMIN.

ROACH, FREDERICK LANCELOT—Corporal, 1st Battn., E.E.F.
ROBERTS, CHARLES.
ROBERTS, NEVILLE.
ROBERTSON, FREDERICK WILLIAM—Returned Medically unfit.
ROMNEY, THOMAS SOLOMON—Sergeant.
ROSTANT, ANDRE—Reported a deserter in Egypt.
ROSTANT, EMANUEL EVAN.
ROSTER, CHARLES.
RUBIN, FELIX.
RUDOLFO, JOSEPH.
RUDOLFO, PHILIP EMANUEL.
RUSSELL, EDMUND EDWARD—Corpl. B. Co., 1st Battn., E.E.F., Egypt.
SAHALU—Returned unfit.
SAMPSON, JONATHAN.
SAMUEL, ALBERT.
SAMUEL, ALBERT.
SAMUEL, THEOPHILUS—CORPORAL, E.E.F.
SAMUEL, JOSEPH.
SAROOPRACHPAUL.
SAVARY, LIONEL.. . . . . . . .DIED 3rd September, 1917.
SCHOON, THOMAS BEGGS.
SCOTT, ARTHUR.
SCOTT, MOSES.
SEALES, JOSEPH SLOAN.
SUBLAL—Returned unfit.
SERRANO, JOSEPH.
SHERIFF, JOHN MILFORD.
SHURLAND, CLIFFORD ALEXANDER.
SIMON, CHARLES.
SIMEON, JOHN GARNET.
SIMMONS, CHARLES.
SINGH, DOUG—Returned unfit.
SKEETE, ZADOK—Private, Egypt.
SMALL, RAPHAEL ARTHUR—Gunner, I Co., 1st Batt., B.E.A.E.F.
SMALL, SIMEON.
SMITH, JOSEPH EMMANUEL. . . . . . .DIED 18th August, 1918.
SOBERS, ALEXANDER.
SOLOMON, ALEXANDER. . . . . DIED 10th October, 1918.
SONGSTER, JAMES LEICESTER.
SONGSTER, SAMUEL. . . . . . . .DIED 12th November, 1916.
SOOGANSINGH—Returned unfit.
SOOJAITKHAN—Returned unfit.
STANFORD, REGINALD ADOLPHUs—Returned Medically unfit.
STEPHEN, JOSEPH.
STEPHEN, LUCIEN. . . . . . .DIED 27th December, 1915.
STERLING, VINCENT MATHIAS.
STEWART, AMBROSE—Returned Medically unfit.
ST. CLAIR, McKAY—Returned Medically unfit.
ST. LOUIS, O'CONAL.

SULTANTSINGH—Returned unfit.
SUTTON, WILMOT ARTHUR.
TAITT, MARTIN LUTHER.
TEIJMUL, JOSEPH—Returned unfit.
TELESFORD, JOSEPH LOUIS.
THOMAS, ABRAHAM.
THOMAS, JAMES.
THOMAS, JOSEPH.
THOMAS, JOSEPH MICHAEL.
THOMAS, MARTIN LUTHER.
THOMAS, RALPH CALAPHAS—Pte. 1st Battn., Egypt.
THOMAS, THEOPHILUS GERMANS.
THOMAS, WILFRED.
THOMPSON, ALFRED WILLIAM.
TITRE, HARRY AUGUSTUS.
TORAILLE, FELIX CHARLES—Returned Medically unfit.
Tota—Returned Medically unfit.
TOUSSAINT, BERNARD RANDOLPH.
TROTMAN, CHARLES EMANUEL.
TROTMAN, ELIAS ALEXANDER JOSEPHUS.
TURPIN, RICHARD—Lce-Cpl. . . . .Distinguished Conduct Medal
VALDEZ, ANDREW.
VALENTINE, ROBERT AUGUSTUS—Sergeant, Egypt.
VANDERPOOL, ALBERT—Returned Medically unfit.
VASCONCELLOS, JULES LOUIS—Lance-Corporal, Egypt.
VIALVA, EDIL.
WAITHE, JAMES JULIEN—Corpl. C. Co., 1st Serv. Battm., Palestine.
WALCOTT, O'DONNELL JOHN.
WALLACE, CHARLES.
WATSON, CHARLES LANCELOT—Returned Medically unfit.
WATSON, EDGAR NEVILLE—Lance-Cpl., Egypt—Now Ag. Co. Qtr. Mstr.
WEEKES, DUNCAN—Returned Medically unfit.
WILFORD, FRANCIS PERCY.
WILLIAMS, HAMILTON JOHN.
WILLIAMS, HENRY HAMILTON—Returned Medically unfit.
WILLIAMS, JAMEs—Sent back for misconduct.
WILLIAMS, JAMES.
WILLIAMS, JOHN—Returned Medically unfit.
WILLIAMS, THOMAS.
WILLIAMS, THOMAS.
WOOD, FITZ HERBERT.
WORRELL, AUGUSTUS.
WORRELL, OSCAR LONGSFORD—Pte. B. Co., 1st Serv. Bat., B.E. Africa.
WRIGHT, ADOLPHUS CHARLES. . . . . .DIED 24th January, 1918.
WYNNE, JOSEPHUS.
YEARWOOD ALBERT.
YEARWOOD, CEPHAS.
YOUNG, JAMES.
ZOE, DONATION.

Trinidadians flock to enlist at the start of the war.
Photograph — G. Duruty.

October 27th, 1914
49 Marine Square,
Port of Spain.

Colonel A. Dueros,

Dear Sir,

Your notice in 'The Times' asking Colonials who wish to join the Colours to write to you or to apply in person at the White City has attracted my attention. And there are many men of good physique and education in the Colony, and throughout the West Indies, who are eager, and who will be proud to enlist. I cabled on Saturday last, the 24th instant, asking if you will accept a contingent from this place. I am awaiting your reply. It is necessary that I should fully explain the object of my cable and facts as they are in these parts.

Trinidad is an Island, the most southern of the British West Indies; a reference to a map will show they are like stepping stones in the Caribbean. The population throughout is very mixed — white, black and all shades, from the weakest cafe-au-lait to the strongest black, East Indians, Chinese, etc.

Those willing to enlist are of the better class and educated. The cables ad papers are read with avidity by them, and so far as West Indians are concerned, the addresses of Lord Kitchener, Messrs. Asquith, Churchill and Lloyd George will not be in vain if their respective local legislatures will but vote the pittance needed to get the men to the Old Country.

We are four thousand and some odd miles from the Old Country and the lowest fare is £17. 10. A few men have left, and a few more are leaving, on their own, but the majority cannot afford it.

I have little doubt that if the services of our men will be accepted by the War Office, our local Government, or public will see that they are sent to the Old Country.

West Indians have realised that it is a fight to a finish, that not only is the existence of the Mother Country at stake, but the very Empire, of which we are all proud to be a part. We should feel not only isolated, but slighted, if our services are declined when men are still wanted to keep the flag flying. In this Colony at least 500 men between the ages of 20 and 40 can be mustered within a few days, men of education and good physique, and I have no doubt 4,000 similar men can be mustered throughout the West Indies in a short time. All we need is just the consent 'Come along.'

In Major de Boissiere, who was one of the contingent at the Diamond Jubilee of the late Queen Victoria and the late King Edward's Coronation, and who has acted as A.D.C. to Her Highness Princess Marie Louise of Schleswig-Holstein, we have a man who commands a following of all classes and colours. He has volunteered for service, but for some reason our Government will not grant him leave of absence. Our men are of no earthly use in these parts, as invasion is most improbable. Transatlantic Zeppelin flight has not yet been dreamt of, and the enemy has no available transport, as their nearest possession is in Africa. We are bottled up here, but we are eager to get out to assist the Mother Country. If you would use your influence in getting our little lot taken into service, this Colony, and the West Indies, will be deeply grateful.

I beg to remain,
Faithfully yours,
ARTHUR A. CIPRIANI.

DAMIEH

Captain A.A. Cipriani

It was on the historic Jordan that the little band of West Indians was destined to cover itself with glory. 'Damieh' — the name that will be always nearest the heart — here it was that we put paid to the Turks and gave the lie to our detractors who said that our men would not stand up under fire. The Battalion, supported by the Auckland Rifles, went into action in artillery formation with the same calm as if they had been on ordinary parade, and in spite of being subjected to heavy fire in the early stages of the advance, never faltered for a single moment, seemingly heedless of the enemy's fire.

This steady advance rather 'put the wind up' the already demoralised Turk, who nothing loath, 'cut sticks' very speedily. Driven from Chalk and Barka Hills he made for the Damieh bridgehead where he came foul of the 1st Batt. Lewis-gunners, who opened such a terrific

Elements of the British Australian and West Indian Forces on the attack in Jordan Valley in the closing months of the war. Illustration from the Graphic, April 1918.

Maj. Harragin, D.S.O.

fire that not a single Turk succeeded in crossing. Failing in this the Turks made their last turn for the Es Salt Hills, the battle resolving itself into a chase.

Earlier in the day, part of the 1st, under Major Harragin, charged up the Damieh hillsides, driving 'Johnnie' from his entrenched position and capturing 200 prisoners and 7 machine-guns, with one killed and six wounded. The 2nd Battalion had 6 killed and 40 wounded in the assault on the Chalk and Barka Hills.

The Turkish army was now in full flight, making their way home up the Es Salt Hills 3,000 feet up and over goat tracks. Our men, flushed with victory, followed without any rest, with little food and water, in the hope of coming up with them again at Amman, where the Divisional Commander had promised them another scrap. After a few hours' rest a forced march through the night brought them to Amman just too late, as our friends the Anzacs had already captured the village.

From this point onward there was no further use for infantry, and the little Regiment that had acquitted itself so well at the first time of asking were thereby deprived of any other chance of showing their mettle. To add insult to injury, our tired and disappointed chaps were ordered back to Jericho to refit, and the march back was left to the Second-in-Command, a Major Bensley, a rare old 'fuss-pot', very intelligent and learned but without an ounce of ordinary horse sense. The men were marched nearly the whole of the next day, without a halt, through a blinding, suffocating dust, and a temperature well nigh 100% in the shade.

Already the effects of that terrible malaria which claimed such a toll from the British forces in Palestine had begun to be felt in the Regiment, and officers and men fell by the road-side like flies. Many who had escaped the Turkish bullets two days previously were now being hurried through Clearing Stations to the nearest hospitals, where a great many paid the supreme sacrifice. Of 2,300 men and 40 officers who took the field on that October morning only 500 returned to Jericho. Nearly 90% had contracted pernicious malaria, and up to this day a great many are suffering from its effects.

The work of the B.W.I. Regiment was a revelation to G.H.Q., who were not slow to mark their appreciation. On the day following the battle General Allenby called in person on our wounded in the hospital at Jerusalem and thanked them for their good work. Recognition from the great soldier in person was a very great compliment, and one which will always be remembered by officers and men.

Major Harragin was awarded the D.S.O., Captain Craig the M.C., Major Thomas bar to the M.C., Sergeant Julien the D.C.M.

Apart from those Mentioned in Despatches, Lieuts. Knaggs, Perkins and Boyd did specially good work and were unlucky not to score a ribbon.

The following was issued to all units:

"I desire to convey to all ranks and all arms of the force under my command my admiration and thanks for their great deeds of the past week, and my appreciation of their gallantry and determination, which have resulted in the total destruction of the 7th and 8th Turkish Armies opposed to us.

Such a complete victory has seldom been known in all the history of war.

EDMOND ALLENBY,
General.
C.-I.-C.

The West India Regiment also known as the Zouaves. By A.B. Ellis.

Spanning a period from pre-Colombian times to World War I The Book of Trinidad now closes. One can't help looking for the significant elements produced by the collective experience of all this. For what emerged out of the 19th century socially, politically, and culturally was strongly influenced by the Afro-French Creole culture as it existed then in this a British Colony. It was this experience that came to fruition in the 20th century. The creole culture produced a singularly dynamic, creative minority who were distinguished in the art, poetry and music of its carnival, calypso and steelband, in its scholarship and sport, which has succeeded in making its mark on the world stage. This creative minority was pivotal in developing the new social and economic dispensation of the post-colonial era.

In a great many respects this was epitomized in the person of Eric Eustace Williams who was to become the greatest figure in Trinidad and Tobago's 20th century history. He was the natural inheritor of the best elements of the black and coloured intelligentsia whose traditions date from the Cedula of Population of 1783. He symbolized to a great number of people their collective hopes and dreams. Their entire colonial experience made flesh.

He was in fact more than merely symbolic. In that he physically embodied it by virtue of being on the one hand a descendant of an illustrious French family, who had settled here before the British Conquest and on the other the product of the African slave diaspora. He was a man of his times.

Ancestry of the Williams Family of Trinidad and Nevis.

Phillippa Sussannah Commissiong & Lt. Col. Sir Charles Felix Smith
apparently light coloured person   *Acting Governor of Trinidad in the 1830s*
reputed to have been rich
"they were married but not churched."

Phillippa Sussanah Smith m John Baptiste Hunt
       Illegitimate son of Col. Le Hunt

Onemia Wilhemenia Jane Hunt   m   Thomas James Williams
born in Trinidad April 1853   born in Nevis April 1855

Disowned by her relatives as a result of this. They had 2 children (that survived childbirth) Henry and Phillippa. Onemia came into contact with her husband through her negro nurse "Da". She (Onemia) looked like a white person, but she said she had coloured blood. She had long, straight, light hair and a straight long nose, spoke French and French-Patois fluently but spoke English with difficulty. Staunch supporter of the R.C. Church (regular church-goer). She came to St. Vincent with her daughter, Phillippa on 22nd April, 1923 and died there on 4th September 1931 and is buried in the Kingston Cemetery (R.C. St. Vincent Section). Certain Trinidad nuns and priests always kept in touch with her through the R.C. Priest, Fr. Charles Veshter, St. Vincent.

Son of Sarah Jane Williams née James (who was of Carib descent (Long straight hair) and born in Nevis in 1830 and died in Trinidad in 1915) and of a negro, nicknamed "OLD KING" who was a turnkey at the Prison in Nevis. — (She, Sarah Williams says she was not born a slave — Staunch Methodist) Old King was also a Methodist. had a good education for that time. Came to Trinidad with Mr. Gaston Johnson — Operated a Real Estate Agency.

Thomas Henry Williams — born in Trinidad 1878 died 1946
Civil Servant attended Tranquillity Boys
m
Eliza Boissiere born 1888 died 1972
Daughter of E. Redford and Jules Boissiere

Eric Eustace Williams the eldest child, born 1911 died 1981.

Compiled by Mr. M. La Borde of St. Vincent
for Mrs. Flora Gittens, sister of The Right Hon. Eric Williams
Former Prime Minister of Trinidad and Tobago

ERIC EUSTACE WILLIAMS

Eric Eustace Williams was indeed exceptional, for he not only excelled academically but was also known as a competent footballer. Born on the 25th September, 1911 he attended Tranquillity Boys Intermediate School where he won a scholarship to the Queen's Royal College. The outcome of his final examinations at Q.R.C. resulted in yet another scholarship this time to the prestigious St. Catherine's Society at Oxford presently known as St. Catherine's College. In 1935 he was awarded his Bachelor of Arts with first class honours. Four years later he obtained his Doctorate of Philosophy in history. He then went to Washington D.C. where he became Assistant Professor of Social and Political Science at Howard University. In 1944 he became the Associate Professor and one year later became Professor.

During the period of 1948 and 1955, because he had specialized in Caribbean Social History, he was appointed to the position of Deputy Chairman of the Research Council of the Caribbean Commission. It was this that brought Eric back to Trinidad. It is of interest to note that his office Kent House, had its headquarters in Rookery Nook, on the very site where his great grandfather John Nicholas Boissiere had lived before.

After he resigned his post as Deputy Chairman in 1955 he directed all his energies into forming the People's National Movement, the party he would lead for the next thirty odd years. It was this party that carried Trinidad and Tobago out of colonialism into Independence and Republicanism. In 1964, Eric Eustace Williams was admitted to the Privy Council. In this period he would refuse a knighthood but accept the more acclaimed award of Companion of Honour. His Alma Mater would bestow on him an Honorary Fellow award and he would become the pro-Chancellor of the University of the West Indies in 1964. Eric Eustace Williams was truly a remarkable man, indeed a child of the 20th century. Photograph — Mrs. Flora Gittens.

EPILOGUE
Bridget Brereton

This 'Book of Trinidad' has tried to portray, in words and in pictures, the historical development of this country from pre-Columbian times to the end of the 19th century. Excerpts from contemporary authors who were eye-witnesses to the events or social institutions which they describe, and old photographs, prints, maps and charts, advertisements and even dance tickets, can often bring a past era to life more vividly than the historian's text, useful and necessary though that always is. There is nothing more evocative of the past than an old photograph, allowing us to imagine the life which its subject, now probably long dead, must have led in a Trinidad very different from our own.

By focussing on the experiences of the successive waves of immigrants who peopled this country – Amerindians, Spaniards, Africans, Frenchmen, British, Indians, Chinese and Syrian/Lebanese – and of their locally-born, Creole descendants, we hope to show the cosmopolitan nature of our society. From the 1780's up to today, this cosmopolitanism, this multi-racial, multi-lingual, multi-religious, hodge-podge, has formed the outstanding characteristic of Trinidad and Tobago. No other Caribbean island is quite like it. 19th Century Trinidad was an almost unbelievable complex society. going from Barbados to Trinidad was like going from the known (English) to the unknown – a still foreign island whose people stubbornly resisted efforts to make the colony British in spirit and in institutions.

Of course, the complexity of Trinidad's society between the 1780's and the early 1900's should not make us lose sight of certain fundamentals. Trinidad was a colony, and its ultimate purpose was to make money for the Europeans or their Creole descendants who owned the land, organised the commerce and ran the affairs of the island. The society was indeed cosmopolitan, but the different racial groups did not enter on equal terms, and colonial life was based on a clear hierarchy, social, political and economic. Europeans and white Creoles owned, governed and managed; people of African and Indian descent worked with their hands as labourers or small farmers (though many of these did own land). Uneasily in between, were the 'people of colour' and the coloured and black middle class of post-slavery times. This racial hierarchy was not seriously undermined until after 1914, though Trinidadians were certainly beginning to challenge it long before that.

Yet, despite the hierarchical structure, society in post-emancipation Trinidad was not without scope for mobility. This was far from a rigid, caste-bound system; in fact, there was a certain fluidity, a restlessness, which we can detect in 19th century Trinidad and which is still a salient feature today. Even at that time, we see the evidence of political consciousness and racial pride among the more educated coloureds and blacks, and the emergence of an upwardly mobile group of Indians who had benefitted from schooling after 1868. In the country-side peasant farmers and labourers of many races were creating a vibrant village life. In the city, black slum folk forged the urban culture which focussed on Carnival and would be the matrix for calypso and steelband. Even the Creole whites, who benefitted most from the colonial economy, saw themselves as true sons of the soil, as deeply rooted local aristocrats, and they often collaborated with blacks and coloureds in political movements, as in the campaigns to reform the Crown Colony constitution in the 1880's and 1890's.

The foundations of Trinidad's modern society were laid, as we have tried to show, in the period between the 1780's and the 1830's. In these decades, after the long Amerindian-Spanish era when the island was barely settled or developed, African and European immigrants (the former coerced, the latter mostly voluntary arrivals) established plantations and created towns, roads, ports, and a lively agricultural and commercial economy. By 1838, when slavery was finally ended, most Trinidadians were of African descent, but the ruling elite was European or white Creole, and there was a significantly large group of 'people of colour', persons of mixed African and European origins. Then in the two generations after Emancipation (1838-1900) the large-scale immigration of people from Asia (India and China) and the Middle East, along with developments among the longer established African and European population groups, further transformed the society. By 1900 Trinidad's social structure and demography was recognisably modern. No new racial group would enter the society after that date, though immigration from India continued until 1917, and many people from China, the Middle East and the Eastern Caribbean would come here in the present century.

At the beginning of the 20th century, then, the composition of Trinidad's population, and its basic social structure, seemed determined. But the island stood poised to enter a period of rapid political and economic development. Indeed, the first World War (1914-18) was something of a watershed here as elsewhere. Economically, the oil industry was about to enter its 'take-off', a development that would soon transform the colonial economy, especially with the collapse of cocoa after 1920. Politically, the post-was period saw a marked rise in political activity and labour organisations which came to challenge both the racial hierarchy of colonial society and the institutions of Crown Colony Government. Middle class reformers and labour activators of all races worked on several different fronts to secure constitutional change and workers' rights. The worker's protests of 1934-37, the agitation of the political leaders and parties from Cipriani onwards, the upheavals of World War Two)1939-45) – all these combined to thrust Trinidad and Tobago into its truly modern (post-1945) era.

This book takes the story up to the eve of the First World War (1914). Later developments – which are within the memory of many of our older citizens – will have to await another book and another time.

THE END